WORKING AMERICANS
1880–2009

Volume X:
Sports & Recreation

by Scott Derks

A Universal Reference Book

Grey House Publishing

PUBLISHER:	Leslie Mackenzie
EDITORIAL DIRECTOR:	Laura Mars
EDITORIAL ASSISTANT:	Jael Bridgemahon
MARKETING DIRECTOR:	Jessica Moody
AUTHOR:	Scott Derks
CHIEF CONTRIBUTOR:	Jim Reindollar
CONTRIBUTORS:	Jimmy Copening, Elizabeth Derks, Marshall Derks, and Lucia Derks
	Sally Gaillard, Caroline Gottlieb, Will Long, Laura Mars, and Josh Wolfe
COPYEDITOR:	Elaine Alibrandi
COMPOSITION & DESIGN:	DSCS—Datastream Content Solutions, LLC
	Composition & Publishing Services

A Universal Reference Book
Grey House Publishing, Inc.
4919 Route 22
Amenia, NY 12501
518.789.8700
FAX 518.789.0556
www.greyhouse.com
e-mail: books@greyhouse.com

Publisher's Cataloging-In-Publication Data
(Prepared by the Donohue Group, Inc.)

Derks, Scott.
 Working Americans . . . / by Scott Derks.

 v. : ill. ; cm.

Title varies.
"A universal reference book."
Includes bibliographical references and indexes.
Contents: v. 1. The working class—v. 2. The middle class—v. 3. The upper class—v. 4. Their children.—v. 5. At war.—v. 6. Women at work—v. 7. Social movements—v. 8. Immigrants—v .9. Revolutionary war to civil war—v. 10. Sports & recreation.
 ISBN: 1-891482-81-5 (v. 1)
 ISBN: 1-891482-72-6 (v. 2)
 ISBN: 1-930956-38-X (v.3)
 ISBN: 1-930956-35-5 (v. 4)
 ISBN: 1-59327-024-1 (v. 5)
 ISBN: 1-59237-063-Z (v. 6)
 ISBN: 1-59327-101-9 (v. 7)
 ISBN: 978-1-59237-197-6 (v. 8)
 ISBN 13: 1-978-1-59237-101-3 (v. 9)
 ISBN: 1-59237-441-7 (v. 10)

1. Working class—United States—History. 2. Labor—United States—History. 3. Occupations—United States—History.
4. Social classes—United States—History. 5. Immigrants—Employment—United States—History. 6. United States—Economic conditions. I. Title.

HD8066 .D47 2000
305.5/0973/0904

PREFACE

This book is the tenth in a series examining the social and economic lives of working Americans. In this volume, the focus is on sports from the perspective of professional and amateur athletes, referees, spectators, hotdog vendors, coaches, cutmen and sports writers. A few of the athletes were highly successful and acclaimed, but most simply loved the pursuit of sport and found ways to arrange their lives around that passion. Their stories include a female archer competing in the chaotic 1904 St. Louis Olympics, a bicycle racer who trained with some of the world's best, a woman who turned from soccer to sailing, a pool player who was willing to share his secrets, an NFL referee who got his start in the peewee leagues, as well as stories about how free substitution in football was about to ruin the game. (How could the game's best player be named if he only played offense or defense, let alone just one position?) Along the way, the evolution of baseball equipment, off track betting, rowing styles, and even the jump shot are explored. Most of the athletes profiled in this book never became famous—although a few did—but for all, the grit and glamour of Americans at play was part of their lives.

The first volume, *Working Americans: 1880-1999: The Working Class,* explores the struggles of the working class through the eyes and wallets of three dozen families. Employing pictures, stories, statistics and advertisements of the period, it studies their jobs, wages, family life, expenditures and hobbies throughout the decades. The second and third volumes, the *Middle Class* and the *Upper Class,* capture the struggles and joys of families possessing progressively greater wealth and their roles in transforming the economy of America from 1880 to 1999. The fourth volume, *Their Children,* builds upon the social and economic issues explored previously by examining the lives of children across the entire spectrum of economic status. The issues addressed include parents, child labor, education, peer pressure, food, fads and fun. *Volume V: Americans at War* explores the life-changing elements of war and discusses how enlisted personnel, officers and civilians handle the stress, exhilaration, boredom and brutality of America's various wars, conflicts or incursions. *Volume VI: Women at Work* celebrates the contributions of women, chronicling both the progress and roadblocks along the way, and highlighting the critical role of women in the frontlines of change.

Working Americans VII: Social Movements explores the various ways America's men and women feel called upon to challenge accepted conventions, whether the issue is cigarette smoking in 1901 or challenging the construction of a massive hydroelectric dam in 1956. *Working Americans VIII: Immigrants* examines the lives of first- and second-generation immigrants with a focus on their journey to America, their search for identity and their emotions experienced in a new land. *Working Americans IX: The Revolutionary War to the Civil War* steps back in time to chronicle the lives of 36 families from the 1770s to the 1860s, detailing their struggles and triumphs whether their occupation was farmer, postal clerk, whiskey merchant, lawyer or cabinetmaker.

Working Americans X: Sports & Recreation tackles the diverse and ever-changing world of competitive sports in America from the viewpoint of the professional, the amateur and the spectator. Along the way, we meet Olympic swimmers, basketball players who rarely played, boxers with extraordinary stamina, weightlifters of unbelievable determination and weekend athletes thrilled by the opportunity to be in the open air. This study profiles both the experiences of an amateur tennis player when girls were an anomaly on the tennis court, as well as an ultimate Frisbee athlete whose freedom to move from sport to sport reflected the impact of Title IX on women's athletics. The impact of technology on motorboat racing and the evolutionary nature of rule changes in football or basketball help us to understand the sports we love. Along the way, we learn the origin of the word "pool" for a billiards table, the work ethic of a cross-country runner and the difficulty of being a championship-level black athlete. To add depth to the profiles, timelines have been constructed for many sports, so readers can fully understand how little or how much their favorite sport has changed. As in the previous volumes, each story is unique as each of us is unique. All the profiles are modeled on real people and events. As in the previous books in this series, most of the names have been changed and some details added based on statistics, the popularity of an idea or writings of the time. The real names of several athletes were used for reasons of visibility, accuracy or sentimentality. They are: Mike Kelly, 1888; Francis Ouimet, 1913; Young Stribling, 1927; Katherine Rawls, 1936; Harrison Dillard, 1952; Jim Bradford, 1960; Jim Rosser, 1983; and Jamie Hagerman, 2006.

Otherwise, every effort is made to profile accurately the individual's sporting experience, home and work life. To ensure that the profiles reflect the mood of each decade and the feelings of the subjects, letters, biographies, interviews, high school annuals and magazine articles were consulted and used. In some cases the people profiled represent national trends and feelings, but mostly, they represent themselves. Ultimately, it is the working Americans and their activities—along with their investments, spending decisions, sports & recreation interests, jobs and passions—that shape the society and the economy of the United States.

INTRODUCTION

Working Americans 1880-2009 Volume X: Sports & Recreation, is the tenth volume in an open-ended series. Like its predecessors, *Sports & Recreation* profiles the lives of Americans—how they lived, how they worked, how they played—decade by decade. Previous volumes focused primarily on economic status or social issues. This volume focuses on individuals with a passion for their game, from Olympic competitors to stadium vendors. It gives equal treatment to professional athletes, amateur players, and those who otherwise support their sport via writing or hawking hotdogs. *Sports & Recreation* covers 21 different activities, including highly competitive team sports like football and hockey, individual sports like archery and tennis, and more recreational activities like fishing and bowling.

Sports & Recreation takes you:

- Into the world of a Yale University oarsman in 1893;
- To France, where YMCA's Robert Meek worked to boast troop morale during World War I by organizing baseball games;
- On a fishing expedition in 1929 during which two friends got lost;
- Up close and personal with New York sportswriter Alan Miller in 1938;
- To the Olympics in Helsinki, Finland in 1952, where Harrison Dillard competed in hurdling;
- Into the St. Louis Cardinal's stadium in 1962, where Charles Plautard sold hotdogs to be close to the game;
- In the boxing ring in 1979 where "cutman" Joe Austin helped boxers stay in the match by working to stop their cuts from bleeding;
- To the high school hockey field where coach Frankie Parsons saw his team win the championship in 1998; and
- On a trip to Las Vegas in 2009 with Alfredo Lenzi's pool team.

Arranged in 12 decade-long chapters, this newest *Working Americans* volume features three **Profiles** per chapter. Each profile starts with **Life at Home**, with enlightening details on family and school life. **Life at Work** summarizes struggles (from discrimination to lack of sleep) and successes (from making the team to winning gold) in a chosen sport. **Life in the Community** details environments that surround the subject, from small rural villages to major cities, and how it helped or hindered each in reaching their goal.

This personal information is followed by historical and economic data of the time. **Historical Snapshots** chronicle major milestones, **Timelines** outline the progress of a variety of sports, and **News Features** puts sporting events and recreational activities in context. These common elements, as well as specialized data, such as **Selected Prices**, punctuate each chapter and act as statistical comparisons between decades. The 36 men and women featured in this volume represent 18 states. In addition, four countries showcase the international community: France, during World War I; and Germany, Finland and Italy during various Olympic games. The Table of Contents provides a detailed list, by decade.

Like the other nine volumes in this series, *Working Americans 1880–2009 Volume X: Sports & Recreation* is a compilation of original research—personal diaries, school records, family histories—plus printed material—government statistics, commercial advertisements, and news features. The text, in easy-to-read bulleted format, is supported with hundreds of graphics, such as photos, advertisements, drawings, awards and badges, and letters.

All ten *Working Americans* volumes are "point in time" books, designed to illustrate the reality of that particular time. Some athletes and recreational players portrayed in this tenth volume were champions and some were not. Many of their stories continue. As one athlete realizes his or her dream, hundreds more begin their own journey.

Praise for earlier volumes—

". . . the Working Americans approach to social history is interesting and each volume is worth exploring . . ."

"these interesting, unique compilations of economic and social facts, figures, and graphs . . . support multiple research needs [and] will engage and enlighten patrons in high school, public, and academic library collections."

Booklist

"The volume 'promises to enhance our understanding of the growth and development of the working class over more than a century.' It capably fulfills this promise . . . recommended for all types of libraries."

Stories from Social Movements *. . . 'succeed in capturing the spirit of the issue and the times . . .'"*

ARBA

"[the author] adds to the genre of social history known as 'history from the bottom up,' . . . Recommended for all colleges and university library collections."

Choice

"this volume engages and informs, contributing significantly and meaningfully to the historiography of the working class in America . . . a compelling and well-organized contribution for those interested in social history and the complexities of working Americans."

Library Journal

TABLE OF CONTENTS

DEDICATION

This work is an expression of thanks and respect for all the coaches, referees and officials who allow sports to thrive, especially Coach Summers, Coach Tritt and referee Jim Rosser.

ACKNOWLEDGEMENTS

As this tenth volume of the *Working Americans* series draws to a close, I must pause and give thanks to publishers Leslie Mackenzie and Dick Gottlieb for birthing and nurturing the concept of describing America through the eyes of ordinary athletes, soldiers, children or even the wealthy. Editor Laura Mars taught it walk and copyeditor Elaine Alibrandi showed it how to skip, run and frolic. For those gifts I am grateful. *Working Americans: Sports & Recreation* was supported by several veteran researchers/writers including Jimmy Copening, Caroline Gottlieb and Marshall Derks. Newcomers who made significant contributions include Jim Reindollar, Will Long, Lucia Derks, Josh Wolfe and Elizabeth Derks. Special thanks for research goes to Joan Wilcox and Marie Concetta Mazzagatti Cloninger. I especially pray that all writers and readers keep an adverb handy at all times—because you never know.

1880–1899

The final two decades of the nineteenth century were an important incubation period for the practice of sport—both amateur and professional. While America was experiencing massive immigration from throughout the world and the key fundamentals of the labor movement were taking shape, exercise and sport were becoming fashionable. Colleges sponsored rowing teams, private tennis clubs were formed, the sale of bicycles rose dramatically and industrial cities became increasingly concerned about providing free space for parks and enjoying fresh air. Sport had its birth at the top and bottom of the economic scale. The affluent embraced croquet, archery and tennis, while boxing, baseball and wrestling became the province of the urban factory worker—including millions of new immigrants crowding the cities.

Baseball was the first major team sport to break into the national scene, and held a dominant position for almost 100 years. Nurtured in thousands of pickup games played in city streets and cow pastures across the nation, baseball by 1871 boasted its first professional league. For the youth of Victorian America, professional baseball offered a glorious career opportunity for both fun and social mobility. The players' decision to don gloves and wear catcher's masks improved play and attracted even more rabid fans. The *St. Louis Post-Dispatch* reported in 1883 that "a glance at the audience on any fine day in the ballpark will reveal telegraph operators, printers who work at night, traveling men, men of leisure, men of capital, bank clerks who get away at 3 p.m., real estate men, barkeepers, hotel clerks, actors and employees of the theater, policemen and firemen on their day off, butchers and bakers."

Boxing, too, emerged as a major sport best symbolized by John L. Sullivan, perhaps the nation's first national sports hero. Heavyweight champion from 1882 to 1892, Sullivan defended his title against James J. Corbett in 1892, drenched in frenetic national newspaper coverage that emphasized that the championship was being held indoors under electric lights, that the fighters' bare knuckles were now encased in boxing gloves and that the event was sponsored by an athletic club—all innovations for the time.

At the same time, while working class America was indulging in sports that paid its players to perform, upper class America was emphasizing that grace and style in tennis, golf or croquet were more important than winning and that cheering was strictly for the "rougher" class. Out of this dichotomy came a tension between amateur and professional sport that would not be resolved until after World War II and would haunt the Olympic Games for much of the twentieth century.

The last two decades the nineteenth century also danced in the reflective glow of the Gilded Age, when the wealth of a tiny percentage of Americans knew no bounds. It was a time of vast, accumulated wealth and abundance of emerging technology—all racing to keep up with the restless spirit of the American people. The rapid expansion of railroads opened up the nation to new industries, new markets and the formation of monopolistic trusts that catapulted a handful of corporations into positions of incredible power and wealth. This expanding technology also triggered a movement of workers from farm to factory, the rapid expansion of wage labor and the explosive growth of cities. Farmers, merchants and small-town artisans found themselves increasingly dependent on regional and national market forces. The shift in the concentration of power was unprecedented in American history. At the same time, professionally trained workers were reshaping America's economy alongside entrepreneurs eager to capture their piece of the American pie. It was an economy on a roll with few rudders or regulations.

Across America the economy—along with its work force—was running away from the land. Before the Civil War, the United States was overwhelmingly an agricultural nation. By the end of the century, non-agricultural occupations employed nearly two-thirds of the workers. As important, two of every three Americans came to rely on wages instead of self-employment as farmers or artisans. At the same time, industrial growth began to center around cities, where wealth accumulated for a few who understood how to harness and use railroads, create new consumer markets and manage a ready supply of cheap, trainable workers. Jobs offering steady wages and the promise of a better life for workers' children drew people from the farms to the cities. A modern, industrial-based workforce emerged from the traditional farmlands, led by men skilled in managing others and the complicated flow of materials required to keep the factories operating. This led to increasing demand for attorneys, bankers and physicians to handle the complexity of the emerging urban economy. In 1890, newspaper editor Horace Greeley remarked, "We cannot all live in cities, yet nearly all seem determined to do so."

Despite all the signs of economic growth and prosperity, America's late nineteenth-century economy was profoundly unstable. Industrial expansion was undercut by a depression from 1882 to 1885, followed in 1893 by a five-year-long economic collapse that devastated rural and urban communities across America. As a result, job security for workers just climbing onto the industrial stage was often fleeting. Few wage earners found full-time work for the entire year. The unevenness in the economy was caused both by the level of change under way and irresponsible speculation, but more generally to the stubborn adherence of the federal government to a highly inflexible gold standard as the basis of value for currency.

Between the very wealthy and the very poor emerged a new middle stratum, whose appearance was one of the distinctive features of late nineteenth-century America. The new middle class fueled the purchase of one million light bulbs a year by 1890, even though the first electric light was only 11 years old. It was the middle class, too, that flocked to buy Royal Baking Powder (which was easier to use and faster than yeast) and supported the emergence and spread of department stores that were sprouting up across the nation.

1883 PROFILE

James Raubach, who lived on a stipend from his father, continually angered and frustrated his parents, who wanted him to settle down, marry, and get serious about his life rather than waste his time playing lawn tennis.

Life at Home

- Twenty-seven-year-old James Raubach lived a life built around one overriding passion: lawn tennis.
- His mother wanted to know why he was not married.
- His father, Frank, was seething that his only son, instead of using his fancy Ivy League education on the nobleness of work, preferred the silliness of play.
- James's older sister, who devoted her time to dresses and fancy balls, always inquired why she doesn't see him at the more fashionable balls.
- Only his younger sister noticed that he was only happy when playing tennis with his friends.
- His father had made his money through hard work in the green grocery business and was lucky enough to pull out of the stock market one month prior to the Panic of 1873 that lasted six years.
- As a result, he had sufficient capital to buy up his competitors and monopolize the wholesale food market in New England.
- But no amount of successful business could distract Frank Raubach from what he saw as his son's complete lack of interest in anything but tennis.
- James had repeatedly told his father that he would settle down and find a girl to marry, but it was hard when all of the British nobility kept coming to America to marry the most eligible girls.

James Raubach preferred playing tennis to just about anything else.

James was only happy when playing tennis with friends.

- Frank told his son that he might have a better chance of finding a girl if he wasn't so busy with his tennis club all the time.
- He had also hinted that unless James settled down, married and got a job, his stipend would end sooner rather than later.
- James's father demanded that he attend the Vanderbilts' ball, known to attract a large number of eligible young ladies.
- Several years earlier, James had bought a house in Harlem on 116th St., a prosperous area where he could live easily off the stipend of $800 his father sent him once a month.
- Thanks to the elevated railroads, installed in Harlem in 1880, an increasing number of people were moving into the area.
- The train also allowed James to get to his club without having to hire a carriage, which made his money go much further.
- He was careful with his allowance.
- He didn't even consider trying any of Mr. Edison's new light bulbs because the cost would force him to get a job.
- James rarely drank, though he did go out with his friends after matches to the bars.
- He rarely dated the women who fluttered around him.
- Before lawn tennis, James' passion was cricket.
- Now he believed tennis was far more dynamic than cricket and had a better chance of success in the United States.

Life at Work

- James Raubach was a founding member of the United States National Lawn Tennis Association, which was a merger of the New York, Boston, and Philadelphia Lawn Tennis Clubs.
- The first meeting of the National Lawn Tennis Association was held at the Fifth Avenue Hotel, New York, on May 21, 1881.
- The impetus for the founding was the inconsistent rules and equipment used around the country.
- These problems became manifest in the 1880 lawn tennis tournament held on Staten Island by the Staten Island Cricket and Baseball Club on September 1.
- The *Richmond County Sentinel* wrote about the tournament, "It will no doubt furnish quite a good deal of amusement to Staten Islanders to see able-bodied men playing this silly game."
- The prize was a silver cup engraved with "The Champion Lawn-Tennis Player of America," worth about $100.
- The first problem arose over the size of the ball.
- Two members of the Beacon Park Athletic Association in Boston complained that the ball, manufactured by Ayres of England, was two-thirds the size of the ball they played with in Boston.
- The judges pointed out that the ball had "Regulation" stitched on it, and that if the two gentlemen did not wish to use the ball, they could pull out of the tournament.
- Another argument erupted about the scoring method of counting to 15, that had been taken from the game of rackets.
- The height of the net caused another argument.
- Afterwards, the National Lawn Tennis Association was created in part to codify the rules of the game.
- Thirty-six delegates, who represented 19 clubs directly, and 16 more by proxy, gathered to inaugurate the association.
- James was a member of the Country Club of Westchester County on 59th Street.
- They decided to hold a national championship in Newport, Rhode Island.
- This was far more successful, although unlike the previous tournament, was open only to club members, not to the public.
- They avoided controversy before the game, announcing that the Ayres ball would still be used.
- The singles game was won by R. D. Sears, an innovator who played the game differently than most.
- Traditionally, players stood close to the net, but Sears played back near the serving line.
- This allowed him more time to reach a ball hit to him and return it.
- James said that it was the most exhausting game of tennis he had ever played, and spent much of the rest of the singles tournament studying Sears's game.
- Since then James had entered every tournament he could, though he never placed very high.
- He thought it was important to check his game against the best in the country.
- It was very hard to practice regularly in the winter because there were very few indoor tennis courts in the country.
- Some were set up in empty halls and armories, but there were almost no covered courts as there were in England.
- He tried to convince his father to let him and his friends practice in his house, but was never successful.
- The next tournament was played at the Newport Casino.

James and his friends believed New York was the place for high society.

- There were still some rumblings about the rules, including the size of the ball and location of the tournaments.
- These issues were expected to be voted on within a few years.

Life in the Community: New York City

- James Raubach and his friends believed New York was the premier city for high society in the nineteenth century: Boston was too insular, Philadelphia had been passed by in the commercial revolution; Washington, DC better served its poor.
- New York had grown very quickly since 1845 when there were only 25 millionaires.
- In 1883, New York City resident John Jacob Astor was the richest man in the United States, with a personal wealth of $25 million.
- The Raubachs where on the margins of this society, having the money but not having made it in that accepted way.
- Frank envisioned that James would marry well and launch the family into full acceptance into society.
- Most upper-class strivers wanted to be part of "The 400," those who were seen at one of Mrs. Astor's balls.
- 400 was the number of people who could comfortably fit into her ballroom, although twice that number were invited to certain parties.
- In 1883, the Vanderbilts put a crimp in Mrs. Astor's domination of the city's elite in a particularly ingenious and expensive way.
- Mrs. Astor had never invited the Vanderbilt girls to any of her balls, even though Mr. Vanderbilt was one of the richest men in New York.
- They were not the right type of people for Mrs. Astor.
- Finally, the Vanderbilts decided to force their way into this high society, by putting on an expensive and luxurious ball of their own.
- It is rumored that the ball cost more than $250,000.
- It was to be the event of the year, expected to compare to the Prince of Wales ball in 1860.
- Mrs. Astor and her daughter were not invited.
- When Mrs. Astor's daughter inquired as to why, she was told that Mrs. Vanderbilt had not had the pleasure of meeting the young girl or her mother.
- In response, a coach was immediately sent for, and the Astors raced to the Vanderbilts' home to pay their respects.
- An invitation was then sent.
- New York had the most gentleman's clubs of any city in the United States.
- Each had its own rules of behavior and many had strict caps on the number of men who could join.
- The Manhattan Club, for members of the Democratic party, stopped accepting members at 600.

Mrs. Astor was famous for her balls for the elite of New York City.

- The creation of these clubs was driven by the explosion of new money.
- When just anyone could make a million dollars, personal wealth was no longer a reliable way to tell who was worthy of being at the top of the social strata.
- Seemingly, every movement of this social class was chronicled in the papers, including parties and invitation lists.
- *The Police Gazette*, taken over by Richard Kyle Fox, a man described as one who knew how to hate, served up an endless supply of upper-class gossip and titillation.
- The city was still reeling from the revolt against Tammany Hall in October of 1881, when the nomination process was changed from a select group of 25 power brokers to over 600 delegates.
- Tammany Hall had controlled New York City politics since the Civil War.
- People hoped that the corruption in New York City government might lessen now that the nomination process had changed.
- Grover Cleveland had become governor of the state in 1882, and there were whispers that he might run for president in the next election.
- A gift from France, the Statue of Liberty was originally slated for completion in 1876 for the Centennial but now it was not expected until some time around 1885, though some worried that the base still would not be built by then.
- The fundraising for the Statue of Liberty's base had been going so slowly that Joseph Pulitzer wrote an op-ed piece in *The World* complaining that the rich were not bearing their share of the cost.
- To help raise money for the project, Emma Lazarus's poem, "The New Colossus," was solicited for an auction of artwork staged by the "Art Loan Fund Exhibition in Aid of the Bartholdi Pedestal Fund for the Statue of Liberty."
- But the statue was only one of several major projects underway.
- After 13 years of construction, the $16 million Brooklyn Bridge was expected to finally connect Manhattan to Brooklyn.
- Twenty lives were lost in the construction of the great bridge, which rose 276 feet into the air.
- Its 86-foot-wide surface accommodated two outer roadways for horse-drawn vehicles, two tracks for trains, and a center walk for foot traffic.
- Showman P. T. Barnum led 21 of his elephants across the span on opening day to assure spectators of its safety and to publicize his circus.
- Only days after the opening ceremony, 12 people were killed in a stampede on the crowded bridge when a rumor circulated that the bridge was about to collapse.
- Electricity was becoming more common in the city, and telegraph and electrical wires between the buildings were hung so thickly that many were afraid the wires would collapse from their own weight.
- Edison had recently completed his filament light bulb to delight of the city's rich.
- On September 4, 1882, Edison finished his new power plant and lit 800 lamps and 50 square blocks of lower Manhattan.
- Orders poured in for Edison to electrify private houses in order for people have the new electric light.

Most of New York's upper class wanted to be seen at one of Mrs. Astor's balls.

HISTORICAL SNAPSHOT
1883

- The Pendleton Civil Service Reform Act established a merit system, including examinations, and the Civil Service Commission worked to end federal employment abuses
- Former Confederate Vice President Alexander H. Stephens was elected governor of Georgia
- The U.S. Supreme Court ruled that the Fourteenth Amendment barred discriminatory action by the states, not by private individuals, rendering two sections of the Civil Rights Act of 1875 unconstitutional
- Abolitionist Sojourner Truth died at Battle Creek, Michigan, at age 86
- Oregon newspaper publisher Abigail Duniway persuaded the state legislature to approve a constitutional amendment providing for woman suffrage, but voters rejected the measure
- U.S. clergymen and liberals organized The Friends of the Indian and held their first conference at the Mohonk Mountain House in New York's Shawangunk Mountains
- New Jersey became the first state to legalize labor unions
- George Westinghouse pioneered control systems for long-distance natural gas pipelines and for town gas-distribution networks
- John D. Rockefeller's Standard Oil Trust monopoly absorbed Tidewater Pipe, bringing the trust's holdings to 20,000 wells, employing 100,000 people
- The Brooklyn Elevated Railroad brought railway service for the first time to America's second-largest city
- The Northern Pacific Railroad was completed with a ceremony at Gold Creek in Montana Territory after 13 years of work
- Chicago meatpacker Philip D. Armour created Armour Car Lines
- U.S. railroads adopted standard time beginning at noon, November 18, as telegraph lines transmitted time signals to all major cities; the decision eliminated more than 100 local time zones
- California-born engineer John Montgomery built a gull-winged glider and made a controlled flight in a heavier-than-air craft
- A machine patented by Massachusetts inventor Jan Matzeliger permitted the upper portions of shoes to be shaped mechanically rather than by hand
- Engineer Hiram S. Maxim patented the first fully automatic machine gun
- *Science* magazine began publication with the backing of Alexander Graham Bell and his father-in-law, Gardiner G. Hubbard
- Robert Koch developed a preventive inoculation against anthrax
- The first direct telegraphic service between the United States and Brazil began
- Thomas Edison pioneered the radio tube with a method for passing electricity from a filament to a plate of metal inside an incandescent light globe
- Joseph Pulitzer of the *St. Louis Post-Dispatch* acquired the *New York World* from Jay Gould
- *Giti, Ladies' Home Journal* and *Life,* a humor magazine, began publication
- More than 3,000 Remington typewriters were sold, up from about 2,350 the previous year
- *Treasure Island* by Robert Louis Stevenson was published

Selected Prices

Bicycle, Columbia. $75.00
Boudoir Safe $100.00
Horse Muzzle $2.50
Illinois Central Railroad Round-Trip $0.25
Lottery Ticket, $30,000 Prize $2.00
Mother's Friend Liniment $1.00
Oil Paint, Tube $0.05
Pistol $20.00
Tooth Extraction $0.25
Tuition, Law School, Two Years $200.00

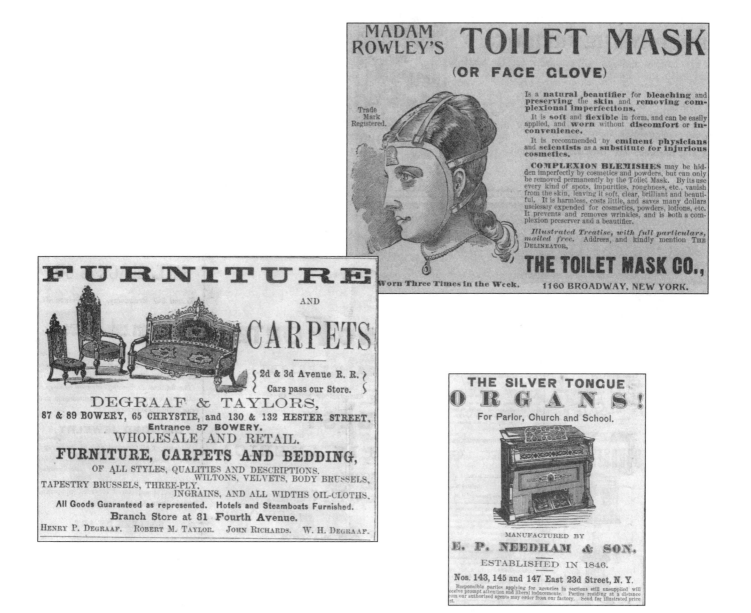

"Croquet and Lawn-Tennis," *Indiana Weekly Messenger* (Pennsylvania), January 11, 1882:

Croquet has lost its popularity, and it is only in remote western towns that one can hear the click of the mallet as it strikes some ball or head or the wail of some too eager girl who has smashed her own foot. Elsewhere croquet has not been played for nearly two years. The croquet mallet has been turned into the beanpole, and the balls have been thrown at vagrant dogs, so that of the 11 million croquet sets formally in the possession of private citizens of the United States, there are now not more than 63 sets which are fit for use.

The disappearance of this pestilent game is a great gain for the cause of morality and public order. Next to horse-dealing, which, according to the Westminster Catechism, "worketh the corruption of the whole nature of him who sells horses," croquet has a far more withering and blasting effect upon what is good in human nature than any other agency. It leads to lying almost as certainly as does trout-fishing. Mr. Herbert Spencer, in his tables and social statistics, asserts that 82 per cent of all ladies who play croquet will systematically claim to have passed hoops they have not passed, and 90 per cent will insist they never stirred the ball which received the stroke of the mallet in that peculiar feat called "croqueting." Of course, those who habitually indulge in flights of the imagination to put it mildly such as those who must inevitably lose all respect for the truth. They who cheat their lovers at croquet will find it easy to deceive their husbands in the game of married life. From cheating to quarreling which in croquet is short and inevitable. In nine games out of every 10 the recording angel is compelled to take notice that Miss Smith has audibly mentioned "it is pretty sickening to see how that Brown girl cheats," and that Miss Brown has openly called Miss Robinson a "mean and hateful thing." In its latter days croquet was characterized not merely by cheating and bad language but by assassination. It was so easy for a quick-tempered and indignant girl to hit her partner over the shins as a rebuke for his bad play, or to strike a faithless lover over the head who had formed a partnership with a hated rival, and perhaps defended her from the accusation of cheating, that mallet outrages became frightfully prevalent. In England alone, in the year 1879, seven had their skulls fractured, 194 were seriously bruised, either in one or both shins, and 605 young ladies were hit in the region of the shoes by mallets thrown by other young ladies. I like to say the state of things existed about the same time in this country, but in the absence of trustworthy statistics it can only be said that all proportion of mallet outrages is as great here as in England. It was this terrible feature of the game which caused a general uprising of all good citizens against it, and led to this substitution of lawn tennis in its place.

The peculiar feature of lawn-tennis is the net which is stretched between the players with a view of preventing adversaries from assaulting one another. The players use a light ball, with which it is impossible to inflict any serious injury, and instead of clubs they play with instruments somewhat resembling the battledore of the last generation, and unfit for offensive purposes except, perhaps, in connection with very young children. The game has commended itself to parents and peaceable people by its apparent safety, and so far it has certainly been unstained by any murderous affrays. Still, it must be evident to everyone that the net commonly used is far too frail. It could be broken down by the rush of a heavy girl, and it would be easy for an agile girl to climb over it. If lawn-tennis is to maintain its reputation as a safe and peaceful game, the net should be made of wire instead of twine; it should be at least a foot higher, and the upper edge should be strewn with broken glass laid in cement or furnished with sharp iron spikes. Sooner or later some mild and imbecile player will madden his adversary to such an extent that nothing but personal violence will be any comfort to her, and she will get over or through the frail twine net with a suddenness that will dazzle the unhappy victim.

"Caught in the Act, The curiosities of pictures of the movements of men and animals," *The New York Times*, June 10, 1883:

Eadweard Muybridge spoke last evening of the "romance and reality of animals and locomotion" to a large and enthusiastic audience in the hall of Union League Club. The lecture was illustrated by stereopticon and zoopraxiscope pictures thrown on a screen and representing horses in motion while trotting, running, and leaping, and oxen, deer, dogs, hounds, and other animals taken while in motion. Similar pictures of men boxing, wrestling, fencing, tumbling, and engaging in various athletic sports were also shown. The practical value of the pictures was shown by the zoopraxiscope, by which the series of pictures instantaneously taken actually reproduced on canvas the gaits of various animals and the movements of men while boxing, jumping, and tumbling.

"Sporting Shot from Iron," *The Cedar Rapids Evening Gazette*, (Iowa) January 12, 1883:

A company has been formed in Iowa for the purpose of manufacturing sporting shot from iron. It is stated that the trials which have been made of the shot have proven it to be fully equal and in some respects superior to lead shot. No tower is required, as the shot is made by the process with less than three feet drop. The company is nearly ready to put the new manufacture into the market, and, as it can be sold at a much lower price than lead shot, the demand will probably soon assume large proportions. It is stated that the iron shot looks well and cannot be distinguished from lead shot by inspection.

"A Losing Book Concern, The American Book Exchange in a Receivers Hands," *The New York Times*, November 27, 1881:

During the past two or three months rumors have been current in business circles of the financial unsoundness of the American Book Exchange, and yesterday the truthfulness of the rumors was demonstrated by the appointment of a receiver for the company. The exact amount of the liabilities is not stated, and there are conflicting reports as to the ability of the managers of the company to extricate themselves from this financial embarrassment. It is conceded by those who are in a position to know all the facts that the Exchange has, since its organization, been doing a very large business on comparatively small capital, and the fact that all of its numerous publications have been put upon the market at extraordinarily low prices has not only aroused the animosity of many rival publishers, but has given rise to quite a general belief that no money is being made by the company.

Other Business Troubles

Dispatches were received in this city yesterday announcing the failure of the well-known house of Dumas and Allen, dealers in cotton and guano, at Forsythe, Georgia. The house was established many years ago, and they did a very large business. They owned a warehouse and real estate valued at $80,000. They owe considerably more in New York, but the full amount of the liabilities is not definitely known.

Reports from St. Louis state that the Missouri Zinc Company had been placed in the hands of Lucian Eaton as receiver. The company was incorporated in 1809 with a capital of $100,000 and eventually was controlled by Messrs. Eaton and Thomas T. Richards, who became the principal owners. Since the suicide of Thomas T. Richards in May, the affairs of the concern have been in bad shape and culminated in the appointment of a receiver.

"Mrs. W. K. Vanderbilt's Great Fancy Dress Ball,"
The New York Times, March 27, 1883:

The Vanderbilt ball has agitated New York society more than any social event that has occurred here in many years. Since the announcement that it would take place, which was made about a week before the beginning of Lent, scarcely anything else has been talked about. It has been on every tongue and a fixed idea in every head. It has disturbed the sleep and occupied the waking hours of social butterflies, both male and female, for over six weeks, and has even, perhaps, interfered to some extent with that rigid observance of Lenten devotions which the Church exacts. Amid the rush and excitement of business, men have found their minds haunted by uncontrollable thoughts as to whether they should appear as Robert le Diable, Cardinal Richelieu, Otho the barbarian, or the Count of Monte Cristo, while the ladies have been driven to the verge of distraction in the effort to settle the comparative advantages of ancient, medieval, and modern costumes, or the relative superiority, from an effective point of view, of such characters and symbolic representations as Princess de Croy, Rachel, Mary Stuart, Marie Antoinette, the Four Seasons, Night, Morning, Innocence, and the Electric Light. Invitations have, of course, been in great demand, and in all about 1,200 were issued.

As Lent drew to a close, everybody having decided what he or she was going to wear, the attention of the select few turned from the question of costumes to the settlement of the details of the ball itself and the practicing of the parts assigned to them in the various fancy quadrilles decided on to make the most conspicuous features of the entertainment. The drilling in these quadrilles has been going on assiduously in Mrs. William Astor's and other private residences for more than a week, while prospective guests not so favored as to be able to witness these preliminary entertainments have had to content themselves with recounting such items of information as could be extracted from the initiated. As early as 7 o'clock last evening, although the ball was not to begin until 11, gentlemen returning from the hair-dressers' with profusely powdered heads were to be seen alighting from coupes along Fifth Avenue, and hurrying up the steps of their residences to complete their toilets. About the same time the passage up the avenue of an express wagon containing the horses for the hobby-horse quadrille attracted a great deal of attention. By 8 o'clock a large crowd of inquisitive loungers was collected in Fifth Avenue and Fifty-second Street watching Mr. Vanderbilt's brilliantly illuminated residence and a group of workmen putting up the awning before the entrance. Inside, long before the ball commenced, the house was in a blaze of light, which shown upon profuse decorations of flowers. These, which were by Klunder, were at once novel and imposing. They were confined chiefly to the second floor, although throughout the hall and parlors on the first floor, were distributed in vases and gilded baskets filled with natural roses of extraordinary size, such as the dark crimson Jacqueminot, the deep pink Glorie de Paris, the pale pink Baroness de Rothschild and Adolphe de Rothschild, the King of Morocco; the Duchess of Kent and the new and beautiful Marie Louise Vassey, but a delightful surprise greeted the guests upon the second floor, as they reached the head of the grand stairway. Grouped around the clustered columns which ornament either side of the stately hall were tall palms overtopping a dense mass of ferns and ornamental grasses, while suspended between the capitals of the columns were strings of variegated Japanese lanterns. Entered through this hall is the gymnasium, a spacious apartment, where supper was served on numerous small tables. But it had not the appearance of an apartment last night; it was like a garden in a tropical forest. The walls were nowhere to be seen, but in their places an impenetrable thicket of fern above fern and palm above palm, while from the branches of the palms hung a profusion of lovely orchids, displaying a rich variety of color and an almost endless variation of fantastic forms. In the centre of the room was a gigantic palm, upon whose umbrageous head rested a thick cluster of that beautiful Cuban vine, vougen villa, which trailed from the dome in the centre of the ceiling.

To make the resemblance to a garden more complete, two beautiful fountains played in opposite corners of the apartment. The doors of the apartment, thrown back against the walls, were completely covered with roses and lilies of the valley.

continued

"Mrs. W. K. Vanderbilt's Great Fancy Dress Ball," . . . *(continued)*

The scene outside the brilliantly lighted mansion, as the guests began to arrive, was novel and interesting. Early in the evening a squad of police officers arrived to keep the expected crowd of sightseers in order and to direct the movements of drivers and cabmen. Before 10 o'clock men and women were wandering about the streets outside of the house and glancing at the windows, or peering under the double canopies which led up to the door. They took up positions on the steps of the houses opposite or stood on the adjacent corners waiting for the carriages to arrive, and then all who could obtain room on the sidewalks crowded at the outsides of the canopies and gazed curiously and enviously at the gorgeously costumed gentlemen and ladies whom the ushers assisted to alight. Carriages containing the more youthful and impatient of the maskers drove past the mansion before 10:30 o'clock, the occupant peering surreptitiously under the curtain to see if others were arriving as he rolled by.

Carriages drove slowly by while the ladies and gentlemen in them, who were not in costume, gazed out of the windows and at the crowds about the house, indicating that curiosity was not confined to the humble walks of life entirely. At 11 o'clock the maskers began to arrive in numbers, and the eager lookers-on in the street were able to catch glimpses through the windows of flashing sword hilts, gay costumes, beautiful flowers, and excited faces. Handsome women and dignified men were assisted from the carriages in their fanciful costumes, over which were thrown shawls, Ulster's and light wraps. Pretty and excited girls and young men, who made desperate efforts to appear blasé, were seen to descend and run up the steps into the brilliantly lighted hall. Club men who looked bored arrived singly and in pairs and quartets, in hired cabs, and whole families drove up in elegant equipages with liveried coachmen and footmen. A great many ladies were accompanied by their maids, who were not allowed to leave the carriages, whereat there was some grumbling. Gentlemen's valets were treated in the same manner, and the ushers insisted that these orders were imperative. At 11:30 o'clock the throng of carriages before the mansion and waiting at the corners was so great that the utmost efforts of the police were necessary to keep the line in order, and many gentlemen left their carriages in adjacent streets and walked up to the canopy which was the entrance to the fairyland. Most of the gentlemen gave orders to their coachmen to call for them at 3 o'clock. Others made the hour as late as 4, and some of the more seasoned and wiser party-goers ordered their carriages as early as 1 and 2 o'clock. The guests had all arrived, save a few stragglers, at midnight, and the crowd began to disperse. A few still remained to wander about in the vicinity of the house, or to gaze into the area windows or up to the more brilliant plate-glass in the stories above. At 1 the police were the sole occupants of the street before the house, with the exception of an occasional wandering belated pedestrian.

The guests on arriving found themselves in a grand hall about 65 feet long, 16 feet in height, and 20 feet in width. Under foot was a floor of polished and luminous Echallion stone, and above them a ceiling richly paneled in oak. Over a high wainscoting of Caen stone, richly carved, are antique Italian tapestries, beautifully worked by hand. Out of this hall to the right rises the grand stairway, which is not only the finest piece of work of its kind in this country, but one of the finest in the world. The stairway occupies a space 30 feet square, the whole structure of the stairway being of the finest Caen stone, carved with wonderful delicacy and vigor. It climbs by ample easy stages to a height of 50 feet, ending in a pendentive dome. Another stairway, also in Caen stone, leading from the second to the third story, is seen through a rampant arch, with an effect which recalls the unique and glorious stairway of the Chateau of Chambord. In the gymnasium, on the third floor, a most beautiful apartment, 50 feet in length by 35 in width, the members of the six organized quadrilles of the evening gradually assembled before 11 o'clock. Lots were drawn Saturday last by the ladies in charge of those quadrilles to decide the order in which they should be danced, it being previously agreed that the ball should be opened by the "Hobby-horse Quadrille," a fantastic set, under the leadership of Mrs. S.S. Howland and Mr. James V. Parker, to which by common consent the privilege was assigned of filling the scene for five minutes and no more.

continued

"Mrs. W. K. Vanderbilt's Great Fancy Dress Ball," . . . *(continued)*

The first place among the more picturesque quadrilles was drawn by the "Mother Goose Quadrille," under the leadership of Mrs. Lawrence Perkins. At a little after 11 o'clock, to the strains of Gilmore's Band, the six quadrilles, comprising in all nearly a hundred ladies and gentlemen, were formed in order in the gymnasium and began to move in a glittering processional pageant down the grand stairway and through the hall.

Winding through the motley crowd of princes, monks, cavaliers, highlanders, queens, kings, dairymaids, bull-fighters, knights, brigands, and nobles, the procession passed down the grand stairway and through the hall into a noble room on the front of the house in the style of Francois Premier, 25 feet in width by 40 in length, wainscoted richly and heavily in carved French walnut and hung in dark red plush. Vast carved cabinets and an immense, deep fire-place give an air of antique grandeur to this room, from which the procession passed into a bright and charming salon of the style of Louis XV, 30 feet in width by 35 in length, wainscoted in oak and enriched with carved work and gilding. The whole wainscoting of this beautiful apartment was brought from a chateau in France. On the walls hang three French-Gobelin tapestries a century old, but in the brilliance and freshness of their coloring seemingly the work of yesterday, and over the chimney-piece hangs a superb portrait of Mrs. Vanderbilt by Madrazo, full of spirit, character, and grace. . . .

"The Education of Children, Importance of Physical Training in Schools," *The Spirit of the Times*, September 15, 1877:

We believe that no system of education can be called complete which does not include physical training as one of its principal branches. The importance of helpful exercise is more generally recognized in the United States now than formerly, and we were gratified recently to hear that a grave professor had thrown his hat in the air in a transport of delight upon learning that his college crew had won a boat race at Saratoga. This proceeding might be considered undignified, but it was much more sensible than if he had frowned upon the enthusiasm of the students for manly and improved exercise. Nearly all the leading colleges of this country have regularly organized rowing clubs, and endeavor to obtain the best possible training. Some of them, we are glad to see, have adopted the rifle as a means of amusement; and no doubt, in a few years, will produce some of the most proficient marksmen in the country. Yet, with all the tendency to outdoor sports, their value as a part of the systematic education is not appreciated as it should be. Rowing and rifle shooting are, comparatively, luxuries only to be enjoyed by young men in college, and are practically beyond the means of the great majority of boys in ordinary schools. Their physical education may be said to be altogether neglected so far as any proper system of teaching is concerned, and depends entirely upon their own inclinations and limited opportunities. How many schools are there in which the master gives the least thought to the bodily health of his pupils, who sit in badly ventilated rooms for hours, deprived of that exercise which is the only relaxation from study? It is not enough to pretend that the boy can play when released from school, for it is not merely play that he wants but muscular development by regular and systematic training. The country boy finds compensation for this want in fishing, riding, farm work, and out-of-door habits generally, but the city boy, as a rule, is without it. Therefore, at the end of the school term, parents are compelled to send pale and sickly children out of town to regain the health they have lost in months of ill-regulated study.

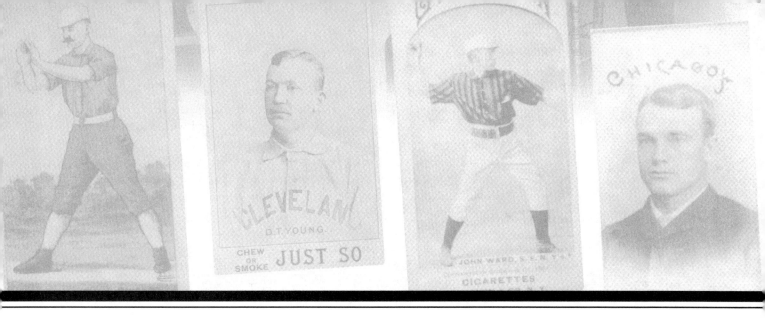

1888 Profile

Mike Kelly experienced a meteoric rise from being an Irish orphan to becoming a legendary baseball hero.

Life at Home

- Mike Kelly's birth in 1857 coincided with the formation of the first legitimate baseball league, the National Association of Base Ball Players.
- For Mike it was a good omen.
- It was also the beginning of a cult of masculinity in America, when men learned new codes of sexuality and competitive sports.
- His parents, Michael Kelly Sr. and Catherine, were members of the Irish famine exodus of nearly one million people, who found a fresh start in the New World.
- Like more than 550,000 Irish immigrants before them, they endured the laughter of Americans when they first stepped off a ship wearing clothes 20 years out of fashion.
- The couple settled in Troy, New York, around other Irish families, where their son was born.
- Unlike other nationalities that came to America seeking open spaces, the Irish chose to huddle in cities, attempting to re-create the close-knit communities they cherished back in Ireland.
- Along with 140,000 other Irish men, Mike's father joined the Union Army in the Civil War when Mike could barely walk, and fought until the war's conclusion in 1865.
- During the war years, the family moved to Washington, DC, so Mike could attend school; there Mike first played baseball.
- After the war was over, Mike's father fell ill and moved the family to Patterson, New Jersey, when Mike was 11 years old.
- Mike Sr. hoped that the climate of New Jersey, coupled with better work in the thriving town, would help speed his recovery.

Mike "King" Kelly

Outfielder/Catcher/Manager

Mike Kelly went from Irish orphan to baseball star in record speed.

17

Ready-made baseballs were hard to come by.

- He never recovered, though, and died a little over a year after moving to Patterson; Catherine became sick as well, and died less than a year after her husband.
- Orphaned, Mike worked during the summers and stayed with a family friend so he could continue attending school and playing baseball.
- Often the baseballs themselves were made from shreds of India rubber wrapped with yarn from a stocking and covered with pieces of an ordinary glove; ready-made baseballs were scarce and much cherished when one could be found.
- A store-bought Willow Wand bat with the words "Home Run" printed in red letters cost $0.15 and was used by both teams.
- No one wore gloves, not even the catcher.
- To support himself, Mike took a job in a textile mill carrying baskets of coal to the top floor for the foreman; Mike could complete the work in a morning and still earn a day's wages.
- He could then spend the rest of his time on the ball field, catching bare-handed and honing his skills.
- That summer, Mike got his first taste of theater when he opened up a playhouse in the cellar of a friend's home.
- A mechanical failure almost killed Mike's friend, Jim McCormick, and slowed the adventure, but not Mike's passion for the vaudeville stage.
- At age 15, the Irish orphan was good enough at baseball to be invited to play on a semi-professional team, the Patterson Keystones, organized by his theater friend's father.
- During his time on the Keystones, Mike played as much baseball as he wanted and was paid a small wage for it, too.

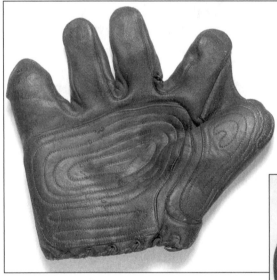

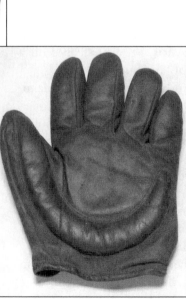

No one on Mike's neighborhood team wore gloves.

- He didn't quit his morning job carrying coal until he was 20 years old, when he was signed to the Cincinnati Red Stockings, the first professional team to pay all of its players.
- Baseball was well rooted into the American culture by 1877.
- Most fans believed baseball to have been invented by General Abner Doubleday in 1839, when in reality it was the culmination of several different games dating back to the 1700s.
- A similar game, rounders, was played at roughly the same time in America, in which the ball was bowled, not pitched, and the batter had to carry the bat while rounding the bases or he was out.
- Baseball was one of the few spectator sports, besides boxing and horse racing, regularly attended by factory workers; the elite leaned toward lawn tennis, croquet, and archery.
- A family-friendly sport, unlike boxing, baseball was attended en masse by many Americans on leisurely Saturday afternoons.
- Its popularity was sufficient to elicit sermons in Protestant churches nationwide, condemning the playing or watching of baseball on Sundays.
- For America's Catholics, baseball was was less of an issue and often followed Sunday services.
- Due to the simplicity of the equipment, baseball was just as accessible to the poor as to the rich; it differed from such sports as tennis or golf, which required special equipment that needed to be purchased.
- Any boy could make a bat out of a decent-sized branch; finding twine and tape for a ball was fairly easy as well.
- Friends would gather in any open field or city street, and a ball game would begin.
- Such was the popularity of baseball that occasionally a shopkeeper might leave the store for an hour to watch the game down the street.
- Even the police were known to take time off their beat to view a good match.
- The winners of a professional game were treated like heroes by their hometown, and afforded respect by the citizens of other towns and cities.
- While playing his first years in Cincinnati, Ohio, Mike developed his skills at catching, which would earn him a reputation as an innovative player, and a handsome paycheck as well.
- The rules of baseball never really concerned Mike, who bent, and even broke the rules to gain the upper hand.
- He paid even less attention to the unwritten rules, and was always waiting for the umpire to turn his back.
- He was also skilled at reading the opposing pitcher, which allowed him to steal bases with deft efficiency.
- Occasionally he would even steal third base from first base without ever even touching second, and then challenge the umpire to show him the rule that prohibited the maneuver.
- His base stealing repertoire also included taking a base by force, sliding high with one leg in an attacking position toward an opposing baseman.
- This slide became one of Kelly's trademarks.

Life at Work

- As a member of the Cincinnati Red Stockings, Mike Kelly was able to play the game he loved, rent his own place for the first time, and pursue acting again.
- Life was good and he did well.

Baseball uniform from the 1880s.

- After a few years in Cincinnati, Cap Anson recruited Mike to the powerhouse team, the Chicago White Stockings.
- Anson taught Mike the value of training well and remaining in shape.
- Mike tried to teach Anson the value of a day's leisure and a healthy pint of ale, without success.
- Nevertheless, they developed a close friendship, and in his autobiography, Mike had nothing but respectful memories of Anson's honest practices and hardworking nature.
- Anson, too, was a baseball innovator, installing baseball fundamentals such as using a third-base coach, having one fielder back up another, signaling batters, and the rotation of two star pitchers to rest their arms.
- Aided by speedy players like Mike Kelly, Anson taught his players to aggressively run the bases, forcing the opposition to make errors.
- Anson was among the first to institute spring training and send his club to warmer climates in the South to prepare for the season.
- During his time as a catcher with the White Stockings, Mike set up a series of "signals" with the pitcher, communicated by gestures he made with his hands; the system proved quite effective and caught on with other pitchers in the league.
- He also arranged a similar system with the outfielders, signaling them to move in on their respective base; he would then throw over the baseman's head, right into the hands of the outfielder.
- The runner, believing the ball had been poorly thrown, would then try to steal the next base, where the outfielder would then relay the ball for an easy out.
- During his final season with the White Stockings, after an away game versus the Washington Olympics, he joined his team on a trip to the White House to meet President Grover Cleveland; the Irish orphan described it as one of the highest honors he had ever received.
- That year, he earned the honor of being the best at bat in the National League.
- In Chicago, Mike sought out the gaudiest and loudest hotel in the city, the Palmer House, dubbed fireproof by its owners and an eyesore by its competitors.
- He spent his money effortlessly, buying the best of everything.
- He ate at expensive restaurants and went to some lengths to impress the ladies.
- His clothes were the latest fashions: Italian leather shoes; ascots with weighty brooches; and suits made of the finest materials.
- One journalist wrote that Mike "whirled his cane around like he owned the city."

- His salary was not exorbitant; he only made enough to push him into the upper middle class, but he spent as if he had millions.
- He drank in expensive bars and rubbed shoulders with the high society of Chicago, who often attended balls thrown for the White Stockings after key victories.
- His drinking came to the attention of his team's owner, A.G. Spalding, who hired Pinkerton Detective Agency to tail him off the field and keep tabs on his late-night drinking sprees.
- When confronted by one detective who accused him of drinking lemonade with his friends at three in the morning, Mike indignantly stated: "it was straight whiskey! I've never had a lemonade at that hour in my life!"
- Mike was often the subject of the tabloids' newest stories, which related his late-night escapades in the company of many young women, even though he was a married man.
- His wife didn't mind the tabloids' claims, she said, even if they had some truth to them.
- Mike was a famous man in Chicago, and he brought home good money, to which she was not at all opposed.
- In 1887, he was traded to the Boston Beaneaters for a record $10,000, earning him the title, the Ten Thousand Dollar Beauty.
- In Boston he was paid a record salary for the professional leagues: $5,000 a year, $2,000 for playing on the team and $3,000 for the use of his picture in team advertisements.
- The advertisement fee was an innovation used to bypass the $2,000 salary cap that the National League put on its players.
- Bostonians were overjoyed to have "stolen" this fantastic and sly catcher and presented him with a pair of white stallions and a carriage to take him from his complimentary house to work at the ball field to show their gratitude for him switching teams.
- The mayor himself held a special banquet for Mike and presented him with a gold watch and chain, among other gifts.
- Mike was unaccustomed to this kind of treatment of a baseball player; in Chicago he was grateful to receive a regular salary.
- In Boston, Mike trained hard every day, but spent his nights in bars and saloons.
- When asked by a reporter if he drank during the game, he replied, "It depends on the length of the game."
- For one season, he successfully captained the Beaneaters, but felt the game's best captain would always be Cap Anson.
- In his autobiography Mike said that if he captained half as well as Anson did, it would be a success in his eyes.
- But that did not diminish a friendly rivalry between the Chicago White Stockings and the Boston Beaneaters, fueled by Boston's acquisition of Mike, whom the White Stockings considered to be their star player.
- It seemed the entire community would turn out for a game between the two teams, who would play more fiercely than usual.
- The home team was spurred by crowd noise to greater heights of courage; the visiting team was ignited by spit from the stands.
- While playing with Boston, Mike continued to look for new chances to take advantage of a play or rule.
- During a game against Philadelphia, knowing the rules stated that a player may enter the game on "notice" to the umpire, Mike jumped out from the dugout, yelled to the umpire, "Kelly catching for Boston," and caught the ball for an out.
- Baseball substitution rules were changed as a result.

As a catcher, Mike didn't start wearing a mask until he played in Boston.

- Mike played various positions but made a name for himself as a catcher; when he began, a rubber mouthpiece was the only protection the catcher had against the fastballs heading his way from the pitching mound just 45 feet from the batter.
- By the time Mike arrived in Boston, a catcher's mask had been developed by a player from Harvard to reduce the chances of "disfigurement," and chest protectors were becoming more common.
- During the off-season, Mike often took jobs on vaudeville stages, acting in short bits and reciting poetry, including his favorite, "Casey at the Bat."
- Audiences loved his recitation and many fans imagined Mike as the cocky protagonist of the poem.
- Occasionally, for laughs, he would replace the subjects of the poem with his own name and team.

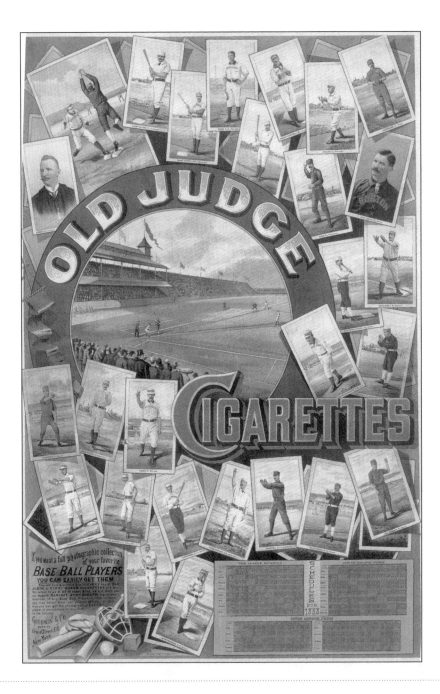

- He loved the laughter of the wintertime theater crowd, which felt different than the whoops and cheers from the baseball grandstands.
- The popularity of both baseball and vaudeville theater were on the rise; cheap productions had very little need for elaborate sets or costumes, so shows could go on at any time.
- That kept the admission cost to a vaudeville production low, and the humor lowbrow.
- Several tobacco companies such as Old Gold Cigarettes began marketing their product using tradable cards depicting baseball players; Mike carried the Allen and Ginter version of himself around for weeks and showed it to everyone.
- The small, sepia-toned photographs were glued onto thick cardboard mounts and distributed widely; over 500 subjects were included—especially the major stars like Mike Kelly, Cap Anson, Connie Mack and Charles Comiskey.
- To further enhance his fame, Mike published his autobiography, the first to be written by a professional athlete.
- Entitled *Play Ball!: Stories of the Ball Field*, the book was introduced and assembled by *Boston Globe* columnist John J. Drohan and published by Emery & Hughes.
- It sold for $0.25 and was published just prior to the 1888 baseball season.
- In the book, Mike retold some of his favorite moments from both baseball and theater, and gave his personal opinion on many of the famous players and managers of the day, most notably Cap Anson.
- He also said that while baseball was an important part of any boy's upbringing, he felt that children ought to stay in school; a good education was the secret to earning a better salary.

Life in the Community: Boston, Massachusetts

- Boston was a thriving city of 350,000 when Mike Kelly was traded from Chicago and became the Ten Thousand Dollar Beauty.
- Bostonians had a rich culture of many different nationalities and ethnicities.
- Visitors to America always sought out Boston, either first or last, in their quest to find a home in the New World.
- Boston's many cultural groups were often at odds with each other, fighting over territorial bounds in the city, politics, and religion.
- War between the Catholics and the Protestants, left behind when they set sail for America, had sparked again, this time between neighbors.
- Featured prominently among the Catholic groups were the Irish.
- The Great Famine of the 1840s and 1850s was still fresh in the minds of many immigrants who had left the Emerald Isle for the freedom of America.
- In 1872, a fire wiped out approximately 776 buildings in the city, destroying countless homes and businesses, and leaving 20 dead and many others wounded.
- This tragedy affected the Irish community more than most, as many Irish-owned businesses were destroyed, putting hundreds of Irish out of work and home.
- Intense adherence to the Catholic faith had helped them through times of need while adapting to the nuances of the New World.
- Their mistrust of Protestants, fueled by their extreme sense of national pride, had caused them to turn to their church for answers.
- The church provided a stern set of rules to be strictly followed no matter the cost.
- The church also presented them with a opening for acting out pent-up aggression through sports.
- The churches would organize baseball and football teams, constituting the first amateur league set up for boys.

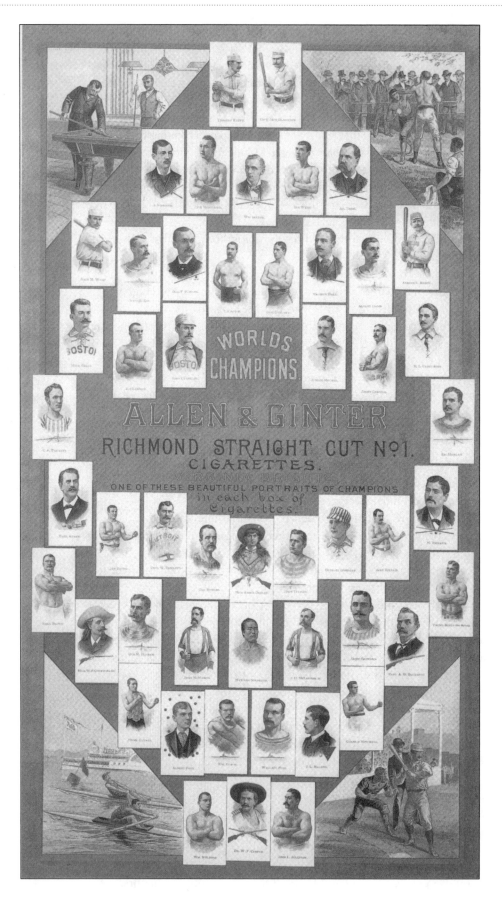

- Many Irish neighborhoods had their own baseball teams by the middle of the 1870s.
- Priests encouraged youths to play sports because it instilled a sense of hard work, fair play, and teamwork.
- It also left room for heroism, a sense self-worth, and a pride in their culture.
- Neighborhood teams staged friendly contests, and often would go to watch the Beaneaters take on challengers from across the country.
- Young Irish boys who came to these games were thrilled by the sly moves and often daring tricks of the catcher, Mike Kelly, whom they saw as an idol.
- Despite their newfound love of baseball, Bostonian Irishmen were becoming increasingly displeased with their unfair treatment, and desired to be further integrated into American society.
- Signs reading "No Irish Need Apply" had been a common sight in Boston, especially during the pre-Civil War era.
- As the Irish gained respect and political power, these signs gradually disappeared, until in 1888 there were barely any left in the city.
- Boston elected their first Irish mayor, Hugh O'Brien, in 1884.
- He was elected again in 1885, and again in 1886 and 1887, when he presented Mike Kelly with his new gold watch and chain, among other presents from the people of Boston.

Baseball was extremely popular in Boston.

SCHLEI, N. Y. NAT'L.   WHEAT, BROOKLYN   COBB, DETROIT

CHANCE, CHICAGO NAT'L   MC GRAW, N. Y. NAT'L   LAJOIE, CLEVELAND   SPEAKER, BOSTON AMER.   KILLIAN, DETROIT

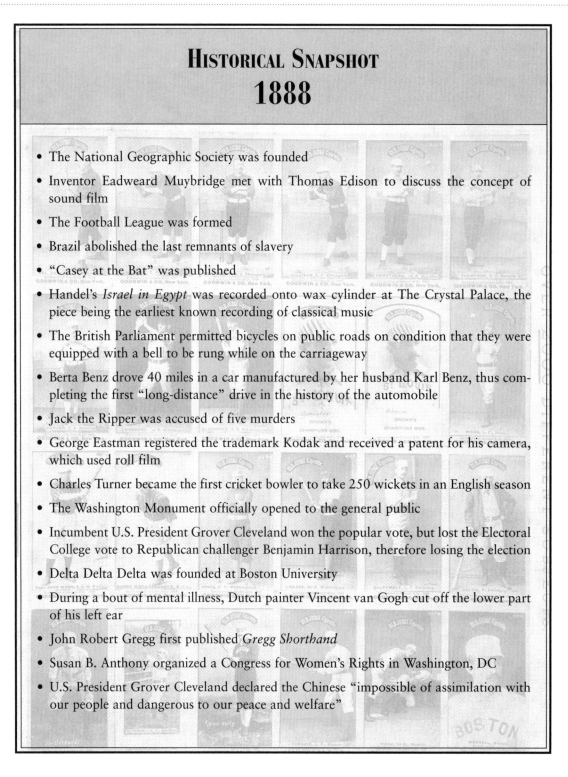

Historical Snapshot
1888

- The National Geographic Society was founded
- Inventor Eadweard Muybridge met with Thomas Edison to discuss the concept of sound film
- The Football League was formed
- Brazil abolished the last remnants of slavery
- "Casey at the Bat" was published
- Handel's *Israel in Egypt* was recorded onto wax cylinder at The Crystal Palace, the piece being the earliest known recording of classical music
- The British Parliament permitted bicycles on public roads on condition that they were equipped with a bell to be rung while on the carriageway
- Berta Benz drove 40 miles in a car manufactured by her husband Karl Benz, thus completing the first "long-distance" drive in the history of the automobile
- Jack the Ripper was accused of five murders
- George Eastman registered the trademark Kodak and received a patent for his camera, which used roll film
- Charles Turner became the first cricket bowler to take 250 wickets in an English season
- The Washington Monument officially opened to the general public
- Incumbent U.S. President Grover Cleveland won the popular vote, but lost the Electoral College vote to Republican challenger Benjamin Harrison, therefore losing the election
- Delta Delta Delta was founded at Boston University
- During a bout of mental illness, Dutch painter Vincent van Gogh cut off the lower part of his left ear
- John Robert Gregg first published *Gregg Shorthand*
- Susan B. Anthony organized a Congress for Women's Rights in Washington, DC
- U.S. President Grover Cleveland declared the Chinese "impossible of assimilation with our people and dangerous to our peace and welfare"

Selected Prices

Baseball Mask	$3.00
Baseball	$1.50
Boxing Gloves	$2.50
Boy's Knee Pants	$1.00
Hotel Room, Cincinnati, Ohio, per Day	$1.00
Men's Shoes, Handmade	$3.00
Men's Suit, Wool	$8.00
Money Belt	$3.00
Pocket Watch	$10.00
Theater Ticket	$0.50

THE POLO GROUNDS NEW YORK

SEASON OF 1887.
HOME GAMES OF THE NEW YORK BALL CLUB FOR THE LEAGUE CHAMPIONSHIP.

April 28, 29,	with Philadelphia,	June 9, 10, 11,	with Washington,	Aug. 22, 23,	with Pittsburg,
May 5, 6, 7,	" Boston,	" 13, 14, 15,	" Philadelphia,	" 25, 26, 27,	" Chicago,
" 9, 10, 11,	" Washington,	July 7, 8, 9,	" Detroit,	" 29, 30, 31,	" Indianapolis,
" 14,	" Philadelphia,	" 11, 12, 13,	" Pittsburg,	Sept. 1, 2, 3,	" Detroit,
" 16, 17, 18,	" Indianapolis,	" 15, 16, 18,	" Chicago.	" 5, 6, 7,	" Washington,
" 20, 21, 23, 24,	" Pittsburg,	" 19, 20, 21,	" Indianapolis,	" 26, 27, 28,	" Boston,
" 26, 27, 28,	" Detroit,	" 23, 25, 26,	" Boston,	Oct. 5, 6, 8.	" Philadelphia
Double by " 30 A.M. & P.M., 31,	" Chicago.				

Letter to Mike Kelly from A.G. Spalding, taken from
Play Ball: Stories of the Diamond Field:

Chicago, Feb. 19,1887.
M. J. Kelly, Hyde Park, N. Y.

Dear Sir—I am in receipt of your picture, in costume and batting position, and the same has been handed to our engraver, with instructions to get out as good a cut as possible for the forthcoming Guide.

I congratulate you on the magnificent salary that I understand you will receive from the Boston club next season, and I hope you will not disappoint them, but will make yourself not only worthy of the amount that you will receive from them, but also of the very large bonus that they have paid the Chicago club for your release. I am just in receipt of a letter from Mr. Billings, from which I quote as follows:

"Kelly did not say a word against you; said the Chicago club was a good one to get money of, when wanted. Anson worked him pretty hard sometimes, when not in condition, and there is where the trouble lies, I think."

I am very glad to know that you have no personal feeling towards me, for I certainly have none towards you, and I do not believe you can truthfully say that either myself or the Chicago club have taken any advantage of you, but have always treated you right and fair. I have placed no credence in the rumors and alleged interviews that have been published in the New York papers, from time to time, knowing, from my own experience, how these interviews are manufactured. As you will, no doubt, be captain of the Boston nine, you will find it necessary, or at least it will be advisable, to set examples to your men in the way of habits and deportment, that will be an incentive for them to follow. . . .

Wishing you every prosperity and success in your new position, I am,

Yours truly,
G. Spalding.

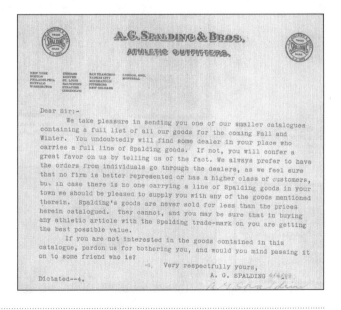

"Casey at the Bat," by Ernest Thayer, 1888

The Outlook wasn't brilliant for the Mudville nine that day:
The score stood four to two, with but one inning
  more to play.
And then when Cooñey died at first, and Barrows
  did the same,
A sickly silence fell upon the patrons of the game.

A straggling few got up to go in deep despair. The rest
Clung to that hope which springs eternal in the
  human breast;
They thought, if only Casey could get but a whack at that,
We'd put up even money, now, with Casey at the bat.

But Flynn preceded Casey, as did also Jimmy Blake,
And the former was a lulu and the latter was a cake;
So upon that stricken multitude grim melancholy sat,
For there seemed but little chance of Casey's getting
  to the bat.

But Flynn let drive a single, to the wonderment of all,
And Blake, the much despis-ed, tore the cover off the ball;
And when the dust had lifted, and the men saw what
  had occurred,
There was Jimmy safe at second and Flynn a-hugging third.

Then from 5,000 throats and more there rose a lusty yell;
It rumbled throuh the valley, it rattled in the dell;
It knocked upon the mountain and recoiled upon the flat,
For Casey, mighty Casey, was advancing to the bat.

There was ease in Casey's manner as he stepped into
  his place;
There was pride in Casey's bearing and a smile on
  Casey's face.
And when, responding to the cheers, he lightly doffed
  his hat,
No stranger in the crowd could doubt 'twas Casey at
  the bat.

Ten thousand eyes were on him as he rubbed his hands
  with dirt;
Five thousand tongues applauded when he wiped them on
  his shirt.
Then while the writhing pitcher ground the ball into his hip,
Defiance gleamed in Casey's eye, a sneer curled Casey's lip.

And now the leather-covered sphere came hurtling through
  the air,
And Casey stood a-watching it in haughty grandeur there.
Close by the sturdy batsman the ball unheeded sped,
"That ain't my style," said Casey. "Strike one," the
  umpire said.

From the benches, black with people, there went up a
  muffled roar,
Like the beating of the storm-waves on a stern and
  distant shore.
"Kill him! Kill the umpire!" shouted someone on the stand;
And it's likely they'd a-killed him had not Casey raised
  his hand.

With a smile of Christian charity great Casey's visage shone;
He stilled the rising tumult; he bade the game go on;
He signaled to the pitcher, and once more the spheroid flew;
But Casey still ignored it, and the umpire said, "Strike two."

"Fraud!" cried the maddened thousands, and echo
  answered fraud;
But one scornful look from Casey and the audience
  was awed.
They saw his face grow stern and cold, they saw his
  muscles strain,
And they knew that Casey wouldn't let that ball go
  by again.

The sneer is gone from Casey's lip, his teeth are clenched
  in hate;
He pounds with cruel violence his bat upon the plate.
And now the pitcher holds the ball, and now he lets it go,
And now the air is shattered by the force of Casey's blow.

Oh, somewhere in this favored land the sun is
  shining bright;
The band is playing somewhere, and somewhere hearts
  are light,
And somewhere men are laughing, and somewhere
  children shout;
But there is no joy in Mudville—mighty Casey has
  struck out.

Baseball Timeline

1700s
Baseball was created by combining rules from other ball games in colonial America.

1791
In Pittsfield, Massachusetts, to promote the safety of the exterior of the newly built meeting house, particularly the windows, a by-law barred "any game of wicket, cricket, baseball, batball, football, cats, fives, or any other game played with ball" within eighty yards of the structure —the first instance of the game of *baseball* being referred to by that name on the North American continent.

1823
A letter in the *National Advocate*, a New York newspaper, refers to "the manly and athletic game of 'base ball'"—16 years before its supposed invention by Abner Doubleday.

1839
Abner Doubleday was credited (falsely) with inventing baseball in Cooperstown, New York.

1856
The New York *Mercury* coined the phrase "the National Pastime."

1857
The National Association of Base Ball Players (NABBP) was formed.

1867
Candy Cummings threw the first curve-ball in baseball.

1869
The Cincinnati Red Stockings became the first officially fully professional baseball club; the following year, with a profit of $1.35, the team disbanded.

1870
The earliest documented use of a glove by a catcher was recorded.

1874
The baseball batter's box was officially adopted.

1876
The National League was established, with William Hulbert as president.

1877
The catcher's mask was first used in a baseball game by James Tyng of Harvard.

1879
Professional baseball adopted the reserve clause, giving teams the right to automatically renew a player's contract at the end of each season.

1882
The American Baseball Association was founded.

1884
The Louisville Slugger, a popular bat, was introduced.

1885
The official rules governing the making and materials of a baseball were written, never to be changed.

1887
Michael "King" Kelly was traded to the Boston Beaneaters from Chicago for a record $10,000.

"The Road to Renown, Indicated by an event in the Illinois Metropolis," *Logansport Daily Pharos*, June 25, 1887

Chicago, June 25—The fuss and feathers kicked up over the presence of the Boston "$10,000 beauty," Mike Kelly, the base ballist, in this city Friday could not have been surpassed had he been some distinguished statesman or philanthropist, and to say that baseball circles were greatly worked up on the occasion is putting it mildly. The noted "all rounder" put up at the Leland, the most "recherché" hotel in the city, and was waited upon as soon after his arrival as could be thought of by a host of admirers of himself and the national game. Reporters in squads hung on his remarks regarding the momentous question as to who would carry off the pennant this year, and other kindred subjects, with ears wide open and pencils poised to catch the full significance of what he said and fix it indelibly on the pages of history as recorded in the daily paper, while a number of the more enthusiastic citizens went to a great expense in procuring a floral offering which was seven feet high and proportionately wide and thick, of the choicest flowers to present to him at the ball park.

As the day wore on, a crowd gathered at the Leland Hotel, where the visitors were stopping. There were four singers in somber raiment in the throng and they sang a meaningless but highly complimentary song to Kelly. Then a cry came for a speech, but the ball player could not speak, owing to a lame leg. The four men in somber raiment sang another song, and then the crowd surged upon the ballplayer and shook his great brown hands. The spectacle was affecting, sublime. A great man was among his friends again. The noon hour had passed when the Chicago players were driven up in front of the hotel to escort Kelly and his colleagues to the park. Flint, Baldwin, Burns and Williamson were in the first carriage. The second vehicle was occupied by Clarkson, Sunday, Darling, and Ryan, and the third by Geiss, Sullivan, Pfeiffer, and Daly. Then came the carriage in which only Mike and Anson were to ride. It was drawn by four bay horses and a long, cadaverous looking man in a funeral plug-hat was on the box.

It was a little after 1 o'clock when the tall drum major in front of Austin's band and all of the carriages slung his staff high into the air. There was an explosion of triumphant melody and the march began amid a roar of cheers. No exalted soldier, fresh from the shot and shell river cities of his enemy, need ask for greater homage than was paid to Mr. Kelly by the baseball cranks of Chicago. A howling, surging mass of humanity swayed against the big banger's barouche, and above the din and uproar of the rabble were exultant shrieks of jeweled cornets and tuneful grunts of tuba and trombone. Anson and Kelly dipped their caps whenever people were wildly demonstrative, and once or twice the man from Boston waved his hand to someone familiar in the crowd. The procession moved west on Madison as far as Throop Street. Crowds lined the sidewalks the entire distance, and at times the cheering was so great as to be almost deafening. It was 2:50 o'clock when the carriages swung into the park from the Throop Street entrance. As the procession, still headed by the puffing musicians, marched towards the diamond over the green turf, a roar of cheers burst from the 12,000 people packed in the stands and encircling the grounds proper. The tumult grew deafening as Kelly's familiar face came nearer the plate, and when he stepped upon the turf near home plate the cheering could have been heard five blocks away.

continued

"The Road to Renown, Indicated by an event in the Illinois Metropolis," . . . *(continued)*

And after all, the first break of the phenomenon when play opened was to muff an easy fly that one of the Chicago boys sent right into his hands. The game was a batter's game from the start. Both clubs put their crack pitchers in the box—Clarkson for Chicago and Radburne for Boston—and Flint and Daly kept watch behind the bat. But the clubs had no respect for the ball tossers, and the fielders were kept busy hunting leather through the game, as the score shows—Chicago: 15, Boston: 18. But Mike was troubled with "Charley-horses."

Hornung was the first man to bat for Boston. The great left fielder hit the ball along the third base line, and Burns juggled it so long that the batsman reached first in safety. Then came only Mike. He hobbled up to the plate and was getting into position when two ushers from the grand stand loped up to the plate with a big floral diamond, across the face of which was the word in immortelles: "Kelly." The piece was surmounted by flags, and was held in place, easel fashion, by two bats. A jockey's cap, made of red, white, and blue silk, accompanied the floral present, which was from the player's friends. The crowd cheered and compelled Kelly to wear his flashy new bonnet. Whether the spectacle Kelly presented boodooed Clarkson will never be known, but it is certain that the Chicago pitcher couldn't place the balls anywhere near the plate, and the batsman was sent to his base. While Kelly was waiting for a ball he could reach, Hornung started out to steal second. Flint hoisted the ball over Pfeiffer's head, and before it could be returned to the diamond the left fielder was on third. Kelly now attempted to duplicate Hornung's performance, but his dickey legs could not carry him to second ahead of Flint's sharp throw to Pfeiffer, and he returned to his bench with an unutterable look of disgust. Flint neither laughed nor smiled. His weather beaten face fell apart from the apex of his nose and slid around the back of his ears. It was the greatest exhibition of facial expression ever seen on a ball field. Wise's foul tip was squeezed by Flint and then Nash reached first on five bad balls and stole second with a rush. With two men on the bases, Morrill popped up a fly which Sullivan pulled down with both hands. For Chicago, Sunday hit sharply to Nash and was thrown out at first. Ryan burled the bat Dunlap gave him against one of Radburne's curves and sent the ball spinning out into left field. The young man then tried to steal second, and was nipped by Daily to Kelly. Sullivan struck out. Just as the Champions were going into the field, Lionel Adams of New Orleans presented Anson with a floral basket inscribed in immortelles: "Old Man."

Salaries must come down or the interest to the public must be increased in some way. If one or the other does not happen, bankruptcy stares every team in the face.

—Albert Spalding, owner of the Chicago White Sox, 1881

Chapter XIV, *Play Ball!: Stories of the Ball Field*, by Mike "King" Kelly, 1888:

There are so many different ways for a man to train, that it is almost utterly impossible for a man to tell which is best. Every athlete has his own idea. The base ball player has his, and he won't change. Neither will the oarsman, the pugilist, the pedestrian, or the other athletes. There are almost as many different ways to train as there are athletes in this country. John L. Sullivan confines his training almost entirely to jogging along roadways, taking short runs, and punching the bag. In this way he generally manages to get himself in very good condition. On the other hand, Hanlan, the oarsman, does his best work in a boat. He rows morning and afternoon, and also takes other exercise. He was the most faithful training man in athletics a few years ago, but of late he has grown stout, and has been inclined to neglect certain things. This may account for his failure to retain championship honors. It is necessary that an athlete should take the very best of care of himself, even when he is not preparing for an athletic event.

There is a class of people who rarely exercise, and it's a fatal mistake. There isn't a man in the world strong enough to live a long life, and be healthy, without taking proper exercise. How many business men we know, who at 50 complain that they haven't any appetite. They complain in the morning that they cannot eat; for lunch, a plate of soup and several glasses of brandy is the best they can do; at night, for dinner, they have a little of this or that, but, as a rule, the soup and the liquors make up the best part of their meal. This should not be so. Every man should exercise in moderation. It is a necessity. Try it, and at the end of a year you will discover how much better you feel. I give a few hints on training, at the urgent solicitation of friends, and because of letters I have received from people I have never met. Do not try them all. Pick out the one you like best. Exercise, even if it's only a two-mile walk each day. . . .

A great many people labor under the idea that training is a fearfully arduous and trying ordeal, and they wonder why men should undertake such a task for the honor to be derived from victory. Such, however, is not the case. To any athlete who likes his work, training is an easy task. The trouble is that too many athletes have, during the intervals between seasons, neglected to take proper care of themselves, and go round dissipating and carousing to such an extent that training to them means little more than hurrying their system in proper condition by ridding it of the alcohol with which they have become saturated. Good, honest training is not a hard task, by any means, but, on the contrary, is a pleasure, as a man never feels so well as when he is in perfect condition.

There is one fundamental rule which must be followed in all training, and that is, to thoroughly cleanse the stomach by a strong purgative. No matter how strong and healthy a man may be, this is the first part which must be accomplished, before anything further can be done. After this is done, the athlete is ready to begin good work.

I will take up the training of the pugilist first. He rises at an early hour, and takes a smart walk of a mile or so before breakfast. This gives him a hearty appetite, and he can eat his breakfast with a relish. A chop or a slice of beef cooked rare is generally given, but oatmeal mush is a nutritious and strengthening article. Breakfast over, a good long walk and jog follows. A suit of heavy clothing is put on, with heavy boots. If the man is fat, and has a lot of superfluous flesh, the heaviest kind of clothing should be put on, while a strip of flannel tied tightly across the stomach will serve to reduce that member. The walk should not be too long, as a wearying journey is likely to bring a reaction, in the shape of loss of vital energy, and staleness, which, above all things, must be avoided. A short distance at a good lively trot is by far the best plan, as fast work draws out the perspiration and hardens the muscles of the legs. On returning, the damp clothes should be taken off as soon as possible, and the skin rubbed down first with rough towels, so as to thoroughly dry the surface, then with bare hands, and finally with rum, alcohol or some other ingredient.

1893 PROFILE

Chet Taylor couldn't wait for the day he could compete as a Yale University student in the Yale-Harvard Regatta, an annual event held since 1859.

Life at Home

- Yale sophomore Chet Taylor was sure of one thing: of all the collegiate sports, rowing made the most stringent demands upon a gentleman's unselfish devotion to his task.
- In baseball and football, there was the stimulus and excitement of frequent, almost daily, games.
- For track athletes there were plenty of brushes with friends or an occasional outside contest to fortify their interest in running, jumping and throwing.
- In boating, although there were many days of enjoyment, the thrill of competition was a one-day event.
- A rower labored for six months, day after day, and the contest was all over in a brief 20 minutes.
- To be prepared for that day and be fit to represent the university, a man had to be willing to go through months of training and hard work when there were no enthusiastic admirers applauding the effort.
- When the weather possessed a twisted vindictiveness against an oarsman, then a show of character and spirit was especially required.
- Chet loved being on the water, the feel of the oars, the muscle strain in his shoulders, and the satisfying sounds of water against the bow.
- He believed that only men of strong character, men in whom perseverance and patience were marked traits, could call themselves collegiate oarsmen with sincerity.

Chet Taylor couldn't wait to compete as a Yale University oarsman.

Chet and his family.

- His father had been an oarsman, and he had taught Chet well.
- Chet grew up learning how to maintain his oars and care for his boats as though they were cherished heirlooms.
- His mother and three older sisters praised him mightily throughout his boyhood whenever he rowed past the family home, racing against himself.
- But despite all the family support, he fully understood that an oarsman was a self-made man.
- A good coach might correct a fault, even an ingrained one, but it was the athlete who got up early, stayed late, and gave his all on the day of the race.
- He also felt very lucky to be at Yale University.
- After a lifetime of dreaming about college, a reversal of fortunes (possibly a bad investment his father would not discuss), threatened to shipwreck Chet's college plans.
- That's when his Uncle Clarence stepped in with the needed financial support.
- Uncle Clarence was a Yale man, who owned more than 250 buildings in the heart of New York's commercial district.
- He was a director of the Chemical Bank and the Metropolitan Opera House, and lived in a New York City mansion envied by all.
- He didn't have a son who could row for Yale in the annual race against Harvard, so Chet became the lucky, substitute son.
- So when he left his home in Pittsburgh, Pennsylvania, Yale-bound Chet knew his college years would include rowing and the opportunity to repay his uncle in the only currency he had: a win over Harvard.

Life at Work

- When Chet Taylor first arrived at Yale his freshman year, he assumed that he would soon be crewing on an eight-oared shell.
- Nothing was prettier or more poetic than the rhythmic swaying of eight bodies dipping eight perfectly balanced oars into the water to propel an exquisitely designed boat to its destination.
- Chet was sure he would win a spot quickly.
- Rowing eight-oared shells, he was told, was a privilege rarely extended to freshmen, especially a 5'5" freshman who had primarily raced singles and fours.
- Racing in singles, they said, while an excellent sport, rarely prepared a man to be a member of the synchronized crew and almost never resulted in a proper gentleman.
- After his hurt feelings healed, he came to realize that paying your dues, waiting your turn, and serving the needs of others, was part of the gentleman boater.
- Chet's first year included graciously wiping down the boats inside and out when they came out of the water, preparing the varsity boat by rubbing it with pumice, smoothing it with soapstone and greasing it with oil and paraffin.
- This was not easy work.
- The eight-oared shell was made of cedar and weighed from 230 to 275 pounds.
- Boat length ranged from 59 to 61 feet.
- They averaged 9" deep from gunwale to keel, with a 4"washboard above the gunwale.
- The middle breadth was typically 20 to 25 inches, narrowing to 16 or 18 inches at the end of the cockpit.
- Oars weighed approximately seven and a half pounds and were eight and a half feet long.
- Early on, Chet decided that he would not participate in sport as a professional, for money.
- He would play for victory.
- The Harvard-Yale Regatta first occurred in 1852 and had been an annual event since 1859.
- The first prize was a pair of black walnut, silver inscribed trophy oars dating back to the inaugural event.
- Originally a three-mile race, it changed into a four-mile sprint in the Thames River, New London, Connecticut, in 1876.
- Two years before Chet arrived, Harvard won in an upstream time of 21 minutes, 23 seconds, 34 seconds ahead of Yale.
- Yale avenged that loss during Chet's freshman year.
- Chet became an oarsman in his sophomore year.
- The race was scheduled for June 30 and, like last year, was to be downstream.
- A crowd of 40,000 turned out to witness the race along the four-mile route; the weather was cantankerous with terrible headwinds and rough water.

Rowing was gaining in popularity.

- As starting time approached conditions grew worse—a gale kicked up white caps on the river.
- When it came time to take his place in the shell, Chet was calm, energized and silent.
- Now was the time, the seniors insisted, when character and training would emerge.
- Harvard jumped out to an early lead with strong and confident strokes in the choppy water.
- The second mile was all Yale, and no one wanted victory more than Chet.
- During the third mile, pain jumped up into his eyes, his shoulders screamed and arms ached; a strong headwind made for a slow time and exhausted rowers.
- In the fourth mile, Chet achieved excellent positioning to maintain the Yale lead.
- Until he crossed the finish line, he didn't hear a single sound from the crowd of 40,000.
- Once Yale won, however, he was engulfed in noise.
- Every whistle in town, on the river and in the harbor, blended with blasts from the railroads and the factories adding to the pandemonium and cheers from the exuberant Yale supporters.
- Experts declared it the hardest race a Yale crew had rowed in years.
- Afterwards the eight were put on a train to New Haven where a reception greeted them, followed by a banquet filled with victory toasts.
- Chet went to bed that night with the sounds of firecrackers and tin horns filling the streets.

NUMBER OF NAMES IN DIRECTORIES PREVIOUS YEARS.

Date.	Volume.	Name of Publisher.	No. of Names.	Increase Names.	Date.	Volume.	Name of Publisher.	No. of Names.	Incre Nam
1840	1	James M. Patten,	2,359		1868	29	J. H. Benham,	14,000	1,
1841	2	"	2,750	391	1869	30	"	14,500	
1842	3	"	2,860	110	1870	31	"	15,081	
1843	4	"	3,000	140	1871	32	"	18,157	3,0
1844	5	"	3,330	330	1872	33	"	19,109	
1845	6	"	3,515	185	1873	34	"	19,476	
1846	7	J. H. Benham,	3,885	370	1874	35	"	20,636	1,
1847	8	"	4,255	370	1875	36	"	20,682	
1848	9	"	4,370	115	1876	37	Price, Lee & Co.	19,567	*1,
1849	10	"	4,294	*76	1877	38	"	20,254	
1850	11	"	5,128	834	1878	39	"	20,915	(
1851	12	"	6,118	990	1879	40	"	21,358	
1852	13	"	7,000	882	1880	41	"	22,171	
1853	14	"	8,244	1,244	1881	42	"	25,048	2,8
1854	15	"	8,246	2	1882	43	"	28,515	3,
1855	16	"	8,619	373	1883	44	"	30,908	2,
1856	17	"	8,280	*339	1884	45	"	31,834	
1857	18	"	9,100	820	1885	46	"	31,843	
1858	19	"	9,216	116	1886	47	"	32,315	
1859	20	"	10,413	1,198	1887	48	"	33,272	9
1860	21	"	11,673	1,260	1888	49	"	35,624	2,
1861	22	"	10,809	*864	1889	50	"	37,574	1,9
1862	23	"	10,956	147	1890	51	"	39,551	1,9
1863	24	"	10,965	9	1891	52	The Price & Lee Co.	41,610	2,0
1864	25	"	11,995	1,030	1892	53	"	44,059	2,4
1865	26	"	12,300	305	1893	54	"	47,148	†3,0
1866	27	"	12,747	447	1894	55	"	49,966	2,0
1867	28	"	12,783	36					

* Decrease. † West Haven included, 975 names.

INCREASE IN POPULATION.

Population of New Haven for 100 years, showing increase and percentage growth at each decade.

Decade.	Population.	Increase.	Per cent.	Decade.	Population.	Increase.	Per ce
1790	4,448			1870	50,840	11,573	29.
1800	5,157	709	15.94	1880	62,882	12,042	23.
1810	6,967	1,810	35.10	1890	85,981	23,099	36.
1820	8,327	1,360	19.52	Lowest percentage, 1800			15.
1830	10,678	2,351	28.24	Highest percentage, 1860			74.
1840	14,390	3,712	34.76	Average percentage for 100 years, 35.			
1850	22,529	8,139	56.56	Average percentage last 50 years, 44.			
1860	39,267	16,738	74.80				

The same increase for the coming as in the past decade, viz.: 36.73 per cent, w

CONTENTS.

New Haven, CT city directory.

Life in the Community: New Haven, Connecticut

- Yale University was in a growth mode in 1893; five buildings were under construction, and its endowment fund exceeded $4 million for the first time.
- Enrollment surpassed 2,000 and many feared the university was becoming too big.
- Yale traced its beginnings to "An Act for Liberty to Erect a Collegiate School," passed by the General Court of the Colony of Connecticut on October 9, 1701, in an effort to create an institution to train ministers.
- Originally called the Collegiate School, it opened in the home of its first rector, Abraham Pierson, in Killingworth; after several moves, the college moved to New Haven, Connecticut in 1716.
- In 1718, Elihu Yale, who had made a fortune while living in India as a representative of the East India Company, donated to the school nine bales of goods which were sold for more than £560, a substantial sum at the time.
- When he donated 417 books and a portrait of King George I, the school changed its name to Yale College in gratitude to its benefactor.
- It was also hoped that he would give the college another large donation or bequest.
- In July 1779, when hostile British forces occupied New Haven and threatened to raze the college, Yale graduate Edmund Fanning, Secretary to the British General in command of the occupation, interceded and the college was saved.
- Yale's gradual expansion included the Yale School of Medicine (1810), Yale Divinity School (1822), Yale Law School (1843), Yale Graduate School of Arts and Sciences (1847), the Sheffield Scientific School (1847), and Yale School of Fine Arts (1869).
- The divinity school was founded by Congregationalists who felt that the Harvard Divinity School had become too liberal.
- In 1887, as the college continued to grow under the presidency of Timothy Dwight V, Yale College was renamed to Yale University.

Wayside Gatherings.

☞ The eve of a great event—Mother Eve when she ate the apple.

☞ Thirty-four pounds of raw sugar make twenty-one of refined.

☞ To accumulate dollars, my son, you must have sense to begin with.

☞ Napoleon the Great was a Mason. He was raised at Malta, 1798.

☞ Prudence is a plume dropped from the wing of some past folly.

☞ Good sense is the best friend a man can have in an emergency.

☞ A false friend and a shadow attend only when the sun shines.

☞ Churches built in the United States in 1891 numbered over eighty-five hundred.

☞ It is the hardest thing in the world to make a Christian out of selfish people.

☞ When a pickpocket pulls at your watch, tell him plainly that you have no time to spare.

☞ The Methodist church needs 1,000 new preachers every year to keep its pulpits supplied.

☞ When a boy is smart, there is a question whether he got it from her folks or his people.

☞ Women of today are on the average two inches taller than they were twenty-five years ago.

☞ Those who occupy the highest stations often think with regret of some pleasanter one they left below.

☞ The wife of a poor manafacturer, living in Ashley county, Tenn., recently gave birth to six children, all boys.

HISTORICAL SNAPSHOT
1893

- The U.S. Marines intervened in Hawaii, resulting in the overthrow of Queen Liliuokalani
- Thomas A. Edison finished construction of the first motion picture studio in West Orange, New Jersey
- Japan adopted the Gregorian calendar
- The first cross-country skiing competition for women took place in Sweden
- The first U.S. commemoratives and the first U.S. stamp to picture a woman, Martha Washington, were issued
- U.S. President Grover Cleveland granted amnesty to Mormon polygamists
- Edward MacDowell's *Hamlet and Ophelia* premiered in Boston
- Webb C. Ball introduced railroad chronometers, which became the general railroad timepiece standard in North America
- Expiration of the first Alexander Graham Bell patent brought a rush of independent exchanges and new systems
- Rudolf Diesel received a patent for the diesel engine
- The first recorded college basketball game occurred in Beaver Falls, Pennsylvania, between the Geneva College Covenanters and the New Brighton YMCA
- A vast section of northern Oklahoma Territory was opened to land-hungry settlers after six million acres were purchased from the Cherokee Indians for $8.5 million
- The World's Columbian Exposition opened in Chicago's Jackson Park to celebrate the 400th anniversary of the discovery of America
- A crash on the New York Stock Exchange triggered a depression known as the Panic of 1893
- Edison's one and a half-inch Kinetoscope was first demonstrated in public at the Brooklyn Institute
- Kokichi Mikimoto, in Japan, developed the method to seed and grow cultured pearls
- Brothers Charles and Frank Duryea drove the first gasoline-powered motorcar in America on public roads in Springfield, Massachusetts
- Colorado women were granted the right to vote
- The American Council on Alcohol Problems was established, along with the Anti-Saloon League and the Committee of Fifty for the Study of the Liquor Problem
- A worker at the De Beers mine at Jagersfontein, Orange Free State, discovered a blue-white diamond weighing about 995 carats
- Marshall Field and Company occupied nearly an entire city block on Chicago's State Street; its wholesale store employed more than 3,000 on 13 acres of floor space
- Sears, Roebuck & Company, a Chicago mail-order firm, racked up sales of $338,000 in baby carriages, clothing, furniture, musical instruments, sewing machines, and a wide range of other merchandise

Selected Prices

Advertising, Full-Page $20.00
Cyclist's Corset $1.00
Diapers, Six $0.05
Fountain Pen $4.00
Hat, Schoolboy's $0.25
Piano Lessons, 24 . . . .$8.00
Roller Skates $7.00
Tooth Soap $0.25
Wrinkle Lotion $1.00
Writing Paper, Linen, 72 Sheets $0.75

"Rowing," *Walter Camp's Book of College Sports*, 1893:

A coach may correct a fault, but faults in rowing are apt to be like the formed habits of mature life, almost ingrained, and to eradicate them requires the steadily fixed and unflagging attention of the individual himself. At first it is a distinct effort at every stroke for him to avoid a lapse into his old or natural way. For days, and it may be weeks, he feels that he must think every time; but then there comes a day when it is more natural and easy to do it the right way than the old way, and his lesson is learned. But this is only one fault, and lucky indeed would be the oarsman who found he had but one fault to correct. In fact, it is a wonder that more men did not become discouraged in their early attempts; but the man who goes in for this sport, and sticks doggedly at it, putting his whole thought and attention upon the instructions he is receiving, reaps in the end the reward for all his labors. To some men, rowing, so far as eventually securing a seat in the varsity boat, is as much out of the question as becoming a varsity ballplayer. There is a knack about rowing as about any other game of skill, but patience and perseverance have made more boatman out of some terribly unpromising material so that one can hardly feel justified in saying to any man, "You'll never be an oarsman." Some of the best men in Harvard and Yale boats have been men who during their first year, yes, even their second year, have been looked upon by the coaches as decidedly doubtful. Besides the monotony of the rowers' training, there must also be considered the fact that in a great final contest, the oarsman does not come into actual contact with his opponent; and so there is lacking the usual stimulus to outdo that so marked in foot-ball, and present to a less extent in the other sports. It is here that the result of the dogged determination is seen; and the same earnest patience which makes the oarsman take kindly to the coach's severest criticisms and put his whole mind into correcting the trivial fault, drives him on when every stroke is a pain and his whole strength seems exhausted. . . . Thus, it is seen that many components—strength, skill, quickness, perseverance, and bulldog pluck, with a cheerful acquiescence to hardships and sacrifices—must be nicely balanced in the oarsman; and the selecting of their men to answer these requirements is the most difficult task of captains and coaches.

"Rowing," *Johnson's Universal Cyclopedia*, 1897:

As a pastime, rowing was introduced into England by the Saxons, and to Alfred the Great was due the introduction of the long galleys of the Mediterranean. On the accession of the Normans, boat-tilting, a passage-at-arms on the water, became popular, and the success of the contestants depended much on skillful handling of the oars. . . .

Although boat-racing in the U.S. is known to have existed since about the beginning of the 19th century, yet no races of importance occurred before 1811 when oarsmen of New York challenged the best of Long Island to a race in four-oared barges with coxswains. The course was from Harsimus, New Jersey, to the flagstaff at the Battery. New York won easily. This race excited so much interest that the winning boat was exhibited for many years in a public museum.

Distinctively amateur rowing was not recognized until 1834, when the Castle Garden Boat Club Association was formed. From this time until 1873, when the National Association of Amateur Oarsmen was founded, the amateur's rating was purely local, being judged by each regatta committee, and it was not an uncommon occurrence for an oarsman to compete as an amateur on one river and as a professional on another. To put an end to this unsatisfactory state of affairs was the main object of the convention of both clubs held in New York on August 28 and 29, 1892, which culminated in the National Association of Amateur Oarsmen of America. . . .

It was not until 1843 and 1844 that boat clubs were formed or boats were owned at either Yale or Harvard. The first intercollegiate race was held at Center Harbor, on Lake Winnipiseogee on August 3, 1852. Harvard was represented by the *Oneida*, while Yale was represented with two boats, the *Shawmut* and *Undine*, all three being eight-oared lapstreaks, rowed on the gunwale and carrying coxswains. The *Oneida* won. . . .

In 1871 the Rowing Association of American Colleges was formed by Harvard, Brown, Massachusetts Agricultural, and the various other colleges with aquatic facilities. Yale refuse to enter, and the races were contested only by the three colleges named above. Massachusetts Agricultural won easily from Harvard in 16:46 1/2 over a straightaway three-mile course. The next year Yale and Cornell entered the Association, which then represented 11 colleges. The race was at Springfield, Mass., was entered by six crews, and was won by Amherst. . . .

Since 1876 the Yale-Harvard race has been an annual occurrence. Of the 19 races rowed, including that of 1894, Yale has won 12 and Harvard seven. The best time was made by Yale in 1888, being 20:10, which stands as a record for eight-oared shells over a four-mile straightaway course. All but the first two of these latter races have been rowed at New Haven, Connecticut, with varying times and wind.

"Gilbert and Sullivan," *Sandusky Daily Register* (Ohio), January 2, 1890:

That famous comic opera-literary-musical co-partnership acting under the firm name of Gilbert & Sullivan has scored another success in their latest production the *Gondoliers, or the King of Barataria*. It was produced at the Savoy Theatre, in London, early in December. The piece, both as to music and play, has been very favorably criticized. Doubtless it will soon be produced in America.

When Gilbert and Sullivan appeared before the public as claimants for attention as comic opera writers, Offenbach was the zenith star. He produced a great number of burlesques. Mme. Aimee was the great medium through which Offenbach's operas became familiar to the American people. The operas were French and so was Aimee. The two went well together. As the dialogue was in a language that few Americans can understand, the operas were not very objectionable. At any rate they took amazingly.

But there was nothing either English or American in Offenbach's operas. The public had become, in a measure, saturated with them when a little cloud, no bigger than a man's hand, appeared which was destined to obscure Offenbach and drive him out of America altogether. *Her Majesty's Ship Pinafore*, a new comic opera, was put on the boards. It was written by Arthur Sullivan and W.S. Gilbert, the latter having published some time before. The work, which showed considerable ability in the comic line, *Pinafore* was English to the core. The music, the words, the action were remarkable and together produced a gem. Besides, there was in it a most delightful satire on the chief lord of the admiralty of the British Navy.

There was something prairie fire-like in the way *Pinafore* took. To have heard it once was nothing. Almost everyone heard it half a dozen times. And many people can say they had listened to from ten to fifteen representations of it. It was the beginning of a new school, and so excellent in all parts that it seemed the public would never grow tired of it.

Then came *The Pirates of Penzance* from the same brains. The novelty was not there, of course; that was all in *Pinafore*, but the public was ready for more, and *The Pirates* was a success. Oscar Wilde was at that time exciting the tension of the people of London, and the next opera Gilbert and Sullivan produced was *Patience*, a satire on Wilde and his followers. It contained a great number of very pretty airs and the music, though not as inspiring as that of *Pinafore*, was very refined. It had an excellent run.

Since then the partners have been bringing out operas almost without limit. *Princess Ida* was based on Tennyson's poem "The Princess," which, something of a satire in itself, gave a favorable opportunity for Gilbert and Sullivan. Since *Princess* there has come out *The Mikado, Ruddygore, The Golden Legend* and others.

"Boating Commands," *Walter Camp's Book of College Sports*, 1893:

"Avast" means stop rowing, and should be called while the oars are in the water, never on the recover except in emergency.

"Hold" means to keep the oar buried at right angles to the side of the boat, thus stopping her progress; the plane of blade being parallel to the surface of the water.

"Back water" means to reverse the motion of rowing, driving the oar in the water from stern to bow instead.

The "Catch" is when the oars take the water on the stroke and the shoulders swing up.

The "Finish" is when the oars leave the water at the end of the stroke.

The "Recover" is the combination of movements through which an oarsman goes from the time to "Finish" until he is again in a position for another stroke, that is, to the position for "Catch" again....

The term "Time" is used technically to indicate the unison of a crew in every movement.

"Bucks" or "Meets the oar" is the expression used to indicate meeting the oar with the body at finish when the arms are pulled in. The body here should be particularly perfectly rigid.

"Slumps." Settles down with shoulders and upper body at the finish, so that the back is crooked and muscles relaxed.

The Panic of 1893

Wall Street stock prices experienced a sudden drop on May 5, 1893; the market collapsed in a panic June 27.

During the ensuing turmoil, 600 banks closed their doors; more than 15,000 businesses failed.

Seventy-four railroads went into receivership; the recession continued for four years.

The 1880s had been a period of remarkable economic expansion in the United States, propelled by the building of railroads.

The overbuilding of railroads and related bankruptcies dragged down the U.S. economy, which worsened when European investors withdrew funds and businesses were starved for capital.

Many companies tried to take over other firms, seriously endangering their own stability; at the same time silver, mined using rail connections, began to flood the market.

An early sign of trouble was the bankruptcy of the Philadelphia and Reading Railroad, which had greatly overextended itself, on February 23, 1893.

The average U.S. worker earned $9.42 per week; new immigrants often received less than $1 per day.

Millions of unemployed workers roamed the streets, begging for help, and children were abandoned.

As the economy worsened, people rushed to withdraw their money from banks.

European investors began to take payment only in gold, depleting U.S. gold reserves and threatening the value of the U.S. dollar, which was backed by gold.

A series of failures followed, including the Northern Pacific Railway, the Union Pacific Railroad and the Atchison, Topeka & Santa Fe Railroad.

17-19 percent of the workforce was unemployed at the Panic's peak, which when, combined with the loss of life savings by failed banks, meant that once secure middle class families could not meet their mortgage obligations.

Many walked away from recently built homes.

Economic conditions forced U.S. railroads to reduce their orders for sleeping cars; the Pullman Palace Car Company reduced wages by one-fourth, while charging full rents in company housing.

George M. Pullman and his executives continued to draw full salaries.

The American Railway Union was founded by socialist Eugene V. Debs.

Lithuanian-born anarchist Emma Goldman urged striking clockmakers to steal bread if they could not afford to buy food for their families.

Congress repealed the 1890 Sherman Silver Purchase Act; the United States returned to the gold standard.

"Under the Elms," *Sketches of Yale Life,* Edited by John Addison Porter, 1885:

Groups under the elm trees! Groups under the elms just after dinner, when everyone prefers a pipe and a comfortable sprawl in the grass, to climbing up four flights of stairs and translating *Undine*, or cramming for Biennial! Under the elms these hot days, where so carelessly, so lazily and so deliciously cool we lie, reading, joking, laughing, smoking, peeping out at times from the thick shade, at the old iron pointers, which spasmodically twitch along towards recitation time and quickly drawing back our heads with the gratifying assurance that we've a half hour yet before beginning the old, old fight with books, the flesh and the Devil!

Under the elms five minutes before the clanging of the remorseless old sentinel and Lyceum belfry! What a fluttering and sometimes cutting of leaves! What a racing through the whole lesson to get some clue which will enable colloquial men to save an inglorious fizzle, and philosophicals to make a triumphant rush! What varied expressions of counte-

nance! Here smiling complacently, there scowls; this man whistles, that one swears; here the serenity of indifference, there the serenity of despair. Now the bell begins to ring. What slow and toilsome ascent up the narrow stairs! What a sudden bolting into the recitation room as the last stroke dies away, and the door closes with a slam behind the last loiterer, and upon a division meekly expectant of the hour's worse contingencies.

"Gentlemen," *Walter Camp's Book College Sports,* 1893:

A gentleman against a gentleman always plays to win. There is a tacit agreement between them that each shall do his best, and the best man shall win. A gentleman does not make his living, however, from his athletic prowess. He does not earn anything from his victories except glory and satisfaction. Perhaps the first falling off in this respect began when the laurel wreath became a mug. So long as the mug was but the emblem, and valueless otherwise, there was no harm. There is still no harm where the mug or trophy hanging in the room of the winner is indicative of his skill; but if the silver mug becomes a solid dollar, either at the hands of the winner or the donor, let us have the laurel back again.

A gentleman never competes for money, directly or indirectly. Make no mistake about this. No matter how winding the road may be that eventually brings the sovereign into the pocket, it is the price of what should be dearer to you than anything else, your honor. It is quite the fashion to say "sentimental bosh" to anyone who preaches such an old-fashioned thing as honor; but among true gentlemen, my boy, it is just as real an article as ever, and it is one of the few things that never rings false.

1877 News Feature

"Athletics: Miller versus Bauer," *The Spirit of the Times, the American Gentleman's Paper,* **July 7, 1877:**

Saturday evening of last week, about 3,000 people, comprising among them many of the leading citizens of this city, gathered at the Empire Rink to witness the second great Greco-Roman wrestling match between Wm. Miller and Bauer. Some months ago these two giants in athletic strength, it will be remembered, wrestled until daylight, and then, overly exhausted, the match was declared a draw, Bauer, on that occasion, winning one fall, more through accident than skilled strength. Since that occasion the feeling between these men has been anything but cordial; in fact, it would not be using too strong language to state that they warmly hate each other, Bauer, with his hot French blood, leading in this pleasant feature. The match this evening grew out of idle banter, the night of the Miller-Christol struggle, was arranged, few days since, for $200 aside, to be governed by the same stipulations as controlled that affair. The winner of that match was to receive the net gate receipts, which, had there been a winner, would have been a handsome sum. The time set for the bouts to begin was sharply 8:30, the men were on hand to the minute, but, unavoidably, there was some trouble in securing a referee. W. Clark, the man agreeable to both athletes, was not on hand, and Pennel, second choice, kept away also. The audience wanted Harry Hill, but Miller for (to him) good reason, strenuously objected. Full 20 minutes' time was lost: Bauer suggested that the audience be the referee; this was received with shouts of derision. At last Capt. Palmer was accepted, a man unknown to both, and equally a stranger to the audience. We believe he was from Utica, and we give him credit for filling the thankless position with entire satisfaction principles, as well as to the audience. The athletes were in superb condition, yet Miller, as the evening waned, proved to be the better; his flesh, hard as a rock, gave no evidence of the tremendous punishment he was receiving, while Bauer's was rosy red in blotches, blushing at the terrible strains to which it was subjected. A more orderly, enthusiastic, or equally divided audience in their friendship, could not have been picked out, each man receiving hearty encouragement for brilliant coups.

At 8:51, all being ready, Whitaker, the omnipresent, announced the terms of the wrestle, and the men cheerfully faced each other for the terrible tussle. From the first loving grasp of the wrist, Bauer evidently was bent upon forcing the battle. Locks and counter-locks were rapidly exchanged; Miller, ever wary, broke instantly choice clinches of his opponent, who showed a decided preference for his favorite neck grip. After about 10 minutes' warm work, the bodies of both being glistened as if they had been covered with diamond varnish, and the perspiration rolled down in continuous streams. Suddenly, with a vicious wrench, Bauer forced Miller on his hands and knees, and worked hard to turn him over. Miller guardedly defended every effort, and seemed willing to allow Bauer to waste his strength in his Herculean efforts to spread out Miller's bulky form. We will state that Miller tipped the beam at 196 while Bauer, more modest, turned, the scale at 175. After fruitless exertions, Miller leapt to his feet, and in a twinkling seized Bauer, and threw him a rattler, but the agile Frenchman was not to be caught napping, and cat-like came down on all fours. It was now Miller's turn to tip him over, but he soon gave it up, allowing Bauer to rise. After half an hour's sharp work, Miller by quick movement got a fierce neck grip and for a full five minutes he held Bauer firmly. The muscles of each now fairly cracked with the tension. Three times did Miller by brute strength bend Bauer's head to the ground. How Bauer escaped choking is a mystery, for his neck was closely circled by the brawny arm. The struggle to free himself was desperate; it was by far the most dangerous grip of the evening, and Bauer showed how he suffered. At last by mighty force, he broke the grip and stood upright. His neck was encircled with a bright red band, which at midnight still gave out carnation tints. As the minutes rolled around, and the close of the hour approached, when a rest was to take place, each redoubled his exertions to secure a fall, and the work was lively. When the moment arrived, the timekeeper called time, and the men were actually forced apart, and retired, as did the majority of the audience, the former to the assiduous attention of their friends, the latter to the equally cheerful greetings of the numerous bars in the neighborhood. Speculation was active that no fall would be gained by either, while others invested freely at evens on the result.

By 10.10 time was called for the second bout. Both men, as they walked in, had cooled out nicely, looked equally as fresh as at the outset, save that Bauer's white skin was adorned with broad welts of red bands, especially his neck, which kept up its protest against the terrible muscular collar which it had been forced to wear for those punishing five minutes. This time honors were easy in the forcing line, the play being fearsome and effective, Bauer evidently willing to give Miller openings which he was not loath to refuse. Suddenly Miller got a tough head and shoulder lock and threw Bauer heavily. He landed on his head, but turned, pivot-like, and came down on his chest. Within five minutes Miller secured the same lock, and this time he was more successful; turning Bauer he fell with him, and, in spite of the ready bridge, he forced him flat to the stage, and, amid great cheering fall No. 1 was announced for Miller. Another intermission of 15 minutes being in order, all hands compared notes, and tested the quality of fair lager and very bad cigars.

At 11.13 time was called for the bout. Miller had now all the advantage, and with common care and shrewd tactics the match was his beyond question. The pile of gate money was within his grasp, and had he used reasonable discretion and kept his wits under control, he might've had the pleasure of grasping it firmly. Of course, it devolved upon Bauer to force the issue; within the remaining 60 minutes he must obtain a fall or the match was lost. He showed that he understood this well, for, after three or four minutes' wrist manipulation, he dashed in to do or die. Here was Miller's opportunity, defensive tactics were chiefly his role, but after getting a crushing fall he lost his temper, became excited, and retaliated by the sharpest defensive work of the evening. Bauer had succeeded admiringly in his ruse. He met the fierce attack of his opponent with wary feints until, with lightning movement he seized an opening, obtained a terrible grip, and, in seven minutes from the call of time, Miller was thrown flat on his back and honors were easy. Nothing but overconfidence and the loss of temper had given Bauer this opening and bitterly good Miller rued his foolishness when too late. It was now anybody's battle; Bauer's stock, rapidly mounting, made him a favorite.

With midnight and Sunday morning rapidly approaching, time was called for the final struggle at 11.18. It was clear that one or the other must win the deciding fall within the next hour or the police present would put a stop to proceedings, and the struggle perforce end in a draw. Both men came out fresh, Bauer alone showing signs of the rough usage he had received. Miller for a few minutes forced the fighting, Bauer acting entirely on the defense. Soon both dropped into this style of proceeding, and the minutes rolled around rapidly. After half an hour Bauer got his neck grip, and strangely endeavored to throw Miller; it was useless, however, although he twisted him about lively. For 20 minutes more was a mere walk around, when 10 minutes of activity ensued, the advantage being equally divided, but no chance of a square fall taking place. The men gave evidence of their waning powers. And 12.18 the ominous call of time, found the men in a fierce grasp, but they were compelled to break and retire. Captain Mount of the police now took charge of the proceedings and commenced his official work of ordering the gas turned down. This told everyone that the fun was over. At the close of the resting spell the men came in again, up went the gas, and the master of ceremonies announced that in the respect of the law, the match could not proceed, that it was a draw; all bets were declared off, stake and game money to be divided. Thus ended the second struggle between these athletes. It is now conclusively proven that these two men are remarkably evenly matched. Bauer's activity and superior science offsetting Miller's advantage of size and strength. Barring carelessness, more evenly matched men never faced each other, and each are a level as to championship honors. We have yet to see the man who can beat either, and we do not believe that either of them can gain any advantage over the other in their present status of muscular power.

1900–1909

The first decade of the twentieth century was marked by dramatic innovation in business and in sport as America's men and women competed to invent a faster automobile or a better bicycle. Colleges across the land became obsessed with football, rowing and cycling. College presidents quickly recognized football's power to bond diverse groups into a single community. Riots, rebellions and drunkenness declined with the introduction of the sport, which quickly became a way to advertise—and differentiate—a school. Mascots and nicknames came into being (for a time Washington College team was known as the Shoo Flies and the University of Nebraska team as the Bug Eaters). But in 1905, the carnage and serious injuries on the college field of play were so high President Teddy Roosevelt threatened to outlaw the game, leading to rule changes and greater safety measures.

The decade also witnessed the formation of adult-managed sports programs arranged through churches, private schools, YMCAs and the public schools. Adult leaders, especially in the cities, concluded that organized boys' sports could build individual character; modern life, many believed, had become too soft and effeminate. Sports could serve as an effective substitute for the lost rural experience. Hiking, birdwatching, camping, rock climbing or simply walking in the new national parks became popular. The invention of the safety bicycle, sporting same-sized pneumatic tires (along with a substantial drop in price) led to a cycling craze, rapidly embraced by women, that put 10 million bicycles on the roads by 1901.

Millions of immigrants flooded the United States, often finding work in the new factories of the New World—many managed by men who came two generations before from countries like England, Germany or Wales. When Theodore Roosevelt proudly proclaimed in 1902, "The typical American is accumulating money more rapidly than any other man on earth," he described accurately both the joy of newcomers and the prosperity of the emerging middle class. Elevated by their education, profession, inventiveness or capital, the managerial class found numerous opportunities to flourish in the new economy. Legislation passed in 1903 and 1907 strengthened the hand of the federal government to enforce immigration laws along the Mexican border. At the time, millions also returned to their homeland to rebuild their lives based on U.S. earnings. And reform was in the air. . . .

At the beginning of the century, the 1900 U.S. population, comprising 45 states, stood at 76 million, an increase of 21 percent since 1890; 10.6 million residents were foreign-born and more were coming every day. The number of immigrants in the first decade of the twentieth century was double the number for the previous decade, exceeding one million annually in four of the 10 years, the highest level in U.S. history. Business and industry were convinced that unrestricted immigration was the fuel that drove the growth of American industry. Labor was equally certain that the influx of foreigners continually undermined the economic status of native workers and kept wages low.

The change in productivity and consumerism came with a price: the character of American life. Manufacturing plants drew people from the country into the cities. The traditional farm patterns were disrupted by the lure of urban life. Ministers complained that lifelong churchgoers who moved to the city often found less time and fewer social pressures to attend worship regularly. Between 1900 and 1920, the urban population increased by 80 percent compared to just over 12 percent for rural areas. During the same time, the non-farming workforce went from 783,000 to 2.2 million. Unlike farmers, these workers drew a regular paycheck, and spent it.

With this movement of people, technology and ideas, nationalism took on a new meaning in America. Railroad expansion in the middle of the nineteenth century had made it possible to move goods quickly and efficiently throughout the country. As a result, commerce, which had been based largely on local production of goods for local consumption, found new markets. Ambitious merchants expanded their businesses by appealing to broader markets.

In 1900, America claimed 58 businesses with more than one retail outlet called "chain stores"; by 1910, that number had more than tripled, and by 1920, the total had risen to 808. The number of clothing chains alone rose from seven to 125 during the period. Department stores such as R.H. Macy in New York and Marshall Field in Chicago offered vast arrays of merchandise along with free services and the opportunity to "shop" without purchasing. Ready-made clothing drove down prices, but also promoted fashion booms that reduced the class distinction of dress. In rural America, the mail order catalogs of Sears, Roebuck and Company reached deep into the pocket of the common man and made dreaming and consuming more feasible.

All was not well, however. A brew of labor struggles, political unrest, and tragic factory accidents demonstrated the excesses of industrial capitalism so worshipped in the Gilded Age. The labor reform movements of the 1880s and 1890s culminated in the newly formed American Federation of Labor as the chief labor advocate. By 1904, 18 years after it was founded, the AFL claimed 1.676 million of 2.07 million total union members nationwide. The reforms of the labor movement called for an eight-hour workday, child-labor regulation, and cooperatives of owners and workers. The progressive bent of the times also focused attention on factory safety, tainted food and drugs, political corruption, and unchecked economic monopolies.

1901 PROFILE

Liam Hanratty fell in love with cycling at an early age and surprised everyone, including his wife's parents, by actually earning a good living at it.

Life at Home

- Liam Hanratty, the son of Irish immigrants, was born in 1881, in the cold month of February, in Worcester, Massachusetts.
- Liam's parents had emigrated four years earlier, eager to join the flourishing, well-established Irish Catholic enclave in that city.
- For more than a decade, Irish immigrants had been flooding into Worcester—a blessing for a city that needed cheap labor to operate their tool and dye shops.
- Even so, longtime residents were unaccustomed to the new-comers' strange customs.
- What united Worcester's citizens was the potential of the safety bike produced in its factories and the freedom it provided riders nationwide.
- Liam received his first bicycle, a used Rover 1890 model, as a birthday present at the age of nine.
- The Rover combined into a single bike J.K. Starley's chain drive system with John Dunlap's innovative pneumatic tires.
- The result was a more comfortable ride, increased speed, and the creation of a whole new industry that employed thousands of machinists and assemblers.
- Like millions of American men and women, Liam fell in love with the speed made possible by the modern bicycle.
- Since the 1890s, advances such as air-filled tires, more durable chains and sprockets, and better design had ignited a cycling craze.
- Customers of the finely made, mass-produced bikes, which sold for between $50 and $100 each, were initially from the more affluent class.

Liam Hanratty (right) was a professional cyclist.

Liam made good money competing.

- But cheaper models and secondhand bicycles made bicycling a democratic activity, and less expensive than keeping a horse.
- The Ideal Bike Company even advertised a $20 bike fit for young and old.
- Dazzled by the speed and flexibility the new cycles offered, entire communities banded together to organize 10-mile speed races from town to town.
- Prized for winners ranged from a silver cup to property suitable for building a house.
- Liam showed substantial skills in the sport, especially the two-mile sprint events.
- He also excelled in his studies at school, giving rise to a parental dream of their son attending the College of the Holy Cross, the oldest Roman Catholic college in New England, founded in Worcester in 1843.
- Liam was torn.
- He didn't want to disappoint his parents, but attending Holy Cross would mean abandoning his beloved cycling.
- When Liam was 16, the college dream ended when his father, Kierman, a railroad lineman, was killed in a work-related accident.
- Almost immediately Liam had to go to work, and care for his mother.
- He found employment as a mechanic in a bike factory, a job that required mechanical skills, as well as extensive testing of new racing models.
- By the time Liam turned 20 years old, was married to Colleen O'Hara, a young schoolteacher whose Irish Catholic parents had immigrated to America in the late 1860s.
- Liam met Colleen at a dance and quickly got the approval of her parents, John and Rhiannon O'Hara, to court.
- They were impressed with the hard-working young machinist who looked after his widowed mother so well, if only he could get over his silly bicycle racing dreams.
- This regret vanished when they discovered that Liam made $1,200 from professional racing that year—almost twice his mechanic's pay.
- Typically, weekend road races paid for first, second and third place finishes; even running second or third, Liam could earn up to $100 per weekend.

Liam and Colleen moved into Liam's mother's house and purchased a state-of-the-art refrigerator.

- That same year, Liam's mother, Kate, took everyone by surprise when she announced her upcoming marriage to grocer Thomas Shea.
- This decision allowed Liam and Colleen to move into Kate's house, and they quickly used their money to buy the latest appliances.
- Their first purchase was a Leonard cleanable refrigerator lined with genuine porcelain enamel, fired on sheet steel that cost the couple $27.50.
- They also purchased an Acme Regal a steel range that was nickel-plated throughout, for $20.55, and an Acme room-heater that used hard or soft coal for $9.95.

Life at Work
- After the tragic death of his father in 1897, Liam Hanratty dropped out of school and secured work as a machinist at the Worcester Cycle Manufacturing Company.
- The company was run by Lewis "Bertie" Monger, a former bicycle racer-inventor, who managed one of the brightest new racing talents in the racing scene, black champion Major Taylor.
- The Bertie Special, Monger's flagship bicycle, was fast, light, elegant and critically proclaimed by racers as a machine built purely for speed.
- The bike had everything, except enough customers.
- With the market already saturated with new inventions and innovative bicycles, Monger's masterpiece sold for $150—more than $50 above its competitors.
- Columbia marketed its own good-quality model at $80.
- New York City alone boasted 1,200 bicycle builders, supporting nearly 7,000 professional riders.
- As bicycle sales diminished at Worcester Cycle, Liam learned that cycling offered dozens of ways to make money, particularly where Major Taylor was concerned.
- Liam turned professional.

- His specialty was the sprints, although he also competed in long-distance races covering 10 to 20 miles.
- He wasn't interested in the continuous race in Madison Square Garden.
- Contestants in this race rode for six days and six nights on the dangerous, steeply banked indoor track, stopping only periodically to sleep.
- This popular competition was attended by more than 5,000 spectators, who filled the air with their cigar smoke, shouts of encouragement and wagers.
- Winner of the $5,000 prize typically clocked nearly 2,000 miles during the six days.
- This race was so arduous, that the health of several riders severely suffered, causing newspapers to call for the race to be banned.
- Liam earned steady money protecting Major Taylor during his races.
- Taylor's calm domination of so many races provoked planned violence against the Negro star including thrown fists, intentional blocking and damage to his bike.
- Liam's job was to keep pace with Major and prevent the assaults.
- Liam had known Major Taylor for years, often riding literally in his shadow during races, but he held no resentment that a black racer dominated the sport.
- Despite rival white riders attempting to sabotage Major Taylor efforts during a race, Taylor broke records in the one-third-mile sprint, as well as the one- and two-mile races.
- Liam took pride in the fact that Taylor depended upon him during important races, but he loved winning his own races best of all.
- Endowed with powerful legs and a light frame, Liam was capable of great bursts of speed as he drew near to the finish line, pushing both himself and his bike to the limit.
- After four years of gaining notice, Liam was sponsored by a closed gear company, and a local tailor designed for him—free of charge—a cycling outfit.
- Liam made sure he looked his best when he raced, and was always impeccably dressed in his racing outfit
- After all, many national newspapers had declared bike racing the most popular spectator sport in America.
- The League of American Wheelmen boasted over 100,000 members, and a highly contested race could draw 20,000 spectators.
- A baseball game typically attracted only 2,500 fans.
- During the wintertime, Liam trained at the Worcester YMCA, which had recently added weights to its facility, allowing Liam to improve his upper body strength.
- The YMCA was a leader nationwide in organizing team games and competitions as a way of absorbing the idle time of city boys and instilling in them the habits of good hygiene, self-discipline and respect for officials.

Life in the Community: Worcester, Massachusetts
- Founded in 1713, Worcester, in central Massachusetts, was the state's second-largest city and a hub of industrial activity at the turn of the century.
- At the dawn of the Industrial Revolution, Worcester's machine and tool industry was one of the nation's largest, making equipment for factories, mills and workshops all over America.

- The city was heavily populated by Irish, Swedish and Armenian immigrants.
- A large Irish Catholic enclave had been established in the late 1700s, and the College of the Holy Cross was founded in Worcester in 1843.
- The city was linked with the bigger commercial centers of New York, Boston and Pittsburgh by excellent railroads.
- Early on, manufacturing towns in New England, including Springfield and Waltham in Massachusetts, and Hartford and New Haven in Connecticut, had provided the skilled labor for the development of high wheel bicycles and the technology that made the safety bike universally popular.
- With a population of approximately 100,000 people, Worcester offered young couples, like the Hanrattys, a full spectrum of social activities.
- To placate his wife, Liam took lessons in the waltz, two-step, polka and the quadrille for $5.00.
- The community was large enough to have hosted a presidential parade for William McKinley, whose re-election bid emphasized prosperity by using the full dinner pail as its symbol.
- Colleen adored children and loved her job as a public school teacher
- Every year, Liam and Colleen took selected children to Buffalo Bill's Wild West and Roughriders show where arena seats could be had for a dollar each.
- The Hanrattys also attended the Great 4-Paw and Sells Brothers Enormous United Circus, featuring Diavolo's Loop the Loop.

Every year the Hanratty's took Colleen's students to Buffalo Bill's Wild West Show.

HISTORICAL SNAPSHOT
1901

- The American yacht *Columbia* defeated British challenger *Shamrock II*, continuing a 50-year winning streak by American yachts in the biennial America's Cup

- The Peace of Peking (Beijing) ended the Boxer Rebellion in China

- At the Pan-American Exposition in Buffalo, New York, deranged anarchist Leon Czolgosz shot President William McKinley, who became the third American president assassinated after Lincoln and Garfield

- Theodore Roosevelt renamed the "Executive Mansion" the "White House"

- Edward Elgar's "Pomp and Circumstance" March premiered in Liverpool

- Field hockey for women made its first appearance in the United States under the tutelage of Candace Applebee, of Vassar University

- Race riots across America, sparked by Booker T. Washington's visit to the White House to dine with President Theodore Roosevelt, killed 34

- The U.S. was given extensive rights by Britain for building and operating a canal through Central America

- The Army War College was established in Washington, DC

- King Camp Gillette, a former bottle-cap salesman, began selling safety razor blades

- Italian scientist and engineer Guglielmo Marconi received the first long-distance radio transmission in St. John's, Newfoundland—2,232 miles

- New York Stock Exchange trading exceeded two million shares for the first time in history

- The American Bowling Congress held its first national tournament in Chicago

- The Automobile Club of America installed directional signs on major highways

- Britain's Queen Victoria died at age 82, after presiding over her empire for nearly 64 years—the longest reign in British history

- Women prohibitionists smashed 12 saloons in Kansas

- The Pan-American Exposition in Buffalo, New York, which featured the latest technologies including electricity and the baby incubator building, attracted nearly eight million people

- U.S. Army soldiers led by Brig. Gen. Frederick Funston captured Emilio Aguinaldo, the leader of the Philippine Insurrection of 1899

- The Oldsmobile plant in Detroit was destroyed by fire

- New York became the first state to require automobile license plates, and charged $1.00 for them

- Walter Reed led the Yellow Fever Commission to Cuba to search for the cause of the disease, where Cuban Dr. Carlos Finlay believed that yellow fever was spread by mosquitoes

- The Wild Bunch, led by Butch Cassidy, committed its last American robbery near Wagner, Montana, taking $65,000 from a Great Northern train

- Hubert Cecil Booth patented the vacuum cleaner

Selected Prices

Bicycle Tire	$2.65
Bicycle, Lady's	$8.95
Palm Reading	$2.00
Pocket Flask, Leather-Covered	$0.80
Range, Acme Regal	$20.55
Rolltop Desk, Oak	$11.95
Sells Brothers Circus	$0.25-$2.00
Spectacles	$1.90
Telephone, Residential Rate, Year	$48.00
Wine, Case	$5.00

Bicycle Racing Timeline

1817

A two-wheel running machine, or velocipede, was invented by German Karl Drais, in response to widespread starvation that led to the slaughtering of horses for food.

1863

A stiff, steel-wheeled bicycle known as the bone shaker, added a front wheel with pedals that was a direct-drive, fixed-gear machine, incorporating one speed.

1870

The introduction of the ordinary or "high wheeler" which featured very large solid rubber tires with long spokes on the large front wheel, popularized the term "bicycle" for "two wheel."

1872

German Friedrich Fischer began the mass production of steel ball bearings, patented by Jules Suriray in 1869.

1876

Browett and Harrison of England patented an early caliper brake.

1878

Scott and Phillott (English) patented the first practicable epicyclic change-speed gear fitted into the hub of a front-driving bicycle.

1879

Henry J. Lawson (English) patented a rear wheel, chain-driven safety bicycle, the "bicyclette."

1880

Thomas Humber (English) adapted the block chain for use with his range of bicycles.

1880s

American women, confined by their long skirts and corsets, rode on an adult tricycle that included rack-and-pinion steering, a differential, and band brakes.

1884

Cyclist Thomas Stevens rode 3,700 wagon trail miles from San Francisco to Boston to complete the first transcontinental bicycle ride.

1888

Pneumatic tires were introduced, dramatically improving the comfort and safety of riding.

1890

Metallurgy improvements led to the popularity of the safety bike, which incorporated chain and sprocket design small and light enough for a human being to power comfortably.

Mass production lowered the cost of bicycles, providing affordable transportation to the average working person, while expanding leisure time choices.

Bicycle manufacturers, sales agencies and private individuals had opened women's riding schools in many northeastern cities; the Metropolitan Academy in New York City set aside a special area for women wishing to learn the mysteries of wheeling, and installed the first athletics-linked shower baths for women in America.

Two and three-day bike tours organized by regional or national cycling groups were common middle class activities; small membership fees and road books provided information about routes, road conditions, hotels, repair shops and "consuls"—club members in towns and cities appointed to answer the questions of touring cycles.

continued

Bicycle Racing Timeline . . . *(continued)*

1892

The song "Daisy Bell," later retitled "A Bicycle Built for Two," gained widespread popularity.

1893

High wheelers were used in competition for the last time.

1894

The number of women riders soared as bicycles became lighter and bloomers came into fashion.

The bicycle messenger business was invented in California when a railway strike halted mail delivery for the San Francisco Bay Area.

1895

Ignatz Schwinn and Adolph Arnold formed Arnold, Schwinn & Company to produce bikes.

The Michaux Club of New York City offered women riding lessons in the morning, indoor riding to music after lunch, and afternoon tea in the clubroom; indoor riding eliminated the possibility of young couples riding off in private, or any chance of immodest exposure of women's limbs.

1898

Major Taylor became the American cycling sprint champion; he was one of the first black athletes to become a world champion in any sport.

"Scarcity of Cyclists, Chance for Second Raters, Revival of Racing Craze in Europe Leads to Exodus of American Riders," *The Salt Lake Tribune* (Utah), March 30, 1902:

From indications, there will be a great demand for bicycle racing men the coming season and this city will not be so well supplied as in former years. Europe has secured the best riders in the United States by offering them big advance money, and with the exception of Frank Kramer from Newark, New Jersey, all have accepted and will sail from New York about May 1st. Iver Lawson, who had decided to remain here until the latter part of June, has been signed by a Paris syndicate and will leave here in a few days for New York. The departure of all the first-class racing men from America to Europe means a gold mine to the second rate man who will be able to get in on some of the big money along the national circuit.

Charles Turville, who has been racing here for the past two years, writes to friends that he will remain in the East this year, having received several good propositions. William King, who came here as an amateur from Los Angeles, California, and later became a professional, has announced his intention to remain in the East and W.E. Samuelson of Provo also will probably remain East for the opening meets. A month ago there were at least a dozen riders in the East anxious to come out, but the majority of them have been signed for Eastern teams.

The amateurs who have been training for the Decoration Day Road Race have been put out very much the past two weeks by the bad weather, which made them return to indoor training. The roads have been in an unrideable condition, and all-wheels have to be hung up for the time being.

"Thriving Organization of Madison County's Metropolis Now Has Membership of 100, Owns Beautiful Clubhouse and Course," *The Post Standard,* Syracuse, New York, April 24, 1904:

The Oneida Golf Club is now one of the most popular organizations in the city of Oneida. The membership is about 100 and will be increased this year. Besides affording such an excellent opportunity for out-of-door exercise, the club is also noted for its social gatherings.

The grounds are situated on the Seneca Turnpike at the head of Broad Street and only a short walk from the end of the streetcar line on Main Street. They comprise the old Ira Chapin farm. In the center of the grounds and on top of the hill is located the Clubhouse.

This week, work has commenced by greenskeeper S. H. Diehl on the fair and putting greens, but the cold weather has retarded the work. From now on the grounds and Clubhouse will be open and it is expected that playing will be commenced as soon as the weather will permit.

Let me tell you what I think of bicycling. I think it has done more to emancipate women than anything else in the world. I stand and rejoice every time I see a woman ride by on a wheel. It gives women a feeling of freedom and self-reliance.

—Susan B. Anthony, 1896

There is a lot of cheap sporting blood in certain of the cycle racers, and it never has shown more clearly than in the case of Taylor, who, as a rider, is really superior to most of them, and as a peaceful, well-behaved athlete, gives far less trouble to his managers than others who feel themselves so much superior to him.

—*New York Journal,* July 1, 1898

Industrial Worcester,
Charles Grenfill Washburn, 1917:

Worcester has developed from a country town to a great manufacturing city in less than 90 years. Within that time the steam engine, the railroad, telegraph and commercial use of electricity have enormously increased the productive power of labor. The improvement in the condition of the laboring classes is no less marked; contrary to the opinion once held, the introduction of labor-saving machinery has advanced instead of lowered wages; has reduced instead of extended the hours of labor . . . many of our mechanics own their own homes, and are naturally deeply interested in the welfare of the city. Avenues for advancement are always open to the capable and industrious. From their ranks will come the leading businessmen for the next generation, upon whom the continuance of prosperity will depend.

The Saturday Evening Post, January 1901

The American love of sports has risen to a pitch never before known. Until the middle of the century just closed we were practically without sports, and even until some 15 years ago there was very little enthusiasm aroused by sports compared with the fever that has within the past decade and a half swept over the country. Year by year the ardent fervor has been increasing, and the coming season promises to be the most enthusiastic of all. . . . This is the era of sport. Practically every man and boy, woman and girl, takes part or wishes to take part in some branch of it. And it is fortunate that the field is broad enough for all. In all this eager devotion to it, there is nothing harmful, nothing that points a warning. On the contrary, it is for individual and national good. It gives health and tone to the system, it clears and freshens the mind by bright exercise and competition in the clear, open air, and drives cobwebs from wearied brains. And thus it is that this era of enthusiastic devotion to sport is good.

1904 Profile

Lydia Ulrich, who was naturally competitive, fell in love with archery as a child and decided to give herself a chance to compete in the Olympics for her twentieth birthday.

Life at Home

- There was an elegance to archery that Lydia Ulrich enjoyed immensely.
- Releasing a perfectly drawn arrow was an act of physical poetry; to actually strike the target exactly where aimed elicited a surge of excitement she didn't fully understand.
- The fifth child and only girl of an affluent New York City banker and his socialite wife, Lydia was pampered, placated and spoiled by all.
- As a toddler she was obsessed with chasing after her older brothers, determined to ride well, skate quickly or run faster to keep up with them.
- Known for her competitiveness, Lydia was especially eager to challenge her brothers the first time she saw an archery tournament during a picnic on her father's estate.
- She had to try it.
- But when it became her turn, she felt clumsy and uncoordinated; the bow was hard to pull and the arrows had a mind of their own.
- Worse yet, her brothers laughed at her.
- It would not happen again.
- While her older brothers concentrated on dozens of sports, including bike racing and football, Lydia focused on one—archery.
- As a result, she became very good and was sought after as an archery partner.
- From age 12, she practiced daily.
- In secret, Lydia lifted paint buckets—two at a time—to strengthen her arms so she could master the smooth drawing back of the bow without a whisper of a waver.

Lydia Ulrich fell in love with archery as a child.

Lydia was hoping to catch a beau with the elegance displayed when drawing her bow.

- She toughened her hands by helping her brothers move rocks.
- She practiced shooting targets from three different distances—each requiring a different adjustment for wind and arrow drift.
- Through the years, she was tempted at times to abandon archery for the emerging excitement of lawn tennis or croquet
- Tennis, however, offered few opportunities to socialize with young men and croquet required stooping, and it was "impossible to look graceful in that position."
- She knew of half a dozen marriages ignited by the beauty of a woman elegantly drawing her bow.
- At 16 years old, she had delightedly scribbled in her journal, "To catch a beau requires a bow."
- She especially loved the romantic history of archery, and enjoyed telling friends that after fire and the wheel, the bow and arrow were mankind's "third invention."
- Early man's survival had depended upon the bow and arrow.
- Genghis Khan's army had conquered worlds with the bow and arrow, and longbow experts of England in the Middle Ages had shaped world history with their expertise.
- The first known archery tournament held in 1583 in Finsbury, England, was said to have attracted 3,000 archers.
- Popular sayings such as point blank, high strung, straight as an arrow, and wide of the mark all originated with archery.
- The oldest continuously held archery tournament still in existence, the Ancient Scorton Arrow, was founded in Yorkshire, England, and dated to 1673.
- Lydia claimed, with a laugh to mask her intensity, that not many sports had that kind of legacy.
- Certainly not cycling, or baseball.
- Besides, in this modern age, the finest outdoor social events included an archery match among men and women.
- Many hostesses believed that recreational archery was the appropriate accompaniment to an impromptu picnic on the lawn or a long anticipated formal dinner.
- What better way to meet men and look good at the same time?
- Even the tools of the trade were attractive.
- Traveling to a meet meant carrying a bow box normally constructed of oak and measuring more than six feet.
- In the box was one compartment with at least two bows, held in position by wooden cradles and leather straps; two compartments for arrows and another with a lid of lead, for accessories such as quiver, spare springs, grease pot, bracer, glove and scorecard.
- When Lydia and her friends all stood together at the shooting line, they looked impressive, which was just as important shooting well.
- For most archery meets, Lydia dressed in the costume of her club—white was favored by the younger women, dark colors preferred by older competitors.

- On the day Lydia turned 19, she wondered out loud whether the corset was truly necessary and began avoiding the most fashionable sporting brassiere because of its excessive weight and discomfort.
- After all, the most critical fashion statement of any self-respecting woman archer was her hat.
- Lydia preferred large, impressive hats with beautiful bird feathers, and occasionally an entire bird, that emphasized her love of nature.
- She believed her hats helped celebrate the beauty of wildlife in America.
- Others wore functional, trendy straw boaters as a way of showing their seriousness and dedication to the sport.
- The one disadvantage to an outdoor sport, Lydia believed, was the tendency of the wind to lick at her skirt and expose her ankles.
- To avoid this embarrassment, especially in that moment when her bow was fully drawn, she wore an anti-Aeolian.
- This contraption of leather straps equipped with lead weights, fitted over her skirts to maintain her modesty and ensure that no gentleman had cause for distraction.
- Gentlemen customarily wore shooting jackets secured at the top by a button.
- Arrows were carried either in a deep, leather-lined pocket or a leather pouch designed to fit within the pocket.

Lydia loved large, impressive hats.

Life at Work

- For almost three years, Lydia Ulrich had been grousing that the 1900 Olympics in Paris had included men's archery but offered nothing for women.
- Where was the fairness in that?
- In fact, archery had a longer, more distinguished resume than many of the permitted sports.
- In addition to swimming events, yachting, gymnastics, and equestrian events, the 1900 games offered ballooning, Fireman's carry, auto racing, tug-of-war, cricket, and live pigeon shooting—but not one arrow for a woman!

Men dominated archery in the Olympics until 1904.

- Baron de Coubertin, founder of the modern Olympic movement, was uncompromising in his view of women as athletes.
- He would do anything to ban them from entering any Olympic activity.
- In 1903, however, he bowed, albeit ungraciously, to include women's archery.
- He had no choice.
- Not only had women successfully competed as archers for at least 50 years, but the host country requested it.
- In 1900 the International Olympic Committee (IOC) had decided that the 1904 Olympics would be held in the United States, with Chicago, St. Louis, and Buffalo all wanting to be the first city in America to hold Olympic games.
- The honor was awarded to Chicago, but organizers of the Centennial of the Louisiana Purchase in St. Louis objected to another international event competing with their exposition.
- In 1903 the IOC changed their minds and awarded St. Louis the Olympic prize.

- James Sullivan, president of the Amateur Athletic Union, was hired to take charge of the Olympics.
- Sullivan held an expansive view of what constituted an Olympic game and promoted events ranging from high school football tournaments to a hurling game waged by two Native American schools.
- Lydia knew before she arrived at the World's Fair honoring the Louisiana Purchase of 1803 that Matilda Howell of the United States would win the archery event.
- Matilda, or Lida, was an experienced, long bow shooting machine, and cool under pressure.
- For competition, the women used a 34-pound draw weight for the longer 50-yard distance and a lighter poundage for the shorter 30-yard distance.
- Lydia's arrows were 26 inches in length and glistened with green tinted feathers, a color of her own choosing.
- She protected her fingers from the string with rubber leather tips, secured by straps to a wristband.
- Since 1878, Peck and Snyder of New York had been marketing archery equipment to women since it was "peculiarly adapted to their habits and nature."
- Women were advised, for example, to look carefully at their clothing, and avoid narrow waists
- They claimed that "A lady who wears a tight corset need not hope for much physical benefit from archery, or, for that matter from anything else."

- The advantages of the sport for women, according to Peck and Snyder, was that a "most fragile young woman, by means of judicious archery practice, developed muscles that, when her arms were flexed, rolled up into balls like a blacksmith's biceps."
- Archers were advised to take an hour's quiet time after eating, or half an hour spent leisurely in the open-air following brain labor and to avoid all smoking pipes until after shooting practice was over.
- *Archery, Its Theory and Practice,* by Horace Ford, advised archers to adopt a comfortable upright but not stiff position, in which the feet are at right angles to the target with the toes some six to seven inches farther apart than the heels.
- He believed the head should be turned toward the target, with a facial expression that was at once "calm, determined and confident."
- Lydia understood these requirements perfectly.
- A respectable showing at the Olympic Games was to be her gift to herself for turning 20 years old.
- What she did not anticipate was the wind, the punishing heat and lighting in Missouri that she wasn't accustomed to.
- Plus, the September event attracted only a handful of spectators but an inordinate number of strange bugs.
- Lydia was uncomfortable.
- During her opening round, her draws were jerky, her release unsure.
- Using a 20-pound pull bow, Lydia was to shoot 24 arrows at a four-foot-diameter target set 30 yards away, then 40 yards away, and then 50 yards away.
- Each distance required different skills, especially when the wind was blowing in unexpected gusts.
- Top score was 10 possible points.
- One point was awarded for the high score at each distance, one point for the high number of hits at each distance, two points for the high total score, and two points for the high total number of hits.
- Lydia's goal was to challenge Lida Howell.
- She didn't come close.
- Unlike other competitions, Lydia was nervous, unfocused, and hot.
- All around her, crowds rushed from one exhibition to another, shouting their excitement.
- The random, uninvited noise caused Lydia to rush her shots, and shoot from an awkward stance.
- She felt as though she acquired someone else's body, someone who didn't understand the rhythm of archery of all.
- She told friends later, that missing the target altogether with her final shot accurately symbolized her Olympic trials in St. Louis, Missouri.

Life in the Community: St. Louis, Missouri
- St. Louis, Missouri, the fourth-largest city in the U.S., considered itself a world-class cultural center.
- The Fair took six years and $15 million to build, and employed 200,000.
- 1,500 buildings were constructed across 1,275 acres of the fairgrounds.
- Scheduled to open in 1903, the centenary of the Louisiana Purchase, the Fair ran behind schedule and was delayed until the following year.
- During the Fair's seven-month run, 20 million visitors attended, often traveling by railroad.

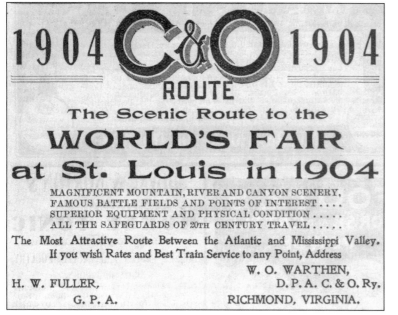

1904 C&O 1904

ROUTE

The Scenic Route to the

WORLD'S FAIR

at St. Louis in 1904

MAGNIFICENT MOUNTAIN, RIVER AND CANYON SCENERY,
FAMOUS BATTLE FIELDS AND POINTS OF INTEREST....
SUPERIOR EQUIPMENT AND PHYSICAL CONDITION.....
ALL THE SAFEGUARDS OF 20TH CENTURY TRAVEL.....

The Most Attractive Route Between the Atlantic and Mississippi Valley.
If you wish Rates and Best Train Service to any Point, Address

W. O. WARTHEN,

H. W. FULLER,   D. P. A. C. & O. Ry.

G. P. A.   RICHMOND, VIRGINIA.

- The Minneapolis and St. Louis Railroad offered two trains daily from Minneapolis, including Pullman sleepers for $25 a person round-trip.
- On April 30, 1904, alone, 187,000 people came to St. Louis and witnessed the grand opening of the Louisiana Purchase Exposition.
- President Theodore Roosevelt opened the Fair from Washington using the same telegraph key with which President Cleveland had opened the Columbian World's Fair in 1893.
- Most of the buildings, structures and statues built for the Fair were demolished after the exposition closed.
- Thomas Edison oversaw the setup of the electrical exhibits, including the Palace of Electricity, which covered seven acres.
- A Moving Picture Theatre gave many Americans their first glimpse of the new medium, and the first opportunity to communicate across thousands of miles by wireless or telephone.
- The Fair demonstrated how food could be cooked in minutes using electricity.
- Over half a million electric light bulbs lit the Fair buildings and water cascades at night.
- The Fair also featured various food sculptures: an 18-foot lighthouse built entirely from salt; a salt sculpture of Lot's wife; a butter sculpture of President Teddy Roosevelt; and a prune sculpture of a bear.
- The 1904 St. Louis Olympic Games, that were spread out over four and a half months, were often forgotten in the chaos of the World's Fair.
- In all, 651 athletes competed in 94 events, including six women and 645 men.
- Although 12 countries were represented, more than 500 competitors were from the United States, and 50 were from Canada.
- European tension caused by the Russo-Japanese War and the difficulty of getting to St. Louis kept many of the world's top athletes away.
- In a number of sports, because there were no competitors from other nations, the U.S. national championship was combined with the Olympic championship.
- For the first time, gold, silver and bronze medals were awarded for first, second and third place competitors.

Thomas Edison supervised the electrical exhibits, including the Palace of Electricity, at the 1893 World's Fair.

The swimming competition about to begin.

- Boxing and freestyle wrestling made their debuts.
- Marathon runners Len Tau and Jan Mashiani, Tswana tribesmen who were in St. Louis as part of the Boer War exhibit at the World's Fair, became the first Africans to compete in the Olympics.
- One of the most remarkable athletes was the American gymnast George Eyser, who won six medals even though his left leg was made of wood.
- American marathoner Fred Lorz received a lifetime ban when it was discovered that he allowed an escort to give him a lift during the grueling 26-mile race.
- In the end, only 14 of the 32 entrants finished the race.

Marathon runners Len Tau and Jan Mashiani were the first Africans to compete in the Olympics.

HISTORICAL SNAPSHOT
1904

- The American Powerboat Association staged the first major powerboat race in America on the Hudson River near New York
- The baseball World Series was canceled after the National League championship team, the New York Giants, refused to play against the American League champion, the Boston Pilgrims
- William Vanderbilt created the Vanderbilt cup race for automobiles, which drew 25,000 spectators and was won by George Heath, averaging 52 miles an hour
- Charles Follis became the first African-American professional football player when he was signed by the Shelby Ohio Blues
- The *Ladies' Home Journal* published an exposé of the popular patent medicine business
- Boston pitcher Cy Young threw the first major league perfect game of the century against the Philadelphia Athletics
- Colgate ribbon dental cream, Campbell's pork and beans, the Caterpillar tractor company, the St. Francis Hotel in San Francisco and offset printing all made their first appearance
- The Supreme Court ruled that Puerto Ricans, while not citizens, could not be refused admission to the United States
- The Broadway drama of Puccini's *Madame Butterfly* was a runaway hit
- In college football, the value of a field goal was reduced from five to four points, a touchdown remained at five points, and a conversion at one point
- Popular books included *Extracts from Adam's Diary, A Dog's Tale* by Mark Twain and *Cabbages and Kings* by O. Henry
- Amanda Clement of Iowa became the first female umpire to officiate a men's baseball game for pay
- First-class passage on the *Lusitania* from New York City to Liverpool, England, was $65
- Ragtime musician Scott Joplin wrote "The Cascades," inspired by the waterfalls at the Grand Basin, specifically for the World's Fair
- John Philip Sousa and his band performed on opening day and several times during the Fair
- Helen Keller, who was 24 and had graduated from Radcliffe College, gave a lecture in the main auditorium

- President Roosevelt dined at the St. Louis Inn in the "Alps," and was entertained by a young lariat-wielding comedian named Will Rogers
- The waffle-style ice cream cone was invented and first sold during the Fair
- Peanut butter, iced tea, and cotton candy, advertised as fairy floss, were first introduced to mass audiences and popularized by the Fair
- Dr. Pepper and Puffed Wheat cereal were first introduced
- J.T. Stinson, a well-regarded fruit specialist, coined the phrase "an apple a day keeps the doctor away" at a lecture given during the exhibition

Selected Prices

Alarm Clock	$2.50
Automobile, Graham Roadster	$850.00
Baseball Calendar	$0.30
Bookcase	$18.25
Buggy	$59.75
Camera	$3.75
Corset	$2.25
Light Bulb	$1.50
Motorcycle	$200.00
Tombstone	$29.00

"Archery to the Fore, Potomac Club getting members in the form for taking part in the international competition to be held the latter part of this month at the World's Fair in St. Louis," *The Washington Post*, September 11, 1904:

The archers of the Potomac Club are putting in the best and most strenuous practice they know preparatory to sending a representation to the forthcoming international meet in St. Louis in the latter part of this month. The practice shooting is being conducted on the Mall opposite the National Museum, and Saturday, and being now a half holiday for most members of the club, is the time for the meet. Three huge targets, now liberally punctured with holes, are set up at ranges varying from 30 to 100 yards; about 1:30 o'clock the first and champion archer is apt to make his appearance on the scene. He is known among his conferees as "the colonel"; in his hair partakes of the gray of the traditional goose feather on the arrows.

The colonel inspects the arrangements that have been made by a hired man, which include a number of bows and arrows enveloped in cases, neatly arranged among the green sward and other paraphernalia of archery, together with a jar of ice water, the latter most welcome, for the sun beats down rather fiercely upon the devotees of the noble sport. The arrows are carefully examined by the colonel, who, finding one of them too heavy, or as he terms it in archery parlance, "slow," proceeds to file it down to the proper weight proportions, explaining meanwhile for novices the skill with which the little sticks are made, the scientific exactness with which the wood, rare South American species, is dovetailed, and the feathers and points put on.

Now another archer makes his appearance and fraternal greetings are exchanged, while two ladies are seen advancing from a distance across the spacious lawn. The colonel explains a great interest is being manifested in archery this year in Washington, as well as other places across the country, the membership of the Potomac club, which has been in existence for the past 20 years, having increased during the last few months by nearly 50 per cent. The parade ground in the Washington Barracks has hitherto formed the scene of the club's practicing, and it is only recently that the Mall has been substituted.

The archers have now assembled to the number of about a dozen, of which some four or five are of the fair sex. The latter are most enthusiastic devotees of the bow and arrow, though inclined evidently to be rather nervous at the start, as indeed are some of the masculine contingent. Of the gentleman, however, two veterans, the colonel, and another military looking personage, display the utmost coolness and sang froid from the very commencement, stringing their arrows to their bows, taking a keen and commanding view of the target, and letting fly with a precision that might be envied by an Indian chief. The colonel puts in three bull's eyes in a dozen shots at a distance of 100 yards, and comes out champion, though closely emulated by the other expert who gets two bull's eyes at the same distance and at the same number of shots. Some of the newer members of the club fly wide of the mark, and their arrows display the most astonishing gyrations, now standing on their heads, striking the target sideways and bouncing up again high into the air.

As the archers get warmed up to their work, the little missiles are let off in confusing numbers, for the most part apparently into space, though they are all eventually recovered by the shooters who, after a certain round has been fired, all go down in a body to count the scores and hunt for the elusive arrows. Not the least trial to the archers in the prosecution of their sport is the ubiquitous small boy who persists in getting in the way and crouching almost under the elbow of the marksman, whom he further irritates with critical remarks noticeable for frankness and volubility rather than admiration and respect.

No sooner are bow and arrow carefully poised and eye and nerves at the nicest tension when the urchin on one side breaks out with, "He's goin' to hit it this time, Bill," while a contemptuous, "No he ain't," from the other accompanies a twinge of chagrin and disappointment across the archer's features as he sees his arrow fly wide of the mark.

Despite drawbacks from this and other causes, the Washington archers are getting into fine form, while the colonel and a few other old and tried shots lead them to hope for a good showing at the forthcoming international contest.

"Full of Thrills, Such will be the International Olympic Games of 1904," *The Mansfield News* (Ohio), October 7, 1902:

Since the revival of the historic Olympic Games by the king of Greece in 1896, 1,600 years after the last ancient games had been celebrated in Greece, a similar event occurs every four years. It was decided by an international committee of 224 representatives of different nations to hold the next in the series in Chicago.

Plans are on a larger scale than ever before attempted and the greater part of September and October will probably be required to carry them out.

World championships will be decided in foot racing, equestrianism, cycling, rowing, swimming, archery and gymnastics. England will be represented by cricket teams, America by base ball, France by boxing with the feet, Germany by fencing and Japan by wrestling. Boomerang-throwing, archery, etc., from the Philippines will also be included.

A novel and exciting feature will be that furnished by a test of horsemanship. Ten wild horses which have never been bridled, saddled or ridden will be numbered and turned loose. Contestants must catch, bridle, saddle and ride them twice around the arena. Forty or fifty minutes are generally required by the winner. These tests are almost as productive of thrills as a Spanish bullfight without the cruelty attending that barbarous past time.

In the evenings historical athletic displays of a spectacular nature will be introduced with the pageantry of ancient Greece and Rome and the knightly tourneys of medieval Europe.

The president publicly expressed an earnest desire that troops from all parts of the world come to strive for supremacy with a large detachment of regular United States soldiers he will send to compete.

At the close an Olympic congress of leading men of the world will discuss sportsmanship, athletics and military matters from the intellectual and scientific side.

As Shining .. Lights ..

From Newspaperdom, July 9, 1903

One does not have to look only to New York for "clean" newspapers. As shining lights of this better class of journalism stand out prominently the Chicago Tribune, the Chicago News, the Detroit Free Press, the **Detroit Times** (formerly "To-Day"), the Cincinnati Enquirer, and many others—every one of them tremendous financial successes.

N. M. SHEFFIELD
Adv. Mgr. The Detroit Times

"Stretching the Long Bow," *The Rake Register* (Iowa), February 19, 1904:

The Olympic Games at St. Louis will bring to the surface something like 57 varieties of sport which flourish in odd corners, far from publicity's searchlight. So little is published regarding archery in the United States, as a current pastime, that there is an air of novelty in the announcement that the meeting of the National Archery Association, to decide the national and international championships, will be held at the Purchase exposition. There will be "night shooting," according to the programme, and this meeting should prove one of the most interesting of the programme of the great athletic carnival. Archery in the United States, says *Illustrated Sporting News,* lost its most persuasive champion in the passing of Murray Thompson, whose book, *The Witchery of Archery,* has sent the youth of a whole generation afield to hunt, as did their forbears in the days of Robin Hood. Sir Conan Doyle is the most attractive living chronicler of stirring tales of the bow of yew and the cloth-yard shaft, as framed in the rousing pages of *The White Company.* To the wholesale out-of-door boyhood, Mr. Ernest Thompson-Stetson is a vigorous missionary of the "bow and arrow" spirit, and the influence of his work, *The Little Savages,* will someday furnish champions for meetings of the National Archery Association of the United States.

"Two Million Kegs of Horseshoes," *The Louisville Courier Journal* (Kentucky), August 12, 1904:

"Two million kegs, containing 100,000,000 horseshoes, are currently used annually in the United States and Canada, approximately speaking," says S.L. Martin of Boston, who represents an iron manufacturing consent of the East.

"That was about the number used last year, and all the hew and cry about rubber shoes and automobiles is raised in the face of the constantly increasing sale of horseshoes. As a matter of fact, the use of rubber horseshoes, which is confined almost altogether to the large cities, is a help to manufacturers. The sale of the old-fashioned shoes goes on increasingly, and in addition to that, manufacturers have an opportunity to make the steel portion of rubber shoes. All so-called rubber shoes have a rim of steel in them, and it is usually a better steel that gives the manufacturer a wider berth for profits than the old-fashioned shoe."

Archery Timeline

2800 BC
The first composite bow was produced by the Egyptians, made from wood, tipped with animal horn and held together with animal sinew and glue; it could be shot 400 yards and would easily penetrate the armor of that time period.

250 BC
The Parthians (from what is now Iran and Afghanistan) would battle with bows from horseback. They developed a technique of pretending to flee, while firing arrows back toward the enemy, which evolved into the phrase "a Parthian shot" and later "a parting shot."

1208 AD
The Mongols used composite bows of approximately 70 pounds.

1307
Legendary William Tell refused to bow toward a hat placed on a pole as a sign of imperial power and was ordered to shoot an apple off of his son's head.

1346
The French army included crossbow men. Their crossbows were fitted with cranks used to draw back the bowstrings.

1520
The musket was invented.

1644
The last battle occurred in which English archers were used; contests of archery skill came into vogue in England.

1800s
The term "first stringer" originated among archers, who saved their best strings for major competitions.

1870s
Forbidden to use guns following the Civil War, former Confederate soldiers employed bows and arrows to hunt, sparking a nationwide archery revival.

1872
Ephraim Morton of Plymouth, Massachusetts, was granted a patent for his wood handled bow with steel rod limbs.

1900
Archery for men was included in the Olympic Games.

1904
Archery for women was added to the Olympic Games.

The sound body is the safest guardian of morality and of civilization. So agree teachers and philosophers as well as physicians. The first decade of the new century finds the world ready to actively support the movement toward intelligent physical training, the principal avenue to which is sane competitive athletics.

—Sportsman James Sullivan,
President of the Amateur Athletic Union

In no place but America would one have dared to place such events on a program, but to Americans anything is permissible.

—IOC president Pierre de Coubertin regarding the "Anthropological Days"
event held during the 1904 Olympic Games

"Sports at the White House," *The New York Times,* May 10, 1904:

The President's encouragement of athletic sports has borne good fruit speedily. The three baseball diamonds that have been laid out in the lot south of the White House are in use constantly, and the grounds are proving an admirable field for the game.

Col. Symons has assigned the various local leagues to the different diamonds and they allot time for their use among themselves. The President has not infrequently gone out to witness some of the games, his sons accompanying him and manifesting great interest in the playing. It has now been decided to give the lovers of quoits a chance to have their sport on the White Lot. Col. Symons has given orders that grounds for the game be laid off in the northwest corner of Monument Field, near Fifteenth and B Streets, where there is a fine turf, with a shade of some magnificent elms.

Archery grounds also have been laid off in the Smithsonian grounds. It is possible that the President will permit golf links to be described through the Mall and the Monument grounds. This is being considered.

"'King' Kelly's Medal Now in Hands of a Pawn Broker," *The Post-Standard,* Syracuse, New York, April 24, 1904:

NEW YORK—In a pawn shop in Park Row is a medal presented to Mike "King" Kelly—"ten thousand dollar" Kelly. Customers ask, who is he? A tragic commentary indeed upon life's little span.

The medal was presented in 1887 by the *Boston Globe* shortly after the baseball world had been electrified by the announcement that the Boston Nationals had purchased Kelly from Chicago for the sum of $10,000. It cost about $250, but now resides in a pawn shop window, tarnished, dusty and forgotten.

Fifteen years ago Michael J. Kelly was conceded to be the best all-around player in the profession, being able to take any position except pitching, and occasionally he even did that. He was born in Troy, New York, and had his first professional engagement with the Olympics of Paterson in 1876-77. . . .

He was regarded in baseball like John L. Sullivan in pugilism. He caught frequently without hat, mask, protector or mouth rubber and was regarded as the best catcher that ever stood behind the bat. He "kidded" a crowd with more audacity than any player before or since. . . .

Kelly stood five feet eleven inches and weighed 180 pounds. He led the league batsman with an average .370, but too many changes in the field make high averages difficult there. Kelly played with New York in 1893, and after that managed a team in Allentown, Pennsylvania. He died November 8, 1894, of acute pneumonia in the Emergency Hospital at Boston.

Medalists—Archery, 1904

Gold
George Bryant—men's double York round
George Bryant—men's double American round
Matilda Howell—women's double National round
Matilda Howell—women's double Columbia round
Matilda Howell, Jessie Pollock, Laura Woodruff, and Louise Taylor—women's team round
Potomac Archers—men's team round

Silver
Robert Williams—men's double York round
Robert Williams—men's double American round
Emma Cooke—women's double National round
Emma Cooke—women's double Columbia round
Emma Cooke and Mabel Taylor—women's team round
Cincinnati Archers—men's team round

Bronze
William Thompson—men's double York round
William Thompson—men's double American round
Jessie Pollock—women's double National round
Jessie Pollock—women's double Columbia round
Boston Archers—men's team round

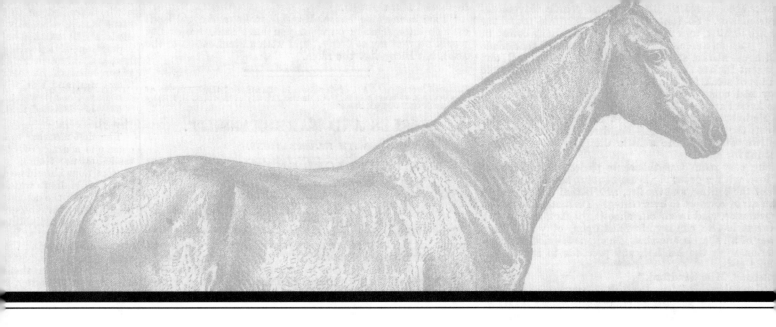

1909 PROFILE

Giuseppe Giacometti grew up in the village of Tresilico, located in the toe of the Italian boot, where old men gambled for fun and horses were raced purely for sport.

Life at Home

- Becoming an American bookmaker was far from the goals of Giuseppe Giacometti when he left the Italian army in 1898.
- He was simply determined to have a better life than his father, who died landless and in debt, leaving seven children and a wife behind.
- Later in life Giuseppe, his parents fourth child and second son, would tell his wife he was born to bookmaking, flamboyantly recounting childhood stories of how he memorized all the names of village elders before he was five.
- Work was difficult to find in Tresilico, where Giuseppe was toiling as a day laborer for a wealthy plantation owner when the itch to emigrate became overwhelmingly tempting.
- While talking with an estate manager in 1899, Giuseppe learned that the Mexican government had come to Italy to hire men to build a railroad in Mexico.
- Italians and Irish had a good reputation for railroad building.
- The Mexican government promised passage of 200 men to Mexico and good wages once they got there.
- Giuseppe and several of his friends were immediately swept up by the excitement, even though for Giuseppe it meant leaving his wife and one-year-old son behind.
- Giuseppe saw this as an opportunity to see the New World, and earn

Giuseppe Giacometti was determined not to pick fruit the rest of his life.

Giuseppe left Italy to work on the railroad in Mexico.

enough money to return to Italy a wealthy man, no longer obligated to take the menial jobs offered by the estate managers.

- It was not the first time Italians had been tempted to leave their homeland in large numbers.
- The first wave of Italian immigration to North America occurred after the unification of Italy in the 1860s, and involved primarily northern Italians who sailed to New York and settled in the Eastern United States.
- By 1880, the Italian population in the U.S. jumped from 4,000 in 1850, to 44,000, and to 484,000 by 1900.
- The second wave of Italian immigration began around 1881 when many southern Italians began to emigrate to the U.S. through the port in New Orleans.

- In America, where cheap land was becoming harder to find, the traditionally agricultural Italians became mostly urban dwellers.
- Starting from the bottom of the occupational ladder, they worked shining shoes, rag-pickers, sewer cleaners, and whatever hard, dirty, dangerous jobs others didn't want.
- Children worked at an early age, as in Italy, at the expense of their education.
- Italians were known for rarely accepting charity or resorting to prostitution for money.
- They earned a reputation for diligence and sobriety as workers, and sought jobs as fishermen, shoemakers, waiters, fruit sellers, and tradesmen.
- Giuseppe took another route entirely, starting his journey to America in Mexico as a railroad man.
- Over the objections of his wife, Giuseppe left Italy in February 1900, planning to help build a railroad from Veracruz to Brownsville, Texas, and return to Italy.
- The Mexican government wanted the work done quickly, but failed to mention the horrendous working conditions, the cholera epidemic or the unbearable heat.
- Two of Giuseppe's fellow villagers died in the first month and three more left during the dark of night, soon after they arrived.
- Giuseppe learned not to trust anyone, especially the Mexicans he worked with.
- The only safe place to keep his money was in the bottom of his shoes, so he slept with his shoes on.
- Despite the difficulties, Giuseppe lived cheaply and mailed his wages home, praying that he would one day return to his homeland.
- At the first opportunity to cross the Rio Grande into Texas, Giuseppe gladly paid $4.00 passage, left railroad building behind, and hopped a freight train to San Antonio.
- There he encountered language barriers and little sympathy.
- Imitating a goat did not get him goat's milk, only laughter, and his desire for olives and cheese went unsatisfied despite a readiness to pay.
- Giuseppe was working harvesting pecans when he was recruited to cleanup after the devastating Galveston hurricane that killed more than 8,000 people.
- Bodies were strewn all over the island, and there was a fear of plague.

Crossing the Rio Grande into Texas.

- Giuseppe was hired to gather the bodies in a pile so they could be burned, a horrible task that paid well.
- Despite being warned to turn in all jewelry found on the bodies, six workers were shot and killed as an example, when they were found with jewelry in their pockets.
- Terrified by what he had seen, Giuseppe eagerly moved to New Orleans in 1901, where he discovered his future—bookmaking horse races within the Italian community.
- Since the beginning of written records, horse racing had been an organized sport in all major civilizations from Central Asia to the Mediterranean.
- Modern horse racing began in the twelfth century when English knights returned from the Crusades with Arab stallions.
- The first racetrack in America was built in Long Island, New York, in 1665, and racing was widely practiced throughout the colonies.
- Organized racing arrived after the Civil War.
- By 1894, when the American Jockey Club was formed to control corruption and illegal betting and doping; there were 340 tracks operating across the country.
- In 1900, a wave of anti-gambling sentiment swept the nation, so that by 1908 the number of racetracks plummeted to just 25.
- Horse racing without betting attracted few fans, and wagering on the race was integral to the appeal of the sport.
- The city of New Orleans encouraged its citizens to have fun in a variety of ways, and Giuseppe found a willing market for his new found profession.

Giuseppe was hired to gather dead bodies from the Galveston hurricane.

Giuseppe stayed away from the brothels in New Orleans.

Life at Work

- Giuseppe Giacometti began his gambling career as a runner, collecting bets around town in the streets and alleyways of New Orleans.
- It wasn't a difficult task, compared to railroad work or hurricane cleanup, consisting of keeping track of little slips of paper for the bookies who handled the bets at the track outside New Orleans.
- Horse racing, known as the Sport of Kings, was no longer entertainment for the wealthy, was becoming popular with the common man as a way to earn a few extra bucks with a well-timed bet.
- Giuseppe averaged between $200 and $300 a day in total gross receipts, with his take five percent—$10 to $15 a day.
- Because gambling was not controlled centrally in New Orleans, the rules often changed, so that it was not uncommon for Giuseppe to fight for his territory with his fists—a task for which he was well suited.
- He worked long hours, and stayed away from the brothels in Storyville.
- By 1905 he was the favored bookie within the Italian enclave of New Orleans, where he spoke the language and displayed an uncanny ability to match names to faces.
- He always remembered who was a winner, and never took a marker from a deadbeat twice.
- By 1906, despite a national movement against gambling, Giuseppe was doing extremely well
- As technology made it possible to make bets on horse races across the nation, the business of gambling business was transformed by electronic wire services.
- Western Union, originally designed as a means of transferring money, quickly became a way for bookmakers to manage a far-flung network of off-track betting.
- Gamblers could place a bet with the bookies anywhere in town, usually in a pool hall.

Pool halls were popular places for gamblers to hear winning lottery numbers.

- Pool halls became popular places for gamblers to hear the winning lottery tickets.
- Lottery tickets were sold all day and results posted late at night, so proprietors of pool halls installed billiard tables to entertain their customers while they waited.
- Eventually the billiard tables took on the name of the pool hall, named for the lottery, or "pooled" tickets.
- With off-track betting on the rise and Western Union moving both information and money across the country, pool rooms became a center for all forms of gambling and owners installed large betting boards for their patrons.
- Thanks to the telegraph, gamblers could follow baseball games inning by inning, "witness" championship boxing matches through round by round descriptions, and place last minute bets on everything from tennis matches in New York to the chance of rain in Denver.
- Advances in the telephone and telegraph allowed an elaborate nationwide syndication network that supported the explosion of racehorse wire, or pool, rooms.
- Gambling brought millions in revenues to the fledgling telephone and telegraph industries.
- Racetracks viewed wire-service reporting as such a threat, because it discouraged patrons from visiting the track, that public phones and visible transmission of results were not permitted at racetracks.
- Gamblers hired spotters to flash detailed information from within the racetrack using complex hand signals to associates nearby, who then wired the information to the sports network.
- Bookies paid a weekly fee for these up-to-the-minute reports from racetracks.
- This is how Giuseppe and his customers tracked jockey changes, scratches and changing odds, and the position of each horse at each quarter post.
- As the results rolled in Giuseppe would read them out loud, in his most dramatic voice, quarter post to quarter post, while his customers cheered, slapped each other's backs and placed more bets.
- During one of these result readings, Giuseppe got an idea.
- Why work for someone else when the Italian community trusts only one person?
- In 1906, Giuseppe used his savings to buy a pool hall with nice furniture, a gigantic map of Italy and a tote board that covered one entire wall.
- He also sent for his wife and eight-year-old son to join him in America.
- Giuseppe quickly gained a reputation for settling wagers swiftly and accurately.
- Although his book accepted bets from a quarter to $25, the average bet was just under $5 per person.
- His pool room was an immediate success.
- His reunion with the wife he had not seen in seven years, was less successful.
- She was frightened by the boisterous sounds of New Orleans, offended by Giuseppe's path to wealth, and shocked that the shy young husband she remembered seven years ago knew everyone he met and talked non-stop in English or Italian—often mixing the two.
- She also objected to the harlots from Storyville hanging around the pool room on their days off.
- Giuseppe's son loved the excitement and quickly learned English, further alienating his mother.
- These years also ushered in the phenomenal success of the 1908 LSU Tigers football team, coached by Edgar Wingard and several business challenges.

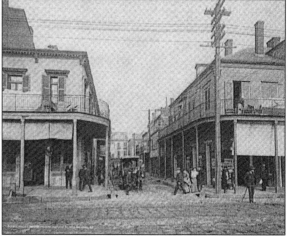

The Italian section of New Orleans was called "Little Palermo."

Giuseppe's wife was not comfortable in New Orleans.

- Giuseppe understood little about college football, but got an expensive education when LSU played their way to a 10-0 record.
- Convinced, every week, that the Tigers would lose big, he took too many bets from LSU supporters.
- This cost him a fortune and a deep dislike of college athletics.
- At the same time, many racetracks, following the model established at the 1908 Kentucky Derby, had begun promoting pari-mutuel betting.
- Developed by Frenchman Pierre Oller, pari-mutuel wagering was a system of betting whereby the winners divided the total amount wagered, after deducting management expenses.
- Giuseppe was convinced that it was a scheme to close down pool rooms like his.
- Already politicians were talking about ways to tax gambling profits and the local police were increasing the pressure—and the cost—of ignoring certain activities.

Life in the Community: New Orleans, Louisiana
- The port city of New Orleans, with a population of 300,000, considered itself "The First City of the South."
- According to *Bay View* magazine, in 1908, "It is among the few cities in our country that can be compared to New York in respect to their metropolitan qualifications, but New Orleans leads all the rest, though in population it is small beside all the others."
- New Orleans boasted an old and exclusive society that supported grand opera, fine theaters and restaurants, and towering church edifices.
- Significantly, its sights were the accumulation of nearly two centuries of Spanish, French and American origin, all blended together.

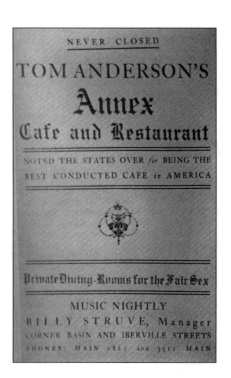

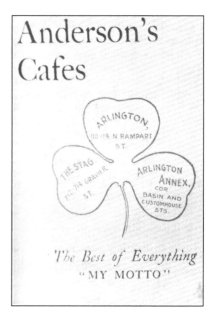

BATTLE OF NEW ORLEANS

- It was an atmosphere irresistible to modern adventure seekers in 1909.
- Louisiana became a French crown colony in 1731.
- Crops, grown on plantations, included indigo, rice, and tobacco; trade was primarily by water and the few roads ran along the levees.
- In 1762, Louisiana was ceded to Spain as a result of the French and Indian War, and Great Britain gained control of Florida, which extended to the east bank of the Mississippi.

New Orleans was home to an exclusive society that supported fine homes and highbrow culture.

- At the same time, Acadians, driven from Nova Scotia by the British, began migrating to Louisiana.
- The Spanish made feeble attempts to offset the growing French population, but were not successful.
- In 1800 Spain returned Louisiana to France by the Treaty of San Ildefonso.
- Although Napoleon I originally intended to establish a new empire in America, he sold Louisiana to the United States in 1803.
- The $15-million Louisiana Purchase represented about 4 cents an acre.
- Louisiana became the eighteenth state on April 12, 1812, comprising the territory south of 33 degrees north latitude, which had been the Territory of Orleans.
- Not until 1819 were the Florida Parishes and the lands west of the Red River added to form the present state boundaries.
- Once the territory became part of the U.S., the Creoles were united in the belief that "Americans" must be kept separate from their far more cultured company.
- The city's Canal Street became the dividing line or "commons area" where the Creoles allowed trade with the Americans, but nothing more.
- By 1860, population exceeded 700,000, and a class system based on plantations with slave labor had developed.
- During the Civil War, the importance of the port of New Orleans and Louisiana's strategic position on the Mississippi made it an early Union target and the state's economy was devastated.
- By 1909 the port of New Orleans was booming with cotton exports and the French Quarter was occupied with tourists seeking adventure.

HISTORICAL SNAPSHOT
1909

- Ernest Shackleton's expedition claimed to have found the magnetic South Pole

- United States troops left Cuba after being there since the Spanish-American War of 1898

- The National Association for the Advancement of Colored People (NAACP) was founded, commemorating the 100th anniversary of President Abraham Lincoln's birth

- The Hudson Motor Car Company was founded

- Popular movies included *Gertie the Dinosaur*, the first animated film; *In a Lonely Villa* with Mary Pickford, and *The Prince and the Pauper*

- William Howard Taft succeeded Theodore Roosevelt as the 27th president of the United States

- Rocky Mountain fever was shown to be transmitted by the tick louse

- Leo Baekeland invented Bakelite, a plastic that wouldn't melt with heat

- The cork-centered baseball was introduced

- The Kewpie Doll, *Vogue* magazine, the electric toaster, Walter Reed Army Medical Center, Western auto supply stores, Castro motor oil and high-strength aluminum alloys all made their first appearance

- America's automakers produced 127,731 automobiles, twice the production of 1908; 34 states adopted a 25 mile an hour speed limit

- Theodore Roosevelt embarked on a post-presidency safari to Africa sponsored by the Smithsonian Institution and the National Geographic Society

- The Sport Club Internacional was founded in Porto Alegre, Rio Grande do Sul, Brazil

- Robert Peary, Matthew Henson, and four Eskimo explorers came within a few miles of the North Pole

- Joan of Arc was beatified in Rome

- The Alaska-Yukon-Pacific Exposition opened in Seattle

- Alice Huyler Ramsey, a 22-year-old housewife and mother from Hackensack, New Jersey, became the first woman to drive across the United States, taking 59 days

- The United States Army Signal Corp Division purchased the world's first military airplane, a Wright Military Flyer built by the Wright Brothers

- The first event was held at Indianapolis Motor Speedway

- Congress banned opium imports except for medical purposes

- The world's first billionaire, John D. Rockefeller, gave away $500 million for medical research

- The U.S. Navy established a navy base in Pearl Harbor, Hawaii

- Two United States warships were sent to Nicaragua after 500 revolutionaries (including two Americans) were executed by order of dictator Jose Santos Zelaya

Selected Prices

Cigarettes, Pack	$0.10
Delivery Wagon	$97.00
Express Mail, Flat Rate	$0.27
False Teeth	$5.00
Plantation, Louisiana	$45,675
Pocket Watch, Gold	$10.50
Telephone	$10.20
Toy Aeroplane	$0.98
Violin	$19.95
Windshield	$25.00

"New Orleans Fire Burns Three Blocks,"
The Nebraska State Journal, August 31, 1908:

Fire which broke out in the center of the commercial district this afternoon swept over portions of the three blocks, destroying a large number of wholesale houses, manufacturing plants and small stores. Originating at Bienville and Chartres streets, the flames worked their way north as far as Oony street and west towards Royal, causing a loss of between one and two million dollars before they were finally subdued.

At the time the alarm was turned in, shortly before 3 o'clock, the New Orleans firemen were in the midst of their annual picnic at a suburban park and the engines and patrols responded with a mere handful of men. It was nearly an hour before the department was able to make anything like a successful fight against the fire, and the horror was added to by an insufficient supply of water.

The fire was one of the most spectacular that has occurred in New Orleans during recent years.

Two warehouses filled with wines and liquors were among the buildings destroyed. Barrels of whiskey and brandy exploded with thunderous roars, which could be heard for blocks and which shook the walls of adjoining buildings and endangered the lives of the firemen engaged in fighting the flames.

It was not until several hours had lapsed that the fire was gotten under control, and even then it continued to burn well into the night.

Site of the fire in New Orleans.

The most common types of bets on horse races include:

- Win—To succeed the bettor must pick the horse that wins the race.
- Place—The bettor must pick a horse that finishes either first or second.
- Show—The bettor must pick a horse that finishes first, second or third.
- Exacta, perfecta, or exactor—The bettor must pick the two horses that finish first and second, in the exact order.

- Quinella or quiniela—The bettor must pick the two horses that finish first and second, but need not specify which will finish first (similar to an exacta box).
- Trifecta or triactor—The bettor must pick the three horses that finish first, second, and third, in the exact order.
- Superfecta—The bettor must pick the four horses that finish first, second, third and fourth, in the exact order.

"McPherson Is Beaten at Billiards," *The Oakland Tribune* (California), December 31, 1910:

McPherson played his last game in the three cushion tourney at the Oakland billiards parlor and met defeat at the hands of Baruch. It was a decisive victory for Baruch, as Mac was handicapped 23 to 30 but could get no further than 14 when Morris had the game won. McPherson can hold his own in individual contests, but fell short of his customary speed under the requirements of tourney play.

Jones and Mann should furnish a fine exhibition in their contest Friday evening. The tourney will, aside from probable ties, come to an end in next week's schedule. John Overlander's welcome face was largely an evidence of the parlors yesterday after an absence of two years. Overlander has been the Oracle for Oakland billiardists and his playing was a delight when seen last. His game is replete with grace and skill, and embodies the nearest technical perfection of any of our prominent cue artists.

"Legislature Worries Fans, Sports Are Anxious As to Fate of Racing and Boxing," Eddie Smith, *The Oakland Tribune* (California), December 30, 1910:

Now that the gathering of the members of the new legislative body of the State of California is about to convene, members of the sports loving fraternity are taking on their regular worried look. . . .

This has always been an occasion of unrest among the lovers of professional sports and this year more than ever the fans of various sports are worrying, the reason being that many of the new members of the body have been elected on what was termed the reform ticket. This reform is taken by some to mean that the state will be ruled by a lot of sanctimonious fools whose every desire will be the elimination of things they do not believe in, but in this case this is not so.

The governor of the state is not the sort of man who falls in love with the sissified young men and is not the type to say that ping-pong is the only good sport for the young to indulge in. I bet my life that Gov. elect Hiram W. Johnson would disown one of his own sons if he was to catch him playing tiddlywinks. And this can be said of many of the other newly elected legislators, this specially applying to those from the northern section of the state. . . .

In regard to the racing situation, it would seem that the movement afoot to establish the use of Pari-Mutuel betting machines is gaining strength and that the appointment of a racing commission is also growing stronger every day. The passage of such a bill would also mean the death knell of the present system of betting and would mean the commission would be appointed that would be none too friendly to the present regime of the racetrack officials. . . .

The people at present in control of the racing games are not in the least in favor of the Pari-Mutuel machines and will no doubt make a fight against the passage of the bill making such betting legal. They insist that they will be very well satisfied with the present situation and can see no reason for a change.

"Gambling: Money Interest Involved," *The Encyclopedia of Social Reform*, 1908:

One of the prime reasons for the continuance of pool rooms, in spite of legislation and the occasional raiding by the authorities, is the enormous financial interest in them which are willing and usually able to pay the largest amounts of immunity from and even protection by the police. The necessity also for the telegraph and telephone to the pool room, to enable it to secure its news from the racetrack, makes the income from the telegraph and telephone companies from the source so valuable that they are willing to go to great lengths to maintain the service and protect the gamblers. Mr. Josiah Flint (author of a series of articles in *Cosmopolitan* magazine, 1907) estimates that the Western Union Telegraph Company and the telephone companies received recently from $5 to $10 million annually from the racetrack and pool room service. Many people believe that if it were made impossible for pool rooms to secure telegraphic service, at least pool room gambling, by far the greatest evil, would be cut off.

"Making of Criminals Through the Race Track," Dr. T. P. Wilson, *Overland Monthly Magazine*, November 1910:

The California Jockey Club, better known, perhaps, as the Emeryville School of Crime, is preparing for the greatest racing season in the history of the state. There will be from 700 to 1,000 more horses entered than ever before, and it is expected that the attendance will average fully, if not over, 5,000 daily during the entire season, which commences in November next, continues until June of next year, a grand total of more than 1,000,000 trackside patrons of the season; there will be six races every day, with an average of about 12 horses in each race. To take care of the several staples and conduct the several departments of business, the services of at least 2,000 employees will be required, and judging by former seasons, the daily betting will be from $200,000 to $300,000, including the outside pool rooms in the Bay area and throughout the state. Perhaps it is safe to say these estimates of the aggregate of the sums of money wagered in California on the Emeryville races each day are all of 25 percent too low, and when it is remembered that nearly every trade center of importance in the United States maintains one or more pool rooms, with special telegraphic services with the racetrack, some idea can be had of the influence for evil the Emeryville racing season exerts upon the whole country.

There should be a vehement and persistent demand all over California for the abolition of the Emeryville racetrack, but not only for the sake of the good name of the state of California, but because the people of this Commonwealth owe it to the country at large to refuse any longer to permit the maintenance of the California Jockey Club's School for Crime, an institution that encourages crime of all degrees and states of degradation in men and women and boys and girls. The people of the other states have the right to measure the moral status and the standard character of social California by the legal aid and comfort of the legal prohibition it throws about Emeryville's open gates and the influence for the encouragement of crime and social divide. . . .

This much is true in any event; no person, young or old, man or woman, could become a devotee, or even an occasional spectator of the events at Emeryville and long maintain his or her self-respect. Everything there tends to lead the mind to lower levels, lower ideals, lower standards of conduct of life, nor is one restraining influence to be found that is born of wholesome domestic or home or commercial life. Only vice is seen in the events of the hour, and such influences as plead for still greater moral degradation are the only arguments in the justification of the track performances therein.

Storyville Classified ads, *Sunday Sun*, New Orleans, Louisiana, 1906:

Miss May O'Brien, proprietress of 1549 Customhouse St., popular with all, has a house full of beautiful young girls and increasing her business daily. May is the Irish Queen, and always has a sweet smile on her face. The many strangers who will come to the city during the Mardi Gras should not fail to visit this establishment.

* * * * * * * * * * * * * * * * * *

Maggie Wilson, a buxom and pretty woman who lives at 1314 Customhouse St., informs the Carnival visitors who are out for a good time to call on her, and she will give them a run for their money and that's no dream.

* * * * * * * * * * * * * * * * * *

Everybody in the sporting world knows Miss Flora Meeker and she knows everybody worth knowing. So it is unnecessary at this time to make any introductory remarks about Miss Meeker, suffice to say she is still at her same old place where she has been for a number of years past, doing a business which she deserves. Miss Flora is well thought of by all and her house is patronized by the best element. Carnival visitors should not overlook this swell mansion where the cream of female loveliness will be found which is situated at number 211 Basin Avenue.

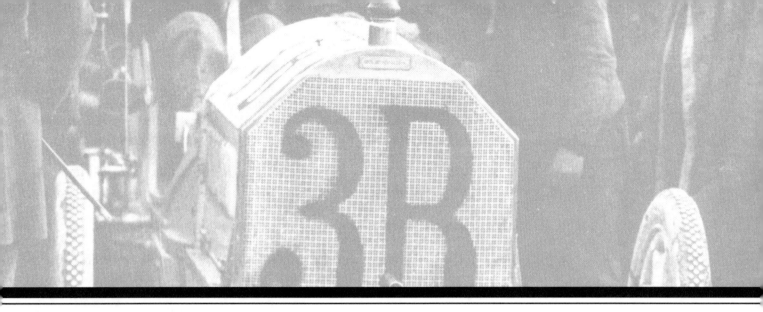

1904 NEWS FEATURE

"The Racing Automobile and Its Relation to the Development of the Pleasure Vehicle," *Scientific American*, January 30, 1904:

To the casual spectator, the side of the huge racing machine dashing around a track at a mile-a-minute clip is in itself an interesting and more or less thrilling spectacle. The higher the speed and the greater the risk run by the operator, the more intense is the excitement as he makes the dangerous turns amid clouds of dust. When several evenly matched cars are running together, rounding the turns at express-train speed and in imminent danger of collision, while the chauffeurs strain every nerve in their efforts to steer them and get out of them the highest speed possible on the straight stretches, one is reminded of the mad excitement of the ancient chariot races of the Romans on the oval track of the great arena.

But apart from the excitement and exhilaration of the race, such competitive speed trials are of the greatest benefit to the automobile designer, first because, sometimes through failure and sometimes through success, they point the way to improvements in construction which, when tested and proven, are incorporated in the regular stock machine; and, secondly, because they give a chance for comparison of different forms of construction under conditions of very severe strain.

Abroad, the benefits of racing have been generally taken advantage of and races have largely been hailed on the highways, which, because of their wide, smooth surfaces, form almost perfect courses for the testing of automobiles at high speeds and over long distances. Generally a circuit 50 or 75 miles in circumference is laid out, and the contestants traverse it several times. The annual race for the Bennett trophy, which is an international affair, has become a classic race abroad; and, if it is ever won by an American machine, it will have the effect of introducing road racing in this country, as the race follows the cup and is always held in the country whose team won the previous year. France, England, and Germany have each had the trophy, and the race next year will be held in the last-named country. The success of the German "Mercedes" machine in 1903 has been attributed by many to the use of ball bearings in the transmission gear and other important parts, and, as a result, many of the foreign manufacturers, as well as some here, have readopted the familiar form of anti-friction bearing on their 1904 machines.

In America, racing has been largely confined to the ordinary racetrack, with occasional straightaway speed trials. During the latter part of the past season, the Winton eight-cylinder racer, which failed to make any showing in the Bennett race last summer, demonstrated the soundness of its principles of construction by winning many races and making new records in various racetracks throughout the country. Driven by Barney Oldfield, it made a mile in 55 seconds; 10 miles in nine minutes, 32 1/2 seconds; and 15 miles in 14 minutes, 21 seconds, all of which are track records for machines weighing over 1,800 pounds. A four-cylinder racer of the same make holds the mile, five-mile, and 10-mile records for machines weighing from 1,200 to 1,800 pounds. . . .

The Ormonde-Daytona Beach on the east coast of Florida is said to be the finest speedway in the world. The second annual race meet, in which the best American, French, and German racers are entered, is being held there this week. New straightaway records were recently made there by the Packard "Gray Wolf" racer, driven by Charles Schmidt, and a Stevens-Duryea chassis, driven by Otto Nestman. The former machine being a 25-horsepower, four-cylinder motor, and weighs 1,400 pounds while the latter has two double-cylinder motors that develop 14 horsepower, and weighs complete 900 pounds. Both have the same size engines as are fitted to their respective firm's regular stock cars. The Packard and 1904 "Voiture Legere" have been directly developed from the experience of the Packard Company with each racer throughout the past season, while the Stevens-Duryea racing chassis was built to demonstrate the speed possibilities of that company's motor. This machine showed its rapid hill climbing abilities at the Eagle Rock, N. J., hill climbing test last Thanksgiving day, by ascending the one-mile hill in 1:37, which was only 1/4 second less than W. K. Vanderbilt, Jr.'s, time. At the most recent attempts to break records with this machine in Florida, it covered a mile in 57 1/5 seconds, thus lowering by nine seconds the previous record for machines of this class, which was made at the same place by the Oldsmobile racer a year ago. . . .

Spurred on by these newly made records on the Florida Sands, Henry Ford next made an attempt to beat them on a specially prepared course on the ice. The trial was made with the reconstructed Ford-Cooper racer, and it was successful. The astonishing time of 39 2/5 seconds was recorded by the official timekeepers, which means a speed of 90 miles

an hour. This new record makes it seem as though the speed of 100 miles an hour will soon be realized. Such speeds are in themselves of no benefit, yet there is no denying the fact that the strains to which they subject the mechanics of the racing car are so far in excess of those met by the everyday runabout or touring cars, that if these are built with practically the same strength of parts, the factor of safety must be very great.

In other words, just as a piece of steel that is incorporated in a modern auto must have several times the strength necessary to withstand the stresses that are likely to be put upon it, so the complete machine should be constructed that it has a large factor of safety. Just how strong to make every part is first somewhat a matter of experiment, and it is far better to risk the life of one man who realizes his danger, than to jeopardize the lives of numerous purchasers who are unconscious of the risks they are taking. Before the development of the racing car and the trying out of parts upon it, the automobilist was liable to serious accidents, such as the breaking of the steering gear or the rear axle; but now, as a result of these exhaustive and machine wracking speed tests, a purchaser buying a car from a firm that has had racing experience is pretty sure to obtain one that is not structurally weak, and with which there is not much chance for a dangerous breakdown.

1910–1919

The recreation movement that emphasized fresh air, exercise and sports blossomed during the second decade of the 1900s. Reformers thought of themselves as being on an exciting new mission to Americanize immigrant children on how to have fun. Increasingly during the decade, sports were organized by age group or size with an emphasis on participation and not always on winning. At the same time, sports stories concerning professionals and amateurs began crowding the daily newspapers while golf gained a foothold in affluent cities across the nation, spurring the building of nine-hole and 18-hole golf courses.

Following the lead of the YMCA, cities around the country founded Sunday school athletic leagues in the years leading up to World War I. Between 1911 and 1917 the number of playgrounds in major cities doubled from 1,543 to 3,940. America's entry into World War I only intensified the enthusiasm for sports. Gen. John J. Pershing asked the YMCA to manage Army facilities employing 12,000 trained physical directors who took charge of athletics in the American Expeditionary Forces in France. In addition, the Knights of Columbus, the Jewish Welfare League and the American Library Association all lent support to the troops. Soon athletics became central to the operations of Army and Navy bases and as a direct result, the American Legion launched its own athletic program in 1925 to "inculcate" good citizenship.

For most of the decade, the economy was strong and optimism was high, especially among the newly emerging middle class—the beneficiaries of improved technology, a stable economy and the unregulated, often unsafe labor of the working class. Jobs were available to everyone; Americans enjoyed full employment, yet hours remained long and jobs were dangerous. Child, female and immigrant exploitation remained, despite a rising level of progressive debate regarding the plight of the underclasses.

Women banded together for full suffrage and against alcohol. Worker-inspired unions battled for better working conditions, and minorities of various origins, colors and faiths attempted to find their voice in the midst of a dramatically changing world. The emerging middle class was proving that it was capable of carrying a greater load of managerial decisions. Millions of dollars were poured into libraries, parks and literacy classes designed to uplift the immigrant masses flooding American shores. The United States was prospering and the elite were re-evaluating America's role as an emerging world power which no longer looked to Britain for approval.

In the midst of these dynamics, the Progressive Movement, largely a product of the rising middle class, began to shape the decade, raising questions about work safety, the rights of individuals, the need for clean air and fewer work hours. Nationwide, communities argued loudly over the right and ability of women to vote and the need and lawfulness of alcohol consumption.

During the decade, motorized tractors changed the lives of farmers, and electricity extended the day of urban dwellers. Wireless communications bridged San Francisco to New York and New York to Paris.

Yet in the midst of blazing prosperity, the nation was changing too rapidly for many—demographically, economically and morally. Divorce was on the rise. The Missouri Christian Endeavor Society tried to ban films that included kissing. The rapidly expanding economy, largely without government regulation, began producing marked inequities of wealth—affluence for the few and hardship for the many. The average salary of $750 a year was rising, but not fast enough for most people.

But one of the biggest stories was America's unabashed love affair with the automobile. By 1916, the Model T cost less than half its 1908 price, and nearly everyone dreamed of owning a car. Movies were also maturing during the period, with 25 percent of the population, including many newly arrived immigrants, going to the nickelodeon to marvel at the exploits of Charlie Chaplin, Mary Pickford, and Douglas Fairbanks, Sr.

The second half of the decade was marked by the Great War, later to be known as the First World War. Worldwide, it cost more than nine million lives and swept away four empires—the German, the Austro-Hungarian, the Russian, and the Ottoman—and with them the traditional aristocratic style of leadership in Europe. It bled the treasuries of Europe dry and brought the United States forward as the richest country in the world.

When the war broke out in Europe, American exports were required to support the Allied war effort, driving the well-oiled American industrial engine into high gear. Then, when America's intervention in 1917 required the drafting of two million men, women were given their first taste of economic independence. Millions stepped forward to produce the materials needed by the nation. As a result, when the men came back from Europe, America was a changed place for both the well-traveled soldier and the newly trained female worker. Each had acquired an expanded view of the world. Yet women possessed full suffrage in only Wyoming, Colorado, Utah and Idaho.

The war forced Americans to confront one more important transformation. The United States had become a full participant in the world economy; tariffs on imported goods were reduced and exports reached all-time highs in 1919, further stimulating the American economy.

1913 PROFILE

Francis Ouimet was fascinated by golfers and their sporting tools, and grew to adulthood at the same time golf was maturing into a visible, competitive sport in America.

Life at Home

- Twenty-year-old Francis Ouimet grew up reading Harry Vardon's book, *The Complete Golfer,* and collecting "Vardon Flyer" golf balls that he discovered on the course near his home.
- Now he was scheduled to play against his hero, a man 23 years his senior, in the most important tournament of his life.
- The newspapers billed the 1913 U.S. Open as a battle between the rising American amateur and the golf star of Britain.
- Francis was born in Brookline, Massachusetts, a Boston suburb that was home to one of the first golf courses in America.
- The Country Club was also his father's occasional employer, providing the French-Canadian immigrant with work as a coachman or gardener.
- The English Protestant oppression from which his father had fled in Canada was replaced by Boston intolerance of immigrant "Frenchies."
- From his two-story clapboard house directly across the street from the Country Club, Francis could see the 17th fairway and green.
- Francis and his brother Wilfred designed their own golf course in an overgrown cow pasture near their house; the first hole required a 100-yard carry off the tee over a creek to a small oval green.
- The second hole was a par three; the third hole crossed back over the creek to a circular green in their own backyard.
- Tin cans from the kitchen served as cups; the two boys carved their own clubs and the badly hit golf shots from the nearby Country Club supplied them with a sufficient number of golf balls.

Francis Ouimet and his older brother, Wilfred.

The Ouimets lived across the street from the Country Club.

- The Country Club first opened its doors in 1882 and added golf six years later to complement an annual horse racing season, archery, tennis, polo, ice-skating and curling.
- The club started with a six-hole course that generated so much interest three more holes were added within a year.
- Twenty sheep were imported from Devonshire, England, to keep the fairways clipped.
- In Brookline, the popularity of the sport was exploding as Francis spent hours watching golfers chip and putt their way past his window while he dreamed of perfecting his swing.
- For most of the nation, however, golf was a curiosity played by the British, the wealthy and powerful.
- Typical 56-hour work weeks left little time for the time-consuming—and expensive—game of golf.
- The cost of lessons, $0.75 an hour, was beyond the reach of Francis, as were custom clubs at $2.50 each or a golf bag at $4.00.
- Rubber tees sold for $0.25 each, and Haskell golf balls cost three for $1.00 at the pro shop.
- When he was eight years old Francis was able to trade three dozen found golf balls at Wright & Ditson's Sporting Goods store for a fairway two wood, called the cut-down brassie.
- His second club was a five iron known as a mashie, followed by a chipping wedge or niblick.
- At age nine Francis began to caddie during the summer, an occupation that not only gave him spending money but an opportunity to study golfers up close in a variety of situations.

Francis caddied at the Country Club, enjoying being around golfers.

- He quickly soaked up an insider's knowledge of the course and its rules.
- His mother was not pleased.
- "No good will come from this, Francis," she said. "Golf can never offer you any kind of life or living."
- When Francis turned 16 he was forced to give up caddying at the Country Club in order to retain his amateur status.
- United States Golf Association rules forbade amateur players from receiving money for any service connected to the sport—including work as a caddie.
- Francis planned to make golf the center of his life, but his father had other ideas.
- After years of frustration, his father demanded that Francis quit school and start work to help the family.
- Golf was never to be spoken of again.
- The captain of the high school golf team, the finest prodigy to emerge from the Brookline Country Club, began work as a $0.10 an hour stock boy.
- At 17 he secretly borrowed $25 from his mother to enter the prestigious National Amateur match to be played in Brookline, but failed to qualify after a summer away from golf.
- It was a pattern that would repeat itself over the next two years, despite a change in jobs and the discovery of Harry Vardon's first book, *The Complete Golfer*.
- He committed the book to memory; it became his Bible.
- Vardon's advice improved Francis's hand action and timing, both of which increased the length of his drives off the tee—when he had time to pursue his passion.

Francis entered the National Amateur match but failed to qualify.

Life at Work

- As 1913 approached, Francis Ouimet was working at the Boston sporting goods store Wright & Ditson, owned by a former professional athlete eager to see his $15 a week sales clerk do well at his passion.
- They both thought winning the National Amateur Golf Tournament—the sport's most coveted American title—was critical and possible.
- Francis was 20 years old and believed the 1913 contest was his final opportunity.
- Together the store owner and Francis formulated a step-by-step tactical plan that emphasized not only the physical side of winning, but the psychological side as well.
- For the first time Francis could practice without fear and with absolute commitment, believing that his shots would fly straight and his putts would fall.
- He qualified for the National Amateur Tournament by winning the Massachusetts Amateur Championship in a walk.
- In the clutch Francis kept his cool and his opponents did not.
- Since its inception in 1894, the National Amateur Tournament had been strictly a match play event that matched hole by hole scoring, not total score.
- In 1913 the prestigious tournament had doubled in size as 141 players had showed up for the competition held at the Garden City Golf Club in Garden City, New York.

Practicing hand action and timing.

20-year-old Francis qualified for the National Amateur Tournament.

- The 6,800-yard course, built in 1898, was renowned for its length, punitive bunkers and small greens.
- The first two days of play reduced the field to 32 golfers.
- Francis was so exhilarated that feeling frightened didn't occur to him, and he easily made the cut.
- Then he was paired in match play against a previous National Amateur champion and won in a close match.
- Francis was eliminated in the quarterfinals, but was invited to play in the U.S. Open, a tournament largely populated by professionals that was scheduled to be played at a familiar place, Brookline Country Club.
- The United States Golf Association's Open Championship began tournament play in 1881.
- Only the Kentucky Derby could lay claim to a longer history of continuous sports contests.
- Francis's hero Harry Vardon was scheduled to play in this year's contest.
- Harry Vardon and Ted Ray arrived with great fanfare, and critics agreed they had an excellent chance to once again capture the U.S. Open trophy for Britain.
- In all, 23 amateurs had been accepted at Brookline, where they were welcome to use the Country Club Clubhouse.
- As an amateur, Francis was allowed to use the Clubhouse, while his hero Harry Vardon was not, following a tradition that excluded professionals, regarded as working class, from the facilities.
- On the first day of the tournament, Francis learned that his regular caddie had deserted him for a more popular, more financially capable pro.
- So for the most important tournament of his life Francis picked a 10-year-old schoolboy, who was playing hooky from school, to be his caddie.

- Covering the event were hundreds of reporters, supported by a crowd of 9,000 who followed Harry Vardon's every move, even though many were watching the first golf match of their lives.
- Course marshals shouted through megaphones to control the stampede on the course, to little avail.
- The crowd watching Francis's round swelled to 1,000, including former President Howard Taft, and 600 automobiles crowded the Country Club lot.
- After overcoming three first hole jitters, Francis posted a 77, six shots behind the leader on the first 18, then a 74 in the afternoon round to finish the first day in fifth place four strokes back.
- The second day was played in a driving rainstorm, which the British golfers considered to be their advantage.
- Francis's mother furtively watched from her house across the street, and his elementary school caddie skipped school again.
- His morning rounds of the second day produced a 74 and the lead, ahead of both Ted Ray and Harry Vardon.
- Francis had shot Friday's lowest round and picked up four strokes on the two best players in the world.
- The press still didn't give Francis a chance of winning the tournament, and with good reason.
- On the final scheduled round of the tournament, Francis allowed his doubts to overpower his confidence, and after the first 10 holes the young amateur had lost his lead and was down two strokes.

Expert players struggled against Francis.

Former President Taft on the golf course.

The crowd was tense as Francis struggled for par.

- The gallery of nearly 10,000 began to smell his defeat, and many wandered away convinced that Francis had lost his golden opportunity.
- Then on the par four, 13th hole, which measured 339 uphill yards, Francis chipped in a birdie from off the green to regain one stroke, causing the crowd to cheer so loudly that his mother could hear it from her front porch.
- On the par three 16th hole, he went for another birdie, but had to struggle for par.
- The newspapers would later describe the crowd as being half mad with tension, when Francis needed one stroke in the next two holes to tie the British champions and be eligible for a playoff the next day.
- The roar of the crowd could be heard two miles away when Francis dropped in a 20-foot putt from above the hole.
- Harry Vardon told the press, "Coming when it did, I count it as one of the master strokes of golf."
- Francis parred the 18th hole and the stage was set for an 18-hole playoff with Ray and Vardon.
- British journalist Bernard Darwin described his own emotions in *The London Times:* "After sober reflection I state my conviction that if I live the length of a dozen lives I should never again be the spectator of such an amazing, thrilling and magnificent finish to an Open championship."
- No amateur had ever won the U.S. Open, and Harry Vardon had never lost to an amateur.
- Even though the rain continued on Saturday, more than 12,000 spectators descended upon the course.
- The three golfers, while polite, barely spoke to each other, and after nine holes all three men were even par 38.
- At the 10th hole, Francis went up by one stoke and for the first time began to imagine that he could defeat the two British stars.
- On the 12th hole the young American went up two strokes.
- His opponents kept waiting for him to crack under the pressure.
- At the 370-yard par four 15th hole, Ted Ray took a double bogey, causing the championship winner between Francis and Harry.
- When Francis teed off on the 17th, he could see his mother watching from her front porch.
- She left the course when the crowd became almost uncontrollable with excitement at the thought that Francis might win the U.S. Open.
- On the 17th green Francis had an 18-foot putt that went downhill and to the right.
- He barely touched it and slowly the ball rolled down the slope and fell in for a birdie three.
- As they approached the final hole, Francis led Vardon by three, Ray by seven.
- Francis fired a perfect drive to the center of the fairway on 18, and his second shot cleared the bunker and landed on the green.

Francis and his fans, after winning the U.S. Open.

- The first putt rolled within nine inches of the cup and, as the second putt dropped in, the entire crowd exploded with excitement.
- Francis was hoisted onto the shoulders of his fans and he was carried to the Clubhouse for the victory ceremony, where he saw his father proudly waving his approval.
- As an amateur, Francis received no compensation, while Harry Vardon's second place finish earned him $300.

Life in the Community: Brookline, Massachusetts

- Originally settled as farmland in the 1630s, Brookline, Massachusetts, was located between the Charles and Muddy Rivers.
- Initially called Muddy River Hamlet, Brookline was incorporated in 1705.
- The town contributed three companies of volunteers for the famous Revolutionary War battles in Lexington and Concord.
- During the 1800s Boston's wealthy merchant class began building summer homes in the area.
- Turnpikes and planked roads from Boston brought the town even closer.
- By the early 1900s Brookline was linked to Boston by an electrified trolley car.
- The USGA offered a total purse of $900 for the tournament, with $300 awarded for first place and $20 for 10th place.
- *The London Times* described the Country Club course as ". . . a very pretty spot (with) picturesque valleys and wooded hills and rocky promontories in one or two places. It's not a big course, yet a very sound one quite difficult enough for any reasonable being."

At home in a wealthy Brookline neighborhood.

HISTORICAL SNAPSHOT
1913

- The International Exhibition of Modern Art at the Armory Show in New York exhibited Marcel Duchamp's *Nude Descending a Staircase, No. 2*

- John Jacob Abel isolated amino acids from blood for the first time

- Sixty movie studios moved to California, leaving 47 in the East

- The ozone layer was discovered by Charles Fabry

- New York's 55-story Woolworth Building, costing $13.5 million, was completed

- Notre Dame achieved a major upset against powerhouse Army in college football, 35-13, by extensively using the forward pass

- Forty members of the newly founded National Women's Party were hospitalized following an attack during a right-to-vote parade in NYC

- President Woodrow Wilson called the Chinese Revolution the "most significant event of our generation"

- University of Chicago coach Alonzo Stagg began experimenting with putting names on football uniforms

- Baby shows, like the "Better Baby Show" gained wide popularity

- A new federal income tax on persons making more than $3,000 a year impacted 600,000 of the nation's 92 million people

- Gilbert's erector set, Quaker Puffed Rice and Wheat, Chesterfield cigarettes and the Toonerville Trolley comic strip all made their first appearance

- Leonardo da Vinci's painting *The Mona Lisa*, which was stolen in 1911, was discovered in Florence, Italy

- U.S. industrial output reached 40 percent of the world's total production

- U.S. beat Britain at tennis in Wimbledon to capture its first Davis Cup since 1902

- Scientists discovered hardening of the arteries in rabbits who ate diets high in cholesterol and fat

- Ty Cobb won his seventh straight batting title in baseball

- Popular songs included "Danny Boy," "The Trail of the Lonesome Pine," "The Curse of an Aching Heart" and "Sit Down, You're Rocking the Boat!"

Selected Prices

Apartment, New York, Weekly	$5.00
Automobile, Franklin 1910	$2,800.00
Baseball	$0.06
Dental Crown	$4.00
Kitchen Cabinet	$23.85
Magazine, *Collier's,* Weekly	$0.05
Ostrich Plume	$18.00
Room, New York, Weekly	$2.00
Teething Powder	$0.25
Water Pistol	$0.21

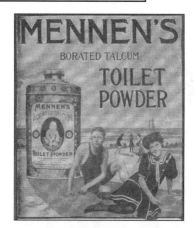

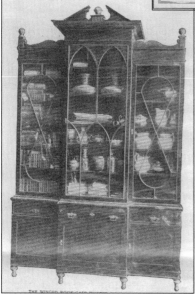

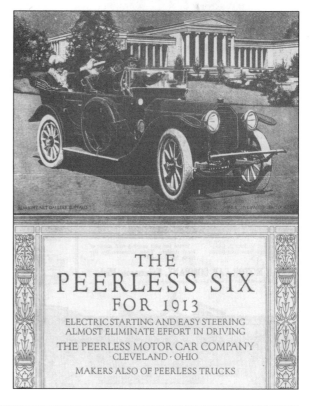

Golf Timeline

1894

The United States Golf Association (USGA) was founded to govern the game.

The size of the cup was standardized at 4.25 inches in diameter.

1895

The first official U.S. Amateur Championship was won by Charles MacDonald.

Spalding became the first American company to manufacture golf balls.

The first U.S. Women's Amateur Championship was won by Mrs. Charles S. Brown.

1896

Harry Vardon won the first of his six British Open titles.

1897

Golf magazine began publication.

Yale University won the first collegiate golf tournament played in the U.S.

The Royal & Ancient Golf Club's Rules of Golf Committee was formed.

William McKinley became the first sitting U.S. president to play the game of golf.

1898

The U.S. Open was expanded from 36 holes to 72 holes.

The term "birdie" was coined during a round at Atlantic City Country Club in New Jersey.

The British Open introduced a cut in the number of golfers eligible to continue after 36 holes of play.

Coburn Haskell invented the "Haskell," a wound, rubber-cored golf ball.

1899

Harvard Dental School faculty member George Grant patented the wooden tee.

The Western Open was played for the first time.

1900

Golf was made an Olympic sport.

Persimmon wood became a popular material for golf club heads.

John B. Coles Tappan, captain of Nassau Country Club in New York, invented the Nassau bet, also known as "best nines."

British champion Harry Vardon's U.S. exhibition tour spurred interest in golf in America.

Goodrich Rubber Company's patented process of winding rubber threads around the core of a Haskell ball, caused a decline in the use of balls made with gutta percha—sap from trees in the Maylay peninsula that is boiled and molded around the rubber core.

1901

Walter Travis won the U.S. Amateur playing a Haskell ball, the first player to win a major using the wound, rubber-core ball.

The first nine holes of what would become known as Pinehurst No. 2 were opened at North Carolina's Pinehurst Resort.

1902

Grooves were added to the clubfaces of irons.

Willie Anderson became the first player to break 300 in a U.S. tournament.

continued

Golf Timeline ... *(continued)*

1903

Walter Travis won the last of his three U.S. Amateur titles.

Oakmont Country Club opened near Pittsburgh, Pennsylvania.

Spalding Company switched from gutta percha to balata to cover their Haskell rubber-core balls, a latex rubber from South American trees.

1904

The British Open format changed from two days of 36 holes each, to three days of 00 holes each.

Walter Travis was the first U.S. citizen to win the British Amateur.

1905

The "Dympl" ball was patented by William Taylor, who discovered that balls with depressions, rather than bumps, fly higher and farther.

The Vardon Grip was explained in Harry Vardon's book, *The Complete Golfer.*

1907

Frenchman Arnaud Massy became the first player from outside the British Isles to win the British Open.

1909

The Royal & Ancient (R&A) Rules of Golf Committee began issuing rulings on what equipment was legal to use in major tournaments.

Dorothy Campbell became the first golfer to win the U.S. Women's Amateur and British Women's Amateur in the same year.

1910

Steel-shafted clubs, developed by Arthur Knight, began replacing hickory in the manufacture of golf club shafts.

The USGA broke from an R&A equipment ruling, by keeping center-shafted putters legal.

1911

The USGA determined par yardages: par three, up to 225 yards; par four, 225-425 yards; par five; 426-600 yards; par six, 601 yards and up.

The Royal & Ancient rejected steel-shafted clubs as illegal.

1913

American amateur Francis Ouimet defeated British stars Harry Vardon and Ted Ray in a playoff for the U.S. Open.

The GOLF GIRLS in The CARNIVAL of SPORTS

"Conditions Favor British," *Naugatuck Daily News* (Connecticut), September 20, 1913:

Outward conditions were favorable for the British contenders Harry Vardon and Edward Ray, when their playoff with Francis Ouimet in their triple tie of the National Open Golf Championship started this morning at the Brookline Country Club. A mist fell, which, along with occasional drizzles all night, made the course softer and more treacherous than yesterday.

There was a tremendous crowd out today. At least 6,000 persons followed the stars from the first tee and hundreds were added at every hole thereafter. The gallery, despite unusual efforts to control it, threatened to upset the contestants in its eagerness to catch all the small points. Vardon was, of course, the favorite, Ray second, and Ouimet third.

Ouimet was in the most blithesome mood of the three before starting, and naturally, since both the foreigners' reputations were at stake, while the boy had nothing to lose.

The contest was at 18 holes.

"Francis Ouimet Hero of the U.S. Golf World," *The Fresno Bee*, September 27, 1913:

Telegrams and letters of congratulations from golf enthusiasts all over the United States are pouring in on Francis Ouimet, the youthful winner of the 19th championship tournament for the United States Golf Association in Brookline, Massachusetts, last week. In keeping the championship in this country Ouimet defeated Vardon and Ray, the leading golf experts of England.

For more reasons than one the victory of Ouimet is noteworthy. This is the first time in the history of golf that an American has defeated the best of England in a championship tournament. And, besides, Ouimet is a mere youth, not yet 21.

Both Vardon and Ray have unstinted praise for the youthful champion. They declare that he beat them fairly and squarely and echo the sentiment of *The London Times* that "all other feelings are extinguished in admiration for the wonderful feat of Ouimet, who proved himself to be one of the game's greatest of golfers."

Ouimet is a native of Brookline. His parents are poor and the boy was forced at an early age to eke out the family income by working as a caddy in the very field where he won the great triumph Saturday. From his 13th year till he graduated from the Brookline High School a year ago, he was a familiar figure in the Brookline links. His play first attracted wide attention in the amateur championship open this year which Jerome D. Travers won.

"Soccer Meeting Next Thursday,"
The Atlanta Constitution, September 28, 1913:

The soccer players of Atlanta will hold a meeting at Spalding's store Thursday night at 8 o'clock for the purpose of perfecting organization for the coming season. All those interested in soccer are invited to be present.

Soccer plans in Atlanta this winter will be on a larger scale than ever before. It is the plan of the soccerites to organize a four-team league and Spalding will give a handsome silver loving cup for the winning team.

The Scottish Society in Atlanta is taking an interest in the game, and the chances are that they will have a team in the league this season.

CAPTAIN C. K. HUTCHISON

A. MASSY

"Golf Ball May Blind Boy,"
Washington Post,
September 3, 1913:

Boyish curiosity to know the composition of a golf ball resulted in an accident last night to Stafford Hawken, the 12-year-old son of Assistant United States Atty. S. McComas Hawken, which may cause the boy the loss of sight of his right eye.

Hawken was unraveling the golf ball at his home on Wisconsin Avenue last night when the sulphuric acid center of the ball exploded and a quantity of the corrosive fluid found lodging in his eye.

Suffering great agony, the boy was taken to the emergency hospital by his father. The eye was found to be in a serious condition.

Do not reflect upon the possibility of defeat; you become too anxious and lose your freedom of style.

—Harry Vardon, *The Complete Golfer*

There are only two types of players—those who keep their nerves under control and win championships, and those who do not.

—Harry Vardon

"President Feels in Better Health, Playing Golf in Sunny Weather," *Titusville Herald* (Pennsylvania), December 31, 1913:

PASS CHRISTIAN, MISSISSIPPI—President Wilson's vacation is greatly improving his health. As he climbed over the bunkers at the golf links today there was a resiliency in his step and a vigor in his walk that revealed to those who have been constantly observing him how much he has been benefited by a week of rest and recreation in the mild gulf climate.

The President played 18 holes of golf again today and seemed to enjoy the exercise. He is growing accustomed to the stubby grass upon the links, with its retarding effect on the roll of drives, and made a much better score today than usual.

"Chum Bob's Talk for the Fans,"
Evening Independent
(Massillon, Ohio), December 31, 1913:

Perhaps one of the most novel golf clubs in the country is being organized out in Tacoma, Washington. The caddies of the Tacoma Golf and Country Club have formed themselves into a mutual organization and are playing the royal and ancient game on a field in the neighborhood of Manitou Park. The new club will be known as the Manitou Park Golf Club. Almost any day after school is out the youngsters may be seen playing over the field.

Remember that the player who first settles down to the serious business of a hard match has the advantage. Concentrated purpose is the secret of victory.

—Harry Vardon, *The Complete Golfer*

America in 1913

Woodrow Wilson was the first Democrat to win the White House since 1892 and the first Southerner since the Civil War.

A man of modest means, Wilson had to borrow money to buy a suit for his own inauguration; the presidency paid $75,000 year, the most he had ever made.

When Wilson delivered the first State of the Union address to Congress in April 1913, he was the first president to make the trip to Capitol Hill since John Adams in 1801.

America boasted 48 states with the recent elevation of the Arizona territory to statehood in 1912.

In all, 97 million people lived in America, 90 percent east of the Mississippi.

Fueled by a surplus of cheap immigrant labor, America's industrial output provided 40 percent of the world's gross production.

Approximately 10 percent of America's 37 million workers belonged to a union.

Annually 30,000 workers were killed on the job; 500,000 were injured at work.

Child labor was largely unregulated.

The average per capita income was $1,200 a year.

Unemployment was at 4.5 percent.

The Dow Jones Industrial Average peaked at 89; less than 1 percent of the population owned any publicly traded stocks.

Nationwide, 23 percent of American homes had a telephone; less than half of Americans lived in a home wired for electricity.

Even though more than 50 automobile manufacturing companies existed, one out of every two cars on the road was a Ford Model T.

The sale of classical music was giving way to popular songs such as Irving Berlin's "Alexander's Ragtime Band," which sparked a nationwide dance craze.

Within the movie industry actors were demanding that their names appear on the screen credits, feeding America's burgeoning appetite for movie stars.

At the Palace Theatre in New York City, where customers were charged an unprecedented $2.00 admission price, aging French actress Sarah Bernhardt and vaudeville veteran W.C. Fields were packing the house nightly.

1914 PROFILE

Sally Waayne was lucky enough to have an enlightened father who helped her perfect her tennis game; her father even devised her own tennis court with a borrowed net and sticky tape.

Life at Home

- Sally Waayne grew up in Zeeland, Michigan, as the only child of a single father.
- Her father, Gordon, was a popular cigar maker in a community dominated by furniture manufacturing.
- Her mother died shortly after Sally's birth, a horrible event that left Gordon devastated and unable to work for weeks.
- His closest friends told him a man couldn't raise a girl and encouraged him to send Sally to his sister's house.
- Possessing a keen mind and a long nurtured ability to do as he pleased, Gordon agreed he couldn't properly raise a girl, so he decided he would raise her as a boy.
- Sally grew up loving baseball, especially the Chicago Cubs, hunting in the deep woods and playing lawn tennis.
- Zeeland was a small, close-knit Dutch community, 20 miles from Grand Rapids, that still clung to its Old World language, customs and traditions.
- Its community leaders were exceedingly proud of its work ethic, cultural roots and intentional isolation.
- They resisted a national move to reduce the typical work week from 54 to 48 hours.
- Zeeland was hardly the ideal environment for a girl who dressed like a boy, knew the vital statistics of base ball players Joe Tinker, Johnny Evans and Frank Chance, and could whip her peers—guys and gals—at tennis.
- Religious leaders from the Dutch community formally took Gordon aside when Sally was eight years old and demanded conformity or banishment from services.
- From that day on, Gordon and Sally faithfully spent Sundays perfecting her backhand, praying for the skills to score aces off first serves.

Sally Waayne was raised a tomboy.

- Because his cigars were of the highest quality, Gordon continued to prosper instead of being boycotted for his actions, and preachers could only grumble.
- In high school Sally attracted the attention of the local newspaper.
- She was 16 when the opportunity of a lifetime landed in her lap.
- Three-time U.S. Open champion—and Sally's idol—Mary K. Browne was planning an exhibition in Grand Rapids, Michigan 20 miles away, and needed some area competition—preferably from local women and girls.
- As a 5′2″ right-hander, Sally was the same height as Mary, who had dominated the U.S. Championships at Philadelphia, scoring triples, singles, doubles, and mixed titles in 1912, 1913 and 1914.
- Now 23 years old, Mary was known for her aggressive play, and her tendency to play more like a "man" than a woman.
- Trained by men players on the unyielding, fast surfaces of California's asphalt courts, she was always prepared, even eager, to settle matters quickly by sharp decisive volleying duels at the net.
- Most of her female opponents preferred a long-volley, backcourt game that emphasized flawless play, not powerful serves and overhead smashes.
- Mary had been tutored by her brother and father and nurtured by a California culture that accepted women's athletics.
- In one of the most demanding days in tennis annals, Mary played 82 games while winning the 1912 singles, doubles and mixed finals all in the same afternoon, much of it in a downpour.
- "The rain was coming down in torrents, and still we went on," Mary had been quoted in the local paper as saying. "Our rackets were mushy and our clothes soaked."
- Sally had never been so excited in her life as when her father told her she was not only going to meet Mary K. Browne, she was going to play a match against the champion.

Life at Work

- Sally Waayne could barely concentrate on school work once she learned she would be opposing Mary K. Browne in a tennis match.
- Sally had never seen a champion play, but imagined it faster and sharper.
- Mary was in the area to compete in the 1914 Western Lawn Tennis Championship at Lake Forest, Illinois, only a train ride away.
- According to the tennis magazine articles, Mary unhesitatingly hit smashes from anywhere on the court and was known to chase down a lob while running backwards, only to crash it back across the net for an easy point.
- Her opponents were amazed to see her so often crashing the net.
- Most of her competitors were graduates of the backcourt school of tennis, where the player stood near the back line and volleyed endlessly until an advantage could be found.
- Stroke for stroke, Mary was known for her sound fundamentals and for understanding the court technique; her returns were hard and accurate.
- She didn't like to lose and she didn't like to play all the time.
- To keep fresh, she intentionally skipped tournaments so that she would always be enthusiastic about the game she loved.
- Everything Sally read about Mary Browne excited her even more.
- Thanks to her dad, she, too, had developed an intimidating serve, a powerful forehand, an adequate backhand and a strong sense of where the ball would be returned.
- Sally's style was said to be unmatched by anyone, except Mary Browne.

Driving to play a match in Grand Rapids was Sally's first long car ride.

- For weeks Sally practiced relentlessly, until blisters swelled her hands and feet.
- When called to help fix supper, her plea was always the same, "Please, just one more serve."
- The day of the match was filled with firsts—her first long car ride, her first trip to Grand Rapids, and her first time to skip school (outside hunting season), and her first official tennis shoes.
- When she fretted about being embarrassed, her dad reminded her that the 1913 Kentucky Derby winner, Donerail, was given a 92.5 to one chance of winning the $5,000 first prize.
- At those odds, he said, he was eager to place a $2 wager on his girl.
- The first serve was the hardest for Sally.
- She rocketed a first ball shot to Mary Browne, then watched in amazement how easily it was returned.
- For Mary, the exhibition match was a chance to promote women's tennis; for Sally the match was a dream come true.
- For the first two sets Sally held her own, displaying a solid ground game combined with a passing shot that left the champion flatfooted.
- The crowded roared to its feet, cheering for the 16-year-old local girl.
- After that, every point was a fierce battle, and Sally had never played someone who dominated the net so completely.
- After Mary graciously won the match, the two met at the net to exchange congratulations.
- Mary looked Sally in the eye and said, "You remind me of myself. Congratulations on a good effort."

Life in the Community: Zeeland, Michigan

- Zeeland, Michigan, was settled in 1847 by a group of Dutch immigrants in search of religious freedom.
- Wealthy landowner, Jannes Van De Luyster, sold all his holdings in the Netherlands in order to purchase the site of the original village, some 16,000 acres, and named the community after a province of the Netherlands.
- Three ships made their way to Michigan, in 1847 carrying 457 immigrants.
- The first building to be assembled was a church, followed closely by a school.
- During the next 25 years, Zeeland acquired a sawmill, a wagon factory, blacksmith shops, grocery stores, and a post office.

- The village officially became a city in 1907 with a population of almost 3,000.
- By that time Zeeland boasted a two-story brick kindergarten building and a two-story brick grade school.
- The city's economy revolved around four furniture factories and one large manufacturing plant.
- Building a public dance hall in the religiously strict community was prohibited.
- Nearby Grand Rapids, which was also settled by the Dutch, became a major lumbering center and premier furniture manufacturing city, during the second half of the nineteenth century.
- It earned the nickname "Furniture City."

Zeeland's economy centered around furniture factories.

Historical Snapshot
1914

- The Federal League, baseball's third major league after the American and National Leagues, expanded to eight teams

- Rookie baseball pitcher George "Babe" Ruth debuted with the Boston Red Sox

- Movie premieres included *The Perils of Pauline, The Exploits of Elaine, Home Sweet Home,* and *Kid Auto Races at Venice*

- Theodore W. Richards won the Nobel Prize in chemistry for his work in the determination of atomic weights

- Thyroxin, the major thyroid hormone, was isolated by Edward Kendall at the Mayo Clinic

- Yale University opened its Coliseum-sized "Bowl" large enough to seat 60,000

- *The New Republic* magazine, passport photo requirements, non-skid tires, international figure skating tournaments, Kelvinator and The American Society of Composers, Authors and Publishers (ASCAP) all made their first appearance

- Pope Pius X condemned the tango as "new paganism"

- Former President Theodore Roosevelt returned from South America with 1,500 bird and 500 mammal specimens and a claim that he had discovered a new river

- Americans condemned the European war as "senseless" and "utterly without cause"

- The writings of Margaret Sanger sparked renewed controversy about birth control and contraception

- Chicago established the Censorship Board to remove movie scenes depicting beatings or dead bodies

- Tuition, room and board at Harvard University cost $700 per year

- Ford Motor Company produced 240,700 cars, nearly as many as all other companies combined

- The outbreak of war in Europe spurred U.S. production of pasta, which had previously been imported

- Popular songs included "St. Louis Blues," "The Missouri Waltz," "Play a Simple Melody," "Fido Is a Hot Dog Now," and "If You Don't Want My Peaches, You'd Better Stop Shaking My Tree"

- In college football, five first team All Americans were from Harvard

- New York was the nation's largest city with a population of 5.3 million, Chicago boasted 2.4 million, Philadelphia 1.7 million and Los Angeles 500,000

Selected Prices

Automobile, Rambler	$1,800.00
Dominoes	$0.33
Fire Insurance, per Year	$6.27
Hotel Room, Boston, per Day	$2.00
House, Seven Rooms, New Jersey	$5,400.00
Ladies' Home Journal, per Issue	$0.10
Suitcase	$4.95
Toupée	$21.65
Vacuum Cleaner	$35.00
Whiskey, Bottle	$1.00

Women in Sports Timeline

1882

The National Croquet Association was formed to revise and standardize the rules.

1883

Matilda Howell won her first national archery title, a feat she would repeat 17 times between 1883 and 1907.

1883

The first baseball "Ladies Day" was held by the New York Giants, where both escorted and unescorted women were allowed into the park for free.

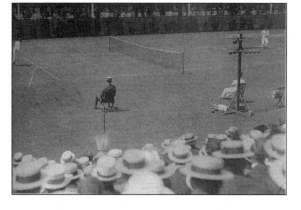

1884

Women's singles tennis was added to Wimbledon.

1885

The Association of Collegiate Alumnae published a study which refuted the widely held belief that college study impaired a woman's physical health and ability to bear children.

Roller skating rinks were built in almost every city and small town around the country at a total cost of $20 million.

1886

The first women's lacrosse game was played.

1887

Ellen Hansell was crowned the first Women's Singles Tennis Champion at the U.S. Open.

1888

The modern "safety" bicycle was invented with a light frame, two equal-sized wheels and a chain drive, encouraging women to join cycling clubs.

The Amateur Athletic Union was formed to establish standards and uniformity in amateur sports.

1889

The first women's six-day bicycle race ended at Madison Square Garden in New York City.

1891

The Shinnecock Hills Golf Club on Long Island opened its doors to women.

1892

The journal *Physical Education*, a publication of the YMCA, said that women needed physical strength and endurance, and dismissed the popular idea that women were too weak to exercise.

Gymnastics instructor Senda Berenson Abbott adapted James Naismith's basketball rules for women and introduced the game to her students at Smith College; the rules confined each player to one-third of the court.

The Sierra Club of California welcomed women members as it organized.

continued

Women in Sports Timeline . . . *(continued)*

1893
Katharine Lee Bates climbed to the top of Pike's Peak and was inspired to compose the poem "America, the Beautiful."

1895
The first Women's Amateur Golf Championship was held, with 13 golfers competing at the Meadow Brook Club, Hempstead, New York.

1895
Frances Willard, president of the Woman's Christian Temperance Union (WCTU), published *A Wheel Within a Wheel,* a best-selling account of learning to ride a bicycle.

The first women's softball team was formed at Chicago's West Division High School.

Volleyball was invented in Holyoke, Massachusetts.

The American Bowling Congress was organized, and established equipment standards and rules.

1896
Women bought 30 percent of all new bicycles.

The first women's intercollegiate basketball championship was played between Stanford and the University of California at Berkeley.

At the first modern Olympics in Athens, a woman, Melpomene, barred from the official race, ran the same course as the men, finishing in four hours, 30 minutes. Baron Pierre de Coubertin, founder of the modern Olympics, said, "It is indecent that the spectators should be exposed to the risk of seeing the body of a women being smashed before their very eyes. Besides, no matter how toughened a sportswoman may be, her organism is not cut out to sustain certain shocks."

1898
Lizzie Arlington became the first woman to sign a professional baseball contract, appearing in her first professional game pitching for the Philadelphia Reserves.

1899
Ping pong, or table tennis, was invented.

1900
Physical education instructors strongly opposed competition among women, fearing it would make them less feminine.

Nineteen women competed in the modern Olympic Games in Paris, France, in just three sports: tennis, golf and croquet.

1901
Field hockey was introduced to women in the United States by Constance M. K. Applebee, a British physical education teacher.

1902
Mrs. Adolph Landenburg introduced the split skirt for horseback riding in Saratoga Springs, New York.

1903
Eleanor Roosevelt enrolled in the Junior League of New York, where she taught calisthenics and dancing to immigrants.

continued

Women in Sports Timeline . . . *(continued)*

1904
Matilda Howell won three gold medals in archery at the St. Louis Olympic Games.

1906
Lula Olive Gill became the first woman jockey to win a horse race in California.

Skater Madge Syers became the first woman world figure skating champion.

1907
The first organized bowling league for women began in St. Louis, Missouri.

1908
The anthem of baseball, "Take Me Out to the Ball Game," was written about a young girl's love of the game.

1910
Dr. Clelia Duel Mosher debunked several popular myths of female health, including one claiming women breathe differently from men, which makes them unfit for strenuous exercise.

For the second consecutive year, Hazel Hotchkiss won the singles, doubles and mixed doubles titles at the U.S. Lawn Tennis Association's championships.

Australia's Annette Kellerman was arrested for swimming in Boston Harbor in an "indecent" one-piece swimsuit exposing her legs.

1911
Helene Britton became the first woman owner of a major league team, the St. Louis Cardinals.

1912
Swimming and diving debuted at the Stockholm Olympic Games, with 57 women from 11 nations competing.

American college women eagerly took up the latest sports craze: wall scaling.

Eleanora Sears completed her first marathon walk of 108 miles in 19 hours and 50 minutes.

1914
The American Olympic Committee formally opposed women's athletic competition in the Olympics.

Women's basketball rules changed to allow half-court play, expanded from the original one-third court rules.

The first national swimming championships were held with women allowed to register by the Amateur Athletic Union (AAU).

"The Greatest Woman in the Courts," Fred Hawthorne, *Outing*, October 1917:

There is a marked divergence in the style of game played by these two feminine wonders in the courts. Miss Browne is distinctly the net player, armed with a brilliant, severe overhead game, the ability to force her openings, to make cunning change of pace. In no single department is she weak, but her greatest effectiveness comes when she operates from just inside the service-court line, there to bring off her sharp overhead shots or to execute low volleys at acute angles across the fore-court, in the style made famous by Frederick B. Alexander.

As a matter of fact, Miss Browne's game is typically a man's. She is always prepared, even eager, to settle matters quickly by sharp, decisive volleying duels at the net, and she can smash wonderfully well from any position in the court. I've seen her more than once take a deep lob while running backwards, as McLaughlin used to do, and then crash it back for a "kill."

Her game is the result of long and careful instruction by such masters of the racket as Tom Bundy, her brother, Nat, and other stars from the Coast, and today the little Californian is a far greater player than when she held the national title.

"Shoulder Socket Is All That Keeps Girl Players from Beating Men Tennis Champions," *Reno Evening Gazette* **(Nevada), July 5, 1915:**

The "lady of the racket and ball" is the belle of the summer season.

You'll meet her everywhere, not only at the country clubs, but in the public parks, and the playgrounds, in vacant back lots, in side streets as well as in private courts on the boulevards.

"High Society" no longer has a mortgage on the good game of tennis. It's every woman's game and almost every woman, and just about every girl you know is playing it this summer.

To be sure, there are men who say that women will never make great tennis players, not that they haven't the brain and the muscle to make McLaughlin, Daugherty and the rest of the men champs notice them. But woman's real handicap on the tennis court is her shoulder socket.

Yep. That's it. Woman's shoulder socket is deeper than man's. That's nature's fault, not woman's. The shoulder ball sets in too far to permit the quick "punchy" cannonball service characteristic of the best men players. No woman, say the main critics, can ever play as well as McLaughlin; her shoulder socket won't let her.

But aside from a little thing like that, the tennis girl is a regular trump in the game of outdoor sports, and judging by the way she's devoting herself to the racket and ball this summer, she'll add to the great glory achieved by Mary Browne of Los Angeles, who is national woman champion, and she'll do it in spite of her funny shoulder socket.

"Woman and the Cost of Living," Editorial, *Christian Herald*, March 2, 1910:

Professor Patten, who fills the chair of Political Economics in the University of Pennsylvania, takes a novel view of the causes of the present high cost of living. In an article in the *Independent* he does not attribute it, as others have done, to gold overproduction, to a decrease in the value of our natural resources, to the undue exploitation of the worker. He believes it arises from three causes: the bad distribution of population, the distance between consumer and producer, and the new status of women. The wife, he says, is no longer a creator of industry in the home, as she was in former days. Now, everything must be purchased outside, and with this increased expense, she has become "often its chief burden." He points out that formerly a $1,000 income sufficed to keep an ordinary home in comfort, as the wife's industry and thrift made it go as far as a much larger sum. Her baking, preserving and dressmaking all saved money. The professor concludes that "the essential conditions of home life cannot be neglected without bringing prosperity to a standstill."

This will appear to most people as a rather one-sided and partial view of the case. Certainly while it may apply to some, it cannot be true of the majority of American homes. But let us hear, through the columns of the *Christian Herald*, what the wives and mothers themselves had to say on this particular phase of the subject. Their letters will prove interesting and helpful reading to many others.

Lyrics to "If You Don't Want My Peaches, You'd Better Stop Shaking My Tree," by Irving Berlin, 1914:

Mary Snow had a beau
Who was bashful and shy
She simply couldn't make the boy propose
No matter how she'd try
Mary grew tired of waiting
So she called her beau to one side
While he stood there biting his fingernails
Mary cried:

If you don't want my peaches
You'd better stop shaking my tree

Let me say that you're mighty slow
You're as cold as an Eskimo

There's a thousand others waiting
Waiting to propose to me

So, if you don't want my peaches
You'd better stop shaking my tree

Mary's Pa and her Ma
Soon came into the room
They took a look at Mary's beau and cried
"You ought to be a groom
Of course, it's none of our bus'ness
But she'd make a lovely bride"
He just answered "I'll think it over" but
Mary cried:

So, if you don't want my peaches
You'd better stop shaking my tree

"The Woman's Game, Tennis for Women,"
Miss Molla Bjurstedt, 1916:

"Take the net as soon as you can and don't let her pass you." I heard this instruction given to a young girl by a man ranking in the first ten. The girl took the advice eagerly as though it were new and unusual. A few weeks later I saw her play; she was faithfully following the principle in so far as reaching the net was concerned, but she was being passed at will. Her opponent, who had not nearly so much tennis ability, was winning rather easily.

The admonition to play the volley game is perfectly sound; the style is most effective if you can play it.

I have never known a girl or woman who could play a net game in singles to three hard sets who could reach the net, volley consistently, and keep the pace. And yet I do not know how many thousands are trying to progress in the style of the game under the impression that first-class tennis is not to be achieved without imitating Mr. Maurice McLaughlin. Mr. McLaughlin, at his best, is a marvelous player; he can do things which an ordinary human being is foolish to attempt. And he must be in the most splendid physical and mental condition to play this particular game. No other man has ever yet been able to put over a railroad serve, follow up to the net, and play the ball almost continuously in the air; it demands more energy and endurance than even the trained man possesses. . . .

If the men in the first flight cannot play the hard serving, smashing game, how foolish it is for the average girl to experiment with it!

"I think that the Lord has brought many of his people to this place, because the language of Canaan is heard widely here. . . . It seems the Lord has preserved this place for the Dutch people. Almost no Americans settle here and also no people with alien beliefs."

—Letter from Jacob Dunnink, Zeeland, Michigan, 1850

Practical Lawn Tennis, James Dwight, 1893:

The choice of a racket is a serious matter. It makes a great deal of difference whether your racket suits you perfectly or not, and it pays to use the same sort of racket all the time. First of all, do not look at any that is not of the simplest make. Have nothing to do with rackets with knobs on the handles or with double stringing or any peculiarity whatever. The best racket is a plain one with a moderate sized head and an octagonal handle. An octagonal handle gives a better hold than a round one and is more comfortable in the hand than a square one. The racket should be practically straight. There may be a slight curve, but it should be very slight.

A very large head seems to me a mistake. If you look at any old racket, you will see that the strings are worn in a little circle in the center of the racket, showing that all the balls have struck there. Therefore, as far as hitting the ball goes, there is no need of a racket more than four inches across. Think how easily such a racket would swing. The trouble would be that the strings would not be long enough to give any spring to the stroke. It would be like playing with the board. All I wish to point out is that as soon as the strings are long enough to give a good spring to the stroke, the head of the racket is large enough, and that the smaller it is the more quickly can it be swung.

New York Evening Mail, July 10, 1910"

These are the saddest of possible words:

"Tinker to Evers to Chance."
Trio of bear cubs, and fleeter than birds,
Tinker and Evers and Chance.
Ruthlessly pricking our gonfalon bubble,
Making a Giant hit into a double
Words that are heavy with nothing but trouble:
"Tinker to Evers to Chance."

1919 PROFILE

As a Secretary for the YMCA, Robert Meek had witnessed his share of horror and casualties in the Great War, even though he himself had never fired a shot.

Life at Home

- Robert Meek had been back from the Great War almost eight months before he decided to talk about his war experiences.
- All around him soldiers young and old were telling war stories of death and destruction, mustard gas and airplane duels.
- The grit and glory of their tales were different from the turmoil, triumph and sadness he had experienced.
- Fighting he witnessed in France was brutish and violent, and left its participants psychologically wounded and mentally exhausted.
- Robert never fired a shot in the Great War, but spent his time, as a Secretary for the YMCA, boosting the morale of the troops playing exhibition baseball games, organizing recreation events and showing films to America's troops.
- This essential role was much praised in Poitiers, France, where he was stationed for 16 months, but it sounded trivial to those in the states who wanted to know how many Germans he had killed and how many French girls he had kissed.
- As a result, he rarely discussed the war.
- Things changed at a dinner party at his uncle's house where three soldiers, who had never left the states, talked about what they would have done had they been in the trenches.
- As though on a lecture circuit, Robert began dictating vital statistics.
- "The YMCA performed 90 percent of all welfare work with American Expeditionary Forces in Europe," he began, "suffering 286 casualties, including six men and two women killed in action working under the YMCA banner."

Robert Meek boasted troop morale as YMCA Secretary in France.

Soldiers in the trenches during WWI.

- "YMCA workers received 319 citations and decorations including the French Legion d'Honneur, the Order of the British Empire, the Distinguished Service Cross and the Distinguished Service Medal."
- The soldiers shifted uncomfortably as Robert continued.
- "In all, 26,000 paid men and women served with the YMCA during World War I, guiding 35,000 volunteers attending to the spiritual and social needs of the troops.
- The YMCA operated 26 R&R leave centers in France that accommodated 1,944,300 American officers and men.
- 4,000 'huts' and tents were used for recreation and religious services."
- Robert paused, took a deep breath and continued with more impressive numbers.
- "The YMCA staffed 8,000 troop trains, mobilized 1,470 entertainers overseas to perform for the troops and is now in the process of distributing 80,000 educational scholarships to veterans of the Great War."
- "We didn't shoot Germans," he said louder than he had intended, "but we did live in trenches, we watched men die and feared for our lives.

YMCA dispensed medication and baked pies for the troops.

FIELD KITCHEN

- We helped the men remember what they were fighting for and that's good enough for me and I hope it is good enough for you."
- With that said, Robert got up, apologized to his uncle for leaving the dinner table early, and walked outside.

Life at Work

- Before the war, Robert Meek lived a dual life—tailor by day and baseball player by night.
- He was passionate about catching ground balls and executing perfect bunts to advance the runner.
- It was his dream to be discovered one day and play in the majors as a lead-off hitting, right-handed shortstop.
- He also enjoyed his work sewing fine men's clothing
- This combination landed him the assignment of YMCA Secretary in France.
- One of his customers was chairman of the YMCA Board who, he told Robert, would be in the thick of fighting before long.

Before the war, Robert played baseball whenever he could.

Robert left his job as a tailor to join the YMCA's war efforts.

- YMCA work dated to the Civil War when 15 YMCA associations formally gathered to coordinate efforts to alleviate the suffering of the sick and wounded.
- When advised of these plans, President Abraham Lincoln wrote to YMCA leaders of his support, stating, "I sincerely hope your plan may be as successful as it is just and generous in conception."
- During its four years of operations during the Civil War, the commission recruited an estimated 5,000 volunteer "delegates" who served without pay in every theater of the war.
- It was the nation's first large-scale civilian volunteer service corps.
- Volunteers served as surgeons, nurses, chaplains and chaplains' assistants, while others distributed emergency medical supplies, food and clothing.
- They built and operated special diet kitchens in hospitals, brought books and prefabricated chapels to soldiers, taught enlisted men to read and write, maintained a hotel for soldiers on furlough, and provided free meals.
- The tradition of serving troops beyond our borders began during the Spanish-American War in 1898, when YMCA staff and volunteers were dispatched to Cuba, Puerto Rico and the Philippines.
- YMCA supplies, including medicine and office materials, reached Cuba before those of the army, and early dispatches from Teddy Roosevelt's Rough Riders were written on YMCA stationery.
- At the beginning of the Great War, General John J. Pershing, appreciative of support from the YMCA during action along the U.S.-Mexican border, would task the YMCA with enormous responsibilities.
- Prior to that war, the YMCA developed mobile canteens and recreational facilities, expanding their expertise in service to the armed forces.
- This expertise blossomed into a massive program of morale and welfare services for the military on the home front, but particularly overseas.
- When war was declared in 1917, the YMCA immediately volunteered its support, and President Woodrow Wilson quickly accepted it.
- They assumed responsibilities on a scale that had never been attempted by a non-profit, community-based organization in the history of the United States.
- Robert's special skills involved listening to homesick soldiers and organizing baseball games.
- He arrived in France during some of the most intense fighting.
- On two occasions he had breakfast with a young man in the morning, only to write a heartfelt "I'm-sorry-about-the-death-of-your-son" letter that night.
- Some days the pace of killing was brutal, while on other days the soldiers were consumed by boredom.
- Robert quickly discovered that a game of catch, with YMCA logo baseballs, would inject new life into the saddest doughboy.
- Twice a year a traveling Army-sponsored baseball team would arrive and play.
- Composed of former professional baseball players and the best amateurs in the Army, they typically won easily.

Sending letters to troops overseas was an important part of the YMCA's work.

War was an international affair.

- These games also created a much needed diversion from the fighting.
- A ballgame was particularly successful if a rivalry was involved, such as when a group of flyboys came into camp with their mechanics.
- Within hours the entire camp knew that the pilots—hotshots of the air—had challenged Robert's nine to a baseball game.
- Bats were in short supply, so both teams shared their gloves and bats.
- Robert led off with a single to left field, stole second and advanced to third on a ground ball to first, while hundreds of soldiers watched.
- Robert's First Sergeant then blasted a shot into deep center, and when the inning ended, Robert's team—American Expeditionary Army—was up 4-0.
- In the fifth inning the game was tied 5-5 and the flyboys had two on and no outs.
- Robert snared a vicious line drive up the middle, stepped on second for out number two and threw out the retreating runner at first for a triple play.

The Army's traveling baseball team.

- The celebration had barely begun when the major arrived to assemble the troops.
- The Germans were on the move again.
- The next day Robert's team lost its catcher by enemy fire.
- The YMCA showed movies that night to help the soldiers forget what they had seen, but most of the team wanted to talk about the game that got cut short.
- If only the game went nine innings, if only Robert was not in position to complete the triple play, if only the catcher had not been in the trench that was shelled.
- Robert tried to concentrate on the movie—*Shoulder Arms*—starring Charlie Chaplin and Edna Purviance, but ended up writing letters home to Sheboygan, Wisconsin.

- The catcher was also from Sheboygan, where the German language was still widely spoken, so Robert wrote the "regrets" letter to his family in German.

America and the Great War

War-ravaged streets.

- The World War began in August 1914, lasted until November 11, 1918.
- It encompassed 28 warring nations with a total population of 1,575,135,000, or 90 percent of the Earth's population.
- The Great War lasted four years, three months, and 15 days, for a total of 1,567 days, and the combined armies in this "gigantic test of civilization" reached a total of 59,176,800 soldiers.
- Battle deaths were 7,781,800, the wounded reached 18,681,200, prisoners and missing comprised 7,081,500.
- Total casualties topped 33,543,500.
- Direct financial cost to all nations was $249 billion, with indirect costs to commerce and trade adding $151 billion.
- America's participation in the war began on April 6, 1917, almost three years after the fighting began, and lasted 19 months, when 4,800,000 men were placed under arms.
- Of these, 2,000,000 men were transported over 3,000 miles across the sea and landed in France in the darkest days of the world crisis.
- On the war effort, America spent $22 billion, loaned its allies more than $10 billion and placed its powerful industrial system at the disposal of the Allied cause.

Fighting in the Great War.

HISTORICAL SNAPSHOT
1919

- Eight members of the Chicago White Sox baseball team were accused of "fixing" the World Series against the Cincinnati Reds

- Heavyweight boxing champion Jess Willard was defeated by challenger Jack Dempsey

- Great Lakes Naval Station defeated Mare Island 17-0 in the Rose Bowl in Pasadena, California, on New Year's Day

- Robert Goddard proposed using rockets to send a vehicle to the moon

- Popular books included *Winesburg, Ohio* by Sherwood Anderson, *Free Air* by Sinclair Lewis; *The American Language* by H.L. Mencken, *Ten Days That Shook the World* by John Reed and *Poems* by T.S. Eliot

- Labor unrest accelerated as unemployment and inflation rose, prompting 2,665 strikes during the year

- President Woodrow Wilson won the Nobel Peace Prize

- Howdy Wilcox won the Indianapolis 500 in a Peugeot racecar

- The 18th Amendment was ratified, prohibiting the sale of alcoholic beverages and approved by Congress despite a veto from President Woodrow Wilson

- Herbert Hoover was named director of the relief organization for liberated countries both neutral and enemy

- More than 30,000 Jews marched in Baltimore to protest pogroms in Poland and elsewhere

- Popular songs included "Baby, Won't You Please Come Home?" "Dear Old Sue," "Daddy Longlegs," "When the Moon Shines on the Moonshine" and "How Ya Gonna Keep 'Em Down on the Farm?"

- The crystal microphone, which permitted high-quality sound at low cost, was produced

- Ernest Rutherford reported the first manmade atomic fission

- Walter Hagan won the U.S. Open in an 18-hole playoff by one stroke over Mike Brady

- Red Sox hitter Babe Ruth broke the baseball single-season home run record, with 29

- President Woodrow Wilson suffered a stroke while on tour promoting the League of Nations

Selected Prices

Bed, Brass	$2.98
Boarding School for Boys, per Year	$700.00
Coffee, Pound	$0.30
Crematory Services	$30.00
House, Brooklyn, New York	$12,000
League Baseball	$0.90
Opera Bag	$3.50
Police Revolver, Colt	$12.50
Seminary, per Year	$250.00
Speeding Ticket, New York City	$10.00

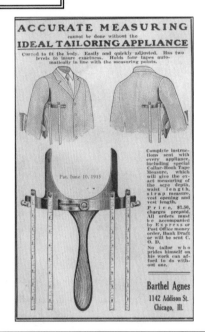

"The Big Brother of the Khaki," *Star Dust from the Dugouts*, William Stidger, 1919:

I've heard of one college president who went into a little outpost to work for the YMCA. The secretary who is in charge there did not know the new man was a college president, and the new man did not advertise the fact. When dinnertime came the first day, the new man asked where he should eat. The Sec. in charge said, "Just follow the men in, and mess with them. Make arrangements with them." So the college president followed the first crowd he saw, and he went in with them. He admits now that he didn't exactly like the food. In fact, it was pretty hard. But he was staying. The men were dressed a little differently from what he expected soldiers to be. They had on white suits, and some of them ate in their shirt sleeves. It appeared to be a sullen gang. Neither fellow on either side of him spoke a word to him for three days. On the evening of the third day he discovered he had been eating in the German prisoners' mess. When the secretary told me this story he added "But he, a college president, had been game enough to do this and stick it out without a word of complaint."

"The Big Brother of the Khaki," *Star Dust from the Dugouts*, William Stidger, 1919:

My friend Dr. A.E. Enyart had two striking examples illustrative of the title of this sketch. One was in the theater in Paris. An American boy sat drinking with a harlot. Secretary Enyart saw him, and motioned for him to come over to where he was standing. They got to talking, and the boy asked him to change $70 in American money into French money. Mr. Enyart said, "No, I won't, for if I did, that girl would get it all before morning, you probably have a wife or mother back there at home, who is a thousand times more entitled to it than she is."

The boy went away, angry at first, but five minutes later my friend was surprised to see the lad at his side again. He didn't say much. He reached out the $70 to the YMCA secretary, gave his mother's address in America, and said, "You are right. Send it to her," and disappeared before the secretary had a chance to get either his name or company address. Mr. Enyart sent the money, and has a receipt for it from the American Express Company, but has never been able to locate the boy.

The remarkable thing about the story to me is the fact that the soldier absolutely trusted that YMCA uniform, so much so, in fact, he handed his money over, with his mother's address, to a "Y" man whom he had never seen before, and left without even suggesting that he be given a receipt for his money.

The YMCA supported the troops in a variety of ways.

"The New Seasons," *Croonborg's Gazette of Fashions*, August 1915:

We are passing through social, political and commercial conditions the like of which the world has never seen.

The situation in Europe and our present relations with pestiferous Mexico, which are rapidly approaching a focus in spite of the peace at any price policy of the Wilson administration, make even the stoutest hearts serious.

It now appears that the great European war may be dragged on indefinitely, or at least to the limit of the borrowing power of the nations engaged in the godless struggle.

There are three ways in which the European holocaust affects every tailor and everyone who wears clothes. Most important of all is the condition that has been brought about in the woolen and fabric markets. Abroad the first care of the warring nations is to provide for the man at the front. Statistics go to show that the life of a uniform is only about six weeks' duration.

English industrial figures show that 80 percent of the woolen mills in Great Britain are monopolized solely for the purpose of clothing the English army and navy. A similar condition exists in other countries.

As far as fashion tendencies are concerned, they lean undeniably toward solid colors and quiet tones. Gone are all the freakish or "flashy" touches in design. The clothes of the fall and winter seasons will reflect the somber minds of American businessmen who view conditions abroad with trepidation and business possibilities at home with some misgivings. . . .

Merchant tailors may build high hopes upon one feature of prevailing conditions, for, while the importation of raw and manufactured woolens has increased to a great extent according to government statistics, there's been a tremendous falling off in the importation of ready-made clothing. This was inevitable, of course, the foreign factories being neither tied up with orders from their own government nor being put out of commission altogether. The foreign-made clothes have enjoyed considerable vogue in this country. There is little doubt that the patrons of the "made in England," "made in Paris" or the "made in Berlin" articles of apparel will turn to the American merchant tailor and custom cutter for more solid comfort and for better style. . . .

It is not generally appreciated that the tailoring trade is the third largest industry in the United States. When it has been thoroughly organized from top to bottom, there is no doubt that it will take its stand amongst the most important organizations in the country.

"Mother of All the Doughboys Is World's Champion Sympathizer,"
Sheboygan Journal (Wisconsin), March 19, 1919:

No soldier that ever went to war has had as many volunteer relatives as the man from the USA. He has "sisters" galore in every one of the YMCA huts here and abroad. They feed him, dance with him and show him the sights in whatever city or country he happens to be in. In England several hundred of his British "cousins" are doing their utmost to give him a good time on leave. He has "brothers" aplenty in every country. He has found "uncles" enough—between paydays. But the American YMCA in London has what it contends is the one and only Mother.

She is Mrs. John L. Raymond, and her home is in New Rochelle, New York. She went to England to be with her husband, who runs a commissary and stores upon which soldiers and sailors depend for the three meals served each day in the Eagle Hut in the Strand. She has remained for about the most important job that has been discovered. As a builder up of morale she has no rival. She is the official Sympathizer.

Over in the corner of the big London hut she sits, always busy with sewing. The needle, however, is mostly camouflage.

A disgruntled-looking doughboy enters. To add to his evident disgust at things in general, there is a tear in his coat. He looks around the hut, sees Mother and makes for her. She glances up with a smile at his torn uniform.

"Certainly I can fix that so you'll hardly know it had happened," she reassures the boy. "Sit down and talk to me while I do it."

In that sentence there is the cue for the doughboy, and he never misses it: "Talk to me." If there's one thing that the American soldier away from home wants to do, it is to talk—providing he finds the right person to talk to. He is not hankering for mere conversation, though when he meets a girl "Y" worker from home much of his reserve disappears. But when he sits down by the woman in the Eagle Hut, he invariably finds himself, before he knows it, telling her the long list of his troubles and his mistakes, and his grudges—everything, in fact, that he wants to get off his chest.

And when the boy has unburdened himself, she says a few words. They are only a few, but they always seem to be the right ones. The soldier or sailor who comes in with a grudge, for which the damages to his apparel only furnish an outlet, goes out, ten to one, with a grin. If it isn't a grin, it is a cheerful, gritty look that is even better. Mother has shaken hands with him, and almost always he has volunteered the promise to write to her, "if she doesn't mind" the first time he has a chance.

This sort of thing takes place not once but a dozen times a day in the "Mother's Corner" of the hut in London. Moreover, the first time the boy has a chance, he does write to Mrs. Raymond. As a consequence, not even a general gets more letters than she does from her big "sons" in France, in Russia, in Italy and—the lucky ones—back here at home. Her mail totals several hundred letters a month.

"Million Letters in the Mails Today Bearing Magic Words 'With the Colors,'" *Cambridge City Tribune* (Indiana), November 22, 1917:

It was evening on the broad Hempstead Plains, Long Island, where the Rainbow division was spending its last night before embarking for France. It had been raining hard in the afternoon—a cold, steady autumn downpour—and there was nothing to suggest the rainbow in the outward aspect of the camp. Lines and lines of sodden canvas housed 27,000 men, gathered from 27 different states. The ground was dotted with tools and quagmires. Under the wet canvas it was damp and cold, with penetrating chill. Lit by flickering candles, tents were far from cheerful shelter from man's last night in his native land.

But there were seven big tents where electric lights and friendliness made the night pleasant. In each of these a soldier was drumming on a piano; others were reading books and magazines; hundreds were writing letters home. Behind the raised counter at one end, three or four young men were busy passing out notepaper and envelopes, selling stamps and weighing parcels, which the men were sending home. One of the soldiers said to me as I stood in the tent used chiefly by men from Iowa: "We came all the way here from the morning, and we're mighty lonely. Then we found this YMCA on the job, and it's been more than a home for us. It gave us what we wanted when we needed it most. We'll never forget it. The boy's best friend is the YMCA.

How close these benches were packed with men, bending over the long tables absorbed in their writing! What an appeal to the sympathies these great groups of soldiers make! Fine, clean-cut, upstanding fellows, some of them mere boys, one thinks immediately of the sacrifice they have made for the rest of us, how precious they are to someone back home. Somewhere, in a far-off farm or village or city street, their parents or brothers or wives who would give all they possess for one glimpse of the sunburned faces as you and I see them on their last night before going across. And it was with the throb of the heart that I watched them, bent over their letter paper, in one after another of those seven big tents.

These were the tents of the YMCA. On that last night in America, the association was serving the soldiers in the best of all ways—giving them an opportunity to write home. On previous nights they had enjoyed boxing bouts, movies, concerts, dramatics and a score of healthy entertainment as well as religious meetings. But on the last night, home ties were strongest. And perhaps that is the keynote of the splendid work the YMCA is keeping among our men in uniform—keeping them in touch with home.

In these times there are some letters that mean more to us than any we have ever read before. They are written on sheets of paper stamped with the stars and stripes and the red triangle of the YMCA, and they bear the magic words, "With the Colors." There are many more than a million such letters in the mail now while you read this. Perhaps one is on its way to you. Each one of our 16 cantonments, where the new national army is being trained, is using more than a million sheets of this paper every month. In the draft army alone that means 16,000,000 filaments of love each month reaching out from the great encampment where the men are being trained into the greatest army this nation has ever dreamed of and binding them to the hearts at home. Multiply that by thinking of all the other places where Uncle Sam has men with the flag—and Navy yards, on the high seas, and arsenals and officers training camps and "over there" in France. In all these places men are writing home. Those unassuming little sheets of notepaper gladden millions of hearts a day.

1913 NEWS FEATURE

"Amateur Athletics, A Poll of the Press," *The Outlook,* February 15, 1913:

When the athletes representing the United States won first honors in the Olympic Games at Stockholm last summer, newspaper comment then showed that all Americans were proud of the American victory. Newspaper comment now shows that all Americans are sorry and chagrined and mortified to learn that something not quite straight aided it in the winning of our honors.

James H. Thorpe, an American Indian, who was a student at Carlisle, gained the most coveted prizes. These gave to America the credit of having developed the world's greatest athlete. More than that, this athlete had been developed from our aboriginal race, the race which once ruled this continent.

The King of Sweden presented the prizes, and Thorpe was the hero of the day. At that time no one suspected Thorpe to be other than an amateur. As a matter of fact, however, he had been, in a very small way to be sure, a professional baseball player. Hence he was not eligible to compete in the Olympic Games, which are for amateurs alone. The American Olympic Committee must now, therefore, apologize to the nations represented at Stockholm and return the prizes unfairly won. This will, of course, require readjustment of the general list of awards. And this, in turn, will lead to a recapitulation of the points won at Stockholm by the competing nations.

Important and impressive in itself, the Thorpe incident is, in the view of the American press, particularly striking because it emphasizes the problem of semi-professional baseball among college men. The question of the eradication of professionalism has troubled all of our colleges and universities ever since their undergraduates began to play the so-called "national game." The basic idea of amateur sports is, as the Philadelphia *Telegraph* says, "that this contest shall be as near even as possible. The professional who follows athletics as a livelihood possesses an unfair advantage over the man who participates in athletics solely for recreational pleasure; therefore, fair play demands that the professional be kept out of amateur sports."

Because of the temptation that college baseball players have to earn a little easy money during the summer playing on minor league teams, and the lukewarm and even indifferent attitude of our colleges and universities, the spread of the evil has become appalling.

It was through the inducements of such agencies that the Indian, Thorpe, fell, and that intercollegiate baseball to-day is honeycombed with semi-professionalism.

Thorpe's plea that he was "not wise to the ways of the world" and "simply an Indian schoolboy" will not, say most newspaper critics, excuse him. The Columbia, South Carolina, *State,* however, thus defends the culprit:

"That Thorpe, therefore, being an Indian, might hardly be held with strict justice to so high a degree of moral accountability as his white competitors properly are, for evasion of the rules governing amateur athletics, is honestly a consideration depleted in his defense at this juncture. His confession of having accepted money for playing baseball in North Carolina while he was a student at Carlisle also sets up a reasonable presumption that he did not at that time realize the effect of that course on his athletic status, though it must be admitted his silence since then concerning the episode has not been perfectly ingenuous."

The Buffalo *Express* discriminates as follows:

"Thorpe certainly knew the difference between honesty and dishonesty when he applied for and received the card from the Amateur Athletic Union, but even so, there appears to be something to say in excuse of his act. He had seen others doing the same thing who, seemingly, had more reason to their training and education to be over-scrupulous in their discriminations."

The Gloversville, New York *Herald* thus reflected the prevailing opinion:

"Every amateur knows he cannot accept money for his services, and even if the Carlisle student did not know when he played in the south, he knew it last summer before going to Stockholm. He took a long chance, got away with, and captured the world championship, now to be stripped of that crowning achievement after a few months' possession of the title. It is a sickening case, and no nation can possibly regret more than the United States does that it permitted a professional to enter the Olympic Games."

In the second place, it is urged that Thorpe did not play professional baseball for a salary, but because he liked to play the game. Says the Buffalo *Express*: "He had an independent income from his property which supplied him with all the money he needed," and the paper adds: "He was not on the diamond to earn a living or his way through college, as many college men are, and there was no profit in the playing for him except that which was derived from the pure pleasure of having an opportunity to gratify his athletic longings."

In the third place many papers note that none of Thorpe's victories at Stockholm can be attributed to what he did when playing baseball. So far as the Olympic Games are concerned, opines the Buffalo *Express*, "He could as well never have seen a ball game, much less played in one." Hence "some will say that the punishment is pathetically excessive," comments the Washington *Herald* "since the offense was the playing of summer baseball in a Southern state." The paper declares: "Thorpe did not become a great runner, jumper, and weight thrower through participation in professional baseball. His professionalism endowed him with no advantage over the college amateurs against whom he won his place in the American Olympic team."

1920–1929

Sports in the decade of the 1920s were deeply impacted by a dramatic rise in the popularity of radio, the falling price of automobiles, especially Fords, and increased coverage of sports by newspapers. The modern sports page began to take shape in the 1880s but did not become a standard feature of all major daily newspapers until the 1920s. By then the percentage of total newspaper space allocated to sport was more than double that of three decades earlier. Even *The New York Times* gave front-page coverage to major prize fights and the World Series. It is one of the reasons cultural historians refer to 1920s as the era of heroes. Ty Cobb and Babe Ruth became household names whose daily statistics were fanatically followed by baseball fans. Fighters Jack Dempsey and Gene Tunney, football player Red Grange and golfer Bobby Jones all made headlines with their accomplishments and exploits. Sports coverage became national in scope: When Dempsey fought Tunney in 1927 for the heavyweight title, 104,000 people attended in person and 50 million Americans followed the action on the 73 stations of the NBC radio network.

The sport of basketball, created in 1891, continued to gain popularity as educators became fascinated with the socializing aspects of physical education and the role of team sports. By the end of the decade, 36 states had adopted physical education requirements for public schools.

The decade following the Great War was marked by a new nationalism symbolized by frenzied consumerism. By the early 1920s, urban Americans had begun to define themselves—for their neighbors and for the world—in terms of what they owned. The car was becoming ubiquitous, zooming from 4,000 registered vehicles at the dawn of the century to 1.9 million 20 years later. Radios and telephones were introduced into millions of homes and some young women felt free to dress as they pleased, wear make-up, and help select the nation's leaders, thanks to the Nineteenth Amendment allowing women's suffrage. This freedom also brought a reaction: decency societies were formed, membership in the Ku Klux Klan grew, and immigration was largely stilled. Simultaneously, aggressive new advertising methods began and were successful. Americans bought and America boomed. With expanded wages and buying power came increased leisure time for recreation, travel and even self-improvement. Although infectious disease was still a killer, an increased emphasis on sanitation, air circulation and early treatment was beginning to chase some of the most feared diseases from the nation's ghettoes.

Following the Great War, America enjoyed a period of expansion and expectation. The role of the federal government remained small during this period and federal expenditures actually declined following the war effort. The 1920 Census reported that more than 50 percent of the population—54 million people—lived in urban areas, the result of increased industrialization and migration of millions of Southern blacks to the urban North.

The availability of electricity expanded the goods that could be manufactured and sold. Radios, electric lights, telephones, and powered vacuum cleaners quickly became essential household items. At the turn of the century, electricity ran only 5 percent of all machinery, and by 1925, 73 percent. Large-scale electric power also made possible electrolytic processes in the rapidly developing heavy chemical industry. Wages for skilled workers continued to rise during the 1920s, putting further distance between the blue-collar worker and the emerging middle class.

Following the war years, women who had worked in men's jobs remained in the workforce, although at lower wages. Women, now allowed to vote, were encouraged to consider options other than marriage. Average family earnings increased slightly during the first half of the period, while prices and hours worked actually declined. The 48-hour week became standard, providing more leisure time.

These national shifts were not without powerful resistance. A bill was proposed in Utah to imprison any woman who wore her skirt higher than three inches above her ankle. Cigarette consumption reached 43 billion annually. The Hays Commission, limiting sexual material in silent films, was created to prevent "loose" morals, and the Ku Klux Klan expanded to repress Catholics, Jews, open immigration, make-up on women, and the prospect of unrelenting change.

Despite a growing middle class, the share of disposable income going to the top 5 percent of the population continued to increase. Fifty percent of the people, by one estimate, still lived in poverty. Coal and textile workers, Southern farmers, unorganized labor, single women, the elderly, and most blacks were excluded from the economic giddiness of the period.

In 1929, America appeared to be in an era of unending prosperity. Industrial production rose 50 percent during the decade as the concepts of mass production were refined and broadly applied. The sale of electrical appliances from radios to refrigerators skyrocketed. Consumers were able to purchase newly produced goods through the extended use of credit. Debt accumulated. By 1930, personal debt had increased to one-third of personal wealth. The nightmare on Wall Street in October 1929 brought an end to the economic festivities, setting the stage for a more proactive government and an increasingly cautious worker.

1925 Profile

Allen Flannery was a miner who worked six days a week in the depths of the Pennsylvania coal mines and gloried in the opportunity to play professional football on the seventh day.

Life at Home

- Allen Flannery was named after Necho Allen, a hunter who discovered the anthracite coal in the region that made Pottsville an important economic community.
- Allen Flannery was a star player on his high school football team, playing several positions, but he excelled on the defensive line, crashing through to stop the run.
- He had hopes of playing football at Lafayette College in Easton, Pennsylvania, but his father died of pneumoconiosis, or "miner's asthma" when Allen was only 16.
- The oldest boy in the family, Allen had to quit school and go to work.
- The mines were the best option, but Pennsylvania law forbade underage miners from working, so his uncle vouched for him as 18, and he went to work.
- When Allen left school, football and baseball went along with it.
- He was now rising at 5:30 every morning, Monday through Saturday, to work underground—often eight to 10 hours per day.
- Each day he would walk deep into the mines, inspecting the buttresses that his lamp lit up in the labyrinth, recalling the death of an older cousin, just one of the more than 2,000 fatalities every year in the U.S. mines.
- Sunday was Allen's only reprieve from work, and much of his day was spent resting.
- At the same time, laboring in the mines had given him arms of steel and he was in the best physical condition of his life.

Allen Flannery abandoned his dream of college football for the dust and darkness of the coal mines.

Coal miners had a grueling schedule.

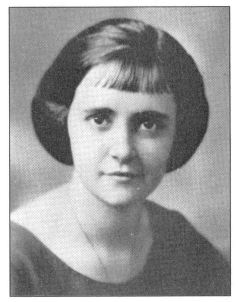

Allen's girlfriend, Ethel.

- When his father was alive, Allen used to watch the local independent football team, the Pottsville Maroons, on Sunday.
- One Sunday afternoon at a community picnic, he became involved in a football game.
- Allen was a talented player, thrilled at the opportunity to play the game he loved so much.
- His skills impressed three players who Allen thought were the best he had ever played against.
- They approached him after the game, saying they were on the Maroons team, and encouraged him to try out for a vacant reserve spot on the 16-man roster.
- Allen made the club, and was one of only two players that had not attended college.
- Allen earned $100 a game, compared to $0.78 an hour for a 48-hour work week in the mines.
- The money allowed him not only to support his family, but also to propose to his girlfriend, Ethel.
- In combination with his miner's wages, his football earnings also allowed him luxuries such as taking Ethel to the Majestic Theater to watch movies.
- They especially loved seeing Harold Lloyd as a human tackling dummy in *The Freshman.*
- The laughter was good for Allen.
- Three years in the mines had aged him, making him appear 10 years older than he actually was.

Life at Work

- Allen Flannery had been hooked on the Pennsylvania Anthracite League football team, the Pottsville Maroons, since their formation in 1920.
- As a high school student, he had a dream of playing for the team someday.
- In the summer of 1925, Dr. John C. Streigel, owner and manager of the Maroons, applied for membership in the budding National Football League, founded in a Hupmobile (an automobile built 1909 to 1940 by the Hupp Motor Company of Detroit, Michigan) dealership in Canton, Ohio, in 1922.
- Streigel had purchased the franchise in 1924 for $1,500.
- The original eight teams had paid $100 to join the league, but by 1925 expansion costs had risen to $500.
- Pottsville was granted a team because the Maroons enjoyed one of the most faithful followings in all of professional football, and because the nearby Frankford Yellow Jackets played their games on Saturday.
- Logistically it would be lucrative for clubs to play Pottsville on Sunday.
- County Blue Laws forbade organized sporting events on Sunday, but the scheduled games were played without interference, and attendance sometimes included police officers, council members, and rumor had it, even the mayor—in disguise!
- While the league was excited about the New York Giants bringing the NFL to America's biggest city, on the field it was Pottsville that garnered the excitement.
- The Maroons boasted several of the league's early stars, stealing them from the three-time champion Canton Bulldogs, making Allen a substitute player always ready to play any one of six positions on offense and defense.
- Allen particularly liked teammate Tony Latone, who had also entered the mines upon the death of his father.
- Tony worked as a slate picker in the mines, developing powerful legs pushing locies—shuttle cars—up the slope.
- On the football field he was physical, powerful and unrelenting.
- During the 1925 season Tony contributed eight touchdowns to a memorable season, leading up to the NFL championship game in Chicago.
- His teammates considered him to be "a one-man gang."
- Coach Dick Rauch, a Penn State football legend who was assisting at Colgate University, was been hired to lead the team.
- For budget reasons, Streigel required players to live locally, which gave Rauch a luxury that no other NFL coach had at the time—scheduled team practices with everyone available to participate.
- After practice, Allen and the team would meet at the fire hall to play cards and drink bottles of locally made Yuengling from the nation's oldest brewery.
- Due to Prohibition, the product was also called "near beer."
- The regular football practices proved fruitful as Pottsville became one of the best teams in the league, with a 9-2 record headed into the last week of the season.
- They played the Chicago Bears, led by rookie sensation Harold "Red" Grange, the "Galloping Ghost," and knocked him out of the game twice.
- After getting knocked out for the second time, Grange said, "The hell with $500 (his pay for the game) it ain't worth it," and walked off the field.
- Their final game was December 6 at Comisky Park in Chicago against the 8-2-1 Cardinals and was billed as "for the championship."
- The swirling snowstorm didn't bother Allen or the Maroons, who dominated the game, winning 21-7.

The Pottsville Maroons played hard and won often.

- The Maroons thought that they had won the championship and in accordance with a new NFL rule, scheduled an additional game against a Notre Dame alumni team, including the "Four Horsemen" who boasted before the Pottsville/Chicago game that they could beat the NFL champion.
- An extra game meant money in everyone's pocket, including Allen's.
- Meanwhile, the Chicago Cardinals wanted to cash in on the popularity of Red Grange and scheduled two games against lesser opponents in order to entice the Bears to play a game against them.
- The Cardinals won the two games with ease, in large part because both teams had disbanded and struggled to find enough players to play the game.
- One of the games against Milwaukee was in danger of being cancelled because Milwaukee didn't have enough players.
- Chicago halfback Art Folson helped the team recruit four high school players in order to field a team.
- The game was a 58-0 slaughter, and when commissioner Joe Carr found out what had transpired, he fined Milwaukee owner Ambrose L. McGurk, who was forced to sell the franchise in 90 days and banned for life from the NFL.
- Art Folson was also banned from the league for his part in the drama.
- Red Grange was injured and following doctor's orders ended his season and the hope of an all-Chicago match.

Thousands of fans turned out for the championship game.

- At the same time, Streigel decided to move the highly hyped Pottsville/Notre Dame game to Philadelphia to better handle the anticipated larger crowd, but the Frankford ownership cried foul, claiming that Pottsville was infringing on their territory.
- Commissioner Carr agreed and telegraphed a warning to Streigel that if they played the game in Philadelphia, there could be consequences.
- The Maroons ignored the warning and played at Shibe Park in front of 10,000 screaming fans, who paid an average of $1 per ticket.
- The game was hard fought with Notre Dame dominating, but Allen made a critical tackle late in the game that gave the Maroons one last chance.
- The contest was won with a dramatic last second field goal, the 9-7 decision bringing respectability to the professional game.
- The Maroons, however, were banned from the league and the Chicago Cardinals were declared the champions.
- The town was outraged at having its championship taken from them, and Allen was confused when he heard the news at the mines.
- Streigel pleaded his case in front of NFL owners, but was denied the championship.
- Chicago owner Chris O'Brien, however, refused the championship based on the circumstances.
- In all the confusion, no vote was taken to declare a champion.

Life in the Community: Pottsville, Philadelphia

- Pottsville, 97 miles northwest of Philadelphia, was an unlikely place for a professional football team.
- Like ancient Rome, the city of 4.2 square miles rests on seven hills.
- Coal mining put the town on the map, helping produce the 150 million tons of the nation's annual coal output, which sold for $3 a ton.
- Pottsville had recently been classified as a third-class city, with more than 20,000 residents.
- Football became a popular sport in the coal mine region of Pennsylvania, and residents loved the quick pace and simple rough and tough game.
- The professional football team, the Pottsville Eleven, became the Maroons in 1924.
- The name change followed delivery of the uniforms, whose maroon color was very impressive.
- The Maroons quickly became the talk of the town after opening the season with a 28-0 drubbing of Buffalo.
- In the Pottsville barbershops, the usual talk of hunting was cast aside in favor of football.
- Dr. Streigel billed the team as a blue-collar club, comprising miners, but in fact many players were signed away from other pro teams with lucrative offers.
- The high school field, Minersville Park, would seat only 5,000, but the devoted fans made the club a financial success.

Pottsville in 1833.

HISTORICAL SNAPSHOT
1925

- *Mein Kampf* by Adolph Hitler, *In Our Time* by Ernest Hemingway, *Manhattan Transfer* by John Dos Passos, *Mrs. Dalloway* by Virginia Wolfe and *The Great Gatsby* by F.Scott Fitzgerald were published

- President Calvin Coolidge declared, "The business of America is business"

- The Model-T Ford sold for its lowest price ever, $260, reduced from $950 in 1909

- Charles David Jenkins produced a working television set

- Alfred Sturtevant of Columbia University demonstrated that developmental effects of genes are influenced by neighboring genes

- Cinema-goers watched *The Phantom of the Opera*, *The Freshman*, *The Gold Rush* and *Ben-Hur*

- Americans spent more than $6 billion on building and construction

- Bootleg liquor prices appeared regularly at the end of the "Talk of the Town" section of *The New Yorker*

- The last fire engine drawn by a span of three horses in Washington, DC, was retired

- Red Grange brought his college fame to pro football, drawing unprecedented crowds as he played 10 games in 17 days

- Walter P. Chrysler introduced the first Chrysler automobile

- John T. Scopes went on trial in Dayton, Tennessee, for teaching the theory of evolution, where he was found guilty and fined $100, though the State Supreme Court set aside the conviction on appeal

- Philip Randolph organized the Brotherhood of Sleeping Car Porters, one of the first black labor unions

- Refrigerator sales reached 75,000 annually, up from 10,000 in 1920

- The National Spelling Bee, dry ice, automatic potato peeling machine, Wesson Oil and Caterpillar tractors all made their first appearance

- *The New Yorker* and *Cosmopolitan* were first published

- Popular songs include, "Swannee," "Tea for Two," "Has Anybody Seen My Gal?", and "Sweet Georgia Brown"

- One in six Americans owned an automobile

- Cosmetics became a $141 million industry

- Nellie Taylor of Wyoming became the first female governor, finishing the term of her late husband

- Greyhound Corporation began with General Motors as its major stockholder

- Trinity College in North Carolina was renamed Duke University after James B. Duke made a $40 million donation

- Having handed over his crime empire to Al Capone, gangster Johnny Torrino retired to Italy with between $10 and $30 million

Selected Prices

Automobile, Chrysler Roadster $1,525.00
Blanket, Wool $4.95
Fishing Reel $4.37
Football Helmet $5.50
Football Pants, Red Grange $3.89
Football, Rawlings $12.00
Golf Tee $0.25
Motorcycle, Harley-Davidson $235.00
Pocketknife $3.50
Wheelbarrow $6.25

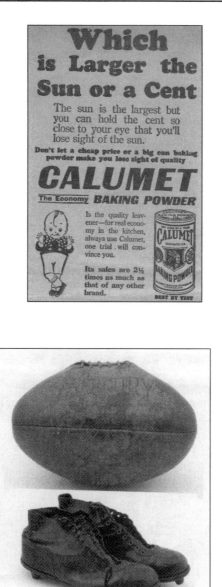

Football Timeline

1820
Old Division football, the earliest form of American football, was played at Dartmouth College; the two sides could have an unlimited number of players.

1874
The universities McGill and Harvard played the first modern American game with an emphasis on running rather than kicking.

1880
Walter Camp of Yale introduced several rule changes to the game, including Scrimmage and Down and Distance.

1893
Joseph M. Reeves of Navy made a protective covering for his head of moleskin.

1895
John Brailler became the first player to openly be declared a professional, when he was paid $10 and expenses to play for Latrobe (Pennsylvania) YMCA versus Jeannette AC.

1896
The Allegheny Athletic Association fielded the first completely pro team but folded after two games.

1896
George "Rose" Barclay added straps and ear pieces to his head gear.

1898
A touchdown changed from four points to five.

1900
William C. Temple of the Duquesne Country Athletic Club became the first individual owner of a team.

1904
A field goal changed from five points to four.

1905
Canton AC, who would later win the first three NFL championships, became a professional team.

President Theodore Roosevelt threatened to shut down football unless changes were made to minimize the violence. "Change the game or forsake it," he said. That year there were 18 fatalities and 159 serious injuries.

1909
A field goal was now worth three points.

1920
The Pottsville Eleven became an independent football team.

1925
Walter Camp, the "Father of American Football" died at age 65.

Knute Rockne coached at Notre Dame for eight years.

"Spikes Report Rockne Will Leave Notre Dame," *The Daily Republican*, Rockville, Indiana, December 12, 1925:

Philadelphia—"Knute Rockne will remain coach at Notre Dame. He has never had any intention of relinquishing his South Bend post. I am authorized to speak for him."

In this statement, J. M. Byrne, eastern representative of Notre Dame University, today sparked reports that Rockne "Groom of the Four Horsemen" and one of the greatest coaches in football history, was considering leaving his berth with the Catholic institution and accepting an offer to coach the Columbia football team.

Rockne and Byrne came to this city to see the Pottsville Maroons battle the "Four Horsemen" and build a team around them at Shibe Park today.

"The overtures made by Columbia never received Rockne's serious consideration," Byrne said. "He has never had any intention of leaving his South Bend post. He had hoped to see the "Four Horsemen" in action here today, but business affairs which I cannot discuss called him to New York this morning."

Rockne was said to have telephoned authorities at the South Bend institution last night denying reports emanating from New York City that he had signed with Columbia.

His eight years at the helm of Notre Dame gave Rockne one of the highest percentages for winning football teams in the history of the sport. His teams have played 75 games, of which they have won 65, tied four and lost six.

"Red Is on the Hospital List," *The Daily Republican,* Rushville, Illinois, December 12, 1925:

Detroit—"Red" Grange is out of professional football for at least 10 days and possibly longer, suffering from a blood clot on his left arm, physicians announced today.

As a result the former Illinois star will not play here today, but may appear on the sidelines. His arm is bound in splints.

The scheduled game between Grange's team, the Chicago Bears, and the Detroit Panthers, however, will be played.

"New York Germans Demand Action to Save Reich from Crumbling," *The World's Work,* December 1923:

The 7,500,000 German-born residents of the United States were urged yesterday to go to the aid of the crumbling German Reich before the Republic was "overwhelmed in the raging seas of international troubles and engulfed by the cruel French bayonets which menaced the Ruhr and the Rhineland and threatened to split Germany into a series of independent units."

The call was heralded by the Rev. Dr. William Popcke, president of the United German Societies under whose auspices German Day was celebrated in the Manhattan Opera House yesterday afternoon and evening. Representatives from German societies in 32 cities participated in the celebration and the Opera House was packed to capacity. The meeting was conducted throughout in the German tongue.

Dr. Popcke said Germans in America must not be content with mere protest, but they should not rest until Germany's present helpless condition has been brought to the attention of not only President Coolidge, but every Senator, Representative, statesman, and politician in the country. The protest, the speaker said, should be addressed in the following terms

The German-born Americans urge you to focus your immediate attention on Germany's condition. The French reign of terror in the Ruhr and Rhineland must be brought to an end before it is too late. . . ."

The audience was asked to cry yea or nay, and amid scenes of intense national feeling, 5,000 rose to their feet and adopted the motion unanimously.

Tony was one hell of a rugged coal miner, and for my money, he was the best football player I have ever seen. I simply cannot imagine anyone who could equal that power play fullback whose leg drive is so unbelievably potent Tony simply knocked the linemen kicking.

—Football great "Red" Grange on Tony Latone, 1931

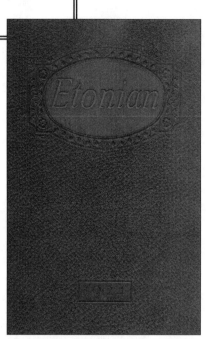

"Athletics," *The Etonian,* yearbook of Elizabethtown College, Elizabethtown, Pennsylvania, 1924:

Throughout the school year we have had among the entire student body the feeling that physical exercise is one of the essential, if not the most essential, phase in an educational career. Consequently there was a need for the development of a proper attitude for this division of school activity. However, great care has been shown in determining how much exercise is needed in order to maintain sufficient body vigor and at the same time to hold the scholastic attainment of the individual in the foreground.

The true sportsman will enter into any kind of athletics wholeheartedly. By playing the game hard he will obtain the greatest amount of value in any game, both from a physical and mental standpoint. This is very evident when we consider any form of group game which requires considerable cooperation among individual players to ensure victory. In this very idea there is something that readily can be applied to everyday life.

We believe that every member of the student body needs some form of physical exercise. Bodily decay and reconstruction are taking place continually. Therefore, if we wish to establish a foursquare educational platform we must not fail to take into the structure a well-founded conception of physical education.

We Americans need to stop and step aside from our daily routine of everyday life and engage in something that will tend to give voice to our bodily systems.

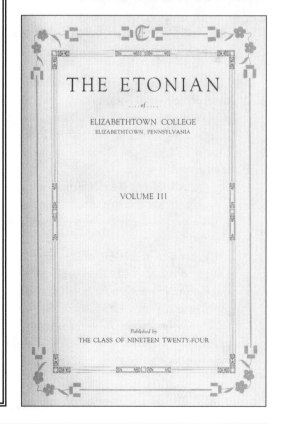

THE ETONIAN
....of....
ELIZABETHTOWN COLLEGE
ELIZABETHTOWN, PENNSYLVANIA

VOLUME III

Published by
THE CLASS OF NINETEEN TWENTY-FOUR

"Sports Briefs," *Alton Evening Telegraph* (Illinois), December 15, 1925:

Because they taught physical exercises in school for salaries, three London young women tennis players have been declared by the Lawn Tennis Association to be professionals and disqualified from competition in amateur matches.

Professional hockey will make its bow in New York tonight with the New York Americans meeting the Canadians of Montréal in the National Hockey League contest. The Governor General's footguard band from Canada and the cadet banned from West Point are the advertised attractions.

The Huddle System of calling basketball signals will replace the method in which the center designates the play when Northwestern opens its floor season tonight against Notre Dame. The Purple will continue the style unless it takes too much time.

Hockey has joined baseball and football in attracting noted players from the ranks of the amateurs

"Billy Evans Says," *Alton Evening Telegraph* (Illinois), December 15, 1925:

I see no reason why colleges should make such a fuss over professional football.

Football is typically a college game. Regardless of the increasing interest in professional football as played by former college men, the sport is in no danger of becoming tainted.

The action of "Red" Grange in leaving college in his senior year for the professional game is the real reason for the drastic measures the colleges have adapted relative to it.

Viewed from certain angles it is to be regretted that Grange did not finish his college career. His action didn't quite conform with college ethics. From a financial tangle, it was a very wise move by the "redhead."

It may be a score of years before the gridiron uncovers another Grange, so it probably would have been best if the college authorities had ignored this action.

"Pro Football Here to Stay, Experts Admit," Edward Derr, *San Mateo Times* (California), December 1, 1925:

Professional football has become so strong that the colleges and universities are powerless to check its advances, according to Maj. John L. Griffith, Commissioner of Big Ten athletics. He predicted that the Western conference athletic directors in their annual meeting here in Chicago Thursday, Friday, and Saturday "will adopt no definite rules against pro football because there is nothing that we can do to stop it."

"We are opposed to professional football, of course," Griffith told United Press in an interview. "But we realize that our hands are tied. About all we can do is to discourage it among the college players. If we could adopt some rules or regulations that would curb it, we probably would do it, but I cannot see how that would be possible."

"Red Grange Took Leading Role When He Cast His Lot with the Professional Men," Henry Farrell, *Galveston Daily News* (Texas), December 28, 1925:

Dartmouth and Michigan, Red Grange and Oberlander made the 1925 football season the most popular and the most interesting in the history of the game.

Attendance records were shattered wherever there was a stadium large enough to provide a record, and Columbus entertained the largest number of paid spectators when 83,000 sat in on the Ohio State-Illinois game in which the great Grange finished his college career.

Grange broke down after joining the Chicago Bears, the professional team. He tried to do something that makes variance trainers say never can be done. He tried to play in five games a week and broke down so badly he had to call a halt.

When he turned professional he was showered with more than $60,000 for various games and stunts and he was on the way to making a millionaire of himself as long as he could keep his hold on the public.

He had been playing only for a little over a week when the cheers turned into jeers. There was no college loyalty in the stands. When he couldn't deliver what the customers had put out their money to see, they gave him the Bronx cheer.

"Many Miners Are Entombed by Blast, North Carolina Disaster Toll May Reach 70, Records Show 59 Men In Mine; 71 Lamps Are Missing," *The Morning Herald,* Uniontown, Pennsylvania, May 28, 1925:

Coal Glenn, N. C., May 27—The fate of threescore or more miners entombed this morning by an explosion below the 1,000-foot lateral of the Carolina Coal Company mine, near here, was undetermined tonight, although rescuers had succeeded in bringing to the surface six bodies and it was feared most of the others had perished.

Records of the mine showed that 59 men, 39 white and 20 negroes, had comprised the crew which went into the mine, while mine officials reported that 71 miners' lamps were missing and it was believed that figure might represent the number entombed.

Hope was expressed, however, by Bion H. Butler, vice president of the mining company, that some of the entombed men might still be alive.

Rescue workers said that the air was clear in the mine below the point where the bodies were found. The fans were kept going all day in an effort to purify the air so that rescuers might be able to penetrate further into the dark recesses that are believed to hold the victims.

Mr. Butler said the best information he had been able to obtain was that the first explosion occurred in the second right lateral of the mine approximately 1,000 feet from the entrance. The two explosions which followed at half-hour intervals were believed by officials to have occurred between the second right shaft and the opening. Mine authorities said the six men whose bodies were found apparently had died only a short time before they were reached.

1927 PROFILE

William Lawrence "Young" Stribling spent most of his childhood in vaudeville with his parents and a younger brother, but in his teenage years became a formidable boxer.

Life at Home

- William Lawrence "Young" Stribling was born to be a prizefighter.
- His birth announcement, in 1904, read: "Born to Mr. and Mrs. W. L. Stribling Sr, a future heavyweight champion of the world, the day after Christmas, to be called William Lawrence Stribling Jr."
- As one of the traveling vaudeville act, "Four Novelty Grahams" (other members were his parents and younger brother Herbert "Babe"), Young Stribling grew up on the road.
- The "Grahams" repertoire consisted of gymnastics and balancing acts that culminated in a boxing match between Young and Babe, who wore oversized gloves.
- It was an enormous hit and never failed to bring the house down.
- Ma and Pa Stribling, both trained acrobats, spearheaded their son's boxing career, including maintaining his physical condition and performance level.
- Pa served as his manager and promoter while Ma actually donned gloves and sparred with Young up until he was 14 years old.
- The Striblings were not a typical, hard-living vaudeville family.
- They prayed and read the Bible together before each show, and attended church every Sunday no matter where they were performing.
- "The Four Novelty Grahams" were so popular that the Stribling family was paid to perform in 38 countries over several years before settling down in Macon, Georgia, just before World War I.
- Macon was called the "Heart of Georgia" because of its location near the Ocmulgee River in central Georgia, home of some of the most impressive Indian mounds in the Southeastern United States.

Young Stribling was born to be a prizefighter.

Clara Virginia Kinney and Young made an unlikely couple.

- Chartered in 1823, Macon was named for Nathaniel Macon, a North Carolina Congressman.
- Young fought his first professional bout in 1921, as a 16-year-old bantamweight in Atlanta, Georgia.
- He fought 75 professional bouts while still in high school and gained the reputation of an up-and-coming pugilist.
- Led by Young as forward, Macon's Lanier High School won the state basketball championship in 1922.
- When the team was invited to the National Interscholastic Tournament in Chicago, Young was ineligible to play because of his status as a professional boxer.
- On his twenty-first birthday Young Stribling married his high school sweetheart, Brenau College student Clara Virginia Kinney.
- She was high society and he was a prizefighter.
- The couple met at Lanier High School and their romance blossomed quickly, from love notes to walking home from school, with Young carrying her books.
- Clara's father was a successful Macon businessman in the cotton industry, and her mother was the first woman elected to the City Council.
- When he was not in serious training for a fight, Young spent considerable time with Clara, often listening to the Crosby radio like many Americans.
- In 1922 the Crosby Radio Corporation had created a radio that relied on simpler vacuum tubes instead of crystals, and it was the first with dials to adjust the volume and tune in to stations.
- Just as important, it was packaged and sold in an attractive wooden case, looking like a respectable piece of furniture in any parlor.
- Together they listened to the *Maxwell House Hour* and the *Midweek Hymn Sing*, both sponsored by Maxwell House Coffee and the *Goodrich Zippers Banjo Ensemble* sponsored by B. F. Goodrich.
- By the time Young was 21, he had earned over one million dollars from his boxing purses.
- He and Clara could afford the best of everything.
- The nation, too, had the appearance of prosperity.
- About 80 percent of American homes had a yearly income of $3,000 a year and could afford electric vacuum cleaners, washing machines, refrigerators and electric ranges.

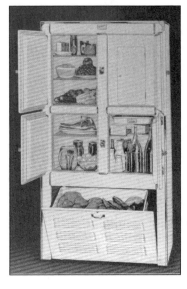

Young and Clara bought the latest appliances.

- A frequent guest of the Stribling household was golfer Bobby Jones, who was born in Atlanta.
- In 1926 Jones became the first golfer to win the British Open and the U.S. Open in the same year, earning him a ticker tape parade.
- Bobby Jones and Young Stribling often walked around Macon wearing "their plus fours, " knickers made from four extra inches of fabric, widely worn by men during activities such as golf.

Life at Work

- Young Stribling took his first shot at a championship title fight when he challenged Irishmen Mike McTigue for the light heavyweight championship of the world on October 4, 1923, in Columbus, Georgia.
- Young was 18 years old.
- McTigue, while a hardened old veteran, discovered that he had seriously underestimated his opponent once he saw Stribling in person.
- McTigue had been led to believe by his manager Joe Jacobs, that Stribling would be easy pickings.
- The handsome, charismatic Young Stribling was considered a scientific boxer who preferred to win on points rather than rely on the knockout.
- He despised what he considered to be the pointless violence of the sport and spoke out against it.
- While witnessing an extremely brutal beating of a young fighter by an older, more experienced boxer, Young Stribling rose from his ringside seat and "threw in the towel," possibly saving the young man from serious injury.
- Young was a poster boy for clean living and never drank, never smoked, and was discriminating in his eating habits.
- He had a mean knockout punch, perhaps because of his clean lifestyle, that knocked half his opponents to the canvas.
- On the morning of the scheduled championship fight, McTigue attempted to use a hand injury to back out, but X-rays showed it to be an old injury, despite the champion's protests.
- Supported by a hometown crowd, Young dominated the light heavyweight championship 10-round fight only to have the referee declare a draw.
- When the 8,000 spectators boisterously challenged his decision, the decision was changed, and Young was announced the winner.
- Three hours later, the referee, hiding out in a secret location, reversed himself again and declared the fight a draw.
- Young had been a champion for three hours.
- Great controversy ensued nationwide.
- After the fight McTigue issued a statement to the press: "I was really surprised this morning when they forced me to go in the ring with only one hand to defend my title. I went into the ring with one hand and I believe I scored more points with that one hand than Stribling did with both of his."
- Despite fighting hundreds of opponents, Young never claimed a title.
- An 18,000-mile barnstorming tour, that included his family, across the country in 1925 earned Young the moniker "King of the Canebrakes," from writer Damon Runyon, reflecting Stribling's popularity in rural areas.
- For the tour the family purchased a bus to give fans in smaller towns an opportunity to see the popular boxer in exhibition bouts.

The Stribling's took the "show" on the road.

Young refused to face black fighters.

- Pa Stribling pitted Young against the local champion at each stop, offering $10 to anyone who could beat his son.
- Young fought 33 matches that year and did much to popularize the sport with his reputation for clean sportsmanship and wholesome living.
- Another cross-country tour in 1927 resulted in his winning 57 straight fights with only one draw and one loss.
- A careful fighter, possessing superb defensive skills, Young never picked up a scar to mar his movie star looks.
- Stribling was loved across Georgia, and served as an Elk, a Kiwanian, a Mason, and a Bible-class teacher who worked with disadvantaged children.
- Black Georgians, though, were less sympathetic to Young for his refusal to face black fighters.

Life in the Community: Macon, Georgia

- When surveyor James Webb laid out the downtown streets of Macon, Georgia, in 1832, he incorporated parks, including 250 acres for Central City Park.
- Citizens were required by ordinances to plant shade trees in their front yards, setting the tone for the shade-soaked city where Young Stribling grew up.
- The land was first inhabited by Creeks and their predecessors 12,000 years before white people arrived.
- In 1806, President Thomas Jefferson had a trading post established there as a peacekeeping and trading site after the Creeks ceded their lands east of the Ocmulgee River.
- Cotton became the mainstay of Macon's early economy as boats, stagecoaches, and, in 1843, a railroad all brought prosperity to Macon.
- During the Civil War, Macon was spared destruction during the Union Army's march to the sea.

Macon, Georgia was a well-planned and prosperous city.

- Following the war and into the twentieth century, Macon continued to build on its agricultural base and became a transportation hub for the entire state.
- Henry Ford's Model T was helping to end the isolation of rural people and transform America into a nation constantly on the move.
- The ubiquitous car was known by a variety of names, including the Tin Lizzie, Flivver, Detroit Disaster, Michigan Mistake, Tacks Collector, Nagivatin' Nancy, and Old Faithful.
- With a production run of 15 million from 1908 to 1927, this four-wheeled contraption had more impact on the nation than the telegraph, telephone, phonograph, radio, electric light and power, or rural free delivery.
- It was powered by a front-mounted longitudinal inline 177ci four-cylinder engine that powered the rear wheels, and its compression ratio (4.5:1) allowed the Model T to run on anything from gasoline to good-grade kerosene.
- The chassis featured a beam axle and transverse springs front and rear, and the planetary transmission, patented by Ford, was integral to the engine.
- The car's 10-gallon fuel tank was mounted to the frame beneath the front seat, and relied on gravity, the Model T could not climb a steep hill when fuel was low.
- Drivers solved this problem by driving up steep hills in reverse.
- The Model T runabout sold for $260 and the touring model was $290.
- The Model A was the second huge success for the Ford Motor Company, starting in 1927, and was available in four standard colors, but not black.
- Prices for the Model A ranged from $385 for a roadster to $1,400 for the top-of-the-line town car.
- The 40-horsepower engine gave the car a top speed of 65 miles per hour.
- The Model A was the first Ford to use the standard set of driver controls, with conventional clutch and brake pedals, throttle and gearshift.

- In cooler climates, owners could purchase an aftermarket cast iron unit to place over the engine's exhaust manifold to bring heated air into the cab, adjusted by a small door that let in the hot air.
- The Model A was the first car to have safety glass in the windshield.
- Young Stribling drove fast cars and motorcycles, and he often flew his own airplane to boxing matches across the country.
- Most barnstorming pilots in the 1920s flew Jenny's surplus Curtis JN 4D trainers, of which thousands were manufactured too late for World War I and, therefore, could be bought for $300 each.
- Young loved flying, and longed for Henry Ford's tri-motor 4 Ats, which was closely patterned on the German Fokker and one of the safest airplanes.
- It had an enclosed cockpit and carried 11 to14 passengers.
- Newspapers were replete with stories about the daring clothes of America's youth, their scandalous dancing, sensual jazz, late-night parties and cynical opinions.
- In most of rural America, however, where Young was a hero, few had come in contact with this kind of lifestyle.
- Based on the words of baseball evangelist Billy Sunday, the world was a "battleground between the children possessed by Satan and the children of God."
- Sunday's son Billy, Jr. had been publicly caught frequenting big city speakeasies, where he danced the night away with women of questionable repute.
- To most country dwellers it was clear that the Devil lived in the big cities, where he was eager to test one's faith.

HISTORICAL SNAPSHOT
1927

- More than 50 million boxing fans listened live to the Jack Dempsey-Gene Tunney matchup over 73 stations on the NBC radio network
- The first trans-Atlantic telephone call was made from New York City to London
- The U.S. Federal Radio Commission began to regulate the use of radio frequencies
- The Roxy Theater was opened by Samuel Roxy Rothafel in New York City
- The Boeing Airplane Company signed a contract with the U.S. Postal Department to fly airmail on the 1,918-mile route between Chicago, Illinois, and San Francisco, California, using the Model 40A mail plane with an air-cooled engine
- The Great Mississippi Flood of 1927 affected 700,000 people in the greatest national disaster in U.S. history
- The Academy of Motion Picture Arts and Sciences was founded
- Charles Lindbergh made the first solo non-stop trans-Atlantic flight, from New York to Paris
- FOX Films acquired the rights to the Tri-Ergon sound-on-film technology, which had been developed in 1919 by three German inventors, Josef Engl, Hans Vogt, and Joseph Massole
- Nearly 600 members of the American Institute of Electrical Engineers and the Institute of Radio Engineers viewed the first live demonstration of television at the Bell Telephone Building in New York
- Golfer Bobby Jones won both the British Open and the U.S. Amateur Championship
- Paul R. Redfern crashed his plane while attempting to fly from Brunswick, Georgia, non-stop to Rio de Janeiro, Brazil
- The Columbia Phonographic Broadcasting System, CBS, was formed and went on the air with 47 radio stations
- The movie *The Jazz Singer* successfully featured sound, marking the end of the silent film era
- New York Yankee baseballer Babe Ruth hit 60 home runs, setting a major league record

- For the second straight year, the Chicago American Giants defeated the Bacharach Giants of Atlantic City, New Jersey, in the Negro League World Series
- The powerful New York Yankees completed a four-game sweep of the Pittsburgh Pirates
- Frank Heath and his horse Gypsy Queen completed a two-year journey of 11,356 miles to all 48 states
- The Ford Motor Company unveiled the Ford Model A as its new automobile
- The musical play *Show Boat*, based on Edna Ferber's novel, opened on Broadway
- The world population reached two billion

Selected Prices

Boxing Gloves $3.95
Cornell University, Annually $1,400.00
Crayons, 24 . . . .$0.30
Cruise, Mediterranean, 71 Days $955.00
Hot Water Heater $55.00
Maternity Corset $6.95
Microscope $16.50
Pipe Tobacco $0.50
Shotgun, Single Barrel $8.95
Waffle Iron $9.75

"Something New in Delivery of Daily Newspaper," *Daily Citizen,* Beaver Dam, Wisconsin, April 20, 1928:

A new era in newspaper service was begun recently by the *Los Angeles Times,* the delivery of the morning paper by airplane on a route north to San Francisco.

The first airplane newspaper delivery was made on Sunday, April 15, according to a letter received by Mr. E. E. Parker, former Beaver Dam resident, who now resides at Altadena, California.

The plane leaves from Los Angeles shortly after the papers are off the press and makes a northerly journey to San Francisco. The plane edition is the same edition that is delivered in Los Angeles, according to Mr. Parker.

"Jones Termed Popular Star, Atlantan Considered One of Greatest Golf Players," *Ogden Standard–Examiner* (Utah), July 11, 1926:

Without a doubt the most discussed golfer in all the world today is Bobby Jones.

His qualifying rounds in the British Open of 36-38-134, followed by the winning of the championship stamped him as one of the greatest golfers of all time.

Recently I received a query from a golf fan asking for some data on Jones; when he started to play in the big tournaments and a brief record of his successes. Here goes:

Jones made his debut in championship golf in Merion in 1916 playing in the amateur championship at the age of 14. At 18 he played in his first open championship at Inverness and finished tied for eighth place.

Eight years after his debut at Merion he won the amateur championship over the same course.

Jones has made a most remarkable showing in the United States open championships.

He finished eighth in his first attempt in 1920. A year later at Columbia, he tied for fifth; at Skokie, in 1922, he had his first big thrill, finishing in a tie for second.

Success finally crowned his efforts at Inwood in 1923 when he tied with Bobby Cruickshanx for first place and won the 18-hole playoff.

The following year he was the runner-up to Cyril Walker at Detroit. Last year at Worcester he tied with Willie MacFarlane. Playing off the tie in an18-hole match the finish found them all even. MacFarlane won out on the second clash over the 18-hole route.

In the last four Open championships Jones has never been farther away than second. His remarkable showing in the British Open makes him the favorite to win at Scioto.

"Movie Review: *The Best Bad Man*," *The Nevada State Journal*, February 1, 1926:

Beginning tonight under new management and with an enlarged orchestra, the Wigwam started the week right with the best picture Tom Mix has ever made. Leaving out much of the wild west hokum that he generally uses, *The Best Bad Man* affords thrills galore and a newcomer to filmdom, Clara Bow. This is not Miss Bow's first appearance in pictures, but it is her best. Just lately she caused considerable comment with an insignificant part in *The American Venus*. Great strides are predicted for her.

The story deals with a crooked land and company manager who steals $100,000 sent by his boss to complete a dam for irrigating several thousand acres of farmland, and tells the ranchers that the big chief is a thief. Water for even domestic purposes is running low and a delegate is sent to tell the wealthy New Orleans idler just what kind of man he is. Mix, playing the big boss, and the idler go to investigate and things begin to happen immediately. In the course of events the supply dam is blown up and a torrent of water rushes down upon the hero, heroine and Sheriff's posse. The villain and his aide also tumble in the angry water. Right here is one of the best water thrills yet. Mix is fast turning into a favorite with the children for they crowded the house during the early performances. If someone isn't careful Tom Mix will turn into an actor yet.

"The Ace of Clubs," Grantland Rice, *Collier's*, August 13, 1927:

Anyone desiring to add to the hubbub of modern sport can do so by coming out boldly and picking some one ball club as "the greatest of all time."

I found this out recently when I quoted the opinions of several rival ballplayers from the American League to the effect that the present New York Yankees could be classed as one of the greatest teams in baseball history.

The rebuttal was somewhat terrific, especially from the old-time fans, but there was a wide difference of opinion.

Ballplayers who have opposed the Yankees point to the offensive power of the team that has Ruth, Gehrig, Meusel, Lazzeri, Combs and others and at the same time backs up this tremendous attack with the best fielding record in the league. And even Wilbert Robinson, who starred with the old Orioles, picks the Yankees as the game's greatest.

But before coming to the ranking of the Yankees there are five great ball clubs to be considered from the story of the past 35 years. These five clubs come in this temporal order: Baltimore Orioles 1894-96; Boston Nationals, 1897-98; Pittsburgh Pirates, 1901-03; Chicago Cubs, 1906-1910; Philadelphia Athletics, 1910-14. . . .

continued

"The Ace of Clubs," Grantland Rice, *Collier's*, . . . *(continued)*

All the clubs mentioned had smart ballplayers, but the ancient and honorable Orioles had more smart ballplayers. They were nearly all smart and if there were any lapses McGraw, Jennings, Robinson, Gleason and Keller made up the difference. They turned out more managers than any lineup in baseball history (McGraw and Robinson are still at the helm), and you might be surprised to know how many letter writing fans prefer headwork to home runs.

Here was one of the smartest and wisest ball clubs of all time. Its members lived baseball, ate baseball, dreamed baseball. The salary matter was unimportant in those days. They were figuring out plays and methods on and off the field, morning, afternoon and evening. The game was everything in their lives. They won three pennants and several of them went to Brooklyn and won two more.

Then came the Boston Nationals with the great catcher in Bergen, a fine outfield in Hamilton, Duffy and Stahl, and one of the greatest infields in Tenney, Lowe, Long and Collins.

Here were four smart, brilliant infielders who all batted well over .300. Many experts still rate this is as the greatest infield of all time. . . .

Pittsburgh from 1901 to 1903 had two good catchers, a star infield and a star outfield. But the strength of this club was a phenomenal pitching staff that carried Jess Tanneyhill, Jack Chesbro, Sam Leever and Deacon Philippe, four pitchers who could make any team look great. . . .

It is still a question as to whether or not the Chicago Cubs from 1906 through 1910 should not be rated as the greatest all-around machine.

This club had a great catcher in Johnny Kling, smart, keen, and a great thrower and a .300 hitter. It had a great pitching staff in "Three-Finger" Brown, Overall, Reulbach, Pfeister and Lundgren.

No one can ever forget the infield (comprised of Chance, Evans, Tinker and Steinfeldt) or the outfield that held Sheckard, Schultz, Hofman and Slagle.

There wasn't a weakness in this Cub organization. In 1906 it cracked a double league record by winning 116 games, a mark that has never been approached. In 1907 it won 107 games and in 1910 it won 104 games.

This Cub team won more games over a stretch of five years than any other team ever listed. They won well over 500 games from 1906 to 1910, and no other club has approached this. It won four pennants in five years. The Athletics did the same, but they never won as many games as the Cubs. . . .

The Yankees of 1927 have shown themselves to be a ball club carrying a cargo of dynamite. No other club ever took more high-power ammunition to the battle field. They have a great outfield in Ruth, Meusel and Combs. They have a slashing, able infield in Gehrig, Lazzeri, Koenig, Morehart and Dugan.

The Yankees have annihilating power at bat (Ruth and Gehrig are the two greatest sluggers any team ever carried). They have the greatest defensive record in their league. But the greatness of no club can be measured by one campaign. It will take at least another year to prove their place—now based on sheer power. No team of recent years has shown anything like the all-around consistency of these mentioned, and this applies in full measure to the old Cubs. But for sheer power the 1927 Yankees must take their place with the elect.

"Sports Done by Brown," *Nevada State Journal*, February 1, 1926:

It begins to look as if the reports circulated last week that Jack Dempsey and Gene Tunney would be meeting in a championship battle at Boyle's Thirty Acres on August 12, is authentic. At least this writer, who enjoys the close acquaintanceship of a personal friend of Dempsey, feels that there is plenty of truth, if not poetry in the matter.

If it is true, then we apparently can kiss "goodbye" any hopes we may have for Dempsey-Willis or Dempsey-Stribling meeting this year, though it is within the range of possibilities that Jack could take on either of the above named, later in the fall after his engagement with Tunney, the ex-marine.

Some sports followers possibly may be surprised at the reference to the Georgia Peach as a possible opponent for Dempsey, but there are not a few astute who certainly believe that the Georgia lad would have more than an even chance with the champion.

Stribling is younger, more active, in better condition than Jack, has a real sock in either paw and we believe would be on the giving end of any setto as well as on the receiving end.

Jack Dempsey and Gene Tunney fight.

"Society Fiancé of Stribling Proud of Him," Malcolm Ellis, *Davenport Democrat and Leader* (Iowa), January 1, 1926:

If the graying ladies with their memories of the days when Sherman cut a swath through Georgia cotton fields, and when Uncle Remus played as a boy in these neighborhood woods, are somewhat shocked over the marriage of the daughter of the Davenports and the Guerrys and the Kinneys to a prizefighter, the younger generation is not the least perturbed.

Truth to tell, there is not among the younger set of this giddy generation enough agitation over the marriage of Young Stribling, contender for the light heavyweight championship of the world, and Miss Clara Virginia Kinney, to make it interesting. The younger set takes it along with the less flamboyant romances. Indeed, to them it is the natural denouncement since the romance has budded and bloomed under the eyes of the town.

Five years ago, Young Stribling was better known as just one of the growing-up kids around town than as a prizefighter. As a basketball player on the high school team he was bidding for stardom, and to the youth of the high school that was far more thrilling than his occasional fights. He came to be the star player on the championship prep and high school basketball team of that state.

It was out of the classroom that this romance emerged, aided by the notes that were slipped surreptitiously while the geometry teacher had his attention centered on proving a theorem. Stribling walked home with Miss Kinney, carrying her books. When influence came he was paying an income tax well up in the five figures, it was in a fast motorcar that they went to the handsome Kinney home in the fashionable Cherokee Heights.

Miss Kinney had dates with other boys, but never eyes for them. She was popular in high school and in college she became the sponsor of a college fraternity and was starred in amateur theatricals.

Of French extraction, from the DuPonts, the same line as the DuPonts of Delaware and the Guerrys, she is dainty and petite, the exemplification of breeding and culture that has existed for multiple generations. Her maternal ancestors were among those French Huguenot settlers who peopled Charleston and made it the South's most aristocratic city. Her paternal ancestors were among the English cavaliers who made Virginia the richest colony. . . .

How will her mother take the match?

"I'm glad Clara is going to have Strib," she said. "He is one of the finest boys I've ever known. I have known him and watched him for years almost as closely as his own mother would. I know they will be happy together. They've been sweethearts since high school days. My daughter could not have picked a better man."

"Tommy Loughran," *In This Corner, 42 World Champions Tell Their Stories*, Peter Heller, 1994:

First time I fought Young Stribling was in New York. . . . I think it was a six-round bout. I think I got $5,000 for it, which was a lot of money in those days. I punched the head off of Stribling. I gave him an awful going over, yet they gave him the decision. . . . It was a one-sided fight. I won easily. Afterward Herman Taylor told me that Damon Runyon guaranteed them the decision. I didn't care about it.

Stribling thumbed my eye. When he did it, I just walked right in and hit him low. I hit him low and kneed him. And the referee came running over and said, "What's wrong, Tommy." I said, "Look at my eye." Blood was running out of it. He said, "Go ahead, the sky's the limit." And Stribling ran like a thief. Any guy that would do that is yellow.

"Mob Charges Ring After Arbiter Calls Bout Draw,"
Davenport Democrat and Leader (Iowa), October 5, 1923:

Although McTigue of Ireland still retains his light heavyweight crown under the third decision rendered by referee Harry Ertie after the Irishman's 10-rounder bout yesterday, his opponent Young Stribling today is the rightful owner, in the opinion of Columbus, Georgia, fight fans. Promoter J. P. Jones of the local American Legion Post so informed Chairman Muldoon of the New York State boxing commission in a telegram sent to him last night demanding a thorough investigation by the commission of yesterday's tumultuous events.

Jones' telegram was sent after referee Ertie, who at first declared the fight a draw and then when the crowd of 8,000 displeased fans charged the ring, changed his decision giving the victory to the 18-year-old Georgia schoolboy, had issued a written statement officially declaring the fight a draw. The statement, issued from the obscurity of a private residence here, contained the assertion that the referee had been threatened with death if he did not give the decision to Stribling and a charge that Major Jones had forcibly held his arm and that of Stribling aloft.

Three hours after the fight Ertie issued a statement that his decision is a draw. Last night, on the eve of the fight, McTigue suddenly claimed that he had a broken thumb. He had doctors to back his claim. He therefore called off the match Wednesday night stating his thumb was broken Monday of this week while training here. This morning 10 of the best surgeons in this state declared after x-ray examination that the injury was an old one and that same injury to the thumb occurred prior to his signing the contract on Labor Day for the bout held today. After much wrangling McTigue agreed to defend the championship. He lost six rounds, carried two, and two were draws. This is the average opinion.

1929 Profile

Best friends John Farley and Donald Sweeney had hiked, fished, hunted and camped together for years. Both were experienced woodsmen, John the expert canoeist, and Don a master fisherman.

Life at Home

- For John Farley and his best friend Donald Sweeney, two trained woodsmen, getting totally lost was embarrassing.
- In fact, if the situation was not so desperate, it would have been completely humiliating.
- Tired, hungry and miles from civilization; John and Don had some decisions to make.
- Should they stick together, even though they disagreed on which path to take, or should they separate and hope that one of them would find help in the endless maze of lakes and islands?
- With each passing hour their decision became more critical.
- The Superior National Forest was a wilderness that saw few visitors.
- John and Don had been friends throughout eight years of competitive swimming, and both had reached the finals of the U.S. Olympic trials—John for the breast stroke, Don for the back stroke.
- Being together fired their competitive juices and they had many adventures together.
- In Chicago, they swam into Lake Michigan on the bet that the first one to look back would concede defeat.
- When Don finally relented, the shore was out of sight and it was dark.
- On a canoe trip, when a loon paddled out in front of them, John told Don to keep the bird distracted while he slipped out the back of the canoe and swam underwater to catch the bird.
- John's attempts to grab the legs of the loon were futile and, eventually, exhausted and out of air, John surfaced.

John Farley and Donald Sweeney were avid outdoorsmen.

The men started their trip while it was still dark.

- Don stopped laughing long enough to tell him the loon had been watching the entire time, and staying out of reach.
- They grew up blocks from each other in Chicago, in families dominated by angry fathers who were frustrated by the difficulties of earning a living.
- Their mothers stretched already meager meals, and the boys had perfected the five-finger discount at the fruit market to keep the hunger away.
- Their trip into Superior National Forest was John's idea, and it was Don's job to provision the trip and predict the number of fish they would catch.
- Canoeing into Superior National Forest the year before, the two men had seen numerous reminders of the old Gold Rush days, and they were eager to return.
- The land was crisscrossed with sloughs and mines, and an ancient wood-burning locomotive rested on rusty tracks on one the many small islands.
- There were no roads and few people, and the wild animals seemed more curious than afraid.
- Sitting quietly and sculling the paddles underwater to avoid the sound of dripping water, they approached deer so close on the shore that Don touched one with his paddle.
- During the trip, four heads peered over a log when the two men pushed off from a portage — two adult and two young otters who swam alongside the men the seven miles to the next portage.
- They also contended with less playful animals.
- During lunch one day, a whiskey jack—a large, gull-like bird with a formidable beak—landed at the campfire and wound up an unwelcome luncheon guest.

Life at Work

- The trip into Superior National Forest had begun ominously.
- Within hours of setting out, John and Don discovered a hiker who had fallen barefoot to the rocks below.
- He was badly cut and in need of medical attention.
- They loaded the man into the canoe and doubled back until they met a family piloting a small inboard boat who agreed to take the young man to the hospital.
- John and Don headed back into the woods, when they encountered the second sign that this would be no ordinary trip—an unexpected swim.
- To make up for lost time, they made a sail for the canoe from a poncho and poles.
- The device was efficient, but not stable, and a side gust blew the canoe over, throwing them in the lake.
- To not to lose any gear, they towed the canoe to a distant island before removing the boat's water, and their wet provisions.
- Secure containers had kept the matches dry; and the compass was fine, but their hydrated foods, salt, sugar and powdered milk were lost.
- A little bacon and rice was all that survived.
- Believing that cooked rice would last longer, they boiled it all and planned on fishing for their main food.
- They wanted a route that traversed the higher land between the lakes.

Manuevering the waterways of Superior National Forest was more than John and Don expected.

It was unclear which lakes were connected.

BEAVER DAM FRUIT
AND GROCERY
MARKET
210 Front St.   Phone 4.   Free Delivery.

STRAWBERRIES	Extra Fancy	23c box
BANANAS	Extra Fancy, Ripe,	4 lbs. 25c
APPLES	Winesaps	4 lbs. 25c
GRAPE FRUIT		4 for 25c
ORANGES	Sweet and Juicy	35c doz.

Tomatoes, extra fancy	20c lb.
Asparagus—California, 2 bunches	25c
Green Onions and Fancy Radishes	5c bunch
Leaf Lettuce	3 bunches 20c
Head Lettuce—the best	3 heads 25c
Spinach	3 pounds 25c
Set Onions	2 lbs. 23c
Cucumbers, extra large	25c each
Rhubarb	3 lbs. 25c
No. 1 Fresh Roasted Peanuts	2 lbs. 29c
Green Peppers—large	6 for 25c
Fresh Turnips	2 bunches 15c
California fresh packed Figs	3 pkgs. 25c
Celery, Carrots, Beets, Parsley, Sweet Potatoes, New Onions	

The provisions they had brought were running low. . .

- Don scaled a tall pine where he could see a chain of lakes about a quarter-mile way, but it wasn't clear whether the lakes were connected.
- For the next several hours, they followed the compass south-west, believing this would lead them to familiar ground, on the alert for the warning slap of a beaver's tail.
- If they weren't careful to stay clear of the beaver dams, sharp sticks within the dam might puncture the canoe.
- Finally they reached a small pond, six feet deep, where they made camp on a flat ledge a few feet above the water.
- Smooth rocks about the size of footballs were scattered about the bottom, behind which they could see the gently waving tails of fish.
- Using a number of different lures, every cast produced a black bass that weighed up to a pound.
- They soon hauled in more fish than they could eat.
- On the afternoon of their fourth day in the forest, they paddled on a wide stream where trout jumped high and the sound of a waterfall could be heard nearby.
- John thought he knew where they were, but wasn't sure.
- A heavy mist was forming, so they decided to camp for the night and fish in the early morning.
- After a good night's sleep, John walked through a dense fog to the rock ledge he had scouted out the night before, sat down and began fishing, his legs extending over the water.
- Almost immediately trout coming upstream began cutting the corner by leaping over his feet—a great start for a glorious day.
- As the fog cleared, he noticed a lynx by a nearby log.
- It crouched motionless as if taking an endless drink of water, when suddenly a trout leaped onto the rocks.
- Before the trout could slip back into the water, the lynx pounced and disappeared with the fish into the woods.
- That afternoon John and Don set out again, carefully comparing the contours of the lake to the map and their compass, as they continued to debate where they were.
- The temperature topped 100 degrees and the supply of rice was disappearing.
- And without salt, sugar, or milk it was a depressing diet.
- They also discovered that the compass was waterlogged, making it erratic and undependable.
- After a few more hours on the lake, they had to admit that they were completely lost.

. . . but trout were plentiful.

- They were even unsure of what lake they were on.
- Don thought he saw the portage about a mile away, but John argued that they should paddle about three miles to the right, looking for the Maligne portage.
- Don insisted so John acquiesced.
- The map showed a trail that led about six miles inland.
- The pair walked two miles along the trail and passed numerous deer tracks, but no signs of camps, no blaze marks, and no room for their 17-foot canoe between the trees.
- Tired and uncertain, they decided to split up.
- They had been gone five days.
- The plan was for Don to take the canoe, the map and basic essentials, find help, and return for John.
- John studied the map to determine how to reach the Indian Reservation 35 miles away if help never arrived.
- The next morning, the pair anointed themselves with scraps of bacon rind for protection from the sun, and reconsidered their plan to split up.
- They launched the canoe together, paddling across the lake, when the west shoreline began to look similar to the contours of Lake Sturgeon.
- In pouring rain, they went from inlet to inlet until, finally they discovered a spot that looked familiar.
- Overcome with intense relief, John suddenly became ill, developing a severe chill causing him to shake violently.
- Don took the lead, building a fire at the edge of the tent and helping John remove his wet clothes as they both crowded near the flames.
- Finally John stopped shaking, but the fever continued and he drifted into a deep sleep.
- When he awoke it had finally stopped raining.
- The next day they traveled west on the Maligne River, through a small lake in the east end of Lac LaCroix.
- They favored the north shore, and about five miles down they finally saw a cabin, that doubled as a store.
- They found no one manning the store, but did find some stale bread and a few canned goods, which the hungry men devoured.
- John's bread tasted like cake, and they both were joyful upon feeling full again.
- When the store trader arrived and saw his supplies gone he was angry at first, but calmed down when John and Don explained their predicament.
- He then provided additional supplies and gave directions to the best routes home.

The men decided it was better to stick together.

A cabin in the distance was a welcome sight.

Life in the Community: Chicago, Illinois

- Chicago, water and transportation were linked throughout the city's history.
- Chicago's first railway, the Galena and Chicago Union Railroad, opened in 1838, which also marked the opening of the Illinois and Michigan Canal.
- The canal allowed steamboats and sailing ships on the Great Lakes to connect to the Mississippi River.
- A flourishing economy attracted residents from rural communities and immigrants from abroad, creating a very diverse city.
- As manufacturing became more dominant among Midwestern cities, Chicago became a center of industry, particularly in meatpacking, with the advent of the refrigerated railcar.
- By 1856, the city of Chicago initiated the United States' first comprehensive sewerage system.
- Untreated sewage and industrial waste had previously flowed into the Chicago River, thence into Lake Michigan, polluting the primary source of fresh water for the city.
- After the Great Chicago Fire of 1871 destroyed a third of the city, including the entire central business district, Chicago experienced rapid rebuilding and growth.
- During this period, Chicago erected the world's first skyscraper in 1885, using steel-skeleton construction.
- The city also invested in many large, well-landscaped municipal parks, which also included public sanitation facilities.
- In 1893, Chicago hosted the World's Columbian Exposition, which drew 27.5 million visitors.

- The 1920s brought notoriety to Chicago as gangsters, including the notorious Al Capone, battled each other and law enforcement on the city's streets during the Prohibition era.
- Chicago had over 1,000 gangs in the 1920s.
- In the 1920s the availability of jobs attracted African Americans from the South.
- Arriving in the tens of thousands during the Great Migration, newcomers had an immense cultural impact, as Chicago became a center for jazz.
- Chicago was located on Lake Michigan, the only one of the five Great Lakes located entirely within the United States.
- Lake Michigan was originally home to lake trout, yellow perch, panfish, largemouth bass, smallmouth bass, carp and bowfin, as well as some species of catfish.

HISTORICAL SNAPSHOT

1929

- Seven gangsters, all rivals of Al Capone, were murdered in Chicago in what was called the St. Valentine's Day Massacre
- The Grand Teton National Park was established by Congress
- *All Quiet on the Western Front* by Erich Maria Remarque, *A Farewell to Arms* by Earnest Hemingway and *Good-Bye to All That* by Robert Graves were all published
- The comic strip *Popeye,* created by Elzie Crisler Segar, appeared for the first time
- The longest bridge in the world, the San Francisco Bay Toll Bridge, opened
- Herbert Hoover was inaugurated as the thirty-first president of the United States, succeeding Calvin Coolidge
- The first Academy Awards were presented at the Hollywood Roosevelt Hotel in Hollywood, California, with *Wings* winning Best Picture
- The first public demonstration of color TV was held at Bell Telephone Laboratories in New York
- Pope Pius XI emerged from the Vatican in a huge procession witnessed by about 250,000 persons, ending nearly 60 years of papal self-imprisonment within the Vatican
- Pablo Picasso painted two cubist works, *Woman in a Garden and Nude in an Armchair,* while surrealist painters Salvador Dali and René Magritte completed several works, including *The First Days of Spring* (Dali) and *The Treachery of Images* (Magritte)
- The Geneva Convention addressed the treatment of prisoners of war
- The Young Plan, which set the total World War I reparations owed by Germany at $26,350,000,000 was finalized
- The Dow Jones Industrial Average peaked at 381.17
- Fritz von Opel piloted the first rocket-powered aircraft, the Opel RAK.1, in front of a large crowd in Frankfurt am Main
- The Wall Street Crash of 1929 wiped out more than $30 billion from the New York Stock Exchange, an amount 10 times greater than the annual budget of the federal government
- Former U.S. Interior Secretary Albert B. Fall was convicted of bribery for his role in the Teapot Dome scandal (Fall had decided that two of his friends should be given leases to drill oil in Naval Reserves without open bidding), becoming the first presidential cabinet member to go to prison for actions in office
- In New York City, the Museum of Modern Art opened to the public
- Joseph Stalin consolidated his power in the Soviet Union by sending Leon Trotsky into exile

Selected Prices

Advertising, Maxwell House, per Year $509,000
Camera $80.00
Corset $1.69
Fishing Line $5.60
Fishing Plug $0.87
Fishing Reel $5.00
Plow, One-Horse $8.25
Radio $39.95
Rifle $25.00
Spark Plug $2.40

"Lakes Lure Visitors to Antrim County Towns," *The Record-Eagle,* Traverse City, Michigan, June 29, 1929:

Emerald green lakes, each in itself a jewel of rare delight, these are the pride and glory of Antrim County.

Elk Lake, Torch Lake, Round Lake, Grass Lake, Clam Lake and Intermediate Lake—where can their like be found in all America or in all the world?

Each is an alluring attraction in itself. Each connected with the others in adding to the diverse charms of these others to its own. Each within a few minutes by auto of the scenic Grand Traverse shore. Favored, indeed, is Antrim.

There is a hill off the main highway north of Elk Lake—it might have been a Signal Hill of the Indians—wherein the cyclorama spread before the beholder, elevated bodies water may be counted. The great bay, largest east shore arm on Lake Michigan; Torch Lake, 18 miles long and 3 miles wide; smaller lakes ranging down to sizable fishing ponds, all of these are within the view.

The north-bound traveler on Federal Interstate Highway U.S. 31 enters Antrim County through an avenue of pines, survivors of the old forest and lusty youths of the new forest. Through the pines to the west comes the glint of the waters of the Grand Traverse Bay.

At the Antrim entryway is Elk Rapids, village of lovely location. Once it was given over to toiling industry, in the days of lumber and charcoal, iron and of isolated smelters. Now it is finding a more agreeable and a more lasting prosperity in the recreation industry that is rising amidst ruins of those other times. . . .

Through Elk Rapids rushes a stream of startling clear water to mingle with the equally clear waters of the bay. In the midst of the stream is an island home, the waters surrounding it like a moat around an ancient castle. Beyond is a dam powerhouse through which the waters purl and boil. Above the dam is a channel, and beyond that channel, water of a strikingly vivid green. It is the water of Elk Lake, clear and crystalline.

Should the traveler go adventuring to Bellaire, there another dam, marks a step to higher waters. More winding, wilderness river and then Intermediate Lake, long, narrow, bending, charming.

At Elk Rapids one may go deep sea fishing. Off the shore, in Grand Traverse Bay, is the range of the large and gamey Mackinaw trout. Exciting sport is offered in angling with pole and copper wire to tempt the huge trout to strike and then wage a thrilling battle to land him. . . .

The streams may be waded or fished from the bank with either flies or natural baits. The ponds may be fished from the shore but more conveniently from a boat. The dry fly is the most popular lure on the ponds, but natural bait gets just as many fish. Electric Pond with its German brown trout, located a mile east of Bellaire, attracts the dry fly casters while Stover Pond, a short run farther east up Cedar River, yields fine catches of "specks" to both the fly casters and live bait soakers.

"Football Extra Saturday," *Daily Globe,* Ironwood, Michigan, October 8, 1929:

To meet the demand of the Globe readers for local, state and national football news, the *Daily Globe* will issue its first football extra of the season next Saturday evening.

Through the changes put into effect several months ago, the *Daily Globe* this season hopes to provide the fans with a greater volume of football news than it has given in previous seasons. Automatic printers will bring the Associated Press news into the *Daily Globe* office at the rate of 60 words a minute. Between three and six o'clock each Saturday afternoon all the football news available will be made ready for the green sheet sports extra. The *Daily Globe* will make every effort to make this year's sports extras better than ever.

"Agree on Program Which Gives Chance to Fish and Fishermen, Declares Convention Speaker," *Sheboygan Journal* (Wisconsin), June 10, 1929:

Dr. Walter Koelz of the University of Michigan urged the members of the Wisconsin Federation of Commercial Fishermen in convention here yesterday to agree upon a program for the regulation of the fishing business, declaring that there is no danger, after such a program is accepted by the fishermen themselves, that legislators will impose drastic or unwise laws for regulating it.

Dr. Koelz is assistant ichthyologist, U.S. Bureau of Fisheries, and a member of the faculty at the Ann Arbor University. For nine years he made an exhaustive study of fish life in the Great Lakes and is generally regarded as an expert in such matters.

His address in part follows:

"The Great Lakes are, as you all realize, bodies of water enormous in size. There are among the world's numerous lakes very few that are closely similar to them. In a discussion of matters pertaining to them it is proper to consider briefly the features that make them so outstanding.

In the first place, their waters are very clear and very pure. The water in the open lakes is safe to drink. They are also very cool and very deep, and before man interfered with them they swarmed with fish. You could probably name a dozen of the inland lakes that had plenty of fish or that were cold and deep, but not many of them have all these characteristics. On the contrary, the best fishing lakes in the state are shallow. Some of them are only a few feet deep and they are warm, weedy and, chances are, even mucky.

The difference between the Great Lakes and the inland lakes, then, is radical. They don't even have the same kinds of fish, and this is as good a place as any to point out that the sportsman who knows all about bass and pike in inland waters is not necessarily an authority in matters that concern the big lakes. In fact, he also often needs to be reminded of John Billings' advice that it is better not to know so much than to know so much that isn't so.

continued

"Agree on Program Which Gives Chance to Fish and Fishermen, Declares Convention Speaker," *Sheboygan Journal* (Wisconsin), . . . *(continued)*

I make a point of this because it has often caused commercial fishermen no end of annoyance and even damage. It is a human trait that anyone who knows quite a little about one thing thinks he knows something about most everything else. 'No,' argues this one, 'if I should set nets in Mud Lake I'd soon clear out the lake because I've seen swarms of fish swimming in the water there.' He doesn't know anything of the sort and if he really set nets in Mud Lake he'd surely be surprised at the small haul he made. It is certain, then, in this man's opinion, that if you allow commercial fishermen at all you're bound to clear out all the fish. We have experience to the contrary.

Here, let me say that the economy body of a body of water is not different in broad aspects from that of a piece of land. A piece of land will raise only so much of a crop and the same is true of a body of water. Some land won't raise anything and some water won't either. If soil on land is heavy and sour it won't do for corn. If the bottom of the lake is stony it won't do for whitefish. If you thin your corn on the hill, you'll get bigger ears; if you thin your fish they'll to grow faster and larger. If you've got a good lake then you will have fish, and up to a certain limit it is a good thing to catch off those fish.

Lake Michigan is a very rich lake and there's nothing wrong with setting nets in it, but let's see what happened to it. When the lake was first fished, the whitefish were about all that were considered fit to eat and therefore worth catching. To offer anyone a sturgeon was an insult. Now the whitefish are cleaned out and the last sturgeon has been caught and we are busy catching bloaters and herring that our grandfathers wouldn't have carried to the cats . . . and I expect to see the day when the fishermen will be marketing shiners which seem to be about the last thing left to catch.

When such things are talked of—I mean the good old days when there were lots of fish and fish for everybody—everyone begins to get mad at the fishermen for catching all the fish, and the fishermen themselves sometimes feel as though they perhaps ought to be sent to jail for it, but there is another way to look at the situation. When fish were common and easy to get, it wasn't always easy to sell what you caught. I remember, and it isn't ancient history either, when the Huron fishermen had to pull out their chub nets because they couldn't fish chubs for 5 cents per pound even though they could get a ton or more at a lift. A man told me once he wasn't interested in increasing the fish supply. He preferred, he said, to handle 100 pounds whitefish at one dollar a pound than to handle a thousand pounds at ten cents. Fresh fish have gone into the luxury class and luxuries are always bought no matter what the cost. Think over the prices you've been getting for your fish and you will see that even making allowances for higher price levels, the price of fish is still climbing.

That doesn't mean the fish business is prospering, but it doesn't mean that it is damned either. If we admit we don't want lots of fish and consequently cheap fish, we must at least be assured of a steady supply. And to be assured of this we must do something at once. Some are fish are done for. Blackfin is very rare; the sturgeon are gone, the whitefish is extinct over vast areas where he used to be common.

Something must be wrong with the way we have run this business. Either we have caught too many fish or they are too small or they were caught at the wrong season or the lake isn't as good for fish as it used to be.

It is indisputably true that a lot of stuff has been dumped in the rivers and the lake that ought not to have been put into it and all that pollution ought to stop, but pollution isn't the main issue before you.

continued

"Agree on Program Which Gives Chance to Fish and Fishermen, Declares Convention Speaker," *Sheboygan Journal* (Wisconsin), . . . *(continued)*

It is perfectly possible that too many fish have been caught. In the first place, there is no excuse for glutting the market in this day and age. Did you ever hear of the orange growers flooding the market with oranges and taking what they could bring? But aside from abnormal or sporadic overproduction, there are too many people in the fishing game. Fishing in our depleted lakes, we can't supply the demand and that's why our prices keep soaring. We've been catching fish that were too small. They don't have a chance to spawn and leave behind successors. We have caught them during spawning season and it prevented them from leaving anything behind.

What is the remedy? How about cutting down operations for a while? Would it be logical to restrict the number of commercial fishing licenses? The Canadian government does it now on their inland lakes. We regulate the number of fish that anglers may take and the number of rabbits and ducks a hunter may kill, and why not regulate the output of the commercial fishermen?

"Bear Onslaughts Encounter Little Resistance in Market," *Salt Lake Tribune,* October 20, 1929:

One of the most powerful bear onslaughts of the year encountered amazingly little resistance in the stock market this week, and sent prices into one of the most precipitous declines in recent financial history. Prices were driven down in bull trading, with the average turnover for full sessions averaging less than 3,300,000 shares until today, when the selling movements reached huge proportions.

Many leading industrials and several rails broke through the low levels of October 4, utilities generally tumbled to the lowest levels on record since early July. The Standard Statistics-Associated Press price index 20 utilities dropped 53.8 points during the week to 280.9 compared to the year's high of 353.1, reached early in September. An index of 50 industrials dropped 17.1 points and better than 20 rails dropped six points. Nearly 60 issues on the New York Stock Exchange drove to new lows for the year or since listing the present shares on that market, including General Motors, Montgomery Ward, United Corporation, United Gas Improvement, Baldwin, Bendix Aviation, Curtiss-Wright, Kennecott, Howe Sound, Marmon Motor, J.I. Case and several of the recently listed investment trusts.

"Motorists, Keep to the Right!" *The Oshkosh Daily Northwestern* (Wisconsin), April 24, 1929:

Quoting portions of a recent editorial in the *Northwestern* to the effect that the "road hog" who sticks to the center of the pavement or drives over on the left side, endangering traffic, was loose again on the highways, the *Merrill Herald* comments:

"It is our observation that the 'highway hog' is growing more numerous as the cars multiply. The highway hog is a very dangerous animal, and something ought to be done to lessen its kind. Just what can be done, we do not know. Perhaps educating him to respect the rights of others when very young might do some good."

Probably the *Merrill* editor is correct. About the only salvation for the careful motorist is a vigorous and continuous campaign of education that will make the hoggish driver see the evil of his ways. But it is not easy to educate a pig, whether it be the farm animal or a human being. It will take a lot of campaigning.

About the best cure would be for the county motorcycle officers to be on the watch for road hogs, arresting them as fast as they can be caught and bringing them into court, to be censured and fined.

The *Eau Claire Leader* says, "Back in the old days when motor chivalry and courtesy were part of the unwritten code it would not have been necessary to call the attention of road hogs to their annoying and unlawful practices. Today it is. Every holiday and every weekend emphasizes the need for some strong arm squad to keep on the right side of the highway the thoughtless and deliberate driver who regards the entire road as his.

"There is a species of mania, akin to that of speeding, that prompts some drivers to hog the road in such fashion that the vehicle in the rear cannot possibly pass. This privilege is guaranteed the trailing car by law, and the refusal to make way for it is a violation of the motor statutes.

"Drivers with a certain grain of courtesy need only a horn toot to make way for the car behind. The other style of driver needs a traffic cop, and the sooner the latter gets into action, the more safe will driving become."

At Superior a campaign was arranged to bring careless and dangerous motoring into disrepute and to focus attention on the need of safe and sane driving now that highway traffic is getting heavy. Stickers were provided upon which was printed the slogan, "KEEP TO THE RIGHT."

If a generous supply of these could be distributed to drivers anxious to spread the word to road hogs, it might help. The strips, with the warning in bold, black letters pasted on the windshield or radiator would meet the eyes of those who usurp the center of the road and they might be ashamed of themselves and move over to the right half of the pavement. The plan is worth trying anyway. Some drivers of trucks are more dangerous road hogs than the operators of pleasure cars.

1924 News Feature

"Sporting Manhattan Fears for Its 'Sport,'" Peter Schuyler,
The Dearborn Independent, **February 9, 1924:**

Frankie Jerome is dead and the heart of sporting Manhattan is sad. He was 25 years old, a veteran of the World War, and one of the best known bantamweights in the East. His courage killed him because he did not know what the word "quit" meant. Injuries he received in a "boxing contest" with another bantamweight sent him to the hospital where he died 36 hours after the referee stopped the bout to save him from further punishment. The medical examiner said he died of intermeningeal hemorrhage caused by the rupture of one of the veins between the surface of the brain and the lining of the skull.

But "sporting" Manhattan is not grief-stricken because Frankie Jerome is dead. Not much! "Sporting" Manhattan is paralyzed with grief because Jerome's death has speeded the movement to kill the boxing "graft" in the city and the state. "It's too bad about Frankie and tough on his mother, but then things'll happen," growls "sporting" Manhattan out of the corner of its mouth. "The hard part of it is the sport is going to be killed and that ain't right."

The possible repeal of the Walker Law, which permits "boxing contests" to be given in New York State in decisions to be rendered, constitutes the element of the tragedy in the death of Frankie Jerome, as far as "sporting" Manhattan is concerned.

It must be understood in the beginning that there is no such thing these days as a prize fight. That is old stuff and belongs to the period when pugilists fought with bare knuckles or skintight gloves which had the cutting power of a razor. Heenan, Morrissey, Kilrain, Sullivan, Mitchell, Fitzsimmons, and Peter Jackson were "fighters." The midgets and the giants who wallop each other in public nowadays are never, never "fighters." Their designation depends on the law of the state or city where they happen to be performing. Where athletic events are permitted within the squared circle, pugilists are athletes. Where "boxing contests" are sanctioned by statute, they are "boxers."

For example, when Mr. Jack Dempsey had a dispute with padded gloves at the Polo Grounds last summer with Luis Angel Firpo, the Wild Bull of the Pampas, everyone who read of the affair knew that a knock down drag out fight was in sight. But since the law of the state of New York forbids prize fights and permits "boxing contests," the million-dollar festivity was camouflaged by the press and the promoters as a demonstration of boxing skill between Mr. Dempsey and the Angel Child of Argentina. So when Mr. Dempsey was smashed through the ropes by a pile-driving blow delivered by Mr. Firpo, it was only a point scored in the latter's favor by the judges and the referee. And when Mr. Dempsey was helped out of the laps of the spectators into which Mr. Firpo's "boxing" craft had punched him and proceeded immediately to knock the representative of South America into costly unconsciousness, he was only exhibiting his finesse as a master of offense. It was only after the money had been collected and the gathering dispersed that either promoters, newspapers, or sporting men forgot their lines and spoke of the function as the "greatest fight every staged."

It must be plain, therefore, that whatever legislative action must take place which will spoil the boxing graft cannot be on the grounds of prize fighting. Even state lawmakers cannot perform impossibilities. They cannot destroy what does not exist and to such a depth of hypocrisy to which we have fallen, that we still refuse to call things by their proper names. . . .

Another coterie which is supposed to be back of the attack and the boxing game is that infinite entity known as the Public, which is an alias for anyone who wants to keep his identity secret. The Public has been charged exorbitant fees for admission to the Garden, so the Public declares. Championship affairs like the "boxing" exhibition between Messrs. Johnson and Renault (from which the former has just recovered) run from $3.30 to $25. Ordinary programs bring from $1.10 to $11 for tickets. In both cases the best seats, in some mysterious way, fall into the hands of speculators. The Public suffers and the Public therefore demands that the Walker Law be repealed or the prices of admission be fixed at a scale which will mean the same thing.

Still another factor has forced public consideration of the graft. That is a succession of astounding decisions rendered by the judges of the contest, the conduct of the "weighing in" process by the officials concerned with that department of the "sport," the summary treatment of representatives of the press and the presence and activities of gamblers at affairs which are, according to law, only presentations of bodily skill conducted with mental co-ordination.

When Benny Leonard and Lew Tendler, the two Jewish exponents of the boxing art in the lightweight division, weighed in before the minions of the boxing law, the newspaper men were excluded from the room although the law says the "weighing in" shall be done in public. Observations had been made that neither Leonard nor Tendler could make the weight limit without sawing off a leg apiece, and to prove they could tip the scales at 135 at two o'clock in the afternoon of the "contest," reporters were kept in outer darkness so they could not look at the beam. Such an uproar was made over that beautiful piece of manipulation that since that time the weighing has been done publicly and will continue to be done until another match of equal importance is staged. . . .

What really underlines the agitation against the "sport" is the contemptuous attitude assumed by its adherents to all considerations of decency. People starve, living expenses soar, human beings suffer privation. On top of these conditions and in the face of them, a hulk of humanity called a champion refuses to pummel another hulk, who wants to be the "champion," unless he gets half $1 million for doing it. Less important bruisers refuse to contribute their services to the cause of the "boxing art" unless they get a stipend for one night equal to the salary of the president of the United States for a year. The managers of "boxers" talk in hundreds of thousands. The promoters of the contest scorn the consideration of anything but millions. A cauliflower-eared, alien-born illiterate, a Jewish mental defective, or a half-brute foreign immigrant who can barely speak English, will appear in public forty-five minutes for $25,000 or a percentage of the gate receipts that will amount to more. For what? The lowest elements of the city, the scum of the state, the refuse of the nation, may enjoy imitation of the Coliseum in Rome any time during the most decadent days of the Empire. Stripped of all its grand pretense, the "boxing" game is nothing but the sight of one man trying to smash another into unconsciousness and being paid to do so by a mob of howling sadists, who, being cowards themselves, are the first to detect the symptoms of faintheartedness in the fighters, and the loudest to yell their discovery to the world.

There are three things in this world which can never be mistaken for anything but what they are. One is the rumble of a circus wagon wheel. Another is the sound which rises from the feet of marching men. The third is a crowd gathered for prize fight—pardon, "boxing contest." And of the three, the last is truly unique. It is the same the world over. It has always been the same and will always be the same. If there are "boxing contests" on Mars, the Martians who support them will look and act and appear just the same as the devotes who swarm to Madison Square Garden.

Meanwhile Frankie Jerome has been killed! "Sporting" Manhattan's only concern now lest the "sport" he died participating in may be finished also. Why should it be? Isn't there money to be made in it? Money talks! Sometimes it rattles—like the bones of dead men. But Manhattan should not worry about that!

1930–1939

The social and economic upheavals of the 1930s took their toll on all sports: attendance plummeted, salaries dropped and baseball rosters were paired down from 25 to 23 players per team. Some athletes fled to Hollywood, including swimmer Johnny Weissmuller, who became filmland's "Tarzan, King of the Jungle," or Buster Crabbe, whose gold medal in the 1932 Olympics helped propel him into the roles of Flash Gordon and Buck Rogers in the movies. Radio broadcasts became a crucial element of the sports environment, cheaply bringing boxing title fights, Army- Navy football games and professional baseball into American homes and revenue into the coffers as Gillette, Ford and Camel cigarettes lined up to be sponsors.

At the same time, women athletes burst into the public arena, primarily as stars of non-contact sports: Babe Didrikson in golf and track, Gertrude Ederle in swimming and Suzanne Lenglen in tennis. Women's baseball and softball were successfully launched. And numerous colleges took tentative steps toward integration by adding black athletes to their track and field teams. In racing, new technology permitted new speed records, and underwater photography was employed to decide swim meet finishes.

Few Americans escaped the devastating impact of the most severe depression in the nation's history. Economic paralysis gripped the country: banks failed, railroads became insolvent, factories closed, unemployment shot upward, and Americans took to the road looking for work, stability and something to believe in. Farmers defied court-ordered evictions, mothers desperate to feed their families staged food riots, and school attendance was back to five months. Fewer couples chose marriage, fewer still had children in this austere environment. And recent immigrants took the opportunity to return to their homeland in hopes of finding jobs. During the entire decade, the United States received a total of 528,000 immigrants, approximately the same number of immigrants who came to America annually in 1911.

By 1934, one in every four farms had been sold for taxes and 5,000 banks had closed their doors, eradicating in seconds the lifetime savings of millions of Americans, rich and poor. President Franklin D. Roosevelt produced a swirl of government programs designed to lift the country out of its paralytic gloom.

Roosevelt's early social experiments were characterized by relief, recovery and reform. The Civilian Conservation Corps (CCC), for example, put 250,000 jobless young men to work in the forests for $1.00 a day. By 1935, government deficit spending was spurring economic change. By 1937, total manufacturing output exceeded that of 1929; unfortunately, prices and wages rose too quickly and the economy dipped again in 1937. Despite some progress, 10 million workers were still unemployed in 1938, and farm prices lagged behind manufacturing progress. Full recovery would not occur until the United States mobilized for World War II.

While the nation suffered from economic blows, the West was being whipped by nature. Dust clouds up to 10,000 feet high swept across the parched Western Plains throughout the 1930s, sometimes with lightning and booming thunder. All human activity halted. Planes were grounded. Buses and trains stalled, unable to race clouds that could move at speeds of more than 100 miles per hour. On the morning of May 9, 1934, the wind began to blow up the topsoil of Montana and Wyoming, and soon some 350 million tons were sweeping eastward. By late afternoon, 12 million tons had been deposited in Chicago. By noon the next day, Buffalo, New York, was dark with dust. Even the Atlantic Ocean was no barrier. Ships 300 miles out to sea found dust on their decks. During the remainder of 1935, there were more than 40 dust storms that reduced visibility to less than one mile. There were 68 more storms in 1936, 72 in 1937, and 61 in 1938.

The people of the 1930s excelled in escape. Radio matured as a mass medium, creating stars such as Jack Benny, Bob Hope, and Fibber McGee and Molly. For a time it seemed that every child was copying the catch phrase of radio's Walter Winchell, "Good evening, Mr. and Mrs. America, and all the ships at sea," or pretending to be Jack Benny when shouting, "Now, cut that out!" Soap operas captured large followings, and sales of magazines like *Screenland* and *True Story* skyrocketed. Each edition of *True Confessions* sold 7.5 million copies. Nationwide, movie theaters prospered as 90 million Americans attended the "talkies" every week, finding comfort in the uplifting excitement of movies and movie stars. Big bands made swing the king of the decade, while jazz came into its own. And the social experiment known as Prohibition died in December 1933, when the Twenty-first Amendment swept away the restrictions against alcohol ushered in more than a decade earlier.

Attendance at professional athletic events declined during the decade, but softball became more popular than ever and golf began its drive to become a national passion as private courses went public. Millions listened to boxing on radio, especially the exploits of the "Brown Bomber," Joe Louis. As average people coped with the difficult times, they married later, had fewer children, and divorced less. Extended families often lived under one roof; opportunities for women and minorities were particularly limited. Survival, not affluence, was often the practical goal of the family. A disillusioned nation, which had worshipped the power of business, looked instead toward a more caring government.

1933 PROFILE

Ben Covington wanted to be the world's speedboat champion, and the best way he could think of doing that was to build his own boats, his way.

Life at Home

- Benjamin Hamilton Woodley Covington VIII was born in 1882, the third oldest of 11 brothers and sisters.
- Ben's father was a ferryboat operator on Lake Osakis in Minnesota, and he often took his son with him to help crew on the ferries.
- As a boy, Ben felt the exhilaration of speed on the water.
- He quickly developed both exceptional mechanical skills and an aptitude for inventing devices to solve mechanical problems.
- Frequently a race between ferry boat operators would emerge and, since a reputation for speed was good for business, the races were often taken seriously.
- Speed and innovation were also taking place on land, as the automobile was the most popular innovation of the time.
- An automobile that operated properly was filled with promises: freedom, romance, and most of all, independence.
- For the first time farmers could pick the church they wished to attend, businessmen could economically distribute goods to a wider area, and families could dream about traveling beyond the boundaries of the county line.
- Geography had been subdued and there was no going back.
- At 29 years old, Ben focused his creative skills on designing mechanical devices for unloading trucks efficiently.
- His patented invention was an immediate success and his startup company exploded with orders.

Ben Covington built boats that went faster than the competition.

Ben's father took him along to help crew on the ferries.

Coming from a large family helped grow his business.

- He was worth millions, practically overnight.
- To meet demand, Ben invited his eight brothers to join him in business.
- They moved operations from St Paul, Minnesota, to Detroit, Michigan, where they established a manufacturing plant alongside other emerging giants Ford, Dodge and Chalmers.
- With his brothers' help and the opportunity afforded to those with new wealth, Ben felt free to explore his first love—speedboat racing.
- A truck was a truck, but a perfectly designed boat that cut through the water barely etching a perfect wake was poetry in its highest form.

Life at Work
- Ben's mechanical genius came natural to him and his business success made him rich.
- But Ben's passion was boat racing.
- He loved his time on the water, challenging his latest creation to defy the rules of physics and go even faster through the water.
- In 1916, at the meeting of the Detroit Powerboat Association, a plea was made for some local Detroiter to help out the syndicate and purchase the powerboat *Miss Detroit I*.
- Ben bought the boat sight unseen.
- After he agreed to purchase *Miss Detroit,* he went to Algonac to see her.
- While he was there he bought the company that built her and began his quest to rob England and France of the bragging rights for the fastest boat in the world.
- During the following 12 years, he broke the speed record five times, the fastest time being 124.860 mph.
- To demonstrate the quality of his boats, Ben not only challenged other boats, but trains as well.
- In 1921 he raced one of his boats against the Havana Special, 1,250 miles up the Atlantic coast from Miami to New York City.
- Ben made the trip in 47 hours and 23 minutes and beat the train by 12 minutes.
- Ben also won five straight powerboat Gold Cup Races between 1917 and 1921, as well as the prestigious international Harmsworth Trophy in 1920 and 1922.

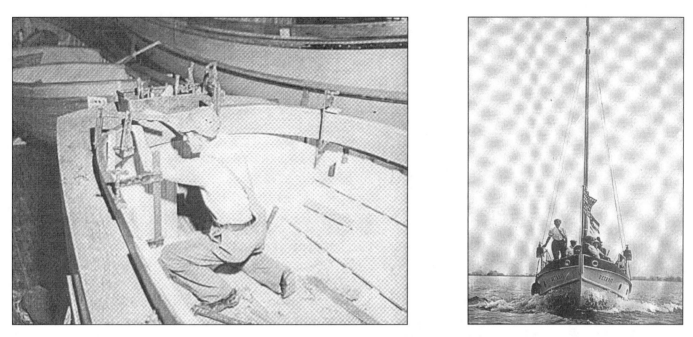

After the stock market crash in 1929, powerboat racing was a hobby only the rich could afford.

- As a result, the rules governing the Gold Cup Races were changed dramatically by the American Powerboat Association.
- The Rules Committee limited engine size, length and configuration of hulls, claiming to encourage "Gentlemen's Runabouts" that could be used for family recreation as well as racing.
- The changes really targeted racers like Ben, whose advanced technology and use of aircraft engines had dominated the Gold Cup.
- Ben's response was to develop an entirely new boat.
- A comfortable, safe runabout with a bottom that incorporated all of the characteristics of his Cup capturing boats was an immediate success.
- Some of America's wealthiest sportsmen—Edward Noble, William Randolph Hearst, John Dodge, Col. Vincent and P. K. Wrigley—were among the first to purchase the new design.
- By the mid-1920s, 60 of the world's most prominent sportsmen were owners of a Ben Covington-built boat.
- America's emerging middle class eagerly joined an army of outboarders, enticed by the economical motors produced by Evinrude, Johnson and others.
- More than 30 companies manufactured boats or motors for the weekend hobbyists.
- What began as an attempt by the American Power Boat Association (APBA) to end Ben Covington's domination of the Gold Cup competition resulted in an entire new line of runabouts that became the playthings of millionaires.
- In 1930 Ben christened a new specialty boat factory designed to produce 1,200 custom, top-quality boats a year.
- Even the 1929 crash of the stock market did not discourage Ben.
- "Quality always sells," he said.
- But it was clear that powerboat racing designed to establish world records was becoming a millionaire's hobby.
- Most racers had either inherited money or owned their own business, and included lumber and sugar barons, and an Evinrude dealer who had powerboats named *Gilmore, Lion Head,* and *Ruth M.*

Some engine manufacturers used extensive advertising.

- Even the weekend waterbug racers began to drive boats built for competition.
- Engines were either Evinrude, Johnson, or Elto models with speeds ranging from 35 to 60 mph, depending on the class.
- Most drivers raced bareheaded, while others wore a leather cap.
- Life jackets were required in competition, but they were not always used properly.
- Ben's assault on the world's speed records was built around his own runabout, powerful engines and a specialized hull.
- In the years before he stopped racing, he had a worthy challenger—his younger brother.
- A race between the two on the Detroit River was billed as a match race between the brothers and English racing record-breaker Kaye Don, driving *Miss England II.*
- Before an estimated record crowd of over a million spectators, Don won the first heat of the race.
- In the second heat, Ben was leading Don, when *Miss England II* suddenly flipped over rounding one of the turns, without injury to Don and his co-driver.
- Ben finished the race first, but both he and Don were disqualified because they had jumped the starter's gun by seven seconds.
- His little brother completed the course without penalty and won the trophy.

Pre-Industrial Detroit

Detroit quickly became a center for innovation and manufacturing.

Life in the Community: Detroit, Michigan

- The industrial city of Detroit, Michigan, began life as a small French trading post in the 1700s.
- Spurred by the opening of the Erie Canal in 1826, the city's Great Lakes location and the increased use of rail transport, Detroit grew rapidly.
- In 1896 Charles B. King drove a horseless carriage on the city streets, inspiring young men to build one for themselves.
- The city already boasted a thriving carriage trade and a supply of talented craftsmen, setting the stage for men like Henry Ford, who built his first automobile factory in Highland Park in 1899.
- Detroit rapidly became a center for manufacturing and innovation, attracting automotive pioneers such as W.C. Durant, Walter P. Chrysler, Ransom Olds and Henry Ford.
- Each established his headquarters in the Detroit metropolitan area, solidifying the city's status as the world's car capital.
- The development of the automobile industry—and boat manufacturing—led to a massive increase in industrial production in the city.
- This in turn led to rising demands for additional labor filled by huge numbers of newcomers from Europe and the American South.
- Poles made up the largest group of foreign-born workers and by 1930 more than 66,000 Poles lived in the city.
- Between 1900 and 1930, the city's population soared from 265,000 to over 1.5 million.
- The landscape of the city also changed dramatically.

Wide tree-shaded avenues gave way to. . .

. . . bustling factory-lined city streets.

- Once known as the "Paris of the Midwest" for its tree-shaded avenues, Detroit grew more blue-collar as its riverfront became lined with factories and grain silos.
- At the same time, Detroit's downtown flourished architecturally, largely under the leadership of Albert Kahn, who designed several dominating, Art Deco skyscrapers.
- During the Great Depression the manufacturing industry was severely shaken, leaving one-third of the workforce out of jobs in 1933.

HISTORICAL SNAPSHOT
1933

- Construction of the Golden Gate Bridge began in San Francisco Bay
- The U.S. Congress voted favorably for independence for The Philippines, against the recommendation of President Herbert Hoover
- Nazi leader Adolf Hitler was appointed Chancellor of Germany by President of Germany Paul von Hindenburg
- *The Lone Ranger* debuted on American radio
- Unemployment reached 15 million, five times higher than in 1931
- The cost of a National Football League franchise topped $10,000
- In Miami, Florida, Giuseppe Zangara attempted to assassinate President-elect Franklin D. Roosevelt, but instead fatally wounded Chicago Mayor Anton J. Cermak
- The magazine *Newsweek* was published for the first time
- Prohibition ended and beer was allowed to be sold nine months before liquor was
- The film version of *King Kong*, starring Fay Wray, premiered at Radio City Music Hall and the RKO Roxy Theatre in New York City
- The Mount Rushmore National Memorial was dedicated
- Newly elected president Franklin D. Roosevelt, proclaimed, "The only thing we have to fear is fear itself" in his inauguration speech
- Jews called for a boycott of German goods to protest Nazi oppression
- President Franklin D. Roosevelt issued Executive Order 6102, making it illegal for U.S. citizens to own gold
- The first modern sighting of the Loch Ness Monster allegedly occurred
- The detection of radio waves from the center of the Milky Way Galaxy was reported in *The New York Times*
- Walt Disney's cartoon *The Three Little Pigs* was released
- *Miss Lonelyhearts* by Nathaniel West, *God's Little Acre* by Erskine Caldwell and *To a God Unknown* by John Steinbeck were all published
- The use of an electric shock to the heart to reverse potentially fatal ventricular fibrillation was developed
- Helen Wills Moody won her second straight Wimbledon title, her sixth overall
- In professional football the goal post was moved to the goal line
- The first drive-in theater opened in Camden, New Jersey
- The *American Totalisator Company* unveiled its first electronic pari-mutuel betting machine at the Arlington Park Racetrack near Chicago
- The first Major League Baseball All-Star Game was played at Comiskey Park in Chicago
- Wiley Post becomes the first person to fly solo around the world, traveling 15,596 miles in seven days, 18 hours, and 45 minutes
- Albert Einstein arrived in the United States as a refugee from Nazi Germany
- The chocolate chip cookie was invented by Ruth Wakefield

Selected Prices

Brace and Bit Set	$2.80
Chifforobe	$18.95
Electric Iron	$1.00
Lathe	$340.00
Radio	$39.85
Sanitary Pads, Five Boxes	$1.00
Sewing Machine	$19.95
Shave Cream	$0.25
Shortwave Receiver	$14.70
Soda	$0.39

"California Ocean Classic in April,"
Syracuse Herald (New York), March 1, 1930:

The second annual fall California long-distance powerboat ocean race will be staged on April 24 to 27, under the auspices of Long Beach Yacht Club, adjacent to Los Angeles. Eleven early entries are on hand for the event, which covers a nautical distance of 446.1 miles and is the longest powerboat race in the world. Besides the Long Beach Club, the St. Francis of San Francisco and Santa Barbara Yacht clubs are cooperating in staging the event. The race is open to cruisers and express cruisers less than 110 feet overall, owned and chartered by recognized yacht clubs.

"Wood Tunes Up His Boat," *The Raleigh Times* (North Carolina), April 11, 1931:

Miami Beach, Florida. With his racing craft tuned to perfection, Gar Wood today was ready for his attempt to wrest the world speedboat crown from Kaye Don, of England.

Wood announced last night he would drive his twin-motored *Miss America IX* over a measured mile course in Indian Creek here today in the hope of bettering the 103.49 miles an hour set by Don in Buenos Aires last week. The Detroit sportsman instructed his mechanics to be ready to put this boat on the course at noon unless strong crosswinds made the water too choppy for speed.

The weather forecast today was for gentle to moderate winds from the east and southeast. The course runs north and south.

Part of the electrical timing apparatus used in checking the exact speed over a measured mile was installed yesterday under the direction of Otis Porter, timer for the American Automobile Association. Porter said the device would be in working order before noon today.

Wood returned to his home in Indian Creek last Sunday to prepare his boat for his attempt to regain the record. He sent the craft roaring over the measured mile course of 102.56 miles an hour March 20 to better the mark established by the late Sir Henry O.D. Segrave on Lake Windermere, England.

"Ruth Is Ready," *The Raleigh Times* (North Carolina), April 11, 1931:

Babe Ruth has served notice on Hank Wilson and other aspirants to homerun honors that he will be very much in the limelight again this year. He has found the range and cracked out three homers during the past three days to tell the fans that he is ready for battle. The doubters every spring come forth with a suggestion that the Babe cannot be as good as last year. But he continues to harass hurlers and please the fans with his long wallops over the fences.

"Studio Test for Details of Opening," *The Raleigh Times* (North Carolina), April 11, 1931:

Possibilities of studio television are to be investigated when New York gets on the air with its first combined sight and sound broadcast.

Program plans are not complete, but the intention is to put on illustrated news items, stock reports, illustrated talks, drama, dancing lessons, vaudeville artists, costumed singers, and other types of entertainment suitable for sight as well as sound.

Following somewhat in the footsteps of Chicago, where "talking movies" of studio presentations have been on the air for some time via the WMAQ and the WIBO and their associated shortwave television stations, the metropolitan area business will have a chance to tune in for visual and aural entertainment coming from the same studio.

Tests of equipment already are under way, with hope that the opening will be presented about April 15, or shortly thereafter.

A broadcasting station, WGBS on 254 meters, is to deliver the sound parts of the program, while W2XCR, Jenkins experimental television transmitter on 147 meters, will deliver the sight. Two receivers will be necessary to bring in the synchronized programs, a broadcast set for sound and the shortwave receiver for television.

The studios are located on the sixth floor of the Fifth Avenue building, not far from the site of the proposed Radio City. They consist of a large room, 14 x 25 feet, the studio proper, or session room, and the control room in the television room.

The studio is fitted acoustically like any broadcast room. At one side is an open window through which the lens of his television "camera" points. In the studio is a portable bank for photoelectric cells, the "microphone" for television.

The camera will use what is known as the "flying spot." That is, a sitter in a darkened room will be bathed with a beam of light directed by scanning disk. The light then is reflected to the photo cells.

"Half of Iowa Homes Buy Sets," *The Raleigh Times* (North Carolina), April 11, 1931:

Iowa has 636,905 families and they own 309,327 radio sets, according to the 1930 census figures released by the Census Bureau. North Dakota has 145,385 families and 59,352 receivers. The bureau is releasing the statistics on each state as rapidly as the count is complete.

Listeners have been active this week in suggesting a name to apply to the owner of a television receiver. From Hartford, Connecticut, comes the word "tellser." A Baltimorean thinks "visual listeners" conveys the proper meaning. Another offers "look-hearers." A resident of Albany suggests "scanners" because then the set owners can say I was "scanning" on the radio last night and saw the most wonderful program.

A Pittsburgher believes that "raduo" is the right name because television compromises a duel service of sight and sound broadcasting. Therefore, the owner would be a "raduoner" and the performer a "raduolist."

"Former Local Man Is Cup Contender," *The New Castle News* (Pennsylvania), September 29, 1933:

Newcastle people are looking to the President's Cup Race in the Pontiac River Friday and Saturday with more than ordinary interest this year. A former New Castle man, George C. Reis, is entered in the race and is considered the leading contender for the cup.

The race is for motor boats of 625 cubic inches displacement. When Calvin Coolidge was in the president's chair he donated a gold cup to be sought for each year. Mr. Reis won the cup two years ago, and tradition says no one wins it twice. That's a tradition he hopes to break.

Mr. Reis has already won two major racing events of the year, the National Sweepstakes at Montauk, Long Island, and the Gold Cup Race in Detroit, which he won the same day Gar Wood kept America supreme in the motor boat racing.

How to Build a Motor Launch, C. D. Mower, 1912:

The motor boat is destined to play a prominent part in the future development of the world. For years man has talked of and longed for a compact, safe power that could be utilized to drive a craft of small dimensions, to take the place of the oar and to relieve him of the irksome toil of rowing. Steam refused even in the hands of the most ingenious to adapt its power to this purpose. This powerful agent when employed in small boats proved to be a wasteful and somewhat dangerous servant.

In the motor driven by the products of petroleum, man has at last found what he has so long waited and toiled for: a safe, economical and trusty engine. It is especially adapted to the propulsion of craft, such as are too small for steam and too heavy to be rowed.

Throughout the world, and remarkably so in this country, there are many bodies of water, lakes, rivers and ponds, that are not navigable by sail-craft, owing to their being surrounded by high banks and having rapid currents. On these waterways, until of late years, nothing could be used but rowboats. It is for voyaging in such waters the motor boat is particularly adapted.

We have had a constant call for book plans for a boat of this description, an easy-to-build, cheap craft, yet one that would look well and run well. This is our reply to that demand, and so far as I can judge the boat herein outlined will prove, if properly built, a handy and speedy craft. . . .

To the man who has already some experience in building, the plans are all you will need. But to the man who has never built a boat before, let me say this: do not attempt to alter or, as some express it, improve upon the plans. Build the boat as here decided, or leave it alone. You cannot change the shape or structure and get a satisfactory result. If you think you can, then take my advice and build a boat wholly from your plans, and not from a distorted conception of ours.

Outboard Racing Timeline

1881
Gustav Trouv described his new electric, portable motor for boats and presented it to the French Academy of Sciences.

1898
The French Yachting Union organized boat races for launches powered by either steam, naphtha or petroleum engines mounted inboard.

1906
Cameron Waterman produced a single cylinder detachable marine motor with its flywheel enclosed in the crankcase called the Waterman Outboard Porto.

1907
The Cameron Waterman Company sold 3,000 outboards in America and Denmark.

1908
Ole Evinrude sold 25 of his single-cylinder, water-cooled outboard motors with 1.5 horsepower for $62 each.

1912
Swedish engineers created the first two-cylinder detachable motor capable of 2.5 horsepower.

1913
The Evinrude Company employed 300 workers to meet domestic and foreign demand.

1920
Thirty outboard motor companies had been created.

1922
The Johnson Brothers introduced at the New York Post Show the Johnson light twin and sold more than 3,000 motors in one year for $140 each.

1923
The Mississippi Valley Powerboat Association sanctioned the first three-mile outboard race to be contested in the United States; it was won by an Elto Twin pushing a displacement hull at an average speed of nine mph.

1924
The American Powerboat Association established a set of rules to apply to boats powered by detachable motors.

1925
The six-horsepower Johnson Big Twin, priced at $190, was introduced.

1926
A 71-mile outboard marathon boat race was staged in New York State; the winner took four hours, 46 minutes.

1927
Bigger engines produced more record-breaking speeds, topping 32 mph.

1928
The Elto outboard set a speed record of 41.7 mph and sold 10,000 units nationwide.

1929
Long 250- mile boat races gained in popularity, often requiring 14 hours on the water.

1930
Hull designs continued to improve speeds, led by the Century Boat Company in Milwaukee, Wisconsin.

1936 PROFILE

Katy "Minnow" Rawls excelled at both swimming and diving, which encouraged her to set her sights on winning Olympic medals in both events—not just difficult, but unusual, even for someone who practically lived in the water.

Life at Home

- In the 1932 Olympics, Katherine Rawls captured a silver medal in the three-meter springboard diving competition.
- With the 1936 Olympics looming, Katy had her sights set on winning medals in both swimming and diving.
- Her chances were good.
- Raised in Florida, Katy started swimming when she was two, began diving at seven, set a world record in the 300-meter individual medley at 13 and won an Olympic medal in diving at 14.
- The oldest in a family of swimmers and divers, Katy and her two sisters were collectively known in Florida as the "Rawls diving trio."
- The children also put on exhibitions as the "Rawls Water Babies."
- Water sports were a natural aspect of growing up in Florida.
- Family stories included Katy's fearlessness on a 25-foot-high platform as a second-grader, and competing at age 13 at the 1931 National Swimming Championships in Bronx Beach, New York.
- Even before the competition in New York, stories began circulating about her athletic prowess.
- She swam freestyle events from sprints to the mile, considered the individual medley her best event, set records in the breast stroke, and dove from both the platform and the springboard.
- But when she arrived for the 300-meter individual medley competition in New York, all spectators saw was a tiny girl, eager to swim one of the most difficult events.
- The individual medley required the swimmer to backstroke for one-third of the distance, breast stroke for a third, and freestyle over the remaining distance.

Katy Rawls' goal was winning not one, but two, Olympic events.

Although Young, Katy proved she deserved a spot on the Olympic team.

- Her principal competitor was superstar Eleanor Holm, the reigning queen of racing who had been winning with frustrating regularity.
- Katy not only won the race, but beat the world record previously set by Eleanor Holm herself.
- The next day Katy enhanced her reputation further by beating champion Margaret Hoffman in the 220-yard breast stroke.
- A year later, as a competitor in 1932 Olympics, Katy was the youngest team member by four years.
- To make the team, she traveled to Jones Beach located on Long Island in New York, site of the U.S. Olympic trials.
- Told by her coach to conserve her energy and aim for a third place finish during the trials of the 200-meter breast stroke, Katy finished a disappointing fourth and failed to qualify.
- Undaunted, she rowed across the water to where the springboard diving competition was underway.
- There she upset champion Georgia Coleman—by a razor thin scoring margin—to win the competition and qualify as an Olympic diver.
- Then she returned to the Casino Pool, a saltwater facility in Fort Lauderdale where she attended high school, before setting out for the Olympics in California.
- Competing in her first international meet, Katy dove well enough against the world's finest in 1932 Olympics in Los Angeles to capture the silver medal—edged out by American Georgia Coleman.
- Georgia captured the springboard diving gold by executing a flawless two and a half front somersault, the first woman to perform the feat in Olympic competition.
- Soon afterwards the International Swimming Federation banned dives it thought too daring for women, including the two and a half somersault.
- That fall, Katy defeated Georgia Coleman in the national championships, one of her four victories during the championship—the maximum number possible in one meet.
- In addition to the springboard diving event, Katy won the 200-meter breast stroke, the 880-yard freestyle and the 300-meter individual medley.
- Katy was hailed as a member of a new youth movement that also included 17-year-old Dorothy Payton.
- As she prepared for the 1936 Olympics, Katy was named *The New York Times* favorite in seven of the nine events in the upcoming Nationals, depending on which she chose to compete in.

Katy and her competitors dove well.

Life at Work

Katy enjoyed competing.

- Faced with the difficult task of making the 1936 Olympic team in both swimming and diving, Katy Rawls chose to concentrate on the freestyle event—her favorite, since the individual medley was not an Olympic event—and springboard diving.
- During tryouts in July at the Astoria Park pool, New York, Katy performed a spectacular layout front somersault dive that gave her an early edge over fierce competition.
- She also executed a forward one and a half with ease.
- Thirty minutes later, she was off the diving platform and preparing for the freestyle event.
- Katy took an early lead and won the event, but had to fight to hold her position in the final five yards of the race.
- She became one of eight athletes to capture a spot that first day.
- Katy also became the only athlete—male or female, runner, swimmer, jumper, fencer or equestrienne—to compete on two distinctly separate Olympic teams before reaching the age of 20.
- Champion swimmer Eleanor Holm Jarrett wasn't so lucky.
- During the nine-day voyage to the Olympics in Berlin, Germany, aboard the *SS Manhattan,* Jarrett, now married and accustomed to an active social life, ignored the strict curfews instituted by the American Olympic Committee.
- Jarrett attended an on-board party that lasted until six in the morning, and continued to drink in public, despite being warned to tone down her behavior.
- Before the ship landed, U.S. officials voted to remove Jarrett from the team, even though she was the defending champion and the favorite to win the backstroke events.
- The decision to dismiss Jarrett caused chaos throughout the swim team.
- At the games themselves, the tradition of the Olympic torch relay before the games was introduced as a way of defining the modern Olympic experience and promoting the new Germany.
- German filmmaker Leni Riefenstahl originally requested that all the torchbearers run entirely in the nude in homage to the athletes of the ancient Olympia.
- The runners preferred to remain dressed.
- The 1936 Olympics also was the first to place the top three finishers in each event on a tiered podium to receive their medals, while the national anthem of the gold-medal winner was played over the loudspeaker.
- Other firsts included freestyle swimmers being allowed to start from diving blocks, and the addition of basketball to the Olympic program.
- In the final basketball game, the United States beat Canada 19-8 in a contest played outdoors on a dirt court in driving rain so severe the teams could not dribble the ball.
- Americans swept the women's springboard diving competition, but not in the order Katy had planned.
- Thirteen-year-old Marjorie Gestring dove flawlessly to become the youngest woman in history to win a gold medal.
- Katy, in a repeat of the 1932 Olympics, captured silver.
- Swimming was even a greater disappointment for Katy.
- As predicted by ousted team member Eleanor Holm Jarrett, the American women were bested by the Dutch who set a new world record.
- Katy finished a distant seventh, but the United States fared well overall.

- American Jesse Owens, one of 10 African American athletes and part of a 66-man track and field squad, won four gold medals in the sprint and long jump events.
- Colorado farm boy Glenn Edgar Morris won gold in the Decathlon.
- Rower Jack Beresford won his fifth Olympic medal, and his third gold.
- The U.S. eight-man rowing team from the University of Washington won the gold, coming from behind to defeat the Germans and Italians with Adolf Hitler in attendance.
- Thanks to extensive preparation, Germany fared better in the games than they did four years earlier.

Life in the Community: Berlin, Germany

- The 1936 Olympic Games in Berlin were carefully scripted long in advance by its German organizers.
- The 1916 Olympics were scheduled to take place in Berlin but WW I caused a change in location, so one could say that the Germans had been preparing for 20 years.
- Prior to canceling events in Berlin, the Reichstag voted to subsidize the Berlin games, the first time such costs were borne by government rather than the private sector.
- Several non-European cities offered to host the 1916 games, including Cincinnati, who promised a half million dollars to help build the stadium and bring European athletes to America but, ultimately, the 1916 games were canceled.
- Germany, as well as several other "aggressor nations," was barred from the 1920 and 1924 Olympics games as unfit for peace-loving enterprises.
- The 1928 the Olympics in Amsterdam included Germany, as well as an American team under the tutelage of Gen. Douglas MacArthur, who considered the games to be a kind of "war without weapons."
- The 1932 Olympic Games in Los Angeles represented the second time the event had been held in the United States.
- The first was in 1904 in St. Louis, Missouri, which was not well attended internationally or remembered fondly.
- Los Angeles was determined to put the city on the map for something other than moviemaking.
- To defray housing costs in the midst of the Depression, Los Angeles created an Olympic Village for men where lodging cost two dollars per day instead of the seven, by more expensive nearby hotels.
- In the Baldwin Hills overlooking the Pacific Ocean, Olympic Village was the perfect setting for movie stars such as Douglas Fairbanks and Will Rogers to walk the grounds signing autographs.
- Women athletes, including the American women's swim team, were assigned to the Chapman Park Hotel downtown.
- Fearing that European athletes would boycott the American Olympics because of the high transportation costs, organizers negotiated, for Olympic participants, a 20 percent discount for transatlantic travel and 40 percent discount for railroad travel within the United States.
- To support its 69 athletes and defray expenses, the Brazilian team attempted to sell bags of coffee at ports along the way at 50 cents a bag.
- They raised enough for 24 members of the team to leave the ship and compete when it reached its destination.
- More than 100,000 people attended the opening ceremonies and the crowds remained respectable for all 14 days of competition.
- The Los Angeles games were the first Olympics to turn a profit, which was approximately $150,000.

- The United States dominated the Olympics, winning 41 gold medals.
- Germany won only three golds, behind Italy, Sweden, Finland, Japan, Hungary and France.
- Newly installed German Chancellor Adolf Hitler denounced the 1932 Olympic Games as a "plot of Freemasons and Jews."
- German Olympic organizers took detailed notes to prepare for the 1936 games, including design of the sports complexes, transportation, housing, publicity, broadcasting, even investigating a Los Angeles department store's claim that its clerks spoke every language represented at the games.
- German newspaper *Volkischer Beobachter,* noted, "Blacks have no place in the Olympics . . . this is a disgrace and a degradation to the Olympic ideal without parallel, and the ancient Greeks would turn over in their graves if they knew what modern man were doing with their sacred national games."
- In 1936, for the first time in modern history, an international protest movement was founded against the designated city of Berlin.
- American Jewish groups branded the Berlin games as the "Nazi Olympics," and wanted the Olympics moved from Germany or for America to boycott the event.

Adolf Hitler's Germany was a contested location for the Olympics.

- Black-owned newspapers pointed out that it is hypocritical for American sports officials to demand equal treatment for German Jews when discrimination against black athletes was accepted at home.
- The movement forced some German reforms, and by the time the games started, only Spain was missing, due to the Spanish Civil War then underway.
- Germany undertook a massive building project including a new stadium that required 2,600 workers to build.
- The Olympic Village in Berlin had its own movie theater, shops, full-sized gymnasium, running track, soccer field, swimming pool and Finnish sauna.
- Every national taste in food was accommodated, including pork for the Czechs, rye bread and blueberries for the Finns, and raw fish and soy sauce for the Japanese.
- Coca-Cola was sold outside the official venues, but German health officials insisted that a warning about its caffeine content be stated on every bottle.
- As in Los Angeles, the Olympic Village was for male athletes only, and the women were housed in a dormitory with tiny rooms near the stadium.
- On opening day, 170 buses brought the athletes to the sports complex, where the airship *Hindenburg* cruised back and forth across the stadium trailing an Olympic banner from its gondola.
- An overflow crowd of 110,000 spectators jammed Olympic Stadium on opening day with 49 nations represented, up from 37 in 1932.
- With great ceremony, the Olympic flame was brought to the stadium by a torch relay from its the starting point in Olympia, Greece.
- Track and field competition, the centerpiece of the modern Olympic Games, dominated the first week of competition and served as a showcase for American star Jesse Owens.
- African American men and women captured 13 medals in track and field, accounting for 83 of America's 107 points in that division.
- These games were the first to have live television coverage by the German Post Office, which broadcast over 70 hours of coverage to special viewing rooms throughout Berlin and Potsdam.

HISTORICAL SNAPSHOT
1936

- Dust storms stripped farmlands of all vegetation in Kansas, Oklahoma, Colorado, Nebraska and the Dakotas

- Lewis Meyer won his third Indianapolis 500 in nine years with an average speed of 109 mph

- Margaret Mitchell's book *Gone with the Wind* sold a record one million copies in six months

- The popular magazine *Literary Digest* predicted that incumbent President Franklin D. Roosevelt would lose the presidential election to Alf Landon

- Jay Berwaner, winner of the Heisman Trophy, was the first pick in the inaugural National Football League draft

- Hit songs included, "I've Got You Under My Skin," "Is It True What They Say About Dixie?," "The Night Is Young and You're So Beautiful" and the "WPA Blues"

- The Boulder Dam, built on the Colorado River, was completed, creating the world's largest artificial reservoir and enough power for 1.5 million people

- The Associated Press began a weekly college football list of the nation's top 20 schools based on a poll

- The first successful helicopter flight was made

- The baseball Hall of Fame inducted its first class: Ty Cobb, Honus Wagner, Babe Ruth, Christie Matheson and Walter Johnson

- Heavyweight German boxer Max Schmeling defeated Joe Louis in 12 rounds

- Polls indicated that 67 percent of Americans favored birth control

- Cleveland Indians rookie pitcher Bob Feller made his first start, striking out 15 St. Louis Browns in a 4-1 victory

- *The Green Hornet* radio show debuted and *The Phantom* made his first appearance in U.S. newspapers

- In violation of the Treaty of Versailles, Nazi Germany reoccupied the Rhineland

- Bruno Richard Hauptmann, convicted of kidnapping and killing Charles Lindbergh III, was executed in New Jersey

- The Santa Fe Railroad inaugurated the all-Pullman *Super Chief* passenger train between Chicago, Illinois, and Los Angeles, California

- Stress was first recognized as a medical condition

Selected Prices

Automobile, Reo	$795.00
Bed and Mattress	$14.95
Bloomers	$0.23
Electric Heater	$1.00
Highway Flare Torches, Dozen	$24.00
Shave Cream	$0.25
Tire	$2.95
Typewriter, Underwood	$49.50
Vacuum Cleaner	$28.95
Wristwatch, Elgin	$33.25

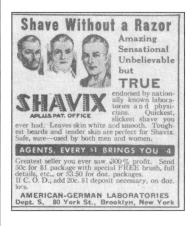

"Sister Acts in Swimming Give Sport Plenty of Life," Harry Grayson, *The Lowell Sun* (Massachusetts), July 27, 1935:

Had the gentleman in the bowler hat who asked the Floradora girl the famous question, "Are there any more at home like you?" been a witness at the national women's AAU swimming championships, he would've found that there are quite a few more, but they didn't stay home, but quite the contrary, swarmed on Manhattan Beach, New York, to help keep the laurels in the families.

There were the Rawls sisters, of Fort Lauderdale—bobbed-haired Katherine, Evelyn, and the youngest and curly-haired Dorothy.

There were the Brooklyn sisters, Elizabeth and Erna Kompa, and the now famous Hoeger girls, of Miami, 11-year-old, 73-pound Mary, the youngest person to ever win a national title of any kind; Ruth, and Helen.

But perhaps it's just as well for mermaids of other lands that Lenoe Kight of Homestead, Pennsylvania, hasn't a sister who swims anywhere near as well as she does. For between stocky Miss Kight, the freestyle luminary who has succeeded the record-wrecking Helene Madison, and the sister acts, women's swimming in America has been swept to its topmost height.

Katherine Rawls, only slightly less formidable than Miss Kight as an all-around star, won the 300-meter individual medley and the 220-yard breast stroke.

The crop-haired, 18-year-old miss has combined with her sisters to win 260 trophies, much to the delight of their father W. J. Rawls, a wholesale produce man.

Like Katherine, Dorothy Rawls, 14, and Neville, 16, are phenomenal backstroke competitors. It was by defeating Eleanor Holm in the backstroke to win her first title that Katherine first attracted widespread attention.

The three Rawls girls have been swimming since they can remember. The gentleman in the bowler no doubt would have agreed that three was quite enough, but would have learned that another Little Rawl Miss Peggy, 8, swan dives, as does Sonny, 10.

The Kompa girls are rising young exponents of the backstroke. They make the finish of 220-yard backstroke strictly a family affair, with Elizabeth barely beating Erna.

The latter only a few days previous had claimed a corner on backstroke fame by shattering a world 220-yard record as old as Mary Hoeger twice in as many days in a New York invitational meet in which she also cracked two American marks.

"Father of Youthful Diver Tells Story of Her Career,"
The Salt Lake Tribune, August 13, 1936:

Only three years ago, at a municipal plunge in Omaha, Nebraska, Marjorie Gestring, then 10 years old, learned to swim—in a very few minutes.

But not until later did she give promise of the diving talent which carried her to the springboard championship in the Olympic games in Berlin Wednesday. She was a puny baby and took gymnastic training on the advice of physicians.

William Gestring, insurance broker, father of the 13-year-old blonde wisp, told about her career after receiving news of her victory.

In addition to her diving virtuosity, she is fairly accomplished at the piano, having given two recitals.

The family was on a vacation visit in Omaha when she learned to swim. That same day, however, her mother, Mrs. Beta Gestring, sent for a music teacher, and a bargain was perfected. For each half-hour Marjorie practiced piano, she would be permitted an hour in the swimming pool.

Within three months, coach Pete Windel in Omaha boasted that exhibitions and a series of radio talks Marjorie made from the poolside in a city park increased the plunge's receipts $400 a week.

Back in Los Angeles, Marjorie continued her diving under the tutelage of coach Fred Cady, now in Berlin. To him, Gestring gave most of the credit for her having won 10 state championships.

She and her mother, who accompanied her to Berlin, will visit the latter's parents in Sweden before returning in time for Marjorie to reenter school, Gestring said.

"Japanese Take Big Lead Over Water Rivals," Gayle Talbot, *Ogden Standard-Examiner* (Utah), August 9, 1936:

The Japanese and Dutch dominated the first day of Olympic swimming competition today, leaving a string of broken records in their wake, and submerging America's hopes to a new all-time low.

The preliminary round saw the little brown men and women establish themselves as exuberant favorites in the men's 100-meter event.

America qualified its two great dash men, Peter Fick of New York and Art Lindegren of Los Angeles, 100-meter semifinal, while all three of its entries in the women's 100, Katherine Rawls, Fort Lauderdale, Florida, Olive McKean, Seattle, Washington, and Bernice Laip, Newark, New Jersey, all survived the opening round. But there didn't look like a winner in the bunch.

In the women's breast stroke, Uncle Sam's flashers finished fifth, fifth, and fourth in three rousing heats.

"Kitty Rawls Trails As New Mark Is Made," *Chester Times* (Pennsylvania), August 10, 1936:

Bearing out the pessimistic predictions of Mrs. Eleanor Holm Jarrett, Dutch women swimmers took the honors in the hundred-meter freestyle event today, with Katherine Rawls, leading American entry, fading out to wind up in seventh place.

As Mrs. Jarrett foresaw, the race went to Rita Mastenbrock of Holland in the new Olympic record time of 1.05.9 with Miss Campbell of the Argentine second in 1.06.4 and Fraulein Arendt of Germany third at 1.06.6.

"Youthful Marjorie Gestring Leads Sweep of Girls Diving Event," *Salt Lake Tribune,* August 13, 1936:

America swept back into the Olympic picture Wednesday when the University of Washington sweepswingers cracked the Olympic record for eight-oared crews wide open, Jack Medica and Marjorie Gestring hung up unexpected triumphs in aquatic competition, and the basketball and boxing teams chalked up new successes.

Surprised by the power of Great Britain, the Huskies from the American Far West stroked by ailing Don Hume had to come from behind to win their trial heat and lower the Olympic record for the 2,000-meter distance to 6.00.8.

Medica lowered the Olympic 400-meter freestyle record to 4.44.5 in scoring an unexpected victory over Shumpel Uto of Japan, while Miss Gestring beat out her teammates Katherine Rawls and Dorothy Poynton Hill for springboard diving honors.

Letter from Swedish International Olympic Committee member Sigfrid Edstrom to Avery Brundage, head of the American International Olympic Committee:

It seems there is some agitation from the American Jews. . . . I cannot understand the reason for this agitation. I understand it's on account of the persecution of the Jews but as to the sport this persecution has not been allowed. Already at the Congress of Vienna in June last year the International Olympic Committee was assured from the highest authorities that there would be no trouble for Jewish athletes in connection with the Olympic Games. Even German Jews would be allowed on the German team. . . .

It is too bad that the American Jews are so active and causing so much trouble. It is impossible for our German friends to carry on the expensive preparations for the Olympic Games if all this unrest prevails. . . .

As regards the persecution of the Jews in Germany, I am not at all in favor of said action, but I fully understand that an alteration had to take place. As it was in Germany, a great part of the German nation was led by the Jews and not by the Germans themselves. Even in the USA the day may come when you will have to stop the activities of the Jews. Many of my friends are Jews so you must not think I am against them, but they must be kept within certain limits.

"Owens Defeats German Sprint Stars Handily," *Salt Lake Tribune*, August 13, 1936:

Jesse Owens, star of the United States Olympic track team, Wednesday night equaled the world 100-meter dash record of 10.3 but disappointed 8,000 spectators by broad-jumping only 7.02 meters (23 feet and 1/2 inches) in losing to Wilhelm Leichum of Germany, who jumped 7.25 meters (23 feet, 9 7/16 inches) in an international track meet.

Displaying Olympic speed despite his third straight night of barnstorming, Jesse outraced two Germans, Gerd Hornberger and Borchmeyer, by two and three yards in the 100.

1938 Profile

It was the greatest job on earth; self-educated sportswriter Alan Miller was paid to watch, discuss and analyze sports on a daily basis.

Life at Home

- Alan Miller dropped out of high school at age 16 so he could accept a full-time sports writer's job at the *Pensacola Journal* newspaper.
- He spent the rest of his life getting a complete education in sports.
- The son of an attorney and one of six children, Al was born in Pensacola, Florida, in 1896.
- He served apprenticeships with the *Dallas Dispatch* and the *Minneapolis* News before turning 20 years old.
- Thanks to his front seat as a reporter, Al was splattered with blood during prize fights, soaked to the bone watching major league baseball in the rain, and threatened with a tennis racket by an athlete unapprecia- tive of his writing style.
- In 1917 at the onset of World War I, he joined the Army as a lieutenant and commanded an infantry platoon fighting in the Argonne Forest.
- He counted himself fortunate to have received only a small shrapnel wound in his foot before returning home from the Great War.
- Al went to New York City in search of work and was hired by the *New York Daily Mail* as a sports reporter specializing in tennis.
- Tennis was capturing nationwide attention as America's men had begun challenging the best France and England had to offer.
- After a few years and an ownership change, the *Daily Mail* folded and Al returned to Europe with four weeks' pay, plus his savings of $500.

Sportswriter Alan Miller and his wife Irene.

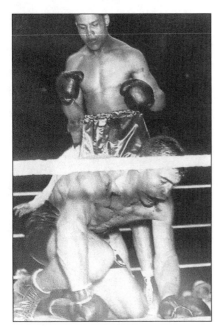

Al was spattered with blood . . .

. . . and threatened with a tennis racket.

Tennis was gaining popularity among women.

- Once his $500 was spent ("on wine, women and the rest foolishly"), Al managed to land a job at the *New York Herald,* Paris edition, where he remained for nine years.
- There he covered The International Lawn Tennis Challenge in Paris, Wimbledon in London, and watched America tennis greats "Big" Bill Tilden and "Little" Bill Johnston develop into international stars.
- The athletic Tilden brought a swashbuckling, masculine style to the game that helped erase its image as a sport for upper-class dilettantes.
- At the *New York Herald* Al gained experience as a rewrite man, night editor, headline writer, reporter and copy reader.
- In 1934 he returned to the United States and joined the sports department of the *New York Herald Tribune.*
- Al loved the noisy clatter of a fully staffed newsroom and cherished the skill required to dictate the essence of a great fight or game to a rewrite man without missing a fact, adjective or comma.
- At the sport's desk, a deadline for one of the newspaper's multiple editions always lurked close by.
- While fans celebrated the latest victory, Al and his ilk were writing for the unseen readers, attempting to "take" them to the game and help them sense its excitement.
- Unlike most reporters, Al did not hide liquor bottles in his desk drawers, his back pocket or in the back of the toilet at work.
- Al had his first drink once his stories were in press, after which he hung out sipping whiskey, talking sports and waiting for the early edition to roll off the presses between 2:00 and 4:00 a.m.
- Only then did he go home.

- Most days he reported to the office after lunch, sometimes before noon but never after 4 p.m.
- He and his wife Irene, an American-born pianist he met in Paris, lived in an apartment in upper Manhattan in New York City.
- The young couple decorated their home in the trendy art deco style which was born in Paris in the 1920s.
- This fresh, streamlined style was exemplified by geometric shapes and patterns celebrating the rise of modern technology and industry.
- Telephones, housewares, furniture and even cars were created in the art deco style.
- Regular movies were the most popular leisure pastime for most Americans during the 1930s, and Alan and Irene were typical in their devotion to film.
- The couple was especially proud of the new Stewart Warner Concert Grand Sheridan model radio phonograph cabinet.
- Together they listened to Orson Welles's radio show of the "invasion" from Mars based on H. G. Wells's *War of the Worlds*.
- The broadcast sounded so authentic, people panicked, believing that Martians had actually landed in New Jersey.

Life at Work

- Early in his career, Al Miller came to the conclusion that reporters were not born, but made by learning through trial and error.
- Getting the facts straight was just the beginning.
- Getting the tone and color correct within the context of a story was the real goal.
- Sports writing was a special calling and Al fully understood that he lived in a Golden Age of sports and sportswriters.
- Ring Lardner, Grantland Rice, Damon Runyon, W. O. McGeehan, Paul Gallico, and Heywood Broun were all tough competitors in the daily sportswriters' game.
- So they could fully exercise their adjectives, these writers were given a great deal of leeway in terms of style and content.
- But the business also was littered with drunks, hacks and layabouts.
- Some sportswriters wrote cynical, witty prose that excoriated everyone, while the "Gee Whiz" group was more romantic and celebrated an athlete's every move—noble or not.
- At some papers, hero worship dominated sports journalism and Al hated it.
- Some sportswriters even took money under the table to report only good news.
- He didn't disparage those who were on the take, because at least they were willing to admit it, Al often said over drinks.
- He surmised that younger reporters suffered from a lack of supervision in the modern era of sports writing and tended to be more interested in the byline than the content of the story.
- His real awakening to good writing occurred in 1925 when he discovered Bernard Darwin, the grandson of Charles Darwin, who wrote for the *London Times*.

Paul Gallico, a successful sportswriter, was tough competition for Al.

Al learned a lot from Bernard Darwin.

- Although Darwin was a golf reporter, he possessed the ability to weave fascinating facts and historical footnotes into the tapestry of his writing.
- Bernard Darwin and Neville Carlos, who reported on cricket, provided high school dropout Al with his education in journalism.
- By relating events as they encountered them, Darwin and Carlos wrote what they thought, unlike the columnist, who attempted to tell the reader what to think.
- When Al returned to New York after a decade in Paris, he was overwhelmed by the sheer number of events available in the city.
- New York City was a daily sports extravaganza.
- Al briefly worked as a columnist with access to any event, but soon decided to direct his energy toward larger, more detailed pieces—especially concerning golf and tennis.
- He gained a reputation for being superbly prepared and capable of conducting in-depth interviews.
- He liked to think of himself as a "word gymnast," but told most people he was simply a "despoiler of good ink."
- After briefly covering hockey at Madison Square Garden, his editor suggested that he write about the forgotten athletes in retirement.
- This marked the turning point in his career.
- Al's features included retired athletes such as Johnny Hayes, who won at the marathon in the London Olympics; Larry Doyle, the great second baseman for the Giants; and a pitcher from the miracle Braves, Dick Rudolph.
- When Al caught up with him, Hayes was the proprietor of a tea and coffee shop in Manhattan.
- Dick Rudolph was an undertaker.
- Al's most popular story concerned Sam Langford, a black boxer who fought in the days before Jack Johnson.

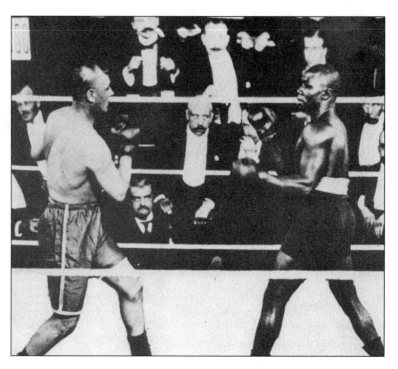

Sam Langford and other "forgotten athletes" benefitted from Al's writing.

- Al found Langford with the help of former Browns football star Fritz Pollard.
- Langford, who was not allowed to vie for the title because of his race, was in a Harlem tenement, blind and living in squalor.
- The story, picked up by the Associated Press, was so moving that Langford received cash donations from all over the country, which he used to set up a fund for former fighters suffering from diabetes.

Life in the Community: New York, New York

- Al Miller loved to watch a good game and participate in a good conversation.
- While in Paris he made the acquaintance of a young up-and-coming writer named Ernest Hemingway who he believed was the most charming young man he had ever met.
- He also attended parties at the house of Gertrude Stein, whom he believed to be "unknowable."
- In New York he was given a window to the world of sports.
- As a sports reporter he had a free pass to the greatest shows in town, in a city that loved to show off.
- He watched Joe Louis regain the heavyweight championship of the world by knocking out Max Schmeling in the first round at Yankee Stadium on June 23, 1938.
- He attended the first National Invitational Basketball Tournament held at Madison Square Garden where Temple defeated Colorado 60-36.
- He was present during the light heavyweight bout at Madison Square Garden when Henry Armstrong became the first man to hold three titles in three weight classes at once.
- He saw amateur Don Budge easily become the first player to complete the Grand Slam in tennis with titles of all four championships.

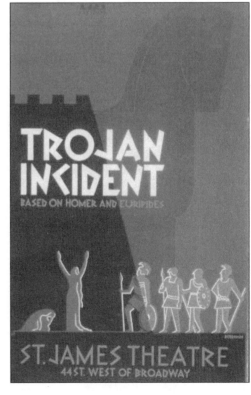

New York City offered a variety of things to do.

- And he witnessed professional football come of age as the New York Giants won the National Football League championship game against the Green Bay Packers 23-17 before 48,120 people in December 1938.
- Despite an ongoing economic depression, New York City had become a Mecca for sports lovers: New York Yankees dominated baseball; Polo Grounds were regular hosts to National Football League championships; top-level tennis was regularly available; college basketball was coming into its own; and boat racing regularly demanded coverage.

HISTORICAL SNAPSHOT
1938

- Seeing eye dogs came into use for aiding the blind
- The Fair Labor Standards Act established the Minimum Hourly Rate at 25 cents
- The Federal National Mortgage Association known as Fannie Mae was established
- Aviator Howard Hughes established a new 'round-the-world record of three days, 19 hours
- The March of Dimes' Polio Foundation was created by Franklin Roosevelt
- A Gallup poll indicated that 58 percent of Americans believed that the United States would be drawn into war; 65 percent favored boycotting German goods
- Seabiscuit defeated War Admiral in their long-awaited race to decide the best horse in America
- Action comics issued the first *Superman* comic

- New York staged a World's Fair called "The World of Tomorrow" which was visited by 25 million people
- Fifty percent of Americans polled selected radio as the most reliable news medium; 17 percent chose newspapers
- Orson Welles's radio adaptation of *The War of the Worlds* was broadcast, causing mass panic in the eastern United States
- Adolf Hitler was named *Time* magazine's "Man of the Year"
- Kate Smith sang her rendition of Irvin Berlin's "God Bless America" for the first time during an Armistice Day radio broadcast
- Disney Studios released *Snow White and the Seven Dwarfs*
- Thornton Wilder's play *Our Town* was performed for the first time
- A toothbrush became the first commercial product to be made with nylon yarn, used for the bristles
- Oil was discovered in Saudi Arabia
- Heavyweight boxing champion Joe Louis knocked out Max Schmeling in the first round of their rematch at Yankee Stadium in New York City
- In the prior five years, 60,000 German immigrants had arrived in America
- Movie box office receipts reached an all-time high and averaged $25 per family per year

Selected Prices

Basketball	.$3.59
Bicycle Tires	.$1.90
Camera, Kodak	.$22.50
Compass	.$1.95
Hotel Room, New York	.$4.00
Laxative, Ex-Lax, Chocolate	.$0.19
Radio	.$17.95
Saddle	.$27.95
Sun Lamp	.$6.75
Target Pistol	.$20.00

"Home Under the Seats," *Pathfinder*, August 27, 1938:

At Columbus, Ohio, Ohio State University's million-dollar stadium—13th largest in the country—seats 75,000 spectators. Distinguished with the fact that it won an important architectural prize when completed in 1921, it is outstanding for yet another reason—eventually, beneath its 75,000 seats, it will house as many as 2,400 students.

This prospect moved closer to reality last week as WPA workers went ahead in making a dormitory out of a third section of the U-shaped stadium's huge understructure. Designed to provide living quarters for 120 young men, the project meant that the number of below-seat residents at Ohio State soon would reach total of 440.

The idea had its birth in the depression year of 1933. At that time, anxious to help needy students remain in school, university officials decided to provide cheap housing for 75 undergraduates by building a dormitory in the fourth floor tower at the stadium's southwest corner. Promptly named the "Tower Club" by those who moved in, the new residential unit was no less successful than it was unique. Accordingly, a year later, the university won the help of the Federal Public Works Administration in making a similar unit out of a section of the underside itself—thus providing a home for 105 additional students. Then, early this year, with the aid of the Works Progress Administration, a second under-section became the home of 140 more. With last week's project, the total expenditure on the "Tower Club" to date was estimated at $172,500, about half of which represented federal funds.

"Excerpt by Al Lacy," *No Cheering in the Press Box,* edited by Jerome Holtzman, 1973:

There is no such thing as a born reporter. You have to learn, just like you have to learn to play the piano. And if you're no different, what's the use? You exist to serve by being capable at the same time being different from other writers, having developed something of your own. I learned by trial and error, by doing it, and having someone throw it back and say "get this down from four pages to one." Or, "look, here's your lead. Put that in front."

One of the reasons sportswriting tends to decline is that the writers, particularly younger ones just beginning, don't have enough supervision, like you find in the city desk. A sportswriter begins to cover things and the first thing he does is sit down at a typewriter and write his own name.

I read the papers, read everything I could, and every time I read a good piece I would say, "Gee, I wish I'd written that." And then I would look at it closer and say, "and if he had done it this way it would have been even better."

Some people are very good writers without having to go through all that. But they aren't good reporters. You have to learn to report, to get the essentials in there and do it well and do it with some charm. I see baseball stories today, and they're too long. The essentials are spread out. Many of the stories I read now, especially in the wire services, are flowery as hell.

"Excerpt by Al Lacy," *No Cheering in the Press Box,*
edited by Jerome Holtzman, 1973:

Of all sports, golf lends itself to writing, to literature. I think it is the best literature. It has attracted many, many fine writers. It's also the last sport where there is still a distinction between professional and amateur. Yet golf writing isn't as good today because of this new tendency to get quotes all the time. It's becoming terrible in golf, really astonishing. Only people who really love golf write good reports anymore. . . .

Golf is a simple game. The ball is stationary. There's only one rule in hitting a golf ball. You bring the club square into the ball and the ball square to the target. That's all there is to it. There's an awful lot of bunk written about golf. In the preface to this golf book I have, *How to Play Golf,* the author says, "I question whether I ought to impose another golf book on the public. There have been so many." The book was written in 1896; since then there've been 5,000 books on how to play golf and how to hit the ball. They make so much to-do about it.

**"Gomez and Ruffing Get Demands, Opening Way to Final Agreements
with Gehrig, DiMaggio, Crosetti, Rolfe, and Others,"**
Lowell Sun **(Massachusetts), March 1, 1938:**

Owner Jack Ruppert of the New York Yankees today is committed to an expenditure of a reported $37,000 for next season for the salaries of two players, namely Lefty Gomez and Red Ruffing, who signed yesterday, but his troubles are not over by any means. In fact, owner Ruppert has about $100,000 go to satisfy all hands.

Having corralled his two best pitchers at what was said to be salaries of $18,500 each, representing a raise of $3,500 a piece, he now is confronted by the task of signing first baseman Lou Gehrig, outfielder Joe DiMaggio, shortstop Frank Crosetti, third baseman Ed Rolfe and pitcher Spud Chandler. Putting it another way, he has everything except a baseball team.

The advance guard started workout yesterday at St. Petersburg in preparation for a quest of a third straight American League pennant and world championship, with the rest of the hands to report the next few days, but two or three of the aforementioned recalcitrants may not be there.

DiMaggio and Gehrig between them are asking about $75,000, and the rest are just as generous as possible with owner Rupert's money in their own behalf, with the result that there may be some absentees when the general spring sessions finally get underway.

"Pictures Show Head Punches Were Ones That Really Won,"
Altoona Mirror (Pennsylvania), June 24, 1934:

You've read and heard a great deal about the "killer instinct" in prizefighters.

Now you can see it if you are so inclined.

The slow motion picture of the 124 seconds of the Joe Louis-Max Schmeling fight is probably the most faithful recording ever made of human savagery.

The picture is much more terrifying to watch than the fight was. In the Yankee Stadium the rapidity with which the butchering occurred, against the background of noise and excitement, prevented anyone from getting a cold and objective view of it. In the quiet darkness of the cold theater where I saw the fight pictures yesterday afternoon, I was appalled by the knowledge that this ruthless, unmerciful killer there on the screen was one and the same man as the Joe Louis whom I had just left a few minutes before—the Joe Louis who talked of ice cream, and trips to Europe, and his new pinstripe suit.

I saw old Joe again after I had seen the pictures and although he was sitting in the same chair and talking in the same low voice, I didn't feel fully comfortable around him. It was as if I had seen a savage tiger behind the bars of the cage suddenly loosed to walk free among the people who had been watching him.

The Louis of the slow motion pictures has no connection with ice cream and pinstripe suits and discussions of the weather. He is a jungle man, as completely primitive as any savage, out to destroy a thing he hates. Even the style of fighting he had been patiently taught was abandoned. He fought instinctively and not by any man-made pattern.

There's one moment in the picture that made me want to turn my head away, and I have seen some pretty dreadful shambles in the ring. This is the moment when Louis sets up the, by then completely helpless, Schmeling for the final blow and then delivers it. This was a right hand smash to the jaw of a falling man—a beaten man who needed only a push to topple him over and not a blow driven home with every ounce of strength in Louis's 200 pounds.

The picture shows very clearly that Louis did hit Schmeling in the kidneys, not once but twice. But it also shows with legal clarity that neither punch was intentional. Schmeling is wrong if he thinks these kidney punches cost him the fight. When he leaves the hospital, let him go to see the film, and he will have to admit that he was a badly beaten man, with no chance of victory, before either kidney punch was delivered. He was on the ropes, out of his head and helpless. And these kidney blows were mere taps compared to the rifle shots that all but tore his head off.

"Rate Budge Number 1 in Tennis Event," *Piqua Daily Call* (Ohio), September 1, 1938:

Don Budge, who already has won the Australian, French and Wimbledon tennis titles this year, will be seeded number one for the U.S. Championships September 8-17 at Forest Hills, New York, when the draw is made today.

Budge stands out like a skyscraper in a wheat field. Yet in spite of his eminence, and in spite of the fact that he is the odds-on favorite to win his second straight national singles title, the tournament promises the best that the United States has to offer, which is considerable.

Heading the invaders will be the Australians, opponents of Budge and Co. in the Davis Cup challenge round. . . .

Since she is ranked number one nationally and has been more active than Helen Jacobs, Alice Marble appears due for the top ranking in the women's single field, which also will have a strong international group.

1938 News Feature

"Seabiscuit Leaves War Admiral Behind in Epichol Race," ***The Helena Daily Independent*** (Montana), November 2, 1938:

Seabiscuit, the Cinderella horse, wrote the most dramatic chapter in his rags to riches story today when he left the great War Admiral struggling far behind with a record-smashing performance in the long-awaited match race at Pimlico.

The one-time selling plater, carrying the red and white silks of Charles S. Howard, of San Francisco, matched the Admiral's famed speed with more speed, stuck to his rival like a leech midway of the backstretch, then pulled away with a final drive that sent him under the wire three lengths in front with a new track record for a mile and three-sixteenths.

The Biscuit, held at slightly more than 2 to 1 as the crowd of 40,000 sent the odds on Samuel B. Riddle's star tumbling to 1 to 4, reeled off the distance in 1:56 3-5. The time clipped one-fifth second off the track record created by Pompoon last spring after Seabiscuit himself hung up a new record of 1:57 2-3 last year.

And so in less than two minutes Seabiscuit settled a year-old argument, won $15,000 and skyrocketed into second place among the world's leading money winning horses.

The clean-cut triumph boosted the Biscuit's earnings to $340,480, only some $36,000 short of Sun Beau's world mark of $376,744, and gave him a record 32 wins, 12 seconds, and 13 thirds in 84 starts during four years campaigning from coast-to-coast. His greatest successes have been since Howard took him out of the Wheatley stable for $8,000 late in 1936 after he had met with little success and spent much of his time as the workhorse for more highly regarded stable mates.

For War Admiral, the defeat meant the loss of the chance to again be acclaimed the horse of the year as he was in 1937, when he nosed out Seabiscuit in a nation-wide poll for sportswriters. It was only the second time in two years that the four-year-old son of Man o' War had bowed his head in defeat.

But it'll not mean the end of the Admiral's racing career. Trainer George Conway, offering no excuses, said he would ship the Riddle star to Narragansett Park for the Rhode Island handicap on November 12. Present plans for the Biscuit call for him to go after the Riggs at Pimlico over the same distance Saturday.

The majority of the crowd came expecting to see a real horse race all the way with Charley Kurtsinger sending War Admiral away and George Woolf of Babb, Montana, trying to catch him with Seabiscuit in the final drive. But actually it was only a duel for three-eighths of a mile. That was on the backstretch when the Admiral moved up and took up a head advantage. For a few strides it looked as if War Admiral was going to pull away, but the son of Hard Tack lived up to his name and refused to give ground.

Coming to the milepost, Kurtsinger sensed the Admiral was weakening and went to the whip, one of the few times in the colt's career that it was necessary to use a persuader. But the Admiral didn't have it. Without once raising his bat, Woolf hand-rode Seabiscuit into a length advantage and with every stride he widened the margin until at the finish he had his rival badly beaten.

Almost as surprising as Seabiscuit's easy victory was the manner in which he outbroke War Admiral after two false starts. The California bay quickly opened up a length and a half advantage, sped past the clubhouse two lengths in front and held his margin until well past the half-mile marker.

Then War Admiral made his move, but three-quarters of a mile further the challenger petered out. A glance at the fractional times showed how Seabiscuit achieved his greatest triumph. He stepped off the first quarter of a mile in 23 3-5 seconds, hit the half-mile post in 47 3-5 and was at the six furlong pole at 1:11 4-5, as fast a time as was turned in during the day by horses going only three-quarters of a mile. He was clocked in at 1:36 4-5 for the mile.

"I have no excuses," said Kurtsinger. "War Admiral simply didn't happen today."

Woolf shouted Seabiscuit was the "best horse in the world" as grooms and stable lackeys nearly tore his clothes off when he returned to the stable.

1940–1949

World War II dominated every aspect of American culture in the 1940s, including sports. In all, 509 active major league baseball players served in the armed forces during the war, some 200 colleges disbanded their football teams because their players went to war and 4,000 boxers including five world champions served in the military. Just as the wartime labor shortage gave women opportunities to work at traditional men's jobs in defense plants, the shortage of men on the playing fields briefly gave women athletes a chance to play in the spotlight. With the threat of cancellation of the 1943 baseball season looming, major league owners created the All American Girls Baseball League as a much-needed morale boost.

After the war, in 1947, Jackie Robinson broke the color barrier in major league baseball, opening the door for other black athletes and closing the door on the future success of the Negro leagues. Professional sports also took its first steps toward becoming big business. A minimum salary of $5,500 a year was established in professional baseball, and owners agreed to establish the first players' pension fund. Auto racing, football, basketball and golf all established players' organizations after the war. Oversight commissions regulated each sport, setting standards of equipment, rules of play, and business practices.

People from every social stratum either signed up for the military or went to work supplying the military machine. Even children, eager to do their share, collected scrap metal and helped plant the victory gardens that symbolized America's willingness to do anything to defeat the "bullies." In fact it was the threat of war that compelled Congress to pass the Alien Registration Act of 1940 that required all non-U.S. citizens within the United States to register with the government and receive an Alien Registration card, which was later known as the "Green Card." In addition, large amounts of money and food were sent abroad as Americans observed meatless Tuesdays, gas rationing and other shortages to help the starving children of Europe.

Business worked in partnership with government; strikes were reduced, but key New Deal labor concessions were expanded, including a 40-hour week and time and a half for overtime. The wartime demand for production workers rose more rapidly than for skilled workers, reducing the wage gap between the two to the lowest level in the twentieth century.

From 1940 to 1945, the gross national product more than doubled, from $100 billion to $211 billion, despite rationing and the unavailability of many consumer goods. From 1943 to the end of the war, the cost of living rose less than 1.5 percent. Following the war, as controls were removed, inflation peaked in 1948 and union demands for high wages accelerated. Between 1945 and 1952, confident Americans—and their growing families—increased consumer credit by 800 percent.

To fight inflation, the Office of Price Administration set price ceilings for almost all consumer goods and distributed ration books for items in short supply. The Selective Service and the War Manpower Commission determined who would serve in the military and when a worker could transfer from one job to another. When the war ended and regulations were lifted, relations between labor and management became strained. Massive strikes and inflation followed in the closing days of the decade, and many consumer goods were easier to find on the black market than on the store shelves.

The decade of the 1940s made America a world power and Americans more worldly. Millions served overseas; millions more listened to broadcasts of the war. The war effort also redistributed the population and the demand for labor. Women entered the work force in unprecedented numbers, reaching 18 million. The net cash income of the American farmer soared 400 percent.

But the Second World War extracted a price. Countries possessed far greater firepower than ever before. In all, the United States lost 405,000 lives to combat deaths at a cost of $350 billion. Following Germany's unconditional surrender on May 4, 1945, however, Japan continued fighting. President Truman dropped atomic bombs on the Japanese cities of Hiroshima and Nagasaki, ending the war and ushering in the threat of "the bomb" as a key element of the Cold War during the 1950s and 1960s.

Throughout the war, soldiers from all corners of the nation fought side by side and refined nationalism and what it meant to America through this government-imposed mixing process. The newfound identity of the American GIs was further cemented by the vivid descriptions of war correspondent Ernie Pyle, who spend considerable time talking and living with the average soldier to present a "worm's eye view" of war. Yet, discrimination continued. African American servicemen were excluded from the marines, the Coast Guard and the Army Corps. The regular army accepted blacks into the military—700,000 in all—only on a segregated basis. Only in the closing years of the decade would President Harry Truman lead the way toward a more integrated America by integrating the military.

Sports attendance in the 1940s soared beyond the record levels of the 1920s; in football the T-formation came into prominence; Joe DiMaggio, Ted Williams, and Stan Musial dominated baseball before and after the war, and Jackie Robinson became the first black in organized baseball. In 1946, Dr. Benjamin Spock's work, *Common Sense Baby and Child Care*, was published to guide newcomers in the booming business of raising babies.

1944 PROFILE

As an observant Jew, Dmitri Berenbaum was deeply committed to becoming to a boxing champion while remaining pious.

Life at Home

- One thing Dmitri Berenbaum made clear to his boxing opponents was, "If you want a whipping, you will have to wait until the sun goes down on Saturday."
- His parents were appalled that their handsome, intelligent son wanted to make his living with his fists.
- They had raised Dmitri to be a doctor or a rabbi.
- How would they answer the question, "What does your son do?"
- Dmitri was much more comfortable with his image as a "ring toiler."
- While growing up, he had read about a Jewish boxer named Barney Ross from Chicago's Maxwell Street ghetto ". . . a riotous dream of Jewish gunmen and bookmakers, fighting furriers and smashed-nose boxers."
- Barney Ross's father was killed in a robbery just before Barney's fourteenth birthday, so Barney started boxing to earn money to free his siblings from an orphanage.
- He went on to be a champion.
- Despite her objections to Dmitri's boxing fixation, Dmitri's mother woke him every morning at 6 a.m. so he could train.
- To show her his appreciation, he strapped tefillin (two small black boxes containing parchment scrolls inscribed with Bible verses) around his arm and forehead before he said morning prayers.
- To schoolchildren, Dmitri talked about the rewards of prayer and the joys of pummeling his opponents into submission.
- At 22 he had fought professionally 17 times, winning 15 bouts, seven by knockout.
- Small and wiry, Dmitri had the ability to snap a long jab with surprising power and then deliver a good combination of blows.
- He was considered sneaky by fight fans and difficult to hit by opponents.
- He had a very busy boxing schedule.

Dmitri Berenbaum was dedicated to becoming a champion boxer.

Dmitri's grandfather taught him to be proud of his Jewish heritage.

Dmitri was a respectful boxer.

- It was not easy being the "Pious Pummeler" or the "Kosher Kid."
- Friday night fights were a staple of the boxing world.
- In total, there were more than 70 Jewish holy days on which he would not fight.
- Each scheduled Saturday night battle required careful planning.
- On the road, he always stayed within walking distance of a synagogue for Friday and Saturday services.
  - He did not drive on the Sabbath and strictly followed Jewish dietary laws.
  - It was a discipline passed down by his grandfather, who was forced to flee Russia to escape the escalating repression of the Jews.
  - Dmitri's family originated in the Russian Empire, which at one time hosted the largest Jewish population in the world.
  - A wave of anti-Jewish repression swept southwestern Russia in 1881, after Jews were wrongly blamed for the assassination of Alexander II.
  - Pogroms (organized persecution of an ethnic group, usually Jews) were initiated in hundreds of Russian towns, during which thousands of Jewish homes were destroyed, and many families were reduced to extreme poverty.
  - During the following three decades, Jews were banned from living in rural areas and towns of fewer than 10,000 people, assuring the slow death of many shtetls (small towns with large Jewish populations).
  - Quotas were placed on the number of Jews allowed into secondary and higher education, and Jews were restricted from many professions.
  - In 1891, most Jews were expelled from Moscow.
  - Tsar Alexander III said, "we must never forget that the Jews have crucified our Master and have shed his precious blood."
  - More than two million Jews fled Russia between 1880 and 1920, a vast majority emigrating to the United States.

A synagogue within walking distance was convenient.

The Russian Empire once home to a large Jewish population.

Jewish persecution left more than 300,000 orphaned.

- Additional pogroms were unleashed during World War I, killing an estimated 70,000 to 150,000 Jewish civilians throughout the former Russian Empire, orphaning more than 300,000 Jewish children.
- In August 1919 Jewish properties, including synagogues, were seized and many Jewish communities were dissolved.
- Rabbis were forced to resign from their posts under the threat of violent persecution.
- Dmitri's grandfather was a rabbi during these troubled times.
- He and his family, including his married daughter and son-in-law, fled to America.
- Dmitri was born sixteen months later in 1922.
- Their first stop was New York City, where thousands of Russian Jews had congregated for decades.
- Miraculously, both Dmitri's grandfather and father were offered positions in Atlantic City, New Jersey, where Dmitri enjoyed a good education and developed his love of boxing.

Many Jews sought refuge in the United States.

Life at Work

- Dmitri Berenbaum, a first-generation American, was proud of his country, especially in time of war—and equally proud of his heritage.
- Shortly after the Japanese attack on Pearl Harbor in 1941, he volunteered for military service in Europe, only to be rejected because of two missing toes on his left foot.
- Now it was his job to entertain factory workers and tourists with his ability to knock cold his opponents.
- It wasn't easy for a boxer to keep kosher, attend shul (or synagogue) almost daily, refuse to fight on the Sabbath and wear a zizith (fringed garment) when not in the ring.
- Dmitri felt alive in the ring, waiting to hit or be hit, and didn't mind these inconveniences.
- Boxing had always lured ethnic audiences—African Americans for Joe Louis, Irish Americans for Jack Dempsey, Italian Americans for Rocky Marciano.
- The natural audience for a Jewish boxer was smaller.
- Jewish boxer Benjamin Leiner changed his name to Benny Leonard so his mother wouldn't discover he had taken up prizefighting.
- When she learned his secret she wailed, "A prizefighter you want to be? Is that a life for a respectable man? For a Jew?"
- By his early twenties, Dmitri was starting to get some attention.
- His last two wins were knockouts in his last two fights and newspapers said he had dynamite in his hands.
- His next bout was a career-maker with an opponent who was more experienced, explosive and better known.
- Fight time was 8 p.m. Saturday, just after sundown.
- This put Dmitri in the spotlight for a good gate, but meant he would have less time to warm up before the fight.
- Dmitri loved the atmosphere of a fight—the smell of tension, the stale sweat of previous boxers, the knowledge that one unfocused moment could result in serious injury.
- When the bell rang to open the first round, the crowd screamed in anticipation.
- "Little Red" a talkative Irishman, had been bragging for weeks he would cut the "kike" down to size in under a minute.
- Dmitri landed the first three blows—two right-hand jabs to the face and a wicked left to the body.
- Little Red didn't like the body shots and grew very aggressive, but collected two more blows to the belly.
- At the end of the first round, Dmitri was still standing, so Little Red was taking a razzing from the New Jersey crowd
- A solid flurry of blows by Little Red quieted the crowd as the round ended.
- As Dmitri sat in his corner, he struggled to clear his head, thinking that Little Red had more power than he first thought.
- Dmitri figured he had two choices—tie up his opponent for most of the second round or move in for a quick kill.
- When the bell rang for the second round Little Red charged across the ring like an enraged bull, determined to capitalize on the blows he had struck at the end of the first round.
- Dmitri, his choice made for him, simply dropped his hands, appeared defenseless and waited for the big swing.
- Dmitri caught Little Red fully exposed across the midsection and struck a right, then delivered two more to the head and a left to the jaw.

- Dmitri then saw the most beautiful sight in the world—an opponent collapsing to the ground already unconscious.
- The crowd was so noisy, Dmitri could not hear the referee's 10-count.
- He did hear the referee announce Dmitri the winner by a knockout, and he also heard his mother say, "I'm proud of you."

Life in the Community: Atlantic City, New Jersey

- Atlantic City had always been a resort town.
- Its location in South Jersey, hugging the Atlantic Ocean between marshlands and islands, was prime real estate for developers.
- The city was incorporated in 1854, the same year train service in the area began, linking this remote parcel of land with Philadelphia.
- The first boardwalk was built in 1870, to help hotel owners keep sand out of their lobbies.
- The idea caught on, and the boardwalk was expanded and modified several times in the following years.
- The length of the boardwalk, before the 1944 hurricane, was about seven miles.

Atlantic City was a resort town.

The boardwalk offered much to see and do.

Boardwalk lights made the city vulnerable at night.

Business owners were happy to cooperate and support the Army.

- Atlantic City was also a shore community vulnerable to attack in 1944 and ready to serve its country in time of war.
- A special police detail was assigned to guarding the water supply 24 hours a day, and prepared to apprehend any stranger who might venture within range of suspicion.
- Hotel owners, at their own expense, made available their artesian wells to the city water mains as auxiliary drinking water supply in case of damage to the main pipelines.
- Indoor swimming pools were kept filled 24 hours a day as another source of water to firemen.
- To prevent lights from the boardwalk making easy targets of passing ships, the Army ordered all lighting fixtures either turned off or altered in such a manner that their illumination would not be visible from the ocean.
- So, 60 percent of all 5,000 neon and other advertising signs were blacked out, while 20 percent of street lights facing the ocean were painted black.
- All Boardwalk lights were also painted black except for a small slit to allow a faint glow toward the 'walk.
- Automobiles on city streets at night were limited to 20 miles per hour and parking lights.
- To house troops during training, 45 hotels were provided for U.S. military occupancy.
- Atlantic City's Convention Hall served as the headquarters for the Army Air Forces Basic Training Center No. 7.
- Facilities were leased by the Army Air Forces at the rate of $1 per day per room, for not less than one year.
- Normally, room rates were $10-$12 per day from May to August and $5-$7 per day in the "off season" from September to April.
- The former Elks Club Building was converted to a radio-operator training center for Coast Guardsmen.
- Before the recruits could function as military personnel, it was first necessary to make sure they could all read and write.
- The 704th Training Group, from Jefferson Barracks, Missouri, came to Atlantic City to assist the newly activated 565th Technical School Squadron.
- It was their mission to see that every recruit reached a fourth-grade reading/writing level within 12 weeks.

HISTORICAL SNAPSHOT
1944

- The first issue of *Human Events* was published
- U.S. troops captured the Marshall Islands
- The U.S. Strategic Air Forces in Europe began handling strategic planning for all U.S. Army Air Forces in Europe and Africa
- The Nazi propaganda film, *The Fuehrer Gives a Village to the Jews*, was filmed in Theresienstadt
- The Japanese launched an offensive in central and south China
- The Nazis executed almost 400 prisoners, Soviet citizens and anti-fascist Romanians at Rîbnita
- In the Polish village of Markowa, German police killed Józef and Wiktoria Ulm, their six children, and eight Jews they were hiding
- The United Negro College Fund was incorporated
- The Germans evacuated Monte Cassino and Allied forces took the stronghold after a struggle that claimed 20,000 lives
- The first line of the poem "Chanson d'automne" by Paul Verlaine was broadcast by the BBC as a coded message to underground resistance fighters in France, warning that the invasion of Europe was imminent
- Rome fell to the Allies, the first Axis capital to fall
- *Operation Overlord*, code named D-Day, commenced with the landing of 155,000 Allied troops on the beaches of Normandy in France, the largest amphibious military operation in history
- Iceland declared its full independence from Denmark
- The deportation of Hungarian Jews to Auschwitz and other Nazi death camps began

- At Camp Hood, Texas, baseball player 1st Lt. Jackie Robinson was arrested for refusing to move to the back of a segregated U.S. Army bus
- Hideki Tojo resigned as prime minister of Japan because of the setbacks in the war effort
- Adolf Hitler survived his forty-second assassination attempt
- A tip from a Dutch informer led the Gestapo to a sealed-off area in an Amsterdam warehouse, where they found Jewish diarist Anne Frank and her family
- IBM dedicated the first program-controlled calculator, known as the Harvard Mark I
- Posters featuring Smokey Bear appeared for the first time
- The *Tsushima Maru*, a Japanese unmarked passenger ship, was sunk by torpedoes launched by the submarine *USS Bowfin*, killing 1,484 civilians, including 767 schoolchildren
- *The Adventures of Ozzie and Harriet* radio show debuted
- German Field Marshal Erwin Rommel committed suicide rather than face execution for allegedly conspiring against Adolf Hitler
- General Douglas MacArthur returned to the Philippines with Philippine Commonwealth President Sergio Osmeña

Selected Prices

Billfold, Leather $2.50
Casserole Dish, Pyrex $0.50
Cemetery Plots, Four Graves $100.00
Fur Coat, Beaver $595.00
Garage Door $7.98
Hostess Pajamas $45.00
Laundry Tub, Concrete $9.85
Opera Ticket, New York $2.00
Pipe $3.50
Saccharin Tablets, 1,000 . . . .$0.54

—if it's Borden's it's got to be good

Elsie says: "Here's my favorite recipe: Take one Axis goose. Cook thoroughly by buying U. S. WAR SAVINGS STAMPS AND BONDS REGULARLY."

"Boxing," *Britannica Book of the Year*, 1944:

Most of the ring champions were in the Armed Forces. Joe Louis, Sgt. in the U.S. Army, occupied himself exclusively to boxing exhibitions for the men in service. Billy Conn, outstanding challenger for the world heavyweight title, was a corporal in the Army, stationed most of the year at Jefferson Barracks, Missouri.

Championships in four divisions where possession was undisputed were frozen. In addition to Louis's heavyweight crown, there were the light heavyweight, middleweight, and welterweight championships. Gus Lesnevich, leader in the light heavyweight, or 170-pound class, was in the Coast Guard. Tony Zale, holder of the middleweight, or 160-pound title, was in the Navy. Freddy Cochrane, champion of the welterweight, or 147-pound class, was in the Navy.

Willie Pep, who shared the position of the world featherweight title, made one defense of his crown, held the title, saw his remarkable streak of victory shattered at 62, and enlisted in the Navy. . . .

Manuel Ortiz, Mexican resident of central California, ruler of the featherweight division, successfully defended his title no less than eight times, a record for championship defense in modern history. . . .

Outstanding among the box office attractions, however, was Beau Jack, who, under his real name Sidney Walker, was originally a caddy and shoeshine boy in his native Augusta, Georgia. He not only contrived to lose and regain his world lightweight title in the states of New York, New Jersey and Pennsylvania, but he shared the distinction for the year's largest gate receipts and established himself as the greatest box office attraction active in the ring.

"Jewish Religious Life," *Britannica Book of the Year*, 1944:

The year 1943 brought to the Jews and Judaism a continued crescendo of horror. In the slaughterhouse of Europe, the struggle of a remnant of Jewry for sheer physical survival left little room for cultivation of Judaism after synagogues and Jewish communities were destroyed and the Nazis "extermination commissions" had annihilated an estimated 4,000,000 Jews.

Yet Jewish refugees were found in mountain caves with their scrolls of the Torah and religious books. Jewish religious life felt a sacrifice in countries such as Holland, Denmark and Italy.

The free Christian world, and even more strikingly Christian prelates and laity in Axis-occupied lands, reacted not only in brave words of protest and denunciation, but also in action, such as in opening monasteries and religious organizations to shelter Jews. The Federal Council of Churches of Christ in the United States set a special day of compassion and prayer for the Jews of Europe, while American Jewry took on itself a six-week period of mourning and intercession. On the favorable side of the ledger, the relaxation of the Soviets' proscription of religion and the influx from Poland into Russia of traditional Talmudic and Zionist Jewish refugees opened up a new chapter in the story of Judaism in Russia.

argus Serves Our FIGHTING FORCES!

FOR more than two years, Argus has been serving our fighting forces, and now, with total war, our efforts have been redoubled to provide sufficient essential materials . . . when and where needed, rather than "too little, too late."

From precision optical units for training, to the vital optical instruments and radio apparatus used on the fighting fronts, Argus equipment is "doing its bit" in helping to preserve liberty and freedom.

argus

SUBSIDIARY OF

INTERNATIONAL INDUSTRIES, INC.
ANN ARBOR • MICHIGAN

"No thanks!"

THIS is the hand of Japan and the dictator nations . . . not a pretty hand.

It offers the world a starvation diet . . . starvation of body and mind and soul.

Boastfully it presents its standard of living and its standard of thinking.

America says "No thanks" with thousands upon thousands of planes and tanks and warships.

We, of The Texas Company, say "No thanks" with millions of gallons of 100-octane gasoline for our war planes. We say "No thanks" by building vast new plants to produce Toluene, vital in making highly explosive TNT . . . and to produce Butadiene, for synthetic rubber.

We have turned the knowledge and skill gained in making Texaco Fire-Chief and Sky Chief Gasolines to the large-scale production of these wartime necessities.

So it has been with all American business. From strength built in peacetime comes the force of the mighty "NO" which today rises from the throat of industry.

"What Women Can Do: Think War, Buy Little, Maintain Our Ideals,"
Life, September 28, 1942:

Up to now the big Jap has pushed everybody around. He has always been in the right spot with the right equipment at the right time, his skin painted the right color. The poor little white men, with wrong plans for using the wrong things in the wrong places (at Singapore even the guns were pointed in the wrong direction) have scurried piteously through the jungles, swatting mosquitoes, leaping over hungry crocodiles and ultimately getting shot or captured. But last week from the far Pacific came a different story. Shortly after the U.S. Marines had taken the airfield on Guadalcanal Island in the Solomons, the Japs landed a force of 750 men at the mouth of the Tenaru River. The Marines closed in and there developed a nasty jungle battle, with the Japs lodged among the trees. Suddenly out of the jungle there appeared the right thing at the right time: a line of Army tanks deliberately headed in the coconut grove where the Japs were concentrated. The Marines let out a roar. As the correspondent described it, "The whole American side of the Tenaru front sounded like the bleachers at Ebbets Field when the Dodgers win." The tanks rushed up and down slaughtering Japs, whose rifle bullets pinged harmlessly against the heavy armor. When all was over not a Jap remained.

The American people would like to fight that kind of war at home too—a war of getting things right to the right places on time. But they aren't doing it. The reason is that in order to fight a war like that . . . you have to think war. And a lot of people responsible for the war effort on the home front in labor, in agriculture, and chiefly in government—are not thinking war.

The problem is this: how can you get this country of 130,000,000 people to act and think like those Marines at Guadalcanal Island? And when you examine the proposition you come to what is perhaps an unexpected answer. The ones on whom this responsibility chiefly falls are the women. Many women have written into the news fronts recently asking what they can do to help the war. This is our reply. If the women of America will take on this war as their own; if they will think war, thoroughly and relentlessly, then this country can begin to look like a real war machine. Then Congress would not dare to play politics with the country's safety; bureaucrats would not dare to fail; and farm and labor leaders would not dare to advance their selfish interests first. Then we might begin to get things right in the right places at the right time. . . .

Action has glamour, but is not necessarily the most important contribution that women can make. Besides, the visible jobs are invisible ones. The most important of these is conservation. This is not limited to the salvaging of fats, tin cans and the like, important though these may be. True conservation goes much further. Despite the fact that merchandisers haven't yet learned to think war, just remember that everything your family consumes retards the war effort. Labor has been required to make it, transport it, retail it. Your money, needed for taxes and war bonds, doesn't fight the Japs when you buy personal comforts. Every luxury you purchase gives Hitler a better chance. Every can you open taxes the war machine just a little more. Try to get the idea in wartime that the resources and products of America are a common trust. This is especially true of your rubber tires, which cannot be replaced but are essential to victory. But it's true also of anything you consume. The old American ideal was abundance, and if we win, that will be our ideal again. But the new American ideal, for winning, is frugality. How much, within the limits of good health, can you do without? That's the test.

Copyright 1942 Life Inc. Reprinted with permission. All rights reserved.

"Horse Racing,"
Britannica Book of the Year, 1944:

Racing in the United States in 1943 reflected the general conditions surrounding it. The immensely increased circulation of money caused by the war effort, combined with a public living under high tension and avid for excitement, sent greater throngs of people to the racetracks than ever before. Despite the ban on pleasure driving, not relaxed until well into the summer, and in some sections, the fall, the national attendance was record-breaking, while the wagering reached figures described as "astronomical." As high as $2,926,702 was bet on a single day at one of the New York tracks, the great centre of the sport. The national total for the year approximated $700,000,000, as a result of which a taxation revenue accrued to some 15 different states of about $35,000,000. In New York alone the amount exceeded $19,000,000. This led to the distribution, in stakes and purses, of the largest amount ever raised for a single year, $18,547,635, as against the previous record of $18,136,118 in 1942.

The richest single race run was the Kentucky Derby, which netted the winner, Count Fleet, $60,725. This three-year-old colt at the close of the season was unanimously voted the "horse of the year."

"Exemptions Removed on Admissions,"
Suburbanite Economist (Chicago, Illinois), September 28, 1941:

Beginning next Wednesday, social, athletic and sporting clubs will be required to pay a federal tax of 11 percent of the dues and assessments of their members if the dues and assessments of the regular members are over $10 a year.

This is one of the new federal taxes which will become effective next Wednesday with the Revenue Act of 1941. The Revenue Act also includes new taxes on admissions, dues and cabaret charges.

Regarding club dues, the act requires that if dues are of a sufficient amount to be taxable, initiation fees of any amount are subject to a tax of 11 percent. If the dues are not taxable, the tax applies only to initiation fees of more than $10.

"Football," *Britannica Book of the Year*, 1944:

The Navy Department granted permission to its cadets in training in the colleges and universities in the U.S. to participate in varsity sports. With few exceptions, the teams were composed predominantly of such trainees in the V-12 and the V-5 programs. Intercollegiate football enjoyed a full season of play that was highly prosperous for many, although there was a general falling off in attendance of 18 percent.

The Army declined to grant such permission to its college trainees, holding that their work program was too heavy to permit them time for varsity competition. As a consequence, the great majority of the colleges with Army training units abandoned intercollegiate football for the duration of the war. . . .

A number of colleges continued to carry on as in peacetime with civilian players under the draft age or classified as IV-4. In almost every instance they suffered defeat after defeat. . . .

It was the colleges with veteran players in the Navy and Marine training units that had the strong teams. Adding to the interest in the season was the fact that many of these players were transferred to other colleges and in numerous instances competed against their former alma maters. In the middle of the season some of them were shipped to other training centres, and there were instances where a player competed against the same opponent a second time after being ordered to another college. As a consequence some teams were considerably weaker in November than they were in October, and others were strengthened by newcomers in the latter half of the season.

"The Master Billiards Player," Chip Royal, Associated Press sportswriter, Kingsport, Tennessee, January 1, 1945:

New York Sports champions may come and go, but Willie Hoppe will always be remembered as the "master" billiard player of the ages.

Willie is the mild-mannered 57-year-old wizard of the ivories who won his first world title when he was 18, defeating Maurice Vignaux in Paris.

As a matter of fact, when you mention billiards, everyone may immediately think of Hoppe. He is to the green baize world what Jack Dempsey is to boxing, Bobby Jones is to golf, Babe Ruth to baseball and Bill Tilden to tennis.

The boy wonder of caroms is still packing them in, whereas the other greats of the "terrific twenties" are only memories. Only recently Willie "played on Broadway" and they had to turn them away. He hasn't forgotten any of the table tricks.

Hoppe always smiles when he recalls the first time he came to the big town. He was only in his teens and had to stand on the box to play his shots. He was promised that, if he won, he'd get a ride in a car that carried the gay blades of little old New York through Central Park.

Somehow, in the excitement of this winning, the promise was forgotten and he hasn't had that rise!

1946 PROFILE

Bob Chaffee, always the tallest kid in class at six feet, nine inches, was a college student who witnessed firsthand a transition in both his hometown and in college basketball.

Life at Home

- Bob Chaffee would have just loved to have a normal conversation with someone.
- He was tired of "How's the weather up there?" and "What did your mother feed you that you got so tall?"
- Bob had always been tall, towering over everyone in his Rhode Island community.
- A reporter covering his high school basketball games said the 6'9″ Bob replaced Jerimoth Hill as the state's highest point.
- Even though Bob's mother came from Norwegian stock, at family reunions he was still the tallest, although some others came close.
- Bob had to sit in the very last pew at the Congregational church his family attended.
- As a result of his height, he took up interests that did not draw attention.
- He was quiet and loved to read, especially mysteries and spy stories.
- Bob read books written by Agatha Christie, Rex Stout, and Ellery Queen.
- On the radio, he listened to *The New Adventures of Sherlock Holmes*.
- He had recently seen an ad for an RCA 10-inch television set, which was retailing for $374.
- His frugal father said, "Not in this lifetime."
- His father agreed with film producer Darryl F. Zanuck, who said, "Television won't be able to hold on to any market it captures after the first six months. People will soon get tired of staring at a plywood box every night."
- In high school, Bob participated in basketball, learning to appreciate the game from his father, who learned the game as a youth at the local YMCA.
- After school, he practiced at the YMCA with friends.
- During World War II, when the basketball season was canceled, he was just one of the boys.

Bob Chaffee's height assured his success in basketball.

- With his friend Vern, Bob often sat in the tower of a local factory with binoculars looking for Japanese and German airplanes that might attack his hometown of Warwick.
- At the waning of the war, Bob was concerned that he would be drafted, but was deemed too tall for military service.
- Instead, he attended Rhode Island State College and made the basketball team.

Life at Work

- Prior to the outbreak of World War II, basketball was a game of speed, but that all changed when the military draft came along in 1941.
- Many of the nation's best players were called into service, forcing some colleges to temporarily halt their sports programs.
- Schools were often stuck with players too slow to succeed.
- Academically, Rhode Island State was an excellent school for Bob Chaffee.
- Its basketball team was known for its speed, rambling offense and lackadaisical defense.
- Bob was 11 inches taller than the school's star player, Ernie Calverley.
- Ernie was the prototype college basketball player before the war—5'10", 145 pounds, and extremely fast.
- He was dubbed the "Splendid Sprinter."
- Ernie had hopes of turning professional, maybe joining the newly founded Basketball Association of America (BAA) that would begin play later in the year.
- During the war, the average age on many pro teams was 18 and a half.
- By the time Bob was a sophomore, he acknowledged to the coach that he was having trouble adjusting to the college game.
- In high school, his smarts made him a star player, but in college, he was lumbering on the court.
- Coach Frank Keaney suggested that Bob try activities like shadow boxing to improve his agility.

Keeping up with the pace of college ball was hard work.

- Bob was a substitute player, but got a lot of playing time because Coach Keaney liked to rotate his players in order to keep them fresh.
- The team was replete with talent and sportswriters were promoting the Rhodies as potential challengers for the National Invitational Tournament or NIT, played at Madison Square Garden.
- With the war now over, school attendance was increasing and basketball was becoming more popular, thanks to some changes to the game.
- New rules eliminated a jump ball after every basket, and new coaching strategies blended quick players with tall players to block shots and shoot over smaller players.
- Bob's confidence grew as the year progressed and the coaches were adjusting to take advantage of his height.
- When NIT selection day arrived, Rhode Island State was the last of the eight teams chosen to play in the coveted tourney.
- In the NIT quarterfinals, Rhode Island State was set to play Bowling Green State.
- Throughout the game the lead rocked back and forth.
- It was the most exciting game Bob had ever played.
- Late in the game, Bowling Green State was up by two and had momentum.
- Bob took the ball and passed it to Ernie, who took a mid-court shot at the basket.
- The 55-foot shot went in and the game was tied, headed for overtime.
- Sportswriters called it, "The shot heard round the world."
- In overtime, Rhode Island State pulled out a victory, 82-79.
- Next up was Muhlenberg, which Rhode Island State easily defeated, 59-49.
- It was time for the championship game.
- Rhode Island State was set to play the Wildcats of Kentucky.
- The game was played at Madison Square Garden in New York City, with 18,475 in attendance.
- Kentucky was favored by 11.5 points, and the experts expected "Big Blue" to trounce the underdog Rams.
- Orthodox Kentucky versus unorthodox Rhode Island State appeared to be a blowout in the making.
- Coach Keaney, however, disagreed.
- After a rousing "us against the world" pre-game speech, he inspired his Rams team just before they hit the hardwood.
- At halftime, the experts were speechless as Rhode Island State led 27-26.
- Bob was playing more than usual.
- Kentucky was blending its size and speed effectively against the much smaller Rams, so Bob, as the tallest Ram, became a signature player on defense this night.
- Ernie was having one of his best games, showing that he was a true all-around team player, passing and setting up his teammates for scores.
- There would be 11 lead changes in the dramatic game, but Kentucky would pull it out in the end, with a 46-45 win.
- As Kentucky coach Adolph Rupp said, as he accepted the NIT trophy, "Who said Rhode Island had no offense? Who said Rhode Island had no defense?"
- Ernie would be named Most Valuable Player in the losing effort, ending his collegiate playing days.
- After showering, Ernie slapped Bob on the back and said, "You were instrumental in keeping us in the game."

Life in the Community: Warwick, Rhode Island

- Warwick, Rhode Island was a city on the mend.
- The once-thriving mill town was hit hard by the 1930s Depression, during which mills closed by the dozens and laid-off workers were everywhere.
- With federal aid, jobs came as schools and roads were built.
- With the war over and the economy rebounding, mills started operating again.
- Warwick was also setting its sights on the future.
- Shopping malls were being built to attract Providence residents who did not want to travel to crowded metropolitan Boston to shop.
- A child of the Depression, Bob was fascinated by department store merchandise.
- During his high school days, he had worked part-time in the stockroom of J.C. Penney and wanted to be a salesperson.
- His dad was skeptical of sales jobs, fearing that another depression could come along.
- Bob liked stocking the neckties, which sold for $1.50, and matching them to the shirts.
- T.F. Green Airport, where Bob's father worked, was trying to be an attractive alternative to Logan International in Boston.
- Begun in 1931, the airport was the first in the nation to be state owned.
- The largest airport in Rhode Island, it was renowned for maintaining schedules—something the larger Logan failed to do.

HISTORICAL SNAPSHOT
1946

- In a speech at Westminster College in Fulton, Missouri, Winston Churchill referred to communism in Europe as an "iron curtain"

- Popular songs included *The Christmas Song, Kentucky Waltz, No One To Cry To,* and *Route 66*

- Approximately 800,000 veterans were enrolled in correspondence courses through the U.S. Armed Forces Institute

- Although the federal government seized control of the railroads to prevent a strike, six days later the workers did strike, and the government relinquished control after three days

- New movies included *The Big Sleep, The Postman Always Rings Twice, Notorious, The Spiral Staircase,* and *It's a Wonderful Life*

- The League of Nations conducted its final assembly in Geneva, Switzerland, turning over assets to the United Nations

- Fifty-three percent of all college students were veterans

- Ten leading Nazis were executed in Nuremberg; Hermann Goering committed suicide two hours before his own scheduled execution

- Over 4.6 million U.S. workers went on strike seeking an 18-cent-an-hour pay raise

- Timex watches went on sale for the first time, with prices starting at $6.95

- Unemployment was 3.9 percent; the Dow Jones high was 212

- The New York Yankees became the first baseball team to travel entirely by air, signing a contract with United Airlines

- Books published included *The Catcher in the Rye, All The King's Men,* and *Animal Farm*

- Actress Rita Hayworth ignited a controversy in the movie *Gilda,* performing a scene in which she strips off arm-length gloves, causing critics and conservatives to deem the movie inappropriate for the viewing public

- Tupperware went on sale in hardware and department stores

- The first mobile car-to-car telephone conversation occurred

- Charles de Gaulle resigned as president of France

- Birth rates were up 20 percent from 1945 as 74 percent of couples had a child within their first year of marriage

- Kenny Washington signed with the Los Angeles Rams, becoming the first black National Football Player since 1933

- The electric blanket was first sold for $39.50

- The Mensa Society was created; the only qualification for an individual to join was to have an IQ in the top 98th percentile

- Percy L Spencer continued work on his recently patented invention, the microwave oven, a six-foot tall, 750-pound appliance that would sell for $5,000

Selected Prices

Aspirin, 100 Count, St. Joseph $0.35
Automobile, Cadillac $3,820
Coffee Percolator $2.95
Fishing Reel $3.79
Movie Ticket $1.10
Oil Burner $268.00
Secretarial School, per Week $1.00
Tattoo $0.25
Washing Machine, Maytag $59.95
Whiskey, Seagram's, Fifth $2.25

"Favorites Win on Free Throw in Last Seconds,"
Syracuse Post-Standard, March 21, 1946:

Ralph Beard sank a free throw with 40 seconds left in the game to give Kentucky a 46 to 45 victory over Rhode Island State in the final round of the national invitational basketball tournament in Madison Square Garden last night. . . .

Beard's one-pointer, coming after Ernie Calverley had charged him as the great Rhode Island center attempted to intercept a pass, gave the top-seeded Lexington quintet the tourney championship.

Until then, the pint-sized quintet from the smallest state in the Union put up a terrific struggle which had the final outcome of the game in doubt until the last seconds.

Holding a halftime lead of 27-26, the rough riding Rams, an 11-point underdog,

saw their slim lead vanish in the first 10 seconds of the second half, but fought back courageously against the taller opponents to regain the lead 31-30 after five minutes.

Four times in the next seven minutes, the Wildcats jumped into the lead, but on each occasion the stubborn Rhody five came back to tie and send the wild-eyed crowd of 18,475 into hysterics. . . .

Rhode Island, publicized for its racehorse style of play which throws defense to the winds, confounded the Lexington five by playing a tight defensive game. Guarding their men closely with a man-to-man defense, the Rams bottled up the Wildcats' fast-break style so completely, the Southerners were held to only nine baskets in the first half and seven in the second.

Another surprise was Calverley, whose 43 points were instrumental in winning the two previous games. Instead of letting go with those famous one handers of his, he contented himself with feeding his mates. He did this so adeptly that Dick Hole was able to sink five baskets and Al Nichols four, mainly because of Calverley's passing, and give the Rams a 27-26 lead at the half.

"Nazis, Japs Agreed to Sink U.S. Ships and Slay Crewmen," Ann Stringer, *The Asheville Times* (North Carolina), January 14, 1946:

NÜRNBERG: The war crimes tribunal heard evidence today that Germany and Japan agreed early in the war to sink U.S. merchant ships without warning to kill as many crewmen as possible, since a shortage of trained personnel would be a major American problem.

Documents were presented from Nazi naval files showing that Adolf Hitler outlined the U-boat campaign against the United States in a talk with Japanese ambassador Hiroshi Oshima soon after the outbreak of war.

An official memorandum said Hitler "hopes to put 20 to 24 U-boats in operation along the coast of the United States" in short order.

"The Fuehrer pointed out that however many ships the United States built, one of the main problems would be lack of personnel," the memorandum said. "For that reason even merchant ships should be sunk without warning with the intention of killing as many of the crew as possible.

"We are fighting for our existence, and our attitude cannot be ruled by any humane feelings. For this reason we must give an order that in no case should foreign seamen be taken prisoner."

Oshima "heartily agreed" and said Japan would be forced to follow the same methods.

"Vatican Denies Defending Axis Partners in War," *The Asheville Times* (North Carolina), January 14, 1946:

The official Vatican organ *Osservatore Romano* said today that the Moscow newspaper *Pravda* "lies" in charging that throughout the war the Vatican defended the Axis.

The *Osservatore* published a full column denial of the charges which were published recently by *Pravda*, the organ of the Communist Party. . . .

The Vatican publication took up point by point the Soviet charges that during the war the Vatican defended Fascist Italy, Nazi Germany and Japan.

The *Osservatore* denied that the pope had asked for the liberation of war criminals. It drew a distinction between political prisoners and war criminals and added: "The pope asks that prisoners of war be treated as men, even though they were conquered."

"Says Baseball in Colleges Needs Help," Harry Grayson, NEA sports editor, *The Asheville Times* (North Carolina), January 14, 1946:

The organized game would do well to work hand in glove with the American Association of College Baseball Coaches, organized to enhance the attractiveness of the sport and reinstate it in the public's affections.

It would be a good trick if they can execute it.

Some 25 years ago baseball held more importance in some schools—Holy Cross, Boston College and Fordham come to mind offhand—than football. Little St. Mary's in California was famous for its products—Harry Krause, Harry Hopper and Duffy Lewis among them—long before Slip Madigan put it on the football map. Holy Cross and Boston College once played to 40,000 spectators in a baseball game at Fenway Park.

Generally speaking, however, interesting college baseball was gradually engulfed in the glamour of the gridiron.

The dearth of grade A major-league material in more recent years can largely be traced to college football.

That is the great college game, and most youngsters will chuck baseball for it. And those men who play both games—well, men like Frank Frisch, Charley Dressen, Mickey Cochrane, Sam Chatman and Snuffy Stirnweiss—are extremely fortunate to come through football in shape to play baseball. Football takes a tremendous toll on muscle-bound mass, breaks and strains.

The college baseball coaches are going to attempt to keep the brighter baseball prospects in baseball. They might never have heard of Ty Cobb, George Sisler, Joe DiMaggio, Ted Williams and Bob Feller, for example, had they played football.

Major-league clubs have for some years strived to knock the football germ out of the heads of perspective baseball stars. The Yankees signed Joe Gordon while he was playing tailback for a high school team in Portland, Oregon, and sent him to Oregon with the stipulation that he confine his athletic activities to baseball.

The college coaches asked the ballclub to lay off their players until they have completed their education. Dick Wakefield banked $52,000 and acquired an automobile for fixing his moniker to Detroit parchment while a Michigan sophomore. . . .

The American Association of College Baseball Coaches has a tremendous job to do and can do a tremendous job for organized baseball.

"Big Expansion for Football Is Seen," *The Asheville Times* (North Carolina), January 14, 1946:

Three other professional football loops have thrown in with the National League in its war against the young All-America Conference. Regardless of how the fight comes out, it now is certain that the play-for-pay game is going to be organized on a nationwide basis. The Dixie League and American Association already back the National Association, and the Texas League is asking for information on it. The entire organization apparently is in the battle against the All-America.

What's more, the All-America now finds itself opposed in all key cities as a result of a switch Saturday night by the National League champion Cleveland Rams to Los Angeles, where the new loop was previously unopposed by the older circuit. The decision by Rams owner Danny Reeves to move his titleholders put the National League squarely against the All-America in New York, Chicago and the California city, the three top "gate" towns in the country, in the now open and all-out war for pro-grid power.

And as the National's club owners headed to the stretch of their annual meeting with schedule kinks to be ironed out and player drafts to be held, it was obvious the moguls were taking the battle a lot more seriously than they were when they first got together last week, and felt they were a lot better prepared for the brawl.

Just how seriously they are now taking the competition was obvious in the fact that they decided to keep their scheduled games and player drafts secret and were willing to make concessions to get the three minor loops into the proposed National Association of Professional Football Leagues. Following baseball's general outline, the National League moguls agreed to recognize territory rights and player contracts for the three loops and will work out plans for player exchanges and working agreements.

Speech by Winston Churchill, House of Commons, August 16, 1945:

There are those who considered that the atomic bomb should never have been used at all . . . that rather than throw this bomb we should have sacrificed a million American and a quarter of a million British lives in the desperate battles and massacres of an invasion of Japan. Future generations will judge this dire decision, I believe, if they find themselves in a happier world from which war has been banished and where freedom reigns, they will not condemn those who struggled for their benefit amid the horrors and miseries of this grim and ferocious epoch.

The bomb brought peace; man alone can keep the peace.

Nothing can stay the course of research in any country, but the construction of the immense plants necessary to transform the theory into action cannot be improvised. So far as we know, there are perhaps three or four years before the great progress in the United States can be overtaken. In those three years, we must remold relationships of all men of all nations in such a way that men did not wish, or dare, to fall upon each other for the sake of vulgar, outdated ambition, or for passionate differences in ideologies, and that international bodies by supreme authority may give peace on earth and justice among men. Our pilgrimage has brought us to a sublime moment in the history of the world.

From the least to the greatest, all must strive to be worthy of these supreme opportunities. There is not an hour to be lost; there is not a day to be lost.

Basketball Timeline

1891

At the Young Men's Christian Association (YMCA) in Springfield, Massachusetts, Dr. James Naismith created the game of Basket Ball, by attaching a peach basket (he had requested a box, but the janitor procured a basket instead) onto an elevated 10-foot track. The ball had to be retrieved after each score.

1892

The first official game was played with nine players, ending in a 1-0 decision, thanks to a 25-foot shot.

1893

The first women's game was played, with rule adaptations by Senda Berenson of Smith College. Men were forbidden to watch.

1894

The free throw line was moved from 20 feet to 15 feet.

1896

The first pro game was played in Trenton, New Jersey.

1897

Teams of five players became standard.

1898

The first professional league, the National Basketball League, was founded and folded five years later.

1906

Metal hoops with backboards replaced peach baskets.

1921

"Basket ball" became "basketball."

1926

Abe Saperstein created the Harlem Globetrotters.

1931

In Peking, China, a three-night tournament was held, drawing 70,000 fans.

1932

The International Basketball Federation was founded with eight teams; Argentina, Czechoslovakia, Greece, Italy, Latvia, Portugal, Romania, and Switzerland.

continued

Basketball Timeline . . . *(continued)*

1936
In the first Men's Olympic Basketball games, the U.S. defeated Canada 19-8 to win the gold medal.

1938
The National Invitational Tournament (NIT) was held at Madison Square Garden in New York City, with six teams invited. Long Island University won and was presented the trophy by Dr. James Naismith.

1939
The National Collegiate Athletic Association (NCAA) championship games began.

1941
The NIT expanded its invitation list to eight teams.

1943
Bob Kurland of Oklahoma State was the first seven-foot-tall player.

1946
In the first televised game, Oklahoma State won the NCAA championship.

The Basketball Association of America was founded, and for the debut game between the Toronto Huskies and the New York Knicks, the Huskies ran an advertisement promoting that any person taller than the 6′8″ player George Nostrand would receive free admission.

Most players earned $2,000 a year on a 60-game regular season schedule.

"America Reels Under Strike That Brings Threats of Hunger," *The Asheville Times* (North Carolina), May 24, 1946:

The nation was struck today by the full impact of the railroad walkout which disrupted the lives of millions, threatened their food supply and dealt commerce and industry the severest blows they ever suffered.

As the most crippling strike in the nation's history spread over the 227,000-mile network of rails, these were the major developments:

1. Millions were stranded, but some roads managed to run a few trains manned by supervisory employees and railroad officials.

2. Steel mills banked furnaces almost immediately and the flow of metal was reduced drastically.

3. Coal mines began closing again and industry spokesmen said 90 percent of bituminous production would be halted by nightfall.

4. Government authorities plan to impose a severe brownout on 21 Eastern and Midwestern states next week if the strike continues.

5. Large cities such as New York and Pittsburgh suffered shortages of fresh foods and meat almost immediately, with the prospect of almost none at all within a day or two.

6. Railroad stations, the scene of milling throngs late yesterday, were deserted today. At Chicago, trains stood in long rows in the silent sheds and yards of the nation's greatest rail center.

1948 Profile

It wasn't easy being an athletic girl, especially Jane "Jeep" Shollenberger, who could throw harder than most guys.

Life at Home

- Jane "Jeep" Shollenberger had been thrown out of half a dozen ball parks in her 17 years—for being a girl.
- Her father began teaching her to throw a baseball when she was eight, alongside two older brothers who saw no reason to coddle their little sister.
- When their father wasn't looking, her oldest brother Hank would fire baseballs at her head to make her leave the field.
- As a consequence, she became a superb defensive player.
- Her other brother would pitch baseballs to her high and inside, then tease her unmercifully if she bailed out of the batter's box to avoid the pitch.
- Jeep's only option was to hit scorching line drives back to the pitcher's mound.
- Line drives that forced her brother to jump out of the way were always a plus.
- Jeep, nicknamed for her height and ruggedness, finally landed a spot on the Industrial Softball League.
- The men didn't run her off because she was good and "they used to think I worked there," Jeep said.
- As tall as most of the men she played with, Jeep struggled to fit in.
- After a game her teammates were never sure whether to kiss her or buy her a beer.
- The war changed everything.
- Suddenly, the men were all enlisting, neighbors were preparing for an invasion and women were being told they needed to work outside the home.
- Factory work—the bane of any nice girl's plan—became respectable and patriotic.
- One day she received two important letters

Jane Shollenberger was a shoe-in for the new women's professional baseball team.

Fans came to see the women field . . .

- The first was from her brothers, who were soldiers since 1942
- The second invited Jeep to play in the All-American Girls Baseball League (AAGBL).
- America needed its morale lifted and women were the answer.
- Baseball owner P. K. Wrigley had received word from President Franklin D. Roosevelt that the 1943 Major League baseball season might be suspended due to manpower shortage.
- He wanted Wrigley to do something to keep the game of baseball going until the men got home from service.
- Athletes such as Jeep Shollenberger were needed for the war effort.
- She was thrilled!
- The newly fashioned league was to be a blend of women's softball and men's baseball.
- Wrigley joined forces with Branch Rickey and several small-town entrepreneurs to create the first professional baseball league for women.
- He used Hall of Fame players Dave Bancroft, Max Carey, and Jimmie Foxx as managers to draw interest in the league.
- That first year, in 1943, the league played a game that was a hybrid of baseball and softball.
- The ball was 12 inches in circumference, the size of a regulation softball (regulation baseballs are nine to nine and a quarter inches).
- The pitcher's mound was only 40 feet from home plate, closer even than in regulation softball and much closer than the baseball distance of 60 feet, six inches.
- Pitchers threw underhand windmill, like in softball, and the distance between bases was 65 feet, five feet longer than in softball but 25 feet shorter than in baseball.
- Major similarities between the AAGBL and baseball included nine-player teams and the use of a pitcher's mound.

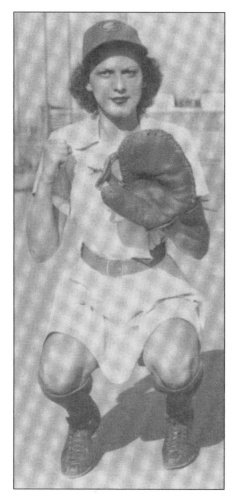

. . . catch . . .

. . . and pitch.

- Over time, the rules were gradually modified to more closely resemble baseball.
- The ball shrank from season to season, the mound was moved back to 60 feet, the base paths were extended to 85 feet and overhand pitching was allowed.
- Runners were allowed to lead off and steal.
- The new game was faster and more exciting for the fans.
- Thirty scouts were hired to find the most outstanding softball players all over the United States and Canada.
- Four teams were started in the AAGBL's first season in 1943.
- In 1944, the All-American Girls Baseball League expanded to six teams.
- Jeep was told she could earn $65 a week playing in the new league.
- She didn't hesitate and traveled by herself to try out with 200 women in Wrigley Field in Chicago.
- For a country girl from Indiana, Chicago was a wonderland of sights, particularly the Cubs' home field.
- After she made the team, she went to Helena Rubinstein classes every morning and practiced baseball every afternoon.
- As she was told repeatedly, "Mr. Wrigley wants ladies, not tomboys."
- The teams generally played in Midwestern cities and frequently moved based on attendance and ownership changes.
- The uniforms were a belted, short-sleeved tunic dress with a slight flare of the skirt.
- Rules stated that skirts were to be worn no more than six inches above the knee, a requirement Jeep routinely ignored so she could run more comfortably.
- A circular team logo sewn on the front of each dress completed the look.
- As a part of the League's "Rules of Conduct," short hair was forbidden and players were required to wear lipstick at all times.
- Fines for not following the League's rules of conduct were $5.00 for the first offense, $10.00 for the second, and suspension for the third.

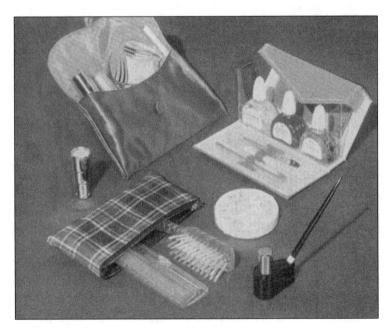

Players were required to look their best at all times.

Life at Work

- Jane "Jeep" Shollenberger's first season was a dream come true.
- She was getting paid to play ball every day.
- Her position was left field, and she was hitting .290.
- The League assigned managers, players and chaperones to teams to balance the talent and make play more competitive.
- Jeep's friends and teammates were traded in mid-season to maintain that balance.
- The regular season ran from mid-May to the first of September and the team that won the most games was declared the pennant winner.
- Jeep's team finished in the middle of the pack, but drew big crowds wherever they played.
- Jeep especially enjoyed honoring her brothers overseas before each game when the entire team lined up in a human "V" for Victory formation.
- Published records showed that the first year's attendance was 176,612 fans, and the press was uniformly amazed at how well the women played ball.
- Indeed, the role of women was changing throughout America in response to the war.
- Women by the thousands had left their homes to support the war effort by taking factory jobs, making munitions and other military machinery.
- This change in traditional attitudes toward women ushered in the acceptance of female professional ball players.
- Going to the ballpark was popular entertainment, and ballpark owners capitalized on the patriotic mood of the country by emphasizing the "All-American Girl" image.
- In effect, the players were symbols of "the girl next door" in spikes.
- The players also played exhibition games to support the Red Cross and the armed forces, and visited wounded veterans at Army hospitals.
- Season two began in Peru, Illinois, with 120 girls, and six managers.
- All League personnel were housed either at the Peru Hotel or at the St. Francis Hotel in Peru's twin city, LaSalle.
- There was access to three baseball diamonds, swimming pools and a gym and the Ruth Tiffany School was contracted to run the nightly charm school.
- The emphasis was on integrating a healthy mind and body, and included the art of walking, sitting, speaking, social skills, clothing selection and make-up application.
- Jeep was in the batting cage at spring training when she learned she had been traded to the Kenosha Comets.
- She never felt comfortable with her new team and thought about quitting, but the thought of returning to mill work kept her playing.
- By 1946, the eight teams in the League were playing 110 games per season, and Jeep was traded to the Racine Belles in Wisconsin.
- To add more excitement to the game, League rules introduced sidearm pitching, which allowed the ball to be delivered toward the batter from a different angle.
- The rule change was decimating the League, as dozens of players found the newly approved pitch impossible to hit.
- Jeep adjusted quickly and found the sidearm delivery helped her clobber more balls with authority.
- At the beginning of each season, Jeep got to know the other girls and helped select nicknames—Bird Dog, Ryecrispe, Curley, or Little Cookie—then it was down to the serious business of winning ball games and avoiding injuries.
- The schedule of 110 games per season required the teams to play single games six days a week, plus double headers on Sundays.
- The only time off was rained-out games, which were made up by playing double headers.

Each team in the League was frequently on the road, playing 110 games per season.

- Right after a game, the team boarded a bus, often arriving in a new city just in time to play the next game.
- The pay schedule was from $55.00 to $125.00 per week.
- By 1948 Jeep was one of the top paid players in the League, earning $125 weekly during the season.
- Expenses were paid by the team, including $2.25 per day for meals.
- In 1948, the League drew a record 910,000 fans for the 10-team League.
- Jeep was having a great year.
- Racine was in a race for the championship, Jeep was in a serious romance with a businessman she had met in Racine, and the major leagues were getting restaffed with quality players.
- Fans had a choice of which league to follow—men's or women's—and some sportswriters thought the women's League could survive, even if the Negro leagues were on their last legs.
- Several women were mentioned as possible players in major league baseball, igniting debates on whether men and women should play together.
- Jeep just wanted to win a championship.
- As the season came to a close she was hitting .315, playing errorless on defense and emerging as a team leader.
- Then came the marriage proposal.
- He was handsome, educated, employed at Johnson's Wax and he loved her even though she was not a traditional girl.
- In the last four games of the season Jeep hit .408 and she had won her championship.
- Within weeks Jeep and her fiance began looking for a house.

Jane's fiancee.

Jane loved her job but looked forward to buying a house and becoming a wife.

Life in the Community: Racine, Wisconsin

- Located on the edge of Lake Michigan, Racine, Wisconsin had its roots in manufacturing and shipping.
- One of the first products manufactured there was fanning mills, machines that separated wheat grain from chaff.
- In 1872 one the world's first automobiles was built there by Dr. J. W. Cathcart, as was the Pennington Victoria tricycle.
- In 1887, malted milk was invented in Racine by English immigrant William Horlick.
- The garbage disposal was invented in 1927 by architect John Hammes of Racine, who founded the company InSinkErator.
- Johnson's Wax, whose headquarters were designed in 1936 by Frank Lloyd Wright, held a large corporate presence.
- And it was home to the Racine Belles, and its live, play-by-play coverage of every home game was an innovation for the League.
- Racine was a blue collar town, ready to cheer for its blue collar team.
- Historically, women in sports were supposed to be women first, athletes second.
- Every effort was made to blend the Racine Belles into both.
- Thanks to the work ethic of the women, the play was exciting and the fans enthusiastic.
- The public liked its girls to be strong and athletic.
- The arrival of the widely publicized "athletic girl" at the turn of the twentieth century had previously brought walking, riding, motoring, cycling, and playing athletic games by women to the forefront.
- It also exposed the paradox of women's sports: how to remain feminine while being athletic.
- Ironically, it was the wealthy women of America who led the way, mostly through social and country clubs where they participated in archery, croquet, tennis and golf.
- It was generally believed that individual sports, as opposed to team sports, were less demanding and more conducive to graceful female physical movements.

- But still, upper-class women were required to show restraint when competing and usually wore full-length dresses including tight-laced corsets.
- A true lady would never consider swinging a mallet between her legs to achieve an accurate croquet shot or drive a tennis ball with an overhand slam.
- Refined sports like archery and tennis did not violate the boundary between proper women and women of other classes.
- The bicycle changed all that.
- The "wheel" allowed all women, especially the middle class, greater freedom to exercise, to ride astride the vehicle wearing shorter, more comfortable skirts, and the independence to go where they pleased.
- Basketball provided women with their next opportunity for freedom of movement and aggressive competition, emerging in the teens as most popular team sport for women.

Babe Didrikson was a sports phenomenon.

- In most cases women played on class teams or in physical education classes, although a substantial number of colleges formed varsity teams.
- By the 1920s the growth of women's athletics spawned numerous female sports heroes such as 20-year-old Sybil Bauer, who broke the men's record in the backstroke, and Gertrude Ederle, who swam the English Channel.
- Stories about female tennis stars became common in the daily sports pages of newspapers—an emerging trend in itself.
- Then came athlete extraordinare Babe Didrikson, who broke Olympic world records in five separate track and field events in the 1930s and then captured headlines as an amateur and professional golfer.
- By the 1930s working-class women discovered sports sponsored by churches, city recreation departments and industrial leagues.
- At the Hawthorne Works of the Western Electric Company in Chicago alone, 500 women participated in bowling, 127 in horseback riding and 96 in rifle shooting.
- Women's softball in particular took the nation by storm.
- In 1946 *The New York Times* estimated 600,000 women's softball teams had been formed to play before 150 million spectators.

Teams in the League were close-knit.

HISTORICAL SNAPSHOT
1948

- Warner Brothers showed the first color newsreel, selecting the Tournament of Roses Parade and the Rose Bowl
- Indian pacifist leader Mahatma Gandhi was assassinated by Nathuram Godse
- The Lions football team was purchased by a Detroit syndicate for $200,000
- The innermost moon of Uranus was discovered by Gerard Kuiper
- Dick Button became the first American to win a figure skating championship in the Olympics
- The Hells Angels motorcycle gang was founded in California
- President Harry Truman signed the Marshall Plan, officially the European Recovery Program (ERP), which authorized $5 billion in aid for 16 countries after World War II
- The 1948 Arab-Israeli War erupted
- The Berlin Blockade began
- Citation won the $117,300 Belmont Stakes to become the eighth horse to win racing's Triple Crown
- The Basketball Association of America expanded to 12 teams when four teams joined from the National Basketball League
- The Negro National League was dissolved, leaving the 10-team Negro American League as the only segregated baseball association remaining
- President Truman initiated a peacetime military draft amid increasing tensions with the Soviet Union and signed Executive Order 9981, ending racial segregation in the armed forces
- Homerun king Babe Ruth died at age 53 from throat cancer
- Heavyweight champion Joe Louis knocked out Joe Walcott in his twenty-fifth defense of his title and then retired

Selected Prices

All-American Girls Baseball Player Salary, per Week . . . . $40-$100
Baseball Player Jackie Robinson's Salary, per Year $17,500
Baseball Player Joe DiMaggio's Salary, per Year $90,000
Baseball Player Ted Williams' Salary, per Year $125,000
Deodorant $0.39
Face Cream $1.39
Hand Cream $1.50
Motorcycle Goggles $3.49
Sunglasses $6.95
Television, General Electric $189.95

OPEN UP AN **OREO** CREME SANDWICH AND TAKE A LICK!

no other chocolate cookie sandwich has the luscious creamy filling of OREO CREME SANDWICH

Nabisco loves cookies! that's why they make 'em so good!

Two mouth-melting chocolate cookies filled *lavishly* with rich vanilla fondant . . . that's an OREO CREME SANDWICH you're loving! It makes a wonderful dessert . . . a perfect between-

OREO

NATIONAL

9-419-M

It does help in times like these

All you need to do to relieve the tension of a World Series game is to ask the butcher boy for a package of

Beech-Nut GUM

"Always Refreshing"

Women's Baseball Timeline

1866
The first organized women's baseball teams in the U.S. were started at Vassar College.

1867
The Dolly Vardens of Philadelphia became the first professional black women's team.

1875
The first women's baseball game for which fans were charged and women players were paid occurred between the Blondes and the Brunettes in Springfield, Illinois.

1876
The Resolutes developed uniforms which included long-sleeved shirts with frilled high necklines, embroidered belts, wide floor-length skirts, high button shoes and broad striped caps.

1890s
Women's "Bloomer Girls" clubs, with an average of three males on them, barnstormed the U.S. and played men's town, semi-pro, and minor league teams; Rogers Hornsby, dressed as a woman, got his start with a Bloomer Girls' team.

1898
Lizzie Arlington became the first woman to sign a professional baseball contract; she signed with the Philadelphia Reserves.

1904
Amanda Clement was the first woman to be paid to umpire a baseball game.

1908
The U.S. baseball national anthem, "Take Me Out to the Ball Game," was inspired by and written about a young girl's love of the game.

1911 to 1916
The St. Louis Cardinals were owned by Helene Britton.

1920s
Philadelphia had factory teams for women, women's leagues, and the Philadelphia Bobbies for non-working women.

1928
Lizzie Murphy became the first woman to play for a major league team in an exhibition game.

1930s
Women baseball players toured internationally, played junior baseball, and signed minor league contracts.

1934
Olympic hero Babe Didrikson pitched exhibition games for the Athletics, Cardinals, and Indians.

1943
The All-American Girls Baseball League (AAGBL) was started by Philip Wrigley, owner of the Chicago Cubs and Wrigley's Chewing Gum.

1946
Sophie Kurys set the stolen base record for the AAGBL with 201 stolen bases in 203 attempts.

1947
The Racine Belles of the AAGBL started the Junior Belles baseball program; 100 girls tried out and 60 were selected to play on four teams.

1948
After five years of play, the AAGBL started throwing pitches overhand instead of underhand.

RULES OF CONDUCT

THE RULES OF CONDUCT FOR PLAYERS AS SET UP BY THE ALL-AMERICAN GIRLS PROFESSIONAL BASEBALL LEAGUE

THE MANAGEMENT SETS A HIGH STANDARD FOR THE GIRLS SELECTED FOR THE DIFFERENT CLUBS AND EXPECTS THEM TO LIVE UP TO THE CODE OF CONDUCT WHICH RECOGNIZES THAT STANDARD. THERE ARE GENERAL REGULATIONS NECESSARY AS A MEANS OF MAINTAINING ORDER AND ORGANIZING CLUBS INTO A WORKING PROCEDURE.

1. Always appear in feminine attire when not actively engaged in practice or playing ball. This regulation continues through the playoffs for all, even though your team is not participating. At no time may a player appear in the stands in her uniform, or wear slacks or shorts in public.

2. Boyish bobs are not permissible and in general your hair should be well groomed at all times with longer hair preferable to short hair cuts. Lipstick should always be on.

3. Smoking or drinking is not permissible in public places. Liquor drinking will not be permissible under any circumstances. Other intoxicating drinks in limited portions with after-game meal only, will be allowed. Obscene language will not be allowed at any time.

4. All social engagements must be approved by chaperone. Legitimate requests for dates can be allowed by chaperones.

5. Jewelry must not be worn during game or practice, regardless of type.

6. All living quarters and eating places must be approved by the chaperones. No player shall change her residence without the permission of the chaperone.

7. For emergency purposes, it is necessary that you leave notice of your whereabouts and your home phone.

8. Each club will establish a satisfactory place to eat, and a time when all members must be in their individual rooms. In general, the lapse of time will be two hours after the finish of the last game, but in no case later than 12:30 a.m. Players must respect hotel regulations as to other guests after this hour, maintaining conduct in accordance with high standards set by the League.

9. Always carry your employee's pass as a means of identification for entering the various parks. This pass is NOT transferable.

10. Relatives, friends, and visitors are not allowed on the bench at any time.

11. Due to shortage of equipment, baseballs must not be given as souvenirs without permission from the Management.

12. Baseball uniform skirts shall not be shorter than six inches above the knee-cap.

continued

RULES OF CONDUCT . . . *(continued)*

13. In order to sustain the complete spirit of rivalry between clubs, the members of different clubs must not fraternize at any time during the season. After the opening day of the season, fraternizing will be subject to heavy penalties. This also means in particular; room parties, auto trips to out of the way eating places, etc. However, friendly discussions in lobbies with opposing players are permissible. Players should never approach the opposing manager or chaperone about being transferred.

14. When traveling, the members of the clubs must be at the station thirty minutes before departure time. Anyone missing her arranged transportation will have to pay her own fare.

15. Players will not be allowed to drive their cars past their city's limits without the special permission of their manager. Each team will travel as a unit via method of travel provided for the League.

FINES OF FIVE DOLLARS FOR FIRST OFFENSE, TEN DOLLARS FOR SECOND, AND SUSPENSION FOR THIRD, WILL AUTOMATICALLY BE IMPOSED FOR BREAKING ANY OF THE ABOVE RULES.

CHARM SCHOOL

FOREWORD

When you become a player in the All-American Girls Baseball League you have reached the highest position that a girl can attain in this sport. The All-American Girls Baseball League is getting great public attention because it is pioneering a new sport for women.

You have certain responsibilities because you, too, are in the limelight. Your actions and appearance both on and off the field reflect on the whole profession. It is not only your duty to do your best to hold up the standard of this profession but to do your level best to keep others in line.

The girls in our League are rapidly becoming the heroines of youngsters as well as grownups all over the world. People want to be able to respect their heroines at all times. The All-American Girls Baseball League is attempting to establish a high standard that will make you proud that you are a player in years to come.

We hand you this manual to help guide you in your personal appearance. We ask you to follow the rules of behavior for your own good as well as that of the future success of girls' baseball.

In these few pages you will find many of the simple and brief suggestions which should prove useful to you during the busy baseball season. If you plan your days to establish an easy and simple routine, so that your meals are regular and well balanced, so that you have time for outside play and relaxation, so that you sleep at least eight hours each night and so that your normal functions are regular, you will be on the alert, do your job well and gain the greatest joy from living. Always remember that your mind and your body are interrelated and you cannot neglect one without causing the other to suffer. A healthy mind and a healthy body are the true attributes of the All-American girl.

BEAUTY ROUTINES

Your ALL-AMERICAN GIRLS BASEBALL LEAGUE BEAUTY KIT should always contain the following:

Cleansing Cream	Mild Astringent
Lipstick	Face Powder for Brunette
Rouge Medium	Hand Lotion
Cream Deodorant	Hair Remover

You should be the best judge of your own beauty requirements. Keep your own kit replenished with the things you need for your own toilette and your beauty culture and care. Remember the skin, the hair, the teeth and the eyes. It is most desirable in your own interests, that of your teammates and fellow players, as well as from the standpoint of the public relations of the League that each girl be at all times presentable and attractive, whether on the playing field or at leisure. Study your own beauty culture possibilities and without overdoing your beauty treatment at the risk of attaining gaudiness, practice the little measures that will reflect well on your appearance and personality as a real All-American girl.

I. SUGGESTED BEAUTY ROUTINE
"After the Game"
Remember, the All-American girl is subjected to greater exposure through her activities on the diamond, through exertion in greater body warmth and perspiration, through exposure to dirt, grime and dust and through vigorous play to scratches, cuts, abrasions and sprains. This means extra precaution to assure all the niceties of toilette and personality. Especially "after the game," the All-American girl should take time to observe the necessary beauty ritual, to protect both her health and appearance. Here are a few simple rules that should prove helpful and healthful "after the game."

1. Shower well and soap the skin.
2. Dry thoroughly to avoid chapping or chafing.
3. Apply cleansing cream to face; remove with tissue.
4. Wash face with soap and water.
5. Apply skin astringent.
6. Apply rouge moderately but carefully.
7. Apply lipstick with moderate taste.
8. Apply eye makeup if considered desirable.
9. Apply powder.
10. Check all cuts, abrasions or minor injuries.

If you suffer any skin abrasion or injury, or if you discern any aches or pains that do not appear to be normal, report them at once to your coach/chaperone or the person responsible for treatment and first aid. Don't laugh off slight ailments as trivialities because they can often develop into serious infections or troublesome conditions that can handicap your play and cause personal inconvenience. See that your injuries, however slight, receive immediate attention. Guard your health and welfare.

continued

BEAUTY ROUTINES . . . *(continued)*

II. ADDITIONAL BEAUTY ROUTINE
"Morning and Night"

In the morning, when you have more time to attend to your beauty needs, you will undoubtedly be enabled to perform a more thorough job. Use your cleansing cream around your neck as well as over the face. Remove it completely and apply a second time to be sure that you remove all dust, grease and grime. Wipe off thoroughly with cleansing tissue. Apply a lotion to keep your hands as lovely as possible. Use your manicure set to preserve your nails in a presentable condition and in keeping with the practical needs of your hands in playing ball.

A. TEETH

Not a great deal need be said about the teeth, because every All-American girl instinctively recognizes their importance to her health, her appearance and her personality. There are many good tooth cleansing preparations on the market and they should be used regularly to keep the teeth and gums clean and healthy. A regular visit to a reliable dentist is recommended and certainly no tooth ailment should be neglected for a moment.

B. BODY

Unwanted or superficial hair is often quite common and it is no problem to cope with in these days when so many beauty preparations are available. If your have such hair on arms or legs, there are a number of methods by which it can be easily removed. There is an odorless liquid cream which can be applied in a few moments, permitted to dry and then showered off.

C. DEODORANTS

There are a number of very fine deodorants on the market which can be used freely all over the body. The most important feature of some of these products is the fact that the fragrance stays perspiration proof all day long. These deodorants can be used especially where excess perspiration occurs and can be used safely and effectively without retarding natural perspiration. The All-American girl is naturally susceptible because of her vigorous activities and it certainly pays dividends to be on the safe side. Deodorant keeps you fresh and gives you assurance and confidence in your social contacts.

D. EYES
"The Eyes Are the Windows of the Soul"

The eyes indicate your physical fitness and therefore need your thoughtful attention and care. They bespeak your innermost thoughts; they reflect your own joy of living or they can sometimes falsely bespeak the listlessness of mind and body. Perhaps no other feature of your face has more to do with the impression of beauty, sparkle and personality which you portray.

A simple little exercise for the eyes and one which does not take much time can do much to strengthen your eyes and add to their sparkle and allure. Turn your eyes to the corner of the room for a short space of time, then change to the other corner, then gaze at the ceiling and at the floor alternately. Rotating or rolling your eyes constitutes an exercise and your eyes will repay you for the attention that you give to them. There are also vitamins prescribed for the care of the eyes. Drink plenty of water and eat plenty of vegetables. We all know well that the armed forces found carrots a definite dietary aid to eyesight. Use a good eyewash frequently and for complete relaxation at opportune moments, lie down and apply an eye pad to your eyes for several minutes.

continued

BEAUTY ROUTINES . . . *(continued)*

E. HAIR

"Woman's Crowning Glory"

One of the most noticeable attributes of a girl is her hair, woman's crowning glory. No matter the features, the clothes, the inner charm or personality, they can all suffer beneath a sloppy or stringy coiffure. Neither is it necessary to feature a fancy or extravagant hairdo, because a daily program for the hair will help to keep it in healthful and attractive condition.

Neatness is the first and greatest requirement. Arrange your hair neatly in a manner that will best retain its natural style despite vigorous play. Off the diamond, you can readily arrange it in a softer and more feminine style, if you wish. But above all, keep your hair as neat as possible, on or off the field.

Brushing the hair will help a great deal more than is realized. It helps to stimulate the scalp which is the source of healthful hair growth. It develops the natural beauty and luster of the hair. And it will not spoil the hairdo. When brushing, bend over and let your head hang down. Then brush your hair downward until the scalp tingles. Just a few minutes of this treatment each day will tend to keep your scalp in fine condition and enhance the beauty of your "crowning glory."

F. MOUTH

Every woman wants to have an attractive and pleasing mouth. As you speak, people watch your mouth and you can do much, with a few of the very simplest tools, to make your mouth invitingly bespeak your personality. Your beauty aids should, of course, include an appropriate type of lipstick and a brush. They should be selected with consideration and care. With your lipstick, apply two curves to your upper lip. Press your lips together. Then, run your brush over the lipstick and apply it to your lips, outlining them smoothly. This is the artistic part of the treatment in creating a lovely mouth.

Patient practice and care make perfect. Open your mouth and outline your own natural curves. If your lips are too thin to please you, shape them into fuller curves. Now, use a tissue between your lips and press lightly to take off excess lipstick. If you wish to have a "firmer foundation," use the lipstick a second time and use the tissue "press" again.

Caution: Now that you have completed the job, be sure that the lipstick has not smeared your teeth. Your mirror will tell the tale and it is those little final touches that really count.

G. HANDS

The hands are certainly among the most expressive accouterments of the body; they are always prominent and noticeable and while feminine hands can be lovely and lily white, as described in the ads, the All-American girl has to exercise practical good sense in preserving the hands that serve her so faithfully and well in her activities. Cleanliness and neatness again come to the fore. Your hands should be thoroughly cleaned and washed as frequently as seems desirable or necessary, and especially after games, they should be cleaned to remove all dust and grime. Soap and water and pumice will do this job to perfection. Then a protective cream should be applied to keep hands soft and pliable and to avoid cracks and overdryness. Your nails should be gone over lightly each day, filing to prevent cracks and splits, oiling for the cuticle.

The length of your nails, of course, depends largely upon the requirements of your play. Keep them neat and clean and your hands will always be attractive.

continued

BEAUTY ROUTINES . . . *(continued)*

H. FACE

"All Beauty Comes from Within"

To the All-American girl, who is exposed to the elements, to the sun, to the wind and to the dust, it is most essential that every precaution be taken for the care of the skin. It should be covered with a protective substance of cream or liquid, depending entirely upon whether your skin is dry or oily. If it is dry, the cream type is recommended and if it is oily, you should use the liquid type. A good cleansing cream can serve as a cleanser, a powder base, a night cream and also a hand lotion. It is a good idea to have such an allaround utility cream on hand at all times and to use it regularly for these purposes.

I. FOR YOUR COLORING

It depends on your particular complexion and whether you have an abundance of natural color tones or need very little coloring. You can determine this in keeping with good taste to acquire the necessary results. People who are naturally pale, of course, need the coloring to help their complexion

III. CLOTHES

Clothes, of course, have always been one of woman's great problems and it might seem so to the All-American girl. However, with the exercising of good taste, the All-American Girls Baseball League player can solve her problem in a tasteful manner and without great expense, without being encumbered with too great a wardrobe for the summer months. The accent, of course, is on neatness and feminine appeal. That is true of appearances on the playing field, on the street or in leisure moments. The uniforms adopted by the League have been designed for style and appeal and there is a tremendous advantage to the girl and to the team which makes the best of its equipment.

From the standpoint of team morale, there is a real "lift" noticeable in the smartly turned out and neatly arrayed aggregation. And from the public appeal standpoint, it is surprising how the crowd will respond to the team that appears on the field with a neatness and "snap" in its appearance. The smart-looking teams invariably play smart ball and you can add to your own drawing power and crowd appeal by looking the part of a ball player on the field. Wear your cap and keep it securely in place. Keep your uniform as clean and neat as possible. Always secure your stockings so that they are smooth and neat and remain in place. Keep your shoes clean and shining. And see if you don't feel better and play better ball.

VICTORY SONG
co-written by La Vonne Paire-Davis and Nalda Phillips

Batter up! Hear that call!
The time has come for one and all
To play ball. For we're the members of the All-American League,
We come from cities near and far.
We've got Canadians, Irishmen and Swedes,
We're all for one, we're one for all,
We're All-American.

Each girl stands, her head so proudly high,
Her motto Do Or Die.
She's not the one to use or need an alibi.
Our chaperones are not too soft,
They're not too tough,
Our managers are on the ball.
We've got a president who really knows his stuff,
We're all for one, we're one for all,
We're All-Americans!

All-American Girls Baseball League, 1948 Results

Eastern Division
Grand Rapids Chicks (77-47)
Muskegon Lassies (66-57)
South Bend Blue Sox (57-69)
Fort Wayne Daisies (53-72)
Chicago Colleens (47-76)

Western Division
Racine Belles (76-49)
Rockford Peaches (74-49)
Peoria Redwings (70-55)
Kenosha Comets (61-64)
Springfield Sallies (41-84)
Play-off Champions: Rockford Peaches

1949 NEWS FEATURE

"The Sideline, A Department for Sports Fans Conducted by Cap Fanning,"
Thrilling Sports, **Spring 1949:**

College football had its biggest season in 1948. It got more publicity and drew more customers to more games than ever before in the eighty-year history of the sport. It also produced a couple of headaches whose potential trouble for players, coaches and rulemakers looms currently like a gargantuan duodenal ulcer.

These headaches in their alphabetical order are 1) pass interference penalty, and 2) the unlimited substitution.

Currently, if the receiver of a forward pass is interfered with physically by one or more defenders, the pass is considered completed at the spot where the interference occurred. If such interference takes place in the end zone the ball is placed on the defender's three-yard line in the possession of the passing team.

The rules made for two highly laudable purposes 1) prevent injury to a player who, intent upon catching the ball might be wide open for a serious spill, and 2) to open up the game by preventing the defense from making the forward pass overdangerous.

It seems to us that assumption of a pass completion merely because the receiver was jolted out of the play is assuming a great deal too much. We have seen entirely too many butterfingered eligibles drop perfectly thrown balls which were right in their grasp. Every football fan has seen the same thing happen again and again—and the more crucial the spot and the greater the pressure upon the receiver, the more apt it is to occur.

What such a referee's completion of a long pass can do to a game or season is something for the sports pages to ponder—and a great many of them have been giving it serious thought. Havoc is a weak word for what he can do to a team in the progress of a tight game. . . .

A thoroughly beaten team, making wild last-minute throws, may find an unearned touchdown in its grasp due to the call in such penalty. Fear of such penalties is one of the causes of the lamentable weakness in pass defense shown during the season just passed.

It is our idea that the penalty should be one of 10 or 15 yards from the line of scrimmage.

This would ensure the team whose pass suffered interference a first down. And, like other such penalties, it would not break up the game for the defense. . . .

As for the other bane in the modern game—unlimited substitutions—its evils and cure are at least as easy to spot diagnosis and cure. Already many coaches, notably General Neyland of Tennessee, are howling against the changes it has wrought to the game.

Most frequently assailed of these is the fact that it has made football a game of specialists. You can no longer call the player of a top-ranking college team a football player. He is today "one of the offense of team" or "on the defense." And in some cases there is even further subdivisions of talent.

As General Neyland recently complained to Grantland Rice, famed sports columnist and picker of all American teams, "How the h--l do you pick an all-star team anymore when none of your players can play the whole game of football?"

The General went on to point out further that only ten percent of the colleges in the country had the manpower to substitute entire teams for attack or defense and that the ruling, instead of allowing low-manpower teams to give their stars more rest, actually increased the disparity between big and small college squads. We think he had something there.

In the old days, of course, there were no substitutions. If a player was hurt, his mates, as in rugby, carried on a man short. Then, for years, a player was allowed to return for the second half after retiring for a substitute in the first. And then this was doubled, permitting the player to enter the same half twice. . . .

It would have been simple to keep the game a contest despite disparities in the numbers of squads had the big shots suggested, instead of unlimited substitutions, a limit on the number of players in the team could use in a game. To our way of thinking twenty-five would be about right. With this number a team would be two deep in every position and have a trio of spares left over.

Such a limitation would not only ease up the cutthroat competition for squad membership at these universities who offer the most liberal athletic scholarships but would result in a better spread of talent throughout the country. And it would save the poor ticket-buying spectator from having to witness many a dreary one-sided rout!

1950–1959

When the decade of the 1950s began, the most significant sports in America were major league baseball and collegiate football. By the end of the decade the National Football League was a major force, the National Basketball Association was stable and attracting rabid fans and the Professional Golf Association was inspiring weekend golfers to join "Arnie's Army" on the golf course. Athletics was viewed as an effective counterweight to the threat of godless communism for a nation in the midst of a Cold War. Participation in Little League Baseball, Pop Warner football, and Biddy Basketball rose dramatically for boys. For girls many of the gains of the 1940s were swept away in a newfound belief that girls could not directly benefit from sports participation.

The 1950s also ushered in the power of television. Fewer than one million families owned television sets in 1949; by 1953 the figure was 20 million; by 1955 two-thirds of all American households owned a television set. And by 1960, 90 percent of American households had a television set. Boxing and baseball became staples of the three available channels. While the Yankees dominated in baseball, winning five straight World Series, the Boston Celtics dominated the National Basketball Association with a run of 11 titles in 13 years, including eight in a row. When the decade began, the West Coast boasted no major league professional teams. Ten years later the Dodgers and Giants were playing baseball in California, along with the Rams and the 49ers in football and the Lakers in basketball.

The consequences of World War II were everywhere in the decade of the 1950s: a population eagerly on the move, industries infused with energy and confidence, plans for interstate highways, hydroelectric dams to power America, a plethora of new national brands made for Americans. As the decade progressed, much of America's energy was focused on family. Television programs that educated and toys that expanded creativity were in vogue. Family travel was considered a necessity and college a definite possibility. Health insurance was common and everyone knew someone who owned a television set. As a result of World War II, the economies of Europe and Asia lay in ruins, while America's industrial structure was untouched and well oiled to supply the needs of a war-weary world.

In addition, the war years' high employment and optimism spurred the longest sustained period of peacetime prosperity in the nation's history. A decade full of employment and pent-up material desires produced demands for all types of consumer goods. Businesses of all sizes prospered. During the 1950s, an average of seven million cars and trucks were sold annually. By 1952, two-thirds of all families owned a television set. Specialized markets developed to meet the demand of consumers such as amateur photographers, pet lovers and backpackers. Shopping malls, supermarkets and credit cards emerged as important economic forces.

This prosperity also ushered in conservative politics and social conformity. The planned community of Levittown, New York, mandated that grass be cut at least once a week and laundry washed on specific days. Divorce rates and female college attendance fell while birth rates and the sales of Bibles rose. Corporate America promoted the benefits of respectable men in gray flannel suits whose wives remained at home to tend house and raise children. Suburban life included ladies' club memberships, chauffeuring children to piano classes, and a newly marketed product known as tranquilizers.

The average wage earner benefited more from the booming industrial system than at any time in American history. In offices, many workers were becoming accustomed to a 35-hour week. Health benefits for workers became more common and paid vacations were standard in most industries. In 1959, 40 percent of American wives worked outside the home. Communications technology, expanding roads and inexpensive airline tickets meant that people and commerce were no longer prisoners of distance. Unfortunately, up to one-third of the population lived below the government's poverty level, largely overlooked in the midst of this prosperity.

The Civil Rights Movement was propelled by two momentous events in the 1950s. The first was a decree on May 17, 1954, by the U.S. Supreme Court which ruled that "in the field of public education the doctrine of 'separate but equal' has no place. Separate educational facilities are inherently unequal." The message was electric but the pace was slow. Few schools would be integrated for another decade. The second event established the momentum of the Civil Rights Movement. On December 1, 1955, African American activist Rosa Parks refused to vacate the white-only front section of a Montgomery, Alabama bus, leading to her arrest and a citywide bus boycott by blacks. Their spokesman became Martin Luther King, Jr., the 26-year-old pastor of the Dexter Avenue Baptist Church. The yearlong boycott was the first step toward the passage of the Civil Rights Act of 1964.

America's youths were enchanted by the TV adventures of *Leave It to Beaver*, Westerns, and *Father Knows Best*. TV dinners were invented; felt skirts with sequined poodle appliqués were the rage; Elvis Presley was worshipped, and the new phenomena of *Playboy* and Mickey Spillane fiction were created, only to be read behind closed doors. Sexual jargon such as "first base" and "home run" entered the language. Learned-When-Sleeping machines appeared, along with Smokey the Bear, Sony tape recorders, adjustable shower heads, newspaper vending machines and Levi's faded blue denims. Ultimately, the real stars of the era were the Salk and Sabin vaccines, which vanquished the siege of polio.

1952 PROFILE

Following in the footsteps of his hero, Jesse Owens, Harrison Dillard overcame the hurdles, literally and figuratively, to win four gold medals.

Life at Home

- At the age of 13, Harrison Dillard gathered with his family around the radio to listen to the 1936 Summer Olympic Games broadcast from Berlin.
- Harrison was especially interested in track and field and the African American superstar, Jesse Owens.
- Owens was a local hero in Harrison's hometown of Cleveland, Ohio.
- Harrison even attended the same high school as Owens, East Tech.
- Jesse Owens was already adored in the black community for his amazing achievements in sports.
- As Owens wowed the Berlin audience and the world press, he shattered the ideal promoted by Adolph Hitler in Germany.
- Hitler had planned to use the games to show the world a resurgent Nazi Germany.
- He believed that German domination of the games would reinforce Nazi propaganda that promoted "Aryan racial superiority" and depicted ethnic Africans as inferior.
- Owens spoiled this plan by winning four gold medals: 100 meter sprint; long jump; 200 meter sprint; and 4 × 100 meter relay.
- After he attended a parade in Cleveland honoring Jesse Owens, Harrison vowed to work harder at becoming faster and stronger.
- Summers came to mean more than just fun, ice cream and fireworks.
- In baseball, he showed his speed and athleticism by constantly stealing bases.
- In track, Harrison got serious about hurdling, a skill he began practicing at 8 years old.

Harrison Dillard worked hard to be like his hero Jessie Owens.

Jesse Owens ran through the same Cleveland streets as Harrison.

- He would practice hurdling using springs from car seats taken from abandoned vehicles.
- Rising at five o'clock, Harrison ran every morning through the quiet streets of Cleveland.
- He ran through his poor neighborhood, encouraged by knowing that Jesse Owens had overcome this tough environment.
- He also knew black athletes had to work harder to succeed— even the great Jesse Owens.
- Jim Crow, state and local racial segregation laws enacted between 1876 and 1965, was still alive and well in many parts of America.
- After a post-Olympic New York ticker-tape parade in his honor, Jesse Owens had to ride the freight elevator to attend his own reception at the Waldorf-Astoria.
- Harrison felt he was blessed to work with Charles Riley, Jesse's old coach, and learn the same way Jesse did.
- In high school, hurdles became his specialty, and he won 82 consecutive events.
- He started Baldwin-Wallace College in Beretha, Ohio, and was drafted two years later, serving in the military until 1946.
- After leaving the military, he tried to qualify for the 1948 Olympics, but came up short in the hurdles.
- He was, however, chosen as a member of the 1948 USA Olympic relay team, which captured a gold.
- Harrison kept at his training and tried again to quality for the hurdle event in the 1952 games in Helsinki, Finland.
- At 5′10″ and 152 pounds, he was considered frail for the Olympics, and was nicknamed "Bones."

Americans had high hopes for track and field.

Life at Work

- As the 1952 Olympics in Helsinki approached, Harrison Dillard was determined to erase the memory of his failure to qualify for the hurdles in the 1948 Olympics.
- His coach pushed hard, putting Harrison through the paces making every step and jump automatic and it payed off when Harrison qualified.
- Helsinki had beaten out Los Angeles, Philadelphia, Detroit, Minneapolis, Amsterdam and Chicago for the opportunity to host the games.
- The Finns were very hospitable, living up to their motto, "You First."
- Some thought so highly of the Finnish nation that there was support to make Helsinki the Olympic destination for all time.
- In all, 5,678 athletes, representing 69 nations, were on hand to participate in 43 events in 19 sports.
- Quivering with anticipation, Harrison lined up, waiting for the starter pistol to fire.
- At the sound of the shot, he came up out of his position and raced down the track.
- He leaped over the hurdles ahead of everyone and managed the 110 meters of the race with grace and fortitude.
- "Bones" crossed the finish line to win the gold, with vociferous cries from the Helsinki crowd.
- The race was a sweep for the U.S., with Jack Davis and Arthur Barnard winning the silver and the bronze, respectively.
- The usually reserved Harrison leaped with joy and exclaimed, "Good things come to those who wait!"
- His Olympics were not over, for he still had the 4 × 100 meter relay.
- The Soviet team was considered a fierce competitor, but Harrison was confident, having been a part of the 1948 gold medal winning team.

Harrison felt a rush as he closed in for the gold.

The Finns' hospitality during the Olympics was welcomed.

Olympians didn't concern themselves with politics.

- Harrison was running the second leg of the relay.
- He took the baton in his left hand from Dean Smith, who carried it in his right.
- Harrison was behind both USSR's Levan Kalyeyev and Hungary's Geza Varasdi.
- He overtook them easily, hearing only the quick, padded slap of his feet on the track and the beating of his heart within his chest.
- He breathed deeply as he rounded the track to make the transfer of the baton to Lindy Remigino's right hand.
- He made the smooth transfer and watched his teammate run ahead of the crowd.
- The seconds seemed like an eternity as the last exchange was made.
- As his teammate crossed the finish line to win the gold, white and black American athletes hugged and celebrated together.
- Harrison had become the first man ever to win Olympic gold medals in both the sprints and the high hurdles.

Life in Community: Helsinki, Finland

- Helsinki, Finland, was originally awarded the 1940 Olympic Games, but due to World War II, the games were canceled and Helsinki was awarded the honor of hosting the 1952 games.
- Germany and Japan, both denied participation in the 1948 games as aggressor nations, were permitted to compete in 1952.
- Much controversy revolved around the USSR, which emerged after World War II as an American foe in the Cold War.
- The media and politicians were obsessed with the potential controversy, wondering what the reaction of the athletes might be in this atmosphere.
- Harrison wasn't worried.
- Having participated in the 1948 games, he knew athletes were not about politics or even ethnicity.
- As an African American athlete, Harrison learned in 1948 that most of the athletes put aside race and worked as a team and a community.
- Athletes from the USSR invited other Olympians to a pre-games party, serving caviar and other fine foods.
- Harrison and his fellow Americans were not interested in Capitalists versus Communists, just being the best athletes they could be.
- The new Russian team felt the same.
- The games brought out goodwill and sportsmanship among the athletes, and Harrison was glad to rise above the political intrigue.
- Not only was there Germany, Japan, and the USSR to create headlines, but also, for the first time ever, Israel was represented.

HISTORICAL SNAPSHOT
1952

- The Federal Reserve Board voted to dissolve the A.P. Giannini banking empire, headed by Transamerica Corporation, which controlled the nation's largest bank, Bank of America
- Popular movies included *High Noon, The Greatest Show on Earth,* and *The African Queen*
- The Metropolitan Opera in New York began charging $8.00 for an evening performance and $30 per seat on opening night
- Books published included *Invisible Man, East of Eden, The Natural, The Old Man and the Sea,* and *Charlotte's Web*
- Vice Presidential candidate Richard M. Nixon declared he was not a quitter in his famous "Checkers" speech
- Jonah Salk at the University of Pennsylvania began testing a vaccine against polio
- W. F. Libby of the University of Chicago dated Stonehenge in England to about 1842 BC

- Reports circulated that the U.S. had exploded a hydrogen bomb
- The transistor radio was introduced by Sony
- Songs included "Walking My Baby Back Home," "Wheel of Fortune," and "Glow Worm"
- Nationwide, 55,000 people were stricken with polio, an all-time high
- The New Revised Standard Version of the Holy Bible was published
- The U.S. Air Force reported 60 UFO sightings in two weeks
- President Harry Truman ordered the seizure of the nation's $7 billion steel industry to prevent a walkout of 650,000 workers; the Supreme Court ruled the move unconstitutional
- *The Today Show* premiered on NBC-TV
- Edward Mills Purcell and Felix Bloch won the Nobel prize in physics for work in the measurement of magnetic fields in atomic nuclei

- The average house cost $9,050
- *Mad Magazine* was introduced, with a circulation of 195,000; 55 percent of college students and 43 percent of high school students voted it their favorite periodical
- Products making their first appearance included the 16 mm home movie projector, two-way car radios, adjustable showerheads, bowling alleys with automatic pin boys and Kellogg's Sugar Frosted Flakes
- Fifty-two million automobiles were on the highways, up from 25 million in 1945
- Thirty-seven-year-old Jersey Joe Walcott knocked out Ezzard Charles to become the oldest heavyweight boxing champion at 37
- An all-white jury in North Carolina convicted a black man for assault, for leering at a white woman 75 feet away

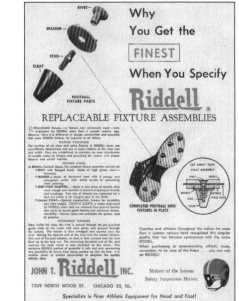

Olympics Timeline

1892

Baron Pierre de Fredi called for a rebirth of the Olympic Games, saying, "It is clear that the telegraph, the railways, the telephone, passionate scientific research, the congresses and exhibitions have done more for peace than any diplomatic convention. Well, I hope athleticism will do even more."

1896

The first games were held in Athens, Greece, with 14 nations participating in nine sports with 245 athletes (all male). Every winner received a silver medal and an olive branch.

1900

In Paris, women competed in four of the 20 sports, including lawn tennis, in which the ladies played wearing hats and long dresses.

1904

The Olympics were held outside of Europe, as St. Louis, Missouri, hosted the games; the low point came when an exposition was mounted to show the inferiority of African Americans and Native Americans.

For the first time, gold, silver, and bronze medals were awarded to the top three contestants.

1912

New technologies included electronic timing devices, photo finishes, and loudspeakers.

1916

No Olympic Games were held, as Berlin, the city awarded the site, was at war.

1920

The oldest medal winner in Olympic history was Sweden's 72-year-old Oscar Swahn, who won the gold in the double shot running deer event.

1924

The Olympic motto, "Citius, Altius, Fortius" (Swifter, Higher, Stronger), was introduced as France became the first nation to host the games twice.

1932

In order to finance their visit to Los Angeles, Brazilians traveled with a cargo of coffee that was sold along the way.

American Peter Mehringer won the gold medal in freestyle wrestling, having learned the sport through a correspondence course.

The Olympics made a profit for the first time, nearly $1 million.

1936

The Berlin Games, intended to be a showcase for Hitler's ideal man, were overshadowed by African American athletes led by Jesse Owens.

continued

Olympics Timeline . . . *(continued)*

1940, 1944
The games were suspended due to World War II.

1948
The Olympics were televised for the first time.

The first political defection occurred when Marie Provaznikova refused to return to Czechoslovakia.

1952
Bill Havens, who declined an Olympic invitation in 1924 for rowing because of his wife being pregnant with their first son, watched his son, Frank, win the gold medal in singles canoeing.

Records Held by Harrison Dillard
World Record: 120 yd. hurdles—13.60 (April 17, 1948-)
Olympic Record: 100 m—10.30 (July 31, 1948-)

Championships
1948 Olympics: 100 m—10.30 (First)
1948 Olympics: 400 m relay (First)
1952 Olympics: 110 m hurdles—13.70 (First)
1952 Olympics: 400 m relay (First)
1947 AAU: 60 yd. hurdles (First)
1948 AAU: 60 yd. hurdles (First)
1949 AAU: 60 yd. hurdles (First)
1950 AAU: 60 yd. hurdles (First)
1951 AAU: 60 yd. hurdles (First)
1952 AAU: 60 yd. hurdles (First)

"America's Speed Classic," H. Wieand Bowman,
Auto Sport Review, April, 1952:

This year will mark the 36th running of the International Sweepstakes at Indianapolis. In an area 13 times as large as the famous Circus Maximus of Rome, 33 cars will try to make 200 circuits of the rectangle track surface at near peak speed. That probably no more than a dozen will complete the entire distance is a foregone conclusion.

Few of the 175,000 or more fans expected to attend this year's go will remember the first "500" run back in 1911 or the number 32 Marmon which carried ex-ribbon clerk Ray Harroun the distance at 74.59 mph average. Ray won a $14,250 b.t. purse for his efforts. And before taxes 14 grand plus with the best steak in town at four bits wasn't just so much mown grass.

Since 1911 a limited few racers have been paid altogether more than two and a half-million dollars in purse and lap monies for their attempts to win the big one. Even with taxes, that ain't hay.

Few spectators on Memorial Day, 1952, would know many of the makes of cars that were entered in the three-day race back on August 19, 1911, when the track was surfaced with oiled dirt. Bob Burman won that first main event, a 250-miler, in slightly more than four and a half hours. His winning car was a Buick pitted against a field comprising three Buicks, a Knox, two Nationals, a Jackson and two Stoddard-Daytons. But the first race ever run at the Speedway was a five-miler earlier that same day, and the winning car was a Stoddard-Dayton.

During the inaugural meet—curtailed after accidents had taken a death toll of a driver, two mechanics and two spectators—Barney Oldfield in a German Benz smashed world records for five-, 10-, 15-, 20-, and 25-mile distances and proved the circuit was fast, if unsafe.

The track was resurfaced with 3,200,000 pressed paving bricks and four more race meets were held before the first annual Memorial Day Classic was conducted in 1911.

In 1925 Peter DePaolo, with Norm Batten as relief driver, was the first race car racer to break the magical 100 mph average mark, winning with a 101.13 mph pace for the distance. DePaolo's mount was an eight cylinder Duesenberg of 121.5 c.i. piston displacement and equipped with a 5-1 ratio centrifugal blower. . . .

A radical increase in cubic inch allowance in 1930 brought in a tremendous array of equipment with representative engines of four, six, eight and 16 cylinders and a top piston displacement limit 366 c.i.s. imposed with superchargers barred on four cycle engines. The 100.448 mph mark of Billy Arnold in the front-drive Miller-Hartz still fell short of DePaolo's 1925 record. Miller's once again outshone the other designs with the first four spots going to Harry Miller's designing genius. . . .

The trend for '52 will be toward lighter chassis weight with increased use of dural and magnesium frame components. Fuel injection systems will largely replace conventional carbureton. Those in the know insist that the 140 mph qualifying mark will be topped and the current combination of the 138.122 mph record holding driver, Walt Faulkner and car owner J.C. Agajanian, may again be the record-shattering combination. It is generally thought that averages of under 132 mph won't make the 33-car starting field and the possibility of 128 mph mark plus average for the distance is high.

"The Week's Mail, Think Machines," *Colliers,* May 16, 1953:

John Lear's article, "Can a Mechanical Brain Replace You?" (April 4) is an excellent presentation of a very difficult subject. Being a computer-systems engineer, I feel that he has done much to enlighten an otherwise uninformed public.

I would, however, like to comment on two points. Mr. Lear stated that a deterrent to the application of digital computer. . . . "is no longer one of learning how to fit numbers to facts, but how to get enough facts to make the equation foolproof." It has been my experience that most repetitive operations, the type most suitable for a mechanical brain to perform, are impossible to make entirely foolproof.

Equations can be readily designed to handle 99 per cent of the problems to be solved by a mechanical brain. The mechanical brain is told to refer the remaining 1 per cent to a human operator who is no longer burdened down by 100 per cent of the operation and can devote his entire time to the remaining 1 per cent.

The second point is the question of where do we go from here? As Mr. Lear indicates, all mechanical brains thus far developed have been designed primarily for the solution of scientific problems. But these represent a relatively small investment in time and money compared to the millions of repetitive clerical operations that must be performed each day by humans.

These jobs will soon start to be replaced by digital computers, not in 10 to 20 years, but commencing within two to five years.

Signed Jerome Svigals, Haddonfield, New Jersey

"48 States of Mind," Walter Davenport, *Colliers,* May 16, 1953:

Mr. L. F. Wheeler reports that to discourage speeding, Houston, Texas, police cars have been equipped with radar. The *Houston Chronicle* discovered that local traffic cops average a mere fraction of more than one violation arrest a day. The *Chronicle* suggested abandoning radar and equipping traffic officers with Seeing Eye dogs.

* *

Pessimistic schoolteacher in Ann Arbor, Michigan, fears that TV is bound to ruin classroom education. Every time a kid comes up with the right answer, she says, he expects an assortment of expensive prizes.

* *

Mildly ominous news from the Hon. John A. Marzall, United States Commissioner of Patents. Mr. Marzall notified the National Association of Manufacturers that applications by Americans for patents have fallen off to the level of 1866. We guess it can't be helped. Russians have invented everything up to and including the year 2053.

"Cover Photo, Frankie Albertson," *Coach and Athlete*, April 1953:

Track fans who witness Tennessee's track meets this spring will be privileged to see one of the smoothest "picture runners" in the country.

He is Frank Albertson, wiry 130-pound Southeastern conference record holder and senior at the University of Tennessee, who will be competing against the nation's best in the half-mile run.

Albertson's easy, relaxed running style has caused more than one critic to exclaim in delight. More important, it has been a prime factor in his becoming the greatest half-miler in Dixie history.

Frankie's diminutive size is probably responsible for his being somewhat limited in running strength, compared to the six-footers he regularly chops down to size. Moreover, he is not exceptionally blessed with speed, although he has gotten down to 50 seconds in the quarter. His saving grace, most observers agree, is the complete efficiency of his form. There just isn't any wasted motion when the black-haired little speedster of Atlantan takes off around the oval.

Handicapped most of last season with a bronchial condition, Albertson rounded into top form late in the season. He broke Alf Holberg's Tennessee state meet record in the half-mile, then took on the best 880-yard field that the SEC has ever seen in its annual meet.

In that race, defending champion John Paris of Mississippi led most of the way. With Albertson close on his heels, Paris passed the quarter-mile post in 54 seconds. This was the order as they went into the home stretch. Here the contest ended. Albertson barreled ahead to win by nine yards, feeling, as he put it, "like new money." His time of 1:52.8 knocked more than a second off the old SEC record set 15 years earlier by Dave Rogan of Kentucky.

COACH & ATHLETE

Vol. XV   *The Magazine for Coaches, Players, Officials and Fans*   No. 8

April 1953
25¢

FRANKIE ALBERTSON
Tennessee

CAMPUS CLOSE-UP
GADSDEN HIGH SCHOOL
Gadsden, Alabama

1956 PROFILE

Bobby Epperson, a stock car racer, was especially good at making up the rules, as a self-appointed member of the "finish first or not at all" school of racing—the only school he had ever enjoyed.

Life at Home

- Bobby Epperson was known for his shy manner, hard drinking and aggressive driving.
- Some people claimed that Bobby managed to be part of more racing wrecks and acquire more fines than any driver in stock car history.
- Bobby didn't care.
- Orphaned at 13, he was raised by his eight brothers and sisters, none of whom had any success in making him go to school.
- Instead, he developed his racing style.
- The family earned a living by growing cotton and corn on 12 acres of worn-out land that their father had left them along the Catawba River near Charlotte, North Carolina.
- Bobby's first job away from the farm was delivering blocks of ice.
- His next job was a two-year stint working in a sawmill.
- Proceeds from stacking lumber financed his first pair of shoes at 16 years of age.
- Bobby drifted from job to job, including working in a pool hall and cotton mill, until he discovered a small dirt track in Hickory, North Carolina.
- There, he talked his way into the driver's seat of a hobby stock car one Saturday night.
- He lasted only two laps before flipping the car, but it was enough for him to become hooked.
- Even though he had only lasted two minutes before wrecking his first race car, he kept on racing.
- On dirt tracks, his power sliding technique, sending his car whipping around corners to line up perfectly for a fast run down the straightaway, was a work of art.

Bobby Epperson was hooked on stock car racing from his first car wreck.

- Many of the tracks were so primitive that the cars literally bounced along the surfaces, moving from one rut to the next.
- Drivers were a mix of devil-may-care adventurers eager to run unbridled behind a powerful engine and accomplished winning drivers hoping to improve their record.
- For Bobby, the strategy at the start of a 100-lapper on a sweltering hot Carolinas summer Saturday night was simple: just smash the pedal to the floor and go.
- As one competitor said, "Driving the cars was like having two mad bulls with one set of harnesses on them and you didn't know where they were going."
- Because of the clouds of dust kicked up on the dirt track, Bobby often could not see where he was driving.
- Sometimes he would pick a landmark—like a parked car—at a point on the track to know when to turn.
- Bobby loved to drive fast and loved having an excuse to do it.
- Driving was as unpredictable as the competition.
- One driver used a plow line for a seat belt, another drove with vice grips for a steering wheel, and another borrowed tires from spectators' cars of spectators when he ran out of spares.
- After the races, "extracurricular activities" often ensued if the drivers disputed the winner or his methods.
- "I've seen 26 drivers fighting in the infield at Greenwood (SC) one time, and 24 of them didn't know what they're fighting for," one driver said. "You kind of made up the rules as you went."
- In 1955 Bobby acquired a regular ride driving a 1934 Ford coupe in the sportsman division.
- His pay jumped from $0.75 an hour to $125 a week—based on his keeping one-third of his earnings on the track.
- On Thursday nights he raced in Columbia SC, Fridays in Cowpens SC, Saturdays in Gaffney SC, and Sundays in Harris NC.
- Off the track, he worked as a well driller and lived a hard life.

Life at Work

- As the 1956 season got underway, Bobby Epperson was determined to make his mark in NASCAR.
- Driver Lee Petty had shown that the series championship could be won through steady consistency that emphasized finishing the race even if he didn't win.
- Tim Flock, who had won 18 races in 1955 driving for millionaire businessman Carl Kiekhaefer, was rolling in money.
- At the same time, Bobby had finished seven races, wrecked nine cars and earned fines totaling $1,780 for aggressive driving.
- Clearly Bobby's method was not producing the kind of income he wanted.
- That year, a total of 56 races were planned, up from 41 just five years earlier.
- In just six years the Grand National racing schedule had migrated from 17 dirt track races and one asphalt-covered track event to a 1956 lineup that featured an almost equal number of dirt and unpaved tracks.
- Bobby needed a new plan to fit into the NASCAR mold if he was to win the big money and keep racing.

Minimal rules and a rough track meant exciting races.

Bobby had stiff competition.

- A decade earlier, mechanic William France Sr., who lived in Daytona Beach FL had promoted the notion that people would pay to watch unmodified "stock" cars—like the ones they drove every day—race against each other.
- In 1947, France decided that racing needed a formal sanctioning organization, standardized rules, a regular schedule and an organized championship.
- On December 14, 1947, France began talks with other influential racers and promoters at the Ebony Bar at the Streamline Hotel in Daytona Beach.
- This resulted in the National Association for Stock Car Auto Racing (NASCAR), which was officially founded on February 21, 1948, with the help of several other drivers.
- NASCAR's first points system was written on a barroom napkin.
- The sanctioning body hosted their first event at Daytona Beach that year, when Red Byron beat Marshall Teague in the Modified Division Race.
- The first NASCAR "Strictly Stock" race was held at Charlotte Speedway on June 19, 1949.
- The cars raced with virtually no modifications to the factory models.
- In 1950, this division was renamed "Grand National."
- Most races were on half-mile to one-mile oval tracks.
- Bobby deeply resented the fact that NASCAR had so quickly become a big business game.

Larger teams with money to spend on uniforms and design usually won.

- Carl Kiekhaefer's team approach was producing consistent wins, but even the fans booed when the big money won.
- Bobby was wise enough to hold his temper so some of the winnings would come his way.
- It happened in a year that pitted Chevrolets and Fords against each other in nearly every race.
- The two car giants collectively had spent better than $6 million to win NASCAR stock car races and sell their products to the motoring public.
- Despite their spending sprees, Kiekhaefer's Chryslers and Dodges still cleaned house, compiling an amazing 16-race winning streak during the early summer.
- NASCAR Grand National season opener at Hickory NC Speedway was marred by a hotel fire that killed a race official the night before the race.
- Bobby had finished out of the money on the familiar track—but he finished with his car intact and was eligible to race another day.
- His fellow drivers knew Bobby and his famous temper well, and had collected a pool betting on how long Bobby could hold his tongue, not wreck his car or avoid a fine.
- During the second race at West Palm Beach, Bobby was running ninth and trading paint with another driver when a tire blew, forcing Bobby to spin into the infield.
- No money, but no wrecks.
- Joe Weatherly and Jim Reed, the first two finishers in the 100-mile race, were both disqualified for technical violations, so Herb Thomas was declared the official winner.
- Bobby was distressed.
- He was driving well, minding his manners, and still running at the back of the pack.
- At Daytona he even finished behind black driver Charlie Scott, who finished in 19th place.
- At least he finished, unlike both Dodge entries, which turned turtle—flipped over—early in the race, eliminating both.
- Then something amazing happened.
- Tim Flock, the winner in Hickory, Daytona Beach and North Wilkesboro, astonished the racing world by quitting the championship Kiekhaefer Chrysler team.

Bobby raced hard and fast on familiar tracks.

- Finally, a break for Bobby, with no more Flock-Kiekhaefer to compete against.
- Short of money and tired of driving politely, Bobby decided to bet all his cards on the 100-mile race in Concord—a track he knew well.
- If he didn't finish in the money, he would not have enough cash to race in Merced, California, next on the list.
- On the 14th lap of the 100-miler, Bobby made a move to join the top 10 drivers.
- On lap 17, he locked bumpers with another driver, causing both cars to slide sideways down the track, resulting in a six-car pileup and blown tires.
- Bobby limped the car back to the pits and climbed out to smoke a cigarette while his crew threw on replacement tires.
- He then roared back onto the track still hearing the curses of his fellow drivers.
- At lap 77 he pulled into the pits for gas, only to learn he was going to be fined and suspended for causing the wreck.
- "Now or never," was Bobby's reply. "Let's see if they will suspend the winner."
- And he roared out of the pits.
- At lap 90 he was third, with his car handling well and his mind clear.
- Bobby was challenging for the lead in the far turn when he ran over metal from an earlier wreck.
- His tire blew immediately and the wall was his next stop, causing the Ford to flip twice.
- When he woke up in the hospital he was greeted by the news that he had not been suspended after all.
- Only later did they tell him that the car was a total loss and he would not be racing for a while.
- "Next time I'll try a Chevy," he said and fell back to sleep.

Life in the Community: Charlotte, North Carolina
- Agriculture attracted the first settlers to the Catawba River region near Charlotte, North Carolina.
- The first industry in the area was a rifle factory, started by two men from Lancaster, Pennsylvania.

- By 1786, the community of almost 300 had a flour and saw mill, a rifle factory, merchants, tailors, weavers, and blacksmiths
- With the invention of the cotton gin by Eli Whitney in 1793, Charlotte became a ginning center, paving the way for its textile industry.
- Charlotte was lifted from its plantation economy by the discovery of gold in 1799, igniting America's first gold rush.
- Production was so heavy that President Andrew Jackson authorized the establishment in Charlotte of a U.S. Mint branch, which was completed in 1837.
- The mint attracted banks to Charlotte, the first of which opened in 1834.
- Growth was also stimulated by the railroad in 1854, turning Charlotte into a transportation hub.
- By 1877, the Carolina Central Railroad stretched from Charlotte to Wilmington, and later expanded from Richmond, Virginia, to Atlanta, Georgia.
- This further fueled the expansion of the textile industry, leading to the creation of department stores, including Belks.
- In 1882, D.A. Tompkins designed and built over 100 cotton mills.
- By 1903, over half of the nation's textile production was located within a 100-mile radius of Charlotte.
- The banking industry developed around the time of the gold rush, and provided capital for new development in the entire Piedmont region.
- The Federal Reserve opened in Charlotte in 1927, bringing prestige and more growth.
- The first NASCAR stock race was held at Charlotte Speedway in 1949; the cars were "strictly stock," with no modifications from the factory.

HISTORICAL SNAPSHOT
1956

- The film version of Rodgers and Hammerstein's *Carousel*, starring Gordon MacRae and Shirley Jones, was released

- Elvis Presley entered the music charts for the first time with "Heartbreak Hotel"

- Nikita Khrushchev attacked the veneration of Joseph Stalin as a "cult of personality"

- Laurence Olivier's film, *Richard III*, adapted from Shakespeare's play, premiered in the U.S. in theatres and on NBC Television, on the same day

- Ninety-six U.S. Congressmen signed the "Southern Manifesto," a protest against the 1954 Supreme Court ruling (*Brown v. Board of Education*) desegregating public education

- The Dow Jones Industrial Average closed above 500 for the first time

- The Broadway musical *My Fair Lady* opened in New York City

- The United Methodist Church granted women the right to full ordained clergy status and also called for an end to racial segregation in the denomination

- The British Rail renamed "Third Class" passenger facilities as "Second Class," which was abolished in 1875, leaving just First Class and Third Class

- General Electric/Telechron introduced the first snooze alarm clock

- President Dwight D. Eisenhower authorized the phrase "under God" to be added to the Pledge of Allegiance

- Baseball pitcher Don Larsen of the New York Yankees threw a perfect game in Game 5 of the 1956 World Series against the Brooklyn Dodgers

- The *Huntley-Brinkley Report* debuted on NBC-TV

- President Eisenhower signed the Federal Aid Highway Act, creating the Interstate Highway System

- Dean Martin and Jerry Lewis performed their last comedy show together

- Elvis Presley appeared on *The Ed Sullivan Show* for the first time

- The hard disk drive was invented by an IBM team led by Reynold B. Johnson

- MGM's screen classic, *The Wizard of Oz*, was shown on television for the first time by CBS

- Soviet troops invaded Hungary to crush a revolt; thousands were killed, more were wounded, and nearly a quarter million left the country

- The United States Supreme Court declared Montgomery, Alabama, laws requiring segregated buses illegal, thus ending the Montgomery Bus Boycott

- Floyd Patterson became the heavyweight boxing champion after the retirement of Rocky Marciano

- Bob Barker made his TV debut as host of the game show *Truth or Consequences*

Take it EASY

EASY to Relax in!
EASY to Look at!
EASY on Budgets!

COMFORTABLY YOURS

BERK-LOCK
3 in 1 CHAIR

SAMMY KAYE
"Wonderfully Restful"

Selected Prices

Acne Cream	$0.59
Automobile, Chrysler New Yorker	$4,243
Face Powder	$1.38
License Plate	$1.00
Mattress, Serta King Size	$79.50
Paneling	$47.00
Pocket Radio	$75.00
Race Car Kit	$2.75
Railroad Fare, Chicago to San Francisco	$63.12
Razor Blades, 20	$0.79

Go **EMPIRE BUILDER** or *WESTERN STAR*
Between Chicago and Seattle-Portland
Convenient Connections to California

GREAT NORTHERN RAILWAY

Business and pleasure DO mix!
Take a Duplex Roomette the
next time. Lounge if you like . . .
work if you must. But arrive
refreshed in a Duplex Roomette.
Privacy . . . for just 10 per cent
more than a lower berth.

GREAT FOR FREIGHT, TOO

GREAT NORTHERN PASSENGER AND FREIGHT OFFICES IN PRINCIPAL CITIES

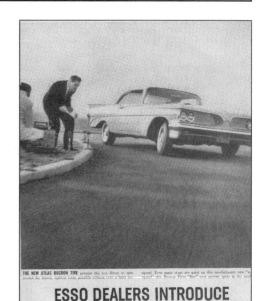

THE NEW ATLAS BUCRON TIRE permits the test driver to spin
around the fastest, tightest turns possible without even a faint hint

ESSO DEALERS INTRODUCE
"NO SQUEAL" ATLAS BUCRON TIRES

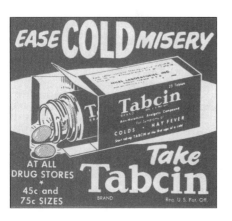

EASE **COLD** MISERY

Tabcin

COLDS . . . HAY FEVER

AT ALL
DRUG STORES
*
45c and
75c SIZES

Take
Tabcin

This way, beer **tastes** better!

(You just add GUINNESS)
Your next beer...*any* beer...is
going to taste different, more
invigorating...if you mix it with
GUINNESS, half-and-half.

This new, "deeper" taste...
mildly bitter but much, much better...is caused by the barley malt
in the GUINNESS. It gives a ruby
color, too.

When you're hosting a party

and want to offer a *variety* of beverages, imported GUINNESS is
"the mixer's mixer." Try a new
"mixed" taste!

Next time you order beer, why
not buy some GUINNESS with it?
Wherever beer is served or at your
food store, delicatessen, super-
market. Try it!

Just ask for GUINNESS !

IMPORTED BY HEUBLEIN FOOD IMPORTING CO., HARTFORD, CONNECTICUT

Racing Timeline

Early 1900s
Stock car racing got its start during Prohibition, with moonshine runners attempting to flee federal tax agents.

December 14, 1947
During a meeting at the Streamline Hotel in Daytona Beach, "Big Bill" France Sr. and a group of ex-moonshiners, gas station owners and local racing boys began talks that led to the forming of the National Association for Stock Car Auto Racing (NASCAR).

February 15, 1948
The first NASCAR race was run at the Daytona Beach Road Course.

February 21, 1948
NASCAR was incorporated.

June 19, 1949
In the NASCAR race run at Charlotte, North Carolina, Jim Roper won in a Lincoln.

September 4, 1950
The Southern 500, NASCAR's first 500-mile race, was held at Darlington Raceway.

1950
"Strictly Stock" series took the name of Grand National.

1951
Jim Flock became the first driver to qualify quicker than 100 mph, driving a Lincoln at the Daytona Beach Road Course.

1953
NASCAR applied the rules by the book and withdrew points to several drivers who had not filled in the inscription form in time.

June 13, 1954
NASCAR's first road race, the International 100, was held at Linden Airport in New Jersey.

"Bobby Allison," *American Stock Car Racers,* Don Hunter and Ben White, 1997:

For (Bobby) Allison to compete as a race car driver, he had to work to raise the money for his first car, which he drove to school during the week and the racetrack on Saturday. This arrangement worked fine until he was required to produce a written parental permission slip to compete.

After night after night of begging his mother for permission, she finally relented. While she thought her blessings were for one race, Allison considered it permission for, as he put it, "at least 100 years."

The odds on a second permission slip were slim, so Allison borrowed the license of a friend, Bob Sunoman, to help launch his career. He used an assumed name, and each time he won, the local newspapers credited the win to "Bob Sunoman."

The sham ended when his father read the newspaper one Sunday afternoon and saw his son's photo and fictitious name accompanying a story announcing another victory. Allison's dad confronted Bobby, saying, "If you're going to race, use your own name," and gave his approval.

"There's Money in Old Cars," *Auto Sport Review,* April 1952:

The only man in America who treats old cars as casually as cards in a filing cabinet is Barney Pollard of Detroit. In the northwestern factory area of Detroit, Mr. Pollard has shed after shed chockfull of valuable autos, so full, in fact, he can't tell you how many autos he owns.

He's not kidding, either. One old-car bug who ventured into this labyrinth of steel emerged after a few hours, drooling about hundreds and hundreds of priceless cars, makes he had never seen before. No one else, though, will venture into Pollard's sheds. Before stacking his cars like cards, Pollard de-rusts the steel portions, rubs linseed oil into the wood and Neatsfoot oil into the leather upholstery. The net result is a greasy jungle no one dares to enter.

Not all of Pollard's cars are stacked up; he usually has several dozen waiting to go into storage at any one time. Just a brief survey is enough to convince anyone that the Pollard collection makes H. Ford looked like an amateur. Of the more than 2,000 makes of automobiles that were made in the US., Pollard has a model of almost every make.

He began collecting, seriously, back in 1939, when he took an old Cadillac as final payment on a long overdue debt. Today, he pursues his hobby with fanatical devotion, covering 400 miles a day when on "hunting expeditions." He scours the Midwestern countryside from the rolling hills of the Ohio River Valley northward into Canada. He has searched as far west as Kansas and, exploring the east, found an old Autocrat on Staten Island, New York.

Into barns, garages, homes, Pollard snoops everywhere. He considers small-town mechanics his best source of tips. Normally, Pollard operates a cinder's business in Detroit, which permits him to pursue this rather expensive hobby. "I don't spend more than 15 minutes with anyone talking about cars. If I can't find out in that length of time whether he wants to sell, I leave him." In some cases, says Pollard, he has waited several years for a "yes" or "no" answer from a car owner.

An old-time auto man, Pollard once worked for Chalmers, then tested (during World War I) Liberty aircraft engines while working for Packard, but has been his own boss since 1918. Detroit is apathetic about old cars, though, says Pollard. "All big cities are poor places in which to find old cars," says Pollard. "Detroit, the world's auto capital, is poorest of them all."

How much does he pay, Pollard won't say, and he has his reasons. "Owners are apt to ask any kind of price, because they've heard so much talk of big prices. Chevrolet and Dodge once gave a new car in trade for an old one, and thus created a lasting impression that old car owners eventually will get an even-Stephen trade-in."

Name your favorite 1907 White Steamer, 1910 Cadillac, 1904 Olds, 1917 Renault Cabriolet, 1910 Stoddard-Dayton, 1911 Flanders 20, 1915 Krit, 1908 Poss truck, Dusenberry, Revere, Grant, Oliver, Pollard's got 'em all!

I had a moonshine car and we started fixing it on Monday to go to race at Darlington (South Carolina). We went down Tuesday and qualified and won the race. I drove the car back home. We took the headlights out and put beefed-up tires on it. There weren't a lot of major changes because what we would do in a car race was about what you'd do to run moonshine, anyway.

—Racing pioneer Junior Johnson

"The Fabulous 1950s," *NASCAR's Wild Years*, Alex Gabbard, 2005:

At the close of World War II in August 1945, GIs were returning home. They arrived with a new spirit seasoned in combat, nerves honed to an edge, and a thirst for adventure that moved them into the workforce and into college during the week, and then out looking for adventure on the weekend. Many went to work in garages and machine shops where they developed speed equipment to be proven on the race track. Tracks from straight lines to road courses to dirt ovals popped up in town after town, drawing droves of paying spectators. . . .

The returning GIs were not happy with the selection of new cars available to them. They had seen the spirited European cars, the small and exciting machines from England, France, and Italy, and many servicemen brought their favorite examples back home with them. This was the beginning of a revolution in the way automobiles were manufactured and marketed in America. . . .

Things got serious in 1949 when both General Motors and Ford Motor Co. introduced entirely new models that left prewar styling in the dust. Fully integrated designs from bumper-to-bumper graced showrooms all across America, and buyers lined up to buy them by the millions. Ford invested over $118 million to design and retool for its new-for-'49 model that sold a total of 821,170 units, over 300,000 more than the year before. Even though Ford's flathead V8 engine was by far the fastest in the low-priced field, buyers flocked into Chevrolet showrooms to set a new sales record, buying 1,031,466 cars. The sleek '49 Chevys were handsome cars with a little more rakish styling than Ford's rather boxy design. . . .

Battle lines for new car sales became more entrenched than ever, and although automobiles had been a major part of the American economy for decades, the influence of a car-hungry postwar buying boom was at a fever pitch, producing a time fertile for innovation. Designers and engineers eyed something new from their competitors and rushed back to their drawing boards to invent something newer. Buick offered buyers the first torque-converter-type automatic transmission, the Dynaflow, in its 1948 models, and then released the rakish convertible-like hardtop for 1949. Both Buick and Cadillac shared this styling advantage with Oldsmobile, and all three introduced overhead valve V8 engines that year. The high-compression Rocket 88 set buyers ablaze with performance never seen before in a car styled so handsomely. Chrysler trumps them all with a simple method of starting their car's engine with an ignition key instead of the key and push button. GM returned in 1950 with Buicks featuring tinted glass. The next year, B.F. Goodrich stepped into the market with "puncture sealing" tubeless tires for top-of-the-line cars. Chevrolet introduced its two-speed power glide automatic with the reliable, if rather stodgy, 105-hp, 235 ci six-cylinder.

"The Fabulous 1950s," *NASCAR's Wild Years*, Alex Gabbard, 2005:

The beginning of Chevrolet's rise to stock car racing began when Jack Radtke entered his Chevy in the February 1955 NASCAR Grand National at Daytona Beach. The beach race had, on occasion, been called when the tide came in and covered the course. It was 4.1 miles around with parallel straights, one on the beach, the other along the adjoining highway, connected at each end by turns through sand. As a whole herd of stockers, usually around 100 cars, came roaring down the hard surface at the start, many didn't make it past the ditch just off the south turn. Radtke started from back in the pack and drove a more cautious race. When he came in 10th overall, a lot of people noticed. . . .

NASCAR's Strictly Stock rules were so restrictive that durability to win was all that was needed, almost. Powerful engines certainly helped, but while both Chevrolet and Ford factory men suspiciously eyed each other on race day, Kiekhaefer's Chryslers cleaned house in '55, and did almost as well the next year. However, in the biggest race of the year, the Southern 500, Chevrolet won the first round, Ford the second.

What gave Chevrolet the edge in '55 was tires. (Driver Mauri) Rose located several sets of special Firestone tires in Dayton, Ohio, left over from Briggs Cunningham's sports car racing days. The better balanced Chevys with softer-compound rubber stuck better than the bigger cars, which simply wore out the tires. The Chevys went by the Oldsmobiles, Buicks, and Kiekhaefer's Chryslers during tire-change pit stops, and after Ford's suspensions collapsed, it was an all-Chevrolet show.

The crowd saw a great race, but few recognized what really happened. It was the first race of the new age, the age of corporate commitment to stock car racing. . . . Manufacturers saw stock car racing as a marketing tool, and NASCAR's "Big Bill" France not only hooked Chevrolet, he snared Ford and got Firestone to boot.

1958 Profile

Martha Lovell, who grew up in the rural South, quickly discovered that she had a natural gift for bowling and a love of competition that spurred her to become better and better at the game.

Life at Home

- Martha Lovell loved and hated the pressure of bowling competition.
- It made her feel alive and energized, but the attention made her feel self-conscious.
- Raised in the rural South, Martha was taught that a respectable woman's name only appeared in the newspaper twice—when she married and when she died.
- Martha did not consider herself upper class.
- She was raised by her mother after her father died in a bar fight when she was 12.
- They sold the family farm and moved into town where her mother Edna worked as a seamstress at a dry cleaner.
- As a child Martha competed to survive.
- She competed against her much younger brother, who was the apple of everyone's eye.
- She competed against the town kids who had more money, more opportunity and better clothes.
- She competed for here mother's attention, when money troubles, work or loneliness sent Edna to her bed for days at a time.
- Martha always took up the slack, helping to raise her little brother, nurse her mother and make good grades.
- Her grades were so good, in fact, that she was admitted to Winthrop College in Rock Hill, South Carolina, on a scholarship in 1943.
- There she met the love of her life—a Yankee no less—who'd been assigned to the all-girl's campus for officer training school to serve his country in time of war.
- Marrying a career military man quickly took her to places she had only read about—Hawaii, California, Japan, Colorado and New York.
- At each stop, they lived in military base housing, drank whiskey sours at the officers' club on Friday nights and joined a bowling league.

Martha Lovell was a natural competitor.

Martha's husband was a pilot in the Air Force.

- Every military base in America, it seemed, was outfitted with a bowling alley—a place Martha could compete without losing her Southern poise or appearing too aggressive.
- She especially enjoyed the mixed leagues when she and her husband could bowl together, and celebrate victory together.
- Now that her husband was a captain and pilot for the Strategic Air Command of the United States Air Forces, their assignment was Homestead, Florida.
- Their children were 10 and seven, a girl and a boy as planned, and both as energetic as their mother and as athletic as their father.
- Prior to meeting her husband Gordon, Martha had never seen a bowling alley.
- Growing up she much preferred an air-conditioned movie theater, the only place to get cool on a Southern Saturday afternoon—even though bowling was an ancient event.
- The history of bowling can be traced back to the Stone Age.
- The first evidence of the game was discovered by the British anthropologist Sir Flinders Petrie and his team of archaeologists in Egypt in the 1930s.
- He unearthed a collection of objects from a small child's grave that appeared to have been a primitive form of the game.
- German historians counter-claimed that the game of bowling originated around 300 AD.
- In Germany, the game had its origin as a religious ceremony for determining absence of sin.
- Introduced by the German monks to the masses, it flourished as a customary test of faith.
- In England, several variations of bowling, such as half-bowls, skittles and ninepins, existed during the mid-1300s.
- The first written mention of the game was made by King Edward III in the year 1366.
- In this reference, he imposed a ban on playing the game because it was distracting the troops from archery practice.
- During the seventeenth century, English, Dutch and German settlers imported their own version of bowling to America.
- At that time, the game, which was regularly played in an area of New York City still known as "Bowling Green," consisted of nine pins.
- Connecticut banned ninepins in 1841 because of its gambling implications.
- The American Bowling Congress was formed in 1895 and is credited with standardizing bowling in the United States and organizing official competitions.
- The Women's Bowling League followed in 1917, under the encouragement of proprietor Dennis Sweeny.
- In 1951 American Machine and Foundry Company (AMF, then a maker of machinery for the bakery, tobacco and apparel businesses) purchased the patents to Gottfried Schmidt's automatic pinspotter, and by late 1952 production model pinspotters were introduced.
- Television embraced bowling in the 1950s, and the game's popularity grew exponentially.
- NBC's broadcast of *Championship Bowling* was the first network coverage of bowling.

- Coverage proliferated with shows like *Make That Spare, Celebrity Bowling,* and *Bowling For Dollars.*
- Martha first discovered bowling during her and Gordon's first overseas assignment in Hawaii in 1947.
- Shy at first, Martha quickly discovered that she had a natural lift that allowed a properly thrown bowling ball to curve perfectly into the pocket.
- When she broke 100, she was hooked.
- When she broke 200, she became a true addict.

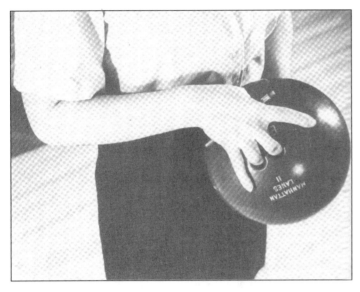

Martha loved the feel of the ball and improved quickly.

Bowling was becoming popular across the country.

Martha felt anxious when Gordon was on assignment.

Life at Work

- Martha Lovell's goal in the spring of 1958 was to bowl well enough to impress her husband, Gordon.
- Rising tensions around the world had kept the Air Forces, particularly the Strategic Air Command, on constant alert.
- There was tension in the house every time Gordon was called out in the middle of the night and ordered to board his B-47 bomber.
- Martha believed that winning the state bowling championship would capture Gordon's attention.
- And dethroning Sarah Middleton from her championship perch would be fun, too.
- Martha planned for the Miami tournament for weeks—babysitters for the children, the perfect outfit and a hairstyle that would hold together through the entire tournament.
- She had only been to Miami twice, which was 25 miles away.
- She went there a third time to practice at the bowling lanes where the tournament was to be held, wanting to leave nothing to chance.
- She had been named city champion in an earlier tournament, earning the right to battle for the state championship and a trip to nationals.
- Martha was so nervous she could not admit she was nervous.
- Gordon was on regular rotation in Morocco the entire month the tournament was to be held.
- Unless she caught someone on a direct duty mission to Sidi Slimane, letters took more than a week.
- A total of 178 teams, a new record, was scheduled compete, which required an elimination round and a chance to test the lanes.
- That first day Martha found the lanes to be fast and predictable, and her confidence was as high as her scores: 201-216-231.
- Her combined score of 648 was not only good enough to secure a return spot, but also designated her as "an up-and-coming star," according to the *Miami Herald*.
- That was thrilling and she desperately wanted to tell Gordon.
- Her two kids were excited for her success but not terribly interested.
- Her daughter was more entwined in the drama surrounding the invitation list for an upcoming birthday swim party.
- Her son wanted to tell her about the latest episode of *Leave It to Beaver*.
- For the second round, Martha dressed carefully, packed carefully and drove carefully to Miami.
- And she was sure that she had selected a perfume that was just right for the occasion.
- She was paired with a woman from Tallahassee who made it clear that military wives should not be allowed to compete in a Florida-sponsored tournament and asked her repeatedly, "Where again are you from, dear?"
- Once again Martha rolled a combined score in excess of 615 and quieted the shrill questioner from Tallahassee.
- By the third round the TV news camera that had been assigned to the event discovered Martha.
- During the first game she rolled a 261, finishing with six strikes.
- During the second game she made few mistakes but still finished with 227.
- It was after she opened the third game with four strikes that the camera moved in and the lights were turned on.
- At first she tried not to notice, but then she couldn't focus.
- With the chance to move to the finals in the balance, Martha made her five-step approach to the line thinking about her hair, her body and who might see her back home.

- The ball never broke, and instead of sliding gracefully into the pocket, rolled listlessly into the right corner picking up only two pins.
- She desperately wanted to cry and send the cameraman away, but she did neither.
- Martha picked up the returned ball in both hands, cradled it as she had been taught, inserted her fingers, set herself up for the approach and picked up the spare with a thunderous clatter.
- Only then did she realize how close she had come to ruining her chances.
- At her seat she rejoiced that the cameraman had stopped filming, only to discover he was waiting for her to bowl again.
- This time, even though she consciously ignored the interruption, she threw too hard and ended with a 7-10 split—a pin in each corner.
- If she was not able to strike the 10 pin hard enough to force it across the lane to take down the 7 pin, she would be left with an open frame.
- With the camera humming in the background and the lights slightly blinding her vision, Martha rolled cross-alley to the 10, which ricocheted back across the lane for a spare.
- The surrounding lanes broke into thunderous applause, and Martha's impossible spare was the clip used by the Miami television station that night, which noted that she had missed the finals by six pins.
- At home, Martha and her friends celebrated—she appeared on television, a victory beyond the championship.
- Her children called her a movie star and ostentatiously bowed when she walked into a room.
- And best of all, Gordon called long-distance to congratulate her.

Martha's nerves sometimes got the best of her during tough shots.

Life in the Community: Homestead, Florida

- Homestead Airfield began as a United States Army Air Forces facility in 1942 when the Army Air Forces assumed control of an isolated airstrip located about a mile inland from the shore of Biscayne Bay.
- The airstrip had been turned over to the government by Coconut Grove-based Pan American Ferries, Inc., which had carved it out of the rocky landscape in the 1940s.
- Returned to civilian control after World War II, it was used as Dade County Airport until January 1953, when the United States Air Force reopened it as Homestead Air Force Base.
- The 379th Bomb Wing was established in 1953, and activated November 1, 1955 at Homestead AFB, Florida.
- It received B-47s and KC-07s in April 1956 and began training for strategic bombardment and air refueling operations.
- Most of its pilots were deployed at Sidi Slimane Air Base, Morocco, starting in 1957.

Homestead Airfield, Florida

HISTORICAL SNAPSHOT
1958

- *Sputnik 1*, launched on October 4, 1957, returned to Earth from its orbit
- Fourteen-year-old Bobby Fischer won the United States Chess Championship
- Hall of Fame baseball player Roy Campanella was involved in an automobile accident that ended his career and left him paralyzed
- Golfer Arnold Palmer was the Professional Golf Association's top money winner for the year at $42,607

- The word *Aerospace* was coined, from the words Aircraft (aero) and Spacecraft (space), taking into consideration that the Earth's atmosphere and outerspace is to be one, or a single realm
- Pope Pius XII declared Saint Clare the patron saint of television
- The peace symbol was designed by Gerald Holtom and commissioned by the Campaign for Nuclear Disarmament, in protest against the Atomic Weapons Research Establishment
- A U.S. B-47 bomber accidentally dropped an atom bomb on Mars Bluff, South Carolina, but no nuclear fission occurred
- The United States launched the *Vanguard 1* satellite
- The U.S. Army inducted Elvis Presley, transforming the so-called King of Rock and Roll into U.S. Private #53310761
- For the eleventh year, Eleanor Roosevelt was first on America's Most Admired Women list
- College tuition topped $1,300 a year, double the cost in 1940
- The first International House of Pancakes (IHOP) opened in Toluca Lake, California
- The U.S. Congress formally created the National Aeronautics and Space Administration (NASA)
- President Dwight D. Eisenhower signed the Federal Aviation Act of 1958, transferring all authority over aviation in the U.S. to the newly created Federal Aviation Agency (FAA, later renamed Federal Aviation Administration)

- New books included *Breakfast at Tiffany's* by Truman Capote; *Dr. Zhivago* by Boris Pasternak; *Kids Say the Darndest Things* by Art Linkletter; *The Affluent Society* by John Kenneth Galbraith; *95 Poems* by e.e. cummings; and *Only in America* by Harry Golden
- *Have Gun, Will Travel* debuted on radio
- The right-wing John Birch Society was founded in the U.S. by Robert Welch, a retired candy manufacturer
- TV premieres included *The Rifleman; Wanted: Dead or Alive; 77 Sunset Strip; The Donna Reed Show* and *Naked City*
- The Baltimore Colts beat the New York Giants 23-17 in overtime to win the NFL Championship in the first title game televised coast-to-coast
- The U.S., USSR and Great Britain agreed to stop testing atomic bombs for three years

Selected Prices

Burger King Whopper $0.37
Food Processor $12.98
Home Permanent $1.50
House, Four Bedrooms, Chicago Area $34,000
Lighter, Zippo $4.75
Magazine, *Life* $0.25
Makeup, Pressed Powder/Foundation $1.35
Photoflash Lamp $0.10
Photostat, Each $0.20
Scotch, Fifth $8.00

Language of the Lanes, compiled by
American Bowling Congress, 1958:

Apple: The ball
Bedposts: The 7-10 split
Benchwork: Conversation intended to upset or disconcert opponents
Big ears: The 4-6-7-10 split
Cheese cakes: Lanes where strikes are easy to get
Cherry: Ball that chops off the front pin of a spare and leaves the pin behind and/or to the right or left standing
Cincinnati: The 8-10 split
Crow Hopper: Clawlike, loose grip on ball noticeable just at release over the foul line
Dead Ball: An ineffective ball
Double wood: One pin directly behind another
Dutch 200: 200 game made by alternate strikes and spares
Foundation: A strike in the ninth frame
Go the route: To finish the game with three or more consecutive strikes
Holding Alley: A lane that resists hook action
Honey: A good ball
Kindling wood: Light pins
Lift: Giving the ball an upward motion with fingers at point of release
Mother-in-law: The number 7 pin
Mule ears: The 7-10 split
Poison ivy: The 3-6-10 setup
Poodle: To roll the ball in the gutter
Rat club: A team that shoots unusually low scores for one game
Short pin: A pin that is rolling on the alley and fails to hit the standing pin
Snow plow: A wide hook that sweeps the pins off the lane
Steal: To get more pins than deserved on a hit
Throwing rocks: Throwing a lot of good strike balls
Turkey: Three strikes in a row
Woolworth: The 5-10 split

If war should ever strike this nation again, our airfields . . . could very well be one of our most precious assets. In an atomic war, the more airfields we have, the better our chances of successful retaliation against an aggressor. More airfields mean more dispersal. More dispersal means more of our retaliatory force can survive an atomic onslaught. More airfields mean more division of an enemy's effort. More airfields could make his job tougher and our job easier.

—Air Force Gen. Nathan Twining, concerning the construction of foreign airfields, 1956

The Woman's Bowling Guide, Sylvia Wene, 1959:

When I was 17 years of age and only 4 feet, 11 inches tall my brother and sister took me on my first visit to a bowling establishment.

"You," my brother stated, "are too small to bowl so you have to sit there and keep score."

The game looked like great fun and I wanted to try my hand. But, as ordered, I sat there and tried to keep score while they bowled.

But the next day I went back to those lanes with my mother to see how I would do. I wasn't very successful. As a matter of fact, I didn't come anywhere near 100. My mother did and, I suppose, that piqued me somewhat.

Anyhow, I decided I was going to roll 100. It took me quite a while. And, by that time, I decided I wouldn't quit till I had rolled 200.

Then, by the time I was able to accomplish 200, I was so crazy about the game, I was not able to give it up.

Now I am still only 4 feet, 11 inches tall.

Yet I am proud of my record:

First woman to bowl a perfect 300 game in a sanctioned East Coast play.

A 206 national recorded average for three straight seasons.

The world record of 11 700 series in one year.

National individual match champion in 1955.

I am making it a point to accent these accomplishments to illustrate to you that stature has little to do with making you a better-than-average bowler.

Consider that there are 25 million bowlers and the national average, for both men and women, is below 150.

There is one major reason for this pin topping deficiency: a scarcity of expert instructors to give individual instruction.

The result is that most bowlers start by simply walking out on the lane with a few words of advice from a friend and roll away. If they approach their friend's peak efficiency, as low as it may be, they are satisfied thereafter to stay in a low-scoring rut from force of copied habit.

I am not trying to tell you that championship bowling is easy. It takes long hours of hard work. But bowling well, which means scoring higher than the national average, isn't at all difficult if you master the basic principles.

And, believe me, it is just as easy to learn the correct basic principles as it is to adopt improper ones.

"Bowling Beauty Tips," *The Woman's Bowling Guide,* Sylvia Wene, 1959:

A woman is known by the aura of femininity that surrounds her. Her perfume, feminine daintiness, and makeup help to make her even more lovely.

Sometimes, in the rush of daily living, we forget some of the details we should remember. But an afternoon or evening of bowling should be something special. So take those few extra seconds to double check.

Wear a light, appealing fragrance, one that whispers and one that definitely doesn't shout. Work out a special makeup, one that is easy to apply, keeps you looking your loveliest, and is natural looking. Use a double amount of deodorant, since activity does speed up body process. All of which will make you feel better, look better, and thus possibly bowl better.

DEODORANTS: nothing spoils the illusion of feminine daintiness and, in a sport such as bowling, makes you feel more conspicuous than unsightly perspiration stains.

Therefore, a good antiperspirant and deodorant should be used. And not only under the arms, but the same antiperspirant should be placed at the bend of the knee and the crook of the arm. There are any number of good antiperspirant deodorants in roll-on, spray, lotion, or cream form. . . .

EYE MAKEUP: apply your eye makeup wisely. Use the eyebrow pencil but keep your eye shadow, if you wish to use it, extremely light.

I would also suggest that you use mascara very sparingly. There are roll-on mascaras which are easily applied and which, being waterproof, resist perspiration.

HANDS AND NAILS: Even if your nails are strong, still be sure to reinforce them with extra coats of nail enamel. A sturdy manicure consists of a base coat, two coats of enamel, and a top coat. To this you may add an additional coat of enamel and a top coat. This builds up a shiny protective coat of armor.

"Bowling Is Top Participant Sport," Oscar Fraley, *Lawton Constitution* (Oklahoma), August 28, 1958:

More than 22 million Americans next week will go back to bowling in palaces straight out of *The Arabian Nights,* Ted Bensinger of Brunswick-Balke-Collender reported today, as the nation's greatest participant sport booms to the billion-dollar mark.

The sport has come a couple of country miles from the cellar establishments of a few decades ago. Among the 9,000 sites the largest is a 66 lane spot in Hicksville, Long Island, complete with cocktail lounge and baby sitters.

One place in Kansas City has a man who does nothing else, at $5,600 a year, but care for the birds whose cages decorate the establishment.

Bensinger, president of the bowling equipment firm, lists these reasons as to why bowling has boomed so tremendously with 35 million people expected to be playing the game by 1966:

1. The attraction it holds as a complete family sport.
2. Increased interest among women.
3. Increased formation of industrial, church and fraternal leagues.
4. The automatic pin setter, which has done away with the need for pin boys and has speeded up the game.

"Women definitely are leading the new boom," he explains. "Women's leagues are growing in membership and the Women's International Bowling Congress has passed one million, meaning it has twice the membership it had a mere eight years ago."

Marian Ladewig, the pert Grand Rapids grandmother who has won just about everything in the woman's bowling world, nodded agreement.

"Men still outnumber women in bowling, about three to one," she estimated. "But more and more women are bowling every year. They find it a great form of relaxation and entertainment and also helps to keep them fit."

For most bowlers, the sport is sheer fun. As an example, during the recent recession there were 400,000 unemployed in Detroit. Yet during that period the number of bowlers in Detroit increased steadily.

And wait 'til the season opens next week.

"Questionnaire Writer Stirs Up Trouble," George E. Sokolski, *The Appleton Post-Crescent* (Wisconsin), March 16, 1959:

The questionnaire writer is still busy stirring up trouble for innocent parents. I have before me a questionnaire used in an American university. The one I have asks only 35 questions but it appears that there is a longer one that has 140 questions. Here are eight samples of the questions asked:

"Have you been embarrassed because of the type of work your father does in order to support the family?

"Has either of your parents insisted on your obeying him or her regardless of whether or not the request was reasonable?

"Do you think your parents fail to recognize that you are a mature person and hence treat you as if you were still a child?

"Have your parents frequently objected to the type of companions that you go around with?

"Is either of your parents easily irritated?

"Have you disagreed with your parents about your life work?

"Was your father what you would consider your ideal of manhood?

"Do you occasionally have conflicting moods of love and hate for members of your family?"

I picked these eight questions out of 35 because nearly every child can answer them affirmatively at some stage. Sure, mother dominates the home! Who else? Otherwise, children would be young anarchists.

In a full family, there is a mother, a father and children. Of course, mother and father sometimes disagree and all children believe that their parents are at times unreasonable. That is part of the process of growing up.

When kids turn on the radio to blare horrible rock-n-roll music, which is an insult to anyone's intelligence, naturally a father or a mother or both will, after a while, complain. Are they unreasonable? The first thing a child must learn, and it is something that is extremely hard to learn, is that when there is more than one person in the house, consideration for others is very important. And that sense of consideration, if lacking, makes of the unfortunate creature a boor whom others avoid.

It has been the good fortune in the United States that it has had no hereditary aristocracy, no landed gentry, no elite by birth. At the beginning of this century, some feared that rich families would combine like fraternity brothers in campus politics, to dominate both the economic and political life in the country. This has not happened.

No aristocracy, not even a monied one, forms itself in this country. New York, and to a degree Palm Beach, Miami, Los Angeles and Beverly Hills, have become playgrounds for the defrocked and evil aristocracy of Europe, some of whom marry Americans for a respite from poverty. Others travel about this country more or less on the cuff, serving as shills for various mercantile enterprises.

Question one in the above questionnaire is therefore not only an irritant in the household but offensive. Before child labor laws put a ceiling on juvenile ingenuity, children who were dissatisfied with family earnings could be newsboys or bootblacks or do a hundred and one odd jobs to show their independence. In this socialistic era, they are required to be idle, listen to rock-n-roll, hang around the soda counter and call themselves beatniks to prove that they hate themselves and the world. Dissatisfied kids should be given an opportunity to work off their beefs.

1956 NEWS FEATURE

"Everyone Gets into the Act," *Sports Illustrated,* **November 26, 1956:**

When the curtain goes up on the TV game of the week between USC and UCLA this Saturday, everyone—even the fan in the highest seat on the tall concrete rim of vast Los Angeles Memorial Coliseum to the patient reserves warming the bench—will be a performer in the biggest, brashest, loudest, greatest show on earth. That adds up to a cast somewhere close to 100,000, a fittingly grandiose spectacle for a production taking place on the outskirts of Hollywood. This will be football western-style—a pageant that is as different from the restrained enthusiasm of the Ivy League as the high-pitched call of the carnival barker from the well-modulated tones to be heard at a literary tea. It is the spontaneous outburst of a city where no service station is christened without a battery of searchlights to sweep the sky. . . .

The football game itself, of course, is much the same as football everywhere. But in the window dressing the influence of neighboring Hollywood has rubbed off on the students who stage the performance, and the TV screens will reflect a good deal of this at halftime. The unique part of the spectacle—the contribution of the West Coast is added to the football extravaganza—is in the meticulously drilled rooting sections which will demonstrate their ingenious animated card tricks while the football teams are resting. . . .

The mechanics of card sections are fairly simple, but first of all they require a warm climate so the rooter can shed his jacket to provide a solid background of white shirts. To begin with, the designs are drawn on graph paper by student managers. Each student in this section is then provided with five cards, colored on each side, his instructions are fastened to the back seat of the seat in front of him. At a signal from a cheerleader the cards are flipped. In the more elaborate productions, they are flipped in sequence to provide motion.

All of this started, oddly enough, in Corvallis, Oregon. Back in 1924, a postgraduate Oregon State student named Linsley Bothwell equipped his 500-man rooting section with cards, and the first animated stunt in history showed a beaver (the OSC mascot) with a big tail standing over a huge lemon yellow O (symbolizing the Beavers' opponent that day, the University of Oregon). At a signal the beaver brought his tail down on the O, demolishing it and providing a source of fun and entertainment which has survived the years. Bothwell, as one might suspect, hailed from Southern California.

Bothwell's pioneering did not go unnoticed and, in 1925, the University of Southern California took a try when their Burdette Henney devised a stunt in which the USC's mascot, the Trojan horse, winked its eye and bucked. By 1931, UCLA was using card stunts, and the following year the Uclans animated their pictures in the growing vogue. UCLA moved a step ahead of the art and science of card pictography in 1935 when Yell Leader Maury Crossman directed 1,000 students in electric displays during the night game against the University of Hawaii. The lights formed a hula girl swaying her hips amid palm trees to the accompaniment of some music from a Walt Disney movie. At the 1954 Rose Bowl game UCLA took cognizance of technical improvements and unveiled what it called a "widescreen UCLArama," in which a total of 3,456 students were card holders. This was the biggest card stunt on record at the time. And next Saturday the UCLA and USC cheering sections will be the largest yet.

1960–1969

The decade of the sixties made quite a reputation for itself through rebellion and protest. No aspect of American society escaped this social upheaval entirely unscathed. The decade included tragic assassinations, momentous social legislation for African Americans, remarkable space achievements, the awakening of a Native American rights movement and some of the nation's largest antiwar protests in its history. Music, hairstyles, the willingness of people to speak out would all be transformed. It was the beginning of the Beatles and the tragic end of the non-violent phase of the Civil Rights Movement. While the nation's "silent majority" slapped "Love It or Leave It" ("It" being America) bumper stickers on their cars, thousands of highly vocal, well-educated middle class citizens carried signs in the streets to loudly protest America's involvement in Vietnam. It was truly a time of wrenching conflict in search of social change.

In the midst of this turmoil, sports, too, underwent a transformation. The burgeoning success of NASCAR was slowed by the death of driver Fireball Roberts in 1960, when manufacturers asked whether the sport had become too dangerous. The appearance of performance-enhancing drugs in football and horseracing captured headlines alongside gambling scandals in the National Football League and college basketball. All the while, salaries continued to rise as television coverage of sports exploded. In baseball, Sandy Koufax and Don Drysdale both made well over $100,000 a year in 1966, although the average player made one-fifth of that amount. Professional golfers Jack Nicklaus and Arnold Palmer routinely made more than $100,000 a year, and quarterback Joe Namath signed with the New York Jets for over $400,000 in 1965 when professional football players routinely make $20,000 a year.

During the decade the National Basketball Association expanded from eight teams to 17 teams and acquired a lucrative television audience eager to watch centers Wilt Chamberlain and Bill Russell define the modern game with their grace and power. In boxing Muhammad Ali captured the heavyweight boxing crown by defeating heavily favored Sonny Liston in 1964.

From 1960 to 1964, the economy expanded, unemployment was low, and disposable income grew rapidly. Internationally, the power of the United States was immense. Congress gave the young President John F. Kennedy the defense and space-related programs Americans wanted, but few of the welfare programs he proposed. Between 1950 and 1965, inflation soared from an annual average of less than 2 percent to 9.5 percent. Upper class investors, once content with the stability of banks, sought better returns in the stock market and real estate.

The Cold War became hotter during conflicts over Cuba and Berlin in the early 1960s. Fears over the international spread of Communism led to America's intervention in a foreign conflict that would become a defining event of the decade: Vietnam. By 1968, Vietnam had become a national obsession. Antiwar marches, grew from a few thousand in 1965, to millions of marchers in New York, San Francisco, and Washington, DC, only a few years later.

The struggle to bring economic equality to blacks during the period produced massive spending for school integration. By 1963, the peaceful phase of the Civil Rights movement was ending. In 1967, 41 cities experienced major disturbances. At the same time, charismatic labor organizer Cesar Chavez's United Farm Workers led a Civil Rights-style movement for Mexican Americans, gaining national support which challenged the growers of the West with a five-year agricultural strike.

As a sign of increasing affluence and changing times, American consumers bought 73 percent fewer potatoes and 2.5 percent more fish, poultry, and meat than in 1940. Factory workers earned more than $100 a week, their highest wages in history. From 1960 to 1965, the amount of money spent for prescription drugs to lose weight doubled. In 1960, approximately 40 percent of American adult women had paying jobs. Their emergence into the workforce would transform marriage, child rearing and the economy. In 1960, women were also liberated by the FDA's approval of the birth control pill.

During the decade, anti-establishment sentiments grew: men's hair was longer and wilder, beards and mustaches became popular, women's skirts rose to mid-thigh, and bras were discarded. Hippies advocated alternative lifestyles, drug use increased, especially marijuana and LSD; the Beatles, the Rolling Stones, Jimi Hendrix, and Janis Joplin became popular music figures; and college campuses became major sites for demonstrations against the war and for Civil Rights. The Supreme Court prohibited school prayer, assured legal counsel to the poor, limited censorship of sexual material, and increased the rights of the accused.

Extraordinary space achievements also marked the decade. Ten years after President Kennedy announced he would place a man on the moon, 600 million people around the world watched as Neil Armstrong gingerly lowered his left foot into the soft dust of the moon's surface. In a tumultuous time of division and conflict, the landing was one of America's greatest triumphs and an exhilarating demonstration of American genius. Its cost was $25 billion and set the stage for 10 other men to walk on the surface of the moon during the next three years.

1960 PROFILE

Jim Bradford, an Olympic weightlifter, trained himself and developed his own technique as a teenager at the local YMCA basketball court.

Life at Home

- Jim Bradford weighed 247 pounds on his fourteenth birthday.
- Until he discovered a copy of the weightlifting magazine *Strength and Health,* he was just another overweight black teen walking the streets of the nation's capital.
- Inspired by the pictures and the personal stories of weightlifters, Jim began working out at home.
- But after a dumbbell mishap in the second-floor bedroom of his home sent plaster crashing upon his family downstairs, Jim was dispatched to the 12th St. YMCA.
- There he began working out, largely training himself, relying heavily on strength, not technique.
- As a result, he taught himself to lift with virtually no split of his legs on the way up, only bending his back as he lifted the bar over his head.
- This technique was developed, he later confessed, from fear of dropping the weights on the YMCA basketball court and getting kicked out for scarring the floor.
- After four years of training and competing on a local level, a very muscular Jim entered his first national event, the 1946 Junior Nationals.
- There he learned some lifting techniques of veteran weightlifters, and made slow progress.
- Four years later at age 22, he won the Junior Nationals and placed third in the Senior National Championship.
- In 1951 he placed second place in the Nationals and earned a spot on the 1951 World Championship Team.
- Here Jim battled aging teammate John Henry Davis, the reigning "World's Strongest Man" and world champion since 1938.
- But John Davis was hurt and Jim Bradford was young and hungry.

Jim Bradford was a self-trained weightlifter.

John Davis was the "World's Strongest Man."

- At the conclusion of the snatch lift, John Davis was in terrific pain, his undefeated reign truly endangered.
- As the clean and jerk competition began, the arena was charged with energy as everyone knew that history was about to be made.
- Jim made his first clean and jerk smoothly and Davis did the same, through the pain.
- Jim answered with an easy second attempt, which was also matched by Davis, who was barely able to leave the stage after the lift.
- Jim knew that if he made his last lift at a still higher weight, Davis would be forced to match him, risking permanent injury.
- A gold medal and the glory of winning the World Championship were in Jim's grasp—a lifetime dream come true.
- But winning meant defeating an injured legend and stripping a team-mate of his undefeated status.
- Jim declined this last lift in the spirit of sportsmanship.
- John Davis retained his title as World's Strongest Man and newspapers heralded Jim's decision as one of the greatest acts of sportsmanship in the history of athletics.
- He won a silver medal at the 1952 Olympics in Helsinki.
- Jim joined the Army, serving in the Korean War, and his weightlifting career was interrupted.
- In 1954, he was called upon to replace an injured member of the World Championship team.
- Jim jumped on an airplane without hesitation and placed second, winning valuable points for the United States.
- By the time the 1960 Olympics in Rome rolled around, he was ready for one more opportunity on the world stage.
- This time he wanted the gold.
- He was 32 years old, married with three children, and earned $56 a week as a documents clerk in the Library of Congress.
- His monthly mortgage was $105—half his income.
- Since paid leave would have jeopardized his amateur status under Olympic rules, he took unpaid leave from his clerk position, which he could barely afford.

Olympic hopefuls.

Life at Work

- Weightlifting was one of the final events at the 18-day-long 1960 Olympics in Rome, and one of the oldest sports of the modern games.
- At the opening parade of nations, African-American Rafer Johnson marched at the head of the U.S. delegation, causing a stir as the first black athlete to carry the American flag in the highly visible ceremony.
- The 305 U.S men looked sharp in the U.S. Olympic team dress uniform: McGregor-Doniger olive green sports coat, Haggar slacks, and Van Heusen beige knit shirt.
- After weeks of anticipation, and the thrill of marching in the opening ceremony, Jim Bradford was brimming with energy.
- The U.S. men's contingent was housed in large buildings in the middle of the village, sharing 50 suites that each held three to eight athletes.
- Americans had their own dining facility open 22 hours a day, from 5 am to 3 am.
- It was operated by an Italian chef with 76 employees who cooked mostly beef, to suit the tastes of Americans.
- Jim loved to travel.
- While at a competition in Warsaw, Poland, the year before, he made a point of meeting locals, attempting their language and eating indigenous foods.
- To the media, the weightlifting competition, which comprised seven weight classes, was the perfect metaphor for the clash of the two superpowers—America and the Soviet Union—in a time of Cold War.
- Americans collected more gold medals during the two previous Olympics in Helsinki and Melbourne, but current momentum favored the Soviet strongmen.
- Jim's American coaches believed that winning the weight contest in Rome "would be our best propaganda weapon" in the Cold War.
- The political tension that invaded the 1960 Olympics had begun two years earlier when a delegation of U.S. track and field athletes became the first team to visit the USSR since the start of the Cold War.
- Russians, cheered on by the home crowd, scored a 172-170 victory, which was interpreted in the wider world as a victory for the Communist way of life.
- A lot more than a gold medal was on the line.
- When it was Jim's turn to compete, the Soviets had won four matches and the team title.
- Jim prepared by spending hours meditating in the Olympic Village, visualizing the handling of immense weights.
- Mental preparation in weightlifting was as critical as the physical.
- In the first round, Jim easily pressed 374.5 pounds, his white clothing a stark contrast to his gigantic black body.
- He made his 396.5 pound press with apparent ease.
- The Soviet opponent, Yuri Vlasov, made his lift, but the judges ruled Vlasov's lift was illegal and the lead went to Jim.
- In the next round, the snatch, Vlasov was the clear winner by 11 pounds.
- Jim's lead was precariously thin and he was concerned.
- It appeared the gold medal would be decided by the clean and jerk.
- That's when the officials announced the initial ruling against Vlasov had been overturned on appeal.
- Jim protested vehemently, but Vlasov was given a comfortable lead going into the last event.
- Eventually, the Soviets claimed the gold.
- Rumors of drug use by the Soviet team didn't bother Jim.
- He came from the old school where excuses didn't count.

Rome was a great background for the 1960 games.

- But to lose because of a judge's ruling was too outrageous for words.
- Officials asked that he not create an international incident—in other words, "Please shut up."
- Silence in the face of injustice was a terrible burden to carry.

Life in the Community: The Olympic Village, Rome

- The Olympic ideal of pure athletic competition, staged once every four years, was designed to rise above the competing ideologies and international disputes currently raging around the world.
- In 1960 the increasingly hot rhetoric of the Cold War was only one of many intrusions.
- One week before the opening ceremony, the American pilot Francis Gary Powers was convicted in a Moscow court on espionage charges after his U-2 reconnaissance plane was shot down in Russia.
- Just days before the closing ceremony, Soviet Premier Nikita Khrushchev staged a dramatic appearance at the UN General Assembly, where he pounded his fist and railed against America and the West.
- Questions were raised concerning which flag East and West Germany would use in the competition, and a major uproar erupted when the athletes from Taiwan attempted to march as the China delegation.
- At the same time, new nations—particularly in Africa—were lobbying for more participants in a wider variety of events, women wanted to run longer distances, and civil rights activists in South Africa wanted the International Olympic Committee to live up to its Olympic Creed and expel the apartheid delegation from South Africa.
- Simultaneously, economic wars were raging over the definition of an "amateur athlete."
- Increasingly, the rigid rules on "amateur" status were being challenged by athletes who saw everyone but themselves making money from the athletes' efforts.
- The 72-year-old Avery Brundage, president of the International Olympic Committee, was the personification of the Olympic movement and the object of considerable ridicule.
- Endorsements, sponsorships and subsidized work programs were all strictly forbidden—although some athletes had begun quietly taking money to wear certain shoes.
- Rafer Johnson, a competitor in the decathlon, was told he would be ineligible for the Olympics because he appeared in *Spartacus,* a film about a slave revolt in ancient Rome.
- The Olympic Committee ruled that Johnson was hired not for his acting ability, but because he was a famous athlete.
- Champion hurdler Lee Calhoun lost his eligibility for a year because he and his wife got married on the *Bride and Groom* TV game show and accepted gifts and a honeymoon.
- All these issues were played out before a worldwide television audience.
- In America, CBS News paid $600,000 for the exclusive rights to the Olympics.

International disputes abounded.

- Under their contract, CBS could broadcast up to 20 hours of programming from August 25 to September 11, or approximately one hour and 15 minutes per day.
- The Italian broadcasting network RAI decided, largely without consultation, which events to cover and provided the necessary camera work, which then required that CBS transcribe the Italian picture, cast at 625 lines per second, into the standard U.S. picture of 525 lines.
- Ponderous TV cameras that weighed more than 60 pounds each lumbered through each broadcast site tethered to cables the circumference of boa constrictors.
- Tapes of each event were flown by commercial aircraft to America, a 9.5 hour trip.
- Jim McKay, a former *Baltimore Sun* police reporter, would then edit the film, write the copy, and provide the voiceover.
- *Encyclopedia Britannica* was a major source of background information for the broadcasts.

HISTORICAL SNAPSHOT
1960

- The National Association of Broadcasters reacted to a payola scandal by threatening fines for any disc jockeys who accepted money for playing particular records

- Four students from North Carolina Agricultural and Technical State University in Greensboro, North Carolina, began a sit-in at a segregated Woolworth's lunch counter, which triggered similar nonviolent protests throughout the Southern United States

- Joanne Woodward received the first star on the Hollywood Walk of Fame

- Adolph Coors III, chairman of the board of the Coors Brewing Company, was kidnapped for $500,000 and later found dead

- The United States announced that 3,500 American soldiers would be sent to Vietnam

- Arthur Leonard Schawlow and Charles Hard Townes received the first patent for a laser

- The United States launched the first weather satellite, TIROS-1

- *Ben Hur* won the Oscar for Best Picture

- A Soviet missile shot down an American Lockheed U-2 spy plane; the pilot, Francis Gary Powers, was captured, tried, and released 21 months later in a spy swap with the U.S.

- President Dwight D. Eisenhower signed the Civil Rights Act of 1960 into law

- The U.S. Food and Drug Administration announced that it would approve birth control as an additional indication for Searle's Enovid, making it the world's first approved oral contraceptive pill

- The nuclear submarine *USS Triton* completed the first underwater circumnavigation of Earth

- In Buenos Aires, four Mossad agents abducted fugitive Nazi Adolf Eichmann, who was using the alias "Ricardo Klement"

- The Soviet Union beat Yugoslavia 2-1 to win the first European Football Championship

- Harper Lee released her critically acclaimed novel *To Kill a Mockingbird*

- The two leading U.S. presidential candidates, Richard M. Nixon and John F. Kennedy, participated in the first televised presidential debate

- Nikita Khrushchev pounded his shoe on a table at a United Nations General Assembly meeting to protest the discussion of Soviet Union policy toward Eastern Europe

- Entertainer Sammy Davis, Jr. married Swedish actress May Britt

- Basketball player Wilt Chamberlain grabbed 55 rebounds in a single game

- Production of the DeSoto automobile brand ceased

- President Eisenhower authorized the use of $1 million toward the resettlement of Cuban refugees, who were arriving in Florida at the rate of 1,000 a week

- The U.S. Supreme Court declared in *Boynton v. Virginia* that segregation on public transit was illegal

- The U.S. Census listed all people from Latin America as white, including blacks from the Dominican Republic, European whites from Argentina, and Mexicans who resembled Native Americans

- The world population was 3,021,475,000

Selected Prices

Board Game, Monopoly $3.33
Bologna, per Pound $0.39
Boy Scout Uniform $10.75
Dictaphone $161.00
Drive-in Movie, per Car $1.50
Driving Lessons $46.88
Fountain Pen $14.95
Microfilm, 100 feet, 16 mm $4.90
Tuition, Augusta Military Academy, Year $1,300
Whiskey, Canadian Club, Quart $7.85

HOW WILL THEY MEASU
AGAINST THE KIDS NEXT

Uncomfortable as the idea is, this is the time to fa
Everyone wants more for his children. And your ch
to compete just as you're competing now in the ar

That's one of the biggest single reasons why so m
have Encyclopaedia Britannica in their home.
Britannica is an easy source of reference the whole
It is the world's most complete collection of facts a
excitingly explained by leading authorities. In it, y
about sports, find a hobby, increase your appreciat
learn about gardening, missiles, philosophy, science
any subject you've ever heard of . . . and thousands

Britannica is more than words—and more than
illustrations. It is a seeking of the mind for truth a
It is priceless for your children. It can be equally in

New edition
ENCYCLOPAEDIA
BRITANNICA
available direct from the publisher on
Book a Month
Payment Plan
you get all 24 volumes now . . . pay later!

There's nothing like a new car—and no compact car like this deluxe Corvair 700.

Corvair
BY CHEVROLET

Our sportsmen represent the new socialistic order where mental health and moral purity are harmonically tied with physical development. Sports and physical development are the habit of the nation. They are the source of the good spirit, happiness, hard work, and long lives of the Soviet people.

—*Pravda*, August 22, 1960

"1,500 Will Cover Olympics," *Pacific Stars and Stripes,* July 31, 1960:

About 1,500 newsmen, photographers, and radio and television commentators will cover the Olympic Games in Rome from August 25 through September 11.

The Italian organizing committee issued 1,200 passes to newsmen from all over the world, and 300 photographers and radio and television men. . . .

Rome's telephone company also has put 2,500 telephones and 500 phone booths at the disposal of the press. The telephones are scattered in various sports arenas and in the main press center. . . .

The organizing committee made several separate accords with various television companies in Europe, the United States and Japan to telecast the games.

Seventy foreign radio organizations have asked the Italian Radio Company (RAI) for technical equipment for their services in connection with radio information in the games.

To meet such a great demand RAI set up a radio center at the Rome Music College near the Foro Italico, which will be the site of many Olympic events. . . .

Technical installations at the radio center include 58 special studios which will be placed at the disposal of various foreign countries for production of their radio programs.

RAI installed more than 800 circuits to ensure links between the radio center and the competition arenas, and to the international center of the Italian State Telephone Company. . . .

More than 250 operators and technicians, from various RAI stations throughout Italy, will be brought to Rome for the games and will be used exclusively for this radio service.

To handle the flood of news copy expected to amount to hundreds of thousands of words a day, special telegraph, cable and radio circuits are being opened between Rome and major cities on every continent.

Olympic Weightlifting Terms

Press: The barbell is lifted from floor to chest and then chest to overhead in two smooth movements with a slight bend but no shifting of the feet.

Snatch: The weight is lifted floor to overhead in one explosive movement; the lifter is allowed to shift his feet.

Clean and jerk: The weight is taken from floor to shoulder height, held there briefly, then lifted overhead with a squat and spring of the legs.

"Former Carbondale Man on Olympic Team,"
Southern Illinoisan, July 10, 1960:

David Lurie, recently chosen member of the U.S. equestrian team, has long dreamed of becoming a star in this last aristocratic Olympic sport.

His father, George Lurie, an executive of Good Luck Glove Company, Carbondale, said his son "decided when he was still young that regular horseback riding was for girls" and that he had his sights set on the more rugged phases of the sport.

Lurie, 20, formerly of Carbondale and who now lives in St. Louis, was named to the Olympic equestrian team that will represent the U.S. in Rome in September after trials recently at Pebble Beach, California.

The phase of riding at which Lurie has excelled is far from being a sissy sport. His father said that the sport takes better conditioning on the part of the athlete than hockey and boxing and is more dangerous.

The three-day equestrian event is made up of three phases: dressage, an endurance test, and stadium jumping. Dressage is where the horse and rider go through intricate maneuvers. The endurance test is a type of steeplechase similar to the Grand National. It is, in effect, a combination of all phases of riding.

Only one horse is allowed to be used for all three phases of the event. The Olympic Committee furnishes the horses to be used but Lurie also owns his own jumper, Capal.

Most of the horses qualified for this event cost from $10,000-$15,000.

The danger that exists is underlined by an accident that kept him out of the Pan American Games in Chicago last year. In a Colorado Springs practice session in 1957, his horse hit a jump and landed on top of him and Lurie suffered a broken collarbone.

In the obstacle course on the endurance test lies the big danger. The course for the Olympic trials at Pebble Beach was specially built for the maximum degree of difficulty. Some of the jumps were 12 to 15 feet in length and about six feet high.

One shuddering jump, called "the coffin" by the horsemen, has a deep ditch behind the jump. The horse must jump both a wall and a ditch after sliding down a deep incline.

The senior Lurie has some fear for his son in the Olympics with reason. In the 1956 Olympics at Stockholm, 53 horses fell on one jump alone and some of the horses had to jump over ones lying injured atop a fence. In 33 obstacles over a five-mile stretch, there were 107 falls and 21 horses that did not make the finish line.

The horse never sees the jumps prior to the race, but the rider can walk around the course ahead of time.

Sample of Apparatus Needed for Olympics, Rome 1960, David Maraniss:

Here is but a small, random sample of what was needed: 12 pole vault uprights, 100 competition hurdles, 384 training hurdles, 40 competition discuses, 165 ash javelins, 40 competition hammers, 138 shots for putting, 96 starting blocks, 110 writing frames for judges, 100 wooden folding chairs, 130 relay batons, 3 mobile luminous indicator boards, 4 special starter pistols, 1,000 metallic torches to fuel the marathon course, 3,000 black competitor numbers on white background for men, 1,500 yellow competitor numbers on black background for women, 300 white competitor numbers on black background for marathon, 110 official basketballs, 60 training balls, six backboards, nine basketball nets, 570 boxing gloves, 580 elastic bandages, 27 speed balls, 47 jump ropes, four brass megaphones for rowing, 40 bicycle carrier frames, 318 plastic armlets, 2 horse slaughter pistols, 100 cockades for horses, 20 electrified blades for sabers, 150 mats for fencing, 480 field hockey balls, 100 sawdust pillows for shooting lines, 60,000 targets for small bore rifles, 50 water polo balls, 153 water polo caps, 262 weights, 39 steel bars for weights, 40 wrestling whistles, 60 protest flags for Finn Class yachting, 400 floating smoke signals, 340 baskets holding 7,200 pigeons, and a fleet of 288 Fiats, 142 buses, 76 Lambretta motor scooters, and 100 Vespas.

"New Grid League Has Troubles," *GRIT*, November 27, 1960:

Owners of clubs in the American Football League are discovering there are plenty of headaches connected with launching a new grid circuit, foremost of which is bucking the established National Football League to the box office. In the battle for the entertainment dollar, the NFL is way out in front.

Crowds of more than 50,000 are common in NFL games, whereas the AFL has few crowds of more than 25,000. On one Sunday alone, five NFL games featured cliffhanging action, out-rivaling any work of fiction. Less than one touchdown separated the rivals, and in just about every case the winning points were scored in the final minutes of play. That's tough competition for a new loop with few "name" players to attract fans.

Tune in to a broadcast of an NFL game and you hear the scores of other league games, but no scores of games in the rival loop. On an AFL broadcast, however, you get scores in both loops. It's a tipoff on which league has the clamp on the Pro football TV fans.

Commissioner Joe Foss, of the AFL, freely admits the new circuit will lose about $2 million this year. Other observers estimate losses will be even higher. And if it weren't for television, the league would lose close to $4 million in its first season. Under a five-year contract with the sponsors, each team in the AFL gets $225,000 yearly from TV. Without this fee, some of the teams might have folded already.

"Negro Singer to Wed White Actress Sunday," *The Danville Virginia Bee,* November 12, 1960:

The Sunday wedding of Sammy Davis, Jr., 34, and Swedish actress May Britt, 26, took on a formal note today with the following communiqué issued by the Negro performer's press representatives:

"Following a private family wedding ceremony, Mr. and Mrs. Sammy Davis, Jr., will go to the Nordic Room of the Beverly Hills Hotel, arriving there at 4 p.m.

"They will remain in the Nordic Room posing for photographs and answering questions from the press for approximately 30 minutes. They will then depart for a private wedding which, for the convenience of their guests, Mr. and Mrs. Davis have requested to be closed to the press."

Newspapers as far away as Stockholm, Miss Britt's hometown, have sent reporters here to cover the rites.

The ceremony will be held at Davis's home above Sunset Strip and will be performed by a rabbi. Frank Sinatra will be Davis's best man and Miss Britt's bridesmaids will include the wives of Davis's business manager and his pianists.

Both Davis and his bride-to-be converted to the Jewish faith.

"Boom in Organized Bowling Continues, No End in Sight," *GRIT,* October 23, 1960:

If you are bowling in one or more leagues this year, you are a member of the fastest-growing participant sport in the nation.

The boom in bowling is so swift that even those who are directing it have difficulty keeping pace with it today.

"Four years ago our membership showed a 10 percent gain," said Frank Baker, executive secretary of the American Bowling Congress. "The next year the gain went up about 12 percent. We look, then, for a leveling off. But for the last two years the surge reached 20 percent."

The progress, said Baker, has been almost incredible since the Second World War. ABC membership in 1946 was 880,000. Today it is 3,500,000 and still growing. It's estimated the total will reach 5,000,000 by 1965.

The interest in the tenpins sport is tremendous. Bowling shows on lanes have contributed to the rapid growth of the sport.

Professional bowlers compete on one TV show for king-size stakes. Six straight strikes are worth from $25,000 up. Frank Clause, of old Forge, Pa., won a $40,000 jackpot on one recent show.

There also is a marked increase in the number of youngsters participating. It is estimated 11,300,000 boys and girls will be firing at tenpins during the new bowling year, most of them taking part in the Junior bowling program of the ABC. This represents an increase of 4,000,000 young bowlers in the two-year period.

"Defending the Jump Shot," Jerry Grunska, coach, Highland Park, Illinois, High School, *Scholastic Coach Magazine,* October 1960:

As a basketball coach, I don't claim to have the antidote to the plague known as the jump shot. I doubt if there is one. If there is, it's certainly a well-kept secret. I know I've never seen anything on the defense of this lethal weapon.

Too many coaches are fatalistic on this score. They're inclined to throw up their hands and say, "What can you do against the good jump shooter?" Other coaches are content to tell the guards to stay close to the jump shooter, force him away from the choice shooting spots, and to nudge him off balance (with the chest) when he goes up for the shot.

Rather than adopt the fatalistic attitude or trust in divine providence (luck), I've attempted to develop a number of skills in blocking the jump shot. These individual techniques have been developed through trial and error by our squad members, observation of college and pro athletes, and analysis of the tactics employed by our opponents.

No question about it, the tremendous challenge of blocking a jump shot stems from the fact that the shooter knows when he is going to jump in the air, while the defense doesn't. Should the defender anticipate the move, he is likely to be faked off his feet. And if his reaction time isn't hair-trigger quick, he'll always be late in timing his leap.

He must respond to the stimuli of the shooter's movement. Admittedly, the simple laws of stimulus and response give the shooter the advantage of prior movement. The defender can hardly avoid being a trifle late in his timing no matter how hard he tries. The process of timing the defensive leap is so complex that I feel it's nearly unteachable. It must be an inherent factor in the athlete's make up, a sort of "sixth sense" in his reflexes.

Even when the timing is right, there's always the big danger of fouling that shooter. Jump shooters nearly always leap straight into the air. They hang at the height of their jump while they shoot and follow through, and usually descend almost straight downward.

The defender usually takes off from a point several feet from the shooter. To have any hope whatever of blocking the shot, he must leap toward the shooter. This will cause his downward progress to be forward as well, so that even if his upward movement hasn't caused contact, his downward flight is likely to.

The defender has one factor in his favor. Whereas the shooter must carry the ball above his head with two hands, the defender can achieve greater extension by using one hand to block the shot. This is his lone advantage. Since he doesn't have the ball and since he uses only one hand, his free arm gives him a chance to gain balance, even while in flight. His jump can be controlled. And it must be to be effective.

1962 PROFILE

Charles Plautard, realizing he didn't quite have what it took to be a professional baseball player, opted to sell drinks and snacks at the games played at Busch Stadium in St. Louis.

Life at Home

- Charles Plautard was born in the central Broadway section of St. Louis, Missouri, the only son of Pierre and Anne-Marie Plautard.
- The Plautard name was first introduced to the area by French fur traders, who built a post on the site of the city in 1764.
- Charlie's father was the owner/operator of a small newsstand on Broadway near Busch Stadium, home of the St. Louis Cardinals baseball team.
- Charlie loved the Cardinals, and most of all loved to follow the exploits of Stan "the Man" Musial.
- Like thousands of young boys growing up in the Gateway City, Charlie dreamed of one day wearing a Cardinals red jersey and being interviewed by *St. Louis Globe-Democrat* sportswriter Bob Burnes.
- Playing highly competitive high school baseball made Charlie realize that, although a decent player, he was no threat to take Stan the Man's job in the Cardinals outfield.
- In 1959, at age 17 and in need of a job, Charlie sought employment at Busch Stadium, relishing the opportunity to simultaneously earn money and root for his beloved Cardinals.
- It was a slow process, with dozens of disappointing trips to the ballpark as he waited his turn for a job.
- His persistence finally paid off when he became a vendor at Busch Stadium.
- He was first assigned to sell the heaviest, least popular drinks, but a baseball barker nonetheless.
- Within two years, he was earning enough money working at the ballpark and at his father's newsstand to rent his own apartment.
- The *St. Louis Post-Dispatch* classifieds advertised "Clean bachelor apartment, completely furnished, $57.50 per month."

Charles Plautard loved the St. Louis Cardinals.

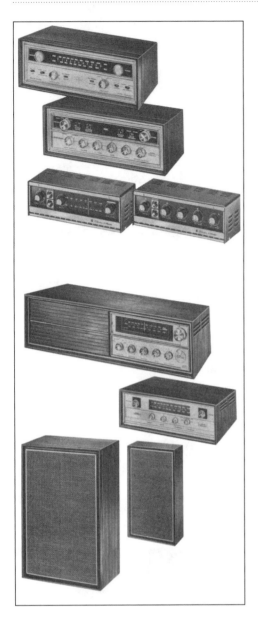

Charlie's new hi-fi allowed him to listen to all the away games.

- One of his first purchases for his new apartment was an Avril playmate hi-fi with long-distance radio so he could listen to the Cardinals away games on the Liberty Mutual Broadcasting network.
- To save money on records, he signed up for the record club where he could have any five of his favorite records mailed to him for $1.97.
- Working as a stadium vendor was physically demanding, so to stay in shape he bought a 110-pound set of final jacketed weights with two dumbbells from Sears Roebuck for $20.
- Charlie was known for his parties, with the music of José Feliciano, a 19-inch GE TV, and lots of Budweiser beer—now with new tabbed aluminum cans.
- Food and beverages have been a part of baseball since 1859.
- During the earliest decades of professional baseball, an array of food was available: peanuts, soft drinks, Cracker Jack, ice cream, cherry pie, cheese, chocolate, hard-boiled eggs, sandwiches, coconut custard pies, planked onions and even tripe.
- Vendors also hawked beer, soda water and chewing gum.
- In fact, a controversy surrounding the selling of beer led to the formation of a new league.
- The National League, sensitive to the image of ballparks—too much drinking, gambling, and generally unsuited for women—tried to eliminate all ballpark alcohol.
- However, Cincinnati Stadium had a long tradition of beer and whiskey sales that averaged $3,000 a season, which supported several of the city's largest industries.
- Rather than face the financial damage of a no-beer ballpark, Cincinnati quit the National League and formed what would later become the American Association, inextricably linking beer and baseball.

Staying in shape helped Charlie to carry all his vending equipment.

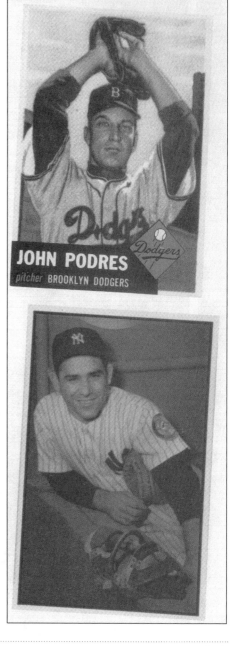

JOHN PODRES
pitcher BROOKLYN DODGERS

Life at Work

- Charlie Plautard was so excited about applying for work as a vendor at Busch Stadium, he arrived two hours before game time, only to be greeted by a throng of other boys and men with a similar goal.
- The year was 1959 and he was 17.
- Unfazed, he joined the rest of the crowd awaiting the arrival of the food concession's manager, who picked from the crowd those who would have the opportunity to sell drinks and snacks during the game.
- The manager would scan the crowd and then point, one at a time, until his daily quota of workers was filled.
- Work as a concessionaire was for one day only, so the selection process was repeated for every new game day.
- The manager possessed a keen memory for faces and work ethic of those he had hired previously.
- He didn't need a fancy evaluation sheet to know who was watching the game when they should be selling, or who attracted so little attention to himself he never made any sales.
- Charlie returned day after day for weeks before he was given an opportunity for the first time.
- He learned to wave and holler to draw attention to himself.
- On the day it happened, he was lined up along the wall with the other prospective workers after the usual veterans had already been hired.
- The boss gave him a look and then pointed in the direction of the other hires.
- Charlie was given a crate of 7-Up and his instructions.
- It was June 21, 1959, and on that day Stan Musial doubled twice—the 652nd and 653rd hits of his career—to break Honus Wagner's National League record during the doubleheader against the Pirates.
- Working two games in a row was exhausting, but exhilarating.

Vendors and stadiums have a long history.

- After that, Charlie was consistently picked on game day.
- Products given to each vendor to sell was determined by seniority
- For those at the top that meant hot dogs.
- They were lighter in weight and far more profitable than soda.
- The hot dog, or red hot, was created by the pioneer concessionaire Harry Stevens on a cold day at the polo grounds in New York when ice cream wasn't selling.
- Harry sent an assistant out for frankfurters, which were sausages sold by the local German groceries.
- He boiled the sausages in water and put them in long buns so the fans could hold and eat them.
- But it was the vendors yelling, "Get them while they're hot, get your red hots here," that attracted the attention of sports cartoonist Tad Dorgan.
- When he published a sketch of the concession workers serving the frankfurters and coined the term "hot dogs," the name stuck.
- As success continued for the Cardinals, so, too, for Charlie
- During his first season as a vendor, he moved up far enough to sell ice cream, and the Red Birds kept winning.
- The popularity of baseball was booming—innovator/owner Bill Veeck added the players' names to their uniforms, and ballparks nationwide were averaging 14,000 fans per game.
- In 1962, after three years of selling, Charlie finally made the big time and was named a hotdog man in Busch Stadium.
- Some vendors developed special tosses or behind-the-back passes to impress the crowd, but Charlie was known for one thing—good service.
- He loved hawking his wares to the crowd using the traditional "red hots here" yell like the vendors of old.

Hearing each crack of the bat while hawking his wares was exciting to Charlie.

- With his booming voice and winning personality, he was popular among the fans and one of the top earners at the stadium.
- The average fan spent between $0.70 to $0.90 per game on drinks and snacks, making the concessions worth $12 million a year.
- The 1962 season began with an 11-4 Cardinal victory over the New York Mets, a team making their baseball debut.
- Stan Musial was on a tear and with each game, it seemed, he shattered another record.
- On June 22, while Charlie watched from the stands, Musial became major league's all-time leader in total bases with 15,864.
- In all, Musial broke four all-time records at Busch Stadium, but he was only one part of a memorable year for Charlie.
- On September 23, the Dodgers' Maury Wills singled and stole second and third to tie Ty Cobb's record of 96 stolen bases in a season, and in the seventh inning, he added one more steal to set a new record.
- Best of all, the Cardinals won the game 11-2.

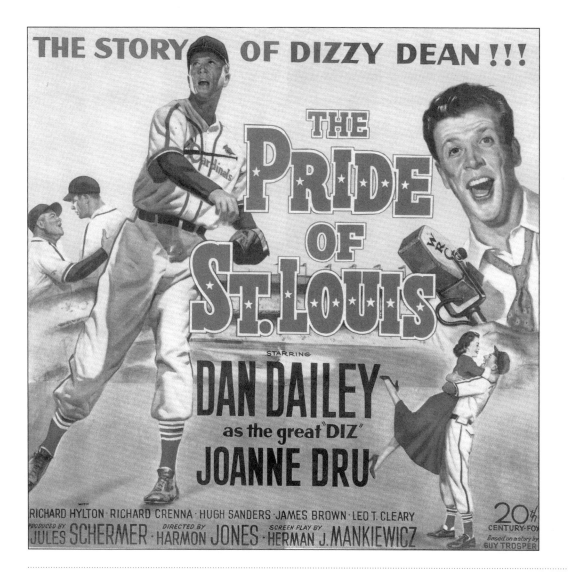

Life in the Community: St. Louis, Missouri

- During the first half of the 1800s, St. Louis was "Gateway to the West," attracting entrepreneurs such as Adolphus Busch, who immigrated to America in 1857 and established a brewing business with his father-in-law Eberhard Anheuser in 1866.
- In 1873 Adolphus Busch discovered a process of pasteurizing beer that allowed the beer to withstand temperature fluctuations.
- This permitted the firm to distribute its beer on a wider basis.
- In conjunction with Carl Conrad, a St. Louis restaurateur, Busch developed a light beer called Budweiser, believing that consumers would prefer it to the darker brews that dominated the market.
- In 1953 Augustus "Gussie" Busch bought the St. Louis Cardinals team and Anheuser-Busch purchased the old Sportsman Park, renaming it Busch Stadium.
- St. Louis quickly developed a reputation as a baseball town.
- Fans rarely booed, always knew the pitch-count, could anticipate a hit-and-run, and appreciated good defensive play—from both teams.
- In keeping with its personal tradition, Busch Stadium fans did not sing "Take Me Out to the Ballgame" for the seventh-inning stretch, but instead clapped along to the Budweiser musical theme.
- "Take Me Out to the Ballgame" was played in Busch Stadium in the eighth inning.

HISTORICAL SNAPSHOT
1962

- Ninety percent of American households owned at least one television set
- ABC began telecasts in color three and a half hours per week
- The world came to the brink of war when America and the Soviet Union faced off over the installation of Soviet missiles in Cuba
- New York City introduced a subway train that operated without a crew on board

- The Beatles' first record, "My Bonnie" with Tony Sheridan, was released by Polydor
- Leonardo da Vinci's *Mona Lisa* was exhibited in the United States for the first time, at the National Gallery of Art in Washington, DC
- *Ranger 3* was launched by NASA to study the moon, but missed it by 22,000 miles
- Captured American spy pilot Francis Gary Powers was exchanged for captured Soviet spy Rudolf Abel in Berlin
- Six members of the Committee of 100 of the Campaign for Nuclear Disarmament were found guilty of a breach of the Official Secrets Act
- First Lady Jacqueline Kennedy took television viewers on a tour of the White House
- John Glenn became the first American to orbit Earth, three times in four hours, 55 minutes, as a member of Project Mercury
- Wilt Chamberlain scored 100 points in a single NBA basketball game
- The U.S. Supreme Court ruled that federal courts could order state legislatures to reapportion seats
- A Cuban military tribunal convicted 1,179 Bay of Pigs attackers
- The Century 21 Exposition World's Fair opened in Seattle, Washington
- The Hulk debuted with *The Incredible Hulk #1* by cartoonists Stan Lee and Jack Kirby
- Dayton Hudson Corporation opened the first of its Target discount stores in Roseville, Minnesota

- Adolf Eichmann was hanged in Israel
- Students for a Democratic Society completed the Port Huron Statement
- The U.S. Supreme Court ruled that mandatory prayers in public schools were unconstitutional
- The Supreme Court ruled that photographs of nude men were not obscene, decriminalizing nude male pornographic magazines
- The first Wal-Mart store opened for business in Rogers, Arkansas
- *Amazing Fantasy #15* featured the superhero character of Spider-Man, created by cartoonists Stan Lee and Steve Ditko

Selected Prices

Air Conditioner, 5,800 BTU $158.00
Apples, Pound $0.10
Baby Food, Three Jars $0.29
Car Seat $6.95
Hi-Fi Phonograph $29.95
LP Record, Peter, Paul and Mary $1.77
Movie Camera, Kodak $1,000
Swimsuit, Woman's $24.00
Tape Recorder $99.95
Television, General Electric, 19 Inch $139.95

"Rube-Barbs," Rube Samuelson,
Pasadena Star News, June 1, 1962:

Using the flying machines and adjusting to all hours of living, major league baseball is now taking a leaf out of pro basketball's book. In other words, operating on PDST [Pacific Daylight Savings Time] one day and EDST [Eastern Daylight Savings Time] the next, a difference of three hours. Adjusting to that setup, sleep-wise, eating-wise, not to mention being ready to play again, is difficult indeed.

The Dodgers can serve as the latest illustration. They flew to Spokane on Monday, played a night game there with their farm club, then flew to New York immediately after. Arrival time in Gotham was around 11 a.m. Fortunately no game was scheduled in New York Tuesday night, and such a schedule is hardly recommended to be ready for Wednesday's doubleheader with the Mets at the Polo Grounds. The Mets themselves provide another example. They arrived by plane at 5:45 a.m. on Wednesday of last week, played three night games against the Dodgers, flew out after the third tilt to arrive in San Francisco at 2 a.m. to get to sleep at 3:30, and played the Giants that afternoon!

All that makes for .330 hitters at best. As Rogers Hornsby, the Mets coach, who rates as the greatest right-handed hitter of all time (he hit .424 in 1924), commented to this writer:

"In my time we played only during the afternoon. While the thing today is to shoot for homers to get the big pay envelopes, the fact remains that night games, rushed air travel, and irregular hours make .400 averages almost impossible."

"Musial Signs for Last Time, Office Job Awaits St. Louis Star,"
San Mateo Times, January 5, 1962:

Stan Musial signed his 1962 contract with the St. Louis Cardinals today saying, "This looks like my last year in baseball."

"I'll try to make this a real good one," Musial said in a morning news conference.

The contract amount was not disclosed. Musial, who said he will be 42 this winter, added, "I don't want to be the oldest player to ever play."

The guess last year was that Musial signed for about $75,000. It was announced that there had been "an adjustment downward."

"That's because of the taxes, and the adjustments amount to very little," Musial said.

"World's Fair Poises for Start Today," *The Salt Lake Tribune,* April 21, 1962:

The Seattle World's Fair, packed with color, culture and science, will open Saturday with President Kennedy pressing a gold telegraph key at Palm Beach, Florida.

This is the same key made of gold nuggets gathered at the Klondike Gold Rush, which President William Howard Taft used to open the Alaska-Yukon-Pacific Exposition in Seattle in 1909.

The World's Fair not only tells the story of man's progress in the last half-century—it also projects man 38 years in the future with a bold forecast of how he'll be living in the year 2000. . . .

A first-day crowd of 90,000 has been forecast by Mayor Gordon Clinton, who wants the entire city to celebrate the moment of the opening by ringing bells, blowing horns and whistles and generally acting as if it were New Year's Eve.

"Huge Salt Cavern in Kansas May Be U.S. Treasure Chest," *GRIT,* November 27, 1960:

A gigantic cavern deep in the Kansas earth is so far beneath the surface the most powerful nuclear bombs could not faze it, and so big that it could contain a whole small town. Some day it may become a vast subterranean fortress—filled with priceless treasures and perhaps even the nerve center that would keep the United States alive in the event of war or some national disaster.

The cavern is the workings of the Carey Salt Company, which for 37 years has been making rock salt out of the vein that runs 400 to 600 feet beneath the surface of the ground around Hutchinson, Kansas. It contains 50,000,000 cubic feet of space, more than triple the area of the Pentagon, the huge headquarters for the American forces at Washington.

First steps have already been taken toward converting this fantastic chamber into a national safety deposit vault.

"Sports Mirror" John Mooney, sports editor,
The Salt Lake Tribune, April 21, 1962:

You may have forgotten all about G.P. (Spike) Arnspiker because it has been a few seasons since he was one of the top riflemen in the area.

But Spike hasn't forgotten about sports.

The other day he called to raise the point.

"You know, a lot of people say 'so what' if the Russians beat us in an athletic competition," Arnspiker challenged. "Well, in the February issue of the *American Legion Magazine,* if you'll check, to see how important it is for the United States to beat the Russians at everything, sports included."

The article he mentioned pictured Soviet newspapers with the following headlines or excerpts from stories:

"Brilliant victory for Soviet sport."

"Sportsmen justify hopes of Soviet people."

"Glory to Soviet sportsmen—heroes of the 17th Olympics."

"The secret of our success—mass work."

Prime Minister Khrushchev boasted, "The triumph of the Soviet sportsmen means a victory for the man of the new socialist society which has already given so much proof of its superiority in the field of science, technology and culture."

Perhaps we have the proper attitude in competing in the Olympic Games for the sheer sport of competing and for the friendships developed among contestants.

But were our athletes as eager to succeed as the Russians, we would enjoy the fun of competition, and still win more events.

There is a fallacy that the sportsmanship award must always go to a loser.

1968 Profile

After 10 years of playing amateur golf, Sally O'Neill turned pro at a time when women's golf was enjoying unprecedented popularity.

Life at Home

- Sally O'Neill's first day at work was a dream come true.
- After a decade of playing amateur golf, Sally O'Neill had turned pro.
- Just standing next to Ladies Professional Golf Association star Kathy Whitworth was a thrill, but learning that she was paired to play a practice round with her hero was both intimidating and exhilarating.
- Sally was only three years old when she first picked up her father's golf club and pretended to take a swing.
- At nine she broke 100, and at 14 she shot 73 on a public course near her house.
- Now she was preparing to be a member of the Ladies Professional Golf Association.
- The 1960s was a time of great expansion for women's golf.
- New courses were popping up everywhere, and earth-moving equipment was allowing golf course designers to create imaginative new contours in the land.
- Riding mowers were making course maintenance less expensive, while encouraging larger and more complex greens and tees.
- Expanded air travel was allowing many to play in faraway courses, especially in the South, where the development of warm weather grasses was creating new opportunities.
- It was also the age of television.
- Golf's premiere moment came in 1953 on the final round of the Men's World Championship of Golf, where a single camera had been positioned atop the grandstand.
- In that setting, Lew Worsham needed a birdie three to reach a playoff with Chandler Harper and win the $25,000 first prize.
- After a perfect tee shot, Worsham faced a wedge approach for roughly 120 yards.
- From there he drove a low shot that continued to roll for 60 feet straight into the hole for an eagle to an outright victory.

Sally O'Neill entered women's professional golf at 26 years old.

Innovative machinery made for more challenging golf courses.

- That historic moment, witnessed by thousands, ushered in coverage of the 1954 Open and the Masters Golf Tournament in 1955.
- By the time Sally was consistently winning tournaments in the early 1960s, every major men's tournament was either on television or preparing to be televised.
- Sally understood the absolute joy of a smooth swing, a soft loft and a perfect landing.
- Her father's friends loved to carp about the frustration that golf engendered, to reassure themselves that golf was a *real* sport even though no one wore helmets.
- Sally also knew how it felt to make those periodic bad swings, but always went back to her father's advice—hold on to the good moments.
- Sally's mother had fallen in love with golf first, then her husband, then her daughter, and then alcohol
- By the time Sally was six, her mother mostly loved alcohol.
- By second grade, Sally learned not to invite friends over to the house
- Her mother spent most afternoons passed out on the living room couch and didn't like the sound of giggly girls.
- Sally found refuge with her great-uncle at the pro shop, where he checked in players, sold equipment and kept the golf merchandise straight.
- On late afternoons, too late to start a round, Sally and her great-uncle would walk the course and swing at a few golf balls.
- First she developed her short game and practiced incessantly, punching the ball onto the green from 30 yards out.
- Only when she had her grip right and her confidence secure was she allowed to pick up a driver.
- Some days her father would arrive at the golf course in time to walk a few holes before they went home.

- Together they would prepare the evening meal and try to coax Sally's mother into eating something.
- Afterwards, they would play board games that emphasized patience, flexibility, planning ahead and keeping your cool.
- In later years, after Sally had left home, she always played board games before a major match because it calmed her nerves.

Life at Work

- Unlike many of the wunderkinds who dominated the Ladies Professional Golf Association, Sally O'Neill was in her mid-twenties before she turned pro.
- But she fully understood what Kathy Whitworth meant when she said, "Golf just grabbed me by the throat. I used to think everyone knew what they wanted to do when they were 15 years old."
- Kathy's parents owned a hardware store in Texas where she grew up as the youngest of three daughters and learned golf using her grandfather's clubs on the nine-hole course built for employees of El Paso Natural Gas.
- Two years after taking up the game at 15, Whitworth won the 1957 New Mexico Women's Amateur golf tournament, a success she repeated the next year.
- Although unpolished, Whitworth had all the shots—from a stellar bunker game to creative recoveries she honed as a teen in New Mexico.
- When she was 20, her father and a couple of local businessmen agreed to subsidize Whitworth's career at $5,000 a year for three years.
- She made $1,217 the first year and came within a hair's breadth of quitting.
- She stayed on the tour after her parents advised, "You have three years. If you don't make it, just come home and we'll do something else."
- It was a story well known to Sally, who didn't have even one year's worth of cushion.
- At 26 she had one shot at making the pro circuit.
- A failed marriage was behind her and she only saw gold ahead.
- On the first tee, Sally positioned herself like a pro, drove like a pro and acted like a pro.
- That lasted through three holes.
- Even though it was only a practice round, Sally was immensely aware that Kathy Whitworth was already ahead by having birdied the first and third holes.
- Sally started to panic—how could she possibly compete at this level every day and make a living?
- On the par four, fourth hole, Sally sliced her tee shot, fired a second shot in the bunker, put the third shot into the back corner of the green, chipped the fourth shot 30 feet beyond the hole, missed the cup on her fifth shot and then dropped in a two-footer for a double bogey six.
- She was so embarrassed, she couldn't even look at Kathy.
- Number five was better, but shaky.
- Number six was a disaster.
- Number seven was even worse.
- On number eight, a par five dogleg, littered with water traps, Kathy teed off first, then stepped beside Sally and said, "Looks like you're trying to copy some of my early rounds when I was just getting started."
- Sally understood.
- She parred the eighth and ninth holes and then fired a 34 on the back nine.
- When Kathy and Sally parted at the end of the day, Kathy said quietly, "I'll be watching you tomorrow."

Harriet (top) and Margaret Curtis

Life in the Community: The Ladies Professional Golf Association (LPGA)

- The early years of the twentieth century were dominated by British women golfers; few American women received major trophies.
- Sisters Harriet and Margaret Curtis, holders of the U.S. Women's Amateur title in 1906 and 1907, played in the British Women's Championship but never dominated.
- Glenna Collett Vare, who captured six U.S. Women's Amateurs between 1922 and 1935, was known for her rhythmic smooth swing that produced long straight shots, but she never won the British Amateur.
- It was not until 1947 that the Women's British Amateur title went to American golfer Babe Didrikson, a superb athlete who had previously won gold medals in 1932 Olympics for the javelin and the 80-meter hurdles.
- In 1950, the Ladies Professional Golf Association was formed with 11 women as its charter members; the effort was underwritten by Wilson Sporting Goods.
- In addition to Didrikson, Patty Berg emerged as a freckled-faced star of the LPGA, serving as its first president.
- By 1952, the LPGA boasted a schedule of 21 events—nearly three times the number of tournaments held just two years before.
- The LPGA Tour prize money reached $200,000 in 1959.
- The LPGA received its first television coverage in 1963 during the final round of the U.S. Women's Open Championship.
- By the end of the 1960s, prize money had grown to $600,000 and the schedule offered 34 events.

Babe Didrikson captured the women's British Amateur title.

HISTORICAL SNAPSHOT
1968

- Johnny Cash recorded *At Folsom Prison*

- The Green Bay Packers won Super Bowl II over the Oakland Raiders 33-14; quarterback Bart Starr was named Most Valuable Player

- *Rowan & Martin's Laugh-In* debuted on NBC

- North Korea seized the USS *Pueblo,* claiming the ship violated its territorial waters while spying

- A civil rights protest staged at a white-only bowling alley in Orangeburg, South Carolina, resulted in the deaths of three South Carolina State College students

- PBS televised the first episode of *Mister Rogers' Neighborhood*

- U.S. President Lyndon B. Johnson mandated that all computers purchased by the federal government support the ASCII character encoding

- President Johnson announced he would not run for re-election after edging out antiwar candidate Eugene J. McCarthy in the New Hampshire Democratic Primary, highlighting the deep divisions in the country over Vietnam

- Congress repealed the requirement for a gold reserve to back U.S. currency

- Howard University students protesting the Vietnam War, the ROTC program on campus and the draft, confronted Gen. Lewis Hershey, head of the U.S. Selective Service System, with cries of "America is the black man's battleground!"

- The film version of Arthur C. Clarke's novel *2001: A Space Odyssey* premiered

- Civil Rights leader Martin Luther King, Jr. was murdered at the Lorraine Motel in Memphis, Tennessee, igniting riots in major American cities across America

- A shootout between the Black Panthers and Oakland police resulted in the death of 16-year-old Panther Bobby Hutton, who was shot by the police over a dozen times after he had surrendered and stripped down to his underwear to prove he was unarmed

- The musical *Hair* opened on Broadway

- The Standard & Poor's 500 Index closed at 100.38, the first time it had ever closed above 100

- U.S. presidential candidate Robert F. Kennedy was shot and killed in Los Angeles, California, by Sirhan Sirhan

- The soap opera *One Life to Live* premiered on ABC

- The semiconductor company Intel was founded

- Police clashed with antiwar protesters in Chicago, Illinois, outside the 1968 Democratic National Convention, which nominated Hubert Humphrey for president and Edmund Muskie for vice president

- Mattel's Hot Wheels toy cars were introduced

Selected Prices

Baseball Cards, 1968 Complete Set	$11.95
Beer, Schlitz, Six Pack	$0.99
Bird Bath	$2.99
Bunk Bed	$69.95
Car Wax	$0.99
Dinette Set	$99.95
Golf Shoes, Women's	$22.00
Range	$299.95
Stroller	$29.95
Tape Recorder, 4-Track	$198.95

"Kathy Whitworth Leads in Tourney," Robert Grimm, *Mansfield News Journal* (Ohio), August 25, 1968:

SPRINGFIELD—Kathy Whitworth, playing her best with big money on the line, fired a three under par 69 Saturday to take a one-stroke lead over Carol Mann after the first round for $35,000 in the Ladies World Series of Golf.

Miss Whitworth, the defending champion in the third annual event, recovered from a bogey on the first hole of the six-woman tournament and played nearly flawlessly the rest of the way.

Her competition faltered in the steamy 90-degree temperature over the 6,194 yard Snyder Park course here.

Miss Mann, recovering on the back nine from an almost disastrous start, was one stroke behind with a 38-32-70 score, followed by Sandra Haynie at even par 72. Susie Maxwell Berning and Sandra Post were at 73 and Mickey Wright was trailing with a six over par 78.

Miss Whitworth played steady golf at one time and at one time on the front nine held a four-stroke lead over Miss Mann. But the six-foot three Miss Mann, leading money winner on the LPGA tour this year, wound up her round in a sensational way, with consecutive birdies on the 16th and 17th holes and an eagle-three on the par five 140-yard 18th hole.

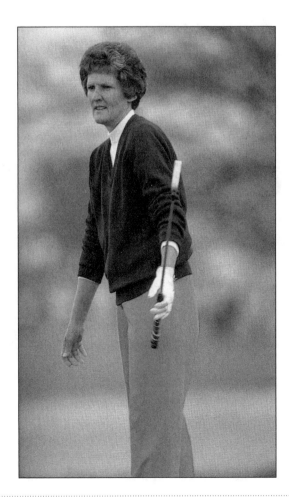

"Census Data," *Britannica Book of the Year,* 1965:

Many authorities believe 1965 marked a historic turning point in worldwide efforts to contain the "population explosion." Encouraged by new policies disclosed during the year by the administration of U.S. Pres. Lyndon B. Johnson, the U.S. and a number of other governments moved at last toward a working consensus that a well-financed attempt must be made to contain or curtail world population growth, particularly in developing lands where the increase of populations continued to outstrip the increase in national wealth. The effect in some emerging countries was to negate even the most strenuous national development schemes to reduce further per capita food supplies.

In 1965 deaths from starvation were reported in parts of India and Pakistan, northeastern Brazil, and in some regions of Africa. The UN estimated that more than half the world population suffered from malnutrition. In 85 countries of Latin America, Africa and Asia, the UN said that about 250 million children were not enrolled in schools, which meant that as many as 20 million persons were added to the illiterate adult population during 1965. About 40 percent of the world population was illiterate.

"The Unwanted Fight," Arthur Daley,
The Winston-Salem Journal (North Carolina), May 11, 1965:

The Cassius Clay-Sonny Liston fight is now in the same category as *Lady Chatterley's Lover* and other works of dubious distinction. It has been banned in Boston.

Like fugitive fighters of ancient days, they have taken it on the lam across state lines and will set up their tent in Lewiston, Maine, 130 miles to the north. It isn't far enough. Labrador would have been better. Then it could have been placed in a deep freeze.

The clock has been turned back half a century or more to the era when pugilists were scrambling to keep at least one step in front of the law.

Those were the days when they fought on barges in secret assembly points. It was a time that Nat Fleischer's *Ring Record Book* now lists with the parenthetical footnote: (police stopped bout). Clay and Liston have loused up a sport that already seemed much too pediculous for further contamination.

Clay could have saved it. When he was winning his Olympic championship in Rome in 1960, he was a likable young man of infinite charm and attractive personality, all the requisites for becoming as popular a heavyweight king as was Joe Louis.

Then he stepped out of character and became a loud-mouthed braggart with his I-am-the-greatest routine and alienated sports followers. It drew attention to him and it moved him up the ladder far faster than if he hadn't been in such a hurry. The worst of it was that his false front became part of his nature.

When Cassius fought Liston for the title in Miami a year ago last February, he should have had everyone rooting for him. Instead, at least half wanted to see Liston jam his big glove into Clay's big mouth. Despite his surly arrogance, disagreeable personality and police record, Sonny-boy actually had people rooting for him.

At the end of the fifth round Clay wanted to quit when some irritating substance found its way into his eyes and blinded him. His seconds pushed him into the ring. At the end of the seventh round Liston wanted to quit, and did, sitting on a stool in abject surrender. His shoulder bothered him, he claimed.

Malodorous though the so-called fight was, the aftermath increased the stench. It was revealed that Clay had joined the Black Muslims and this further alienated the public. Another development was that the Liston camp secretly signed Clay to a return bout after his promotional aegis in the event that he won, a happenstance that didn't allay suspicions that hanky-panky of some sort was involved in the strange ending of their first bout.

When the heat grew intense at the peculiar setup of Intercontinental Promotions, Inc., Liston gave away half his stock to an erstwhile benefactor who just happened to be a friend of Frankie Carbo and a business partner of Blinky Palermo. Later the other half was sold to someone else. But Boston willingly agreed to stage the Clay-Liston rematch last November. On the virtual eve of the fight, Cassius had undergone an emergency hernia operation. Eventually the match was rescheduled for the same Boston Garden on May 25.

However, a new governor was in the state house by then and the climate had changed. Garrett Byrne, the Boston district attorney, began some legal moves and local gendarmes began harassment of Liston in his training camp. That was not too unusual. Liston always had troubles with cops.

Since the tail wags the dog in boxing's present method of doing business, the live gate is of minor consequence compared to the theater-TV. The closed-circuit boys took a stab at Cleveland, which wanted no part of it.

"We'll hold it on barges, if necessary," said the theater-TV boys.

This would have completed the cycle of a total throwback to yesteryear. Lewiston spared them this embarrassment. The bold talk is that Lewiston, a depressed area with a 5,000-seat arena, might draw almost as much live gate as was expected in the Boston Garden, which is almost thrice its size. That's nonsense. The big thing still is theater-television, some $4 million of it.

Clay, now known as Muhammad Ali, will continue training in Chicopee, Massachusetts, while Liston, now laundered to Boy Scout respectability, will shift his camp on Wednesday to Poland Spring near Lewiston. So the fight game has gone tank town like a struggling road show.

Trends in Sports Television

- Nothing was more central to the history of organized sports during the second half of the twentieth century than television.
- With the advent of television, the fan base of every team expanded dramatically—no longer bound by geography.
- To attract more viewers, television added graphics, music and ex-athlete announcers to create a sporting experience unavailable to the fan in the stands.
- Television also changed the rules of several sports, including arbitrary timeouts for commercials and the scheduling of kickoff or tee-off times based on the perceived needs of the viewing public.
- In the 1950s and early 1960s, technology dictated the effectiveness of televised sports.
- Television cameras could follow the two men in the boxing ring but struggled to capture the excitement of a baseball hit into deep left field.
- At the same time, television stole the live audience that supported boxing (and minor league baseball) and wiped out more than half of the fight clubs located in smaller cities.
- ABC was the first of the big three networks to dramatically embrace sports programming.
- For the first time, cranes and helicopters were used to obtain unique views of the stadium; handheld cameras brought close-up shots of cheerleaders to the television audience for the first time and the crowd became part of the performance.
- By the late 1960s, fans carried banners to the games and ran onto the field to catch the attention of television cameras.
- In 1961 ABC began production of *Wide World of Sports*, which offered a potpourri of athletic events and stimulated national interest in sports as diverse as snow skiing, track events and the demolition derby.
- The advent of television also elevated football, which overtook baseball in popularity.

"Home Television by Satellite," editorial,
The Winston-Salem Journal (North Carolina), May 11, 1965:

The demonstrations of live trends—Atlantic Television, reliably relayed by the Early Bird satellite—have been impressive. But the satellite that really threatens to revolutionize television is yet to be built.

That satellite will not simply relay signals across oceans from one transmitting area to another. It will receive signals from the ground to the public. One satellite, hovering 22,000 miles above the equator, could reach nearly all the homes in the nation—or indeed the North and South American continents.

The company that built the Early Bird, Hughes Aircraft Company, says such a satellite will be in orbit within two years after someone puts up the money to pay for it.

The effect of a broadcasting satellite on television could be tremendous. One such satellite would be at least the equivalent of a complete network of local broadcasters. Three of them could offer the public approximately the same national programming services now offered by NBC, CBS and ABC. Six can effectively double the present network services. And there could be far more than six broadcasting satellites.

These orbiting transmitters certainly would not come cheaply. We might make a guess, based on limited information, that one would cost about $20 million. That would be a bargain price for television networks and is well within the range of private capital resources.

But when we go beyond the technical and economic practicality of broadcasting satellites, we run into extremely difficult problems of public policy. The biggest of these is: What happens to local television?

National programming could reach the public more cheaply via satellite; the local stations would have a tough time surviving. These stations represent a huge investment, as well as a source of employment for thousands of persons and communities across the nation. Also they serve as windows for the cultural, political, social and economic activities in their communities. Loss of most or all of these stations would be a grave one indeed.

To be weighed against the losses are the potential gain and viewing choice of the public that several network-operated satellites could provide. The present three-way split of the networks is not enough, apparently, to permit such specialization, and most programs are designed for mass appeal.

So far, there has been no battle on the question of satellite TV. The television industry is faced with more immediate issues, such as the growth of cable television, to concern itself about an innovation that is not far off the drawing boards.

Moreover, satellite TV will take some time in coming. Aside from the task of building orbiting transmitters, there would be the probably slow process of converting receivers to bring in the signals from space. Hughes Aircraft estimates this would cost $140 for each receiver, $40 of which would go for special antennae.

Broadcasting via satellite obviously has fast money-making potential—and such opportunity should not go neglected. Satellite TV could become a reality, and a very public issue, sooner than some of us may suspect.

1960 NEWS FEATURE

"The Boys With the Horse-Sized Job," Ernest Havemann, *Sports Illustrated*, May 23, 1960:

The thoroughbred racehorse, though a noble steed, can be a sore trial to the people around him. Even the shyest little two-year-old, gazing at the world through his gentle and liquid eyes, weighs around 1,000 pounds, mostly in bone, hoof, muscle and teeth. Some horses are grouchy and some are friendly. The symptoms for both are distressingly similar. Whether in anger or in play, the horse knows only a few ways of expressing himself, and these take such forms as rearing, bucking, kicking, jumping and biting. The average $2 bettor, it can be safely said, would be thrown into utter terror by any close contact with the racehorse, affectionate or otherwise.

Being bred for speed and not necessarily for intelligence, furthermore, the comprehension of the modern racehorse of his role in society is sometimes rather limited. Some horses hate to run while others are so enamored of running that they would gladly turn every morning gallop into a speed contest. Some horses love to have the rail at their flanks and keep trying to lug in. Others (the great Whirlaway was one of them) hate the very sight of the rail and try to lug out. Some are lazy and like to lean against the starting gate, a habit that makes them come out sideways when it opens. Some refuse to stand in the gate at all and have to be shipped back to the breeding farm or trained for jumping races where no starting gate is used.

Most horses, however, do get to the track if they have the speed for it, and once there, learn how to behave on it. That they do so is a great tribute to the racehorse trainer, who has always received a great deal of credit and fame—and to the exercise boy, who has heretofore received practically none.

The exercise boy is racing some unsung hero, practically worth his weight (around 120 pounds) in gold. He is out at the stable at dawn, when these frightening creatures are at their friskiest. He puts the exercise saddle on the horse, rides him at a walk to the track, steadies him with the feel of his confident hands on the reins and withers, calms him, reassures him, hangs on when he bucks or shies, teaches him manners, corrects his bad habits, gets him used to standing up straight in the starting gate, gallops him a slow mile or gives him a fast workout that is a marvel of split-second timing. Then he takes the horse back to the stable.

For some exercise boys this is the major part of the job. For others, the day has just started. The boy walks his mount in a circle for half an hour and until his sweat has dried, his hide is cool and he is ready to go back to the stall without danger of pneumonia. After that the boy repeats the process, usually with two more horses. In the afternoon, if one of the horses is racing, the exercise boy leads him into the paddock, helps saddle him, and then turns him over to a jockey who will get all the glory if he wins. Win or lose, the exercise boy reassures the horse while he is unsaddled and led back to the stable, then walks him around again until he cools off.

The exercise boy may be busy at the track until 6 p.m., a little over 12 hours after he first showed up. He works seven days a week all year round, a nomad who follows the horses south in the winter and north in the summer. For this, if he is lucky enough to work for one of the big stables, he gets around $75 a week.

Under the circumstances, nobody sets out deliberately to become an exercise boy. Practically all of them are would-be or has-been jockeys, getting experience or getting fat. Some of the young ones will make the grade as jockeys. Some of the older men will develop into trainers. The others will someday find what little local glory they enjoy slipping through their fingers. Even if an exercise boy can keep his weight within bounds, he is likely to get too cautious in his forties to be much good. In the final analysis his profession is a battle of will and daring between the 120-pound rider and the half-ton horse. A middle-aged man, especially if he has picked up a wife and children along the way, begins to see the discrepancy in the contest and loses his stomach for the bolts, the falls and the bruises. He can then either become a mere stable hand, which is a come down, or leave the racetrack altogether, which is by that time unthinkable.

Most of the really good exercise boys grew up with horses. One such was Freeman McMillan, a long, lean Oklahoman who spent nine years galloping horses for Calumet Farm and included among his protégés Armed and Citation, winners of nearly $2 million between them. McMillan was acknowledged to be just about the best of them all, especially with strong and ambitious horses like these two—who would certainly have busted out from under any ordinary rider and perhaps ruined their careers by exhausting themselves.

Besides his talent for making a headstrong horse behave, McMillan was noted for his judgment of pace. Once he exhibited Citation in a workout between races at Hollywood Park in California. The trainer, Calumet's Jimmy Jones, told them to go a mile in around 1:37. An official clocker at the finish line caught the workout at 1:36 3/5.

Citation, being such a great animal, is not conceded by anyone concerned to have any bad habits. McMillan likes to say: "He had more sense than any horse that ever looked through bridle."

When pressed, McMillan will admit this beautifully mannered horse once kicked him in the stomach. Fortunately the blow landed due center of the stopwatch McMillan was wearing in his trousers watch pocket. The watch was completely flattened but McMillan received only superficial bruises.

Another fine exercise boy, famed among horsemen if not among the public, was Bernie Everson, a tall, dark, serious young man who worked for the Alfred G. Vanderbilt stables. He is chiefly noted as the boy who handled Native Dancer.

Boy met horse in peculiar fashion. The Dancer was one of 11 yearlings freshly broken to saddle who were shipped from the farm to join the Vanderbilt stable at Santa Anita in November 1951. On the day they first went out for a gallop, Everson was riding another of them—he has forgotten which—and another boy was up on the Dancer. They had barely taken the track when the Dancer exhibited some of the playful mannerisms, which he was to retain for his entire racing career. He reared up, fell backward, dumped his rider and took off on a solo exploration of the Santa Anita scenery.

The next time out, Trainer Bill Winfrey asked Everson to take over the Dancer. This was a high compliment, but Everson took a fairly dim view of it at the moment. He had just come off a series of misfortunes. Once, while exercising a gelding named Band Concert at the Laurel track, he had run into a loose horse and wound up with a broken back that kept him in the hospital for months. Soon after he returned to action an unruly 2-year-old threw him and broke his back again. All in all, he was tired of hospitals and full of unpleasant memories—and he could not help recalling that Band Concert, who started it all, had been a gray just like the Dancer. "People ask me if I knew the minute I got up on Native Dancer that I had a great horse," he says. "The truth is, all I was thinking at the time was that I was probably in for a rough ride."

The ride was not as rough as expected, although at the end of it the Dancer got up on his hind legs and pranced lightly off the track in a near-vertical posture, as if trying to live up to his name. This was a routine he kept following whenever leaving the track, presumably in sheer joy at having done his work so well. He also developed a trick of suddenly dropping his left shoulder to get rid of his rider. All in all, he threw Everson off his back six times, and on numerous other occasions he tossed Everson around like a sack of wheat when being walked to cool out.

Native Dancer meant a good deal to Everson. For one thing, he got a percentage of the purse money, and, all in all, the Dancer earned Everson close to $4,000 in extra pay. And having a champion means even more than money. Everson, though he dislikes being considered sentimental, will concede that he had tears in his eyes the day he watched the Dancer lose the Kentucky Derby—and again on the day at Belmont Park when the Dancer said farewell to racing and was shipped home to the farm.

At the opposite pole from the Dancer in Everson's affections stands a deceptively pleasant looking bay colt named Cousin, who went to the races a year before the Dancer and for a time seemed equally promising. In August 1951 Cousin won three 2-year-old stakes at Saratoga, including a length-and-a-half victory over the great Tom Fool in the Hopeful. In the process, however, he developed an abiding distaste for race tracks and began refusing to set foot on them in the training hours. "You couldn't coax him or threaten him," says Everson. "You'd say go and he'd stop; you'd say stop and he'd go. Except he wouldn't go on the track no matter what you said."

Cousin's last race that season was the Futurity at Belmont. He reared at the start, almost throwing his jockey, and finished eighth. The stable retired Cousin but persevered with him over the winter and managed to get him on the track the following spring. He ran poorly a few more times and eventually was sent to England where he became a jumper. As Everson puts it, "Cousin just got the best of everybody. He won out."

The best thing in an exercise boy's life is a champion, like the Dancer. The worst is a horse that could have been great but refused.

1970–1979

Sports on television was very big business in the decade of the 1970s, dramatically impacting salaries, scheduling, and in some cases, regulations on the field of play. In football, baseball, basketball, boxing, auto racing, golf and tennis, athletes began to make millions of dollars a year. The change came because of television money and the sweeping away of archaic rules that claimed athletes belonged to the teams that had drafted them and could be traded at the discretion of the owners. To meet financial demands and expectations of viewers, television executives instituted an increase in the number of games played in the season and even dictated playoff schedules to maximize potential viewership.

The political high water mark for the decade came in 1972 with the passage of Title IX in the federal education amendments. This far-reaching regulation provided a legal basis for structural changes in women's physical education and athletics. Significantly, Title IX established the legal understanding that boys and girls have the same rights to athletic facilities and programs, coaches and instructors, uniforms and transportation.

With the Vietnam War still raging, interest in the environment rising and America's troubled cities deteriorating, the turbulent legacy of the 1960s flowed into the 1970s. Racial unrest rampaged through the public schools, and books, movies, and magazines tested American mores, while protests against the Vietnam War continued. Mix in a volatile economy that caused the cost of living to climb and the result was an America stripped of its ability to dominate the world economy. A scandal-plagued president was driven from office, and another found his presidency—and the nation—held hostage by Iran. Gas prices skyrocketed when Arab oil producers declared an embargo on oil shipments to the United States, setting off shortages and gas rationing for the first time in 30 years. The sale of automobiles plummeted, unemployment and inflation nearly doubled, and the buying power of Americans fell dramatically.

The economy, handicapped by the devaluation of the dollar and inflation, did not fully recover for more than a decade, while the fast-growing economies of Japan and western Europe, especially West Germany, mounted direct competitive challenges to American manufacturers. The value of imported manufactured goods soared from 14 percent of U.S. domestic production in 1970 to 40 percent in 1979. The inflationary cycle of recession returned in 1979 to disrupt markets, throw thousands out of work and prompt massive downsizing of companies. A symbol of the era was the pending bankruptcy of Chrysler Corporation, who could not compete against Japanese imports. The federal government was forced to extend loan guarantees to the company to prevent bankruptcy and the loss of thousands of jobs.

The appointment of Paul Volcker as the chairman of the Federal Reserve Board late in the decade gave the economy the distasteful medicine it needed. To cope with inflation, Volcker slammed on the economic brakes, restricted growth of the money supply, and curbed inflation. As a result, he pushed interest rates to nearly 20 percent—their highest level since the Civil War. Almost immediately the sale of automobiles and expensive items dropped. The decade was also marred by the deep divisions caused by the Vietnam War. When U.S. involvement ended, the Vietnam War had been the longest war in American history, having cost $118 billion and resulted in 56,000 dead, 300,000 wounded, and the loss of American prestige abroad.

The decade was a time not only of movements, but also of moving. In the 1970s, the shift of manufacturing facilities to the South from New England and the Midwest accelerated. The Sunbelt became the new darling of corporate America. By the late 1970s, the South, including Texas, had gained more than a million manufacturing jobs, while the Northeast and Midwest lost nearly two million. Rural North Carolina had the highest percentage of manufacturing of any state in the nation.

The largest and most striking of all the social actions of the early 1970s was the Women's Liberation Movement. It fundamentally reshaped American society. Since the 1950s, a small group of well-placed American women had attempted to convince Congress and the courts to bring about equality between the sexes. By 1972, the National Organization for Women (NOW) multiplied in size, the first issue of *Ms.* magazine sold out in a week, and women began demanding economic equality, the legalization of abortion, and the improvement of women's role in society. "All authority in our society is being challenged," said a Department of Health, Education and Welfare report. "Professional athletes challenge owners, journalists challenge editors, consumers challenge manufacturers . . . and young blue-collar workers, who have grown up in an environment in which equality is called for in all institutions, are demanding the same rights and expressing the same values as university graduates."

The decade also included the flowering of the National Welfare Rights Organization (NWRO), founded in 1966, which resulted in millions of urban poor demanding additional rights. The environmental movement gained recognition and momentum during the decade and the growing opposition to the use of nuclear power peaked after a near calamity at Three Mile Island in Pennsylvania in 1979. As the formal barriers to racial equality came down, racist attitudes became unacceptable and the black middle class began to grow. By 1972, half of all Southern black children sat in integrated classrooms, and about one-third of all black families had risen economically into the ranks of the middle class.

1977 Profile

Sonny Howell credited hard work for his success in the National Hockey League, saying that only winning, beating a man to the puck, and having the stamina in the last period to make a perfect pass mattered.

Life at Home

- One of seven children, Sonny Howell grew up playing basketball in Walpole, Massachusetts, where playing hockey was serious business.
- His three older brothers were basketball players, but most of Sonny's friends were obsessed with hockey.
- At first, Sonny followed his brothers' lead, and didn't play organized hockey until he was 13 years old.
- Then, almost overnight, he became fascinated by the angles and speed of the game.
- He skated on the bantam team as a high school freshman, followed by three years of varsity hockey.
- Never a great goal scorer, Sonny's size and versatility allowed the team to employ him in numerous positions—particularly on defense—to stop the competition's best player.
- It was a strategy that produced team wins, but did not endow Sonny with a total command of a single position.
- "They were always looking for someone who was big enough to play defense, so I was shifted from position to position; but I was sure I was still good enough to play at the college level."
- But it was football that brought Sonny to Colgate University in Hamilton, New York, on an athletic scholarship.
- Sonny was most interested in Colgate because of its academic standing, with athletics a means to an end.
- After a successful freshman year in football as a defensive halfback, Sonny was offered the chance to play hockey.
- The collegiate football and hockey seasons overlapped, so a choice had to be made: hockey defenseman or football defensive halfback.

Sonny Howell chose hockey over all other sports.

- Sonny chose hockey and developed into a spectacular player—the type that always hustled, always anticipated the next pass and never tired of being physical.
- Fortuitously, three Boston Bruins scouts were spectators at the Invitational Tournament during his senior year at Colgate.
- Sonny played well enough to get a tryout invitation with the Bruins.
- All he had to do was work hard and his career would be launched.

Sonny was a versatile player and always hustled on the ice.

Life at Work

- Sonny Howell, at six foot two and 205 pounds, worked for months getting ready for the Boston Bruins training camp.
- "I ran, skated a couple of times a day, lifted weights—just everything I could think of from sun-up to sundown to get ready for the tryouts."
- Friends worked out with him in shifts—one in the morning, one in the afternoon and one in the early evening.
- Sonny's high energy and determination required three athletes to keep up with his training regimen.
- On the first day of training camp, Sonny was sure he was prepared.
- Within the first hour, he realized how much work he still had ahead if he wanted to be a professional.
- Camp was brutal.
- It seemed that everyone was faster and smarter.
- But no one worked harder.
- Time in the American Hockey League would be required before he was ready to handle the power moves and stick play of the National Hockey League.
- The American Hockey League was tough, populated by players desperate to move up to the NHL or terrified that they were about to be moved out of hockey altogether.
- Friendships were fluent and moods were mercurial.
- On the long bus rides from game to game, Sonny read history books—especially concerning World War I.
- His grandfather had fought in the Great War and had returned from France with a limp, a souvenir rifle and an incurable wanderlust.
- After the war, the day-to-day duties on the farm paled beside the uncountable possibilities of travel and adventure.
- Sonny's father had grown up on the road, moving with his restless father every few years.
- The traveling stopped when the car his grandfather was driving through the mountains failed to make a turn and hurdled 1,200 feet to the canyon floor.
- Sonny believed that the secret to his grandfather's emotional life was concealed in the muddy trenches of WWI France.
- So before every away game, he checked another book out of the public library and studied his personal history.
- At the end of the first season with the Rochester Americans, Sonny had played well enough to earn the opportunity to make it in the big leagues.
- Sonny played 10 exhibition games with the pros, but lost his chance to move up on the last day.
- He was assigned to another season in the AHL.
- It was a huge disappointment.
- He had been so sure that he made the team that he told his father to buy season tickets to the big league club.

- So, based on his background, only one path was available: more hard work.
- His next opportunity came as a substitute for an injured player in the 1977 NHL playoffs.
- He played well and the team continued to win, so Sonny stayed and someone else moved down to the American Hockey League.
- With a reluctant nod from his pregnant wife, Sonny bought a house in Hamilton, New York, home of Colgate University.
- Even if his 30-year mortgage outlasted his career by 29 years, he and family would have a home.

Life in the Community: Hamilton, New York

- The village of Hamilton is about 10 miles from the geographic center of New York State, in the rolling hills of the Chenango Valley, approximately five hours from New York City.
- Hamilton was founded in 1795 by Elisha Payne and incorporated in 1816.
- By 1820, Hamilton was an active trading center for an extensive farming area and boasted two taverns, several stores, a schoolhouse, church, newspaper, grist mill and sawmill.
- For Sonny Howell and his family, the biggest attraction Hamilton had to offer was Colgate University.
- For many years, Hamilton's major industry had been the university.
- In addition, Hamilton was a charming and essentially rural community that had changed little in either size or character during the past 100 years.
- The college got its start in 1817, when 13 men—six clergy and seven laymen—had met with "13 dollars, 13 prayers, and 13 articles."
- In that meeting, the men founded the Baptist Education Society of the State of New York, the cornerstone in the foundation of what would become Colgate University.
- The state chartered the Baptist Education Society in 1819, choosing Hamilton as the location for its school.
- In 1823, Baptists in New York City—soapmaker William Colgate among them—consolidated their seminary with the Hamilton School to form the Hamilton Literary and Theological Institution.
- By 1846, the institution was renamed Madison University and, through a state charter, was given the right to grant degrees.
- Madison became Colgate in 1890, recognizing nearly 70 years of continuous involvement and service by the Colgate family.
- The Theological Division merged with the Rochester Theological Seminary in 1928 to become the Colgate Rochester Divinity School, and Colgate became nonsectarian.
- The university became coeducational in 1970.
- By 1977, Colgate was a highly selective, independent, coeducational liberal arts college enrolling approximately 2,700 undergraduates.
- With a population of 2,500, the village of Hamilton was roughly the size of the student body of Colgate.
- Approximately 85 percent of the university's faculty members lived within 10 minutes of its campus.

HISTORICAL SNAPSHOT
1977

- President Jimmy Carter pardoned Vietnam War draft evaders
- The TV miniseries *Roots* was phenomenally successful on ABC
- Record company EMI sacked the controversial U.K. punk rock band the Sex Pistols
- Approximately a dozen armed Hanafi Muslims took over three buildings in Washington, DC, for two days, killing one person and taking more than 130 hostages
- Focus on the Family was founded by Dr. James Dobson
- Optical fiber was used to carry live telephone traffic for the first time
- *Star Wars* became the highest grossing film up to that time
- A.J. Foyt became the first driver to win the Indianapolis 500 a record four times
- The first Apple II computers went on sale
- After campaigning by Anita Bryant and her anti-gay "Save Our Children" crusade, Miami-Dade County, Florida voters overwhelmingly voted to repeal the county's gay rights ordinance
- Spain held its first democratic elections, after 41 years under the Franco regime
- The Supreme Court ruled that states were not required to spend Medicaid funds on elective abortions
- Elvis Presley performed his last concert at Market Square Arena in Indianapolis, Indiana, shortly before he died
- The Tandy Corporation TRS-80 Model I computer was introduced
- President Carter signed legislation creating the United States Department of Energy
- The Big Ear, a radio telescope operated by Ohio State University, received a radio signal from deep space
- In treaties between Panama and the United States, the U.S. agreed to transfer control of the canal to Panama at the end of the twentieth century
- *Courageous,* skippered by American Ted Turner, swept *Australia* in the 24th America's Cup
- The United States and the Soviet Union signed a Nuclear Non-Proliferation Act (NNPA), along with 15 other nations
- The modern Food Stamp Program began
- Pelé played his final professional soccer game as a member of the New York Cosmos
- The Atari 2600 game system was released
- Reggie Jackson blasted three home runs to lead the New York Yankees to World Series victory
- The 2060 Chiron, the first of the outer solar system asteroids known as centaurs, was discovered by Charles Kowal
- Egyptian President Anwar Sadat became the first Arab leader to officially visit Israel when he met with Israeli Prime Minister Menachem Begin to seek a permanent peace settlement
- A DC-3 charter plane carrying the University of Evansville basketball team crashed, killing 29 people, including 14 members of the team and head coach Bob Watson

Selected Prices

Airfare, Round-Trip, NY to San Francisco $252.00
Briefcase $52.00
CB Radio $269.99
Drapes $9.96
Motor Oil. $0.39
Motorcycle Helmet. $30.99
Stereo Wall System $199.00
Sunglasses. $7.99
Telescope $129.95
Tricycle. $16.99

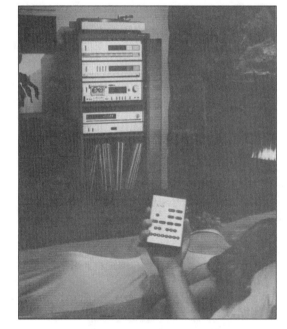

Hockey Timeline

1877
The first known rules for hockey were published by the *Montréal Gazette*.

1888
The Amateur Hockey Association of Canada was formed, with four teams in Montréal, one in Ottawa and one in Quebec City.

Circa 1892
The first women's hockey game was played in Ottawa or Barrie, Ontario.

1893
Frederick Arthur (Lord Stanley of Preston and Governor-General of Canada) donated a trophy to be called the Dominion Hockey Challenge Cup, which later became known as the Stanley Cup.

1894
The first artificial ice rink opened in Baltimore.

1895
College athletes from the United States and Canada played the first international series of matches; the Canadians won all four games.

1896
The Winnipeg Victorias became the first team from Western Canada to win the Stanley Cup.

1900
The goal net was introduced.

1904
Five teams in the United States and Ontario formed the International Hockey League, the first league of professional teams; it lasted three seasons.

1910
The Montréal Canadiens played their first game after joining a new league called the National Hockey Association.

1911
Teams in Western Canada formed the Pacific Coast Hockey Association (PCHA) and introduced several innovations: blue lines were added to divide the ice into three zones, goaltenders were permitted to fall to the ice to make saves, forward passing was allowed in the neutral zone and the 60-minute game was divided into three 20-minute periods.

1912
The number of players allowed on the ice was reduced from seven to six per team.

1917
Four NHA teams reorganized to form the National Hockey League.

The Seattle Metropolitans of the PCHA became the first American-based team to win the Stanley Cup.

1920
An ice hockey tournament was played at the Summer Olympics, with Canada winning.

1923
Foster Hewitt called the first hockey broadcast for radio, an intermediate game between teams from Kitchener and Toronto.

continued

Hockey Timeline . . . *(continued)*

1924

The Boston Bruins defeated the Montréal Maroons 2-1 in the first NHL game played in the United States.

The NHL increased the regular season schedule from 24 to 30 games; players on the first-place Hamilton Tigers refused to compete in the 1925 playoffs unless they were paid for the extra games played.

Ice hockey debuted at the Winter Olympics, with Canada winning the gold medal.

1926

The New York Rangers, Chicago Black Hawks and Detroit Cougars (later renamed the Red Wings) joined the NHL.

The Western Hockey League disbanded and sold most of its players to the new NHL teams, leaving the NHL as the undisputed top hockey league in North America.

1929

The first offside rule was introduced.

1934

Ralph Bowman of the St. Louis Eagles scored the first penalty shot goal.

1936

The New York Americans defeated Toronto 3-2 in the first game to be broadcast coast-to-coast in Canada.

Great Britain won the Olympic gold medal, marking Canada's first significant loss in international ice hockey.

1937

A rule to deal with icing was introduced.

1942

The Brooklyn Americans withdrew from the NHL, leaving the Canadiens, Maple Leafs, Red Wings, Bruins, Rangers and Black Hawks.

1945

The NHL season began in October for the first time.

1946

Babe Pratt became the first NHL player suspended for betting on games.

Referees began using hand signals to indicate penalties and other rulings.

1947

Billy Reay of the Montréal Canadiens became the first NHL player to raise his arms and stick in celebration after scoring a goal.

1949

The center red line first appeared on the ice.

1952

Hockey Night in Canada made its television debut.

1955

NHL officials wore striped sweaters for the first time.

The Zamboni made its NHL debut when Montréal hosted Toronto.

1956

Jean Beliveau was the first hockey player to appear on the cover of *Sports Illustrated*.

The USSR competed in Olympic ice hockey for the first time, winning the gold medal.

continued

Hockey Timeline . . . *(continued)*

1957

The first NHL Player's Association was formed with Detroit's Ted Lindsay as president.

CBS became the first U.S. television network to carry NHL games.

1958

Willie O'Ree of the Boston Bruins became the first black player in the NHL.

1961

The Hockey Hall of Fame opened in Toronto.

1963

The first NHL amateur draft was held in Montréal, with 21 players selected.

1967

The NHL doubled in size, adding franchises in Pittsburgh, Los Angeles, Minnesota, Oakland, St. Louis and Philadelphia.

1970

The Buffalo Sabres and Vancouver Canucks joined the NHL.

1972

The World Hockey Association began play, outbidding NHL teams for several star players.

Star Bobby Hull became hockey's first million-dollar man when he left the Chicago Black Hawks and signed a 10-year, $2.75 million contract with the World Hockey Association (WHA) Winnipeg Jets.

The Atlanta Flames and New York Islanders joined the NHL.

1974

The Kansas City Scouts and Washington Capitals joined the NHL.

The USSR won the first World Junior Hockey Championship.

A second Canada-Soviet exhibition series took place, featuring Canadians from the WHA against the Soviet national team.

1975

Soviet club teams played in North America for the first time when the Central Red Army and Soviet Wings played a series of exhibition games against NHL teams.

1976

Two franchises moved: the California Seals became the Cleveland Barons and the Kansas City Scouts became the Colorado Rockies.

"Foreword, 1968," *Ice Time*, Jay Atkinson, 2001:

I had two upbringings. Coming of age in Methuen, Massachusetts, a small bowtie-shaped community on the New Hampshire border, my buddies and I went to public school, attended Mass on Sunday, and joined a benign paramilitary organization known as the Cub Scouts. For fun, sometimes we threw rocks at cars or rode around on our Stingray bicycles, singing "Hey, hey, we're the Monkeys!" Among the densely packed three-deckers, in a neighborhood bounded by asphalt, we played football and baseball on the street, sewer cap to sewer cap. As far as we knew, this was life.

In the summer of 1968, just after I turned 11, my father got a new job and we moved across town to Central Street: larger, more well-appointed houses and within half a mile radius, two small ponds and a tree-lined swamp. When the leaves fell off the trees as November passed into December, the swamp froze over, and I was introduced to a different world from the one I had known. Here the sport of choice was ice hockey (and when the ponds melted, street hockey). Dad bought me a pair of skates and a straight-bladed Victoriaville stick. I was in business.

But what sets hockey apart from sports like football and baseball is that you can't simply go out there and play. Of course, you're welcome to try, in the sense that, theoretically, you can climb into the family jalopy and enter the Indy 500. It's just that your chances of being competitive are pretty slim. To excel at hockey—to sail over the ice throwing body checks, dodging your opponents, and blasting the puck into the net—you have to first master the rudiments of skating. An odd and esoteric skill, perhaps, but one that's completely necessary.

Most of the kids in my new neighborhood had been skating for two or three years, and some had been lacing up blades even longer than that. They swooped across Lynch's swamp in graceful arcs, like they had a special dispensation to reduce gravity. Eventually I gained the courage to join them, wobbling around in a little half-circle as players from both teams whizzed past on either side. But there was something strangely invigorating about all that cold, clean air, and the echo sticks and pucks make against the snow-packed hillside.

One night a certain kid failed to show up, and they asked me to play goalie. At the end of the swamp closest to the streetlight, there was a "net" that someone had knocked together from two by fours and rusty chicken wire. I was handed a pair of battered sofa cushions for leg pads, an old catcher's mask and a first baseman's mitt. The game began and one of the players on the other team streaked straight toward me. He rifled a shot on goal, and I came sliding out and knocked it aside. My teammates cheered as the loose puck was gathered up and they all went zooming the other way. Using the blade of my stick, I cleared the shavings from in front of the net, just like an old pro. In that instant, I discovered my passion for the sport.

"Stanley Cup Well Running Dry for Flyers," Paul Giordano, *Bucks County Courier Times* (Pennsylvania), May 14, 1976:

PHILADELPHIA—The Philadelphia Flyers had everything going for them last night, but the final score.

First off, the Montréal Canadiens were 0-5-1 at the Spectrum in their last six games.

Secondly, the Flyers, since the start of the 1974 playoffs, had won 22 of 24 playoff games at the Spectrum.

And last but by no means least, since she couldn't be there in person, Kate Smith's "God bless America" was played as her smiling picture, arm raised in salute, appeared on two gigantic projection screens hung from the rafters at each end of the ice.

The final score read: Montréal 3, Philadelphia 2. And the Canadiens were three up in the best-of-seven Stanley Cup finals.

It all started at 3:17 of the first period when Montréal's Steve Shutt curled what looked like a knuckleball by Wayne Stephenson from 70 feet out. The puck just hung in mid-air and then dropped in the net. A power play goal.

"Right at the end of the shot," Stephenson said, "it dropped. It hit the back of my glove and went in."

The Flyers, however, came on strong with a pair of goals by Reggie Leach, who had been shut out in the first two games. Leach scored on a power goal at 8:14 of the first, whipped the puck through goalie Dan Dryden's legs to give the Flyers a 2-1 lead as the first period ended.

"I'm the first one," Leach said. "He (Dryden) had his left side covered. He gave me about six inches of the net to shoot at and I kept it low."

The second?

"He (Bill Nyrop, Montréal defenseman) was trying to take a pass that wasn't too good. I took it from him and put it between Dryden's legs."

But it wasn't enough.

Gary Dornhoefer drew a two-minute penalty for elbowing with one second to play in the first period. Then, at 1:09 of the second, Shutt scored his second power play goal of the night and the game was knotted at 2-all.

It remained deadlocked until 9:16 into the third period when Pierre Bouchard tallied on a 50-footer.

"It either hit (Rick Chartraw, who was in the slot) who was screening," Stephenson said, "or something. It jumped to the right and changed direction."

"Just a routine shot," Fred Shero said. "We've scored a lot like that, too. Some may say the first and third Montréal goals were luck, but luck wasn't a factor. They just outplayed us."

"Colgate Seeks Win over Clarkson in SIT," Joe Robbins, *Syracuse Post Standard*, December 26, 1973:

Colgate's hockey team will oppose Clarkson in his second game in Syracuse invitational tournament Friday night, and they hope to reverse last year's result which saw Clarkson win 6-4. The Red Raiders are 3-4-1, while Clarkson's Golden Knights are 4-3 going into the tournament. . . .

The 1973-74 season has been one of ups and downs for Colgate. They opened with a 4-2 triumph over Sir George Williams, but dropped games to Province 6-2 and Northeastern 4-1. . . .

Colgate coach Brad Houston has promised a new look from his Raiders and may make some dramatic lineup changes in the SIT. Junior defenseman Dan Desmond, who has one of the best slap shots in collegiate circles, leads the team scoring with nine points.

1978 Profile

Jane Fisher crewed on a J24 sailboat that had won the District D Championship, and now had a spot to crew in the 1978 World Championship in Annapolis, Maryland.

Life at Home

- Unlike most of her contemporaries and competitors, Jane Fisher had not been sailing since childhood.
- For most people, sailing was an obsession that captured them early in life, giving them plenty of time to gradually unravel the complicated beast known as wind.
- Growing up, Jane had pursued other sports and passions including soccer and rafting.
- Throughout college she'd worked as a raft guide on the Ocoee River in Tennessee and competed in raft races on the Gauley River in West Virginia.
- One year, her all-girl team qualified for the National Raft Race in Colorado.
- Rafting down treacherous rivers and choking on crashing whitewater demanded lightning quick decision-making and superior upper body strength.
- Lazy decisions, hidden rocks or obstreperous currents could send a rafting team into the water.
- At 26 years old, this veteran of numerous nasty, rock-laden swims—including two near drownings and dozens of stitches required for her head—Jane decided she'd had enough of whitewater.
- One evening while going to meet friends at a local Columbia, South Carolina bar, Jane met a man who asked if she'd like to go sailing.
- Blessed with a total ignorance of sailing, but a love of water, she agreed.
- The following Saturday she met up with the owner of the boat, Brad, and his Ranger 29.
- She and the rest of the crew were racing in the Saturday races held at Lake Murray, a 50,000 acre manmade lake near Lexington, South Carolina.

Jane Fisher traded whitewater rafting for sailboat racing.

Work as a raft guide was fun but could be dangerous.

- Jane's first day of sailing was hectic—wind was blowing hard, people were yelling and she had no idea what was going on.
- She only knew that it was cold and she didn't want to fall into the water.
- After the race, she instinctively knew she'd found her new sport as she felt the familiar adrenaline and sported a huge grin.
- Jane spent the next couple of Saturdays with this crew, learning fundamentals of the sport, names of the boat parts, and trying not to get yelled at.
- Only after Jane went to the library and checked out several sailing books did the boat's many functions begin to make sense.
- Her research taught her the names of all the lines and why they were used.
- She also discovered that at five feet one inch tall and 105 pounds, she was very small for sailing, a sport that demands strength, endurance and quick decision-making under pressure.
- At the gym, she focused on lifting weights to strengthen her shoulders, back, arms, abs, and legs so that all parts of her body could be utilized.
- She ran, rowed and pedaled a stationary bike to keep up her endurance.
- Jane also read voraciously—anything that she could find that contained tactical racing tips and quizzes that tested her knowledge.
- Finally, Jane sailed at every opportunity.
- By watching the water and reading the wind, figuring out how to set the sails to maximize boat speed became her new assignment.
- Jane sailed with Brad and his crew for almost a year.
- One spring day in 1975 a boat with two men in it sailed by and asked if Jane wanted to come aboard.

Brad introduced Jane to her new sport.

Teamwork was crucial.

Jane's team made it to four races.

- Jane already knew that in this male-dominated sport, females had to be on their toes, but she was interested in talking to one of the men who spoke with reverence about sailing.
- These two men, Joe and Chip, were on Chip's J24 and looking to put together a group of five people who trained and raced together, traveling to different events.
- Jane literally jumped ship and began a new assignment on a J24.

Life at Work
- When Jane Fisher was asked to be part of the program as a J24 foredeck person, she had no idea what that job entailed.
- Joe and Chip said, "No problem, we'll teach you."
- Jane's weight of 105 pounds was perfect for the role: light crew were needed in the foredeck position so the bow of the boat did not dig into the water and slow the boat down.
- On the day Jane came on board, two others were picked up: Steve as cockpit, and Mac as middle.
- Joe was to drive the boat, Chip was to trim the sails—both the genoa and the spinnaker.
- Steve balanced the boat, trim the tweens and help raise and lower the spinnaker.
- Mac kept the boom vang, outhaul, topping lift, cunningham and downhaul in check.
- Jane raised and lowered the genoa, adjust the genoa cunningham, put the pole up and down and raise and lower the spinnaker.
- Unfortunately for Jane, almost all of her work was required in the space of mere minutes.
- She called it the impossible dance because there were so many steps.
- Joe told her there was one way to do it right and a billion ways to mess it up.

- A "mess-up" slowed the boat down at crucial moments and the race could be lost.
- As the season progressed, Jane and Steve became fast friends, studying the mechanics and theories of sailing together and talking over all the nuances of the race.
- Steve got her a T-shirt that proclaimed her membership in the Foredeck Union with a rude graphic indicating when she would be getting around to their complaints on the back.
- Steve figured that since Jane was destined to be yelled at and expected to have six hands to do her job, she needed an outlet to vent.
- Jane soon learned that even though most of the problems occurred at the back of the boat, she would always be blamed in the heat of the moment.
- The team made it to four races, taking a third, second, first and second before the chemistry on the boat between Chip and Joe made the team fall apart.
- In the spring of 1976 Jane joined another team, one of whom was a former Olympic sailor from Russia, aboard a San Juan 31.
- She and Steve continued to be friends and hone their skills separately and apart.
- Jane had started to get noticed around the clubhouse and in the Southeastern circuit because of her size, skills and smile.
- Every year in the spring, the local yacht club held an Easter Regatta in which boats from as far away as Canada traveled to compete.
- Jane was asked to crew on a boat from Florida as their middle mast person because of her "local knowledge" of the lake.
- This was where she became fully aware of the sexism in this predominately male sport.
- In addition to her foredeck duties, it was assumed that she would make all of the lunches for the crew and do all of the shopping for the drinks and food.
- Her need to use the restroom—a bucket—while sailing for eight hours at a time was viewed with disgust.
- The more boats Jane sailed, the more she realized how personalities on shore would transform on the water in the midst of a heated race.
- She began to recognize those with whom she would enjoy sailing and those with whom she would not.
- Jane also discovered the joy of sailing at sunset and letting the wind purify her soul.
- But rough-water sailing was also inspirational.
- Once while Jane was sailing in Annapolis, Maryland, a tempestuous storm blew through and tore up the main sail, forcing her team to limp back into the harbor.
- No one was hurt, but the adrenaline rush was huge.
- Big wind or "Blowing Like Stink" was great fun, while one of the most challenging scenarios was sailing in light air.
- The entire crew must be spread out and balanced precisely to keep the boat flat or sometimes in a windward heel in order to keep the boat moving in light air.
- Typically in a sailboat race, since one cannot sail directly into the wind and must sail close to 45 degrees off the wind, the sailor is looking for the shortest course to the mark.
- When the wind is very light, one must sail for the wind and not to the shortest course.
- It is often slow and very hot when there is no breeze.
- Jane had many times walked off the boat with a concentration headache from peering so hard into the horizon for wind.
- Her reputation within the circuit continued to grow over the next two years, and Jane found herself sailing on a J24 whose owner lived in Wrightsville Beach, North Carolina.
- The trimmer lived in St. Augustine, Florida, the tactician in Jacksonville, Florida, the mast in Charlotte, North Carolina, and Jane in Columbia, South Carolina.

Each regatta win brought the team closer to the Nationals.

- Teams normally do better when they sail together all the time, but this team would only get together for big national regattas and when they could earn spots to bigger regattas.
- Somehow, after the first two races, the team gelled and worked together very well.
- Their first race was in 1978 at Oriental, North Carolina, a spot where the Neuse River and the ocean meet.
- With much laughter, combined with great finishes, the team finished first and earned a spot in the Nationals.
- The entire crew was aware that more work lay ahead if they were to compete against the "big boys" or professional sailors to win the Nationals.
- Throughout that spring, summer and fall they traveled all over the East Coast, competing in whatever regatta was open to J24s and fine tuning their movements and minds.
- In the process, Jane became fully cognizant of how beaten up she was getting on the bow of the boat.
- During one Saturday in Jacksonville, Florida, the bay was very choppy and the work difficult.
- During the first leg of the first race on a six-leg day, Jane lost her shoe.
- To try and balance on the bow of a boat with only one shoe was very difficult.
- Later that day Jane lost her balance and hit her temple very hard on the spinnaker ring, but managed to finish the race before making her way to the back of the boat.
- Since Jane rarely complained of her injuries, she was ignored until the skipper realized she was green and gritting her teeth.
- When asked what was the matter, Jane said she was trying not to throw up.
- The crew wanted to know why she hadn't said anything.
- When she said that she lost her shoe and then hit her head, they stared at her in amazement knowing they had also won the regatta.
- Next stop, the Nationals.
- Teams from all over the world would travel to see who could take home that year's world title in an event being held in Annapolis, Maryland, at a premier venue, the Chesapeake Bay.

Life in the Community: Lake Murray, South Carolina

- Lake Murray, where the Columbia Sailing Club was headquartered, was a 50,000-acre manmade lake in the Midlands of South Carolina.
- It covered approximately 78 square miles of land with 647 miles of shoreline, and provided electricity for South Carolina's entire Midlands region.
- Lake Murray was completed in 1930 and gradually became renowned for striped bass fishing and summer water sports.
- In order to build Lake Murray, the Lexington Water Power Company relocated 5,000 citizens and removed three churches, six schools, and 2,000 graves.
- The first sailing club on Lake Murray was established in the 1930s, but dissolved when the winds of war blew across the world.
- The re-founding of the Columbia Sailing Club occurred in 1957; that year 19 members agreed to pay dues of $5 per quarter.
- The 1958 regatta resulted in strong media coverage, and the club was launched.
- Sailboat racing had arrived at Lake Murray.
- Columbia, located in the center of South Carolina, was that state's most populated city, the state capital, the home of the University of South Carolina's main campus, and the site of the South Carolina State Fair each October.
- Columbia was named for Christopher Columbus, and it was South Carolina's first planned city.
- Despite this, Columbia did not have a single paved street until Main Street was surfaced in 1908.

HISTORICAL SNAPSHOT
1978

- The Copyright Act of 1976 took effect, making sweeping changes to United States copyright law
- The Holy Crown of Hungary was returned to Hungary from the United States, where it had been held since World War II
- Electrical workers in Mexico City discovered the remains of the Great Pyramid of Tenochtitlan in the middle of the city
- Charlie Chaplin's remains were stolen from Corsier-sur-Vevey, Switzerland
- *Annie Hall* won Best Picture at the Academy Awards
- President Jimmy Carter decided to postpone production of the neutron bomb—a weapon which kills people with radiation but leaves buildings relatively intact
- Volkswagen became the second non-American automobile manufacturer to open a plant in the United States; it produced the Rabbit in New Stanton, Pennsylvania
- The U.S. Senate voted 68-32 to turn the Panama Canal over to Panamanian control on December 31, 1999
- St. Paul, Minnesota, became the second U.S. city to repeal its gay rights ordinance after Anita Bryant's successful 1977 anti-gay campaign in Dade County, Florida
- Pete Rose of the Cincinnati Reds got his 3,000th major league hit
- Mavis Hutchinson, 53, became the first woman to run across the United States; her trek took 69 days
- Resorts International opened the first legal casino in the eastern United States, in Atlantic City, New Jersey
- California voters approved Proposition 13, which slashed property taxes nearly 60 percent
- Cricketer Ian Botham became the first man in the history of the game to score a century and take eight wickets in one inning of a test match
- The comic strip *Garfield* made its debut
- In *University of California Regents v. Bakke,* the Supreme Court barred quota systems in college admissions but affirmed the constitutionality of programs which gave advantages to minorities
- The Camp David Accords were signed between Israel and Egypt
- Giuseppe Verdi's opera *Otello* made its first appearance on *Live from the Met*
- President Carter signed a bill that authorized the minting of the Susan B. Anthony dollar
- The New York Yankees clinched their 22nd Baseball World Series Championship, defeating the Los Angeles Dodgers 7-2 and winning the Series four games to two
- In Guyana, Jim Jones led his People's Temple cult in a mass murder-suicide that claimed 918 lives, 909 of them at Jonestown, including over 270 children
- The first U.S. Take Back the Night march occurred in San Francisco

Selected Prices

Apartment, NY, 3½ Rooms, Month	$240.00
Bedspread	$34.96
Calculator, Pocket	$29.00
Cocktail Table	$139.00
Floor Lamp	$78.50
Life Vest	$20.59
Movie Ticket	$0.75
Perfume, Chanel No. 19	$9.50
Slow Cooker	$13.79
Stationery, 100 Sheets, Envelopes	$6.95

"Intrepid Joins Bich Team as French Hone for 1980,"
Newport Daily News, August 17, 1978:

The note scribbled on the silver tape around *France I*'s winch drum said in bold, black letters—"Ficker isn't quick as Bich."

Little did the crews on *France I* or *Intrepid* know how true it was. Baron Marcel Bich glanced at the wording as he climbed on board the 12-meter Sunday, laughed a little and that was that. Not a word.

Four hours later Bich was instructing the sailboat's tender, *Nanny,* to fetch *Intrepid.* "I suggest you pick up the *Intrepid,* which is approximately 1/2 hour behind France," Bich said in his decidedly French accent. The tickle in his voice was hard to disguise.

Bill Ficker, who etched his mark in America's Cup fame at the helm of *Intrepid* in 1970, was at the wheel again. But this time around, it was not a Cup summer, it was not a Cup race, the crew was not wearing Cup foul weather gear and their dreams were not silver lined. However can you explain the French beating the Americans? Un grand faux pas?

Baron Bich, the Bic pen and lighter entrepreneur, has returned to Newport this summer for four weeks of intensive crew and technical training. It is a means to an end. That end, of course, is winning the America's Cup in 1980.

All the stops have been pulled out of the French 12-meter hole. Bich failed in 1970 and 1974 with *France I.* He built a new *France II* for the 1977 skirmish, but ended up losing the challenge after substituting *France I* at the last minute.

He has another 12-meter on the drawing table for 1980—to be made this time out of aluminum instead of his traditional wood designs.

Bich usually sails his fleet of 12-meters, which now includes *Intrepid,* in Hyeres, along the southern coast of France. But his dream of winning the next America's Cup has closed the door on summers at home. Bich apparently has decided that the key to winning is practice on the other team's field.

"It's our only chance," Bruno Bich, the second-oldest Bich son, said this week. "The Americans fight so hard among themselves. For us, training here gives us the best chance to get used to the waters.

"This summer, we are enjoying ourselves sailing with Americans, but it is also giving us the chance to sail against another boat."

France I and *Intrepid* are towed out from the Newport Offshore Ltd. dock together each morning, but there the parallel ends. *Intrepid* is manned by Americans, many of whom are veterans of past America's Cup races. Lowell North, skipper of *Enterprise* during most of the last Cup defense competition, has taken a turn this summer at the helm of *Intrepid.* So has Gerry Driscoll, skipper of *Intrepid* in 1974 and scores of other veterans. . . .

Bruno Bich described the daily races, divided into two 14-day sessions, as instructive for everyone. The plan is to give the French and Americans a chance to redefine 12-meter sailing in a non-Cup summer. "We have no intention of having any Americans sailing with us in the 1980s," he said. "In fact, I can tell you, we're planning not to do it."

Ficker looks at it as a learning session, too. "It's a chance to keep your hands in it," he said after *Intrepid*'s epic loss to Bich Sunday. "It's a lot of fun to race hard for two weeks. The 12-meter world is very tight—the people in it are awfully well trained.

"It's also an opportunity for us to look at the fellows who might help us out in our 12-meter program. It gives us a chance to try different things."

"Sail Racing: A Gamble Against the Elements," Liz Larcom, *Del Rio News-Herald* (Texas), September 3, 1978:

"We're gonna gamble," announced Mike Dungan, skipper of a Catalina 25 owned by Fred and Frankie Lee Harlow.

Still tied to the dock, he was already devising his tactics the fifth weekend of racing in Amistad Yacht Club's summer series.

His decision: to use the big 170 sail, gambling that the winds during the two-hour race would not come up so much that the big sail would not heel the boat over to an inefficient sailing angle.

His wife and sole crew member, C.J., dug out the big sail from the cabin of Lake Amistad's oldest sailboat (nine years), and soon the pair maneuvered the craft into the harbor of the Mexican marina.

"I had a cotton mouth on the start," confessed Mike.

With six sailboats circling the still harbor, stopwatches to check, and the signal flags of race official Jim Williams to watch, there was plenty to give a skipper cotton mouth.

Crossing the starting line early would draw a foul, but crossing even seconds late could cost a skipper the race in competition that is sometimes determined by split-seconds.

Today's course had been announced by Williams only 15 minutes earlier. Now he stood on the deck of his anchored sailboat, beside the starting (and finishing) line. At the sound of the horn the race was on.

"Fifteen seconds late!" exclaimed Mike, but as the boat headed out across the lake, five other sailboats trailed behind.

Mike had the helm while his only crew member C.J. trimmed the sails. Both watched the knot meter, wind direction, sails and other boats.

The course would cover only a corner of Lake Amistad's 85-mile length. With its broad expanses, varied destinations, and steady winds, uncrowded Amistad provides ideal sailing without the complication of tides....

"It's easy to get distracted," said Mike, eyes sweeping the knot meter as the boat skimmed along toward a distant buoy it must round. "You get busy watching the buoy and all the other boats and forget to watch your sails."

"Look at George come," said C.J., pointing at George Hall's Ericson 29 that was fast closing in behind. Soon the boats were dueling, the Ericson trying to pass on the upwind side. But the Catalina made the marker first and made a neat turn around it.

Next, the course headed for Chuy Island, back near the Mexican shore.

"We'll take it high," decided Mike. "I think there will be a good wind coming off the land just as we get there. If my theory is right I don't want to get caught too far downwind."

The boats spread out across the lake now, but the race outcome was far from evident. With the Portsmouth system, each model of boat had its handicap, so the boat out front would not necessarily be the winner.

"Sailing is relaxing," said C.J., who only minutes before had been using every ounce of muscle to pull on a rope. "It's work," she laughed. "But it's not like 'at work'." She paused, then added as she trimmed the sail a bit, "It's exciting!"

continued

"Sail Racing: A Gamble Against the Elements," . . . *(continued)*

As Mike and C.J. approached Chuy Island, the breeze indeed picked up, but not much. It was clear the J24 owned by John Haire was reaching the island first.

As Mike and C.J. sought to keep *Kaylea* just far enough from Chuy Island to avoid running aground, the J24 maintained its lead and Woody, behind, took down the spare sail to ready for the last leg.

The wind was up as the helmsman aimed for the buoy that is Marker 7. Heeled over, Mike regretted the choice of the big sail as he watched John Haire's J24 sailing ahead of him.

The last buoy approached. "Now!" said the skipper, and the pair swung the sail around to the other side at the precise moment the boat rounded the buoy.

The finish line was next. Finishing with an unfavorable wind, the boats glided in. The race had taken about two hours.

Calculations the next day would determine the points winner, but first across the line was the only race-designed sailboat in the field, the J24. The Ericson 29 also preceded the *Kaylea*.

"The 170 didn't pay," said Mike, referring to his gamble with the big sail. But it hadn't lost him much either. Results the next day showed the Ericson 29 first, Mike and C.J. second, and the J24 third.

A pair of long sighs were heard as the Dungans stowed away the sails of the *Kaylea*. They nodded agreement when competitor Bonnie Chambers proclaimed from the dock, "I'm exhausted!"

Oliver Lorenz, skipper of a San Juan 21, said of sailing, "You're challenging other people, but you're challenging natural forces, too.

"You could go out on the lake and water ski, and you have done it all of five minutes. But a lot of tactics go into sailing a boat. I learn something new every time. You could sail forever and still learn something new every time."

1979 Profile

Although as a teenager, Joe Austin dreamed of being the greatest lightweight boxer in the world, eventually he realized that he lacked the power to become a real contender.

Life at Home

- Joe Austin grew up in an Ohio mill town, whose rhythms were dictated by the shift whistle's morning and afternoon calls to work.
- Invariably, the men of the town checked their pocket watches—to make sure they were correct—when the whistle blew for the second shift.
- It was a tough town, just outside of Cleveland, where every young boy had to prove himself with his fists.
- A child of the Great Depression, Joe had ample opportunities to fight simply to stay alive.
- He was better than most and gained a fierce reputation for fighting through pain even when he was losing—which wasn't often.
- When he was in junior high school and still weighed less than 100 pounds, the high school kids would organize fistfights just to see how much he could take.
- On more than one occasion, his father left work early so he could wager on his son.
- When Joe turned 16, he took his fighting skills to the Army, where he became an exhibition boxer, exempted from some of the more tedious drill exercises.
- Even when the Korean War broke out, he spent his time traveling from base to base putting on a lightweight boxing show.
- Often he was matched against the "girls" who had joined the "sissy" Air Force or the musclehead Marines.
- And when the fighting turned dirty, he knew those rules very well.
- In 1954 he turned pro.

Joe Austin's boxing career was as a boxer cutman.

- His first fight was in Spokane, Washington, where the liquor flowed freely and the rules were relaxed.
- His opponent was a tall, inexperienced country boy who was unaccustomed to being hit, but who had a powerful left hand.
- The fight lasted three rounds, and afterwards Joe had to help stop the bleeding he had caused.
- His next six fights were also victories.
- Then he met a true pro who pounded him unmercifully for four rounds before he was knocked out.
- Joe's hospital stay would have lasted two weeks, but he checked himself out so he could be in the ring the following Friday night.
- For the next decade, he was a fixture on fight cards throughout the Midwest—sometimes taking two fights a week.
- "I fought to eat," he recalled. "Fighting fed every part of me."
- Rarely did his bout receive—or deserve—top billing.
- Eventually, his sharp cheek bones that caused him to bleed easily, and a slow left hand that never delivered enough power, got in the way of his dream.
- So Joe, desperate to stay in the fight game, migrated to the role of cutman—an overlooked, but crucial assignment in the world of Blood Inc.

Life at Work

- For three decades, Joe Austin had made his living pressing his long thin fingers into the wounds of professional boxers—some great and some less than good.
- Through the years he had fought against having a nickname.
- While others loved to be called "Stitch" or "Doc," Joe wanted to remain invisible and not draw attention to himself.
- He cherished his privacy, and after a fight never hung out with the fight crowd or chased women.
- He had been married for 26 years.
  - By nature most cutmen are vagabonds who rambled from fight to fight and arena to arena to earn two percent of the fighter's purse for the night.
  - Some were clowns and some were brilliant, but for all, the job description was the same: perform miracles in an instant.
  - Between rounds he had quickly and efficiently closed thousands of bloody cuts, gashes and noses.
  - To learn his craft, he spent hours cutting himself and experimenting with different mixtures to close the wound.
  - Some of his greatest discoveries became legend.
  - In the early days, many of the best cutmen refused to share their secrets—even those who had enough work.
  - But with experience and clever hands, Joe learned how to fix one brutal cut at a time, often working on a bleeding boxer between rounds and surrounded by a chorus of screaming fans.
  - By definition, a cutman's job during a fight is to stop any bleeding from the face or nose and to reduce swelling around the boxer's eyes by applying cold pressure.
  - The goal is to keep the boxer eligible and fighting.
  - Blood flowing from the eyebrows must be kept out of the eyes if the fight is to continue.

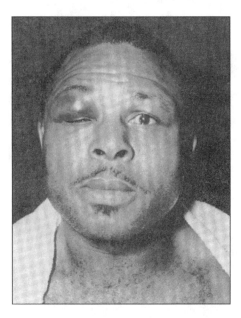

Cutmen had techniques to treat gashes and bruises.

- The tools of a cutman's trade vary from a lubricant like Vaseline, used to help keep facial skin elastic to avoid cuts, to more exotic chemicals that coagulate the blood quickly.
- Even the application of Vaseline requires skill.
- Just enough helps a boxer, but too much will get on the opponent's gloves, and then into the eyes of the cutman's fighter.
- Another tool of the trade is an endswell, a flat piece of steel, rounded at the edges, which is either kept on ice or filled with ice to keep it cold.
- Direct pressure with an endswell helps the cutman treat swelling, often called "a mouse."
- Chemicals such as epinephrine are used on cotton-tipped swabs to coagulate the blood and stop bleeding.
- After the bleeding is controlled, the cut is filled with Avitene, a powder that forms a sort of instant scab.
- Adrenaline hydrochloride on a cotton-tipped swab inserted into the nostrils stops the bleeding once the nose is pinched shut on it, thus saturating the area with the medicine.
- Joe was thrilled when he could stopped nosebleeds that so the fight could continue.
- During one fight, he was working the corner of a promising middleweight contender who received a terrific gash above his left eye early in the first round.
- As the round ended, Joe immediately jumped into the ring and begin working on the cut, applying pressure over the wound between his fingers and palm.
- After he applied a special coagulant, the ringside physician was in his face and wanted to look at the cut.
- In the old days, Joe would have let him do so while also blocking the view.
- These days, blocking the physician's view is frowned on, and can get a cutman banned.
- The physician looked at the facial rip and said, "I'll give you another round to control the bleeding; if not, I'm going to stop the fight."
- The bleeding started to slow down between the second and third rounds, and by the fourth round Joe had the cut completely under control.
- His fighter won the bout and ended up receiving 40 stitches after the fight.
- It was a rough 32 minutes of extreme stress that drew a commendation from the New York State Athletic Commission doctors.
- But the praise must go to the fighter, also, Joe insisted.
- After all, his ringside handiwork would have been undone if the middleweight had not remembered to keep his hands up and protect his eye.
- To stop the fight, the ringside doctor must determine that the bleeding is uncontrollable.
- Joe believed it was important for the fighter's sake that the cutman had sufficient time to work on the cut—possibly one to three rounds, depending on the severity.
- In the end, it comes down to the cutman's skill.
- During one fight a cut was so bad it went in two different directions—across the eyebrow and down the side of the fighter's face.
- "He was so bad I had to pinch it with both hands; he literally had two flaps of skin hanging from his face," said Joe.

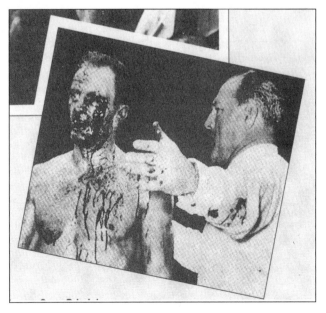

Sometimes not even Joe could stop the bleeding.

- Joe used Avitene, which he pushed into the cut.
- By the fifth round he had the cut under control, and his boxer got a split decision by the judges.
- Afterwards, the boxer was transported to the hospital, while Joe went to the airport and caught a flight home.

Life in the Community: St. Louis, Missouri

- During his travels as a cutman, Joe Austin had worked in a number of large American cities.
- Tampa, Florida, felt too transient, Chicago too cold, and Albuquerque, New Mexico, too foreign.
- For some reason, St. Louis, Missouri, the city struggling to regain its feet after 75 years of decline, felt just right.
- For most of the twentieth century, the rise and fall of St. Louis was inextricably linked to its role as a commercial center near the confluence of the Mississippi and Missouri rivers.
- Founded as a trading post in 1764 and named for King Louis IX of France, the city gained prominence in the 1800s as the capital of the Louisiana territory.
- St. Louis was a departure point for explorers Lewis and Clark, and as the community matured, it promoted itself as a gateway to the west.
- At the time of the 1904 World's Fair, which was visited by an astounding 20 million visitors in seven months, the city's total population topped 600,000.
- Then, in the 1950s, when postwar Americans wanted to live in their own homes, thousands fled to the suburbs.
- The metropolitan area grew to contain 2.4 million people, 12th largest in the nation, but the city itself was neglected.

1904 World's Fair, St. Louis, Missouri

- Downtown St. Louis became a shabby collection of old stores and offices; some homes had only dirt floors and no hot water.
- Revival began in the 1980s, when major corporations led by young executives from outside St. Louis decided to revitalize the once proud city.
- One of the first items on the agenda was construction on the waterfront of the towering stainless steel archway, rising 630 feet and becoming a major tourist attraction.
- Anheuser-Busch Brewery, which bought the Cardinals baseball team when its owner sought to move the franchise out of town, won support to build a new stadium.
- Private investment in condominiums and luxury homes followed.
- Joe Austin particularly enjoyed the ethnic ties that held many sections of the town together: the Italians in the Hill area of south St. Louis; the descendents of German and Dutch settlers who always kept their brick homes neat and clean; and the Jewish influence that led much of the renovation.
- Much of the change was fueled by federal redevelopment money—$34 million—which jumpstarted the main mall, the Midwest's biggest retail center under one roof, and the development of DeBaliviere Place for joining the cities near Forest Park, site of the World's Fair in 1904.
- It was there that Joe purchased for $60,000 a condominium that had been renovated from the shell of an abandoned apartment building.
- It gave him both the rustic old look he adored and the convenience of a modern home.
- A condominium demanded no attention to maintenance as he traveled the country attending to cutman chores.

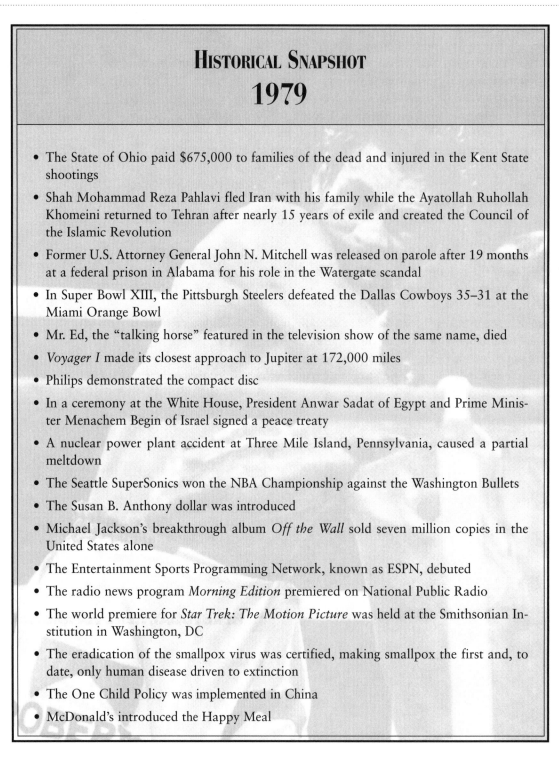

HISTORICAL SNAPSHOT
1979

- The State of Ohio paid $675,000 to families of the dead and injured in the Kent State shootings
- Shah Mohammad Reza Pahlavi fled Iran with his family while the Ayatollah Ruhollah Khomeini returned to Tehran after nearly 15 years of exile and created the Council of the Islamic Revolution
- Former U.S. Attorney General John N. Mitchell was released on parole after 19 months at a federal prison in Alabama for his role in the Watergate scandal
- In Super Bowl XIII, the Pittsburgh Steelers defeated the Dallas Cowboys 35–31 at the Miami Orange Bowl
- Mr. Ed, the "talking horse" featured in the television show of the same name, died
- *Voyager I* made its closest approach to Jupiter at 172,000 miles
- Philips demonstrated the compact disc
- In a ceremony at the White House, President Anwar Sadat of Egypt and Prime Minister Menachem Begin of Israel signed a peace treaty
- A nuclear power plant accident at Three Mile Island, Pennsylvania, caused a partial meltdown
- The Seattle SuperSonics won the NBA Championship against the Washington Bullets
- The Susan B. Anthony dollar was introduced
- Michael Jackson's breakthrough album *Off the Wall* sold seven million copies in the United States alone
- The Entertainment Sports Programming Network, known as ESPN, debuted
- The radio news program *Morning Edition* premiered on National Public Radio
- The world premiere for *Star Trek: The Motion Picture* was held at the Smithsonian Institution in Washington, DC
- The eradication of the smallpox virus was certified, making smallpox the first and, to date, only human disease driven to extinction
- The One Child Policy was implemented in China
- McDonald's introduced the Happy Meal

Selected Prices

Coatdress, Polyester	$21.00
Dryer, Kenmore	$149.00
Golf School	$650.00
Jeans, Men's	$13.00
Jumpsuit, Women's	$31.99
Motorcycle, Kawasaki	$699.00
Phone Rate, U.S. to Europe, Three Minutes	$6.75
Sweatercoat	$140.00
Tie	$10.00
Weight Bench	$35.87

"Will Destiny Match Leonard and Duran?"
The Indiana Gazette (Pennsylvania), November 28, 1979:

The next big money bout in boxing likely will be Sugar Ray Leonard meeting Robert Duran and the clash of the most exciting personalities in the ring today—counting even the heavyweight division.

It's a fight that could be worth at least $2 million for each boxer, a miraculous purse for welterweights. And it signals the ultimate Renaissance of the little man in boxing, virtually shut out since the Mohammad Ali (aka Cassius Clay) era began 15 years ago.

Leonard, who emerged from the Montréal Olympics as a colorful reincarnation of the young Sugar Ray Robinson, has been groomed carefully for the welterweight championship since he turned pro on February 5, 1977.

Undefeated in 25 bouts—capped by a sensational one-round knockout of Andy (Hawk) Price here in late September—he has never been seriously pushed.

But Leonard must beat Wilfred Benitez for the World Boxing Council version of the welterweight title on November 30 before a Duran confrontation can be translated into millions of dollars.

Duran is a spectacular former lightweight champ who has lost only one bout in his 12-year career—and that was seven years ago. He graduated to the welterweight division because, at age 28, he could no longer make the 135-pound weight limit. In fact, he balloons so much between bouts, he may have trouble getting in under 147.

Their meeting, if destiny isn't detoured, promises the classic matchup of a flashy boxer (Sugar Ray) against the thunderous, aggressive clouter (Duran).

This is the kind of interest generated by John L. Sullivan versus Gentleman Jim Corbett, or Jack Dempsey versus Gene Tunney, or Joe Frazier versus Mohammad Ali.

Leonard, effusive and cocky, is a tribute to hype. He talks like Ali: "I've been ready for a championship fight from the time I turned pro. The time of reckoning is now. . . . When I start throwing punches, I hate to count. It's like counting money . . . I'll be glad to accommodate any champion as long as he's not a heavyweight."

But like Ali, Leonard backs it up with flashy ability. Astutely maneuvered by Angelo Dundee, who worked Ali's corner all those years, he ascended into the championship range under a bunch of setups, wearing them down more with a blizzard of punches than with devastating power.

"New Oxford's Powers Keeps Getting Better," Jim Loose, *The Gettysburg Times,* February 1, 1979:

For someone in her first year of playing basketball, Elecia Powers isn't having a bad season. In fact, the New Oxford center is having the kind of season that many experienced players envy.

Powers, a junior, is averaging 8.6 points per game and more than 12 rebounds per game. Within the Blue Mountain League, however, she has scored 119 points for an average 11.9 points per game. She has scored in double figures in eight of her last nine starts. Just the other day against Biglerville the 5-11 Powers scored 21 points and pulled down 18 rebounds. That was coming off a game against Littlestown in which she grabbed 19 rebounds.

"Yes, I was really surprised," said Powers when asked about her statistics. "I knew I could jump but I didn't know I could get all the rebounds. As far as the points, I wasn't really expecting as many as I have got this year."

Although Powers has played basketball since she was little, she has never competed on a cage team before this season. Her prior team competition was in volleyball, which she readily admits is her favorite sport.

"I was so used to playing volleyball I had to get everything together for basketball," she said. "It wasn't really hard. I just had to get adjusted to it."

One person who is glad she has made the adjustment is new Oxford coach Jeff Topper. Topper was more than pleased to have someone standing 5-11 around for the team, although he wasn't sure what to expect when Powers struggled through the first several games.

"I started to worry," Topper said. "It was kind of a letdown. But she started working at it hard and has now been a real pleasant surprise. She's helped us through this good streak we've been having (six straight wins). . . ."

One of Powers's biggest contributions this season, according to Topper, has been to take some of the pressure off the team's leading scorer, Theresa "Peep" Kuhn.

"Probably directly I would say rebounds [have been her greatest asset]," Topper said. "But her ability to score on some follow-up shots has helped. We weren't getting them early in the year; that was hard on Peep. With her [Powers] in there being big, it takes the pressure off the other inside people."

"Rodgers Could Taste Third Boston Marathon Victory," *Aiken Standard* (South Carolina), April 17, 1979:

BOSTON—Hometown boy Bill Rodgers, superstar marathoner with the fiery will to win, has renewed his claim to the elusive title as the world's top runner of the grueling road race.

"I could taste the third win," the 31-year-old former schoolteacher said Monday after wearing down Japan's Toshihiko Seko to set an American record in winning the 83rd Boston Marathon. "I don't want someone to take it away."

The five foot nine, 128-pounder from Melrose, Massachusetts, ran away from Seko on the famed "Heartbreak Hill" to win his third Boston event in two hours, nine minutes and 27 seconds. It broke the U.S. record he set in 1975.

The victory Monday, by 45 seconds over Seko, was a near breeze down the home stretch through cold rain. Rodgers won the 1978 race in 2:10:13 by only two seconds over Jeff Wells of Dallas in the closest 26-mile, 385-yard event on record.

Seko, 23-year-old college student in Japan, and the winner of the Fukuoka International Marathon in his homeland last December, ran with Rodgers for 20 miles before his legs went numb on the third of a brutal series of hills in Newton, Massachusetts.

Rodgers, who has won the Fukuoka race along with back-to-back victories in New York City's young but prestigious marathon, was beaten by Seko last December.

On the run from rustic Hopkinton to Boston, Rodgers said athletes tend to get overconfident, explaining, "You have to restrain yourself. Then you have to make your move at the right time."

For the victorious Connecticut native, now operator for a running store located along the Boston Marathon route, that charge came as Seko was struggling uphill.

Rodgers blasted 15 yards ahead in the big incline and widened his lead. Police escort motorcycles had to move quickly to stay ahead of the hard driving champion, whose goal is to win an Olympic gold medal at the Moscow Olympics.

1972 NEWS FEATURE

"Avery Repeats Stop Winter Olympics View," *Pacific Stars and Stripes*,
February 13, 1972:

SAPPORO, Japan—Avery Brundage, veteran president of the International Olympic Committee (IOC), said the Winter Olympic competition should be stopped because it is "not universal" and played with scandal.

In an exclusive interview with United Press International, the 84-year-old Chicago millionaire who has headed the IOC for 20 years took pains to praise the organization of the XI Winter Olympics at Sapporo.

At the same time, however, he repeated his contention that there should be no Winter Games at all.

"The Winter Games are not universal," he said. "There's also the problem of weather, location and ski scandals which have been with us for the last 10 years." Brundage often has said many top Alpine skiers are, in fact, professional, and as such should not be allowed to participate in the Olympics, which are for amateurs only.

He said, "The arrangements for the Sapporo Games are almost perfect. The facilities are excellent, while there is an abundance of snow, something we have not had in the past.

"Indeed, some of the sites are really beautiful. The biathlon course, for instance, is one of the prettiest I've seen. And, of course, events get off exactly as scheduled."

He said, "The Japanese deserve to be congratulated for the staging of a highly successful Games."

Brundage, an archrival of the Winter Games primarily because of the cost and commercialization of Alpine skiing, added: "But we must look at the Winter Games from the overall points of view.

"I understand the Japanese have spent nearly $600 million in these Games. Not all the money has gone to the Games sites, but a very substantial part of it has. This is excessive for 10 days of winter sports involving some 1,500 athletes, especially when you consider only 15 odd countries are represented in all the events. Two Filipino skiers can hardly be called a team, by way of example," he said.

Brundage, who has been president of the IOC since 1952, and plans to retire from the post at the conclusion of the Summer Games in Munich, took on the question of Austria's Karl Schranz, the 33-year-old superstar of the Alpine circuit who was booted out of the

Games before he could compete for the Olympic gold medal that has eluded him in 18 years of competition.

Brundage said, "Mr. Schranz earned his living from skiing for 18 years. I believe that speaks for itself and proves my points.

"Mr. Schranz did not need to compete in the Games. He has capitalized on his Olympic fame. The reception he received on his return to Vienna from members of the Austrian government shows that sport has become a political factor in that country.

"We [IOC] do not like when an Austrian Minister contacts his counterparts in other countries in an effort to take over the Olympic Games. No sir, we do not like it."

Reminded that Schranz is not alone in violating Olympic rules, and that similar cases can be brought against those who compete in the Summer Games, Brundage said: "There may be isolated cases; we need proof of these, but none are so blatant."

Asked whether he thought the International Ski Federation (FIS) was trying to conform to IOC rules, now that it is investigating Annie Famose for doing a radio commentary on Alpine events for a European station, Brundage said: "It's a good sign, but a very mild one in view of the enormous violations over the years."

Brundage charged the FIS with being dishonest. "We are not through with the FIS. They allow athletes to violate the rules through the years and tell us unofficially the rules have been broken. Then they force athletes to sign entry forms claiming they have competed within the rules. We don't like it. I call that dishonest," he said.

Asked if he agreed with the charge that Denver, which hosts the 1976 Games, had been dishonest in its presentation when it won the right to play host at Amsterdam in 1970, Brundage said, "No."

"FIS has agreed to the change in Alpine and Nordic skiing sites. They should have looked at the possibilities before giving their sanction. Now we feel it's too late to take the Games away, especially after the expenditure the Denver people have been put to.

"They have guaranteed us the Games will be held under Olympic rules and we are satisfied on this point."

Looking back on his 20 years as president of the IOC, Brundage said: "Apart from the scandals in Alpine skiing, the Olympic movement is recognized as one of the great social forces in the world. It is not perfect but we do our best. I am proud of this fact."

Pressed about the fact that most Olympic medalists are not amateurs in the true sense of the word, Brundage said, "If a sport requires the training of athletes to the exclusion of their studies and their business, then it should be excluded from the Games."

Brundage rejected suggestions that some athletes train as many as eight hours a day. "Nobody needs to train for that time. I tried it when I was a competitor. The result was I became stale and my performance suffered."

1980–1989

America went sports crazy in the 1980s, fueled by big television contracts. Outfielder Dave Winfield began the decade by signing a record-setting 10-year contract with the New York Yankees for $22 million; basketball player Earvin "Magic" Johnson signed with the Los Angeles Lakers for $1 million a year for 25 years. Sports historian Benjamin Rader believes "nothing was more central to the history of organized sports during the second half of the 20th century than television." This included placing the television spotlight on lesser known sports such as beach volleyball, Olympic luge and professional soccer.

In playgrounds across America, children of all ages and ethnicities found joy in playing sports. Many embraced more than one sport, including soccer, which grew dramatically in popularity during the decade. African American athletes, long prominent in basketball and football, captured greater visibility and endorsement money, but were rarely represented at the "thinking positions": coach, quarterback or catcher.

The decade of the 1980s suffered an unpropitious beginning. Interest rates and the rate of inflation reached a staggering 18 percent. Unemployment was rising. America was in its deepest depression since the Great Depression of the 1930s. The two-career family became the norm; more than half of all married woman and 90 percent of female college graduates worked outside the home. This economic instability, paired with the rising number of women in the workforce, injected new energy into the movement for social change. America loudly questioned the role of nuclear weapons in world affairs, grappled with the abortion question, and furiously wrestled with the conflicting needs of the economy and Mother Nature. By the end of the decade, thanks in part to the productivity gain proved by computers and new technology, more Americans entered the rarified atmosphere of the millionaire and felt better off than they had in a decade.

Convinced that inflation was the primary enemy of long-term economic growth, the Federal Reserve Board brought the economy to a standstill in the early days of the decade. By 1984, the tight money policies of the government brought inflation to 4 percent, the lowest level since 1967. The plan to strangle inflation succeeded and Americans prospered. The decade came to be symbolized by self-indulgence.

At the same time, defense and deficit spending roared into high gear, the economy continued to grow, and the stock market rocketed to record levels. In the center of recovery was Mr. Optimism, President Ronald Reagan. The Reagan era, which spanned most of the 1980s, fostered a new conservative agenda of good feeling. During the presidential election against incumbent President Jimmy Carter, Reagan joked, "A recession is when your neighbor loses his job. A depression is when you lose yours. And recovery is when Jimmy Carter loses his."

The economic wave of the 1980s was also driven by globalization, improvements in technology, and the willingness of consumers to assume higher and higher levels of personal debt. Although 42 percent of all American workers were female, their median wage was 60 percent of that of men. The rapid rise of women in the labor force, which had been accelerating since the 1960s, brought great social change, from married life, to office culture.

The rising economy brought greater control of personal lives; homeownership accelerated, choices seemed limitless, debt grew, and divorce became commonplace. The collapse of Communism at the end of the 1980s brought an end to the Old World order and set the stage for a realignment of power. America was regarded as the strongest nation in the world and the only real superpower. At the end of World War II, the U.S. economy accounted for almost 50 percent of the global economic product; by 1987, the U.S. share was less than 25 percent as American companies moved plants offshore and countries such as Japan emerged as major competitors. This need for a global reach inspired several rounds of corporate mergers as companies searched for efficiency, market share, new products, or emerging technology to survive in the rapidly shifting business environment.

The 1980s were the age of the conservative Yuppie (Young Urban Professional). Business schools, investment banks, and Wall Street firms overflowed with eager baby boomers who placed gourmet cuisine, health clubs, and high-performance autos high on their agendas. Low-fat yogurt, high-fiber cereals and Jane Fonda workout videos symbolized much of the decade. As self-indulgence rose, concerns about the environment declined. Homelessness increased and racial tensions fostered a renewed call for a more caring government. During the decade, genetic engineering came of age, and personal computers were still in their infancy.

The sexual revolution, undaunted by a conservative prescription of chastity, ran head-on into a powerful adversary during the 1980s with the discovery and spread of AIDS. The right of women to have an abortion, confirmed by the Supreme Court in 1973, was hotly contested during the decade as politicians fought over both the actual moment of conception and the right of a woman to control her body. Cocaine also made its reappearance, bringing drug addiction and a rapid increase in violent crime. The Center on Addiction and Substance Abuse at Columbia University found alcohol and drug abuse implicated in three-fourths of all murders, rapes, child molestations, and deaths of babies suffering from parental neglect.

1983 PROFILE

Jim Rosser was a National Football League referee on weekends, on top of working a full-time position as director of personnel for American Furniture Company in Martinsville, Virginia.

Life at Home

- In 1960, Jim Rosser got his first taste of officiating during a newly formed midget league football game in Mooresville, North Carolina.
- The league had been formed following a disastrous 0-10 season, and Mooresville High School had hired a new football coach who believed in building a solid foundation for the future.
- He wanted to develop a midget age (six to 12 years old) football program that would supply him with quality players and he needed referees; Jim gave it a try and loved it.
- He earned $10 for calling the first game.
- A year later he was calling high school football games every Friday night, and by 1967 he had broken into the college ranks, refereeing freshman games in the Atlanta Coast Conference.
- By 1970, he was elevated to Atlantic Coast Conference (ACC) varsity games, traveling each week to a different setting and rivalry.
- His regular Saturday stage was a stadium filled with thousands of screaming fans desperate for another win.
- The college ranks, he quickly learned, was a place where the speed of the players and the pace of the game accelerated dramatically.
- "One of the first things I learned was to swivel my head"; otherwise, he would miss a call, and Jim hated to make mistakes or draw attention to himself.
- Football officials always wanted to be invisible, even wearing stripes.
- Major games between in-state rivals could be nerve wracking.
- But as a gangly 6'4", 175-pound tackle for the 1952 Anniston High School football team in Alabama, Jim got some advice to live by from his coach: "if you ever pull on your jockstrap and don't have butterflies in your stomach, take it right back off."
- Nervousness was simply part of the players' preparation.

Jim Rosser juggled a full-time job with refereeing for the NFL.

- When he graduated high school, Jim was an all Calhoun County, Alabama footballer, captain of the Anniston basketball team and sixth man on the golfing team.
- At Auburn University he played freshman basketball, but a bad shoulder ended his collegian athletic career and the scholarship; Jim waited tables to pay the $31-a-quarter tuition.
- After graduation, he was off to Quantico, Virginia, and Camp Pendleton, California, for a stint as a Marine Corps reconnaissance officer.
- In civilian life he found his calling as a personnel director and referee.
- Life was good.
- Jim served seven years as a football official in the Atlantic Coast Conference and was first scouted by the NFL during the 1974 Bluebonnet Bowl and again in the 1977 Orange Bowl.
- On the third play of the Orange Bowl game, Jim was accidentally knocked to the ground; he was then helped to his feet by Ohio State coach Woody Hayes, one of the toughest taskmasters in the game.
- But referees are often remembered best for their mistakes, and Jim had one he would always recall.
- In 1974 he was suspended for a game for blowing a call at Duke.
- He had counted twice and was convinced there were 12 men on the field before he threw the flag.
- The film showed only 11 men on the field.
- So the next week he watched the University of North Carolina-North Carolina State game from the stands instead of the field.
- "It was one of the hardest things I've ever had to do," he said.

Life at Work

- Jim Rosser's first assignment as a National Football League referee was in St. Louis on August 2, 1977—a pre-season game.
- As a rookie referee, he made $325 a game.

Jim was excited to make the move from college football to the NFL.

- Just as it was the job of 22 highly paid professional football players to do bodily harm to each other on over 100 plays a game, it was Jim's job to control the chaos one play at a time.
- "You have to consciously think about every play. You try to get set mentally on every play. Before the play starts you review what can happen. The first time you don't, something weird happens."
- The NFL first began scouting Jim as a NFL referee four years earlier, conducting extensive background checks, psychiatric testing, FBI-style investigation and comprehensive interviewing.
- He also had a veteran NFL mentor guiding him through the rigorous process.
- Every year more than 120 college referees were considered for five or six slots.
- Initially, Jim was told his application had been rejected; two months later Jim received a phone call from Art McNally, supervisor for NFL officials, who informed him that he been selected to fill a position which had opened unexpectedly.

The officiating crew was a tight-knit group.

- To prepare for his first game as a back judge, Jim watched game films provided by the NFL until deep into the night.
- "First I watched clips of a rookie back judge making key calls; then I watched films of their best back judge making calls. The NFL trains its officials well."
- Back judge is one of the most physically demanding positions in officiating, especially as the pass has come to dominate the professional game.
- Normally, he started 17 yards beyond the line of scrimmage and went full length down the field with the receiver and some of the fastest players in the league.
- Yet, he was supposed to beat them to the goal line.
- During an average game, a back judge will run up to 11 miles.
- Unlike baseball umpires, whose crews rotated positions from game to game, football officials specialized.
- When Jim joined the NFL in 1977, there were six on-field officials: the referee, who lines up behind the offensive backfield; the umpire, who is positioned in the middle of the field behind the defensive line; the head linesman and the line judge, who are on opposite sidelines on the line of scrimmage; the field judge, who stands on the sideline in the defensive backfield, and the back judge, who is positioned in midfield behind the defensive backs.
- A seventh official, the side judge, an across-the-field complement to the field judge, was added in 1978.

Referees had to be physically and mentally fit.

- The additional judge provided assistance to Jim and passing plays, whose area of responsibility was 18 to 20 yards ahead of scrimmage.
- Each official played a particular role on every play; officials had to wait for the play to come to them.
- Every call was graded, including his no calls.
- Jim's part-time role as arbitrator in one of professional sports' most violent pastimes was on top of his full-time position as director of personnel for American Furniture Company in Martinsville, Virginia.
- Typically he worked a five-day week and dropped by the office on Saturday mornings to clean up paperwork before flying off to whatever NFL city he was assigned that week.
- Game assignments and locations were made on a weekly basis; Jim was never able to plan his travel in advance.
- Once in the NFL city of the week, he would join the rest of the officiating crew for a meeting, break for dinner and meet again at 9 p.m. to go over game film from the previous week's game.
- The crew, who worked together all season, also ate breakfast together on Sunday mornings to once again go over the basic mechanics of the game.
- Jim then returned home late Sunday night or early Monday morning, after attempting to get some sleep on the plane so he could report to work on Monday morning.
- The NFL flew referees first-class, which was seldom heavily booked on Sunday nights, so he could stretch out across two seats and get some sleep.
- It was the same routine for 107 referees, most of them holding full-time jobs.
- Only 10 NFL officials played pro football themselves.
- Their average age was 48, with 24 years of officiating experience; the NFL required a minimum of 10 years' experience to even be considered.
- To remain eligible, NFL referees were required to complete an exhausting battery of tests annually.
- In addition, a four-day clinic was held each summer that included game films of each official, which were reviewed and offered for critique.
- A 175-question test was taken each spring; the first year Jim missed 18 of the first 20 questions.
- "The test was open book, so you might guess how in-depth each question must be," he explained.
- He also ran daily to keep in shape; Jim hated to lift weights and rarely did.
- He quickly learned that during the game it was not the physical fatigue that wore him down, but the mental wear and tear.
- "It takes total concentration to follow the action; you can't let up, not even for a moment," he remarked.
- With 3,000 plays to watch each year, and each taking only seven seconds on average, a blink of the eye could result in a missed call.
- "It is hard to have a good game officiating a bad blowout game," he said.
- During his second year in the league, a rule change allowed defensive men to chuck or bump a potential pass receiver once near the line of scrimmage, and then only when the receiver was within five yards.
- Another rule change allowed offensive linemen to leave their hands open to block when protecting the passer.
- Jim believed the rule changes made the game safer.
- In 1978, a study on the use of instant replay as an officiating aid was made during seven nationally televised pre-season games.
- And the popularity of the game continued to explode.

Jim had only been hit twice during his career.

- Bolstered by the expansion of the regular-season schedule from 14 to 16 weeks, the NFL paid attendance exceeded 12 million for the first time.
- The per-game average of 57,017 was the third-highest in league history and the most since 1973.
- In 1980, Pittsburgh defeated the Los Angeles Rams 31-19 in Super Bowl XIV in a game that was viewed in a record 35,330,000 homes.
- CBS, with a record bid of $12 million, won the national radio rights to 26 NFL regular-season games, including *Monday Night Football,* and all 10 post-season games for the 1980-83 seasons.
- Television ratings in 1980 were the second-best in NFL history, trailing only the combined ratings of the 1976 season.
- All three networks posted gains, and NBC's 15.0 rating was its best ever.
- CBS and ABC had their best ratings since 1977, with 15.3 and 20.8, respectively.
- But the 1982 NFL season, the 63rd regular season of the National Football League, included a 57-day-long players' strike that reduced the season from a 16-game schedule per team to nine games.
- Because of the shortened season, the NFL adopted a special 16-team playoff tournament.
- Division standings were ignored: eight teams from each conference were seeded 1-8 based on their regular season records.
- The season ended with Super Bowl XVII, when the Washington Redskins defeated the Miami Dolphins.
- During the prior six years in the league, Jim had only been hit twice during a game.
- Both were accidental, but painful.
- As the 1983 season got underway, Jim had come to believe that most NFL officials performed for the love of the game.
- "I can't think of anyone who does it for the money, not anyone," he commented.

Furniture making was a major industry in Martinsville, Virginia.

Life in the Community: Martinsville, Virginia

- The furniture industry, along with textiles, was the lifeblood of Martinsville, located in southern Virginia.
- Founded by American Revolutionary War General, Indian agent and explorer Joseph Martin, Martinsville and its surrounding county boasted a population of 75,000 by the early 1980s and claimed to have more millionaires per capita than any city in the state.
- The city's first major industry in the 1800s was the manufacture of plug chewing tobacco; the area became known as the "Plug Tobacco Capital of the World."
- Thanks to the entrepreneurial efforts of several families, the city's main industry for a century was furniture construction, boasting companies such as Bassett Furniture, American Furniture Company, and Gravely Furniture Company.
- Shortly after World War II, DuPont built a chemical manufacturing plant.
- DuPont later built a large manufacturing plant for producing nylon, a vital war material, which made the city a target for strategic bombing during the Cold War.
- This nylon production jumpstarted the growth of the textiles industry in the area.
- For several years Martinsville was known as the "Sweatshirt Capital of the World."
- Martinsville is also home to the Virginia Museum of Natural History, an affiliate of the Smithsonian Institution and founded by Martinsville native Dr. Noel Boaz, and the Piedmont Arts Association, an affiliate of the Virginia Museum of Fine Arts.
- Martinsville was also present at the birth of NASCAR, possessing a small, half-mile round racetrack that was home for the beginning drivers of the sport like Junior Johnson, Richard Petty, Rex White and Windale Scott.

HISTORICAL SNAPSHOT
1983

- The musical *Annie* was performed for the last time after 2,377 shows at the Alvin Theatre on Broadway
- Apple Inc. released the Apple Lisa personal computer
- Björn Borg retired from tennis after winning five consecutive Wimbledon championships
- Lotus 1-2-3 was released for IBM-PC compatible computers
- Congress released a report critical of the United States' practice of Japanese internment during World War II
- The final episode of *M*A*S*H* was aired and set a record for the most watched episode
- President Ronald Reagan announced plans to develop technology to intercept enemy missiles, which the media dubbed "Star Wars"
- Michael Jackson performed the dance move known as the "moonwalk"

- Hezbollah terrorists bombed the U.S. Embassy in Beirut, killing 63 people
- *Pioneer 10* became the first manmade object to leave the solar system
- Sally Ride was the first American woman in space, on the space shuttle *Challenger*
- Vanessa Lynn Williams became the first African American to be crowned Miss America
- Australia won the America's Cup
- Richard Noble set a new land speed record of 633.468 mph, driving *Thrust 2* at the Black Rock Desert, Nevada
- The Baltimore Orioles defeated the Philadelphia Phillies 5-0 in game 5 to win the series four games to one for their third World Championship
- At the 17th General Conference on Weights and Measures, the metre was defined in terms of the speed of light as the distance light travels in a vacuum in 1/299,792,458 of a second
- Simultaneous suicide truck bombings destroyed both the French and the United States Marine Corps barracks in Beirut, killing 241 U.S. servicemen, 58 French paratroopers and six Lebanese civilians
- Microsoft Word was first released
- President Reagan signed a bill creating a federal holiday on the third Monday of every January to honor American civil rights leader Martin Luther King, Jr.

- The first United States cruise missiles arrived at Greenham Common Airbase in England amid protests from peace campaigners
- United Nations Resolution 37 demanded that the Soviet Union withdraw from Afghanistan
- *Flashdance* and *Return of the Jedi* were box office hits

Selected Prices

Automobile, Honda Civic	$7,517
Beer, 12-Pack	$3.19
Bicycle	$179.99
Circus Ticket	$8.50
Knee Pads	$5.99
Rollerblades	$24.99
Skate Helmet	$15.99
Turntable, Sony	$200.00
Video Game	$54.95
Videotape, *Italian Cookbook*	$42.50

Not long ago we had a game where a receiver in the backfield was hit on a pass play. It was an early hit but not a vicious one. The fans were screaming for pass interference, but since the play occurred behind the line of scrimmage, it wasn't pass interference and we didn't call it. That was an example of a good "no call."

—NFL Veteran Referee Jerry Markbreit

NFL Rules Timeline

1950
Unlimited free substitution was restored, opening the way for the era of two platoons and specialization in pro football.

1951
The Pro Bowl game, dormant since 1942, was revived under a new format matching the all-stars of each conference at the Los Angeles Memorial Coliseum.

A rule was passed that no tackle, guard or center would be eligible to catch a forward pass.

1955
The sudden-death overtime rule was used for the first time in a pre-season game between the Rams and Giants at Portland, Oregon.

A rule change declared the ball dead immediately if the ball carrier touched the ground with any part of his body except his hands or feet while in the grasp of an opponent.

1956
Grabbing an opponent's facemask (other than the ball carrier) was made illegal.

Using radio receivers to communicate with players on the field was prohibited.

A natural leather ball with white end stripes replaced the white ball with black stripes for night games.

1960
The AFL adopted the two-point option on points after touchdown.

continued

NFL Rules Timeline . . . *(continued)*

1962

Both NFL and AFL leagues prohibited grabbing any player's facemask.

The AFL voted to make the scoreboard clock the official timer of the game.

1966

Goal posts offset from the goal line, painted bright yellow, and with uprights 20 feet above the crossbar were made standard in the NFL.

1967

The "sling-shot" goal post and a six-foot-wide border around the field were made standard in the NFL.

1969

The AFL established a playoff format for the 1969 season, with the winner in one division playing the runner-up in the other.

1970

The merged 26-team league (NFL) adopted rule changes of putting names on the backs of players' jerseys, making a point after a touchdown worth only one point, and making the scoreboard clock the official timing device of the game.

1972

The inbounds lines, or hashmarks, were moved nearer to the center of the field, 23 yards, one foot, nine inches from the sidelines.

Tie games, previously not counted in the standings, were made equal to a half-game won and a half-game lost.

1973

A jersey numbering system was adopted: 1-19 for quarterbacks and specialists, 20-49 for running backs and defensive backs, 50-59 for centers and linebackers, 60-79 for defensive linemen and interior offensive linemen other than centers, and 80-89 for wide receivers and tight ends.

Players who had been in the NFL in 1972 could continue to use old numbers.

1974

One sudden-death overtime period was added for pre-season and regular-season games.

The goal posts were moved from the goal line to the end lines.

Kickoffs were moved from the 40- to the 35-yard line.

After missed field goals from beyond the 20, the ball was to be returned to the line of scrimmage.

Restrictions were placed on members of the punting team to open up return possibilities.

Roll-blocking and cutting of wide receivers were eliminated.

The extent of downfield contact a defender could have with an eligible receiver was restricted.

Penalties for offensive holding, illegal use of the hands, and tripping were reduced from 15 to 10 yards.

Wide receivers blocking back toward the ball within three yards of the line of scrimmage were prevented from blocking below the waist.

continued

NFL Rules Timeline . . . *(continued)*

1976
Owners adopted the use of two 30-second clocks for all games, visible to both players and fans, to note the official time between the ready-for-play signal and snap of the ball.

1977
A 16-game regular season, four-game pre-season was adopted.

1978
A second wild-card team was adopted for the playoffs beginning in 1978, with the wild-card teams to play each other and the winners advancing to a round of eight post-season series.

Defenders were permitted to make contact with eligible receivers only once.

The head slap was outlawed; offensive linemen were prohibited from thrusting their hands to an opponent's neck, face or head.

Wide receivers were prohibited from clipping, even in the legal clipping zone.

Rule changes permitted a defender to maintain contact with a receiver within five yards of the line of scrimmage, but restricted contact beyond that point.

The pass-blocking rule was interpreted to permit the extending of arms and open hands.

continued

NFL Rules Timeline ... *(continued)*

1979

Rule changes prohibited players on the receiving team from blocking below the waist during kickoffs, punts and field-goal attempts.

The wearing of torn or altered equipment and exposed pads that could be hazardous was prohibited, and the zone was extended in which there could be no crackback blocks.

Officials were instructed to quickly whistle a play dead when a quarterback was clearly in the grasp of a tackler.

1980

Rule changes placed greater restrictions on contact in the area of the head, neck and face.

Under the heading of "personal foul," players were prohibited from directly striking, swinging or clubbing on the head, neck or face.

1981

It became illegal for players to put adhesive or slippery substances such as the product "stickum" on their bodies, equipment or uniforms to make it easier for them to catch a pass.

The penalty for an ineligible receiver who touched a forward pass became a loss of down.

The penalty for illegal use of hands, arms or body (including holding) was reduced from 15 yards to 10 yards.

The penalty for intentional grounding was modified: loss of down and 10 yards penalty from the previous spot, or if the foul occurs more than 10 yards from the line of scrimmage, loss of down at the spot of the foul.

1982

The penalty for incidental grabbing of a facemask by the defensive team was changed from five yards and an automatic first down to just five yards.

The penalties for illegally kicking, batting or punching the ball were changed from 15 yards to 10 yards.

The league discontinued the 1979 numbering system for officials and reverted back to the original system in which each NFL official was assigned a different number.

1983

In the last 30 seconds of a half, with the defensive team behind with no more timeouts, a defensive foul could not prevent the half from ending except for the normal options that were available to the offensive team.

Pass interference would not be called if there was incidental contact, or if players made simultaneous attempts to catch, tip, block or bat the ball.

A player was not allowed use a helmet that was no longer worn by anyone as a weapon to strike an opponent.

"It's Open Season on the Zebras,"... *(continued)*

The question is whether a mere human being or seven mere human beings (the current size of an officiating crew) can bring law and order to a vast field populated with 22 speeding giants joined in hand-to-hand combat. Predictably enough, (Pete) Roselle is not quick to criticize his officials or even to admit that they are any more or less given to error. "Yes, there have been mistakes, but there were mistakes last year, too," he says. "The officials have literally thousands of opportunities for error in each game." To arrive at the number of potential calls an official might be faced with in a given game, he says, you multiply the average number of plays per game, about 160, by the number of players on the field, 22. That comes to 3,520 different instances which may require a judgment by a single official. "However, that's low," he adds, "since there are other complicating factors involved, such as emotionalism on the sidelines and maybe some improper understanding of the rules by players or coaches. Besides the sheer magnitude of possible judgment, the biggest problem is how to see what's happening with 22 huge bodies, any one of which might come into your line of vision. At field level, you have only one angle of vision. There are problems. We've added the seventh official, and it helps."

1985 PROFILE

Paul Howe overcame his lack of stature to fulfill his desire to play professional football for 11 teams spanning three leagues.

Life at Home

- Born in Lexington, Massachusetts, in 1951, Paul Howe grew up with a love for sports that blossomed after his father, Charles, a sales engineer, took him to a Boston Patriots game on Paul's tenth birthday.
- Boston had been awarded the eighth and final franchise in the new American Football League in 1959, and Lou Saban had been named the team's first head coach.
- Paul was giddy with excitement to be going and was ready for the game two hours early.
- He knew all about the team, its players and its plans.
- He had even submitted dozens of entries when the team asked the public to name the team; thousands of entries were submitted and 74 fans suggested the winning name, the Boston Patriots.
- Boston Globe artist Phil Bissell then drew a cartoon of a Minuteman preparing to snap a football; team owners liked the drawing so much "Pat Patriot" was selected as the team logo.
- The team's regular season home opener came on September 9, 1960, when 21,597 fans at Boston University field watched the team lose to the Denver Broncos 13-10.
- Paul's game was a whirlwind of noises, tastes and sounds; his father bought him a souvenir banner, three hot dogs and a drink.
- Paul was deliriously happy, even though his team lost.
- He slept all the way home.
- After that, Paul would rather play football than watch television, unless a game was on.
- As an athlete, Paul developed a team-first attitude that impressed his coaches and teammates, who voted him team captain of both the high school football and hockey teams.

What Paul Howe lacked in size he made up for in perseverance.

When Paul didn't make the NFL draft, he tried out for the World Football League.

- The local newspaper promoted him as a college prospect, but the team's 5 and 5 season didn't draw much attention to a six-foot, 210-pound defensive lineman.
- Paul played his college ball at the University of Pittsburgh while majoring in physical education.
- Most colleges had passed on Paul because he was deemed undersized for both an offensive and defensive lineman, but Pitt used an innovative speed-based defense that allowed undersized linemen to be aggressive.
- Paul set his sights on the pro game; however, he went undrafted in the NFL's 12-round Annual Selection Meeting; most teams were interested in big, space-eating defensive linemen.
- He signed with the Atlanta Falcons, but was cut before the 1974 season began, because he was considered too small to play the run.
- He then tried the rival World Football League.
- He signed with the Chicago Blitz, but again failed to make the final cut.
- It pained him to get the phone call that he was to turn in his playbook.
- Year round, Paul painted houses to make ends meet as he continued to work out and prepare himself for the pros, writing letters to teams hoping to receive an invitation to training camp or to replace an injured player.
- Paul spent two years as a nomad in training camps with the Washington Redskins, the WFL's Charlotte Hornets, and back to the NFL with the New England Patriots.
- His life consisted of sweating in the summer sun of training camp, moving from city to city, learning new playbooks, and finding himself a stranger in every locker room.
- Logic told him to surrender his dream, face facts, and get a job coaching high school sports, but his heart wouldn't let him give up.
- He sharpened his focus and in 1976 his perseverance paid off as he landed on the roster of the Denver Broncos.

- He impressed head coach Robert "Red" Miller with his special team skills and attitude, but the Broncos famous "Orange Crush" defense was talented and deep, so Paul was moved to the offensive line.
- He stayed late, learning every spot on the line, working at all five positions to make himself a more attractive backup.
- Paul made the team and was part of the Denver Broncos 1978 Super Bowl team, a career high for him.

Life at Work

- Paul Howe enjoyed life in the Mile High City with its year-round golfing, skiing and hiking.
- And he had felt financially secure enough to marry Nancy, a sales associate at a sporting goods store he frequented.
- But every season it was a struggle to make the roster as the 12-round draft brought younger, cheaper competition to challenge his roster spot.
- A coaching change in 1981 and a new pass-oriented scheme that didn't fit Paul's abilities left him with only his special team skills to make the team.
- In the NFL, if you are not a starter, you must earn your keep on special teams.
- Special teams were beginning to come to attention in the early 1980s, thanks to players like Bill Bates and Andre Waters, who played with reckless abandon, sacrificing their bodies for the sake of making a tackle.

Paul's wife, Nancy stayed in Denver when he was traded to the Colts.

- Some players did not report concussions for fear of losing playing time or not making the team at all.
- Paul used his hockey experience to help him play aggressively, but under control, so as not to receive the brain damage that prematurely ended the careers and even the lives of players.
- Undersized for a lineman, but with speed and tenacity, Paul became a hero on special teams.
- Coach Red Miller called his style of play "hell-bent."
- His teammate, the tough, undersized linebacker Tom Jackson, gave him the nickname "Thumper."
- "Whenever I made a hit, Tom said I *thumped* somebody."
- Paul's prowess for special team play was not only appreciated by his coach and teammates, but also the fans.
- The Bronco fans loved and identified with his blue-collar background and rooted for him to make the roster each year.
- Some fans wore T-shirts that had "Howe's Herd" emblazoned on the back, turning Paul into a cult hero.

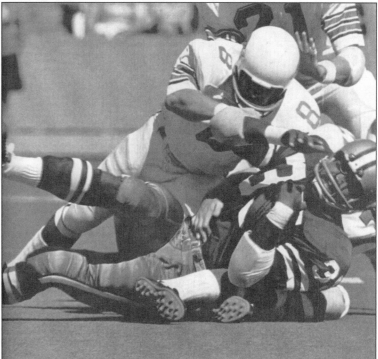

"Thumper" was Paul's nickname.

- Mile High Stadium would shake as fans stomped their feet to a Howe tackle.
- But loyalty was a rare commodity; Paul was traded to the Baltimore Colts in 1982, just as the league went on strike.
- With Nancy in Denver and no locker room fellowship, Paul increased his drinking, going to bars and making bets with customers who wanted to try and outdrink a tough guy pro football player.
- When the season began, the marriage was strained and Paul found himself depressed, which kept his drinking at a dangerous level.
- His on-field performance suffered and the Colts dumped him, but he signed with the Chicago Fire of a new World Football League.
- But the WFL had financial difficulties, and some teams even had their uniforms confiscated by sheriff's deputies.
- Things grew worse at home as Nancy admitted to having an affair; Paul felt helpless.
- The next football season, Paul jumped at a chance to return to Denver and play for his old Broncos head coach, Red Miller, now in charge of the Denver Gold of the United States Football League (USFL).

- Miller was fired four games into the season due to difficulties with ownership, and new coach Darrell "Mouse" Davis preferred a wide open passing offense.
- After the 1984 spring USFL season ended, Paul was released and no team came calling.
- He was losing his wife, about to lose his home, and knew he was going in the wrong direction.
- His never-give-up attitude aided him in the difficult challenge of turning his life around, as one day he said to himself, "Paul, you're a bum and you weren't raised to be a bum."
- He told Nancy he wanted to get back together; he promised to quit drinking and join a church support group.
- They began attending church regularly and vowed to make a new start.
- Word of getting his act cleaned up got back to the Broncos, who signed him to the biggest contract he had ever received.
- In a job where only 215 out of every 100,000 high school senior football players make it to the NFL and with an average career length of only 3.5 years, Paul felt blessed to celebrate his tenth year in professional football.

Paul was drawn to Colorado's natural beauty.

Life in the Community: Denver, Colorado

- Like Paul Howe, visitors have long been attracted by Colorado's frontier past, informal living and breathtaking scenery.
- Admitted to the Union in 1876, Colorado holds the title of the highest of the 50 states and has an average of 300 days of sunshine each year.
- Although gold started Colorado's road to statehood, crude oil, natural gas and coal now played a critical role in the economy of the state.
- In addition, Colorado was the major source of steel hardening minerals such as molybdenum and tungsten.
- Originally known as the "Queen City of the Plains," Denver is now recognized as the "Mile High City."
- Denver spreads over nearly 100 square miles, with the city and surrounding areas claiming more than one million people.
- Dominating the Denver skyline is the gold-domed state Capitol building, which is topped with solid 28-carat gold leaf from the mines of the Rockies.
- More than 200 federal bureaus, agencies and regional offices are located in Denver, giving rise to its claim of being the "Western Washington, DC."
- Military facilities in and around Denver house more than 52,000 people, providing an annual federal payroll of more than $700 million.

HISTORICAL SNAPSHOT
1985

- Agriculture Minister Mikhail Gorbachev, 54, became premier of the Soviet Union

- Actor Rock Hudson became the first celebrity to die of AIDS, raising awareness of the disease

- Thirty-eight people died during a riot by soccer fans at the European Cup finals in Brussels

- The first Live-Aid concert was watched on television worldwide by 1.6 billion viewers, raising $70 million for famine relief in Ethiopia

- The song "We Are the World" raised $50 million for African famine relief

- New Zealand refused to allow a U.S. warship entry into its waters on the grounds that it contained nuclear arms

- Boxer Mike Tyson knocked out Hector Mercedes to win his first professional fight

- The U.S. Rabbinical Assembly of Conservative Judaism accepted women rabbis

- The Pulitzer Prize-winning novel, *Lonesome Dove,* by Larry McMurtry, was published

- The income for video cassette rentals equaled movie box office income for the first time

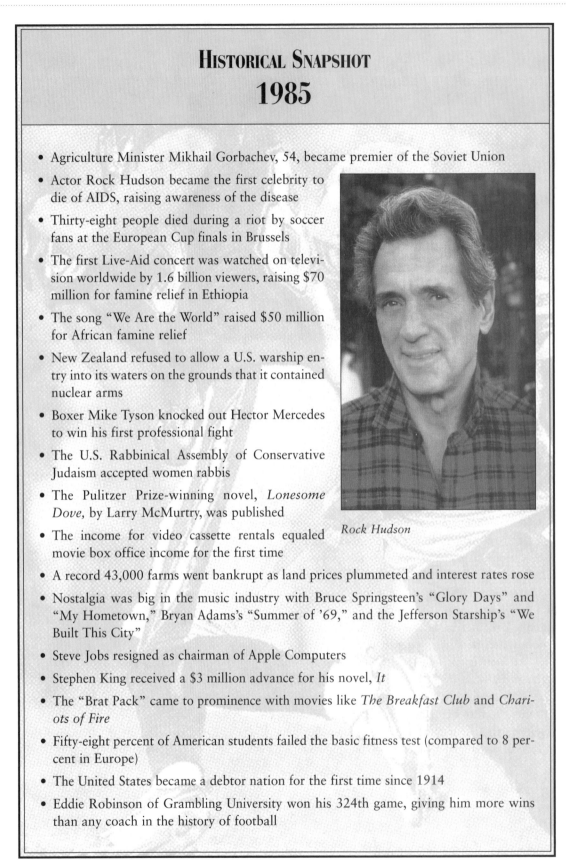

Rock Hudson

- A record 43,000 farms went bankrupt as land prices plummeted and interest rates rose

- Nostalgia was big in the music industry with Bruce Springsteen's "Glory Days" and "My Hometown," Bryan Adams's "Summer of '69," and the Jefferson Starship's "We Built This City"

- Steve Jobs resigned as chairman of Apple Computers

- Stephen King received a $3 million advance for his novel, *It*

- The "Brat Pack" came to prominence with movies like *The Breakfast Club* and *Chariots of Fire*

- Fifty-eight percent of American students failed the basic fitness test (compared to 8 percent in Europe)

- The United States became a debtor nation for the first time since 1914

- Eddie Robinson of Grambling University won his 324th game, giving him more wins than any coach in the history of football

Selected Prices

Clogs $19.95
Computer $895.00
Disposable Diaper, Each $0.21
Guitar $89.99
Light Bulb $4.00
Microwave $199.99
Movie Ticket $4.00
Pen Set $30.00
Shirt, Men's $15.88
Sweatshirt $19.95

Pro Football Trends: 1985

- The NFL was experiencing serious competition for the first time since the AFL-NFL merger of 1970.
- The World Football League (WFL) and the United States Football League (USFL) challenged the NFL for fans.
- The WFL was on its second attempt after a failed try in the mid-1970s.
- The USFL was a more serious threat, with big spending owners like Donald Trump and Disney.
- It also took chances that the NFL was hesitant to take, such as the two-point conversion and a salary cap.
- The USFL stole players from both the college ranks and NFL rosters.
- Among the USFL's many star players were Jim Kelly, Steve Young, Doug Flutie, Herschel Walker, Reggie White, and Sam Mills.
- Chicago Bears running back Walter Payton, the NFL's top player, even considered a contract with the Chicago team rather than his Bears team.
- Thanks to the competition of the USFL, the average salary of an NFL player more than doubled between 1982 and 1985 from $90,000 to $190,000.
- In 1985, the USFL voted to go from a spring league to a fall league with the hope of merging with the NFL.
- The plan failed and the expense cost the league $163 million in losses due to its reckless spending and a TV feud with the NFL.
- The USFL sued the NFL for having a monopoly on pro football in the United States and won the case, receiving their court costs plus a financial compensation to cover their debts.
- The jury ruled that the league should receive $1, incorrectly believing that the judge would adjust the amount to a sum he deemed fair.
- According to U.S. law, this amount was to be tripled, and so, with interest, the NFL wrote a check to the USFL for $3.76.
- The check has never been cashed.

NFL Timeline

1892
The Allegheny Association of Pittsburgh paid guard Pudge Heffelfinger, a three time All-American at Yale, $500 to play a game against Pittsburgh AC. Heffelfinger won the game when he recovered a fumble and ran for a touchdown, the game's only score, in a 4-0 win.

1893
Players were offered season-long $50 contracts.

1906
The forward pass was introduced.

1909
A touchdown was now worth six points, a field goal three.

1921
Fritz Pollard became the first African American coach, leading the Akron Pros.

continued

NFL Timeline . . . *(continued)*

1922
The NFL was born; opening day attendance of the eight games was a combined 22,500 fans.

1936
The very first NFL Annual Selection Meeting was held with the Philadelphia Eagles selecting halfback Jay Berwanger of the University of Chicago. He never signed with team and used his Heisman Trophy as a doorstop in his library.

1940
Walter "Red" Barber paid $2,500 for the rights to broadcast the NFL championship game on 120 radio stations on the Mutual Broadcasting System. The game was the most decisive in league history as the Chicago Bears defeated the Washington Redskins 73-0.

1943
Due to losing players in World War II, the Philadelphia Eagles and the Pittsburgh Steelers combined to form a team, the Phil-Pitt Steagles.

Helmets became mandatory.

1950
The free substitution rule came into effect, allowing teams to have players who don't play both sides of the ball.

1956
NBC-TV paid $100,000 to replace the Dumont Network for the title game.

1958
The "Greatest Game Ever Played," a sudden death overtime spectacular championship game between the New York Giants and the Baltimore Colts was a television sensation.

1967
The first Super Bowl was played. The Green Bay Packers defeated the Kansas City Chiefs 35-10. Attendance was 61,946, not a sellout since fans found the $12 ticket price exorbitant.

1970
The AFL and the NFL merged.

1972
The Miami Dolphins had a perfect season, culminating in their 14-7 Super Bowl win over the Washington Redskins; 90,000 fans attended, while 75 million watched on television.

1985
In Super Bowl XIX, the San Francisco 49ers defeated the Miami Dolphins 38-16. A record $40 million was wagered on the game through Las Vegas odds makers. The game had a $113 million impact on the San Francisco area economy.

Television revenues were NFL, $17 million per team; USFL, $2.1 million per team.

"Football Fanatics Set Record Straight," *Salina Journal* (Kansas), December 12, 1985:

They are football's dedicated detectives, historians who enjoy the sport not only on television, but on microfilm monitors that transport them to the halcyon days of professional football.

They're 150 members of the loosely knit professional Football Researchers Association scattered across the country. Most are mere spectators; some, including former all-pro guard Joe Kopcha of the Chicago Bears, are former players. All are fans.

Bob Carroll, for instance, is a Pittsburgh area researcher and illustrator with an encyclopedic knowledge of football's forgotten heroes. Lido Starelli, a San Francisco plasterer, has missed only one 49ers game in 43 years and has every game program to prove it.

The amateur researchers specialize in debunking the myths and mysteries of the sport's sometimes nomadic and often misunderstood past.

"It's amazing how much of the myth and lore associated with pro football don't stand up under research," said Carroll, 49, the editor of *The Coffin Corner,* the PFRA's semi-monthly newsletter. "Much of what has been written even in encyclopedias isn't always accurate."

For example, it has long been accepted that the National Football League was formed September 17, 1920, as the legendary George Halas and other founding fathers squatted on Hupmobile running boards in a Canton, Ohio, auto dealership. An illustration of the historic meeting hangs in a prominent place in the Pro Football Hall of Fame in Canton.

But, Carroll said, Canton newspaper headlines blared "New League Is Formed" more than a month before, and that the car dealer meeting may have served merely to formalize plans for a league that later would capture the imagination of the nation.

Carroll, citing the fruits of research, offered these tidbits:

- Only several years before the historic 1958 Baltimore Colts-New York Giants overtime championship game, "pro football was only about as popular as indoor soccer is today."
- Just six years before that game, "the turning point in NFL history," the Colts were called that Dallas Texans and "were so bad, they wound up finishing the season in Hershey, Pennsylvania."
- Even in the early 1950s, newspaper columnists frequently wrote that an average college football team could beat any pro team.
- Pro football's first great passing quarterback wasn't the revolutionary Sammy Baugh, but a highly underrated former Michigan All-American named Benny Friedman who once threw 18 touchdown passes in a single season with a ball "more like a watermelon than a football. . . ."

"Broncos, Saints Inspire Opposite in Fans," *The Capital* (Annapolis, Maryland), November 15, 1985:

Dan Reeves knows the two sides of Denver Broncos fans. Some of them, after all, wanted his head after the Broncos had the affront to lose again to Seattle last season and fell to 11-2 after 10 straight wins.

But after Reeves' Broncos beat the San Francisco 49ers Monday night, he gave them full credit.

"When they come out in this kind of weather and cheer us on like they did, that's showing terrific support," he said. "They helped us win the game."

More precisely, one snowball-throwing fan helped them win the game.

The missile in question, one of numerous snowballs flung from the stands in Mile High Stadium during the game, landed in front of San Francisco's Matt Cavanaugh as he was about to spot the ball for Ray Wersching's 19-yard yard field-goal attempt. The best Cavanaugh could do was pick up the ball and heave it awkwardly (and unsuccessfully) into the end zone.

The 49ers ended up losing 17-16. The police ended up escorting five people from the stadium on what Detective Ken Chaves said was a charge of "throwing missiles."

And the incident tarnished Denver's image. As Dan Gayer of Commerce City, Colorado, said after the game: "It makes us look bad, especially when it's on national television."

Yesterday, the young man whose snowball may have cost the 49ers the game, called the *San Francisco Examiner* to apologize. He turned down a $500 reward offered for his story. . . .

Denver fans are probably the most blindly loyal in the National Football League: 73,173 of them showed up Monday in 20-degree weather despite a 30-10 defeat in San Diego the previous week. They would have been there had the Broncos entered the game 3-6 instead of 6-3.

The waiting list for season tickets is as long as the waiting list in Washington and New York, where the population base is millions larger. There have been divorce cases in which the battle for custody of Broncos tickets is more bitter than the battle for custody of the kids.

And memories linger. Lou Saban, who hasn't coached the Broncos since 1971, is still known there scornfully as "half a loaf," because he played for a tie against the Dolphins that season and excused his actions by saying: "Half a loaf is better than none."

"Defense Key in Playoffs," *The Capital* (Annapolis, Maryland), December 26, 1984:

Nobody in professional football appreciates defense more than Pittsburgh coach Chuck Noll, who assembled the Steel Curtain that produced four Steelers Super Bowl championships.

So Pittsburgh goes into Sunday's American Football Conference semi-final game with proper respect for the Denver Broncos, who allowed only 241 points all season, second lowest in the National Football League.

Noll was not surprised that the wild-card victories of the New York Giants and Seattle Seahawks were constructed by stifling defense that simply shut down the Los Angeles Rams and Los Angeles Raiders.

"Defense has been important in championship football games as long as I can remember," Noll said. "Before you can win, you have to not lose."

Denver didn't lose very frequently, dropping only three games all season. And the opportunistic Bronco defenders scored eight touchdowns after forcing fumbles and picking up passes. Noll, a connoisseur of defense, was suitably impressed.

Bronco coach Dan Reeves knows the Steelers' reputation for being stingy with yards and points and spent much of the last week drilling Denver on defending against the blitz.

Nobody, however, blitzes more than the Chicago Bears, who led the league in rushing defense, total defense, and set a record with 72 quarterback sacks. The Washington Redskins, hoping for a third straight trip to the Super Bowl, must control the Bear defenders as well as handle Walter Payton, the NFL's all-time rushing leader.

1989 PROFILE

Carlos Piccolo, built to be a runner, began running at a very early age, trained hard, and carefully kept track of his progress.

Life at Home

- For Carlos Piccolo there was no high like a runner's high.
- He was first swept away by the runner's sensation at an early age, before he was 12, but did not remember the exact moment.
- Starting when he was 13, Carlos began keeping a runner's journal, logging his times, distances and feelings ("legs sore, hot day, ran 4.5 miles").
- His older brother possessed a massive, powerful chest and legs like tree trunks; even as a small boy everyone expected him to be a football player.
- Carlos, on the other hand, was shaped like a second-grader's hand-drawn crayon stick figure.
- With long pipe cleaner legs attached to a frame that would never conquer 150 pounds, Carlos was a genetic aberration in an aggressive family that once destroyed the living room sofa when it was used as a football blocking dummy.
- Carlos's grandparents brought the family to America when they left Mexico in 1929 seeking better opportunities for their growing family; they settled in Albuquerque, New Mexico, two years later.
- His grandfather tended horses, managed ranch maintenance and dreamed that his children would one day graduate from high school.
- Carlos's father filled that expectation, and while still in his twenties opened his own store that sold fresh fruits and vegetables, quality meats and many, many tobacco products.
- Even the white people of Albuquerque, some of whom spoke very little Spanish, would drive across town to shop for his special hand-rolled cigars and top-grade chewing tobacco.
- The Piccolo family also loved to talk loudly, long and often; shouting over each other was acceptable, even expected, by everyone.
- Everyone, that is, except Carlos.

Carlos Piccolo loved to run.

The Piccolo family store was well known for quality produce and tobacco.

- He learned early that he could best do his talking with his feet, especially after his football linebacker brother lost a bet and had to train with Carlos for a week.
- His brother said simply, "I'll never bet against you again."
- Training for a cross country meet was not Carlos's biggest problem, though; relaxing was.
- In the final five minutes before a high school race, Carlos's brain was bombarded by his past mistakes—poor pacing, moves made too late, running out of energy, missing a turn or failing to anticipate the late strength of a competitor.
- Besides, cross country meets were unpredictable since they were staged on an open course over rough terrain.
- The high school 5km courses often combined routes that incorporated grass, mud, asphalt, rocks, steep inclines, woodlands, and even water.
- On race days, Carlos normally rose at 5:30 a.m. to be prepared—but Carlos was always prepared.
- He only stopped ironing his underwear because his brother teased him so unmercifully.
- He planned what and when he would eat, the level and pace of his water intake and his sleep patterns.
- He knew from experience that when the pain struck, he would "man up" and run through the agony; he always wanted to be ready.
- The question was whether he could run through his own anxiety and stay focused on winning, not on failing.
- He had become successful enough that his parents actually came to see him run in cross country meets, proud that he once ran the mile in under 4:20 and could consistently maintain 5:35 per mile splits on the 3.2-mile courses.
- They also realized that running could be Carlos's ticket to college, if the college recruiters were to be believed.
- Carlos only went on one college recruiting trip.
- At an altitude of 7,700 feet, Western State College's campus among the Colorado Rocky Mountains in Gunnison, Colorado, was so beautiful and inspiring, it sold itself.
- Carlos knew immediately that this was the perfect place to test his limits within the rugged alpine playground.
- The beauty of the place reminded him of the runner's adage, "If you're not enjoying the journey, you probably won't enjoy the destination," and agreed to attend the 2,000-person campus.
- His first year was good, his second year better.
- As a junior, Carlos was expected to challenge the best that Colorado, Stanford, and the University of Arkansas had to offer and then win his division.

Life at Work

- At Western State College Carlos Piccolo's teammates hailed from seven different states and all had been proclaimed as cross-country heroes in high school, assuming local newspapers even knew the sport existed.
- Cross country was difficult for most reporters to explain, especially when the runners disappeared into the woods near the starting line and often did not re-emerge until they neared the finish line.
- Besides, who in their good senses would voluntarily run 95 miles a week to earn the right to run some more.

- At least in baseball, exhausting fitness work made the players eligible to hit a baseball or in football to hit each other.
- But long-distance running was the niche Carlos had claimed for himself and now he wanted to prove himself at a collegiate level at Western State College.
- During the previous summer, Carlos had trained extensively in high-altitude conditions until he could comfortably run a five-mile aerobic threshold in less than 26 minutes; in addition, he ran 100 miles weekly.
- At the college level, meet distances were usually 8 km (5 miles) for men and for women, 6 km at regional and national competitions.
- Carlos's very first qualifying meet was staged at the University of Colorado and attracted some 250 runners from 16 colleges.
- The University of Colorado had signed a contract with Nike, permitting each runner to receive Terra Humma training shoes, cross-country racing flats, track flats, shorts, long sleeve and short sleeve T-shirts, sweatpants, sweatshirts, wristbands and headbands.
- Schools the size of Western State rarely received that level of endorsement support and resented the slight; Carlos saw the Nike logo as a personal snub directed against him and his team.
- Cross-country was an intensely individualistic sport whose scoring was entirely dependent on team results.
- Points were awarded to the individual runners, equal to the position in which each crossed the finish line (first place got one point, second place got two points, etc.).
- Only the first five runners in for a team were counted toward that team's score; the points for these runners were summed, and the teams were ranked based on the total, with lowest being best.
- The lowest possible score in a five-to-score match was 15 (1+2+3+4+5), achieved by a team's runners finishing in each of the top five positions.
- In the first invitational meet of Carlos's junior year, his goal was to improve on his personal best time and finish in the top five.
- A hamstring injury was too fresh to take extraordinary risks on the first meet.
- But once the gun sounded and his competitive juices began to cascade, Carlos decided it was crucial that he win the race against the big schools and make a statement.
- His coach tried to slow him down, but Carlos would not listen.
- After three miles he was third; on the steep hill on mile four he took second, and after his finishing kick for the final 800 yards he was first.
- Winning was why he ran nearly 20 miles a day in all kinds of weather.
- When the race ended he was first, proud and re-injured.
- The pain was nauseatingly intense.
- He couldn't walk, he couldn't think, and he had another meet in three weeks.
- The coach called for rest; Carlos was convinced he could run through the pain and make a statement to Division II champion South Dakota State.
- For 20 days he stretched carefully, underwent massage therapy daily on his leg and ran through the pain.
- A routine day of jogging always seemed to end in a full bore run.
- On the day of the race, Carlos was unable to get out of bed; his thigh was swollen dramatically, the pain terrific.
- At a distance he could hear the other teams arriving, but he was still unable to stir from his bed.

Runners often ran in packs.

Life in the Community: Albuquerque, New Mexico

- Albuquerque, New Mexico, which embraces roughly half of the population of the state, is bordered on its eastern side by the Sandia Mountains and divided by the Rio Grande, which flows through the city, north to south.
- Albuquerque's enticing charm was born from its deep roots, starting with the Native Americans who lived there for thousands of years before the city's official founding by the Spanish.
- The Rio Grande Valley had been populated and cultivated since as far back as 2000 B.C.
- The Pueblo people who lived in the area when Europeans arrived had a sophisticated culture and advanced skills in stone masonry, ceramics and a wide range of arts and crafts.
- The first Spanish explorers arrived in Albuquerque in approximately 1540 under General Francisco de Coronado.
- In 1706, a group of colonists were granted permission by King Philip of Spain to establish a new city and chose a spot at the foot of the mountains where the Rio Grande River made a wide curve, provided good irrigation for crops and a source of wood from the cottonwoods, willows and olive trees.
- The early Spanish settlers erected a small adobe chapel where today's San Felipe de Neri Church still stands in Albuquerque's Old Town.
- Its plaza was surrounded by adobe homes clustered close together for protection.
- Albuquerque's dry climate brought many tuberculosis patients to the city in search of a cure during the early 1900s, and several sanitaria sprang up on the West Mesa to serve them.
- The establishment of Kirtland Air Force Base in 1939, Sandia Base in the early 1940s, and Sandia National Laboratories in 1949, made Albuquerque a key player of the Atomic Age.
- The city continued to expand outward onto the West Mesa, reaching a population of 384,736 in 1989.

Albuquerque is situated on the Rio Grande.

Sandia National Laboratories in Albuquerque was established in 1949.

HISTORICAL SNAPSHOT
1989

- Scientists speculated that the New World Peruvian architecture could be as old as the Egyptian pyramids
- Baseball commissioner Bart Giamatti banned baseball star Pete Rose for life from the game for allegedly betting on major league baseball games
- The longest peacetime period of economic expansion reached its 85th month in December; per-capita income was up 19 percent since 1982
- Television's top programs included *Roseanne, The Cosby Show, Cheers, A Different World, The Wonder Years* and *The Golden Girls*
- Congress passed a $166 billion bailout to assist the savings and loan industry
- Cocaine and crack cocaine use was up 35 percent over 1985
- Sony purchased Columbia Pictures, sparking concerns about a Japanese invasion of Hollywood
- Chinese demonstrators at Tiananmen Square carried a Styrofoam statue of liberty as part of their protest against the Chinese government
- A private U.S. satellite, Comedy Cable Television, the pregaphone to talk to a fetus, and a girl playing in the Little League World Series all appeared for the first time
- The movie *Batman* grossed $250 million, the fifth-highest in movie history
- *The Heidi Chronicles* by Wendy Wasserstein won both the Tony award and the Pulitzer Prize
- In women's fashion, Calvin Klein's lean and refined look included soft fabrics with little or no jewelry
- *The Joy Luck Club* by Amy Tan, *The Satanic Verses* by Salman Rushdie, *The Temple of My Familiar* by Alice Walker, *The Oldest Living Confederate Widow Tells All,* by Allan Gurganus and *A Brief History of Time* by Stephen Hawking were bestsellers

- In Chicago, veterans protested at the Art Institute where the American flag was draped on the floor
- "Wind Beneath My Wings" by Bette Midler won a Grammy award for best song
- *Field of Dreams; When Harry Met Sally; Glory; Driving Miss Daisy; Sex, Lies and Videotape;* and *Roger and Me* premiered at movie theaters
- George H. W. Bush succeeded Ronald Reagan as the 41st U.S. president
- Barbara Clementine Harris was consecrated as the first female bishop of the Episcopal Church in the United States
- Union Carbide agreed to pay US$470 million to the Indian government for damages it caused in the 1984 Bhopal disaster
- Iranian leader Ruhollah Khomeini encouraged Muslims to kill *The Satanic Verses* author Salman Rushdie
- The first Global Positioning System satellite was placed into orbit
- The Soviet Union announced that all of its troops had left Afghanistan

Selected Prices

Alcohol, Double Martini	$1.08
Ballet Ticket	$18.00
Bicycle Child Carrier	$14.99
Camcorder	$893.00
Chicken Pot Pies, Three	$0.99
Exercise Machine, Nordic Track	$399.99
Olive Oil	$8.28
Sofa Bed	$799.00
Television, Sony Watchman	$95.00
Vacuum Cleaner, Mini-Vac	$44.88

"Looking for Dedication? Cross Country Sets the Pace," Bob Frisk, *Chicago Daily Herald*, November 11, 1988:

There was a time when cross country was a sport designed primarily to get you in shape for a more glamorous activity like basketball.

That's certainly the way it was when I was in high school. The rewards really appeared meager in comparison with the time and exertion put into the endeavor.

The changes have been dramatic. A fitness revolution ran across the country. Dedicated coaches worked in developing successful training techniques, and high school cross country programs were, well, off and running.

Today, the cross country runner in this area is a big man or woman on campus.

Saturday's hero may not always be a football player. Saturday's real hero may be that young person who is running over the river and through the woods and not just to grandmother's house.

Last weekend, the Mid-Suburban League (MSL) completed another amazing double in state cross country.

Schaumburg's boys and Conant's girls just added to an incredible record of accomplishments for this remarkable high school sports conference.

Mid-Suburban boys now have won three state cross country championships in the past four years and five overall. Mid-Suburban girls have won six titles in the past seven seasons and seven overall.

Remarkable? Yes. Surprising? Not really.

You just have to look at the caliber of coaches down the line throughout the MSL, the important continuity of most staffs and the impressive feeder systems to develop early this talent.

Nevertheless, it still can be difficult telling young people, particularly incoming freshmen, that there is satisfaction in a sport where you run, run, run, run. Run until it hurts and then run some more.

I've always admired cross country coaches because they are faced with the daily challenge of keeping their practices interesting.

Reprinted by permission of the Daily Herald, Arlington Heights, Illinois.

continued

"Looking for Dedication?
Cross Country Sets the Pace," . . . *(continued)*

"Well, athletes, let's see. I think we'll . . . run."

Meets take care of themselves because of their importance, runners jockey for position as they near the chute, but it has to be extremely difficult for a coach to motivate these athletes through their arduous, daily workouts.

There's so much more to this sport than just a crisp fall run, but a cross country coach must be surrounded with believers. So many young people are just waiting for someone to guide them and care about them.

No, it doesn't take a great athlete to be cross country runner. You may not need the coordination of the basketball player or the agility and speed of a halfback or the strength of a tackle.

But you definitely need desire and dedication and endurance. You can work on endurance, but you must have desire and dedication to succeed.

Do you know what really impresses me at any cross country meet?

I watch those young runners, boys and girls, who are laboring far behind the field, struggling with every move, obviously aching.

I stood at the Mid-Suburban League meet and marveled at the tenacity of these young people as the field spread out, dramatically separating the levels of ability.

Those runners hundreds of yards behind the leaders were hurting. It showed. Many could barely see the competitors in front of them. The distance was that great.

This was not a glamorous time for a young athlete. You couldn't hide out there when you're so far behind. Everybody lining the course can see you. It's certainly a different kind of spotlight.

I just had to stand there that day and applaud this kind of determination. This is truly the dedicated high school athlete in action.

The only real reward may be the personal satisfaction you get from passing another runner in the final few yards to finish 80th instead of 81st, or from knocking a second off your best time.

These runners may be in as good or better shape than the athletes who finish well in front, but each individual has his or her own limitations, and that's what makes this sport such a thrilling competition.

Cross country takes a very special kind of desire and dedication, those intangible traits that can be so hard to define.

Although this area may be extremely proficient at collecting state trophies in cross country, the biggest rewards for most of our young runners are not to be reaped in high school.

Those rewards will come later in life, when that incredible dedication needed in cross country day after day after day in a very lonely sport carries over into the real world and leads to something which others, less dedicated, might miss.

I don't know about you, but I certainly would look at a high school cross country background as a big plus in anyone's job application.

"Securing Participants Keeps Coaches on the Run," Ira Josephs, *Doyleston Intelligencer* (Pennsylvania), August 27, 1989:

Cross country, a sport that flourished in the Bucks-Mont area as recently as the early 1980s, may have reached a numbers crossroads as the calendar turns toward 1990.

For although a handful of area teams and individuals enjoyed success in both the district and state level in recent years, Bucks-Mont area coaches say it has become more and more of an uphill climb to maintain that top-flight level of performance in the long run.

Declining numbers, they say, appear to be taking their toll on specific programs in some cases, and on the sport in general in others.

But veteran coaches aware of the cyclical nature of the sport also noticed that the quantity and quality, two key ingredients in a program's success, have tended traditionally to fluctuate from year to year, rising and falling due to a variety of different factors.

It is a sport of peaks and valleys. Not just on the course, either.

Said Central Bucks East head coach Paul Wilson: "It's really hard to predict trends."

But it has not been hard for coaches to notice the dwindling cross-country numbers in many area schools. Said William Tennent head coach Andy Warren, the Warminster school is no exception.

"In the late '60s and '70s, we had teams of 35 or 40," Warren said. "The last three years, we've been anywhere from 20 to 25. A big school squad for a public school is 25."

The decline of participants is more noticeable at Pennridge where Dick Leight is entering his 29th year as coach this fall.

"In the late '70s and early '80s we had 23 kids on the team," Leight said. "They were kids who ran since they were in 10th grade.

"Last year I had 20, but many of them were seniors who were running cross country for the first time. That's not the way to be a successful cross-country runner.

"I'm confident that if I have a kid for three years, by the end of those three years he'll be a respectable runner. It's the kids who come out for three years that make the team."

1983 NEWS FEATURE

"Old Plugs for New Bass," Robert A. Hedeen, *Fur-Fish-Game,* February 1983:

Back in the 1940s when I first started fishing seriously for bass with artificial lures, any plug that weighed less than five-eights ounce was considered a light lure. In fact, many of the popular plugs of that era tipped the scales at a much greater weight, and they seem to be especially true of surface plugs. They were all large.

Over the years, however, lighter and smaller plugs have evolved as the use of spinning and bait-casting equipment gradually replaced the stiff casting rod of four or five feet in length and the free-spool, level-wind reel. With this type of heavy artillery, it was almost impossible to cast plugs lighter than a half ounce. Likewise, with the long, flexible sticks and light lines we use today, it is especially awkward to properly propel a bait that weighs in excess of a quarter ounce.

Reflecting on the matter, I think bait casters of yore adopted their tackle and techniques to the large plugs because they were the only size available. All of this may go back to an evening in the 1890s when a man by the name of James Heddon was passing a lazy afternoon by reposing on the banks of Dowagiac Creek in Michigan and whittling a piece of wood. According to legend, Heddon grew tired of whittling and nonchalantly tossed the bits of wood into the slowly moving current. Supposedly, a huge bass exploded out of the depths and knocked the scrap of wood a foot or so into the air. Heddon was astounded and immediately rushed home to his workshop where he proceeded to whittle another scrap of wood into the shape of a cigar. He sharpened one end and affixed a pop bottle cap in which he had punctured a hole. He attached hooks and a piece of line and rushed back to the banks of the Dowagiac, where he cut a willow pole and cast his invention to the eagerly awaiting fish. As the story goes, the lunker bass that smashed into his lure was hooked and landed, and the first Heddon lure was born. Appropriately, this first Heddon lure was a surface plug and weighed more than two ounces

During the '40s and early '50s I collected almost every bass plug that came on the market, and my constantly depleted bank account gave testimony to the fact there were plenty to choose from. I learned to catch bass on many of them, and it didn't take me long to start believing the old axiom, "If they strike on the surface, they fight on the surface." The thrill of witnessing the strike and the subsequent open-air battle was infinitely more stimulating than taking fish on a subsurface bait, where the fish usually does not surface until the end of the battle. At one time during this period I found it necessary to transport my lures in two large, cumbersome tackle boxes as it seemed new lures were constantly making an appearance on the market. I made it a practice to replace any successful lures that I lost in some lake or stream.

Many of the lures I collected proved to be ineffective—(maybe I did not learn to use them correctly)—and when one of them was left hanging on an underwater smack, I was not always unhappy with the prospect of opening up a previously occupied spot in one of the boxes. Come to think of it, I believe many of the lures I purchased were designed to catch the fishermen rather than the fish. I recall one plug I acquired that consisted of a bare-chested mermaid with hooks attached. Needless to add, I had no luck with this so-called fish lure and was not disappointed when a friend "forgot" to return it after trying it out.

As time passed I followed the trend of most fishermen: first in the spinning and later in the spincasting. New types of reels and long flexible glass rods replaced my short and stubby bait casting rods and free-spool reels. The large and ponderous plugs gave way to ultra-light spinners and unbelievably small pluglike lures. By 1960 I was able to carry my tackle in one box, and the large plugs that had formerly been proven producers were gradually placed in old shoe boxes, shoved further and further back into the attic and forgotten. Forgotten, that is, until a few months ago when I happened upon a cache of them while searching for another item.

As I gazed fondly at the angling antiques of yesteryear, all of which happened to be surface plugs, many fond memories returned. Suddenly a thought occurred to me: "If they did the job then, will they do the job now?"

Fortunately, I still had an old bait casting rig that was in fairly good condition, so I decided to give the "over the hill gang" another chance to justify my purchase of them years before. Calling the role of those present, I found I had the following: Heddon's Crazy Crawler and Chugger, the Aborgast Hula Popper and Jitterbug, a South Bend Babe Oreno, and a Whopper Stopper Topper, which I believe was manufactured by the Bomber Company.

Early the next morning I was filled with anticipation as I launched my pram into the beautiful and historic Pokomoke River on Maryland's eastern shore. The Pokomoke River is bounded by the most northern stand of bald cypress in the United States, and some say it is the deepest river east of the Mississippi. This is also a bass fisherman's bonanza and is the site of an annual bass fishing contest which attracts anglers from up and down the eastern seacoast. In addition to large mouth bass, the Pokomoke serves as the residence for a large population of chain pickerel, yellow perch, white and black crappie and channel catfish. . . .

My excitement grew as I guided the boat into the small oxbow where I enjoyed considerable success in the past. I had my six lures laid out on the seat of the boat, and as I

glanced down at them my eye caught the Hula Popper. I think I have caught more bass on the surface with this lure than any other—the newer and smaller baits notwithstanding—so I selected it to go first. I remembered to tie the line directly to the eye of the plug, since I had learned many years ago that a snap swivel, no matter how small, will frequently interfere with the inherent action of many lures. As the Hula Popper sailed outward toward an open space in the dense cover of lily pads that protected the shoreline, it suddenly stopped in flight and shot straight backwards on a line for my head. I'd forgotten to thumb the reel to prevent the revolving spool from overrunning the outgoing line, and the result was the nemesis of all anglers that use those reels—the backlash. As I ducked my head, the Hula Popper zipped past, missing my ear by an inch or two.

My next cast, though somewhat clumsy, miraculously landed close to the target area, and I hastened to reel in the excess line. Many fishing pros insist one should let the surface lure lie perfectly still for 30 seconds or longer, but I have always been too impatient to follow that advice. As I had done so many times in the past, I raised the rod tip to get a little twitch after a few seconds. The familiar "glug" made on the Pokomoke was the same sound it made in the Colorado River in central Texas some 20 years earlier, and a wave of pleasant nostalgia swept over me. . . .

With any surface lure, the idea is to hoodwink the bass into believing the plastic or wood is really a small animal struggling in the water. Frequently the sporadic action resulting from twitching the rod will give such an illusion, but sometimes a slow retreat is necessary to fool the fish. If neither tactic worked on the first cast, I tried again. I cast to the same spot in the lily pads, and, just as the ripples made by the splashdown were dissipating into wider and wider circles, the bass struck while the plug was resting quietly on the surface.

I was so taken by surprise that I momentarily lapsed into a state of shock and was incapable of reacting to the situation. I had not really expected a hit, and was, in fact, considering where I should cast next. After a few moments my wits returned, and I reeled frantically to take in the slack line. Eventually I felt the fish on the line, and as he made a run to the right I applied pressure to turn him back. This seemed to infuriated him, and he leapt clear of the surface and did a sort of tail dance an inch or so above the water as he shook his head and body in a violent attempt to throw the hook. He jumped two more times before his fighting spirit was broken, and I was eventually able to guide him alongside the boat. As I hoisted him over the gunwale with my thumb and forefinger grasping his jaws, he rattled his head again, and the hook popped free from the plug! The hasp which had connected the hook to the body of the bait for so many years had deteriorated with rust and finally fractured. I was in luck to have landed that bass.

He was about18 inches in length, and I guessed he would weigh in the vicinity of three pounds—truly a beautiful fish with coalescing green and silver colors on each side of the dark, pronounced lateral line. His mouth was so large I could almost insert my closed fist into it.

As this large mouth was not injured in any way, I removed the hook with the aid of a hemostat and returned him to the river. With a swish of his tail he disappeared into the coffee-colored water—hopefully to live and fight another day.

The excitement of the catch was unabated as I proceeded to another location to give the next plug a chance. This time I tied on the red and white Chugger and remembered how, on another river at another time, I had taken three bass on four casts with the same lure. I cast this old ally toward a large rock that jutted out of the shoreline, and having remembered to thumb the reel this time no backlash resulted. . . .

At home later that evening, I recounted how my collection of geriatric plugs had reproven their fish-taking ability. I decided then and there to retire the old fellows for good. The chance of losing one of these old friends was so great that any additional fishing with them would not be worth the risk. But, who knows, maybe in a few years I will remove them from the special box in which they are now stored, sharpen the hooks, touch up the colors, and try them again. If I do, I feel confident these old soldiers will come through again with flying colors.

1990–1999

The business of sports ran on stimulants most of the 1990s as the Michael Jordan-led Chicago Bulls won six championships in the National Basketball Association, steroid-influenced homerun hitting dominated major league baseball and the world came to Atlanta, Georgia, for the twenty-sixth Olympiad. There Carl Lewis won his ninth Olympic gold medal and sprinter Michael Johnson made breaking records look easy. Free agency within the professional ranks, which enabled players to sign with any team, left fans confused as players moved from team to team. And for the first time since 1904 the baseball World Series was canceled in 1994 because striking players couldn't agree with stubborn owners about how to divide billions of dollars in revenue.

In the process, television's reach expanded exponentially: cable television carved out niches like the Golf Channel just in time for African American golfer Tiger Woods to burst onto the golf scene in 1996. The U.S. women's soccer team won the World Cup on American turf in 1999. The success of women athletes was best exemplified by the National Basketball Association's decision to create the Women's National Basketball Association in 1997, the excitement created by speed skater Bonnie Blair in the XVI Winter Olympics or the three NCAA National Championships captured by the University of Tennessee's Lady Vols basketball team.

The economy limped into the 1990s under the gloom of recession, but quickly exploded into the Era of Possibilities. This robust economy empowered and emboldened the nation's traditionally less well off. The ranks of the African American middle class swelled; women filled half of all seats at the nation's law and medical schools, and Hispanic workers immigrated in droves to chase the dream of economic prosperity in a foreign land. Predictably, this growing population Spanish-speaking workers ignited raucous rounds of debate concerning America's immigration policy—especially as it related to immigrants arriving by way of Mexico.

America's disabled gained new rights and more respect, and America's Christian fundamentalists found their political voice. And as wealth grew, the possibilities flourished. Colleges became overcrowded, while the buying power and media attention paid to America's youth exploded. Personal computers, fully capable of competing with television and its rapidly expanding array of specialized channels, became a fixture in millions of homes. The 1990s were characterized by steady growth, low inflation, low unemployment and dramatic gains in technology-based productivity. The resulting expansion was particularly meaningful to computer companies and the emerging concept known as the Internet—a technology that would revolutionize business, media, consumer buying and interpersonal relations in the opening years of the twenty-first century.

As the 1990s opened, America was struggling with a ballooning national debt and the economic hangover of the savings and loan industry. Media headlines were dominated by stories of rising drug use, crime, racial tensions and the increase of personal bankruptcies. Family values became a political touchstone. Guided by Federal Reserve Chair Alan Greenspan's focus on inflationary controls and a declining deficit, the U.S. economy soared, producing its best economic indicators in three decades. By the end of the 1990s the stock market was posting record returns, job creation was at a 10-year high and businesses were desperately searching for qualified workers in a technologically savvy world. As a result, the 1990s gave birth to $150 tennis shoes, condom boutiques, pre-ripped jeans, digital cameras, DVD players, and 7.7-ounce cellular telephones. The decade was also a time of debate, much of it powered by 24-hour programming on television channels and the resurgence of talk radio. Americans publicly debated limits on abortion, tougher criminal enforcement, the role of affirmative action, bilingual education, food safety and Internet child pornography.

1995 Profile

As a professional strongman, Mark Strahorn had done it all—often on national television; at six foot two inches and 300 compact pounds, Mark boasted the kind of body capable of wrestling an anchor chain to a standstill.

Life at Home

- In competition Mark Strahorn had dragged a Mack truck up a ramp, flipped an 800-pound tire a dozen times across a football field and lifted a 400-pound Atlas stone (a concrete ball with lead cores) and still failed to win America's Strongest Man Contest.
- On some cable channels—especially those in the high two figures, he was a regular at 2 a.m. when repeats of the World's Strongest Man Contests received their most consistent exposure.
- Despite years of competition and television publicity, Mark was best known as the friendly barkeeper at the Elk's Horn in Jackson Hole, Wyoming.
- The total earnings from strongman contests were less than $20,000.
- Growing up in upstate New York, Mark was the son of a welder and an emergency room nurse.
- His parents had a good marriage and liked, but did not worship, their three children.
- From an early age, Mark was expected to work beside his father, always relegated to grunt work and was ignored when he complained.
- His dad also built him his first set of weights from scrap metal.
- Only an average athlete growing up, Mark was too small to play football, weighing only 156 pounds in the 10th grade.
- And then, after graduating high school and working on construction, he began to grow.
- He also continued lifting weights.
- Three years later he entered a competitive bodybuilder contest long before made-for-TV strongman specials became a feature of late-night television.

Too small to play football as a boy, Mark grew to a compact 300 pounds.

An 800-pound tire was no match for Mark.

Life at Work

- When he wasn't working, Mark Strahorn, 33, was training for the next strongman competition.
- Nearly everyone in the sport was required to hold a full-time job: in previous years the title of America's Strongest Man had been held by a cop, a salesman for a nutrient supplement company and a bartender.
- In Eastern Europe, stronger men were national celebrities; in America, most were just big, big guys.
- Mark figured, "That's life."
- There was no room for introspection in the midst of the dead lift when it felt like battery cables were hooked to his sciatic nerve.
- Or during a seated rope pull, when his vertebrae popped like firecrackers; deep down he knew he would pay for this abuse one day.
- Or even when he read about a fellow strongman—and friend—who had died suddenly in the midst of a strenuous workout.
- The media always blamed steroids.
- Mark understood that a gigantic dead lift could exert enough physical pressure to kill.
- It's also the point that the exhilaration of adrenaline kicked in.
- One strongman reported, "Six hundred seventy-five pounds for eight reps, last set was pretty cool, shins were bleeding, nose was bleeding, couldn't hear out of my right ear for 30 seconds, acid reflux, fun all the way around."
- In all, Mark lifted six days a week—anything that was heavy—Atlas stones, lead cylinders, barbells, cars, anything.
- Monday was bench/back, Tuesday was hips and thighs (squats), Wednesday was GPP/conditioning work, typically some sled-dragging or weighted walks.
- "I also hit my core hard on this day," he remarked.
- Thursday he did Olympic lifts: snatches/cleans and jerks, front squats in that order.
- Friday was more conditioning work, Saturday was event work; "Sunday I'm off completely."

- Strongman competition workouts legitimately took 45 minutes; shorter if he pushed his pace.
- "I just find that working more often helps my recovery, and I'm too obsessive-compulsive to just stay away," he explained.
- Strongman contests have their roots in early twentieth-century circuses, the American West, and stone lifting in ancient northern Spain.
- Modern strongman contests officially date to 1977 when Bruce Wilhelm won the first World's Strongest Man competition.
- Since then the strongest men on the planet have come together annually in a series of unique tests of strength to determine the World's Strongest Man.
- The competitions have been held in a variety of locations including Zambia, Iceland, Mauritius, Malaysia, Morocco, China and the U.S.
- Many of the gigantic competitors received their training as Olympic weightlifters or, as in the case of British champion Geoff Capes, an Olympic shot-putter.
- The reigning champions were both from Iceland: Jon-Pall Sigmarsson, who earned four championships between 1984 and 1990, and Magnus ver Magnusson, who had won in 1994 and was favored in 1995.
- Mark understood that at 33 he was running out of time; it's one of the reasons he became part owner of the bar in Jackson Hole.
- "I'll know when it's time," Mark said. "My back will tell me in a loud voice."

Life in the Community: Jackson Hole, Wyoming

- Jackson Hole, Wyoming, had become a tourist town.
- Archeologists claimed that people had been visiting the valley for 12,000 years.
- During those prehistoric times, no one tribe claimed ownership to Jackson Hole, but Blackfeet, Crow, Gros Ventre, Shoshone and other Native Americans used the valley during the warm months.
- Severe winters prevented habitation.
- Between 1810 and 1840, the area was a crossroads for the six main trapper trails that converged in Jackson Hole.
- Mountain men held annual summer rendezvous, or trade shows, there, where they sold their furs or traded them with companies like the Hudson Bay Company and the Astoria Fur Company for winter supplies.
- These gatherings also allowed the trail-weary mountain men a chance to eat, drink and exchange tales with other trappers.
- By 1845 the fur trade had ended, as the fashion of men's beaver hats back East gave way to silk hats.
- Then the passage of the Homestead Act of 1862, which allowed settlers to acquire land at the cost of improvement, attracted homesteading families along with a sizable influx of Mormon settlers.
- The inhospitable climate with its very limited growing season soon caused some homesteaders to sell out, while others grew hay and 90-day oats and raised beef cattle as cash crops.
- For many, outfitting and guiding became a means of supplementing family income as wealthy Eastern visitors traveled to the valley.
- Ranchers quickly determined that wrangling city dudes was easier and more profitable than wrangling cows.
- In the early twentieth century, economic downturns further encouraged the development of dude ranches.

Geographic beauty attracted tourists to Jackson Hole.

- Tourism became a significant business in the valley after the formation of Grand Teton National Park and the designation of other federal lands, including Yellowstone National Park.
- The expansion of Grand Teton National Park in 1929, 1943 and 1950 spawned a different type of tourism.
- Tourists from all over the world, numbering as many as three million annually, visited the area for the scenery, the wildlife, the recreational opportunities, the geographic features, and the romance of the American West.
- Through the years, the many movies made in Jackson Hole have added to the valley's fame, including an early version of *Nanette of the North* in 1921, *Shane* and *Spencer's Mountain* in 1963.

HISTORICAL SNAPSHOT
1995

- America boasted 720,000 physicians and 190,000 dentists
- The movies *Braveheart* with Mel Gibson, *Apollo 13* with Tom Hanks, *Leaving Las Vegas* with Nicholas Cage and *Dead Man Walking* with Susan Sarandon all premiered
- Fifty-seven million viewers watched the murder trial of O.J. Simpson, accused of killing his estranged wife Nicole Brown Simpson and her friend Ronald Goldman
- Top record singles for the year included "Can You Feel the Love Tonight" by Elton John, "Gangsta's Paradise" by Coolio and "Dear Mamma'" by Tupac Shakur
- The frozen body of a 500-year-old Inca girl was found bundled in fine wool in the Peruvian Andes
- Two Americans were arrested for the Oklahoma City terrorist bombing, which killed 169 people and left 614 injured

- Research showed that three ounces of salmon a week reduced the risk of fatal heart arrhythmias by 50 percent
- Businesses nationwide introduced casual Fridays, allowing employees to wear less formal attire
- The Centers for Disease Control reported a leveling off of teen sexual activity; reportedly, 52.8 percent used condoms
- Blue M&Ms, custom-made coffins, Pepcid AC and the computer language Java all made their first appearance
- More than seven million people subscribed to online computer services such as America Online, CompuServe and Prodigy
- Hollywood's most expensive film, *Waterworld*, which cost $200 million to make, was a box office flop
- Louis Farrakhan led a "Million Man March" on Washington, attracting 400,000 men who pledged to take greater social and family responsibility
- The 104th United States Congress, the first controlled by Republicans in both houses since 1953 to 1955, convened
- At Super Bowl XXIX the San Francisco 49ers become the first National Football League franchise to win five Super Bowls, as they defeated the San Diego Chargers
- Mississippi ratified the Thirteenth Amendment, becoming the last state to approve the abolition of slavery
- The New Jersey Devils swept the heavily favored Detroit Red Wings to win their first Stanley Cup in the lock-out shortened season

Selected Prices

Apple Personal Computer	$1,099.00
Armoire	$899.00
Automobile, Lincoln Mark VIII	$20,292
Comforter	$160.00
Exercise Equipment, Treadmill	$299.96
Hotel Room, Chicago	$160.00
Low Flush Toilet	$270.00
Luggage, Samsonite	$399.99
Videotape, *Lethal Weapon*	$15.99
Water, 1.5 Liter	$0.49

"Charles County Sheriff's Office Hosts Strong Man and Woman Contest," *Southern Maryland News,* September 1, 2004:

To help combat domestic violence and raise awareness of this important issue, the Charles County Sheriff's Office and the North American Strongman Society hosted the fourth annual Strong Man and Woman Contest August 7 at White Plains Regional Park.

Four weight classes—200 pounds, 231 pounds, 265 pounds and heavyweights—competed in six events. The first event in the competition was the axle press for max weight, which required competitors to raise a weighted truck axle over their heads. The winner for this event was Jeremiah DiRuzzo in the 200-pound class, Adam Keep in the 231-pound class, Jedd Johnson in the 265-pound class and Mark Lehman in the heavyweight class.

The next event was the stone load where competitors had to lift six stones weighing from 235 to 329 pounds from the ground onto barrels standing from 47 inches to 52 inches off the ground. Only two competitors from the 231-pound class—Joe Snarly and Keith Pickey—were able to successfully place all six stones on the barrels. Johnson and Lehman of the 265-pound class and heavyweight class, respectively, were able to also place all six stones on the barrels.

In the third event, the farmer's walk and keg carry, competitors must carry 250 pounds in each arm for 20 yards to a cone, turn around, walk back to the starting point and carry a 250-pound keg for 30 feet, all in the fastest time. Kevin Senato won the 200-pound class, Snarly won the 231-pound class and Johnson and Lehman won their respective classes.

The next event was the sandbag carry-yoke walk, where competitors were required to carry a sandbag ranging from 225 to 245 pounds 50 feet, then pick up and carry a 640- to 770-pound yoke back. Winners were Rob Lemerise in the 200-pound class, Graham Bartholomew in the 231-pound class, Dan Cenidoza in the 265-pound class and Lehman in the heavyweight class.

The tire flip was the next competition and required competitors to flip a 680-pound tire. Winners included Senato in the 200-pound class, Bartholomew in the 231-pound class, Cenidoza in the 265-pound class and Lehman in the heavyweight class.

The last competition was Conan's Wheel, where competitors were required to walk between 525 to 625 pounds in a circle, approximately 80 feet. Winners included Senato in the 200-pound class, Keep in the 231-pound class, Johnson in the 265-pound class and Lehman in the heavyweight class.

Competitive World's Strongest Man Events

Carry and Drag (Anvils, Anchor and Chain)

Competitors carry two 130 kg anvils a set distance, and then drag an anchor and chain weighing 300 kg a further set distance until the whole anchor and chain crosses the finish line. The winner is the athlete who covers the most distance in the shortest time.

Giant Log Lift

The athlete stands with his back facing a 380 kg tree trunk and lifts it over his head as many times as possible within the designated time. The winner is the athlete who successfully completes the most repetitions within the time limit.

Pillars of Hercules

The athlete stands with arms extended, gripping handles that restrain two pillars, one at each side. Timing will stop when the athlete is no longer able to hold the 150 kg weights. The winner is the athlete who holds the Pillars in the correct position for the longest time.

Fingal's Fingers

The five large poles are lifted in ascending order of weight and flipped over 180 degrees. The winner is the fastest to flip all the fingers, which vary in length from 3.5 m-5.5 m and in weight, 200/225/250/275/300 kg.

Truck Pull

The athletes wear a harness and pull a Mack cab truck and trailer, with the help of a rope, along the road, facing the direction of the finishing line throughout the pull. The winner is the athlete who completes the course in the fastest time, or who covers the most distance in the fastest time.

Dead Lift (Barrels)

Competitors are required to lift a number of heavy barrels, which are dropped one by one into a frame. On completion of a good lift, another barrel is loaded automatically, until time runs out or all the barrels are lifted. The athlete lifting the most weight in the shortest time wins. Start weight: 1st Barrel 260 kg, 2nd Barrel 275 kg, 3rd Barrel 285 kg, 4th Barrel 300 kg, 5th Barrel 320 kg, 6th Barrel 335 kg.

Squat Lift

The competitors stand under the bar and must squat down until they are below parallel and lift the weight back up to the fully erect position; each time they return to the erect position, more weight will be added to the apparatus. The winner is the athlete who successfully lifts all weights in the fastest time, or the most weight in the time allowed (75 seconds).

Overhead Lift (For Reps)

Athletes lift a wooden log from the ground and then raise it overhead as many times as possible in the time limit, returning the weight back to the floor in a controlled fashion before attempting to do the next lift. The winner is the one who completes as many lifts as possible within the time limit. Weights: 115 kg—Time limit: 75 seconds.

Atlas Stones

The athlete picks up the lightest stone first and places it onto a platform, and continues until all five have been put on the wall or until his time has run out. The winner is the athlete who places the most stones onto the platforms in the quickest time. Weights: 100, 112, 120, 140, 160 kg.

continued

Competitive World's Strongest Man Events *(continued)*

Giant Farmer's Walk
The competitor carries a weight in each hand over a marked course as quickly as possible. Weights: 2×160 kg.

Dead Lift (For Reps)
A car is positioned on a frame which has handles extending from underneath the car. The athlete grips the handles and lifts the car to the "knees locked" position and places the car down on the ground again. The winner is the athlete who completes the most lifts in a given amount of time. Weight of an average car (approximately 1,800 kg).

Fridge Carry
Athletes carry a yoke that holds two fridge freezers on their shoulders over the course as quickly as possible within the time limit. The winner is the athlete who completes the course in the shortest time or, failing that, the one who travels the farthest in the quickest time. Weights: 415 kg/904 lbs—Course: 30 metres—Time Limit: 60 seconds.

Plane Pull
The competitors pull a plane, with the help of a harness and rope, along a set course. The winner is the athlete who covers the complete course in the fastest time or, failing that, who covers the biggest distance in the shortest time. Length of course: 30 metres—Time Limit: 75 seconds—Weight: approximately 70 tons.

Africa Stone
Athletes must wrap their arms around the stone, interlocking their fingers. They remove the stone from the stand and walk as far as possible along a course until they cannot carry it any further. If the athlete drops the stone on the ground, or steps out of the designated lane, the attempt will be terminated. The winner is the athlete who carries the stone the farthest distance. Weight: $+/-175$ kg—Course: for distance.

"Steroids Don't Cause Rage Outbursts, Study Says," *Syracuse Herald Journal,* July 4, 1996:

Body builders already believed it, and science has finally proved it: Steroids make big muscles. But researchers found no evidence that steroids make users prone to outbursts of anger known as "roid rage."

The carefully controlled study showed convincingly for the first time a few weeks of male sex hormone injections substantially beef up arms and legs and increase strength.

In addition, psychological tests and questioning of the men's spouses found no evidence that steroids made them angrier or more aggressive.

Steroids are widely thought to cause violent mood swings, and people charged with violent crimes have pleaded roid rage as a defense.

But among steroid users who are mentally healthy, "testosterone doesn't turn men into beasts," said Dr. Shalender Bhasin of Charles H Drew University in Los Angeles. Bhasin left open the possibility that in people who are mentally unbalanced to begin with, steroids can make them worse.

Possession and distribution of steroids without a prescription is a federal crime, punishable by up to a year in prison and a fine of at least $1,000.

Doctors have warned that potential side effects include sterility, testicular shrinkage, acne, abnormal liver function, baldness, high blood pressure and heart disease.

Bhasin and his colleagues said the results in no way legitimize steroid use by athletes, but suggested steroids may be a good way to help AIDS patients and others whose muscles waste away because of disease.

"Legend in Making, Minors Alan Again Player of the Year," Mark Pierce, *Alton Telegraph* (Illinois), July 7, 1994:

Corrie Alan is quickly becoming the stuff of a legend.

That's a strong word legend but it fits. How else to describe a softball pitcher who has a career record of 63-4? How else to describe a hurler who was 23-2 last season with a 0.27 ERA?

Well, you can describe her as the player of the year. Again.

For the second straight season, the last these 5 foot seven Junior has been tabbed Telegraph Prep Softball Player of the Year.

In saving with a repeat performance, Alan said her 1994 campaign but there is similar to what she accomplished in 1993.

"I didn't really do much different this season," Alan said. "We had another good season."

The Minors, 24-2 this year, continued to be the dominant Class A softball squad in the area and earned a second consecutive berth in the Class A state tournament.

"Media Making Racket over Glen Ellyn's Dynamic Duo of Tennis," *Chicago Daily Herald*, September 28, 1995:

If the name Engel sounds familiar lately, perhaps it is because of the mini-media blitz we have been seeing in recent weeks for the sibling tennis players Marty and Adria Engel of Glen Ellyn.

They have been featured in the media for their tennis prowess and it's doubtful the name will leave the public's eye anytime soon.

Marty, 22, a fifth-year senior at Northern Illinois University, appeared in a "Faces in the Crowd" segment of the September 18 issue of *Sports Illustrated* after winning the men's singles title at the Intercollegiate Tennis Association Summer Collegiate Championships. He also appeared in the September 21 issue of *Tennis Week*. The title also gave him an automatic berth in the U.S. Open tryouts.

While Marty was gracing the inside pages of national magazines, Adria, 15, was featured in a Sports Channel segment last Friday evening. It was Adria's first time on television, but it's doubtful it will be the last. This sophomore at Glenbard West is traveling down a path leading to professional tennis. And she's taking the scenic route.

"This year I started playing pro tennis just to see how I would do out there," she said. "In March I went to Mexico for a month. I played four tournaments there and the last tournament was the Masters. It's a lot of fun. A good experience and really good competition. I like it more than Juniors."

Although Adria has chosen not to play on her high school tennis team to concentrate on tournament play, she has also decided not to forsake her high school years as some aspiring players have done in the past. She's content to do it her way and is quite proud of her world ranking of 755.

"The truly cool to see you have a professional ranking in the world," she said. "I think I'm really lucky to be able to be doing all that I'm doing. I'm just really excited."

Reprinted by permission of the Daily Herald, Arlington Heights, Illinois.

1998 PROFILE

When Frankie Parsons did not make the high school varsity soccer team his junior year, he turned to coaching to stay involved with the game.

Life at Home

- Frankie Parsons began his soccer career at age six.
- He played for the Prince William County (Virginia) REC League; they were called the Skyrockets and wore royal blue shirts.
- Frankie mostly played defense; his main job was to stop the forward from scoring goals.
- After one season, his family moved to Summerville, South Carolina, and he began playing for the Summerville YMCA youth league, where he continued to stop the forwards from advancing to the goal.
- For six years he toiled in the YMCA league before being recruited by the Summerville Soccer Club.
- Three years later he made its Classic team, composed of the highest skilled players who traveled the southeast playing on weekends.
- During his junior year of high school, Frankie was recruited by the area rival Hungryneck Soccer Club, where he played marking back for the men's Under-19 team.
- But to his deep disappointment, he did not make the high school varsity team his junior year.
- Frankie turned to coaching to stay involved with soccer, taking on a coed under-10-years-old team for the Summerville Soccer Club.
- He earned his first coaching certification license that year: the US Soccer F license.
- He also began to draw on the coaching philosophy he learned at the Ralph Lundy summer soccer camp and applied it to his team.
- In addition, Frankie enrolled in the teacher cadet program, designed to get students interested in being teachers.
- Frankie taught fourth and eighth graders; the eighth grade class he taught reunited him with his own eighth grade teacher, Mr. Clark.

Frankie Parsons decided to coach soccer instead of play.

His coaching career began in high school.

- The fall of his senior year, he was asked to coach the Summerville Soccer Club's boys REC U-12 team.
- During his search for colleges that year, he concentrated on quality schools where he might play soccer.
- He also wanted a small school, and mainly concentrated his search to Division III schools.
- He decided to go to Erskine College in Due West, South Carolina, because it was an in-state school where he could use a tuition grant that made the school affordable.

Life at Work

- Frankie Parsons was a walk-on for Erskine College's soccer team; his first year he compiled 35 minutes of playing time.
- After that, he returned to coaching.
- His training sessions (practices) were organized around the Ralph Lundy Method; the skill is displayed, then the players break into groups and practice the skill demonstrated.
- He worked to avoid unproductive habits such as singling out players, which can break down the team culture, allowing players to be apathetic.
- Frankie believed that quality team culture demanded that everyone respect one another.
- Players didn't have to be friends, but they did have to respect every team member.
- It was the coach's job to teach the players how to be better and work their hardest at every task.
- As a coach, Frankie learned how to be a leader and a mentor, not a buddy, and not to acknowledge favorites, which fostered a poor team culture.
- After college Frankie moved to Columbia, South Carolina, for graduate school and continued his soccer coaching career.

Frankie made sure he treated all players the same.

- He was told by his new club that if he got his South Carolina Youth Soccer Association D Coaching license, he would be paid $750 per season.
- The first semester of graduate school, Frankie began coaching the U-12 Lightnings for the Irmo Soccer Association.
- It was the club's only girls' team.
- The assemblage of players was a hodgepodge of 8-12-year-olds of varying skill levels.
- He knew immediately he had his work cut out for him.
- Frankie also quickly learned the difference between coaching boys and girls: boys you pushed, girls you guided—especially younger girls.
- Girls were also much more social and had to be guided to keep their focus; girls also wanted to develop personal friendships with the coach, which allowed Frankie to figure out the different motivators for each girl.
- At their first game, the Lightnings won 4-1.
- It was the first of many wins.
- In the spring of 1995, Frankie's team found themselves in the State Finals, in a strange twist of fate, against the Hungryneck Hurricanes.
- The game ended in a tie and was decided by penalty kicks; Frankie's team lost by one.
- After the game the goalkeeper and the player who had missed her penalty kick were inconsolable.
- Frankie and his assistant coach did their best to stay positive and felt it was time to lead by example.
- He told the team they played great and that they were champions, even though they'd not won their last game.
- After all, they were better than every other team in the state.
- Frankie reminded his girls how much they'd improved and how much fun they had all had together.
- He emphasized how impressed their parents were in the amount of progress they'd made in one season.
- Overall, it had been a great season.

The Lightnings were a champion team.

Frankie coached the newly-named Nightmares.

- That fall, he was rehired to coach the U-12 girls' team; they renamed themselves the Nightmares.
- That year Frankie made another discovery: parents can be one of the worst parts of youth sports.
- One parent secretly paid his child to score goals, which disrupted the team mentality; another parent was loudly abusive to referees, opposing players and fans.
- And Frankie kept on winning, including a six-state tournament in Jacksonville, Florida.
- He also got a boost from the 1996 Summer Olympics and the U.S. Women's team gold medal win that significantly spurred interest by girls to the sport of soccer.
- In the spring of 1997, Frankie went to the next level and began coaching the junior varsity girls at Cardinal Newman, a small private school in Columbia.
- He was invited to coach the girls through a connection he'd made in the area's soccer network.
- Here, too, he had his work cut out for him; newly found enthusiasm for soccer did not necessarily equal skilled players with years of experience.
- By the spring of 1998, Frankie was coaching the Cardinal Newman JV team and the U-13 Nightmares.
- Older players did not play in the spring, as that is when high school soccer is in season.
- He was also helping two other coaches with a U-10 girls' advanced REC team, working to create a feeder system of talent.
- During the spring of 1998, Frankie took his U-13 girls to a tournament in Johnsonville, Tennessee, where they lost to a team from Ann Arbor, Michigan.
- One of the traditions at soccer tournaments was for each team to exchange club patches, embroidered with each club's logo.
- Although his girls had many patches from other teams in previous tournaments, the highlight of this one was to receive a patch from a team that was from so far away.

Cardinal Newman High School's JV team.

Frankie and his assistant coach were proud their team made it to the tournament.

- The league also decided to pay for Frankie to get his National Soccer Association Class C coaching license: $1,000 dollars for an eight-day residential clinic at an out-of-state sports complex.
- The National Class C clinic consisted of morning classroom time and a field session, an afternoon classroom and field session, and an after-dinner two- to three-hour field session.
- The last day of the clinic, the coaches were required to do a main field assessment, which was an assessment of tactical and technical training techniques and an oral and written exam.

Clinic exercises were grueling.

- Not everyone who attended the clinic was certified as a Class C coach by the National Soccer Association.
- Frankie passed his exams and was certified by the reigning body of U.S. soccer as a National Class C coach.
- After he received his certification, he was asked to be the director of soccer for the club, giving him a $10,000 raise in addition to his $2,300 per team he coached.

Life in the Community: Columbia, South Carolina

- Columbia was home to the main campus of the University of South Carolina, which was chartered in 1801 as South Carolina College.
- The city itself had a population of 116,278.
- It was founded in 1786 as the site of South Carolina's new capital and was one of the first planned cities in the United States.
- Located at the confluence of two major rivers, Columbia grew rapidly with cotton as its economic lifeblood.
- Columbia's First Baptist Church hosted the South Carolina Secession Convention on December 17, 1860, where the delegates approved a resolution in favor of secession, 159-0.
- In February 1865, during the Civil War, much of Columbia was destroyed by fire while being occupied by Union troops under the command of General William Tecumseh Sherman.

The National Soccer Association certified Frankie as a coach.

In 1865, fire destroyed much of Columbia.

Columbia in 1872.

- According to legend, Columbia's First Baptist Church barely missed being torched by Sherman's troops.
- The soldiers marched up to the church and asked the groundskeeper if he could direct them to the church where the declaration of secession was signed.
- The loyal groundskeeper directed the men to a nearby Methodist church; thus, the historic landmark was saved from destruction.
- During Reconstruction, journalists, travelers and tourists flocked to South Carolina's capital city to witness a Southern state legislature whose members included ex-slaves.
- Columbia had no paved streets until 1908, when 17 blocks of Main Street were surfaced.
- There were, however, 115 publicly maintained street crossings at intersections to keep pedestrians from having to wade through a sea of mud between wooden sidewalks.
- In 1917, the city was selected as the site of Camp Jackson, which grew into the U.S. Army's largest training facility.
- On August 21, 1962, eight downtown chain stores served blacks at their lunch counters for the first time.
- The University of South Carolina admitted its first black students in 1963.
- As many vestiges of segregation began to disappear from the city, blacks attained membership on various municipal boards and commissions, and a non-discriminatory hiring policy was adopted by the city.
- These and other such signs of racial progression helped earn the city the 1964 All-America City Award for the second time, and a 1965 article in *Newsweek* magazine lauded Columbia as a city that had "liberated itself from the plague of doctrinal apartheid."
- By 1990 the Columbia metropolitan population reached 470,000.

HISTORICAL SNAPSHOT
1998

- Smoking was banned in all California bars and restaurants
- Russia began to circulate new rubles to stem inflation and promote confidence
- Ramzi Yousef was sentenced to life in prison for planning the first World Trade Center bombing
- Nineteen European nations agreed to forbid human cloning
- Researchers in Dallas, Texas, presented findings about an enzyme that slowed aging and cell death
- Veteran astronaut John Glenn returned to space aboard Space Shuttle *Discovery*
- Paula Jones accused President Bill Clinton of sexual harassment
- The Denver Broncos became the first American Football Conference (AFC) team in 14 years to win the Super Bowl, as they defeated the Green Bay Packers, 31–24
- President Clinton denied on national television that he had "sexual relations" with former White House intern Monica Lewinsky
- Compaq bought Digital Equipment Corporation
- Ford Motor Company announced the buyout of Volvo Cars for $6.45 billion
- Dale Earnhardt won the Daytona 500 on his twentieth attempt

- Osama bin Laden published a *fatwa,* declaring *jihad* against all Jews and Crusaders
- The U.S. Supreme Court ruled that federal laws banning on-the-job sexual harassment also applied when both parties were of the same sex
- NASA announced that the *Clementine* probe orbiting the moon had found enough water in polar craters to support a human colony and rocket fueling station
- At the Academy Awards, the movie *Titanic* won a record 11 Oscars

- The Food and Drug Administration approved Viagra for use as a treatment for male impotence, the first pill to be approved for this condition in the United States
- Citicorp and Travelers Group announced plans to merge, creating the largest financial-services conglomerate in the world, Citigroup
- The Chicago Bulls won their sixth NBA title in eight years, defeating the Utah Jazz 87–86 in Game 6 on a fadeaway jumper by Michael Jordan
- The Detroit Red Wings swept the Washington Capitals in four games in the 1998 Stanley Cup finals
- Microsoft released Windows 98
- The National Distance Running Hall of Fame was established, inducting five members in its initial class
- France defeated Brazil 3-0 to win the 1998 FIFA World Cup
- Biologists reported in the journal *Science* how they sequenced the genome of the bacterium that causes syphilis, *Treponema pallidum*
- The United Kingdom banned the importation of land mines
- Terrorist bombings of the United States embassies in Dar es Salaam, Tanzania, and Nairobi, Kenya, killed 224 people and injured over 4,500

Selected Prices

Blender	$49.99
Camera, Canon, 35 mm	$1,900.00
Cat Food, Purina, 20 Pounds	$7.99
Deodorant, Old Spice	$1.79
Film, Kodak	$6.00
Hotel Room, South Carolina	$260.00
Shampoo, Vidal Sassoon	$2.50
Soccer Ball	$69.95
Soccer Cleats	$129.95
Television, 19-Inch Zenith	$139.00

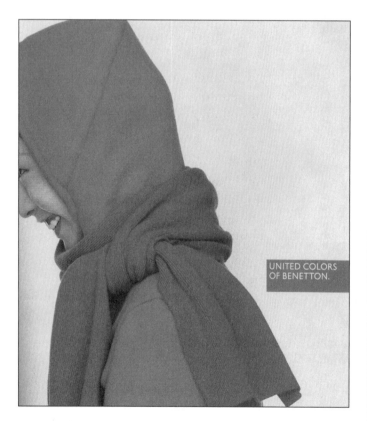

American Soccer Timeline

1620
In the original Jamestown settlement, Native Americans played a game called pasuckuakohowog, with goals one mile apart and as many as 1,000 people participating at a time.

1820
A form of soccer was played among the Northeastern universities and colleges of Harvard, Princeton, Amherst and Brown.

1830
The modern form of soccer originated among working-class communities and was seen as a way of keeping young and energetic kids out of trouble at home and in school.

1848
In England, the first Cambridge Rules were drawn up.

1862
The Oneida Football Club was formed in Boston, the first soccer club anywhere outside of England.

1883
The four British associations agreed on a uniform code and formed the International Football Association Board.

1885
The first international match was played between teams (U.S. vs. Canada) outside of Great Britain.

1888
The penalty kick was introduced.

1904
The Olympic Games of 1904 in St. Louis included soccer as an official Olympic sport where club teams competed under the national team banner.

Delegates from France, Belgium, Denmark, The Netherlands, Spain, Sweden and Switzerland established FIFA (The Federation Internationale de Football Association) at a meeting in Paris.

1914
The United States Football Association (USFA) was granted full membership in FIFA at the annual congress at Oslo.

1916
The first United States Football Association (USFA) Men's National Team traveled to Norway and Sweden; the Americans played six matches, finishing 3-1-2.

1920
The Dick-Kerr's Ladies Professional Team (England's unofficial team) spurred interest in the sport.

1921
The American Soccer League (ASL) was born when franchises were granted to Fall River (MA), Philadelphia, Jersey City Celtics, Todd Shipyard of Brooklyn, New York FC, Falcons FC of Holyoke (MA), and JP Coats of Pawtucket (RI).

1926
The Hakoah team from Israel played before 46,000 fans at the Polo Grounds against an ASL select team.

continued

American Soccer Timeline . . . (continued)

1930

The U.S. was one of 13 nations to compete in the first FIFA World Cup competition in Montevideo, Uruguay.

1932

At the 10th Olympic Games in Los Angeles, soccer was eliminated due to a controversy between FIFA and the International Olympic Committee (IOC) over the definition of an amateur athlete.

1933

The National Collegiate Athletic Association (NCAA), the governing body of college athletics in the United States, released an official rulebook covering all intercollegiate soccer in the U.S.

1950

Joe Gaetjens' goal gave the USA the win over England, 1-0, at the World Cup in Brazil; it was called the biggest upset ever in international soccer.

The first college bowl game was played in St. Louis; Penn State tied the University of San Francisco 2-2.

The Philadelphia Old-Timers Association organized the National Soccer Hall of Fame with 15 inaugural inductees.

1967

Two new major professional leagues in the U.S. began which became the North American Soccer League (NASL).

The Hermann Trophy award for the college player of the year was initiated with. Dov Markus of Long Island University as the first recipient.

1975

The New York Cosmos of the NASL signed Pelé for a reported $4.5 million.

1977

The NASL signed a seven-game contract for national television.

1978

The New York Cosmos became the first NASL team to break one million in home and away attendance.

The Major Indoor Soccer League (MISL) started with six franchises: Cincinnati Kids, Cleveland Force, Houston Summit, New York Arrows, Philadelphia Fever and Pittsburgh Spirit.

1981

The United States Under-20 National Team competed in its first World Youth Championship in Australia; the U.S. team lost to Uruguay 3-0, tied Qatar 1-1, and lost to Poland 4-0.

1982

The National Soccer Hall of Fame and Museum opened in the Wilber Mansion, Oneonta, New York.

1985

The first U.S. Women's National Team competed internationally in Italy.

1988

The United States was awarded the 1994 World Cup during the FIFA Congress in Zurich.

1989

For the first time since 1950, the U.S. Men's National Team qualified for the 1990 World Cup after a 1-0 victory over Trinidad and Tobago.

continued

American Soccer Timeline . . . *(continued)*

1990

The U.S. Men's National Team competed in the World Cup in Italy for the first time in 40 years.

The U.S. Women's National Team qualified for the world championship.

The WSL and the ASL merged to form the American Professional Soccer League.

1991

The U.S. Men's National Team won its first-ever regional championship.

The U.S. Women's National Team won the first-ever FIFA Women's World Championship in China after beating Norway 2-1 in the final.

The United States Under-23 team won the gold medal at the Pan Am Games in Cuba.

1992

The U.S. Men's National Team won the inaugural U.S. Cup.

The Major Indoor Soccer League folded after 15 years in existence.

The U.S. Futsal Team won the silver medal at the FIFA World Championship in Hong Kong.

1994

The United States hosted the 1994 FIFA World Cup, attracting over 3.5 million in attendance, a World Cup record.

The Women's National Team won the Chiquita Cup, an international tournament with four national teams of Germany, China, Norway and the United States.

1995

The U.S. Men's National Team won the U.S. Cup, defeating Nigeria, tying Colombia and outplaying Mexico to a 4-0 victory.

1996

FIFA awarded the 1999 Women's World Cup to the United States.

The U.S. Women's National Team won the first-ever gold medal in the Olympic Games in Atlanta, defeating China 2-1 in the championship game.

Major League Soccer was launched, providing the United States with its first Division I outdoor pro league since the North American Soccer League folded in 1985.

"Preface," *A Parent's Guide to Coaching Soccer*, Jack McCarthy, 1990:

"Hey, coach, I can't make baseball practice tomorrow because I have a soccer game, okay?"

I looked down at the robust, freckle-faced kid, and remember wondering what this red-blooded American boy saw in soccer.

It was 1978, not so long ago. My attitude reflected the ignorance of an entire generation of American parents. We grew up in a culture where football was the number one game. I had no idea what soccer was really about. I knew it was played all over Europe, and I figured Europe would come to our way of thinking sooner or later. It was a dark age here for soccer, and I was a dinosaur.

A few years later, my daughter developed an interest in playing sports. She tried a year of baseball, but never really got into it. Our town had just started a soccer team for girls a bit older than my daughter. I called the president of the local soccer club and asked why there was no team for younger girls. He said, "There is no coach." I answered, "You have a coach now; what do I do?" He said, "Get on the phone and put together a team." A month later we were on the field.

Fortunately for me, none of the girls had ever played soccer. They never knew how little I knew and neither did their parents. I had coached and played other sports before, so I could fake it, but I really knew nothing. Little did I know that I was on the threshold of my most rewarding coaching experience, and that I was about to become part of one of the greatest games in the world. The soccer explosion of the 1980s is a clear testimony to its growing popularity.

I figured the first step was to get a book on soccer. As I stated in my earlier book, *A Parent's Guide to Coaching Baseball,* there were plenty of baseball books, but none that really helped the novice. Well, what I found when looking for something on soccer was even worse. I couldn't find any books at all.

Fortunately, there were coaching clinics available throughout our state soccer organization, and I learned the fundamentals. There just wasn't anything that really brought the concept of soccer home to me, or that clearly showed me how to develop a kid's skills. I felt very much alone. Most coaching materials assume the reader has played the game. But, like most American parents, I had not. . . .

How did my girls do? We lost our first game 17-0 against a team that had been together for three years. So I set our goals realistically. The next game we decided to keep the other team below 10 goals, and we succeeded. Then our goal was to score, and we succeeded. Finally, our goal was to win a game, and we were successful in that, also. Two years later the girls went undefeated, and then became the first-ever girls' varsity team at Hillsboro High school in New Jersey. Then I dropped out to coach my younger son in soccer for a few years. During my years coaching soccer, I played the game myself on weekends, pick-up games for coaches and parents at our high school field. It is hard to learn the sport as an adult, but the skills are slowly coming.

The Girls of Summer, The U.S. Women's Soccer Team and How It Changed the World,
Jere Longman:

Like representative government, soccer has been imported from England and democratized in the United States. It has become the great social and athletic equalizer in suburban America. From kindergarten, girls are placed on an equal footing with boys. In the fall, weekend soccer games are as prevalent in suburbia as yard sales. Girls have their own leagues, or they play with boys, and they suffer from no tradition that says women will grow professionally to be less successful than men. . . .

Soccer has become the fastest growing sport in the country in both high school and college. From 1981 through 1999, the number of women's collegiate soccer teams grew from 77 to 818, propelled by Title IX. There are now 93 more women's teams than men's teams at the university level. Soccer is serious enough now

as a sport that coaches are fired for poor performance, the big football schools are showing increased interest, and a few of the top women's collegiate programs now use private planes for recruiting. Chris Petrucelli, who won a national championship for Notre Dame, was lured to Texas in early 1999 by a contract worth $180,000 annually and by a $28 million soccer and track facility.

On the high school level, there were 257,586 girls registered to play soccer in 1998-1999, compared with 11,534 in 1976-77. Of the 18 million registered soccer players the United States, 7.5 million, or 40 percent, were girls and women, according to the Soccer Industry Council of America.

1999 Profile

Mike Lincoln was a basketball player from Indianapolis, Indiana, who walked-on to a basketball team in one of the most competitive conferences in the country—the Big Ten.

Life at Home

- Unlike the fairy tales of old, there was no magical moment when Mike Lincoln discovered basketball; he dreamed of playing Division One college basketball all the time.
- In school during math class, he daydreamed about hitting the winning shot just as the buzzer sounded; on the court after school, he carefully crafted the perfect pass, and in bed at night, he repeatedly executed a spectacular dunk before a roaring crowd.
- And when his mother needed Mike at suppertime, she always knew where to find him—on the basketball court behind the house.
- There he practiced constantly the skills needed in a game: squaring his shoulders before a leaping shot from the corner, dribbling confidently with his left hand as he exploded past a defender in the lane or shooting with consistency no matter the circumstance.
- One summer, on his way to basketball camp, Mike and his father even compiled a list of schools Mike dreamed of attending.
- When they reviewed the list, they discovered the colleges were all Division I schools and they were all in the Big Ten.
- Basketball was everything for Mike, whose parents were supportive of his every decision as long as his grades were solid.
- Spring meant one thing: the arrival of wall-to-wall televised games in an athletic festival of happiness known as March Madness.
- Over a matter of weeks, the nation's best teams would battle for the right to play for the national championship.
- The stated rules were simple: one loss and your tournament was over—no second chances, no voting, no appeals.
- Mike could not imagine a life better spent than watching the likes of Illinois, Indiana, Michigan, Northwestern, Purdue or Wisconsin in a battle for domination above the rim night after night.

Mike Lincoln grew up dreaming of playing Division I basketball.

A basketball court was Mike's favorite place to be.

- Mike's personal opportunity at greatness occurred after his sophomore year of high school, when he attended the Pittsburgh session of Five Star Basketball Camp.
- There, under the experienced gaze of Howard Garfinkle, for three minutes that July Mike played a perfect game.
- Howard Garfinkle was the director of the famed Five Star Basketball Camp.
- Employing a formula that had produced over 320 NBA players, his camps emphasized the fundamentals of the game and offered players the opportunity to play in front of college coaches.
- The daily schedule included stern lessons in everything from how to effectively handle a half-court trap to how to properly set up a defender before using a screen.
- Unaware that Garfinkle was watching, Mike played aggressive, smart basketball, drilling a series of mid-range jumpers.
- Garfinkle became a fan and remained one even after the country's Division I coaches did not bother to recruit Mike.
- Several small colleges invited Mike for visits that could have resulted in a basketball scholarship, but he wanted an academically challenging institution, preferably noted for its engineering program, where he could play basketball.
- The idea for Mike to walk-on to a college basketball team had come from Howard Garfinkle.
- He called Mike during his senior year of high school and asked if he was willing to walk-on to a team since no scholarships had come his way.
- Mike had no problem walking on, and the University of Illinois was selected as the perfect place; after Garfinkle placed a call to the coach, Mike was offered a spot.
- To prepare himself, the summer before his freshman year of college Mike worked out with several ex-college players who helped him prepare for the quickness and physicality of college basketball.

- In Division I everyone was fast, physical and fit; Mike learned there would be no rest breaks after a drill, and time in the weight room was intense.
- Before he ever set foot on the Illinois campus, he was exhausted.

Life at Work

- When Mike Lincoln arrived at the University of Illinois, he was a 6′2″, 175-pound shooting guard without a scholarship or reputation.
- Of the 14 players on the basketball team, only two were non-scholarship walk-ons; Mike had an immediate sense of being an outsider.
- In the immediate run-up to the basketball season, Mike participated with the rest of the squad in open gyms.
- Open gyms were run by the players without coaches present.
- Mike was told to pass the ball to gain respect from the older players, even though Mike had built his entire basketball repertoire around highly consistent, pinpoint shooting.
- But he quickly discovered that he had been given good advice.
- During the open gyms, Mike was startled by the speed of play and the size of the players.
- Everyone was bigger and quicker than he.
- He had to exert much more energy than the other players just to keep up.
- Some of his finest moves resulted in impressive blocks by his older teammates.
- There were no "gimmes" in Division I basketball.
- After being the go-to player in high school, Mike found it difficult to come to terms with his new role as a basketball player.
- After the acclaim of high school and numerous awards, Mike had to face the fact that he was smaller, slower and a non-scholarship player who was often overlooked and rarely a recipient of the perks of being a basketball player.
- Few of his teammates even bothered to learn his real name; he was habitually referred to by his teammates as Buddy.
- "Buddy, go rebound for those guys," or "You take Buddy on your team."
- Living hours away from his parents took an adjustment; they had attended every game he ever played.
- He was also challenged by the pressures of the classroom.
- The time demands of being a student-athlete were rigorous.
- To ensure that eligibility was not lost, the basketball players had an academic advisor who kept close tabs on the players, their grades and their attendance of classes.
- Some professors did not even understand that Mike was on the team—thus the reason for an absence.
- In a similar fashion, the first time Mike entered the team locker room he was dazzled, until he made his way to his locker.
- That's when he realized that, unlike the others, his locker did not have his name and number, only masking tape with the number 20 written on it.
- Walk-ons didn't always last, he was told; he would earn his name on the locker by and by.

Mike needed to stay healthy, fast and fit.

In high school Mike was one of the best players.

Sometimes Mark's role was to cheer his team-mates on from the bench.

- Then, in October of Mike's freshman year, everyone in the basketball program met at the coliseum to have the team picture taken.
- It was an exciting time, marking the end of pre-season and the beginning of the regular season.
- When Mike walked into the locker room, there were only jerseys for the 12 scholarship players.
- His heart trembled as he walked out of the locker room without a jersey.
- It was a lesson in life as a walk-on.
- After games, the players would walk back out to the arena to meet friends and family.
- There were always kids waiting for autographs.
- Because Mike played so little, he often didn't have to shower after games and was the first out to the arena.
- There, kids would ask if he was a player, then ask for an autograph.
- Just as Mike would put the pen to paper, the kids would see one of the stars of the team and run to him instead.
- Hitting a game-winning shot was not even a possibility, Mike realized by mid-season.
- He was the one player on the team who could not dunk the basketball, but on occasion he would slap the backboard on the way in for a lay-up.
- He was the player at the end of the bench who always cheered on his teammates.
- If he checked in, the fans knew the game was over.
- Yet he stayed on the team, despite rumors of coaching changes, a severe case of shin splints, and the open disdain of one senior player who repeatedly challenged Mike's right to a place on the team.
- "It's about character, not points," Mike's father told him after freshman year ended.
- "No," Mike replied. "It's about proving points, playing time and proving everyone wrong about me."

Life in the Community: Urbana, Illinois

- The University of Illinois was created through the Morrill Act of 1862, which granted each state in the United States a portion of land on which to establish a major public state university, one that could teach agriculture, mechanic arts and military training "without excluding other scientific and classical studies."
- After a fierce bidding war among a number of Illinois cities, Urbana was selected as the site for the new "Illinois Industrial University" in 1867.
- The campus became known for its landscape and architecture and was identified as one of 50 college or university "works of art" by T.A. Gaines in his book *The Campus as a Work of Art.*
- The main research and academic facilities were divided almost exactly between the twin cities of Urbana and Champaign.
- The campus has four main quads, which compose the center of the university and are arranged from north to south and regarded as a world-leading magnet for engineering and sciences, both applied and basic.
- In 1952, the university built the Illinois Automatic Computer, the first computer built and owned entirely by an educational institution.
- Its reputation was such that the university recently celebrated January 12, 1997, as the "birthday" of HAL 9000, the fictional supercomputer from the novel and film

2001: A Space Odyssey; in both works, HAL credited "Urbana, Illinois" as his place of operational origin.

- The University of Illinois was also the site of the Department of Energy's Center for the Simulation of Advanced Rockets, an institute which has employed graduate and faculty researchers in the physical sciences and mathematics.

- It performs materials science and condensed matter physics research, and is home to the Frederick Seitz Materials Research Laboratory.

- Since 1957, the Illinois Transportation Archaeological Research Program has conducted archaeological and historical compliance work for the Illinois Department of Transportation.

- It serves as a repository for a large collection of Illinois archaeological artifacts numbering over 17,000 boxes, including 550 boxes from the famous Cahokia Mounds, an ancient Indian city and the oldest archaeological site in the U.S.

- The university had also developed one of the largest Greek systems in the world by membership with 69 fraternities and 36 sororities on the campus.

- Of the approximately 30,000 undergraduates, about 3,330 were members of sororities and about 3,370 were members of fraternities.

- Among university libraries in North America, only the collections of Harvard, Yale, the University of California, Berkeley, and the University of Toronto were larger than those of the University of Illinois.

HISTORICAL SNAPSHOT
1999

- The Denver Broncos won their second Super Bowl in a row, defeating the Atlanta Falcons 34–19

- The last ice hockey game was played at the historic Maple Leaf Gardens in Toronto

- Dr. Jack Kevorkian was found guilty of second-degree murder for administering a lethal injection to a terminally ill man, igniting a national debate concerning assisted suicide

- The rapidly rising Dow Jones Industrial Average closed above the 11,000 level for the first time

- In Laramie, Wyoming, Russell Henderson pled guilty to kidnapping and felony murder for the hate crime killing of Matthew Shepard because he was gay

- Two Littleton, Colorado, teenagers, Eric Harris and Dylan Klebold, opened fire on their teachers and classmates at Columbine High School, killing 12 students and one teacher, and then themselves

- Two Libyans suspected of bringing down Pan Am flight 103 in 1988 were handed over to Scottish authorities for eventual trial in the Netherlands

- Nancy Mace became the first female cadet to graduate from The Military College of South Carolina

- *Star Wars Episode I: The Phantom Menace* was released in theaters and became the highest grossing Star Wars film

- After 22 years of restoration work, Leonardo da Vinci's *The Last Supper* was placed on display in Milan, Italy

- Cathy O'Dowd, a South African mountaineer, became the first woman to climb Mount Everest from both the north and south sides

- Napster, a music downloading service, debuted

- NATO suspended its air strikes after Slobodan Milosević agreed to withdraw Serbian forces from Kosovo

- Apple Computer released the first iBook, the first laptop designed specifically for consumers

- USA soccer player Brandi Chastain scored the game winning penalty kick against China in the FIFA Women's World Cup

- The world's population reached six billion people

- The U.S. Senate rejected ratification of the Comprehensive Test Ban Treaty

- The Exxon-Mobil Corporation merger was completed, forming the largest company in the world

- The U.S. turned over complete administration of the Panama Canal to the Panamanian Government, as stipulated in the Torrijos-Carter Treaty of 1977

- Boris Yeltsin resigned as president of Russia, leaving Prime Minister Vladimir Putin as the acting President

Selected Prices

Audio Tape $5.00
Camcorder $2,700.00
Ceiling Fan $190.00
Cell Phone $199.00
Computer, Compaq Presario $1,999.00
Fur Coat $2,595.00
Printer, Epson $279.00
Radar Detector $199.00
Software, Microsoft Office 4.2 . . . .$248.99
VCR $240.00

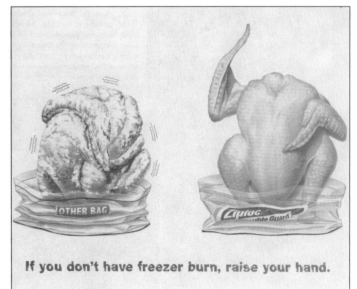

If you don't have freezer burn, raise your hand.

Walk-On: Life from the End of the Bench,
Alan Williams, 2005:

"I was a freshman in study hall. Between fervent attempts to begin studying, some of the scholarship players began to give another teammate a hard time, flippantly poking fun at how much time he was spending with his new girlfriend. It seemed harmless at the moment, so I decided to throw in my two cents. While I found that my contributions yielded temporary rewarding laughter from much of the room, it was only a matter of time before I saw the noticeably large fist coming in the direction of my face.

"It hurt. That night in study hall, I came to the conclusion that, as a freshman walk-on, I wasn't allowed to joke around with our seven-foot center from Germany just yet."

Practices were my games, but when it came to the real games, I knew not to look at the coach unless we were up by a sizable margin. During my freshman year, we were up at least 25 points at the University of Virginia at home, so, with good reason, I began to look down the bench at Coach Odom.

After a little pressure from the crowd, Coach walked down toward my end and signaled with his hand it was time for me to go in. So all in one motion, I got up, took off my warm-ups, and sprinted to the scorer's table. I was ready, or was I?

As I took a knee for the next dead ball, Coach Odom signaled me back to the bench. I walked back over to him, and as I got close enough, he put his arm around me, looked me in the eye, and said, "Alan, who are you going in for?" I thought for a second and then looked back at him with an honest face: "I don't know, Coach." Coach smiled back at me: "It always helps to know that, doesn't it?"

"Campus Life: Illinois Basketball Team Penalized After Recruiting Inquiry," *The New York Times*, November 11, 1990:

The University of Illinois men's basketball team will enter the 1991 recruiting fray hobbled by National Collegiate Athletic Association penalties imposed last week.

But the head coach, Lou Henson, said the damage would be minimal. "The high school coaches in this state, I think, are more behind us now than ever," Mr. Henson said at a team practice on Thursday, adding that coaches have told him they will continue listing Illinois as a choice for their athletes.

The Fighting Illini finished in the Final Four of the NCAA basketball tournament in 1989, before the NCAA began investigating its recruiting techniques.

These are the penalties, which restrict both the coaches and the university:

- The team cannot play in the March 1991 NCAA championship tournament.
- The university cannot offer more than two basketball scholarships in each of the 1991-92 and 1992-93 academic years.
- In calendar year 1991, basketball coaches are prohibited from recruiting off campus; no more than two basketball coaches will be permitted to recruit off campus the following year.
- The university is barred from paying for official campus visits by potential student athletes during 1991.
- The team is prohibited from playing outside the continental United States in 1991.

It could have been worse, said Chuck Smrt, the NCAA associate director of enforcement, who said the so-called death penalty could have been imposed for two years—and, in his opinion, should have been imposed—effectively eliminating the university's basketball program.

But Mr. Henson maintains that the penalties are too severe. He said, too, that the NCAA's Infractions Committee finding that the university lacked "institutional control" over athletic programs was wrong.

"If we have problems because of basketball, I think that's my responsibility," he said, "and the chancellor of the university, or the president or the athletic director cannot follow the basketball coaches all the time."

Still, Mr. Henson, who is in his 17th year as the head coach, said he viewed the restrictions as a challenge, not an obstacle.

"I'd retire in a year or two, but now I'm more motivated than ever," he said at a news conference on Wednesday. "I might coach another 10 years."

The NCAA said that significant violations occurred in the school's recruiting procedures, but added that the evidence did not substantiate the most serious allegations: that Illinois offered large sums of cash and cars to lure leading recruits.

The inquiry centered on an allegation that Deon Thomas, a Chicago high school student, told the University of Iowa that an Illinois assistant coach, Jimmy Collins, had offered him $80,000 and a Chevrolet Blazer to attend Illinois. The athletic association also investigated allegations that Illinois offered to help buy a house for Mr. Thomas's grandmother and for the mother of another high school athlete, LaPhonso Ellis, who now plays basketball as a junior at the University of Notre Dame. The NCAA did not reveal who made the allegations.

"Players Give New Coach Enthusiastic Thumbs Up," Bob Logan, *Chicago Daily Herald*, June 10, 2000:

Illinois players gave their new coach, Bill Self, a thumbs-up greeting Friday, pleased that the uncertainty was over.

Self stepped up in class after taking Tulsa to the top of the Western Athletic Conference, racking up a 74-22 record in just three years there. Seated near the Assembly Hall podium for Self's media bow, the players perked up noticeably when he talked of the kind of season (32-5) the Golden Hurricanes had under him in 1999-2000, reaching the quarterfinals in the NCAA tournament.

"All of the five games we lost came down to the last shot, and we still had a chance to win or tie, Self said. "That's the kind of basketball I expect to play with these talented (Illini) guys."

Maybe that was Self-promotion, of a sort, but it had an impact. So did Self's Friday morning meeting with the team, first as a group and then one-on-one.

"I told them they had a right to feel any way they wanted about the situation," Self said. "I'm a player's coach. I set tough standards, but I care about them as individuals."

Reprinted by permission of the Daily Herald, Arlington Heights, Illinois.

"Victory over Michigan Boost for Chukwudebe," *Alton Telegraph* (Illinois), January 27, 1998:

Victor Chukwudebe felt quite comfortable Sunday at the Assembly Hall in Champaign.

No wonder. The 6-foot-7, 230-pound sophomore/center from Springfield is brimming with confidence.

"Victor has a terrific work ethic and a great attitude," University of Illinois basketball coach Lon Kruger said. "All he needed was a shot of confidence."

Chukwudebe, a Springfield Lanphier High product, gave his self-esteem a big boost with a 10 point, six rebound performance against Michigan. Chukwudebe's play was a key factor in Illinois' 64-53 Big Ten conference win.

"He always gives us good rebounding and defense," said Illini senior guard senior Kevin Turner, "and Sunday he provided some offense (10 points) that wasn't expected. He gave us a lift.

"Our job out front was to pick up the guards early and make it difficult for them to pass deep," Turner said. "We knew we had to double if the big guys got inside, but it didn't happen very often. Our guys kept them out of the lane most of the time."

Chukwudebe, sharing time with 6-foot-8, 240-pound senior Jarrod Gee in the middle, held his own against 300-pound Robert Traylor of Michigan.

"He's the strongest guy I've been up against," said Chukwudebe. "You have to use your quickness and anticipation to prevent him from getting the spot he wants. If you can force him off the lane, he's not as effective."

Sunday's win enabled Illinois to improve to 13-7 overall and 5-2 in conference play. The Illini are locked in a fight with Purdue, Indiana and Michigan for second place in the Big Ten. Surprisingly, Michigan State leads the pack at 6-1.

Mike Lincoln's Pre-season Freshman Schedule

AM
5:30 Wake up, eat a piece of bread, and drink some OJ
5:40 Walk over to Athletic Center to stretch and get loose
6:00 Run three miles with team and coaches
6:30 Weights
7:45 Breakfast with teammates
8:30 Shower and get ready for class
9:00 Spanish
10:00 English
11:00 Religion

PM
12:00 Health and exercise requirement
1:00 Grab salad and sandwich
1:30 Study hall (required)
3:00 Individual workouts (four players and four coaches)
4:00 Weights
5:00 Pick up games
6:00 Shower
6:30 Dinner
7:00 Study hall
9:00 Complete reading assignment for class
10:00 Extra shooting
11:00 Open hour, free time
12:00 Bed, lights out

1994 NEWS FEATURE

"Texas Lutheran's Own 'Fab Five,' Players have bonded like sisters during four years at TLC," Barry Halvorson, *The Sequin Gazette-Enterprise* (Texas), October 30, 1994:

A handful of freshmen arrived together in Texas Lutheran College in the fall of 1991, coming into a tradition-rich volleyball program that was in need of a boost.

Injecting the energy and enthusiasm of youth and a considerable amount of talent, Dana Krueger, Jessica Szymanski, Christy Clawson, Stacie Matheson and Natalie Rundell quickly became known as "The Fab Five." And what England's "Fab Four," the Beatles, did for rock 'n roll, these five players have done for volleyball in Sequin—made it a red hot product.

The success started almost from day one with two of the five—Krueger and Szymanski, who were in the starting lineup—and the rest seeing considerable playing time off the bench. The five also found a mentor that first year in former TLC All-American Michelle Henniger, then a senior on the team. That season the team finished 21-17, were Hearts of Texas co- champions, and finished one game short of returning TLC to the NAIA National Championship Tournament for the first time since 1985.

They were on their way.

"That first year, we were really just a scrappy bunch of players," Szymanski, a Sequin High graduate, said. "And Michelle made a big contribution to our development. She really showed us a lot about playing at the college level."

Helping to ease the adjustments was the way their personalities blended immediately. Szymanski and Matheson are the most outgoing and quickest to respond to questions from the press. Clawson, the setter, served much the same role in the interview, passing things around to make sure everyone got a chance to respond. Krueger and Rundell are two of the quietest players both on and off the court, but are also two of the most dangerous players.

All five arrived literally at the same time, each attending the same tryout camp, each feeling confident she had made the team, and each ready to go to college.

"We all came in together," Krueger said. "I think that helped us a lot because we could support each other."

Such a verbal outburst brought jokes from her teammates.

Teamwork is important in volleyball.

"One of the first things that I noticed," Szymanski said "was that while the rest of us like to talk, Dana didn't."

"We lived together, ate together, just really hit it off from that first (tryout)," Matheson said. "I had a feeling right then that we were all going to make it."

Their second year was not quite as successful. They had some doubts about college and aspects of their personal lives, but they never questioned the support they would receive from the rest of their recruiting class.

"After our freshman year there were some doubts about being here," Matheson admitted. "I considered going somewhere else, but personally I stuck it out for everyone else. I didn't want to let them down."

"I had some questions, too," Clawson said. "I asked myself what I would do without volleyball and I couldn't come up with an answer, so I stayed."

"These ladies are my sisters," Szymanski said. "I never had any doubts about becoming a close-knit family. During that year is when we really got to know each other. We learned about our weaknesses and our strengths and we learned to play to our strengths."

"We have all had to lean on each other," Matheson adds. "They have leaned on me and I on them. One of the big advantages we have is that we are all strong in own own way so that no player has had to carry this team. If one person is having a bad night, the rest of us realize it and pick up our own games."

Szymanski says each has her own understood role in helping to motivate the others.

"I can't yell at Christy or she gets mad at me," she laughed. "We will just look at each other and touch hands. It's different with Stacie. She can yell at all of us. She's the one that gets us fired up on the court. She's got a way of yelling at you that doesn't get you mad at her, just gets you going."

Season three of the "Fab Five" in Texas Lutheran was the most successful as a group. They finished the season with a 41-10 record as they earned a return trip to the NAIA National Championship Tournament and finished the season as the number nine-ranked team in the NAIA.

It was a big payoff for a group of girls who had a wide variety of interest only a few years earlier when they were starting out in high school.

Krueger, whose mother is a highly successful high school coach at John Jay High School in San Antonio, was always a volleyball player.

"Ever since I was real little, I've always been hanging around in gyms," she admitted. "My mother never pushed me into athletics; it was kind of expected of me. I enjoyed it so much that it really didn't matter."

Rundell and Matheson both preferred basketball to volleyball early and both admitted to missing the other game. Szymanski played both volleyball and basketball in high school, but always harbored a dream to be on the dance team, while Clawson preferred soccer and softball.

Each admits they had to give up some of their other passions to make it in their chosen sport.

"I never understood why they (sports and dancing) couldn't coexist," Szymanski said. "That's been one of the big changes ever since I graduated from high school. Today girls are getting to do both.

"I was given a choice in high school of playing volleyball or basketball and eventually chose volleyball," she said. "But I never thought I should have had to (make that decision)."

Another social change the five have observed is a newfound popularity as the girls that guys want to be with. Breaking a certain mold, all are attractive, but none allowed herself to be pigeonholed into the typical high school pastimes which were reserved for the "pretty girls."

"We are the female jocks," Matheson laughed. "We're the ones without makeup. When you see us after practice you'd wonder why anyone would look at us. But back when we started, people were unfamiliar with that idea. In junior high, athletics were not for girls. You were kind of a social outcast because the boys wanted pretty girls."

"Things have changed now, Clawson said, picking up the argument. "A lot of guys don't want 'prissy.' We have the guys from the soccer, basketball and baseball teams always coming up to us wanting to know how to set or spike or how to make a particular serve. They recognize us for being athletes as well as women."

"I think some of it has to do with the fact that we are more fit than most," Krueger contributed." "In the U.S. there is more of an emphasis on healthy lifestyles and people now find it more attractive."

The trip to the national tournament has resulted in more interest in the TLC volleyball team this year, an attention that the "Five," now seniors, are relishing.

"The effect of going to the national tournament has been fantastic," Matheson said. "With the coverage we got, people are more aware of what is going on. I have seen every professor I have at games this season and most have been very supportive. And that helps because the volleyball team at TLC has always been noted for staying eligible, and when they see us play, they understand that we are working hard. But we also don't skip any classes, because professors are going to notice that as well."

Two the most outspoken members of the team on the extra attention are the two shy ones.

"I like to know that people have an interest in what we are doing," Rundell said. "Before it would be people saying, 'Oh you had a game last night' to asking 'What was the score?' to now going to the match themselves."

"There is a great deal of motivation for us in the fact that people were behind what we were trying to do," Krueger said. "It makes it feel not like we're doing it just for ourselves but for the school and all the graduates we have around the country. It's a real motivation."

So far this season, the Lady Bulldogs are right on schedule to return to the national tournament and right on schedule to graduate as their sport has helped them gain the self-confidence of winning, but also made them better overall students and people.

"Athletics teaches you a lot about life," Rundell said. "To be able to combine volleyball with college, you have to be more responsible, more organized in your life and set priorities. I have benefited a lot in other areas because of playing volleyball."

2000–2009

History will record that the new century began in the United States on September 11, 2001, when four American commercial airliners were hijacked and used as weapons of terror. After the tragedies at the World Trade Center in New York; Shanksville, Pennsylvania; and the Pentagon in Washington, DC, Americans felt vulnerable to a foreign invasion for the first time in decades. America's response to the attacks was to dispatch U.S. forces around the world in a "War on Terror." The fist stop was Afghanistan, where a new brand of terrorist group known as al-Qaeda had planned and executed the attacks under the protection of the country's Taliban rulers. America's technologically superior weaponry was impressively displayed as the Afghan government was quickly overthrown, although capturing al-Qaeda leader Osama bin Laden and stabilizing a new government proved more vexing. With the shell-shocked economy in overall decline and the national debt increasing at a record pace, the United States rapidly shifted from Afghanistan to Iraq. Despite vocal opposition from traditional allies such as Germany and France, President George W. Bush launched Operation Iraqi Freedom with the goal of eliminating the regime of Saddam Hussein and his cache of weapons of mass destruction. The invasion resulted in worldwide demonstrations, including some of America's largest protest marches since the Vietnam War. As in the invasion of Afghanistan, the U.S. achieved a rapid military victory, but struggled to secure the peace. When no weapons of mass destruction were found, soldiers continued fighting while an internal, religious civil war erupted; support for the war waned and vocal protest increased.

Despite the cost of the war, the falling value of the dollar and record high oil prices, the American economy began to recover by 2004. Unemployment declined, new home purchases continued to surge, and the full potential of previous computer innovation and investment impacted businesses large and small. Men and women of all ages began to buy and sell their products on the Internet. eBay created the world's largest yard sale; Amazon demonstrated, despite sneering critics, that it could be the bookstore to the world; and we all learned to Google, whether to find the exact wording of a Shakespearian sonnet or the menu at Sarah's Pizza Parlor two blocks away. At the same time, globalization took on a new meaning and political import as jobs—thanks to computerization—moved to India, China or the Philippines, where college-educated workers were both cheap and eager. American manufacturing companies that once were the centerpiece of their community's economy closed their U.S. factories to become distributors of furniture made in China, lawn mowers made in Mexico or skirts from Peru. The resulting structural change that pitted global profits and innovation against aging textile workers unable to support their families resulted in a renewed emphasis in America on education and innovation. If the U.S. was to maintain its economic dominance, the pundits said, innovative ideas and research would lead the way.

As the decade drew to a close, after eight years of the presidency of George W. Bush, America's economy was in recession—the victim of its own excesses: too much consumer borrowing, extensive speculation in the housing market and widespread use of "exotic" financial instruments that failed to reduce risk. In the wake of the economic crash, some of the most respected firms on Wall Street disappeared through mergers or collapse, unemployment topped 12 percent and consumer confidence plummeted. When newly elected President Barack Obama took office in 2009, America was at war in Iraq and Afghanistan, the federal government was spending billions of dollars to save the banking system and the price of oil was on the rise. President Obama made universal health care a key element of his first year in office, igniting controversy and exposing the deep divisions that existed nationwide.

Sports during the first decade of the twenty-first century became a 24/7 obsession for many. With the dramatic expansion of the Internet, cell phones, the addition of new cable channels and a plethora of new sporting events, America was clearly addicted to sports—including many whose lure was tinged with danger. NASCAR expanded its geographic reach and began challenging football for most viewers, the Williams sisters brought new life to professional tennis and Tiger Woods continued his winning ways on the golf course. Despite a decade of falling television ratings, NBC paid an astonishing $2.3 billion for the combined rights to the 2004 in 2008 Summer Games and the 2006 Winter Games.

The incredible achievements of cyclist Lance Armstrong captivated racing and non-racing fans alike as he won the Tour de France an unprecedented seven consecutive times. Baseball's Boston Red Sox finally shook the "Curse of the Bambino" to win a World Series and Barry Bonds slugged 73 home runs for the San Francisco Giants in 2003, only to be accused of improper drug use as the decade came to an end.

Professional women, who for decades had struggled to rise past the glass ceiling in their companies, began to find bigger opportunities in the 2000s. Significantly, the promotion of a woman to a top slot in a Fortune 500 company ceased to make headlines. Some top female CEOs even began to boldly discuss the need for more balance in the workplace. Yet surveys done at mid-decade showed that more Americans were working longer hours than ever before to satisfy the increasing demands of the marketplace and their own desire for more plentiful material goods. In some urban markets the average home price passed $400,000; average credit card debt continued to rise and the price of an average new car, with typical extras, passed $20,000.

2001 PROFILE

Lola Martin participated in many sports such as soccer, basketball and rock climbing, but the activity she loved the most was the fastest-growing outdoor sport of Ultimate Frisbee.

Life at Home

- Lola Martin was raised in Greenville, South Carolina, the youngest of three children.
- Though her parents divorced when she was seven, she did not feel different from her classmates and enjoyed the opportunity to get to know both parents.
- Her father, as a basketball player, baseball player, and track runner in high school, encouraged all of his children to try different sports.
- Her mother, also athletically talented and a lover of the outdoors, encouraged her children to explore nature independently.
- As the youngest, Lola felt the need to keep up with her brother, three years older, and sister, seven years older.
- She started playing soccer at age eight on a coed team and soon joined a newly emerging all girls' team at age nine.
- An all girls' team was touted as progressive at the time, although other states had long ago created similar programs, making South Carolina a few steps behind even neighboring states like North Carolina and Georgia.
- She thought she would play soccer for the rest of her life, and did until her freshman year of college.
- In high school, she also played basketball, rock-climbed, and ran track and cross-country.
- In all, her teams won four state championships—one in soccer, one in basketball and two in track.
- She also found the time to play in one Ultimate Frisbee tournament, having been recruited for her ability to run and catch.
- Her previous experience with Ultimate Frisbee was at summer camp, where she enjoyed the constant movement but hated the tendency of the boys to rarely pass to the girls on the team.

Lola's love of sports stemmed from her parents.

Ultimate frisbee showcased all Lola's athletic abilities.

- But at the tournament she was able to showcase all her athletic talents and had a ball.
- She also realized how much there was to learn about the rules, the throwing motion, when to cut and when to huck the disc (throw long).
- Ultimate, as it was more appropriately termed (Frisbee is a brand name), involved a field similar to that of a football field (40 yards wide by 70 yards long with 25-yard end zones on either end).
- With seven players per team on the field at a time, the players' movements were a combination of soccer, basketball and football.
- The rules also mimic other sports: the need to establish a pivot foot was borrowed from basketball, the interference calls on receivers from football.
- In Ultimate, running with the disc was not allowed.
- Therefore, a team must move the disc down the field by throwing and catching with the eventual goal of catching the disc in the end zone to score.
- If the disc touched the ground during this progression, barring a foul, possession changed to the other team who then tried to score in the other end zone.
- Lola especially appreciated the multiple strategies that could be employed, including zone defenses, set plays on offense, various cutting strategies—all familiar because of her participation in basketball and soccer.
- The most unique aspect of the sport to Lola was the lack of official referees.
- Field conduct was regulated by "Spirit of the Game," a term used to describe each individual player's responsibility to uphold the rules and play with sportsmanship.
- Therefore, players must know all the rules of the game and call them when they felt there had been a violation.
- The opposing player had an opportunity to agree or disagree.
- There was a level of trust that each player would not cheat with rule calls to gain an unfair advantage.

- In higher-level games, official observers were used as passive referees; if there was a dispute on the field, the players asked the observer for his/her opinion, which was final.
- Since its conception, players have established the rules.
- Ultimate began with the invention of the disc, which World War II veteran Fred Morrison called the "Whirlo-Way" in 1948.
- By 1949 the disc was being marketed in the midst of the UFO craze as plastic flying saucers useful for tossing on America's beaches.
- Then, in 1955, Wham-O (best known for the hula hoop) provided national distribution and in 1957, the name Frisbee.
- By 1968 New Jersey high schools were experimenting with a variety of rules, and in 1972 Princeton and Rutgers Universities staged a collegian contest before 2,000 students.
- Also on hand were a local TV station, a reporter for *The New York Times* and a mention in *Sports Illustrated*.
- Twenty years later as many as 100,000 athletes were participating in organized games, mostly connected with colleges and universities.
- When Lola entered college, Ultimate was played in over 42 countries and was government sponsored in Sweden, Norway and Japan.

Life at Work

- Lola Martin entered college with high expectations.
- Her plan was to study hard and play college soccer; after a summer of intense training and weightlifting she was in superb shape.
- But after discovering the pitfalls of no social life and a disagreeable coach at a Division I Soccer varsity program, Lola searched for another athletic outlet.
- She remembered her one Ultimate Frisbee tournament and thought that developing her skills in a new sport would be fun.
- Soon, she was hooked.
- She also found that her switch from soccer to Ultimate was not uncommon; many new college Ultimate players migrated from sports such as soccer, basketball and volleyball.
- Her college's women's team was formed only three short years earlier.
- So Lola believed she would have an opportunity to help the program build on itself.
- At the end of her freshman year, she was elected captain for the following year and soon began gaining regional recognition for her aggressive play.
- She also discovered the difficulties that came with balancing a leadership position and rigorous university classes.
- While varsity players enjoyed the support of professional tutors and some sympathy from professors, Ultimate players practiced four to five times a week without similar support or recognition.
- She even found that most people thought her sport involved a dog, was some variation of golf, or that marijuana-smoking hippies were the only people that played.
- Though she enjoyed the liberal attitudes that the sport attracted, Ultimate was much more intense than the majority of people thought.
- When deciding on a major, she was naturally drawn toward teaching.
- She initially knew that she loved teaching, but was also drawn to the flexibility of scheduling, allowing her to play Ultimate when she pleased.
- Many of her older Ultimate role models were teachers and advised her as to which avenues to pursue to maximize her ability to play and complete her studies.

Lola loved to compete and was elected captain.

- With her increasing recognition, she was scouted by club teams in the area to play Ultimate outside of school.
- The club season was primarily from the middle of the summer through the fall, and the college season was mostly during the spring semester, though there were tournaments for both divisions all year.
- The club division was composed of open (men's), women's, mixed (coed) and masters' (men over 30) categories.
- Lola found herself recruited to play on mixed teams, but also one of the top women's teams in the country.
- With a lighter schedule her senior year, she switched from playing mixed to women's Ultimate, committing to coast-to-coast travel for tournaments and rigorous practice on the weekends.
- Because the women's team was not close by, she had to travel over two hours and would often stay at a teammate's house after practice on Saturday night before Sunday morning practice.
- She did not mind though; Ultimate was her life, and her best friends were her teammates.

The game was much more demanding than most people thought.

- By the end of her senior year, her team had qualified for nationals for the first time in school history, and she was being mentioned on blogs by people from across the country.
- Though her team did not finish strongly at nationals, she was honored in an awards ceremony as being voted the fifth best college player (called the Callahan award) in the U.S. and Canada by other female college players.
- She was pleasantly surprised, since East Coast players and players from smaller schools tended not to rank very high in other female players' minds.
- Shortly after she graduated, tryouts for her club team began, along with track practices, agilities workouts, and weekend practices, a never-ending cycle.
- Sometimes she felt overwhelmed.
- But then she picked up a disc and hucked it downfield and smiled to herself.
- She loved this sport.

Life in the Community: Greenville, South Carolina

- Greenville, South Carolina, was part of the Cherokee Nation's protected grounds after the Treaty of 1763, which ended the French and Indian War.
- No white man was allowed to enter, though some families already had settled just within the boundary, and white traders regularly crossed the area.
- During the American Revolution, the Cherokee sided with the British.
- After a campaign in 1776, the Cherokee agreed to the Treaty of DeWitt's Corner, ceding territory that includes present-day Greenville County to South Carolina.
- Originally called Pleasantburg, Greenville County was created in 1786.
- In the early to mid-1900s, with Greenville being known as the "Textile Center of the South," an Exposition Hall for the textile industries was built.
- Beginning in the 1970s, then-Mayor Max Heller spearheaded a massive downtown revitalization project.
- The first and most important step in changing downtown's image was the streetscape plan, narrowing the street's four lanes to two and installing angled parking, trees, and decorative light fixtures, as well as creating parks and plazas throughout downtown.
- As the largest city in the Upstate area, Greenville is home to theaters and event venues that regularly host major concerts and touring theater companies.
- Four independent theaters each present several plays a year, while the Greenville County Museum of Art is noted for its collections of work by Andrew Wyeth, Jasper Johns, Andy Warhol and Georgia O'Keeffe.
- Greenville's economy, formerly based largely on textile manufacturing, had been transformed by substantial investments by foreign companies.
- The city is the North American headquarters for Michelin and is the sole manufacturing location for BMW in the Americas.

Greenville is Michelin's North American Headquarters.

HISTORICAL SNAPSHOT
2001

- Noah, a gaur, became the first individual of an endangered species to be cloned
- The U.S. Federal Trade Commission approved the merger of America Online and Time Warner to form AOL Time Warner
- Wikipedia, the online encyclopedia, was launched on the Internet
- President Bill Clinton awarded former President Theodore Roosevelt a posthumous Medal of Honor for his service during the Spanish-American War
- George W. Bush became the 43rd president of the United States
- The Baltimore Ravens defeated the New York Giants 34–7 to win their first Super Bowl title

- The submarine *USS Greeneville* accidentally struck and sank the Japanese fishing vessel *Ehime-Maru* near Hawaii
- The 73rd Academy Awards selected *Gladiator* as the year's Best Picture
- In The Netherlands, the Act on the Opening up of Marriage allowed same-sex couples to marry legally for the first time in the world since the reign of Nero
- *Soyuz TM-32* lifted off from the Baikonur Cosmodrome, carrying the first space tourist, American Dennis Tito
- The Colorado Avalanche won their second Stanley Cup
- The world's first self-contained artificial heart was implanted in Robert Tools
- FBI agent Robert Hanssen was arrested and charged with spying for Russia for 15 years
- NASCAR legend Dale Earnhardt died in a last-lap crash in the 43rd annual Daytona 500
- President George W. Bush limited federal funding for research on embryonic stem cells
- The U.S. Justice Department announced that it no longer sought to break up software maker Microsoft, and would instead seek a lesser antitrust penalty
- Almost 3,000 were killed in the September 11, 2001, attacks at the World Trade Center in New York City; the Pentagon in Arlington, Virginia; and in rural Pennsylvania
- The 2001 anthrax attacks commenced as letters containing anthrax spores were mailed from Princeton, New Jersey, to ABC News, CBS News, NBC News, the *New York Post*, and the *National Enquirer*; 22 people in total were exposed and five of them died
- Barry Bonds of the San Francisco Giants broke the single season home run record with 72 home runs for the year
- The U.S. invaded Afghanistan, with participation from other nations in retaliation for the September 11 attacks
- Enron filed for Chapter 11 bankruptcy protection five days after Dynegy canceled an $8.4 billion buyout bid, triggering the largest bankruptcy in U.S. history

Selected Prices

Advil, 50 .... $3.99
Binoculars $29.99
Champagne $15.99
Compass $7.99
Dishwasher, Maytag $429.00
Frisbee $12.00
Pepper Grinder $12.99
Pizza, Little Caesar's $12.95
Sleeping Bag $29.96
Tape Measure $19.99

"Bolts in Rocks Have Climbers Screaming from Mountaintops," Dean Starkman, *The Wall Street Journal,* June 11, 2003:

Patrick Seurynck was scaling a dangerous 400-foot granite cliff near Aspen, Colorado, last June when his partner above yelled down some disturbing news: "The anchors are gone!"

The 48-year-old Mr. Seurynck, who has been climbing rocks for 10 years, had just spent weeks drilling in place numerous stainless-steel bolts for securing ropes. He knew immediately what had happened: A bolt cutter had struck. He climbed down safely, fuming.

"It was just arrogant audacity," says Mr. Seurynck, still riled.

Whether to bolt or not is a smoldering question in rock climbing these days as the sport comes to grips with growing popularity. Once the domain of a scruffy few that embraced an ethic of self-reliance, conservationism and risk, rock climbing is being overrun by a new generation less connected to its daring past. The result: a culture clash on the rocks.

Traditional, or "trad," climbers favor passive protection gear metal nuts and spring-loaded retractable metal wedges called cams. These are slipped into cracks and then removed by the last climber to make an ascent. Climbers say newcomers put up permanent bolts merely to make hard climbs easier.

"They are entirely and utterly for the convenience of climbers, who, in my view, have just gotten incredibly lazy," says Richard Goldstone, a Poughkeepsie, New York, math professor, who has argued for fewer bolts in the Mohonk Preserve, a traditional climbing Mecca 80 miles north of New York.

The less-fastidious new-schoolers, sometimes called "sport climbers," dismiss the critique as elitist. They say bolted routes allow relatively safe climbs on even advanced routes and along the lines that otherwise could not be climbed at all. Besides, they say, bolts are becoming the norm. . . .

With at least 450,000 regulars now on the rocks in the U.S., up from 200,000 a decade ago, land managers fear that bolting is getting out of hand. "All of them are looking to prevent the proliferation," says Randy Kaufman, a National Park Service official. . . .

The nation's main rock-climbing group, the Access Fund, in Boulder, Colorado, is pro-bolt and favors leaving it up to climbers to decide when to place them. The group fears bureaucracy, so it is hoping the agencies provide "timely authorizations" for anchors, the spokesman says.

But a minority of climbers, including some big names in the sport, believe restrictions are needed. The anti-bolters echo the position of environmental groups that say permanent bolts degrade rock, look bad and allow climbers to disturb raptors' nests.

"'Ultimate Frisbee' Among Growing Outdoor Sports," Jennifer Anderson, Associated Press, *Kerrville Times* (Texas), September 7, 2000:

PORTLAND, Oregon: The plastic disc soars through the sky, tracing a long arc with a translucent glow before it floats for a frozen moment above the heads of two young men who leap to greet it.

Fwap! One claps the Frisbee between his hands while a player on defense lands on his feet and vows to knock it down the next time.

But there's no time for waffling.

"Stall one, stall two," he yells in Ultimate Frisbee lingo, counting the seconds his opponent has to fling the disc downfield in hopes of scoring the game point.

Before his defender can shout "stall three," he whips a hammer throw (Frisbee slang for a long vertical toss) into the end zone where a ponytailed teammate dives into the grass to catch it with her fingertips.

"Nice grab! Game!"

To these athletes, the familiar Frisbee that started as a toy more than 50 years ago has become a game enjoyed competitively by at least 100,000 people worldwide, about half in the United States.

Ultimate Frisbee—first played in 1968 by high school students in Maplewood, New Jersey—is a fast-paced non-contact sport that combines the speed of soccer, the objective of football and handling skills of basketball.

But what makes the sport unique is there is no referee, official scorekeeper or timekeeper.

Ultimate Frisbee relies on a "Spirit of the Game" rule, which, as defined in the game handbook, places responsibility for fair play on the player. It says that highly competitive play is encouraged, but never at the expense of the pure joy of the game.

"The people who play Ultimate really are virtuous people and play honestly," said Deana McMurrer, co-captain of Portland's only all-woman team, which last year took second place in the national tournament in San Diego and the world tournament in Scotland.

"It's a great quality that we can carry over to our lives."

Perhaps because of the game's emphasis on fun and fair play, Ultimate is especially embraced in the laid-back Pacific Northwest.

"The spirit of the game is alive and well here," said Mark Aagenes, Missoula, Montana-based coordinator for the Northwest region's Big Sky section, which includes Utah, Idaho, Montana, part of Wyoming and Alberta, Canada.

"People play because they like each other and want to have fun with it". . . .

"Frisbee Fans Get Fitness, Fun," *Winnipeg Free Press,* June 4, 2001:

It's just a round piece of plastic, but a Frisbee is the ultimate sport and fitness toy for growing fanatics like Jill Goddard.

Two nights a week, Goddard, a Toronto public health nurse, "hucks" and "backhands" a Frisbee at school and other fields, an oh-so-cool way to have fun, socialize and exercise.

Goddard is among Canadians who play Ultimate Frisbee, the trendy disc-throwing team sport that combines the nonstop running of soccer, the non-contact rules of basketball and the passing of football.

"You need to have good reflexes and you don't have to be a fitness freak, but you need a good cardiovascular base as there's lots of running around," the 28-year-old said before joining her coed team, the Limp Diskits, for a Monday night game against an opposing team at a Toronto high school.

A huck, as Ultimate jargon goes, is a long throw, and sometimes Goddard is guilty of a "swill," a bad throw.

But she was on a high after scoring three points in her team's 14-4 win to open the spring-summer season at the beginning of May, her first year in the Ultimate Frisbee adult coed league run by the Toronto East Sport Social Club. There are about 30 teams in two divisions, for beginners and advanced players.

Ultimate, sometimes called Frisbee football, is said to have been invented by New Jersey high school students in 1968 (although some say that it has its roots in Eastern colleges in the '50s). The Frisbee was conceived in 1948 by a California army pilot who molded plastic in the shape of pie tins, which kids and soldiers had been playing catch with decades. . . .

Ultimate has since become an international phenomenon, and there are world championships and competitive bodies like the U.S.-based Ultimate Players Association. The sport makes its debut as a medal sport in the 2001 World Games in Japan this August as the only self-officiated sport of the Games. There's also talk of it in the Olympics.

The beauty of Ultimate Frisbee is that it's a cheap form of fitness: all you need is a disc, which costs a few bucks, the players and a field . . .

"Ultimate is for people who want exercise, fresh air, to run around and blow off some steam after a hard day at work," said Michael Lichti, a coordinator for the Toronto East Sport Social Club, which charges $400 for a team with 10 players to join the league. "There's also the social aspect, meeting people on your own and on other teams."

After games, for instance, Goddard and her teammates go out for drinks and bites and to conduct a friendly game of postmortem.

"What I like is that Ultimate isn't as competitive as some of the other sports I do," says Goddard, who is also into running, hiking and paddling. "And most of the people in the league are of the same mindset, young professionals who are fit and into other sports, but who don't have the idea it's the be-all and end-all to win."

2006 PROFILE

Taught how to skate as soon as she could walk, Jamie Hagerman grew up to become a powerhouse hockey player—eventually landing on the U.S. Women's Olympic ice hockey team in 2006.

Life at Home

- Jamie Hagerman was born in 1981 in Deerfield, Massachusetts, the third child, with two older sisters, Casey and Kully; her younger sister Whitaker was born in 1987.
- Her parents both worked at the local preparatory high school, Deerfield Academy.
- Her father Dave was the head of athletics at the school, and her mother Parny was the director of admissions.
- Jamie's father was a hockey player at the University of New Hampshire and a hockey coach at Deerfield, so it was only natural that his children would play as well.
- Jamie hit the ice at age three.
- As she was learning to take her first strides on the ice, Jamie and her family relocated to another prep school, Hotchkiss School, in Lakeville, Connecticut.
- There, in the northwest corner of the state, she joined her first ice hockey team, becoming a "Cub" in Salisbury Youth Hockey.
- The Lakeville/Salisbury area had a small-town feel.
- The children with whom Jamie skated often attended the same school and church.
- Jamie attended the local public school, Salisbury Central School, up through eighth grade; just over 300 students attended the school.
- As she progressed through Salisbury Central, she also progressed through the different levels of youth hockey.
- After her three years as a Cub, she became a Mite, then a Squirt, Pewee, and finally a Bantam—spending about two years at each level.
- Jamie always made the "A" team—or the best team—at each level, going toe to toe with boys her age; she typically played right wing.

Jamie learned to skate as a toddler.

As a "cub," Jamie was the only girl on the Youth Hockey team.

- She was usually the only girl on her youth hockey team; her parents were careful not to point out her unique position on the team.
- Some of her favorite memories on the youth hockey team were playing on the frozen lakes in January with her Salisbury Youth Hockey teammates, who were also her best friends.
- In addition to playing in the youth hockey league, Jamie would practice with the Varsity girls' team at Hotchkiss School, which helped her become an even stronger player.
- The first time gender ever became an issue was when Jamie was 10.
- She was dressed in her hockey gear, eating at the dining hall at Salisbury School, where her dad was now working, when a boy walked up to her and said, "What are you doing?" She responded, "Going to hockey practice." The boy said, "Don't you know hockey is for boys and not for girls?"
- After graduating from Salisbury Central School, Jamie went to Deerfield Academy for high school from 1995 to 1999.
- While at Deerfield, she joined an all-girls' hockey team in Cromwell, Connecticut, called the Polar Bears, and also played on Deerfield's own girls' ice hockey, soccer and lacrosse teams.
- At Deerfield, she switched from playing right wing to defense.
- Starting at 14, she went to the USA Hockey camps, which were designed for the best hockey players, broken down by age groups.

Jamie loved playing with her friends on her neighborhood's frozen lake.

- Schoolwork at Deerfield did not come easy to Jamie.
- She had to work incredibly hard to master the subjects she was studying—if she didn't understand a topic or problem the first time, she'd try a second or third time until she eventually understood it.
- Her hard work endeared her to teachers at the time, and she became a top student at the school.
- By her senior year, she was captain of the hockey, lacrosse and soccer teams and was heading to Harvard to play hockey as well as lacrosse.
- Harvard was an essential step to her ultimate goal: to play hockey for the United States at the Winter Olympics.

Jamie was a natural at playing hockey.

Life at Work

- Jamie Hagerman thrived at Harvard.
- She loved her coaches and her teammates; in her freshman year, she was named to the conference All-Rookie team.
- Her second year at the school, she tore her anterior cruciate ligament, or ACL, during lacrosse practice.
- Her doctor told her she did not need surgery to play ice hockey since hockey is gentle on players' knees, but she could no longer play lacrosse.
- While she was at Harvard, she was once again selected to go to the USA camp for the best female players.
- At this level—the senior women's team—Jamie was being scouted for the Olympics.
- She also made it into the two critical tournaments a year—the Four Nations Cup in November, and the World Championships in April.
- She graduated from Harvard in 2003 and promptly moved to Canada to further her training for the Olympics.
- She was hoping to make one of the professional women's league teams in Canada.
- Only two Americans were allowed on each team, and there were eight teams in the country.
- In all, there were about 100 American girls fighting for those 16 spots.
- Jamie beat the odds and made a team in Toronto.
- She couldn't earn money in Canada for visa reasons, so she worked hard to save up money during the summer so she could financially survive the hockey season.
- When she headed up to Toronto, she was told by the team that she and the other American player needed to live with the Canadian Olympians until they got them their own house.
- The two women lived in an unfinished basement for four months—turning on the dryer at night to keep warm.
- Jamie moved back to the United States in April 2004 and made the World Championship Team, which brightened her hopes of making the 2006 Women's Olympic team.
- During this time, she moved back to Boston and worked as assistant coach on the women's hockey team at Harvard.
- She loved returning to her alma mater, her role as a coach, and the opportunity to stay in shape and practice for her possible Olympic bid.
- In the summer of 2005, she made the summer camp for the top 40 players in the country.

Jamie was excited to be a part of the Olympic team.

- Over the summer, the 40 Olympic competitor candidates were then cut to 25 hockey players.
- Those players then skated together from August to December, when the 25 were then cut to 20.
- Her family nervously awaited the announcement of the final roster outside the locker room of one of the exhibition games leading up to the Olympics.
- Jamie left the locker room in tears.
- Her parents thought the tears were because she did not make the team, but they were actually tears of joy—she was going to the Olympics.
- The 2006 Winter Olympic Games in Turin, Italy, were the third time women's ice hockey appeared in the Winter Games.
- Jamie and her team first played Switzerland and then Germany, beating both teams handily: 6-0 and 5-0, respectively.
- The third game against Finland was a bit tighter, but the United States came out on top, 7-3.
- After a three-day break, the women's hockey team headed into their semi-final game against Sweden.
- The United States had a 25-0 record against Sweden, so the odds were in their favor.
- The United States took the lead in the game, 2-0, with a goal in the first and second period each.
- But the Swedes caught up, scoring two goals little more than three minutes apart.
- Despite outshooting the Swedes 39-18, the United States could not get past the Swedish goalie Kim Martin, leaving the score tied through the third period and overtime.
- Now the teams were headed into a shootout.
- The United States failed to score during the shootout, and the Swedes scored their final two shots, leading them to victory and a spot in the finals against Canada.
- Brokenhearted at their loss, the United States gathered themselves for their bronze-medal game against Finland.
- Beating Finland 4-0, the United States team showed they could bounce back—playing stronger, with sharper passes and deft puck handling.
- Jamie and her teammates were awarded a bronze medal for their victory against Finland.
- Although she did not win the gold, it was a thrilling experience for Jamie to be on the Olympic team.
- It was also a special moment for her father, Dave.
- After playing goalie at the University of New Hampshire, her father was good enough to attend the U.S. National Team training camp, in preparation for the Olympics.
- Before he even got to go to the camp, he was drafted to fight in Vietnam.
- Jamie not only fulfilled her dream of going to the Olympics, but also her father's.
- After the Olympics, she discovered she had torn her ACL again.
- She knew she had injured herself during the Olympics, but decided to keep quiet about the injury so she wouldn't jeopardize her chances to make the team.
- She had surgery on her knee.
- After the big win at the Olympics, she headed to Washington, DC, to teach advanced placement psychology in high school.
- But hockey was not left behind.
- During the summer, she taught at ice hockey camps, sharing her Olympic story with a new generation of female skaters.

Life in the Community: Salisbury, Connecticut

- Salisbury, Connecticut, is located in the northwest corner of the state, on the borders of New York and Massachusetts.
- The town of Salisbury was incorporated in 1741, and it includes the villages of Salisbury and Lakeville, and the hamlets of Amesville, Lime Rock and Taconic.
- Salisbury is a rural area of rolling mountains, dotted with lakes and crisscrossed by the Housatonic River.
- During the Federal period, Salisbury was known for its iron production.
- Because the town was not near a river large enough to ship raw iron, the town instead handled much of the labor on their own—working the iron into wrought iron that was of such high quality it could be used for gun barrels.
- Salisbury iron became the choice iron for Connecticut's early nineteenth-century arms industry.
- Many of the arms were shipped South to be used by the Union army during the Civil War.
- Over the course of the twentieth century, Salisbury moved away from the iron industry and became a more upscale area, known as a weekend destination for New Yorkers.
- In 1999, Salisbury had a population of 3,977.

HISTORICAL SNAPSHOT
2006

- NASA's Stardust mission successfully returned dust from a comet
- United Airlines emerged from bankruptcy after being in that position since December 9, 2002, the longest such filing in history
- In Super Bowl XL, the Pittsburgh Steelers defeated the Seattle Seahawks 21–10
- The Blu-ray Disc format was released in the United States
- Massive antiwar demonstrations, including a march down Broadway in New York City, marked the third year of war in Iraq
- Warren Buffett donated more than $30 billion to the Bill & Melinda Gates Foundation

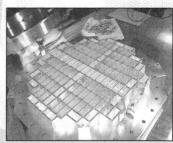

Stardust spacecraft

Collector tray to collect interstellar dust particles.

- The Military Commissions Act of 2006 was passed, suspending habeas corpus for "enemy combatants"
- A Pew Research Center survey revealed that 81 percent of Americans believed it was "common behavior" for lobbyists to bribe members of Congress
- More than a million immigrants, primarily Hispanic, staged marches in over 100 cities, calling for immigration reform
- Liquids and gels were banned from checked and carry-on baggage after London Metropolitan Police made 21 arrests in connection with an apparent terrorist plot to blow up planes traveling from the United Kingdom to the United States
- The International Astronomical Union defined "planet," demoting Pluto to the status of "dwarf planet" more than 70 years after its discovery

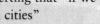

- Two stolen Edvard Munch paintings, *The Scream* and *Madonna,* were recovered in a police raid in Oslo, Norway
- President George W. Bush used the fifth anniversary of the September 11, 2001, attacks to emphasize the link between Iraq and winning the broader war on terrorism, asserting that "if we give up the fight in the streets of Baghdad, we will face the terrorists in the streets of our own cities"
- Google bought YouTube for $1.65 billion
- *Pirates of the Caribbean: Dead Man's Chest* became the fastest film in Hollywood history to reach the billion-dollar mark worldwide in box office receipts
- Former Iraqi leader Saddam Hussein was sentenced to death by hanging after an Iraqi court found him guilty of crimes against humanity
- Massachusetts enacted Universal Health Coverage, requiring all residents to have either public or private insurance
- PlayStation 3 and Wii were released in North America
- Smoking was banned in all Ohio bars, restaurants, workplaces and other public places

NO SMOKING

To report violations call
1-866-559-OHIO (6446)
in accordance with Chapter 3794
of the Ohio Revised Code.

Selected Prices

Beach Towel $20.00
Concert Ticket $40.00
Disposable Camera, Kodak $7.99
Gas Grill $134.99
Plastic Surgery, Liposuction $2,578.00
Private School, Hotchkiss, Annual $24,500
Radio/CD Player, Bose $499.00
Sirius Satellite Radio $100.00
Telephone, Motorola $79.95
Tires and Wheels $449.00

MINI300PE

AM/FM Shortwave radio and flashlight

Compact and power-packed
- Multi-function LCD screen
- Clock, alarm, and sleep timer functions
- Receives 7 International Shortwave bands
- Telescopic and internal ferrite bar antennas
- Built-in speaker and earphone input
- 5 colors to choose from

Trends in Women's Hockey

- The first organized all-women's hockey game took place in Barrie, Ontario, in 1892, two decades before the formation of the National Hockey League.
- In 1894, a female club team formed at Queen's University in Kingston, Ontario, known as the "Love-Me-Littles," incurred the wrath of the school's archbishop, who did not want women to play.
- Within two years, teams had formed at McGill University and in the Ottawa Valley.
- The first women's hockey championship for the province of Ontario was held in 1914.
- In 1916, the United States hosted an international hockey tournament in Cleveland, which featured both American and Canadian players.
- The Great Depression and World War II knocked the wind out of the gaining popularity of the sport; women did not start getting back into ice hockey until the 1960s.
- In 1967, the Dominion Ladies Hockey Tournament was held in Brampton, Ohio.
- The Dominion Ladies Hockey Tournament featured 22 teams, with players from ages nine to 50 competing.
- By the 1970s, several Canadian provinces moved to establish associations to govern female hockey teams.
- At the same time, American colleges and high schools started to form varsity and club teams for women.
- Canada held its first national championship for women's hockey in 1982.
- Eight years later, it hosted the first Women's World Ice Hockey Championships.
- Two years later, after the second world championships were held in Finland, the International Olympic Committee voted to include women's hockey in future Olympics.
- Women's ice hockey made its Olympic debut in 1998, at Nagano, Japan.
- With the World Ice Hockey Championships, and the introduction of the sport at the Olympics, women's ice hockey grew in popularity across the world.
- Canada and the United States still have the most female ice hockey players, and typically the most talented ones.
- In 1990-1991 season, there were 6,036 registered female hockey players in the United States; by 2001, there were 39,693—a 580 percent increase.

"These Bears on the Cutting Edge; State's Top Girls' Hockey Program Is Making Its Mark Nationally," Matt Eagan, *Hartford Courant,* December 1996:

When Maurice FitzMaurice started the Connecticut Polar Bears girls' ice hockey team, the prevailing wisdom was there were no female hockey players in the state. At least as far as colleges were concerned. A girl from Connecticut who wanted to play hockey ended up on a boys' team, limiting her playing time and her exposure to college scouts.

That has changed.

The Polar Bears have played in 10 national championship games, winning five, since FitzMaurice started the club 12 years ago. And the holiday tournament, which started in the first year, has grown from a one-day, four-team event at Loomis Chaffee School in Windsor into a tournament with seven divisions and 63 teams. Major college scouts have flocked to seven rinks in Connecticut since Thursday to see the nation's top talent.

The tournament will end today with semifinals and finals in each division. The Polar Bears Midget 1 team (under-19) will play Team California in a semifinal at Tri-Town Sports Center (12:50 p.m.). The other semifinal has Massachusetts teams Assabet Valley and Chelmsford at Loomis (1:15). The final is at Tri-Town (6:10 p.m.).

The Polar Bears Squirt 1 (under-12) also qualified for the semifinals and will play Team Michigan at Tri-Town (9:20 a.m.). The winner advances to the 3:10 p.m. final at Tri-Town against Assabet Valley 84 or Assabet Valley 85, who play at Loomis (9:30 a.m.).

"It's come a long way since 1985," said FitzMaurice, an attorney who lives in Wethersfield. "Every major college has been here. We've been getting the attention for the last seven or eight years and that also is attracting teams because your West Coast girls don't get as much exposure because it's a long way to go for coaches to find them."

Teams from California started appearing three years ago. This year, the tournament features three California teams, one from Seattle, and teams from Michigan, Washington, DC, and the Northeast.

The level of play also attracts the scouts.

"I've been to a lot of these tournaments," said Roy Holinges of Needles, California. "We go to Canada and around the [U.S.], I follow the California teams a lot, and this is as good as the competition gets."

Connecticut has 12 members of the U.S. National Junior group, which is the top 50 in the country. Another, Angela Ruggiero of Choate-Rosemary Hall School in Wallingford, is on the U.S. National Team which is going to China next week and is a forerunner to the 1998 U.S. Olympic team.

The idea for the tournament came shortly after the Polar Bears started their first season. Said FitzMaurice: "The idea was to start to bring in some other girls because all we did is play boys back in those days. There were no girls' teams close by and we wanted to see how we would match up in the nationals."

The Polar Bears wound up winning the national championship. Since then, they have become one of the country's elite programs against heady competition such as Minnesota, which has just one select team.

The sport has changed since that first national championship in the spring of 1986. FitzMaurice said most players on his team also play other sports and all lift weights, something that wasn't common in the 1980s.

Some of the state's top players in other sports play for the Polar Bears. Jen Wiehn is an all-state soccer player at Tolland. Meaghan Cahill was a top soccer player at Kingswood-Oxford in West Hartford.

Also, more girls are becoming interested and college-level women's hockey programs are becoming more common, a trend FitzMaurice hopes will continue after the sport makes its debut in the 1998 Olympics.

"I think people will be shocked once they see the game," FitzMaurice said. "Once that happens, some parents will start to say 'I've got a good athlete, why don't I get her started on hockey?'"

There are plenty of opportunities. Polar Bears Wiehn and Liz Macri will be attending Dartmouth; Jordan Rettig will attend Princeton. Two others are being considered by Cornell, another by Yale.

"The whole reason we started this team was to get kids exposure and educational opportunities," FitzMaurice said. "At this point, it's an emerging sport, even though the competition is getting better every year, in this state there may be 10,000 female soccer players and fewer than 100 female hockey players.

"Plus it's a team sport with high endurance and kids, as part of the tournament process, get to travel and bond with their teammates who they learn as much from as coaches and teachers or anyone else."

"Women's Hockey Semifinal; Sweden 3, USA 2 (Shootout); Progress Stings," Rachel Blount, *Star-Tribune* (Minneapolis, Minnesota), February 2006:

They had seen the movie *Miracle* so many times that some of them could recite the lines. In the hours before Friday's Olympic semifinal against the United States, Swedish forward Maria Rooth and some of her teammates decided the time had come to give women's hockey its own version of that legend.

Sweden's 3-2 shootout victory will go down as a landmark in the women's game. While Rooth and her teammates hurled themselves into a blue-and-yellow pile on the Palasport Olimpico ice, the U.S. women bit their lips and felt the sting of a day they knew would come. As far back as September, coach Ben Smith warned that Finland and Sweden were at the doorstep of a historic upset. The Finns came close, and the Swedes made it happen, finally widening the women's hockey world beyond the U.S.-Canada axis.

The Americans had gone 73-0-2 against the six Olympic participants other than Canada. That included a 25-0 record against Sweden. In the past, Rooth said, her team never quite believed it could crack the icy wall that separated the North American powers from everyone else—until they arrived at the place where miracles are born.

"We said [Thursday] we were going to make a new miracle," said Rooth, a former Minnesota Duluth player who scored the shootout winner and both of Sweden's goals in regulation. "If we just believed we could beat them, we thought it could happen. Everyone was so committed. Everyone believed."

Except on the American side. The U.S. players felt only disbelief at losing their first Olympic semifinal. As Sweden's players got high-fives from NHL stars and countrymen Peter Forsberg and Mats Sundin, goalie Chanda Gunn fought a losing battle with tears, and Angela Ruggiero couldn't grasp the reality of playing for a bronze medal.

That will happen Monday against Finland, 6-0 losers Friday to Canada.

"I'm in shock right now," Ruggiero said. "It's a huge day for Sweden. It hurts, but we have to stay positive, because we can still win a medal.

"Everybody talks about the USA and Canada, but this may just open the world's eyes to the fact that there are other teams out there. We're back on our heels right now. But if you can take something positive away from this, maybe that's it."

Swedes' confidence grew.

Four years ago, Sweden's Olympic committee considered keeping its women's hockey team home for fear it would not be competitive in the Winter Games. The Swedes had finished fifth in the 1998 Olympics, the first to include women's hockey, and surprised with bronze in 2002.

Goalie Kim Martin was only 15 when she played in the Salt Lake City Games. Friday, her brilliance in the net provided the foundation for Sweden's greatest victory. Martin made 37 saves and thoroughly frustrated the Americans with her nimble, assured play.

continued

"Women's Hockey Semifinal; Sweden 3, USA 2 (Shootout); Progress Stings," . . . *(continued)*

The United States outshot Sweden 39-18, but the players' faces reflected the anxiety created by frequent miscues and breakdowns—and by Martin's impenetrability. Former UMD forward Erika Holst stripped the puck from Gophers' defenseman Lyndsay Wall behind the U.S. net and fired it to the charging Rooth for the tying shorthanded goal. The Swedes intercepted several passes deep in the American zone, and countless U.S. scoring chances sailed wide, struck the goal cage or banged off of sticks.

The United States also went 2-for-11 on power plays, including a two-player advantage that lasted more than three minutes in the second period.

"We had a lot of good opportunities on the power plays," forward Katie King said.

"We didn't put them home, and that's what hurts. We were maybe too pretty on plays and lost it a few times, and they capitalized."

A distinctly Swedish vibe began to take over the arena as Rooth's goals, little more than three minutes apart, negated a 2-0 U.S. lead. ABBA played on the sound system. Fans with horns and Tre Kroner jerseys outblared their American counterparts. The tension swelled through the scoreless third period, the overtime and the shootout.

The first five shooters missed or were stopped. Pernilla Winberg beat Gunn with a wrist shot to the stick side, and Rooth followed in similar fashion to cement one of the defining moments of these Olympics.

"When it was over, I had to ask people what happened," Holst said. "Tonight, we said, `This is our night. We're going to win. No one can take this away from us.'"

"A breakthrough"

As Canada and the United States buried their opponents in pool play, their coaches were forced to answer questions about whether their sport belonged in the Olympics. A paucity of competitive teams recently got women's softball bounced from the Summer Olympics program.

The North American rivals had faced off in every world championship and Olympic final in history. It seemed a foregone conclusion that they would do so again, but even through their tears the U.S. players were able to acknowledge the impact their upset will have on the sport.

"It's a breakthrough for them and their program," said U.S. forward Natalie Darwitz of Eagan. "I wish it wasn't us, but it's great for women's hockey. It shows there's a lot more than the U.S. and Canada."

Sweden's coach, Peter Elander, said he took a cue from the late Herb Brooks in preparing his team. Like Brooks, who famously kept his players on the ice after a tie and made them skate to exhaustion, Elander drove his team relentlessly for the past three months.

Which goes to show that even American hockey movies have influenced the women's game abroad. Elander thanked the United States and Canada for playing the Swedes so often, allowing them to learn and develop. Many European players also are refining their games with U.S. college teams, including nine Olympians who have played for or been signed by Minnesota Duluth.

Sweden's victory resulted from its fearless and aggressive defense, a smart game plan, improved speed and conditioning, and a new attitude. Years of losses to the North Americans have affected the psyches of some opponents; the Finns, after seizing a 3-1 lead on the United States in pool play, tightened up and lost. By getting over that hurdle, the Swedes have opened a window of possibility for others.

Elander and his players speculated that Friday's upset will stimulate the growth of the game in Sweden. At the very least, it promises to give hope to hockey's have-nots.

"We said at the beginning that people were going to be surprised at how competitive this tournament was," said forward Jenny Potter of Edina. "This is disappointing, and it's hard. It's all you dream about. But they beat us. What else can you say?"

"Today's Players See Brighter Tomorrow; Growing Coaching Sorority Part of Long-term Hockey Plan," Jill Lieber, *USA TODAY*, February 2006:

TORINO—Sometimes, Jamie Hagerman, a defenseman on the U.S. women's ice hockey team, feels like a stranger in a strange land.

When she's not devoting energy to winning a gold medal, she's committed to her job as an assistant women's ice hockey coach at Harvard.

The Crimson are one of six NCAA Division I women's ice hockey programs with female head coaches—and the only Division I school with an all-female coaching staff.

"At Harvard, we talk about it a lot: 'We are the only all-women staff. Why?'" Hagerman says.

The rest of the time, Hagerman feels like one of the crowd, playing one of the fastest-growing women's sports, with participation up 400 percent in the USA in the last decade, according to USA Hockey. She is one of seven women on the Olympic team who are, or have been, coaches of women's or girls' teams.

They include Katie King, an assistant at Boston College; Courtney Kennedy, head coach at Buckingham Browne and Nichols School in Cambridge, Mass.; and Jenny Potter, who coached at a Minnesota high school.

Also: Kathleen Kauth, a former volunteer assistant coach at Brown; Tricia Dunn-Luoma, a former assistant coach at New Hampshire; and Chanda Gunn, a former Massachusetts youth league coach.

"For a while, it was a male-dominated sport," Hagerman says. "It used to be women playing a men's sport. Now it's women playing hockey. A couple of years ago you couldn't make ends meet coaching. As a part-time first assistant at Harvard, I made $20,000 my first year. Now women can make a living."

Dave Ogrean, the executive director of USA Hockey, says increasing the pool of experienced female head coaches, especially at the national and international level, is a priority.

"We need to do a better job immediately," he says. In fact, Ogrean says his goal is to generate a list of women capable of coaching the 2010 or 2014 U.S. Olympic team. (The Canadian Olympic women's team is coached by Melody Davidson, on leave as head coach at Cornell.)

Ben Smith, in his third Olympics, became the first full-time head coach of the U.S. women's national and Olympic teams in 1996. He coached the USA to the Olympic gold medal in 1998 and silver in 2002. His contract is up after Torino.

Ogrean says he understands why none of the players from those first two U.S. Olympic teams are coaching at an elite level: "They're a collection of highly educated, high-achieving, exceptional women, not just women hockey players." But he hopes, over time, some team alumni will pursue coaching.

"When we sit down to talk about the next four years and the four years after that, I want there to be a lot of women whose names legitimately jump to mind as coaching candidates," Ogrean says.

From USA TODAY, a division of Gannett Co., Inc. Reprinted with permission.

2009 PROFILE

Alfredo Lenzi grew up in an Italian neighborhood, in a large family of first- and second-generation Italians. He learned how to hustle for what he wanted, and developed a competitive edge that served him well as a winning pool player.

Life at Home

- Alfredo—Al to his friends—Lenzi learned at an early age that it was who you knew that mattered.
- Al knew plenty of the right people.
- He never had to look far for a way to make a buck.
- Like any college student, Al came home during school breaks and summers.
- Unlike most college students, however, his jobs usually found him.
- One of Al's uncles—he had eight—belonged to the bartending union, so Al bartended.
- Similar connections got him jobs on a railroad crew and Highway Department.
- His father owned a waste removal company and worked long hours.
- His mother was the firm hand of this middle class Italian family, and Al's two older sisters often took her lead.
- But Al was the "baby," the only boy, and spoiled rotten.
- He was given two rules growing up—be home for dinner and stay out of trouble.
- He loved all sports in high school but football was his passion.
- Al was a start quarterback at Notre Dame High School in West Haven, Connecticut, where he developed a competitive nature, believing that winning was everything.
- Coming close was like a boy kissing his sister—it didn't count.
- He became interested in pool at age 14 after watching the 1960 film *The Hustler.*
- He read *Willie Mosconi on Pocket Billiards,* and Mosconi became his hero.
- When he wasn't on the football field, Al hung around pool halls.
- He learned from watching the older men play.
- There wasn't much mentoring—pool players weren't about to give away their secrets.

Al had that competitive edge necessary for pool players.

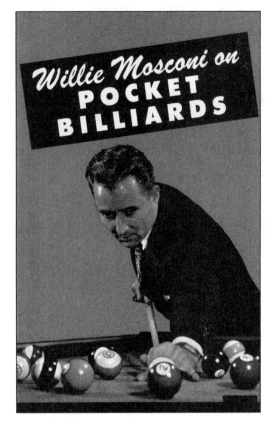

Willie Mosconi was Al's hero.

Al spent time learning from the pros.

- Al had his best lessons by challenging the old pros for a dollar or two a game.
- He was a quick study and perfected his game of straight pool—in which each player received one point for each ball pocketed.
- When he started college, Al began playing pool in earnest.
- In addition to straight pool, he became a pretty good 8-ball player—a game where you shot either the seven solid balls or the seven striped balls, and then the 8 ball.
- He learned which bars had the fastest tables and the drunkest crowds—Al rarely drank while playing and made money by betting on winning the game.
- On a good night, he could make $60, betting $3 or $4 a game.
- Al perfected two sure-fire strategies for winning—sharking and hustling.
- Sharking was startling your opponent to the point of making him miss a shot.
- This included coughing, dropping something, or walking into your opponent's line of vision when he was down on a shot.
- Hustling was tricking your opponent into thinking that you were not very good—and losing a few games to prove it.
- The key was getting him to bet the farm on you losing, after which, of course, your luck miraculously turned and you won it all.
- These schemes might sound easy, but they can be dangerous.
- If your opponent became wise to your strategy, you risked getting into a fight or being banned from the bar.
- All in all, Al found pool a profitable pastime.
- Always generous with his time, Al once accompanied a college buddy to New Orleans to find a car he had "lost" during Mardi Gras.
- They were determined to find the car and drive it back.
- They found the car, but ran out of money.

- Al's pool playing skills came in handy in a Bourbon Street bar, where he hustled an Oklahoma City man for $75, at $5.00 a game.
- The pair quickly got into the car and drove back to college.
- After graduating college, Al joined the Navy.
- He was stationed in Virginia Beach, where he found the best pool bars, but also found himself the victim of the "double hustle."
- This is when you think you are hustling an unassuming opponent, only your opponent is hustling you better.
- Not liking being suckered, Al sharpened his intuition skills after that.
- He continued to practice pool in Bremerton, Washington, where his submarine, the *Patrick Henry*, was stationed for a maintenance overhaul.
- Al became pool buddies with Slim, an old-time road pool player who lent Al a custom pool stick, inlaid with mother of pearl, to use in the Northwest Regional Straight Pool Tournament at the Navy Base on Widbey Island.
- Generally, Al played with house sticks.
- Hustlers never carried their own stick; that was a dead giveaway that you were good.
- Not only did he win first place with Slim's borrowed stick, but he developed an appreciation for expensive pool sticks.

Al joined the Navy after college.

Life at Work

- After the Navy, Al Lenzi married his high school sweetheart and they followed a job to Great Barrington, Massachusetts, 125 miles north of Manhattan.
- There he taught physical education at the local high school and coached football and wrestling.
- His wife concentrated on her hair stylist career while they raised their two sons.
- In 1995, Al retired early from teaching and worked as a stylist in their beauty salon—a surprisingly successful second career for him.
- His marriage wasn't as successful, however, and ended in divorce.
- His newfound freedom drew him back into the pool playing circuit.
- But finding places to play and decent competition wasn't easy in Great Barrington.
- Al encouraged a bar owner in a neighboring town to start a pool league.
- As the league grew, area bars and restaurants installed pool tables.
- League officers would create detailed schedules, alternating weekly matches among a number of available places.
- Over the next 10 years, Al would play in several leagues at once—cutting hair by day and playing pool as many as four nights a week.
- As the captain of his teams, he coached his players to win season after season.
- His beauty salon doubled as his trophy room.
- Alone and with his teams, he traveled up and down the East Coast to compete in eight- and nine-ball tournaments.

In Great Barrington, Al taught high school.

- Tournaments were often double elimination, two-day affairs.
- If a player lost one match, he was put in the loser's bracket and kept playing until he lost the second time.
- Al won his fair share of these tournaments, but he never stopped practicing.
- Unlike his younger days, winning now felt better when he played his best, not when his opponent made mistakes.
- There were often long waits in between matches, encouraging side games and individual betting.
- Official cash payouts for these tournaments could be as much as several thousand dollars.
- Al was a voracious collector of pool equipment, gadgets and supplies.
- He owned dozens of custom pool cues, including specialty break cues to break the balls at the beginning of a game, and jump cues to jump the cue ball over another ball.
- While at pool tournament trips, Al was on the prowl for the latest and greatest pool thing, including instructional videos and pool books.
- He had hundreds of instructive videos and books that he would often lend out to anyone who wanted to improve his or her game.
- Before an important match, Al would practice with members of his team at his home on his professional nine-foot table.

Pool tournament trips combined playing pool and shopping.

Al's team competed nationally.

Well-maintained sticks were important.

- They would review rules and practice certain shots over and over.
- Al's team often would win a trip to Las Vegas to compete in the national tournament.
- These tournaments included hundreds of teams from all over the country.
- Rules were strictly enforced—no jeans, sandals, flash photography or smoking.
- He and other team members would often play in single contests as well as the team event.
- Players would watch the bracket board to see where and when their friends were playing, so they could be on hand to support them during a match.
- In addition to playing in matches, Al would take advantage of the pool vendors at the tournament and get his sticks serviced.
- They did it all, from cleaning and smoothing to putting on new tips and new wraps.
- Al also looked forward to seeing his favorite professional players, like Johnny Archer and Corey Deuel, compete in Las Vegas.
- He loved watching them make great shots, and when they missed, he was reminded that even the pros make mistakes.

Johnny Archer

Corey Deuel (left)

Great Barrington is home to typical New England beauty.

Life in the Community: Great Barrington, Massachusetts

- The Berkshire Mountains in Massachusetts are composed of 15 rural New England towns including Great Barrington.
- Berkshire County was a popular vacation spot for New Yorkers, with a variety of cultural events, including Tanglewood—the summer home of the Boston Symphony Orchestra—world class museums, art galleries and theaters.
- In 1978, the population of Great Barrington was 3,000; 35 years later Great Barrington's second-home population was nearly 9,000.
- Great Barrington had the enviable combination of scenic beauty, sophistication and trendy fashion.
- It was also home to a wide variety of food, from organic farm markets to fine dining that rivaled the best Manhattan restaurants.
- Still, Al complained that he couldn't find "good, Italian food."
- Menus were too creative and portions too small for his taste.
- When he won the lottery, he would open an Italian restaurant and pool hall in town.
- The Berkshires also offered a variety of education choices, from progressive nursery schools and private prep schools to award-winning public schools.

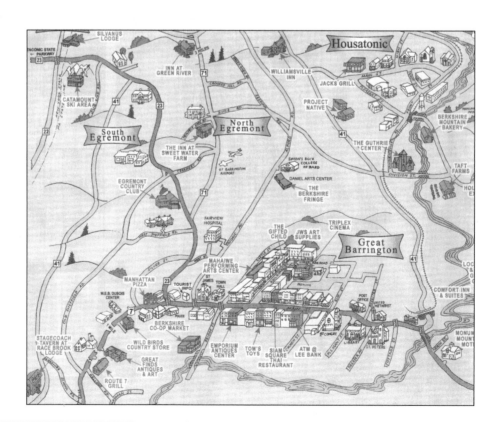

HISTORICAL SNAPSHOT
2009

- Barack Obama was inaugurated as the forty-fourth president of the United States, the first African American to hold the office

- U.S. Airways Flight 1549 made an emergency landing in the Hudson River after colliding with a flock of Canadian geese, with everyone on board saved due to the efforts of Captain Chesley "Sully" Sullenberger, the co-pilot and crew

- North Korea announced a successful nuclear test in North Hamgyong

- The H1N1 Virus, also known as swine flu, was classified as a pandemic

- President Obama, in support of women's rights, signed an equal pay law as his first piece of legislation

- Iran's presidential election triggered accusations of election rigging that resulted in weeks of violent protests which the Iranian Government quickly suppressed

- Michael Jackson died under suspicious circumstances; his death was later ruled a homicide

- Supreme Court Justice Sonia Sotomayor, the first Latina to serve on the Court, was confirmed

- NASA launched the Kepler Spacecraft to find Earth-size planets in the habitable zones of stars

- The International Criminal Court issued a warrant for the arrest of Omar Hassan al-Bashir, president of Sudan, for crimes against humanity and war crimes in the Darfur region

- Former President Bill Clinton went to North Korea to save two American journalists Laura Ling and Euna Lee, after they had been sentenced to 12 years' hard labor for "committing hostilities against the Korean nation and illegal entry"

- President Obama signed an order to close Guantanamo Bay Prison within a year

- Servicing Mission 4 (SM4) to repair the Hubble Space Telescope was completed

- Albania and Croatia joined NATO

- Johanna Siguroardottir became the prime minister of Iceland and the first openly lesbian head of a government

- President Obama committed himself to passing comprehensive health care reform in his first year to ensure high-quality, affordable health care for all Americans

- President Obama won the Nobel Peace Prize

- Elinor Ostrom, an Indiana University professor, was the co-winner of the Nobel Prize in Economics and the first woman to win the award

Selected Prices

Beer, Budweiser 12-Pack $8.99
Fireplace Gas Logs $399.00
Lawn Mower $219.00
Microwave $64.99
Pool Ball Set $57.00
Pool Cue $100.00
Pool Table $1,899.00
Recliner $799.00
Scooter $79.97
Vitamins, Centrum, 130 .... $7.99

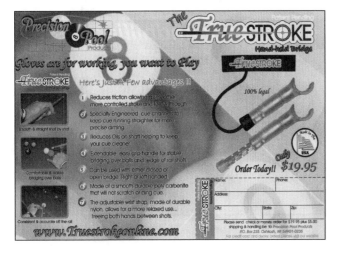

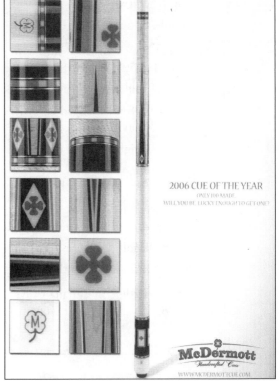

Glossary of Pool Terms

Action: Playing pool for money.

Angled: When the corner of a pocket prevents a player shooting the cue ball directly at an object ball.

Angled Shot: A shot that requires the cue ball to drive the object ball at an angle rather than straight ahead.

Apex of Triangle: The position in the grouping of object balls that is on the *foot spot,* the front ball position of the *pyramid* or *rack.*

Bad Hit: Hitting the wrong ball, also considered an illegal hit.

Ball in Hand: After an opponent's bad hit, being allowed to put the cue ball anywhere on the table.

Bank Pool: A game where a pocket must be designated, and all scored balls must rebound off one or more cushions before being pocketed.

Billiard: When the cue ball contacts an object ball and goes on to contact a second object ball, also known as carom.

Break: The initial shot of a pool game, when the cue ball separates the rack of object balls.

Bridge: The stick used to extend a player's reach, usually located underneath the rails on either side of the pool table.

Bridge Hand: The hand that is placed on the table to support the shaft of the cue stick.

Bye: A situation in which a tournament player has no opponent in a preliminary match.

Calcutta: A separate prize fund during tournaments that is created by selling pool players through an auction to tournament spectators who win money on their winning players.

Call: A situation in which a ball is given to a player with a condition that the player must declare when and where he or she is playing that particular ball.

Closed Bridge: When the forefinger and thumb enclose the shaft of a cue stick.

Combination: When two or more object balls are involved in pocketing the last ball in that sequence.

Cosmo: A simple layout of balls for an easy run with easy position play throughout.

Dab it: Playing pool with a high degree of excellence.

Diamonds: Inlaid spots that are positioned symmetrically on the rails of a pool table to serve as a guide for players to adjust to different table conditions.

Draw Shot: When the cue ball backs up from the ball it hits.

Duck: A defensive play.

English: The left or right spin that's applied to the cue ball.

Flow Chart: A listing of tournament players, their opponents, scores, payouts, time of their next match, and table assignments.

Foot Spot: A quarter-sized circular patch adhered to the cloth on a pool table where the front ball sits when the balls are racked.

Foul: Something illegal in the game, such as scratching, moving a ball, hitting the wrong ball, etc.

Goalie: A player who doesn't score, or tries to prevent others from scoring.

Hanger: An easy, tap-in shot.

continued

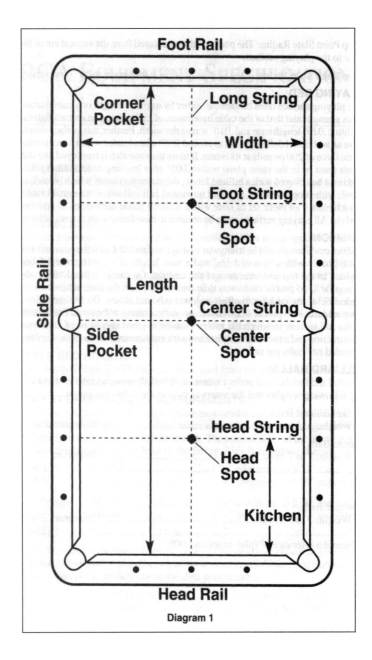

Diagram 1

Glossary of Pool Terms *(continued)*

Head Stringhead Spot: The line or spot on the breaking end of the pool table, behind which is called the kitchen.

Hooked: Having no clear path from the cue ball to the object ball to be hit.

Hot Seat: Being the undefeated player remaining in a double elimination tournament, waiting to play the winner of the loser's bracket to determine the champion.

Jelly Roll: To give someone out of the action (money) a percentage of your action.

Juiced Table: A table with an embedded wire designed to pull off-track a magnetized ball (usually the cue ball).

Kick Shot: Hitting one or more cushions with the cue ball before contacting a desired object ball.

Lady's Aide: The wooden bridge that supports the shaft of a cue stick, and allows a woman—or a short man—to shoot long, stretch shots.

Lock Down: A situation in which an opponent can't possibly win.

Masse: Extreme English created by a downward stroke into the cue ball, which causes it to sharply curve.

Miscue: A bad stroke that causes the tip of the cue stick to slip off the side of the cue ball.

Oil: An offensive shot that leaves an opponent with no shot.

On the Hill: Being within one game of winning a match, or within one ball of winning a game.

On the Wire: Spotting a player a certain number of games to his or her credit before the match begins.

Open Bridge: When the cue stick is supported by an open, flat bridge hand.

Orange Crush: To spot someone the 5-ball (orange) and the break (crush).

Out of the Air: Playing one-handed, and not being allowed to rest the shaft of the cue stick on anything.

Pinch: Shooting a shot with a slight angle to the pocket, twisting the object ball into the pocket by applying English on the cue ball.

Pocket Billiards: A slang term for pool; since the cue ball is not intentionally played to carom (or billiard) off an object ball into a pocket, technically, there is no such game as pocket billiards.

Position: When one pockets a ball and controls the cue ball to be in the desired location for the next shot.

Race: A designated number of games to win, as in a race to nine.

Rags: The cloth of the rail or cushion.

Rake: Another term for Bridge, Crutch, or Lady's Aide.

Rail: The outermost portion of a pool table.

Regulation Table: Before World War II, most pool tables in Northern states were 5′ × 10′ and in Southern states 4′ × 8′. After the war a compromise settled the size of table used for championships: 4.5′ × 9′ tables. By true definition, a regulation table is any table, regardless of size, that is twice as long as it is wide.

Road Rack: Leaving spaces between balls in a rack so as to prevent an opponent from making a ball on the break.

Rolling the Cheese: A desperate attempt to pocket the 9-ball by blasting it around the table, hoping that it will drop into a pocket.

continued

Glossary of Pool Terms *(continued)*

Roll Out/Push Out: When a player pushes or rolls the cue ball anywhere on the table, giving the opponent the option of passing the shot back or attempting to execute a legal shot; this is only an option on the first shot after the break.

Scratch: When the cue ball goes into a pocket.

Set: A certain number of games a player must gain ahead of the opponent.

Shark: One who interferes with a player's performance with unexpected movements, noise or psychological manipulation.

Shortstop: A good shooter whose skill level is below that of a top player.

Snap: The break shot.

Snooker: To position the cue ball behind an object ball that blocks the path of the shot.

Spot: A handicap given to a player, or a specific spot on a pool table.

Stall: Slowing down the pace of the game enough to cool off a hot opponent.

Stiff: To make the cue ball stop on a shot that has a slight angle, or to shorten the angle of a bank shot with English.

Straight Pool: Played with 15 balls and technically called 14.1 Continuous Straight Pool, it is played by shooting 14 balls off the table, which are then racked without the remaining ball, allowing continuous play.

The Draw: A drawing of numbers that occurs before a tournament begins to determine the order of players listed on a flow chart and their opponents.

The Line: The line between the middle diamonds on the breaking end of the pool table, covering one quarter of the playing surface, also known as the kitchen.

Throw: The effect caused by friction between two dry balls in a close combination shot.

Traffic: The object balls that a cue ball must travel through for position on the next ball.

Tuck and Roll: Body English, or a swing of the cue stick in the direction of the side spin that's applied to the cue ball.

Wild: Winning the game by pocketing the 8-ball and 9-ball at the same time.

Wrinkle: A stroke that produces a slight curve in the path of the cue ball.

"Archer's Arrow Falls True at Glass City Open,"
Pool & Billiard Magazine, January 2006:

Tom Gearhart and Tom Elder celebrated their fourth successful year running the Glass City Open, and as a longstanding event with men who love pool behind it, we can all hope for 40 more!

Eighty-eight players filed in this year including defending champion Charlie Bryant, but a loss at the hands of local fan favorite, Dan Wardrop, sent him quickly to the one loss side.

By Friday, fans had their eyes on Filipino Al Lapena, who defeated Corey Deuel in a hill-hill thriller, followed by a big win over Danny Basavich, 10-5.

But Lapena fell to the sharp-shooting talents of Earl "The Pearl" Strickland, a former Glass City Open champion who was fast looking like a favorite to win after defeating both Lapena and arch-nemesis Johnny Archer. Strickland, sponsored by Cuetec Cues, was the first to the point and a guaranteed spot in the final battle. He defeated Steve McAninch to get there, then sat waiting as things played themselves out on the one loss side.

Johnny Archer, sponsored by Cuestix International, might have suffered a battle wound at the hands of the Pearl, but it wasn't fatal. He fought through Mark Jarvis, Danny Basavich, Brandon Ashcroft, Shawn Putnam and McAninch to earn a Strickland rematch.

The finals were everything you go to a pool tournament to see! Two amazing players duking it out for cash and bragging rights. They kept it close throughout the match until Archer finally made his move. With the score tied six games apiece, Johnny, the "Scorpion" wiggled up to an 8-6 lead.

Earl fought back to 8-7. Archer reached the hill first to lead 9-7. Earl again closed the gap to 9-8. Archer played a brilliant rack that began with a bank combo (1 to the 4), Left tough on the one ball, he sliced it in to get in line for the two.

Earl must have seen his own fate as he rose from his chair to rake in the remaining balls and concede the game/match/set to a jubilant Johnny.

U.S. vs. WORLD: 1-5

With giant fields from all over the planet, the annual World Pool Championship 9-ball event may be the most accurate gauge of national performance. Here's how the U.S. has fared since 2000, including Americans who reached the top 8.

YEAR	WINNER	U.S. IN TOP 8
2000	Fong-Pang Chao (Taiwan)	2 (Cory Deuel and Earl Strickland, T-3rd)
2001	Mika Immonen (Finland)	1 (Jeremy Jones, T-5th)
2002	Earl Strickland (USA)	2 (Strickland; Johnny Archer, T-5th)
2003	Thorsten Hohmann (Germany)	1 (Earl Strickland, T-3rd)
2004	Alex Pagulayan (Philippines)	1 (Johnny Archer, T-5th)
2005	Chia-Ching Wu (Taiwan)	1 (Rodney Morris, T-3rd)

"APA Members Take Home $300,000 at National Singles Championship," *InsidePOOL Magazine*, July/August 2006:

Over $300,000 in cash and prizes went to American Poolplayers Association (APA) members at the APA National Singles Championships, held April 27-29 in Las Vegas, NV, at the Riviera Hotel & Casino. The National Singles Championships consisted of both the 8-Ball Classic and 9-Ball Shootout Singles Championships, and both events were sponsored by Cuetec Cues, Valley Tables, Valley Ultra Teflon Cloth, and Aramith Billiard Balls. The final round of the 9-Ball Shootout featured three championship matches, one for each skill level tier, with two shooters in each match competing for $10,000 in cash and prizes.

In the Green Tier (Skill Levels 1-3), Andrea De Rossett of Woodstock, GA, defeated Brian Gannon of Bayonne, NJ. De Rossett advanced to the finals after a semifinal-round victory over Melissa Casanova of Winter Park, FL, while Gannon advanced after defeating Curtis Dixon of Oklahoma City, OK.

Following her victory, De Rossett was at a loss for words. "This has just been such a highlight to a great weekend—thanks to the APA for putting on such a spectacular event!" De Rossett exclaimed.

After besting Monica Clark in the semifinal round, Lee Cox of Richmond, VA, bested Jameson Newton of Largo, FL, 38-20 in the finals of the White Tier (Skill Levels 4-5) for the championship. Newton advanced to the finals by defeating Angela Flores of Norcross, GA.

"I didn't come here expecting to win it all, but I felt I had as good a shot as anybody," said an elated Cox after the match.

The finals of the Black Tier (Skill Levels 6- 9) featured defending champion Brian Parks of Bakersfield, CA, against Gary Wheeler of Apache Junction, AZ, and Parks was able to keep his title another year by winning over Wheeler 75-45. Wheeler advanced to the finals after defeating Robert Stiles of Marietta, GA, in the semifinals, while Parks advanced after a victory over Edward Marriott Jr. of Rock Hill, SC, in the semifinal match of the Black Tier.

Reprinted with permission.

continued

"APA Members Take Home $300,000 at National Singles Championship," ... *(continued)*

After the win, Parks said the key to defending his title was patience. "I got behind early on in the match, but I was able to keep my composure, wait for my chance . . . and I came back," stated Parks.

Each of the three champions received a prize package worth $10,000. The runners-up in each of the three tiers took home a prize package worth $5,000.

Over 12,000 amateur shooters attempted to qualify for the 2006 APA 9-Ball Shootout Singles Championship in their local league area, and more than 1,900 pool players made it to the regional level of the 9-Ball Shootout before the field was whittled down to 136 men and women competing for 9-ball crowns in each of three skill level tiers.

More than 40,000 shooters attempted to qualify for the 2006 8-Ball Classic. Over 5,000 pool players made it to the regional level before the field was narrowed to 364 men and women competing for 8-ball crowns in each of three skill level tiers.

In the finals of the 8-Ball Classic, three champions each took home a prize package worth $15,000 for their performances.

In the Blue Tier (Skill Levels 2-3) of the 8-Ball Classic, it was Ron Shippert of Las Vegas, NV, defeating Frank Titus-Rogan of Springfield, VA, 3-2 in the final match. Shippert defeated Crystal Hefferman of Cocoa, FL, in the semifinals to advance, while Titus-Rogan defeated Dennis Larson of Loranger, LA.

"This is just incredible," exclaimed Shippert. "I played smart and played good defense, and that made the difference."

The finals of the Yellow Tier (Skill Levels 4-5) saw Armando Leal of Live Oak, TX, defeat Brian Holgate of Camby, OR, 4-0 in the finals. Leal advanced to the finals by defeating William Grubbs of Bluff City, TN, earlier in the day in the semifinal round, and Holgate defeated George Van Zandt of Metairie, LA, in the semifinals.

continued

"APA Members Take Home $300,000 at National Singles Championship," . . . (continued)

"I was happy just to qualify [for the National Singles Championships]. This was my first time out here, so it was an experience in itself. Winning it all was just over the top," said Leal with excitement after his win.

The finals of the Purple Tier (Skill Levels 6-7) pitted former U.S. Amateur Champion Robert Hall of Huntsville, AL, against William "B.J." Hastings of Pasadena, MD. Hall bested Hastings in the finals 5-1, having defeated Dave Dreidel of Utica, NY, in the semifinal round. Hastings advanced after defeating Melinda Huang of Los Angeles.

"It just feels great. It really capped off my goals as an APA member of winning the U.S. Amateur Championship and now this," said Hall.

First-place champions in each of the three tiers received cash and prizes worth $15,000. The runners-up in each of the three tiers received cash and prizes worth $9,000.

In conjunction with the National Singles Championships, APA conducted the annual Jack & Jill Doubles Championship in the MiniMania Tournament Room. Champions Larry and Lisa Overstake of Fayetteville, OH, defeated Mike Jones and Chrissi Moore of Mobile, AL, capturing the first-place title. The Overstakes took home a $5,000 cash prize, and runners-up Jones and Moore took home a $3,000 cash prize.

Sportsmanship awards were presented to Meghan Barrette of Chapel Hill, NC, and Kim Steinle of Mansfield, TX, for their outstanding conduct throughout their matches in the 9-Ball Shootout and 8-Ball Classic, respectively.

2005 NEWS FEATURE

"Casting Cull, Examining the Process Used to Spot Potential Superstars," Mike Hembree, *NASCAR Illustrated*, April 2005:

Somewhere across these United States, there is a great racecar driver waiting to be discovered. With weekly short track dotting the landscape from big cities to off-the-beaten-path hamlets, drivers who might have the right stuff are being trained in every corner of the country.

It is a statistical fact, however, that only a handful of the thousands who might have potential will make it to Nextel Cup, to the big show. With only 43 spots available in every Cup starting grid (and a few dozen others to be filled in NASCAR's other major series), the chances of any given driver who happens to have a reputation as Johnny Runfast at the local track making it to the Daytona 500 are very slim, at best.

Still, many of the best seemed to move through the system and eventually get a realistic shot at the big time. How does that happen? How do team owners and managers find the needles in a haystack? How does Driver A get from Podunk to Pocono?

There is no standard answer, but one thing seems to be of utmost importance in the process: Drivers hoping to land in the Nextel Cup should try to keep their names in print and in general conversation wherever racers gather.

The process is more structured in other professional sports. Drafts define the order in which teams select new players. In NASCAR, the field is wide open to harvest. Everybody's eligible. Although participants must be at least 18 years old to drive in NASCAR's leading series, drivers much younger can be signed to contracts and placed in development roles, a practice that has become almost standard in big-time stock car racing.

Short of sitting beside the cradle when parents named Andretti or Wallace bring home Baby from the hospital, how do team owners identify the potentially gifted? In baseball, grizzled old scouts with well-worn caps and cigar ashes falling between their teeth roam the countryside with radar guns and practiced eyes, sitting at American Legion games in high school playoffs in search of the Next Great Name. There is no equivalent to the baseball scout in racing. Instead, it's more about group enterprise.

Todd Kluever of Wisconsin survived a 400-resume competition at Roush Racing to win a ride in a Roush Craftsman truck this year.

"I really don't know how they got my name," Kluever says. "I was driving Late Models back home for (team owner) Gerry Gunderman. Mark Martin, Jimmy Fennig, Matt Kenseth—they all know him. I got a call from Gunderman, and he said he'd just gotten off the phone with a lady from Roush Racing who was asking a lot of questions about me."

That lady was Stephanie Smith, who was among the Roush officials working on the driver search.

"I called her, and she said they had heard things about me and wanted to see my resume," Kluever says. "I sent it. A couple days later, they called and said they wanted me to attend a test at North Wilkesboro."

Kluever was one of two dozen drivers picked from the group of 400 resumes to test at North Wilkesboro Speedway, a North Carolina short track that was part of the Cup series for many years. The top 10 drivers from that test advanced to Darlington Raceway in South Carolina for round two of what team owner Jack Roush calls the Gong Show. Kluever was the winner or, as he puts it, the survivor.

"Todd had a higher hurdle than anybody who's come to our program," Roush says. "There was more scrutiny to pass. The deal for the Gong Show last year was to consider resumes with at least three different recommendations from people we thought were credible—track owners, other drivers whom we respect, media people. We had 400 credible resumes.

"When we got it down to 10 at Darlington, there probably were at least eight you couldn't say no to. But Todd stood the straightest and the tallest."

Jack Bickford perhaps created the template for pairing the young driver for profitable future in motorsports. Stepfather of four-time Cup series champion Jeff Gordon, Bickford put together a grand plan during Gordon's preschool years to give him the best possible shot at being a successful racer. It's not surprising that Bickford receives more than the occasional phone calls about the process.

"It's the subtle little things that work together," Bickford says. "There's not a true scouting system out there, but people have confidence in other people. Rick Hendrick asks me questions about the development of kids. Over the years Richard Childress has said, 'John if you could find me someone who has had Earnhardt drive. . . .' It's all about word-of-mouth.

"In 2000 Ray Evernham and I drove down to Daytona. We said, 'Let's go to the sprint car races.' We show up at Volusia County Speedway (near Daytona Beach) and there's Kasey Kahne getting ready to qualify. I pointed to Ray and said, 'Watch him drive this car.' So Kasey gets the quick time. I said, 'Watch him. You'll be racing against him if you don't have him racing for you.'"

Kahne won rookie of the year honors for Evernham last year and is considered one of NASCAR's brightest rising stars.

One of the most experienced driver search individuals in NASCAR is Ganassi Racing team manager Lorin Ranier, whose father, Harry, was the original owner of the team that is now Robert Yates Racing. Lorin, now in charge of finding hot young drivers for Ganassi, brought future champion Tony Stewart from sprint cars and open wheel racing into the NASCAR fold.

"I've been around for so long I've kind of developed an eye for it," Ranier says. "It's easy to separate the really, really good ones from the good ones. There are guys that are good and guys that are really good. The ones who are really good—there's such a small number.

"It's that way in any sport. Look at the NBA. All those players were really great when they were kids. But there is a select few—Magic, Jordan, Shaq—who are just world-class. That's all we're trying to find, and they're not all going to be that. But we want the ones we pick to have the potential to be that."

Where does Ranier look? He doesn't spend his weekend on the short track circuit.

"I do a lot of research on the Internet," he says. "I watch all the (television) racing shows. I see who's doing what. I follow the feeder series. Enough is good to be good. You know who's going to be good. When I brought Tony Stewart down here, I said, 'I can't believe there aren't 20 owners trying to hire this guy.'"

INDEX

Italic page numbers indicate images. **Bold** page numbers indicate profile subjects.

Italic page numbers indicate images. **Bold** page numbers indicate profile subjects.

Italic page numbers indicate images. **Bold** page numbers indicate profile subjects.

Italic page numbers indicate images. **Bold** page numbers indicate profile subjects.

Italic page numbers indicate images. **Bold** page numbers indicate profile subjects.

Italic page numbers indicate images. **Bold** page numbers indicate profile subjects.

Italic page numbers indicate images. **Bold** page numbers indicate profile subjects.

Italic page numbers indicate images. **Bold** page numbers indicate profile subjects.

Italic page numbers indicate images. **Bold** page numbers indicate profile subjects.

Italic page numbers indicate images. **Bold** page numbers indicate profile subjects.

Italic page numbers indicate images. **Bold** page numbers indicate profile subjects.

Italic page numbers indicate images. **Bold** page numbers indicate profile subjects.

Grey House Publishing gratefully acknowledges the following books and periodicals
for use of the excerpts and articles reprinted in this edition.

Business Information ◆ Ratings Guides ◆ General Reference ◆ Education ◆
Statistics ◆ Demographics ◆ Health Information ◆ Canadian Information

Grey House
Publishing

The Directory of Business Information Resources, 2009

With 100% verification, over 1,000 new listings and more than 12,000 updates, *The Directory of Business Information Resources* is the most up-to-date source for contacts in over 98 business areas – from advertising and agriculture to utilities and wholesalers. This carefully researched volume details: the Associations representing each industry; the Newsletters that keep members current; the Magazines and Journals - with their "Special Issues" - that are important to the trade, the Conventions that are "must attends," Databases, Directories and Industry Web Sites that provide access to must-have marketing resources. Includes contact names, phone & fax numbers, web sites and e-mail addresses. This one-volume resource is a gold mine of information and would be a welcome addition to any reference collection.

"This is a most useful and easy-to-use addition to any researcher's library." –The Information Professionals Institute

Softcover ISBN 978-1-59237-399-4, 2,500 pages, $195.00 | Online Database: http://gold.greyhouse.com Call (800) 562-2139 for quote

Hudson's Washington News Media Contacts Directory, 2009

With 100% verification of data, *Hudson's Washington News Media Contacts Directory* is the most accurate, most up-to-date source for media contacts in our nation's capital. With the largest concentration of news media in the world, having access to Washington's news media will get your message heard by these key media outlets. Published for over 40 years, Hudson's Washington News Media Contacts Directory brings you immediate access to: News Services & Newspapers, News Service Syndicates, DC Newspapers, Foreign Newspapers, Radio & TV, Magazines & Newsletters, and Freelance Writers & Photographers. The easy-to-read entries include contact names, phone & fax numbers, web sites and e-mail and more. For easy navigation, Hudson's Washington News Media Contacts Directory contains two indexes: Entry Index and Executive Index. This kind of comprehensive and up-to-date information would cost thousands of dollars to replicate or countless hours of searching to find. Don't miss this opportunity to have this important resource in your collection, and start saving time and money today. Hudson's Washington News Media Contacts Directory is the perfect research tool for Public Relations, Marketing, Networking and so much more. This resource is a gold mine of information and would be a welcome addition to any reference collection.

Softcover ISBN 978-1-59237-407-6, 800 pages, $289.00 | Online Database: http://gold.greyhouse.com Call (800) 562-2139 for quote

Nations of the World, 2009 A Political, Economic and Business Handbook

This completely revised edition covers all the nations of the world in an easy-to-use, single volume. Each nation is profiled in a single chapter that includes Key Facts, Political & Economic Issues, a Country Profile and Business Information. In this fast-changing world, it is extremely important to make sure that the most up-to-date information is included in your reference collection. This edition is just the answer. Each of the 200+ country chapters have been carefully reviewed by a political expert to make sure that the text reflects the most current information on Politics, Travel Advisories, Economics and more. You'll find such vital information as a Country Map, Population Characteristics, Inflation, Agricultural Production, Foreign Debt, Political History, Foreign Policy, Regional Insecurity, Economics, Trade & Tourism, Historical Profile, Political Systems, Ethnicity, Languages, Media, Climate, Hotels, Chambers of Commerce, Banking, Travel Information and more. Five Regional Chapters follow the main text and include a Regional Map, an Introductory Article, Key Indicators and Currencies for the Region. As an added bonus, an all-inclusive CD-ROM is available as a companion to the printed text. Noted for its sophisticated, up-to-date and reliable compilation of political, economic and business information, this brand new edition will be an important acquisition to any public, academic or special library reference collection.

"A useful addition to both general reference collections and business collections." –RUSQ

Softcover ISBN 978-1-59237-273-7, 1,700 pages, $175.00

The Directory of Venture Capital & Private Equity Firms, 2009

This edition has been extensively updated and broadly expanded to offer direct access to over 2,800 Domestic and International Venture Capital Firms, including address, phone & fax numbers, e-mail addresses and web sites for both primary and branch locations. Entries include details on the firm's Mission Statement, Industry Group Preferences, Geographic Preferences, Average and Minimum Investments and Investment Criteria. You'll also find details that are available nowhere else, including the Firm's Portfolio Companies and extensive information on each of the firm's Managing Partners, such as Education, Professional Background and Directorships held, along with the Partner's E-mail Address. *The Directory of Venture Capital & Private Equity Firms* offers five important indexes: Geographic Index, Executive Name Index, Portfolio Company Index, Industry Preference Index and College & University Index. With its comprehensive coverage and detailed, extensive information on each company, The Directory of Venture Capital & Private Equity Firms is an important addition to any finance collection.

"The sheer number of listings, the descriptive information and the outstanding indexing make this directory a better value than …Pratt's Guide to Venture Capital Sources. Recommended for business collections in large public, academic and business libraries." –Choice

Softcover ISBN 978-1-59237-398-7, 1,300 pages, $565/$450 Lib | Online DB: http://gold.greyhouse.com Call (800) 562-2139 for quote

---

Business Information ◆ Ratings Guides ◆ General Reference ◆ Education ◆
Statistics ◆ Demographics ◆ Health Information ◆ Canadian Information

The Encyclopedia of Emerging Industries

*Published under an exclusive license from the Gale Group, Inc.

The fifth edition of the *Encyclopedia of Emerging Industries* details the inception, emergence, and current status of nearly 120 flourishing U.S. industries and industry segments. These focused essays unearth for users a wealth of relevant, current, factual data previously accessible only through a diverse variety of sources. This volume provides broad-based, highly-readable, industry information under such headings as Industry Snapshot, Organization & Structure, Background & Development, Industry Leaders, Current Conditions, America and the World, Pioneers, and Research & Technology. Essays in this new edition, arranged alphabetically for easy use, have been completely revised, with updated statistics and the most current information on industry trends and developments. In addition, there are new essays on some of the most interesting and influential new business fields, including Application Service Providers, Concierge Services, Entrepreneurial Training, Fuel Cells, Logistics Outsourcing Services, Pharmacogenomics, and Tissue Engineering. Two indexes, General and Industry, provide immediate access to this wealth of information. Plus, two conversion tables for SIC and NAICS codes, along with Suggested Further Readings, are provided to aid the user. *The Encyclopedia of Emerging Industries* pinpoints emerging industries while they are still in the spotlight. This important resource will be an important acquisition to any business reference collection.

"This well-designed source…should become another standard business source, nicely complementing Standard & Poor's Industry Surveys. It contains more information on each industry than Hoover's Handbook of Emerging Companies, is broader in scope than The Almanac of American Employers 1998-1999, but is less expansive than the Encyclopedia of Careers & Vocational Guidance. Highly recommended for all academic libraries and specialized business collections." –Library Journal

Hardcover ISBN 978-1-59237-242-3, 1,400 pages, $325.00

Encyclopedia of American Industries

*Published under an exclusive license from the Gale Group, Inc.

The Encyclopedia of American Industries is a major business reference tool that provides detailed, comprehensive information on a wide range of industries in every realm of American business. A two volume set, Volume I provides separate coverage of nearly 500 manufacturing industries, while Volume II presents nearly 600 essays covering the vast array of services and other non-manufacturing industries in the United States. Combined, these two volumes provide individual essays on every industry recognized by the U.S. Standard Industrial Classification (SIC) system. Both volumes are arranged numerically by SIC code, for easy use. Additionally, each entry includes the corresponding NAICS code(s). The *Encyclopedia's* business coverage includes information on historical events of consequence, as well as current trends and statistics. Essays include an Industry Snapshot, Organization & Structure, Background & Development, Current Conditions, Industry Leaders, Workforce, America and the World, Research & Technology along with Suggested Further Readings. Both SIC and NAICS code conversion tables and an all-encompassing Subject Index, with cross-references, complete the text. With its detailed, comprehensive information on a wide range of industries, this resource will be an important tool for both the industry newcomer and the seasoned professional.

"Encyclopedia of American Industries contains detailed, signed essays on virtually every industry in contemporary society. ... Highly recommended for all but the smallest libraries." -American Reference Books Annual

Two Volumes, Hardcover ISBN 978-1-59237-244-7, 3,000 pages, $650.00

Encyclopedia of Global Industries

*Published under an exclusive license from the Gale Group, Inc.

This fourth edition of the acclaimed *Encyclopedia of Global Industries* presents a thoroughly revised and expanded look at more than 125 business sectors of global significance. Detailed, insightful articles discuss the origins, development, trends, key statistics and current international character of the world's most lucrative, dynamic and widely researched industries – including hundreds of profiles of leading international corporations. Beginning researchers will gain from this book a solid understanding of how each industry operates and which countries and companies are significant participants, while experienced researchers will glean current and historical figures for comparison and analysis. The industries profiled in previous editions have been updated, and in some cases, expanded to reflect recent industry trends. Additionally, this edition provides both SIC and NAICS codes for all industries profiled. As in the original volumes, *The Encyclopedia of Global Industries* offers thorough studies of some of the biggest and most frequently researched industry sectors, including Aircraft, Biotechnology, Computers, Internet Services, Motor Vehicles, Pharmaceuticals, Semiconductors, Software and Telecommunications. An SIC and NAICS conversion table and an all-encompassing Subject Index, with cross-references, are provided to ensure easy access to this wealth of information. These and many others make the *Encyclopedia of Global Industries* the authoritative reference for studies of international industries.

"Provides detailed coverage of the history, development, and current status of 115 of "the world's most lucrative and high-profile industries." It far surpasses the Department of Commerce's U.S. Global Trade Outlook 1995-2000 (GPO, 1995) in scope and coverage. Recommended for comprehensive public and academic library business collections." -Booklist

Hardcover ISBN 978-1-59237-243-0, 1,400 pages, $495.00

Business Information ◆ Ratings Guides ◆ General Reference ◆ Education ◆
Statistics ◆ Demographics ◆ Health Information ◆ Canadian Information

Grey House
Publishing

The Directory of Mail Order Catalogs, 2009

Published since 1981, *The Directory of Mail Order Catalogs* is the premier source of information on the mail order catalog industry. It is the source that business professionals and librarians have come to rely on for the thousands of catalog companies in the US. Since the 2007 edition, *The Directory of Mail Order Catalogs* has been combined with its companion volume, *The Directory of Business to Business Catalogs*, to offer all 13,000 catalog companies in one easy-to-use volume. Section I: Consumer Catalogs, covers over 9,000 consumer catalog companies in 44 different product chapters from Animals to Toys & Games. Section II: Business to Business Catalogs, details 5,000 business catalogs, everything from computers to laboratory supplies, building construction and much more. Listings contain detailed contact information including mailing address, phone & fax numbers, web sites, e-mail addresses and key contacts along with important business details such as product descriptions, employee size, years in business, sales volume, catalog size, number of catalogs mailed and more. *The Directory of Mail Order Catalogs*, now with its expanded business to business catalogs, is the largest and most comprehensive resource covering this billion-dollar industry. It is the standard in its field. This important resource is a useful tool for entrepreneurs searching for catalogs to pick up their product, vendors looking to expand their customer base in the catalog industry, market researchers, small businesses investigating new supply vendors, along with the library patron who is exploring the available catalogs in their areas of interest.

"This is a godsend for those looking for information." –Reference Book Review

Softcover ISBN 978-1-59237-396-3, 1,700 pages, $350/$250 Lib | Online DB: http://gold.greyhouse.com Call (800) 562-2139 for quote

Sports Market Place Directory, 2008

For over 20 years, this comprehensive, up-to-date directory has offered direct access to the Who, What, When & Where of the Sports Industry. With over 20,000 updates and enhancements, the *Sports Market Place Directory* is the most detailed, comprehensive and current sports business reference source available. In 1,800 information-packed pages, *Sports Market Place Directory* profiles contact information and key executives for: Single Sport Organizations, Professional Leagues, Multi-Sport Organizations, Disabled Sports, High School & Youth Sports, Military Sports, Olympic Organizations, Media, Sponsors, Sponsorship & Marketing Event Agencies, Event & Meeting Calendars, Professional Services, College Sports, Manufacturers & Retailers, Facilities and much more. The Sports Market Place Directory provides organization's contact information with detailed descriptions including: Key Contacts, physical, mailing, email and web addresses plus phone and fax numbers. *Sports Market Place Directory* provides a one-stop resources for this billion-dollar industry. This will be an important resource for large public libraries, university libraries, university athletic programs, career services or job placement organizations, and is a must for anyone doing research on or marketing to the US and Canadian sports industry.

"Grey House is the new publisher and has produced an excellent edition...highly recommended for public libraries and academic libraries with sports management programs or strong interest in athletics." -Booklist

Softcover ISBN 978-1-59237-348-2, 1,800 pages, $225.00 | Online Database: http://gold.greyhouse.com Call (800) 562-2139 for quote

Food and Beverage Market Place, 2009

Food and Beverage Market Place is bigger and better than ever with thousands of new companies, thousands of updates to existing companies and two revised and enhanced product category indexes. This comprehensive directory profiles over 18,000 Food & Beverage Manufacturers, 12,000 Equipment & Supply Companies, 2,200 Transportation & Warehouse Companies, 2,000 Brokers & Wholesalers, 8,000 Importers & Exporters, 900 Industry Resources and hundreds of Mail Order Catalogs. Listings include detailed Contact Information, Sales Volumes, Key Contacts, Brand & Product Information, Packaging Details and much more. *Food and Beverage Market Place* is available as a three-volume printed set, a subscription-based Online Database via the Internet, on CD-ROM, as well as mailing lists and a licensable database.

"An essential purchase for those in the food industry but will also be useful in public libraries where needed. Much of the information will be difficult and time consuming to locate without this handy three-volume ready-reference source." –ARBA

3 Vol Set, Softcover ISBN 978-1-59237-361-1, 8,500 pages, $595 | Online DB: http://gold.greyhouse.com Call (800) 562-2139 for quote

The Grey House Performing Arts Directory, 2009

The Grey House Performing Arts Directory is the most comprehensive resource covering the Performing Arts. This important directory provides current information on over 8,500 Dance Companies, Instrumental Music Programs, Opera Companies, Choral Groups, Theater Companies, Performing Arts Series and Performing Arts Facilities. Plus, this edition now contains a brand new section on Artist Management Groups. In addition to mailing address, phone & fax numbers, e-mail addresses and web sites, dozens of other fields of available information include mission statement, key contacts, facilities, seating capacity, season, attendance and more. This directory also provides an important Information Resources section that covers hundreds of Performing Arts Associations, Magazines, Newsletters, Trade Shows, Directories, Databases and Industry Web Sites. Five indexes provide immediate access to this wealth of information: Entry Name, Executive Name, Performance Facilities, Geographic and Information Resources. *The Grey House Performing Arts Directory* pulls together thousands of Performing Arts Organizations, Facilities and Information Resources into an easy-to-use source – this kind of comprehensiveness and extensive detail is not available in any resource on the market place today.

"Immensely useful and user-friendly ... recommended for public, academic and certain special library reference collections." –Booklist

Softcover ISBN 978-1-59237-376-5, 1,500 pages, $185.00 | Online Database: http://gold.greyhouse.com Call (800) 562-2139 for quote

Business Information ♦ Ratings Guides ♦ General Reference ♦ Education ♦
Statistics ♦ Demographics ♦ Health Information ♦ Canadian Information

Grey House Publishing

The Environmental Resource Handbook, 2008/09

The Environmental Resource Handbook is the most up-to-date and comprehensive source for Environmental Resources and Statistics. Section I: Resources provides detailed contact information for thousands of information sources, including Associations & Organizations, Awards & Honors, Conferences, Foundations & Grants, Environmental Health, Government Agencies, National Parks & Wildlife Refuges, Publications, Research Centers, Educational Programs, Green Product Catalogs, Consultants and much more. Section II: Statistics, provides statistics and rankings on hundreds of important topics, including Children's Environmental Index, Municipal Finances, Toxic Chemicals, Recycling, Climate, Air & Water Quality and more. This kind of up-to-date environmental data, all in one place, is not available anywhere else on the market place today. This vast compilation of resources and statistics is a must-have for all public and academic libraries as well as any organization with a primary focus on the environment.

> *"...the intrinsic value of the information make it worth consideration by libraries with environmental collections and environmentally concerned users." –Booklist*

Softcover ISBN 978-1-59237-195-2, 1,000 pages, $155.00 | Online Database: http://gold.greyhouse.com Call (800) 562-2139 for quote

New York State Directory, 2008/09

The New York State Directory, published annually since 1983, is a comprehensive and easy-to-use guide to accessing public officials and private sector organizations and individuals who influence public policy in the state of New York. *The New York State Directory* includes important information on all New York state legislators and congressional representatives, including biographies and key committee assignments. It also includes staff rosters for all branches of New York state government and for federal agencies and departments that impact the state policy process. Following the state government section are 25 chapters covering policy areas from agriculture through veterans' affairs. Each chapter identifies the state, local and federal agencies and officials that formulate or implement policy. In addition, each chapter contains a roster of private sector experts and advocates who influence the policy process. The directory also offers appendices that include statewide party officials; chambers of commerce; lobbying organizations; public and private universities and colleges; television, radio and print media; and local government agencies and officials.

> *"This comprehensive directory covers not only New York State government offices and key personnel but pertinent U.S. government agencies and non-governmental entities. This directory is all encompassing... recommended." -Choice*

New York State Directory - Softcover ISBN 978-1-59237-358-1, 800 pages, $145.00
Online Database: http://gold.greyhouse.com Call (800) 562-2139 for quote
New York State Directory with *Profiles of New York* – 2 Volumes, Softcover ISBN 978-1-59237-359-8, 1,600 pages, $225.00

The Grey House Homeland Security Directory, 2008

This updated edition features the latest contact information for government and private organizations involved with Homeland Security along with the latest product information and provides detailed profiles of nearly 1,000 Federal & State Organizations & Agencies and over 3,000 Officials and Key Executives involved with Homeland Security. These listings are incredibly detailed and include Mailing Address, Phone & Fax Numbers, Email Addresses & Web Sites, a complete Description of the Agency and a complete list of the Officials and Key Executives associated with the Agency. Next, *The Grey House Homeland Security Directory* provides the go-to source for Homeland Security Products & Services. This section features over 2,000 Companies that provide Consulting, Products or Services. With this Buyer's Guide at their fingertips, users can locate suppliers of everything from Training Materials to Access Controls, from Perimeter Security to BioTerrorism Countermeasures and everything in between – complete with contact information and product descriptions. A handy Product Locator Index is provided to quickly and easily locate suppliers of a particular product. This comprehensive, information-packed resource will be a welcome tool for any company or agency that is in need of Homeland Security information and will be a necessary acquisition for the reference collection of all public libraries and large school districts.

> *"Compiles this information in one place and is discerning in content. A useful purchase for public and academic libraries." –Booklist*

Softcover ISBN 978-1-59237-196-6, 800 pages, $195.00 | Online Database: http://gold.greyhouse.com Call (800) 562-2139 for quote

Business Information ♦ Ratings Guides ♦ General Reference ♦ Education ♦
Statistics ♦ Demographics ♦ Health Information ♦ Canadian Information

The Grey House Safety & Security Directory, 2009

The Grey House Safety & Security Directory is the most comprehensive reference tool and buyer's guide for the safety and security industry. Arranged by safety topic, each chapter begins with OSHA regulations for the topic, followed by Training Articles written by top professionals in the field and Self-Inspection Checklists. Next, each topic contains Buyer's Guide sections that feature related products and services. Topics include Administration, Insurance, Loss Control & Consulting, Protective Equipment & Apparel, Noise & Vibration, Facilities Monitoring & Maintenance, Employee Health Maintenance & Ergonomics, Retail Food Services, Machine Guards, Process Guidelines & Tool Handling, Ordinary Materials Handling, Hazardous Materials Handling, Workplace Preparation & Maintenance, Electrical Lighting & Safety, Fire & Rescue and Security. Six important indexes make finding information and product manufacturers quick and easy: Geographical Index of Manufacturers and Distributors, Company Profile Index, Brand Name Index, Product Index, Index of Web Sites and Index of Advertisers. This comprehensive, up-to-date reference will provide every tool necessary to make sure a business is in compliance with OSHA regulations and locate the products and services needed to meet those regulations.

"Presents industrial safety information for engineers, plant managers, risk managers, and construction site supervisors..." –Choice

Softcover ISBN 978-1-59237-375-8, 1,500 pages, $165.00

The Grey House Transportation Security Directory & Handbook

This is the only reference of its kind that brings together current data on Transportation Security. With information on everything from Regulatory Authorities to Security Equipment, this top-flight database brings together the relevant information necessary for creating and maintaining a security plan for a wide range of transportation facilities. With this current, comprehensive directory at the ready you'll have immediate access to: Regulatory Authorities & Legislation; Information Resources; Sample Security Plans & Checklists; Contact Data for Major Airports, Seaports, Railroads, Trucking Companies and Oil Pipelines; Security Service Providers; Recommended Equipment & Product Information and more. Using the *Grey House Transportation Security Directory & Handbook*, managers will be able to quickly and easily assess their current security plans; develop contacts to create and maintain new security procedures; and source the products and services necessary to adequately maintain a secure environment. This valuable resource is a must for all Security Managers at Airports, Seaports, Railroads, Trucking Companies and Oil Pipelines.

"Highly recommended. Library collections that support all levels of readers, including professionals/practitioners; and schools/organizations offering education and training in transportation security." -Choice

Softcover ISBN 978-1-59237-075-7, 800 pages, $195.00

The Grey House Biometric Information Directory

This edition offers a complete, current overview of biometric companies and products – one of the fastest growing industries in today's economy. Detailed profiles of manufacturers of the latest biometric technology, including Finger, Voice, Face, Hand, Signature, Iris, Vein and Palm Identification systems. Data on the companies include key executives, company size and a detailed, indexed description of their product line. Information in the directory includes: Editorial on Advancements in Biometrics; Profiles of 700+ companies listed with contact information; Organizations, Trade & Educational Associations, Publications, Conferences, Trade Shows and Expositions Worldwide; Web Site Index; Biometric & Vendors Services Index by Types of Biometrics; and a Glossary of Biometric Terms. This resource will be an important source for anyone who is considering the use of a biometric product, investing in the development of biometric technology, support existing marketing and sales efforts and will be an important acquisition for the business reference collection for large public and business libraries.

"This book should prove useful to agencies or businesses seeking companies that deal with biometric technology. Summing Up: Recommended. Specialized collections serving researchers/faculty and professionals/practitioners." -Choice

Softcover ISBN 978-1-59237-121-1, 800 pages, $225.00

Business Information ✦ **Ratings Guides** ✦ **General Reference** ✦ **Education** ✦
Statistics ✦ **Demographics** ✦ **Health Information** ✦ **Canadian Information**

The Rauch Guide to the US Adhesives & Sealants, Cosmetics & Toiletries, Ink, Paint, Plastics, Pulp & Paper and Rubber Industries

The Rauch Guides save time and money by organizing widely scattered information and providing estimates for important business decisions, some of which are available nowhere else. Within each Guide, after a brief introduction, the ECONOMICS section provides data on industry shipments; long-term growth and forecasts; prices; company performance; employment, expenditures, and productivity; transportation and geographical patterns; packaging; foreign trade; and government regulations. Next, TECHNOLOGY & RAW MATERIALS provide market, technical, and raw material information for chemicals, equipment and related materials, including market size and leading suppliers, prices, end uses, and trends. PRODUCTS & MARKETS provide information for each major industry product, including market size and historical trends, leading suppliers, five-year forecasts, industry structure, and major end uses. Next, the COMPANY DIRECTORY profiles major industry companies, both public and private. Information includes complete contact information, web address, estimated total and domestic sales, product description, and recent mergers and acquisitions. *The Rauch Guides* will prove to be an invaluable source of market information, company data, trends and forecasts that anyone in these fast-paced industries.

"An invaluable and affordable publication. The comprehensive nature of the data and text offers considerable insights into the industry, market sizes, company activities, and applications of the products of the industry. The additions that have been made have certainly enhanced the value of the Guide." –Adhesives & Sealants Newsletter of the Rauch Guide to the US Adhesives & Sealants Industry

Paint Industry: Softcover ISBN 978-1-59237-127-3 $595 | Plastics Industry: Softcover ISBN 978-1-59237-128-0 $595 | Adhesives and Sealants Industry: Softcover ISBN 978-1-59237-129-7 $595 | Ink Industry: Softcover ISBN 978-1-59237-126-6 $595 | Rubber Industry: Softcover ISBN 978-1-59237-130-3 $595 | Pulp and Paper Industry: Softcover ISBN 978-1-59237-131-0 $595 | Cosmetic & Toiletries Industry: Softcover ISBN 978-1-59237-132-7 $895

Research Services Directory: Commercial & Corporate Research Centers

This ninth edition provides access to well over 8,000 independent Commercial Research Firms, Corporate Research Centers and Laboratories offering contract services for hands-on, basic or applied research. Research Services Directory covers the thousands of types of research companies, including Biotechnology & Pharmaceutical Developers, Consumer Product Research, Defense Contractors, Electronics & Software Engineers, Think Tanks, Forensic Investigators, Independent Commercial Laboratories, Information Brokers, Market & Survey Research Companies, Medical Diagnostic Facilities, Product Research & Development Firms and more. Each entry provides the company's name, mailing address, phone & fax numbers, key contacts, web site, e-mail address, as well as a company description and research and technical fields served. Four indexes provide immediate access to this wealth of information: Research Firms Index, Geographic Index, Personnel Name Index and Subject Index.

"An important source for organizations in need of information about laboratories, individuals and other facilities." –ARBA

Softcover ISBN 978-1-59237-003-0, 1,400 pages, $465.00

International Business and Trade Directories

Completely updated, the Third Edition of *International Business and Trade Directories* now contains more than 10,000 entries, over 2,000 more than the last edition, making this directory the most comprehensive resource of the worlds business and trade directories. Entries include content descriptions, price, publisher's name and address, web site and e-mail addresses, phone and fax numbers and editorial staff. Organized by industry group, and then by region, this resource puts over 10,000 industry-specific business and trade directories at the reader's fingertips. Three indexes are included for quick access to information: Geographic Index, Publisher Index and Title Index. Public, college and corporate libraries, as well as individuals and corporations seeking critical market information will want to add this directory to their marketing collection.

"Reasonably priced for a work of this type, this directory should appeal to larger academic, public and corporate libraries with an international focus." –Library Journal

Softcover ISBN 978-1-930956-63-6, 1,800 pages, $225.00

**Business Information ♦ _Ratings Guides_ ♦ General Reference ♦ Education ♦
Statistics ♦ Demographics ♦ Health Information ♦ Canadian Information**

**Grey House
Publishing**

TheStreet.com Ratings Guide to Health Insurers

TheStreet.com Ratings Guide to Health Insurers is the first and only source to cover the financial stability of the nation's health care system, rating the financial safety of more than 6,000 health insurance providers, health maintenance organizations (HMOs) and all of the Blue Cross Blue Shield plans – updated quarterly to ensure the most accurate information. The Guide also provides a complete listing of all the major health insurers, including all Long-Term Care and Medigap insurers. Our _Guide to Health Insurers_ includes comprehensive, timely coverage on the financial stability of HMOs and health insurers; the most accurate insurance company ratings available–the same quality ratings heralded by the U.S. General Accounting Office; separate listings for those companies offering Medigap and long-term care policies; the number of serious consumer complaints filed against most HMOs so you can see who is actually providing the best (or worst) service and more. The easy-to-use layout gives you a one-line summary analysis for each company that we track, followed by an in-depth, detailed analysis of all HMOs and the largest health insurers. The guide also includes a list of TheStreet.com Ratings Recommended Companies with information on how to contact them, and the reasoning behind any rating upgrades or downgrades.

> _"With 20 years behind its insurance-advocacy research [the rating guide] continues to offer a wealth of information that helps consumers weigh their healthcare options now and in the future." -Today's Librarian_

Issues published quarterly, Softcover, 550 pages, $499.00 for four quarterly issues, $249.00 for a single issue

TheStreet.com Ratings Guide to Life & Annuity Insurers

TheStreet.com Safety Ratings are the most reliable source for evaluating an insurer's financial solvency risk. Consequently, policy-holders have come to rely on TheStreet.com's flagship publication, _TheStreet.com Ratings Guide to Life & Annuity Insurers_, to help them identify the safest companies to do business with. Each easy-to-use edition delivers TheStreet.com's independent ratings and analyses on more than 1,100 insurers, updated every quarter. Plus, your patrons will find a complete list of TheStreet.com Recommended Companies, including contact information, and the reasoning behind any rating upgrades or downgrades. This guide is perfect for those who are considering the purchase of a life insurance policy, placing money in an annuity, or advising clients about insurance and annuities. A life or health insurance policy or annuity is only as secure as the insurance company issuing it. Therefore, make sure your patrons have what they need to periodically monitor the financial condition of the companies with whom they have an investment. The TheStreet.com Ratings product line is designed to help them in their evaluations.

> _"Weiss has an excellent reputation and this title is held by hundreds of libraries. This guide is recommended for public and academic libraries." -ARBA_

Issues published quarterly, Softcover, 360 pages, $499.00 for four quarterly issues, $249.00 for a single issue

TheStreet.com Ratings Guide to Property & Casualty Insurers

TheStreet.com Ratings Guide to Property and Casualty Insurers provides the most extensive coverage of insurers writing policies, helping consumers and businesses avoid financial headaches. Updated quarterly, this easy-to-use publication delivers the independent, unbiased TheStreet.com Safety Ratings and supporting analyses on more than 2,800 U.S. insurance companies, offering auto & homeowners insurance, business insurance, worker's compensation insurance, product liability insurance, medical malpractice and other professional liability insurance. Each edition includes a list of TheStreet.com Recommended Companies by type of insurance, including a contact number, plus helpful information about the coverage provided by the State Guarantee Associations.

> _"In contrast to the other major insurance rating agencies...Weiss does not have a financial relationship worth the companies it rates. A GAO study found that Weiss identified financial vulnerability earlier than the other rating agencies." -ARBA_

Issues published quarterly, Softcover, 455 pages, $499.00 for four quarterly issues, $249.00 for a single issue

TheStreet.com Ratings Consumer Box Set

Deliver the critical information your patrons need to safeguard their personal finances with _TheStreet.com Ratings' Consumer Guide Box Set_. Each of the eight guides is packed with accurate, unbiased information and recommendations to help your patrons make sound financial decisions. TheStreet.com Ratings Consumer Guide Box Set provides your patrons with easy to understand guidance on important personal finance topics, including: _Consumer Guide to Variable Annuities, Consumer Guide to Medicare Supplement Insurance, Consumer Guide to Elder Care Choices, Consumer Guide to Automobile Insurance, Consumer Guide to Long-Term Care Insurance, Consumer Guide to Homeowners Insurance, Consumer Guide to Term Life Insurance, and Consumer Guide to Medicare Prescription Drug Coverage_. Each guide provides an easy-to-read overview of the topic, what to look out for when selecting a company or insurance plan to do business with, who are the recommended companies to work with and how to navigate through these often-times difficult decisions. Custom worksheets and step-by-step directions make these resources accessible to all types of users. Packaged in a handy custom display box, these helpful guides will prove to be a much-used addition to any reference collection.

Issues published twice per year, Softcover, 600 pages, $499.00 for two biennial issues

Business Information ♦ **Ratings Guides** ♦ **General Reference** ♦ **Education** ♦
Statistics ♦ **Demographics** ♦ **Health Information** ♦ **Canadian Information**

TheStreet.com Ratings Guide to Stock Mutual Funds

TheStreet.com Ratings Guide to Stock Mutual Funds offers ratings and analyses on more than 8,800 equity mutual funds – more than any other publication. The exclusive TheStreet.com Investment Ratings combine an objective evaluation of each fund's performance and risk to provide a single, user-friendly, composite rating, giving your patrons a better handle on a mutual fund's risk-adjusted performance. Each edition identifies the top-performing mutual funds based on risk category, type of fund, and overall risk-adjusted performance. TheStreet.com's unique investment rating system makes it easy to see exactly which stocks are on the rise and which ones should be avoided. For those investors looking to tailor their mutual fund selections based on age, income, and tolerance for risk, we've also assigned two component ratings to each fund: a performance rating and a risk rating. With these, you can identify those funds that are best suited to meet your - or your client's – individual needs and goals. Plus, we include a handy Risk Profile Quiz to help you assess your personal tolerance for risk. So whether you're an investing novice or professional, the *Guide to Stock Mutual Funds* gives you everything you need to find a mutual fund that is right for you.

> *"There is tremendous need for information such as that provided by this Weiss publication. This reasonably priced guide is recommended for public and academic libraries serving investors." -ARBA*

Issues published quarterly, Softcover, 655 pages, $499 for four quarterly issues, $249 for a single issue

TheStreet.com Ratings Guide to Exchange-Traded Funds

TheStreet.com Ratings editors analyze hundreds of mutual funds each quarter, condensing all of the available data into a single composite opinion of each fund's risk-adjusted performance. The intuitive, consumer-friendly ratings allow investors to instantly identify those funds that have historically done well and those that have under-performed the market. Each quarterly edition identifies the top-performing exchange-traded funds based on risk category, type of fund, and overall risk-adjusted performance. The rating scale, A through F, gives you a better handle on an exchange-traded fund's risk-adjusted performance. Other features include Top & Bottom 200 Exchange-Traded Funds; Performance and Risk: 100 Best and Worst Exchange- Traded Funds; Investor Profile Quiz; Performance Benchmarks and Fund Type Descriptions. With the growing popularity of mutual fund investing, consumers need a reliable source to help them track and evaluate the performance of their mutual fund holdings. Plus, they need a way of identifying and monitoring other funds as potential new investments. Unfortunately, the hundreds of performance and risk measures available, multiplied by the vast number of mutual fund investments on the market today, can make this a daunting task for even the most sophisticated investor. This Guide will serve as a useful tool for both the first-time and seasoned investor.

Editions published quarterly, Softcover, 440 pages, $499.00 for four quarterly issues, $249.00 for a single issue

TheStreet.com Ratings Guide to Bond & Money Market Mutual Funds

TheStreet.com Ratings Guide to Bond & Money Market Mutual Funds has everything your patrons need to easily identify the top-performing fixed income funds on the market today. Each quarterly edition contains TheStreet.com's independent ratings and analyses on more than 4,600 fixed income funds – more than any other publication, including corporate bond funds, high-yield bond funds, municipal bond funds, mortgage security funds, money market funds, global bond funds and government bond funds. In addition, the fund's risk rating is combined with its three-year performance rating to get an overall picture of the fund's risk-adjusted performance. The resulting TheStreet.com Investment Rating gives a single, user-friendly, objective evaluation that makes it easy to compare one fund to another and select the right fund based on the level of risk tolerance. Most investors think of fixed income mutual funds as "safe" investments. That's not always the case, however, depending on the credit risk, interest rate risk, and prepayment risk of the securities owned by the fund. TheStreet.com Ratings assesses each of these risks and assigns each fund a risk rating to help investors quickly evaluate the fund's risk component. Plus, we include a handy Risk Profile Quiz to help you assess your personal tolerance for risk. So whether you're an investing novice or professional, the *Guide to Bond and Money Market Mutual Funds* gives you everything you need to find a mutual fund that is right for you.

> *"Comprehensive... It is easy to use and consumer-oriented, and can be recommended for larger public and academic libraries." -ARBA*

Issues published quarterly, Softcover, 470 pages, $499.00 for four quarterly issues, $249.00 for a single issue

TheStreet.com Ratings Guide to Banks & Thrifts

Updated quarterly, for the most up-to-date information, *TheStreet.com Ratings Guide to Banks and Thrifts* offers accurate, intuitive safety ratings your patrons can trust; supporting ratios and analyses that show an institution's strong & weak points; identification of the TheStreet.com Recommended Companies with branches in your area; a complete list of institutions receiving upgrades/downgrades; and comprehensive coverage of every bank and thrift in the nation – more than 9,000. TheStreet.com Safety Ratings are then based on the analysts' review of publicly available information collected by the federal banking regulators. The easy-to-use layout gives you: the institution's TheStreet.com Safety Rating for the last 3 years; the five key indexes used to evaluate each institution; along with the primary ratios and statistics used in determining the company's rating. *TheStreet.com Ratings Guide to Banks & Thrifts* will be a must for individuals who are concerned about the safety of their CD or savings account; need to be sure that an existing line of credit will be there when they need it; or simply want to avoid the hassles of dealing with a failing or troubled institution.

> *"Large public and academic libraries most definitely need to acquire the work. Likewise, special libraries in large corporations will find this title indispensable." -ARBA*

Issues published quarterly, Softcover, 370 pages, $499.00 for four quarterly issues, $249.00 for a single issue

Business Information ✦ **Ratings Guides** ✦ General Reference ✦ Education ✦
Statistics ✦ Demographics ✦ Health Information ✦ Canadian Information

TheStreet.com Ratings Guide to Common Stocks

TheStreet.com Ratings Guide to Common Stocks gives your patrons reliable insight into the risk-adjusted performance of common stocks listed on the NYSE, AMEX, and Nasdaq – over 5,800 stocks in all – more than any other publication. TheStreet.com's unique investment rating system makes it easy to see exactly which stocks are on the rise and which ones should be avoided. In addition, your patrons also get supporting analysis showing growth trends, profitability, debt levels, valuation levels, the top-rated stocks within each industry, and more. Plus, each stock is ranked with the easy-to-use buy-hold-sell equivalents commonly used by Wall Street. Whether they're selecting their own investments or checking up on a broker's recommendation, TheStreet.com Ratings can help them in their evaluations.

"Users... will find the information succinct and the explanations readable, easy to understand, and helpful to a novice." -Library Journal

Issues published quarterly, Softcover, 440 pages, $499.00 for four quarterly issues, $249.00 for a single issue

TheStreet.com Ratings Ultimate Guided Tour of Stock Investing

This important reference guide from TheStreet.com Ratings is just what librarians around the country have asked for: a step-by-step introduction to stock investing for the beginning to intermediate investor. This easy-to-navigate guide explores the basics of stock investing and includes the intuitive TheStreet.com Investment Rating on more than 5,800 stocks, complete with real-world investing information that can be put to use immediately with stocks that fit the concepts discussed in the guide; informative charts, graphs and worksheets; easy-to-understand explanations on topics like P/E, compound interest, marked indices, diversifications, brokers, and much more; along with financial safety ratings for every stock on the NYSE, American Stock Exchange and the Nasdaq. This consumer-friendly guide offers complete how-to information on stock investing that can be put to use right away; a friendly format complete with our "Wise Guide" who leads the reader on a safari to learn about the investing jungle; helpful charts, graphs and simple worksheets; the intuitive TheStreet.com Investment rating on over 6,000 stocks — every stock found on the NYSE, American Stock Exchange and the NASDAQ; and much more.

"Provides investors with an alternative to stock broker recommendations, which recently have been tarnished by conflicts of interest. In summary, the guide serves as a welcome addition for all public library collections." -ARBA

Issues published quarterly, Softcover, 370 pages, $499.00 for four quarterly issues, $249.00 for a single issue

TheStreet.com Ratings' Reports & Services

- Ratings Online — An on-line summary covering an individual company's TheStreet.com Financial Strength Rating or an investment's unique TheStreet.com Investment Rating with the factors contributing to that rating; available 24 hours a day by visiting www.thestreet.com/tscratings or calling (800) 289-9222.
- Unlimited Ratings Research — The ultimate research tool providing fast, easy online access to the very latest TheStreet.com Financial Strength Ratings and Investment Ratings. Price: $559 per industry.

Contact TheStreet.com for more information about Reports & Services at www.thestreet.com/tscratings or call (800) 289-9222

TheStreet.com Ratings' Custom Reports

TheStreet.com Ratings is pleased to offer two customized options for receiving ratings data. Each taps into TheStreet.com's vast data repositories and is designed to provide exactly the data you need. Choose from a variety of industries, companies, data variables, and delivery formats including print, Excel, SQL, Text or Access.

- Customized Reports - get right to the heart of your company's research and data needs with a report customized to your specifications.
- Complete Database Download – TheStreet.com will design and deliver the database; from there you can sort it, recalculate it, and format your results to suit your specific needs.

Contact TheStreet.com for more information about Custom Reports at www.thestreet.com/tscratings or call (800) 289-9222

Business Information ◆ Ratings Guides ◆ General Reference ◆ **Education** ◆
Statistics ◆ Demographics ◆ Health Information ◆ Canadian Information

Grey House
Publishing

The Value of a Dollar 1600-1859, The Colonial Era to The Civil War

Following the format of the widely acclaimed, *The Value of a Dollar, 1860-2004, The Value of a Dollar 1600-1859, The Colonial Era to The Civil War* records the actual prices of thousands of items that consumers purchased from the Colonial Era to the Civil War. Our editorial department had been flooded with requests from users of our *Value of a Dollar* for the same type of information, just from an earlier time period. This new volume is just the answer – with pricing data from 1600 to 1859. Arranged into five-year chapters, each 5-year chapter includes a Historical Snapshot, Consumer Expenditures, Investments, Selected Income, Income/Standard Jobs, Food Basket, Standard Prices and Miscellany. There is also a section on Trends. This informative section charts the change in price over time and provides added detail on the reasons prices changed within the time period, including industry developments, changes in consumer attitudes and important historical facts. This fascinating survey will serve a wide range of research needs and will be useful in all high school, public and academic library reference collections.

"The Value of a Dollar: Colonial Era to the Civil War, 1600-1865 will find a happy audience among students, researchers, and general browsers. It offers a fascinating and detailed look at early American history from the viewpoint of everyday people trying to make ends meet. This title and the earlier publication, The Value of a Dollar, 1860-2004, complement each other very well, and readers will appreciate finding them side-by-side on the shelf." -Booklist

Hardcover ISBN 978-1-59237-094-8, 600 pages, $145.00 | Ebook ISBN 978-1-59237-169-3 www.greyhouse.com/ebooks.htm

The Value of a Dollar 1860-2009, Fourth Edition

A guide to practical economy, *The Value of a Dollar* records the actual prices of thousands of items that consumers purchased from the Civil War to the present, along with facts about investment options and income opportunities. This brand new Third Edition boasts a brand new addition to each five-year chapter, a section on Trends. This informative section charts the change in price over time and provides added detail on the reasons prices changed within the time period, including industry developments, changes in consumer attitudes and important historical facts. Plus, a brand new chapter for 2005-2009 has been added. Each 5-year chapter includes a Historical Snapshot, Consumer Expenditures, Investments, Selected Income, Income/Standard Jobs, Food Basket, Standard Prices and Miscellany. This interesting and useful publication will be widely used in any reference collection.

"Business historians, reporters, writers and students will find this source... very helpful for historical research. Libraries will want to purchase it." –ARBA

Hardcover ISBN 978-1-59237-403-8, 600 pages, $145.00 | Ebook ISBN 978-1-59237-173-0 www.greyhouse.com/ebooks.htm

Working Americans 1880-1999
Volume I: The Working Class, Volume II: The Middle Class, Volume III: The Upper Class

Each of the volumes in the *Working Americans* series focuses on a particular class of Americans, The Working Class, The Middle Class and The Upper Class over the last 120 years. Chapters in each volume focus on one decade and profile three to five families. Family Profiles include real data on Income & Job Descriptions, Selected Prices of the Times, Annual Income, Annual Budgets, Family Finances, Life at Work, Life at Home, Life in the Community, Working Conditions, Cost of Living, Amusements and much more. Each chapter also contains an Economic Profile with Average Wages of other Professions, a selection of Typical Pricing, Key Events & Inventions, News Profiles, Articles from Local Media and Illustrations. The *Working Americans* series captures the lifestyles of each of the classes from the last twelve decades, covers a vast array of occupations and ethnic backgrounds and travels the entire nation. These interesting and useful compilations of portraits of the American Working, Middle and Upper Classes during the last 120 years will be an important addition to any high school, public or academic library reference collection.

"These interesting, unique compilations of economic and social facts, figures and graphs will support multiple research needs. They will engage and enlighten patrons in high school, public and academic library collections." –Booklist

Volume I: The Working Class Hardcover ISBN 978-1-891482-81-6, 558 pages, $145.00 | Volume II: The Middle Class Hardcover ISBN 978-1-891482-72-4, 591 pages, $145.00 | Volume III: The Upper Class Hardcover ISBN 978-1-930956-38-4, 567 pages, $145.00 | www.greyhouse.com/ebooks.htm

Working Americans 1880-1999 Volume IV: Their Children

This Fourth Volume in the highly successful *Working Americans* series focuses on American children, decade by decade from 1880 to 1999. This interesting and useful volume introduces the reader to three children in each decade, one from each of the Working, Middle and Upper classes. Like the first three volumes in the series, the individual profiles are created from interviews, diaries, statistical studies, biographies and news reports. Profiles cover a broad range of ethnic backgrounds, geographic area and lifestyles – everything from an orphan in Memphis in 1882, following the Yellow Fever epidemic of 1878 to an eleven-year-old nephew of a beer baron and owner of the New York Yankees in New York City in 1921. Chapters also contain important supplementary materials including News Features as well as information on everything from Schools to Parks, Infectious Diseases to Childhood Fears along with Entertainment, Family Life and much more to provide an informative overview of the lifestyles of children from each decade. This interesting account of what life was like for Children in the Working, Middle and Upper Classes will be a welcome addition to the reference collection of any high school, public or academic library.

Hardcover ISBN 978-1-930956-35-3, 600 pages, $145.00 | Ebook ISBN 978-1-59237-166-2 www.greyhouse.com/ebooks.htm

Business Information ✦ Ratings Guides ✦ General Reference ✦ **Education** ✦
Statistics ✦ Demographics ✦ Health Information ✦ Canadian Information

Grey House
Publishing

Working Americans 1880-2003 Volume V: Americans At War

Working Americans 1880-2003 Volume V: Americans At War is divided into 11 chapters, each covering a decade from 1880-2003 and examines the lives of Americans during the time of war, including declared conflicts, one-time military actions, protests, and preparations for war. Each decade includes several personal profiles, whether on the battlefield or on the homefront, that tell the stories of civilians, soldiers, and officers during the decade. The profiles examine: Life at Home; Life at Work; and Life in the Community. Each decade also includes an Economic Profile with statistical comparisons, a Historical Snapshot, News Profiles, local News Articles, and Illustrations that provide a solid historical background to the decade being examined. Profiles range widely not only geographically, but also emotionally, from that of a girl whose leg was torn off in a blast during WWI, to the boredom of being stationed in the Dakotas as the Indian Wars were drawing to a close. As in previous volumes of the *Working Americans* series, information is presented in narrative form, but hard facts and real-life situations back up each story. The basis of the profiles come from diaries, private print books, personal interviews, family histories, estate documents and magazine articles. For easy reference, *Working Americans 1880-2003 Volume V: Americans At War* includes an in-depth Subject Index. The Working Americans series has become an important reference for public libraries, academic libraries and high school libraries. This fifth volume will be a welcome addition to all of these types of reference collections.

Hardcover ISBN 978-1-59237-024-5, 600 pages, $145.00 | Ebook ISBN 978-1-59237-167-9 www.greyhouse.com/ebooks.htm

Working Americans 1880-2005 Volume VI: Women at Work

Unlike any other volume in the *Working Americans* series, this Sixth Volume, is the first to focus on a particular gender of Americans. *Volume VI: Women at Work*, traces what life was like for working women from the 1860's to the present time. Beginning with the life of a maid in 1890 and a store clerk in 1900 and ending with the life and times of the modern working women, this text captures the struggle, strengths and changing perception of the American woman at work. Each chapter focuses on one decade and profiles three to five women with real data on Income & Job Descriptions, Selected Prices of the Times, Annual Income, Annual Budgets, Family Finances, Life at Work, Life at Home, Life in the Community, Working Conditions, Cost of Living, Amusements and much more. For even broader access to the events, economics and attitude towards women throughout the past 130 years, each chapter is supplemented with News Profiles, Articles from Local Media, Illustrations, Economic Profiles, Typical Pricing, Key Events, Inventions and more. This important volume illustrates what life was like for working women over time and allows the reader to develop an understanding of the changing role of women at work. These interesting and useful compilations of portraits of women at work will be an important addition to any high school, public or academic library reference collection.

Hardcover ISBN 978-1-59237-063-4, 600 pages, $145.00 | Ebook ISBN 978-1-59237-168-6 www.greyhouse.com/ebooks.htm

Working Americans 1880-2005 Volume VII: Social Movements

Working Americans series, Volume VII: Social Movements explores how Americans sought and fought for change from the 1880s to the present time. Following the format of previous volumes in the Working Americans series, the text examines the lives of 34 individuals who have worked -- often behind the scenes --- to bring about change. Issues include topics as diverse as the Anti-smoking movement of 1901 to efforts by Native Americans to reassert their long lost rights. Along the way, the book will profile individuals brave enough to demand suffrage for Kansas women in 1912 or demand an end to lynching during a March on Washington in 1923. Each profile is enriched with real data on Income & Job Descriptions, Selected Prices of the Times, Annual Incomes & Budgets, Life at Work, Life at Home, Life in the Community, along with News Features, Key Events, and Illustrations. The depth of information contained in each profile allow the user to explore the private, financial and public lives of these subjects, deepening our understanding of how calls for change took place in our society. A must-purchase for the reference collections of high school libraries, public libraries and academic libraries.

Hardcover ISBN 978-1-59237-101-3, 600 pages, $145.00 | Ebook ISBN 978-1-59237-174-7 www.gale.com/gvrl/partners/grey.htm

Working Americans 1880-2005 Volume VIII: Immigrants

Working Americans 1880-2007 Volume VIII: Immigrants illustrates what life was like for families leaving their homeland and creating a new life in the United States. Each chapter covers one decade and introduces the reader to three immigrant families. Family profiles cover what life was like in their homeland, in their community in the United States, their home life, working conditions and so much more. As the reader moves through these pages, the families and individuals come to life, painting a picture of why they left their homeland, their experiences in setting roots in a new country, their struggles and triumphs, stretching from the 1800s to the present time. Profiles include a seven-year-old Swedish girl who meets her father for the first time at Ellis Island; a Chinese photographer's assistant; an Armenian who flees the genocide of his country to build Ford automobiles in Detroit; a 38-year-old German bachelor cigar maker who settles in Newark NJ, but contemplates tobacco farming in Virginia; a 19-year-old Irish domestic servant who is amazed at the easy life of American dogs; a 19-year-old Filipino who came to Hawaii against his parent's wishes to farm sugar cane; a French-Canadian who finds success as a boxer in Maine and many more. As in previous volumes, information is presented in narrative form, but hard facts and real-life situations back up each story. With the topic of immigration being so hotly debated in this country, this timely resource will prove to be a useful source for students, researchers, historians and library patrons to discover the issues facing immigrants in the United States. This title will be a useful addition to reference collections of public libraries, university libraries and high schools.

Hardcover ISBN 978-1-59237-197-6, 600 pages, $145.00 | Ebook ISBN 978-1-59237-232-4 www.greyhouse.com/ebooks.htm

Business Information ◆ Ratings Guides ◆ General Reference ◆ **Education** ◆
Statistics ◆ Demographics ◆ Health Information ◆ Canadian Information

Working Americans 1770-1896 Volume IX: From the Revolutionary War to the Civil War

Working Americans 1770-1869: From the Revolutionary War to the Civil War examines what life was like for the earliest of Americans. Like previous volumes in the successful Working Americans series, each chapter introduces the reader to three individuals or families. These profiles illustrate what life was like for that individual, at home, in the community and at work. The profiles are supplemented with information on current events, community issues, pricing of the times and news articles to give the reader a broader understanding of what was happening in that individual's world and how it shaped their life. Profiles extend through all walks of life, from farmers to merchants, the rich and poor, men, women and children. In these information-packed, fun-to-explore pages, the reader will be introduced to Ezra Stiles, a preacher and college president from 1776; Colonel Israel Angell, a continental officer from 1778; Thomas Vernon, a loyalist in 1776, Anna Green Winslow, a school girl in 1771; Sarah Pierce, a school teacher in 1792; Edward Hooker, an attorney in 1805; Jeremiah Greenman, a common soldier in 1775 and many others. Using these informationfilled profiles, the reader can develop an understanding of what life was like for all types of Americans in these interesting and changing times. This new edition will be an important acquisition for high school, public and academic libraries as well as history reference collections.

Hardcover ISBN 978-1-59237-371-0, 660 pages, $145.00

The Encyclopedia of Warrior Peoples & Fighting Groups

Many military groups throughout the world have excelled in their craft either by fortuitous circumstances, outstanding leadership, or intense training. This new second edition of *The Encyclopedia of Warrior Peoples and Fighting Groups* explores the origins and leadership of these outstanding combat forces, chronicles their conquests and accomplishments, examines the circumstances surrounding their decline or disbanding, and assesses their influence on the groups and methods of warfare that followed. Readers will encounter ferocious tribes, charismatic leaders, and daring militias, from ancient times to the present, including Amazons, Buffalo Soldiers, Green Berets, Iron Brigade, Kamikazes, Peoples of the Sea, Polish Winged Hussars, Teutonic Knights, and Texas Rangers. With over 100 alphabetical entries, numerous cross-references and illustrations, a comprehensive bibliography, and index, the *Encyclopedia of Warrior Peoples and Fighting Groups* is a valuable resource for readers seeking insight into the bold history of distinguished fighting forces.

"Especially useful for high school students, undergraduates, and general readers with an interest in military history." –Library Journal

Hardcover ISBN 978-1-59237-116-7, 660 pages, $135.00 | Ebook ISBN 978-1-59237-172-3 www.greyhouse.com/ebooks.htm

The Encyclopedia of Invasions & Conquests, From the Ancient Times to the Present

This second edition of the popular *Encyclopedia of Invasions & Conquests*, a comprehensive guide to over 150 invasions, conquests, battles and occupations from ancient times to the present, takes readers on a journey that includes the Roman conquest of Britain, the Portuguese colonization of Brazil, and the Iraqi invasion of Kuwait, to name a few. New articles will explore the late 20th and 21st centuries, with a specific focus on recent conflicts in Afghanistan, Kuwait, Iraq, Yugoslavia, Grenada and Chechnya. In addition to covering the military aspects of invasions and conquests, entries cover some of the political, economic, and cultural aspects, for example, the effects of a conquest on the invade country's political and monetary system and in its language and religion. The entries on leaders – among them Sargon, Alexander the Great, William the Conqueror, and Adolf Hitler – deal with the people who sought to gain control, expand power, or exert religious or political influence over others through military means. Revised and updated for this second edition, entries are arranged alphabetically within historical periods. Each chapter provides a map to help readers locate key areas and geographical features, and bibliographical references appear at the end of each entry. Other useful features include cross-references, a cumulative bibliography and a comprehensive subject index. This authoritative, well-organized, lucidly written volume will prove invaluable for a variety of readers, including high school students, military historians, members of the armed forces, history buffs and hobbyists.

"Engaging writing, sensible organization, nice illustrations, interesting and obscure facts, and useful maps make this book a pleasure to read." –ARBA

Hardcover ISBN 978-1-59237-114-3, 598 pages, $135.00 | Ebook ISBN 978-1-59237-171-6 www.gale.com/gvrl/partners/grey.htm

Encyclopedia of Prisoners of War & Internment

This authoritative second edition provides a valuable overview of the history of prisoners of war and interned civilians, from earliest times to the present. Written by an international team of experts in the field of POW studies, this fascinating and thought-provoking volume includes entries on a wide range of subjects including the Crusades, Plains Indian Warfare, concentration camps, the two world wars, and famous POWs throughout history, as well as atrocities, escapes, and much more. Written in a clear and easily understandable style, this informative reference details over 350 entries, 30% larger than the first edition, that survey the history of prisoners of war and interned civilians from the earliest times to the present, with emphasis on the 19th and 20th centuries. Medical conditions, international law, exchanges of prisoners, organizations working on behalf of POWs, and trials associated with the treatment of captives are just some of the themes explored. Entries are arranged alphabetically, plus illustrations and maps are provided for easy reference. The text also includes an introduction, bibliography, appendix of selected documents, and end-of-entry reading suggestions. This one-of-a-kind reference will be a helpful addition to the reference collections of all public libraries, high schools, and university libraries and will prove invaluable to historians and military enthusiasts.

"Thorough and detailed yet accessible to the lay reader. Of special interest to subject specialists and historians; recommended for public and academic libraries." - Library Journal

Hardcover ISBN 978-1-59237-120-4, 676 pages, $135.00 | Ebook ISBN 978-1-59237-170-9 www.greyhouse.com/ebooks.htm

Business Information ◆ Ratings Guides ◆ General Reference ◆ Education ◆
Statistics ◆ Demographics ◆ Health Information ◆ Canadian Information

Grey House
Publishing

The Encyclopedia of Rural America: the Land & People

History, sociology, anthropology, and public policy are combined to deliver the encyclopedia destined to become the standard reference work in American rural studies. From irrigation and marriage to games and mental health, this encyclopedia is the first to explore the contemporary landscape of rural America, placed in historical perspective. With over 300 articles prepared by leading experts from across the nation, this timely encyclopedia documents and explains the major themes, concepts, industries, concerns, and everyday life of the people and land who make up rural America. Entries range from the industrial sector and government policy to arts and humanities and social and family concerns. Articles explore every aspect of life in rural America. *Encyclopedia of Rural America*, with its broad range of coverage, will appeal to high school and college students as well as graduate students, faculty, scholars, and people whose work pertains to rural areas.

"This exemplary encyclopedia is guaranteed to educate our highly urban society about the uniqueness of rural America. Recommended for public and academic libraries." -Library Journal

Two Volumes, Hardcover, ISBN 978-1-59237-115-0, 800 pages, $250.00

The Religious Right, A Reference Handbook

Timely and unbiased, this third edition updates and expands its examination of the religious right and its influence on our government, citizens, society, and politics. From the fight to outlaw the teaching of Darwin's theory of evolution to the struggle to outlaw abortion, the religious right is continually exerting an influence on public policy. This text explores the influence of religion on legislation and society, while examining the alignment of the religious right with the political right. A historical survey of the movement highlights the shift to "hands-on" approach to politics and the struggle to present a unified front. The coverage offers a critical historical survey of the religious right movement, focusing on its increased involvement in the political arena, attempts to forge coalitions, and notable successes and failures. The text offers complete coverage of biographies of the men and women who have advanced the cause and an up to date chronology illuminate the movement's goals, including their accomplishments and failures. This edition offers an extensive update to all sections along with several brand new entries. Two new sections complement this third edition, a chapter on legal issues and court decisions and a chapter on demographic statistics and electoral patterns. To aid in further research, *The Religious Right*, offers an entire section of annotated listings of print and non-print resources, as well as of organizations affiliated with the religious right, and those opposing it. Comprehensive in its scope, this work offers easy-to-read, pertinent information for those seeking to understand the religious right and its evolving role in American society. A must for libraries of all sizes, university religion departments, activists, high schools and for those interested in the evolving role of the religious right.

" Recommended for all public and academic libraries." - Library Journal

Hardcover ISBN 978-1-59237-113-6, 600 pages, $135.00 | Ebook ISBN 978-1-59237-226-3 www.greyhouse.com/ebooks.htm

From Suffrage to the Senate, America's Political Women

From Suffrage to the Senate is a comprehensive and valuable compendium of biographies of leading women in U.S. politics, past and present, and an examination of the wide range of women's movements. Up to date through 2006, this dynamically illustrated reference work explores American women's path to political power and social equality from the struggle for the right to vote and the abolition of slavery to the first African American woman in the U.S. Senate and beyond. This new edition includes over 150 new entries and a brand new section on trends and demographics of women in politics. The in-depth coverage also traces the political heritage of the abolition, labor, suffrage, temperance, and reproductive rights movements. The alphabetically arranged entries include biographies of every woman from across the political spectrum who has served in the U.S. House and Senate, along with women in the Judiciary and the U.S. Cabinet and, new to this edition, biographies of activists and political consultants. Bibliographical references follow each entry. For easy reference, a handy chronology is provided detailing 150 years of women's history. This up-to-date reference will be a must-purchase for women's studies departments, high schools and public libraries and will be a handy resource for those researching the key players in women's politics, past and present.

"An engaging tool that would be useful in high school, public, and academic libraries looking for an overview of the political history of women in the US." –Booklist

Two Volumes, Hardcover ISBN 978-1-59237-117-4, 1,160 pages, $195.00 | Ebook ISBN 978-1-59237-227-0
www.gale.com/gvrl/partners/grey.htm

Business Information ♦ Ratings Guides ♦ General Reference ♦ **Education** ♦
Statistics ♦ Demographics ♦ Health Information ♦ Canadian Information

An African Biographical Dictionary

This landmark second edition is the only biographical dictionary to bring together, in one volume, cultural, social and political leaders – both historical and contemporary – of the sub-Saharan region. Over 800 biographical sketches of prominent Africans, as well as foreigners who have affected the continent's history, are featured, 150 more than the previous edition. The wide spectrum of leaders includes religious figures, writers, politicians, scientists, entertainers, sports personalities and more. Access to these fascinating individuals is provided in a user-friendly format. The biographies are arranged alphabetically, cross-referenced and indexed. Entries include the country or countries in which the person was significant and the commonly accepted dates of birth and death. Each biographical sketch is chronologically written; entries for cultural personalities add an evaluation of their work. This information is followed by a selection of references often found in university and public libraries, including autobiographies and principal biographical works. Appendixes list each individual by country and by field of accomplishment – rulers, musicians, explorers, missionaries, businessmen, physicists – nearly thirty categories in all. Another convenient appendix lists heads of state since independence by country. Up-to-date and representative of African societies as a whole, An African Biographical Dictionary provides a wealth of vital information for students of African culture and is an indispensable reference guide for anyone interested in African affairs.

"An unquestionable convenience to have these concise, informative biographies gathered into one source, indexed, and analyzed by appendixes listing entrants by nation and occupational field." –Wilson Library Bulletin

Hardcover ISBN 978-1-59237-112-9, 667 pages, $135.00 | Ebook ISBN 978-1-59237-229-4 www.greyhouse.com/ebooks.htm

American Environmental Leaders, From Colonial Times to the Present

A comprehensive and diverse award winning collection of biographies of the most important figures in American environmentalism. Few subjects arouse the passions the way the environment does. How will we feed an ever-increasing population and how can that food be made safe for consumption? Who decides how land is developed? How can environmental policies be made fair for everyone, including multiethnic groups, women, children, and the poor? *American Environmental Leaders* presents more than 350 biographies of men and women who have devoted their lives to studying, debating, and organizing these and other controversial issues over the last 200 years. In addition to the scientists who have analyzed how human actions affect nature, we are introduced to poets, landscape architects, presidents, painters, activists, even sanitation engineers, and others who have forever altered how we think about the environment. The easy to use A–Z format provides instant access to these fascinating individuals, and frequent cross references indicate others with whom individuals worked (and sometimes clashed). End of entry references provide users with a starting point for further research.

"Highly recommended for high school, academic, and public libraries needing environmental biographical information." –Library Journal/Starred Review

Two Volumes, Hardcover ISBN 978-1-59237-119-8, 900 pages $195.00 | Ebook ISBN 978-1-59237-230-0
www.greyhouse.com/ebooks.htm

World Cultural Leaders of the Twentieth & Twenty-First Centuries

World Cultural Leaders of the Twentieth & Twenty-First Centuries is a window into the arts, performances, movements, and music that shaped the world's cultural development since 1900. A remarkable around-the-world look at one-hundred-plus years of cultural development through the eyes of those that set the stage and stayed to play. This second edition offers over 120 new biographies along with a complete update of existing biographies. To further aid the reader, a handy fold-out timeline traces important events in all six cultural categories from 1900 through the present time. Plus, a new section of detailed material and resources for 100 selected individuals is also new to this edition, with further data on museums, homesteads, websites, artwork and more. This remarkable compilation will answer a wide range of questions. Who was the originator of the term "documentary"? Which poet married the daughter of the famed novelist Thomas Mann in order to help her escape Nazi Germany? Which British writer served as an agent in Russia against the Bolsheviks before the 1917 revolution? A handy two-volume set that makes it easy to look up 450 worldwide cultural icons: novelists, poets, playwrights, painters, sculptors, architects, dancers, choreographers, actors, directors, filmmakers, singers, composers, and musicians. *World Cultural Leaders of the Twentieth & Twenty-First Centuries* provides entries (many of them illustrated) covering the person's works, achievements, and professional career in a thorough essay and offers interesting facts and statistics. Entries are fully cross-referenced so that readers can learn how various individuals influenced others. An index of leaders by occupation, a useful glossary and a thorough general index complete the coverage. This remarkable resource will be an important acquisition for the reference collections of public libraries, university libraries and high schools.

"Fills a need for handy, concise information on a wide array of international cultural figures."-ARBA

Two Volumes, Hardcover ISBN 978-1-59237-118-1, 900 pages, $195.00 | Ebook ISBN 978-1-59237-231-7
www.greyhouse.com/ebooks.htm

Business Information ◆ Ratings Guides ◆ General Reference ◆ **Education** ◆
Statistics ◆ Demographics ◆ Health Information ◆ Canadian Information

Political Corruption in America: An Encyclopedia of Scandals, Power, and Greed

The complete scandal-filled history of American political corruption, focusing on the infamous people and cases, as well as society's electoral and judicial reactions. Since colonial times, there has been no shortage of politicians willing to take a bribe, skirt campaign finance laws, or act in their own interests. Corruption like the Whiskey Ring, Watergate, and Whitewater cases dominate American life, making political scandal a leading U.S. industry. From judges to senators, presidents to mayors, *Political Corruption in America* discusses the infamous people throughout history who have been accused of and implicated in crooked behavior. In this new second edition, more than 250 A–Z entries explore the people, crimes, investigations, and court cases behind 200 years of American political scandals. This unbiased volume also delves into the issues surrounding Koreagate, the Chinese campaign scandal, and other ethical lapses. Relevant statutes and terms, including the Independent Counsel Statute and impeachment as a tool of political punishment, are examined as well. Students, scholars, and other readers interested in American history, political science, and ethics will appreciate this survey of a wide range of corrupting influences. This title focuses on how politicians from all parties have fallen because of their greed and hubris, and how society has used electoral and judicial means against those who tested the accepted standards of political conduct. A full range of illustrations including political cartoons, photos of key figures such as Abe Fortas and Archibald Cox, graphs of presidential pardons, and tables showing the number of expulsions and censures in both the House and Senate round out the text. In addition, a comprehensive chronology of major political scandals in U.S. history from colonial times until the present. For further reading, an extensive bibliography lists sources including archival letters, newspapers, and private manuscript collections from the United States and Great Britain. With its comprehensive coverage of this interesting topic, *Political Corruption in America: An Encyclopedia of Scandals, Power, and Greed* will prove to be a useful addition to the reference collections of all public libraries, university libraries, history collections, political science collections and high schools.

> *"...this encyclopedia is a useful contribution to the field. Highly recommended."* - CHOICE
> *"Political Corruption should be useful in most academic, high school, and public libraries."* Booklist

Two Volumes, Hardcover ISBN 978-1-59237-297-3, 500 pages, $195.00 | Ebook ISBN 978-1-59237-308-6
www.greyhouse.com/ebooks.htm

Religion and Law: A Dictionary

This informative, easy-to-use reference work covers a wide range of legal issues that affect the roles of religion and law in American society. Extensive A–Z entries provide coverage of key court decisions, case studies, concepts, individuals, religious groups, organizations, and agencies shaping religion and law in today's society. This *Dictionary* focuses on topics involved with the constitutional theory and interpretation of religion and the law; terms providing a historical explanation of the ways in which America's ever increasing ethnic and religious diversity contributed to our current understanding of the mandates of the First and Fourteenth Amendments; terms and concepts describing the development of religion clause jurisprudence; an analytical examination of the distinct vocabulary used in this area of the law; the means by which American courts have attempted to balance religious liberty against other important individual and social interests in a wide variety of physical and regulatory environments, including the classroom, the workplace, the courtroom, religious group organization and structure, taxation, the clash of "secular" and "religious" values, and the relationship of the generalized idea of individual autonomy of the specific concept of religious liberty. Important legislation and legal cases affecting religion and society are thoroughly covered in this timely volume, including a detailed Table of Cases and Table of Statutes for more detailed research. A guide to further reading and an index are also included. This useful resource will be an important acquisition for the reference collections of all public libraries, university libraries, religion reference collections and high schools.

Two Volumes, Hardcover ISBN 978-1-59237-298-0, 500 pages, $195.00 | Ebook ISBN 978-1-59237-309-3
www.greyhouse.com/ebooks.htm

Human Rights in the United States: A Dictionary and Documents

This two volume set offers easy to grasp explanations of the basic concepts, laws, and case law in the field, with emphasis on human rights in the historical, political, and legal experience of the United States. Human rights is a term not fully understood by many Americans. Addressing this gap, the new second edition of *Human Rights in the United States: A Dictionary and Documents* offers a comprehensive introduction that places the history of human rights in the United States in an international context. It surveys the legal protection of human dignity in the United States, examines the sources of human rights norms, cites key legal cases, explains the role of international governmental and non-governmental organizations, and charts global, regional, and U.N. human rights measures. Over 240 dictionary entries of human rights terms are detailed—ranging from asylum and cultural relativism to hate crimes and torture. Each entry discusses the significance of the term, gives examples, and cites appropriate documents and court decisions. In addition, a Documents section is provided that contains 59 conventions, treaties, and protocols related to the most up to date international action on ethnic cleansing; freedom of expression and religion; violence against women; and much more. A bibliography, extensive glossary, and comprehensive index round out this indispensable volume. This comprehensive, timely volume is a must for large public libraries, university libraries and social science departments, along with high school libraries.

> *"...invaluable for anyone interested in human rights issues ... highly recommended for all reference collections."*
> - American Reference Books Annual

Two Volumes, Hardcover ISBN 978-1-59237-290-4, 750 pages, $225.00 | Ebook ISBN 978-1-59237-301-7
www.greyhouse.com/ebooks.htm

To preview any of our Directories Risk-Free for 30 days, call (800) 562-2139 or fax (518) 789-0556
www.greyhouse.com books@greyhouse.com

Business Information ◆ Ratings Guides ◆ General Reference ◆ **Education** ◆
Statistics ◆ Demographics ◆ Health Information ◆ Canadian Information

Grey House
Publishing

The Comparative Guide to American Elementary & Secondary Schools, 2008

The only guide of its kind, this award winning compilation offers a snapshot profile of every public school district in the United States serving 1,500 or more students – more than 5,900 districts are covered. Organized alphabetically by district within state, each chapter begins with a Statistical Overview of the state. Each district listing includes contact information (name, address, phone number and web site) plus Grades Served, the Numbers of Students and Teachers and the Number of Regular, Special Education, Alternative and Vocational Schools in the district along with statistics on Student/Classroom Teacher Ratios, Drop Out Rates, Ethnicity, the Numbers of Librarians and Guidance Counselors and District Expenditures per student. As an added bonus, *The Comparative Guide to American Elementary and Secondary Schools* provides important ranking tables, both by state and nationally, for each data element. For easy navigation through this wealth of information, this handbook contains a useful City Index that lists all districts that operate schools within a city. These important comparative statistics are necessary for anyone considering relocation or doing comparative research on their own district and would be a perfect acquisition for any public library or school district library.

"This straightforward guide is an easy way to find general information.
Valuable for academic and large public library collections." –ARBA

Softcover ISBN 978-1-59237-223-2, 2,400 pages, $125.00 | Ebook ISBN 978-1-59237-238-6 www.greyhouse.com/ebooks.htm

The Complete Learning Disabilities Directory, 2009

The Complete Learning Disabilities Directory is the most comprehensive database of Programs, Services, Curriculum Materials, Professional Meetings & Resources, Camps, Newsletters and Support Groups for teachers, students and families concerned with learning disabilities. This information-packed directory includes information about Associations & Organizations, Schools, Colleges & Testing Materials, Government Agencies, Legal Resources and much more. For quick, easy access to information, this directory contains four indexes: Entry Name Index, Subject Index and Geographic Index. With every passing year, the field of learning disabilities attracts more attention and the network of caring, committed and knowledgeable professionals grows every day. This directory is an invaluable research tool for these parents, students and professionals.

"Due to its wealth and depth of coverage, parents, teachers and others… should find this an invaluable resource." -Booklist

Softcover ISBN 978-1-59237-368-0, 900 pages, $145.00 | Online Database $195.00 | Online Database & Directory Combo $280.00

Educators Resource Directory, 2007/08

Educators Resource Directory is a comprehensive resource that provides the educational professional with thousands of resources and statistical data for professional development. This directory saves hours of research time by providing immediate access to Associations & Organizations, Conferences & Trade Shows, Educational Research Centers, Employment Opportunities & Teaching Abroad, School Library Services, Scholarships, Financial Resources, Professional Consultants, Computer Software & Testing Resources and much more. Plus, this comprehensive directory also includes a section on Statistics and Rankings with over 100 tables, including statistics on Average Teacher Salaries, SAT/ACT scores, Revenues & Expenditures and more. These important statistics will allow the user to see how their school rates among others, make relocation decisions and so much more. For quick access to information, this directory contains four indexes: Entry & Publisher Index, Geographic Index, a Subject & Grade Index and Web Sites Index. *Educators Resource Directory* will be a well-used addition to the reference collection of any school district, education department or public library.

"Recommended for all collections that serve elementary and secondary school professionals." –Choice

Softcover ISBN 978-1-59237-179-2, 800 pages, $145.00 | Online Database $195.00 | Online Database & Directory Combo $280.00

Business Information ◆ Ratings Guides ◆ General Reference ◆ Education ◆
Statistics ◆ Demographics ◆ Health Information ◆ Canadian Information

Grey House
Publishing

Profiles of New York | Profiles of Florida | Profiles of Texas | Profiles of Illinois | Profiles of Michigan | Profiles of Ohio | Profiles of New Jersey | Profiles of Massachusetts | Profiles of Pennsylvania | Profiles of Wisconsin | Profiles of Connecticut & Rhode Island | Profiles of Indiana | Profiles of North Carolina & South Carolina | Profiles of Virginia | Profiles of California

The careful layout gives the user an easy-to-read snapshot of every single place and county in the state, from the biggest metropolis to the smallest unincorporated hamlet. The richness of each place or county profile is astounding in its depth, from history to weather, all packed in an easy-to-navigate, compact format. Each profile contains data on History, Geography, Climate, Population, Vital Statistics, Economy, Income, Taxes, Education, Housing, Health & Environment, Public Safety, Newspapers, Transportation, Presidential Election Results, Information Contacts and Chambers of Commerce. As an added bonus, there is a section on Selected Statistics, where data from the 100 largest towns and cities is arranged into easy-to-use charts. Each of 22 different data points has its own two-page spread with the cities listed in alpha order so researchers can easily compare and rank cities. A remarkable compilation that offers overviews and insights into each corner of the state, each volume goes beyond Census statistics, beyond metro area coverage, beyond the 100 best places to live. Drawn from official census information, other government statistics and original research, you will have at your fingertips data that's available nowhere else in one single source.

"The publisher claims that this is the 'most comprehensive portrait of the state of Florida ever published,' and this reviewer is inclined to believe it...Recommended. All levels." –Choice on Profiles of Florida

Each Profiles of… title ranges from 400-800 pages, priced at $149.00 each

America's Top-Rated Cities, 2008

America's Top-Rated Cities provides current, comprehensive statistical information and other essential data in one easy-to-use source on the 100 "top" cities that have been cited as the best for business and living in the U.S. This handbook allows readers to see, at a glance, a concise social, business, economic, demographic and environmental profile of each city, including brief evaluative comments. In addition to detailed data on Cost of Living, Finances, Real Estate, Education, Major Employers, Media, Crime and Climate, city reports now include Housing Vacancies, Tax Audits, Bankruptcy, Presidential Election Results and more. This outstanding source of information will be widely used in any reference collection.

"The only source of its kind that brings together all of this information into one easy-to-use source. It will be beneficial to many business and public libraries." –ARBA

Four Volumes, Softcover ISBN 978-1-59237-349-9, 2,500 pages, $195.00 | Ebook ISBN 978-1-59237-233-1
www.greyhouse.com/ebooks.htm

America's Top-Rated Smaller Cities, 2008/09

A perfect companion to *America's Top-Rated Cities*, *America's Top-Rated Smaller Cities* provides current, comprehensive business and living profiles of smaller cities (population 25,000-99,999) that have been cited as the best for business and living in the United States. Sixty cities make up this 2004 edition of America's Top-Rated Smaller Cities, all are top-ranked by Population Growth, Median Income, Unemployment Rate and Crime Rate. City reports reflect the most current data available on a wide-range of statistics, including Employment & Earnings, Household Income, Unemployment Rate, Population Characteristics, Taxes, Cost of Living, Education, Health Care, Public Safety, Recreation, Media, Air & Water Quality and much more. Plus, each city report contains a Background of the City, and an Overview of the State Finances. *America's Top-Rated Smaller Cities* offers a reliable, one-stop source for statistical data that, before now, could only be found scattered in hundreds of sources. This volume is designed for a wide range of readers: individuals considering relocating a residence or business; professionals considering expanding their business or changing careers; general and market researchers; real estate consultants; human resource personnel; urban planners and investors.

"Provides current, comprehensive statistical information in one easy-to-use source… Recommended for public and academic libraries and specialized collections." –Library Journal

Two Volumes, Softcover ISBN 978-1-59237-284-3, 1,100 pages, $195.00 | Ebook ISBN 978-1-59237-234-8
www.greyhouse.com/ebooks.htm

Profiles of America: Facts, Figures & Statistics for Every Populated Place in the United States

Profiles of America is the only source that pulls together, in one place, statistical, historical and descriptive information about every place in the United States in an easy-to-use format. This award winning reference set, now in its second edition, compiles statistics and data from over 20 different sources – the latest census information has been included along with more than nine brand new statistical topics. This Four-Volume Set details over 40,000 places, from the biggest metropolis to the smallest unincorporated hamlet, and provides statistical details and information on over 50 different topics including Geography, Climate, Population, Vital Statistics, Economy, Income, Taxes, Education, Housing, Health & Environment, Public Safety, Newspapers, Transportation, Presidential Election Results and Information Contacts or Chambers of Commerce. Profiles are arranged, for ease-of-use, by state and then by county. Each county begins with a County-Wide Overview and is followed by information for each Community in that particular county. The Community Profiles within the county are arranged alphabetically. *Profiles of America* is a virtual snapshot of America at your fingertips and a unique compilation of information that will be widely used in any reference collection.

A Library Journal Best Reference Book "An outstanding compilation." –Library Journal

Four Volumes, Softcover ISBN 978-1-891482-80-9, 10,000 pages, $595.00

Business Information ✦ Ratings Guides ✦ General Reference ✦ Education ✦
Statistics ✦ **Demographics** ✦ Health Information ✦ Canadian Information

The Comparative Guide to American Suburbs, 2007/08

The Comparative Guide to American Suburbs is a one-stop source for Statistics on the 2,000+ suburban communities surrounding the 50 largest metropolitan areas – their population characteristics, income levels, economy, school system and important data on how they compare to one another. Organized into 50 Metropolitan Area chapters, each chapter contains an overview of the Metropolitan Area, a detailed Map followed by a comprehensive Statistical Profile of each Suburban Community, including Contact Information, Physical Characteristics, Population Characteristics, Income, Economy, Unemployment Rate, Cost of Living, Education, Chambers of Commerce and more. Next, statistical data is sorted into Ranking Tables that rank the suburbs by twenty different criteria, including Population, Per Capita Income, Unemployment Rate, Crime Rate, Cost of Living and more. *The Comparative Guide to American Suburbs* is the best source for locating data on suburbs. Those looking to relocate, as well as those doing preliminary market research, will find this an invaluable timesaving resource.

"Public and academic libraries will find this compilation useful…The work draws together figures from many sources and will be especially helpful for job relocation decisions." – Booklist

Softcover ISBN 978-1-59237-180-8, 1,700 pages, $130.00 | Ebook ISBN 978-1-59237-235-5 www.greyhouse.com/ebooks.htm

The American Tally: Statistics & Comparative Rankings for U.S. Cities with Populations over 10,000

This important statistical handbook compiles, all in one place, comparative statistics on all U.S. cities and towns with a 10,000+ population. *The American Tally* provides statistical details on over 4,000 cities and towns and profiles how they compare with one another in Population Characteristics, Education, Language & Immigration, Income & Employment and Housing. Each section begins with an alphabetical listing of cities by state, allowing for quick access to both the statistics and relative rankings of any city. Next, the highest and lowest cities are listed in each statistic. These important, informative lists provide quick reference to which cities are at both extremes of the spectrum for each statistic. Unlike any other reference, *The American Tally* provides quick, easy access to comparative statistics – a must-have for any reference collection.

"A solid library reference." -Bookwatch

Softcover ISBN 978-1-930956-29-2, 500 pages, $125.00 | Ebook ISBN 978-1-59237-241-6 www.greyhouse.com/ebooks.htm

The Asian Databook: Statistics for all US Counties & Cities with Over 10,000 Population

This is the first-ever resource that compiles statistics and rankings on the US Asian population. *The Asian Databook* presents over 20 statistical data points for each city and county, arranged alphabetically by state, then alphabetically by place name. Data reported for each place includes Population, Languages Spoken at Home, Foreign-Born, Educational Attainment, Income Figures, Poverty Status, Homeownership, Home Values & Rent, and more. Next, in the Rankings Section, the top 75 places are listed for each data element. These easy-to-access ranking tables allow the user to quickly determine trends and population characteristics. This kind of comparative data can not be found elsewhere, in print or on the web, in a format that's as easy-to-use or more concise. A useful resource for those searching for demographics data, career search and relocation information and also for market research. With data ranging from Ancestry to Education, *The Asian Databook* presents a useful compilation of information that will be a much-needed resource in the reference collection of any public or academic library along with the marketing collection of any company whose primary focus in on the Asian population.

"This useful resource will help those searching for demographics data, and market research or relocation information… Accurate and clearly laid out, the publication is recommended for large public library and research collections." -Booklist

Softcover ISBN 978-1-59237-044-3, 1,000 pages, $150.00

The Hispanic Databook: Statistics for all US Counties & Cities with Over 10,000 Population

Previously published by Toucan Valley Publications, this second edition has been completely updated with figures from the latest census and has been broadly expanded to include dozens of new data elements and a brand new Rankings section. The Hispanic population in the United States has increased over 42% in the last 10 years and accounts for 12.5% of the total US population. For ease-of-use, *The Hispanic Databook* presents over 20 statistical data points for each city and county, arranged alphabetically by state, then alphabetically by place name. Data reported for each place includes Population, Languages Spoken at Home, Foreign-Born, Educational Attainment, Income Figures, Poverty Status, Homeownership, Home Values & Rent, and more. Next, in the Rankings Section, the top 75 places are listed for each data element. These easy-to-access ranking tables allow the user to quickly determine trends and population characteristics. This kind of comparative data can not be found elsewhere, in print or on the web, in a format that's as easy-to-use or more concise. A useful resource for those searching for demographics data, career search and relocation information and also for market research. With data ranging from Ancestry to Education, *The Hispanic Databook* presents a useful compilation of information that will be a much-needed resource in the reference collection of any public or academic library along with the marketing collection of any company whose primary focus in on the Hispanic population.

"This accurate, clearly presented volume of selected Hispanic demographics is recommended for large public libraries and research collections."-Library Journal

Softcover ISBN 978-1-59237-008-5, 1,000 pages, $150.00

Business Information ♦ Ratings Guides ♦ General Reference ♦ Education ♦
Statistics ♦ Demographics ♦ **Health Information ♦ Canadian Information**

Grey House
Publishing

Ancestry in America: A Comparative Guide to Over 200 Ethnic Backgrounds

This brand new reference work pulls together thousands of comparative statistics on the Ethnic Backgrounds of all populated places in the United States with populations over 10,000. Never before has this kind of information been reported in a single volume. Section One, Statistics by Place, is made up of a list of over 200 ancestry and race categories arranged alphabetically by each of the 5,000 different places with populations over 10,000. The population number of the ancestry group in that city or town is provided along with the percent that group represents of the total population. This informative city-by-city section allows the user to quickly and easily explore the ethnic makeup of all major population bases in the United States. Section Two, Comparative Rankings, contains three tables for each ethnicity and race. In the first table, the top 150 populated places are ranked by population number for that particular ancestry group, regardless of population. In the second table, the top 150 populated places are ranked by the percent of the total population for that ancestry group. In the third table, those top 150 populated places with 10,000 population are ranked by population number for each ancestry group. These easy-to-navigate tables allow users to see ancestry population patterns and make city-by-city comparisons as well. This brand new, information-packed resource will serve a wide-range or research requests for demographics, population characteristics, relocation information and much more. *Ancestry in America: A Comparative Guide to Over 200 Ethnic Backgrounds* will be an important acquisition to all reference collections.

"This compilation will serve a wide range of research requests for population characteristics
... it offers much more detail than other sources." –Booklist

Softcover ISBN 978-1-59237-029-0, 1,500 pages, $225.00

Weather America, A Thirty-Year Summary of Statistical Weather Data and Rankings

This valuable resource provides extensive climatological data for over 4,000 National and Cooperative Weather Stations throughout the United States. Weather America begins with a new Major Storms section that details major storm events of the nation and a National Rankings section that details rankings for several data elements, such as Maximum Temperature and Precipitation. The main body of Weather America is organized into 50 state sections. Each section provides a Data Table on each Weather Station, organized alphabetically, that provides statistics on Maximum and Minimum Temperatures, Precipitation, Snowfall, Extreme Temperatures, Foggy Days, Humidity and more. State sections contain two brand new features in this edition – a City Index and a narrative Description of the climatic conditions of the state. Each section also includes a revised Map of the State that includes not only weather stations, but cities and towns.

"Best Reference Book of the Year." –Library Journal

Softcover ISBN 978-1-891482-29-8, 2,013 pages, $175.00 | Ebook ISBN 978-1-59237-237-9 www.greyhouse.com/ebooks.htm

Crime in America's Top-Rated Cities

This volume includes over 20 years of crime statistics in all major crime categories: violent crimes, property crimes and total crime. *Crime in America's Top-Rated Cities* is conveniently arranged by city and covers 76 top-rated cities. Crime in America's Top-Rated Cities offers details that compare the number of crimes and crime rates for the city, suburbs and metro area along with national crime trends for violent, property and total crimes. Also, this handbook contains important information and statistics on Anti-Crime Programs, Crime Risk, Hate Crimes, Illegal Drugs, Law Enforcement, Correctional Facilities, Death Penalty Laws and much more. A much-needed resource for people who are relocating, business professionals, general researchers, the press, law enforcement officials and students of criminal justice.

"Data is easy to access and will save hours of searching." –Global Enforcement Review

Softcover ISBN 978-1-891482-84-7, 832 pages, $155.00